lonely planet

Coastal California

Alexis Averbuck, Alison Bing, Celeste Brash, Anita Isalska, Amelia Mularz, Julie Tremaine, Ryan Ver Berkmoes, Wendy Yanagihara

CONTENTS

Plan Your Trip

The Guide

STEPHEN MOEHLE/SHUTTERSTOCK, ILYA KHAYN/SHUTTERSTOCK

Redwood National & State Parks (p266)

Toolkit

Storybook

Pinnacles National Park (p305)

SANDRA FOYT/SHUTTERSTOCK

Morro Bay (p331)

COASTAL CALIFORNIA

THE JOURNEY BEGINS HERE

Moving to San Francisco was a leap of faith. 'It's just for a year or two,' I told family and friends, unsure how my new life in the US would unfold. Most of what I knew about California came from movies; maybe I'd be cruising down the Pacific Coast Highway in a convertible before the year was out. Life in the Bay Area isn't cinematic, it turns out – it's riotous! The energy of its creative and ambitious population buoyed my own aspirations, and years passed in a blur of Dolores Park picnics and tech startup gossip over dirty martinis. Traveling along the coast has been a balm for frenetic city life. Watching waves thrash the shore became a form of meditation. Every spring, I hike to see coastal beauty spots like Montaña de Oro (p330) blazing with California's distinct orange poppies. I added poppies to my tattoo collection; California is forever under my skin.

Anita Isalska

@lunarsynthesis

Anita is a UK-born writer who has spent several years getting lost along the US West Coast. Anita wrote the Central Coast chapter.

My favourite experience is idling around **Morro Bay** (p331). From kayak trips beneath its huge volcanic rock to wandering along the pier, there's always a mystical interplay of light and fog that inspires daydreams.

WHO GOES WHERE

Our writers and experts choose the places which, for them, define Coastal California.

FROM LEFT: NITO/SHUTTERSTOCK, SUNDRY PHOTOGRAPHY/ SHUTTERSTOCK, T.TSENG/FLICKR/CC BY 2.0 ©

Once in **San Francisco** (p43), wandering through Chinatown into City Lights (pictured), I noticed a sign painted by a 1930s cult: 'I am the door.' It's true. SF is the threshold between fact and fiction, past and future, body and soul.

Alison Bing

@AlisonBing (X)

Alison wrote the San Francisco chapter.

I may have spent my life traveling the world, but for me the drive between Santa Cruz and **Pacifica** (p159) on Hwy 1 will always be the most beautiful in the world.

Ryan Ver Berkmoes

@ryanvb (Bluesky)

Ryan wrote the Marin County & Bay Area and Los Angeles chapters.

Growing up in **Oakland** (p132), I know anything can happen in the Bay Area, from a seafront oyster lunch with local wine and a good friend, to a night out dancing.

Alexis Averbuck

alexisaverbuck.com

Alexis wrote the Napa & Sonoma Wine Country chapter.

FROM LEFT: DOGLIKEHORSE/SHUTTERSTOCK, NICUHL23/SHUTTERSTOCK, NURIA KREUSER/SHUTTERSTOCK

Mendocino Village (p234) is one of my favorite destinations in California. It's a logging town that was saved from economic disaster by artists in the 1960s.

Amelia Mularz

@ameliamularz (Instagram)

Amelia wrote the North Coast & Redwoods chapter.

You don't have to be rich to reap the wealth of surfing Rincon Point, hiking Montecito's front country or picnicking with locally made, world-class pinot. This is the beauty of **Santa Barbara** (p344).

Wendy Yanagihara

@wendyyanagihara

Wendy wrote the Santa Barbara chapter.

The first time I drove down **Pacific Coast Highway** (Hwy 1; p308), I felt like I was home. A million sunny days later, I still get the same thrill from driving the stunning stretch of coastline.

Julie Tremaine

@julietremaine

Julie wrote the Disneyland & Orange County and San Diego chapters.

CONTRIBUTING WRITERS

Dylan Lalanne-Perkins

dylanlalanneperkins

Dylan covered the Castro and Haight in the San Francisco chapter.

Margot Seeto

@beyondmeato

Margot covered Downtown, Nob Hill and Day Tripsi n the San Francisco chapter.

North Coast
Behold epic views, redwoods and cool clifftop towns (p228)

Russian River Valley
Float along the river while sipping top vintages (p215)

Napa
Wine and dine in California's iconic vineyards (p170)

San Francisco
Treasure the Golden Gate thrills and neighborhood hills (p43)

OREGON
IDAHO
0 200 km
0 100 miles
Crescent City
Klamath River
Lava Beds National Monument
Goose Lake
Redwood National Park
Weed
Mt Shasta (14,179ft)
Alturas
Arcata
Eureka
Shasta Lake
Lassen Volcanic National Park
Redding
Susanville
Red Bluff
Chico
Oroville Reservoir
Sacramento Valley
Sacramento River
Mendocino
Nevada City
Truckee
Clear Lake
Grass Valley
Lake Tahoe
South Lake Tahoe
Davis
Sacramento
Sierra Nevada
Santa Rosa
Sonoma
Napa
Sutter Creek
Berkeley
Stockton
Sonora
Yosemite National Park
Mono Lake
San Francisco
Oakland
Palo Alto
San Jose
Mammoth Lakes
Bishop
White Mountain (14,252ft)

Santa Cruz
Surf, SUP and sip microbrews (p284)

Big Sur
Embrace high drama on the most spectacular road trip (p306)

Cayucos
Sashay around an unspoiled beach town (p312)

Monterey
Eyeball jellyfish tanks and seal-speckled shores (p294)

La Jolla
Snorkel in a dazzling marine wonderland (p494)

Los Angeles
Combine celebrity glam with diverse neighborhoods (p375)

Channel Islands National Park
Sail to whale-filled waters and remote hiking trails (p368)

Laguna Beach
Celebrate the artsy anchor of SoCal's best beaches (p466)

Santa Cruz
Monterey
Fresno
Kings Canyon National Park
Mt Williamson (14,380ft)
Sequoia National Park
Mt Whitney (14,505ft)
NEVADA
Death Valley
Death Valley National Park
Diablo Range
Big Sur
Paso Robles
Cambria
Cayucos
Morro Bay
San Luis Obispo
Bakersfield
Mojave
Mojave National Preserve
ARIZONA
Barstow
Needles
Santa Barbara
CHANNEL ISLANDS
Channel Islands National Park
Santa Monica
Pasadena
Los Angeles
Newport Beach
Laguna Beach
CATALINA ISLAND
Oceanside
La Jolla
San Diego
Tijuana
SAN CLEMENTE ISLAND
Palm Springs
Indio
Blythe
Salton Sea
Imperial Valley
Colorado Desert
Yuma
Mexicali
MEXICO
PACIFIC OCEAN

GASTRONOMIC DELIGHTS

What does California's coast taste like? Salt air, seafood and peaches, ripe to bursting. Up and down the coast fish is hauled from the Pacific and into dishes like cioppino (seafood stew) and clam chowder – you'll find them everywhere from fish markets to swanky restaurants. Seafood aside, vegetarian-friendly Coastal California is proud, perhaps obsessed, by its local fruits and veggies. Artichokes, garlic and avocados are so revered they get their own festivals; you'll soon see why.

FROM LEFT: JENIFOTO/SHUTTERSTOCK, EDDIE-HERNANDEZ.COM/SHUTTERSTOCK, BENJAMINHEATH/LONELY PLANET

Tacos Galore

Slow-cooked meat, crispy battered seafood or perfectly seasoned veggies folded into a tortilla...it's all art! Outstanding tacos abound; LA and San Diego are highlights.

Farmers Markets

Wipe-the-mud-off vegetables and tempting plums, cherries and tomatoes, depending on the season. Markets usually have food trucks, baked goods and takeaway treats.

Abundant Produce

More than three-quarters of US nuts and fruits are grown in California, along with more than one-third of all veggies. Fill that tote bag!

Ferry Building (p64), San Francisco

BEST FOODIE EXPERIENCES

Duck inside SF's ❶ **Ferry Building** (p64), a landmark for good taste with local, sustainable producers and a legendary farmers market.

Go on a culinary adventure in Napa and Sonoma wine country. Start in downtown ❷ **Napa** (p170)and roam out to smaller spots like Healdsburg.

Mingle with hipsters, office jockeys and visitors at ❸ **Grand Central Market** (p393), a gourmet food hall in Downtown LA going strong since 1917.

Feast on sustainable seafood straight from the source, from clam chowder to rich crab-festooned cioppino, overlooking the ocean in ❹ **Monterey** (p294).

Satisfy your cravings for Korean flavors at minimalist-chic ❺ **San Ho Won** (p97) in San Francisco, starting with ribeye bulgogi.

OUTDOOR ESCAPADES

For surfers, snorkelers and kayakers, California's 840 miles of coast are a playground of rolling waves and glittering coves. But these marine antics are entirely outclassed by the locals: the acrobatic seals, sea otters and dolphins who share the waters everywhere you go. Thrills continue inland, like marching along rocky ridges in Pinnacles National Park or steering a 4WD along Big Sur's Old Coast Road. Adventurers of all experience levels will find something to get their adrenaline surging.

Surfing Paradise

Learn to surf at easygoing spots like La Jolla and **Santa Cruz** (p288; pictured), or just watch the pros hang ten on legendary surf breaks like Trestles and Steamer Lane.

Hiking Trails

Almost endless walking routes spiderweb along California's coast, from day hikes in the Bay Area to miles of shore in stirring **Montaña de Oro State Park** (p330; pictured).

Enchanting Forests

Mighty redwoods thrive in the cool ocean-kissed air. Roam beneath giants as tall as 380ft along the **North Coast** (p228), or feel like a giant yourself among the dainty trees at **Elfin Forest Natural Area** (p332) in Los Osos.

FROM LEFT: NATALIE GERDING/SHUTTERSTOCK, JOOJOOB27/SHUTTERSTOCK, KELLYVANDELLEN/GETTY IMAGES

Pinnacles National Park (p305)

BEST OUTDOOR EXPERIENCES

Set sail to remote ❶ **Channel Islands National Park** (p368) to hike through spectacular flora and snorkel a kelpy wonderland.

Paddle a locally made redwood outrigger canoe through the estuary near ❷ **Mendocino** (p237) in search of harbor seals and harmony.

Pick from the bounty of coast-hugging state parks in ❸ **Big Sur** (p306) for rambles among redwoods and a waterfall that tumbles right onto the beach.

Go where there are no roads: hiking trails on the ❹ **Lost Coast** (p251) duck and dive along a pristine part of California with coastal views and occasional elephant seals.

Hike and scramble through ❺ **Pinnacles National Park** (p305) exploring boulders, spires and bat-filled talus caves.

LIBERATING ROAD TRIPS

Fill the gas tank and buckle up – road trips allow you delicious spontaneity and California's coast will kindle the wildest part of your soul. Steer through sun-splashed wine country, along sinuous coastal roads and deep into rugged ranches and historic inland towns. Plot out your start and end points, then let curiosity guide you to quaint towns and 'wait, pull over!' beach lookouts. Just make sure your rental car has unlimited miles – you'll need 'em.

FROM LEFT: LUCENTIUS/ISTOCK, SOPHONK/GETTY IMAGES, FEEL4NATURE/SHUTTERSTOCK

Pacific Coast Highway

Snaking along California's coast for 656 glorious miles, the legendary **Pacific Coast Highway** (Hwy 1; p526) has unfathomable views of bluffs and beaches.

Avenue of the Giants

This incredible 32-mile road (p256) on the North Coast is canopied by the world's tallest trees – redwoods, some of which were seedlings during the Roman Empire.

Roadside Attractions

Don't resist the photo op! Break up your journey with wacky sights like the gravity-defying **Mystery Spot** (p289) in Santa Cruz.

Bixby Bridge, Big Sur (p308)

BEST ROAD TRIP EXPERIENCES

Cruise along the most famous section of Hwy 1 through ❶ **Big Sur** (p306), a curvaceous road skirting perilous bluffs and mystical forests.

Follow old-growth redwoods and fog-kissed shores along the ❷ **Sonoma Coast** (p212) from Bodega Bay to Mendocino.

Witness California at its wildest by driving north from ❸ **Eureka** (p259) to Trinidad's dramatic headlands and through Redwood National & State Parks.

Drive to inland wonders by following Hwy 101 from the vineyards of ❹ **Paso Robles** (p323) to San Miguel's evocative mission and the martian landscape of Pinnacles.

Explore Central California's lesser-developed coastline from Gaviota to ❺ **Ventura** (p365) for stirring views of wide-open ranches, coastal bluffs and the Santa Ynez Mountains.

CALIFORNIA CURIOSITIES

New Age mysticism, eclectic artists...Coastal California feels wickedly weird, and oh, how quickly you'll embrace your inner oddball! San Francisco and Los Angeles are a marvel-a-minute, from eerie tiki bars to morbid museums, but remote areas are where your eyebrows will rise highest.

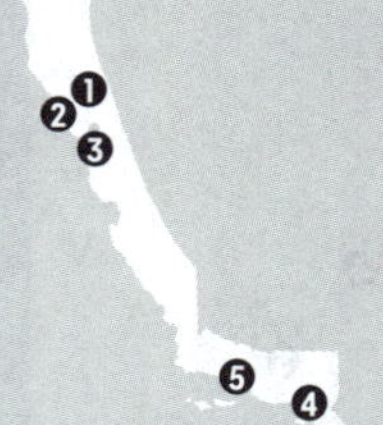

BEST OFFBEAT EXPERIENCES

Slather thick volcanic mud right up to your neck then hose it off with mineral water at the venerable ❶ **mud baths** (p188) in Calistoga. Relax and hydrate!

Marvel at artistically repurposed tin cans and cutlery by ❷ **Patrick Amiot** (p203), in a delightful gallery in Sebastopol.

Step into the darkness of a geodesic dome in San Francisco's ❸ **Exploratorium** (p57) and rely on your senses to navigate through.

Cabinet of curiosities or elaborate spoof? Hurtle from crying ants to a microscopic Pope at the ❹ **Museum of Jurassic Technology** (p411) in Los Angeles.

Gaze up at the largest-known Torrey pine in existence (around 130ft tall) in ❺ **Carpinteria** – (p353) it's home to rare nesting snowy egrets.

FROM LEFT: WYNN WYGAL/SHUTTERSTOCK, DADEROT, CC 0, VIA WIKIMEDIA COMMUNS ©

Over-the-Top Architecture

There's a glint of unhinged genius at showpiece buildings like **Hearst Castle** (p316; pictured), complete with free-roaming zebras, and the incomparably pink **Madonna Inn** (p328).

Unique Museums

Hundreds of vintage mechanical amusements delight (and terrorize) visitors at San Francisco's **Musée Mécanique** (p54; pictured), a must-see for its fortune-telling wizard and toothpick Ferris wheel.

Little Denmark

Demolish Danish pastries and admire straight-outta-Europe architecture in quaint **Solvang** (p354), a Scandi-style city in the Santa Ynez Valley.

PER BREIEHAGEN/GETTY IMAGES

Humpback whales, Monterey Bay (p296)

WILDLIFE WATCHING

Wildlife is everywhere in California: thrilling glimpses of whales breaking the surface, the furry faces of sea otters popping up in a seaweed bed, monarch butterflies in eucalyptus groves and skies filled with migrating birds. Guided excursions get you closer but you can see many wildlife wonders simply by walking around.

BEST WILDLIFE EXPERIENCES

Sight playful dolphins in cobalt-blue ❶ **Monterey Bay** (p294), or admire rays and isopods in the crowd-pleasing aquarium.

Kayak among sea otters and chubby little seals in the wildlife-rich estuary at ❷ **Moss Landing** (p292) near Santa Cruz.

Listen to grunting elephant seals at ❸ **Año Nuevo State Park** (p161), where thousands of hefty beasts come to flirt, philander and pick fights.

Roam the peninsula of ❹ **Point Reyes National Seashore** (p128) and glimpse migrating whales offshore. Got binoculars?

Witness a menagerie of marine mammals and flocks of roosting seabirds on hikes in ❺ **Point Lobos State Natural Reserve** (p302).

Underwater Wonders

Commune with coral-reef creatures and giant colonies of pinnipeds while hiking, snorkeling or kayaking offshore at places like the uninhabited **Channel Islands** (p368).

Whale-Filled Waters

Whether you want to see migrating gray whales or somersaulting humpbacks, all the ocean's giants come to feed in the krill-rich waters of **Monterey Bay** (p296).

FAMILY FROLICS

California is brimming with activities to inspire wide-eyed wonder in grown-ups and kids – and fortunately for parents, they aren't all shriek-inducing theme park rides. Family-friendly boardwalks and piers in Santa Cruz and Santa Monica bring innocent pleasures to life. Mellow beaches with gentle waves are easy to find, and the further south you travel, the warmer the water.

BEST FAMILY-FRIENDLY EXPERIENCES

Enjoy sunshine and surf in ❶ **San Diego** (p475), then head to **Legoland** (p498) in Carlsbad to see California in miniature.

Meet the most unusual residents of San Francisco: precocious sea lions at ❷ **Pier 39** (p55) and bison in **Golden Gate Park** (p105).

Saddle up for a family adventure on horseback along the Ventura River in ❸ **Ojai** (p370).

Cycle the recreational trail, gawp at sharks or take a guided kayak tour – ❹ **Monterey** (p294) is made for family hi-jinks.

Look down when you skywalk through the towering redwoods at ❺ **Sequoia Park Zoo** (p261) in Eureka.

FROM LEFT: MEHMETTEKE/SHUTTERSTOCK, V_E/SHUTTERSTOCK

Beach Scenes

Endless summers are fueled by Ferris wheels and carnival games, coupled with soul-stirring sunsets in **Santa Monica** (p421; pictured), **Venice Beach** (p427) and **Santa Cruz** (p286).

Theme Parks

Summon the cartoon heroes and cue the special effects! Kids love action-packed days at **Disneyland Resort** (p446), **Universal Studios Hollywood** (p430; pictured) and more, with movie-themed rides and live shows.

Bring the Dog

Outdoorsy destinations like **Huntington Beach** (p462) and **Laguna Beach** (p466) welcome dogs with open paws. Some wineries and breweries allow furry friends outside – ask first.

KONSTANTIN YOLSHIN/SHUTTERSTOCK

Alcatraz (p55)

RICH HISTORIES

It's been a wild ride for California from the days of mammoths to becoming the world's fourth-largest economy. Hike to centuries-old Native American cave art, confront the mission system, reflect upon the frenzied rush for gold and finish with a martini at Prohibition-era bars where the walls can talk.

BEST HISTORICAL EXPERIENCES

Watch Clint Eastwood in *Escape from Alcatraz* before visiting ❶ **The Rock** (p55) – a former military prison and penitentiary – on a tiny history-rich island rising in the San Francisco Bay.

Roam Downtown ❷ **Los Angeles** (p386) from Olvera St to Chinatown (two of them!) and Little Tokyo, soaking up some of California's founding cultures.

Dive deep in ❸ **Sonoma** (p192) history as far back as the 1820s at an adobe mission and taste the wine that inspired the breakaway Bear Flag Republic.

Walk in the footsteps of author John Steinbeck (p304) in ❹ **Salinas**, the 'Salad Bowl' of the US.

Visit the garage where Bill Hewlett and David Packard kicked off the Silicon Valley revolution in ❺ **Palo Alto** (p148).

Cultural Collisions

Native American tribes, Spanish Colonial *presidios* (forts) and Catholic missions, Mexican *pueblos* (towns) and mining ghost towns have all left traces here for you to find.

Land Back

California increasingly supports the return of thousands of acres of stolen ancestral lands to Native Americans – from the Lost Coast to Little Sur and beyond.

REGIONS & CITIES

Find the places that tick all your boxes.

North Coast & Redwoods

PEEK BEHIND THE REDWOOD CURTAIN

Lumber barons wised up and conserved primeval redwood forests along the misty, rugged and wild North Coast. Let your offbeat flag fly in Humboldt County, and swap seafaring stories at spectacular coastal fishing villages like Elk and Mendocino, as you explore some of California's most majestic landscapes.

Napa & Sonoma Wine Country

WHERE VINEYARDS AND REDWOODS MEET THE OCEAN

The sun-washed valleys and cool coastal fog make Napa and Sonoma Counties the state's most iconic wine-growing regions. But local ranches and hippie free-thinking also thrive, yielding bountiful farm-to-table meals, unusual small towns and interesting blends of luxe and laid-back, with a killer coastline to boot.

North Coast & Redwoods p228

San Francisco

CALLING ALL FREE SPIRITS HOME

San Francisco, with its charming streets and cable cars, keeps pushing boundaries through trendsetting food, social movements, art and technology. This city is defined by bold moves and rich history, with multicultural influences and its iconic landmarks like the Golden Gate Bridge keeping life fresh and inspiring.

Central Coast

WILD SHORES FOR WANDERING SOULS

Surf south from eclectic Santa Cruz with its old-timey beach boardwalk, stop to whale-watch at wildlife-rich Monterey Bay, then hike past Big Sur's coastal waterfalls and gawk at Hearst Castle en route to spirited San Luis Obispo and its bountiful Paso Robles wine country.

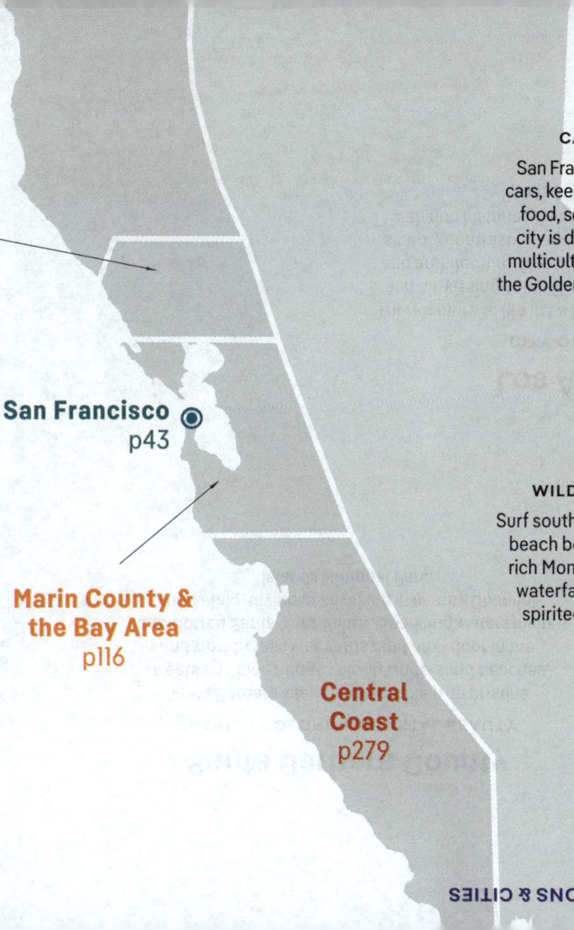

Marin County & Bay Area

WHERE THE COAST MEETS THE BAY

Outdoorsy people love Marin and San Mateo Counties for their beaches, forests, wildlife and hiking and cycling trails – but city slickers will appreciate the counterculture hubs of Berkeley and Oakland with their vibrant food and arts scenes, along with the manicured streets of world-dominating Silicon Valley.

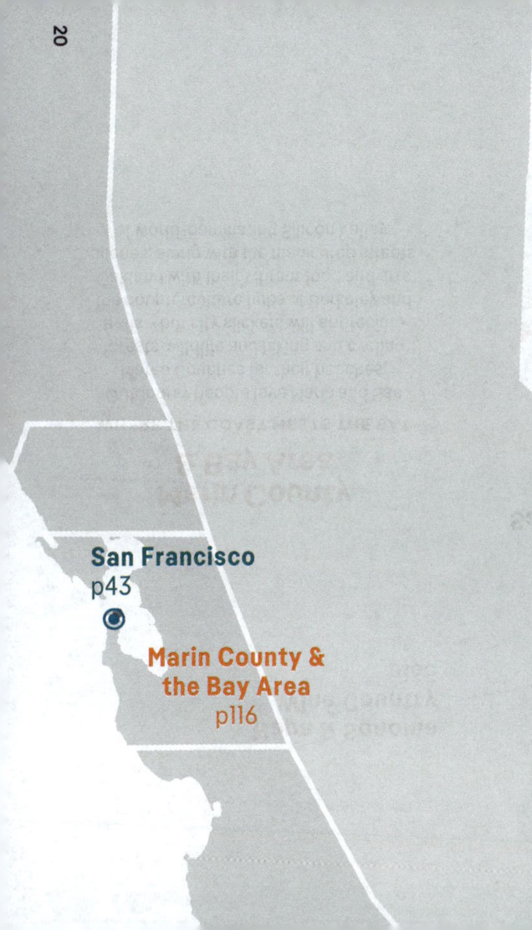

San Francisco
p43

Marin County & the Bay Area
p116

Santa Barbara County

SPANISH COLONIAL COASTAL BEAUTY

Santa Barbara keeps a low profile with pristine streets and high hedges along white-sand beaches, and world-class vineyards right next door in the oak-dotted Santa Ynez Valley. Sparkling waters invite snorkeling, diving or kayaking in nearby Channel Islands National Park.

Los Angeles

CITY OF DREAMS

There's more to life in La La Land than sunny beaches and air-kissing celebrities. Explore its bounty of art and architecture, feast on eclectic cuisines and visit sharply contrasting and lively neighborhoods, each with rich histories dating from the earliest days of Spanish colonization.

Disneyland & Orange County

A QUINTESSENTIALLY CALIFORNIA EXPERIENCE

The OC's beaches are packed with strapping surfers, volleyball champions and retouched reality stars. If you think this scenery is surreal, check out the hyper-reality of the Disneyland Resort and the rest of the theme parks that keep the kids enthralled, meeting life-size characters from their favorite flicks.

San Diego & Around

CALIFORNIA'S MOST LAID-BACK CITY

California's southernmost city seems like it's on permanent vacation, with a near-perfect year-round climate on its beaches and a booming craft-brewery scene. Explore further with Balboa Park's quirky museums and the architecture along El Prado promenade, or wander laid-back beach towns seeking the ultimate fish taco.

ITINERARIES

San Francisco to Redwood Forests

Allow: 7 days **Distance:** 330 miles

You can spend a lifetime exploring San Francisco's steep streets and rainbow-colored neighborhoods. But tear yourself away to Northern California's fog-curtained coast and titanic trees. The roads resemble leafy tunnels as you drive to meet some of the biggest redwoods on the planet, with a few sips of wine country en route.

Bartholomew Estate Winery (p195)

1 SAN FRANCISCO 2 DAYS

There's no wrong way to explore the City by the Bay (p43). Ride cable cars to dim sum in Chinatown then hike up to Coit Tower. Sail away on a prebooked tour of Alcatraz or delve into eclectic Haight-Ashbury. If nothing else, eat outstanding tacos in the Mission then hit Dogpatch's breweries or the Castro's (pictured) LGBTQ+ bars.

Detour: *Take BART to the East Bay for diverse attractions in* ***Oakland*** *(p132). ½ day*

2 MARIN HEADLANDS & SAUSALITO 1 DAY

Drive across the Golden Gate Bridge to the **Marin Headlands** (p124), where panoramic views reward hikes in the hills. Calves well stretched, relax with lunch in picture-perfect harbor town **Sausalito** (p122) and take a stroll to admire boutiques and colorful houseboats.

3 SONOMA WINE COUNTRY 1 DAY

Drive on to heritage buildings and dozens of wine-tasting rooms in **Sonoma** (p190). Sip gewürztraminer at mid-19th-century Gundlach-Bundschu and picnic with zinfandel at Bartholomew Estate. Sleep it off in a charming inn or B&B. Book ahead and take the shuttle from Sausalito to Muir Woods to avoid parking stress.

Detour: *Another kingdom of chardonnay awaits just 20 minutes' drive east in world-famous* ***Napa Valley*** *(p170). 1 day*

FROM LEFT: JAY L CLENDENIN / LOS ANGELES TIMES VIA GETTY IMAGES, OVERSNAP/GETTY IMAGES

Trinity Alps Wilderness
Arcata
Weaverville
Six Rivers National Forest
Hayfork
Redding
Humboldt Redwoods State Park
6 END
Weott
Platina
Shasta-Trinity National Forest
Red Bluff
2h
Yolla Bolly-Middle Eel Wilderness
Paskenta
Leggett
Covelo
Mendocino National Forest
Black Butte Lake
Westport
Eel River
Fort Bragg
Snow Mountain Wilderness
Caspar
Willits
5 Mendocino
Albion
Upper Lake
Ukiah
Elk
Philo
Clear Lake
Hopland
Boonville
Kelseyville
Clearlake
Point Arena
Cloverdale
Gualala
Lake Berryessa
2 3/4h
Muir Woods
4
Napa
1h
Phillip Burton Wilderness
Sonoma Wine Country
1h
3
2
Marin Headlands & Sausalito
1
30min
San Francisco
START
Oakland
San Mateo
PACIFIC OCEAN
Half Moon Bay
0 50 km
0 25 miles

4

MUIR WOODS 1 DAY

When sunshine glints through the forest canopy and bathes tremendous tree trunks in light, **Muir Woods National Monument** (p126) feels like an almost-sacred refuge. Step out along the Main Trail Loop (1 mile), or commune with redwoods on a longer hike. Make sure you reserve and pay in advance (and avoid busy weekends if you can). Drive onward to Mendocino in the late afternoon.

5

MENDOCINO 1 DAY

The further north you drive, the more magically tree-lined your route becomes. By the time you join coastal Hwy 1, you're in an otherworldly forest realm. Once arrived, get out on the water: **Catch a Canoe & Bicycles, Too** (p237) loans canoes that you can paddle into the redwood-fringed estuary. Take a stroll on the **Mendocino Headlands Trail** (p234) for flower-studded meadows and views of surf crashing into the rocks.

TRISTAN BRYNILDSEN/SHUTTERSTOCK

6

HUMBOLDT REDWOODS STATE PARK 1 DAY

The grand forested finale is **Humboldt Redwoods State Park** (p256). Take the Avenue of the Giants (pictured) exit and make stops along the 32-mile scenic drive to goggle at trees that rise 370ft high; short hikes (less than a mile) are signed along the way. Tomorrow you'll drive back to San Francisco – unless arty Eureka and the Lost Coast tempt you further north.

OSPREY CREATIVE/SHUTTERSTOCK

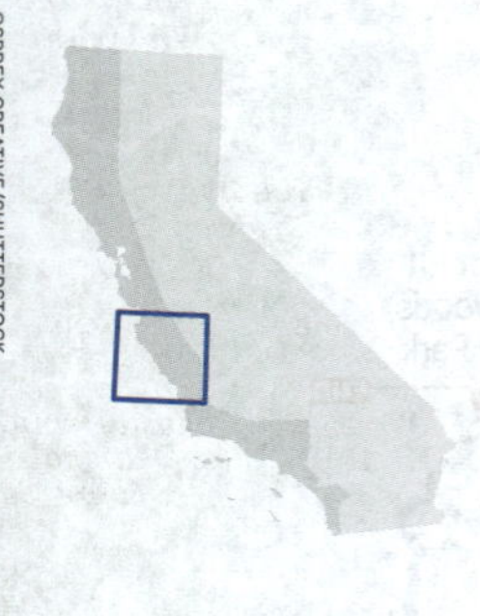

McWay Falls (p309)

ITINERARIES

Big Sur & Central Coast Loop

Allow: 6–9 days **Distance:** 185 miles

The most iconic section of California's coastal Hwy 1 is in Big Sur, where road trip fantasies become reality: dizzying cliffs, wave-smashed beaches and barely trammeled backcountry. A loop from marine haven Monterey lets you drive this legendary road with stops in chic Carmel-by-the-Sea, quaint beach towns and Paso Robles' lesser-known wine country.

1

MONTEREY ⏱ 2 DAYS

Start in **Monterey** (p294), where oceanside family amusements and a whopping aquarium can easily consume a day or two. Take a whale-watching tour to see giants somersault in the bay, or spot wildlife from a stand-up paddleboard or kayak. Historic Cannery Row and Old Fisherman's Wharf warrant a nostalgic ramble, and 17-Mile Drive is a pint-sized circuit by car or bike.

2

CARMEL-BY-THE-SEA ⏱ 1 DAY

What's this: a golden, swimmable beach in easy walking distance of a fairy-tale town and abundant wine tasting rooms? **Carmel-by-the-Sea** (p302) is pinch-me pretty and eminently walkable. Don some shades and book a brunch spot – you've made it to the California good life.

Detour: *Stop off at* ***Point Lobos State Natural Reserve*** *(p302) to walk wild cliffs and spot seabirds. ½ day*

3

BIG SUR ⏱ 2 DAYS

Big Sur (p306) is the showreel that flies through your mind when someone says 'California road trip.' Stop wherever the mood takes you: the dreamy lookout at Painters Point, wild Garrapata Beach and its blufftop walk, bridges you might recognize from Instagram, and McWay Falls tumbling straight onto the beach. Staying overnight grants you full immersion into this remote place; book ahead.

4 CAMBRIA & CAYUCOS 2 DAYS

If Hwy 1 is open, you can coast straight through to Cambria and Cayucos. Along the way gaze out at the vast ocean from appropriately named Ragged Point and watch elephant seals causing a ruckus in San Simeon. Then pick a town and flop on the beach: chic, gourmet **Cambria** (p312) or old-school-cool **Cayucos** (p312).

Detour: *Hwy 1 isn't always open through to Cambria due to bad weather and landslides. If it's closed, take the long route via Hwy 101, stopping at literary* ***Salinas*** *(p304) and the pinot-rich* ***River Road*** *(p304). 1 day*

5 SAN LUIS OBISPO 1 DAY

SLO down in **San Luis Obispo** (p326). Downtown is defined by outdoor dining, farm-to-table food and arty boutiques. If that sounds too relaxing, you're in easy reach of hilly state parks and blustery shores that beg to be rambled.

Detour: *Rent a paddle in* ***Morro Bay*** *(p331) and share the water with otters and a big volcanic rock. ½ day*

6 PASO ROBLES 1 DAY

A ranching town turned upscale wine-making hub, **Paso Robles** (p317) offers a taste of cowboy country through a haze of fruity syrah. Check out a quirky museum or two then hit the urban tasting rooms of Tin City or a wine-sipping excursion into the Adelaida District. Once your trunk is clanking with take-home bottles, loop back to Monterey via the northbound Hwy 101.

ALEKSEI POTOV/SHUTTERSTOCK

Torrey Pines State Natural Reserve (p494)

ITINERARIES

SoCal for the Family

Allow: 7–9 days **Distance:** 265 miles

The kids are squealing for Disneyland. Meanwhile the grown-ups need a little more convincing: perhaps Hollywood glamor and a small splash of wine country would do the trick? This road trip checks all the boxes with classic SoCal attractions and oceanside pleasures that all age groups will relish.

1

SANTA BARBARA 1 DAY

Begin in elegant beachfront **Santa Barbara** (p344; pictured). Paddle gentle beaches, stroll pedestrian-friendly State St and bike along the waterfront Cabrillo Bike Path. Hands-on museums like the Sea Center and MOXI amuse all ages and some wine-tasting venues have lawns and games to keep kids occupied.

***Detour:** Venture to Danish-influenced **Solvang** (p354), 50 minutes from Santa Barbara. ½ day*

2

LOS ANGELES 2 DAYS

Time to go big in **LA** (p375). Stroll the Hollywood Walk of Fame, tour Paramount Pictures, then gaze out at the Hollywood sign from Griffith Observatory. Nibble everything from loaded pickles to ice cream at the Original Farmers Market and spend an afternoon at crowd-pleasing Santa Monica Pier (pictured) with its fairground attractions and paddle-friendly waters.

3

NEWPORT BEACH 1 DAY

Set out early to drive east of LA to **Newport Beach** (p458). Then the fun begins! Head to Newport Beach Pier (pictured) or the Balboa Fun Zone for oceanside amusements and embark on a sunset sail from Mariners Mile.

***Detour:** Thirty minutes' drive east is **Crystal Cove State Park** (p469), 3.2 miles of glorious shore (and great snorkeling). ½ day*

FROM LEFT: THOMAS BARRAT/SHUTTERSTOCK, KENKISTLER/SHUTTERSTOCK, GABRIELE MALTINTI/SHUTTERSTOCK

4 DISNEYLAND ⏱ 1 DAY

Devote your day to Disneyland; avoid tears by planning ahead with a park reservation and tickets. At **Disneyland Park** (p446) adults will sigh with nostalgia at the first glimpse of Sleeping Beauty's Castle (pictured). **Disney California Adventure** (p449) is across the plaza, a newer park with recreations of more recent kid favorites like *Cars* and *The Incredibles*.

5 SAN DIEGO ⏱ 2 DAYS

Sprawling **San Diego** (p480) is chock-full of fresh-air attractions. Start in huge Balboa Park for myriad museums and the enormous San Diego Zoo (pictured) with its big cats, bears and more. Get a dose of open-air history by walking through the Old Town and enjoying photo ops at restored wagons and 19th-century shopfronts – fit everyone in a selfie, we know you can do it.

6 LA JOLLA ⏱ ½ DAY

Who's that languid character hogging the beach? That would be one of the famous sea lions or seals (pictured) of **La Jolla Cove** (p494). Nearby, descend into a secret grotto in the Sunny Jim Sea Cave Store, then find a beach of your own – perhaps family-friendly Windansea or Torrey Pines.

FROM LEFT: DISNEYLAND RESORT, STEPHEN MOEHLE/BARTFETT/500PX, MICHAEL J MAGEE/SHUTTERSTOCK

WHEN TO GO

There is no bad time to be in Coastal California, especially for wildlife and walking – pick your region and plan accordingly.

Despite California's sunny reputation, the climate can differ dramatically by season and region – and weather patterns on the coast are especially changeable. Bright green meadows and blooming wildflowers come alive in spring (roughly March to May), especially after the winter rains, which ease off in mid-April. Summer (June to August) varies from sweltering inland to comfortably cool in San Francisco. Summer is high season almost everywhere, with school holidays and tourists arriving from around the state, nation and world. Temperatures are comfortable in fall (September to November), when abundant sunny and cloudless days are outstanding for hikers. However, the drier months from summer through November have become what's known as 'fire season,' and wildfires can break out as early as late spring, especially in SoCal. Be vigilant about fire dangers – no open flames, ever – and keep an eye on the news. Winter (December to March) brings rainstorms, cooler temperatures (especially in the mountains) and a superabundance of migrating birds and whales.

Looking for a Bargain?

During the summer (June to August) accommodation prices are 50% to 100% higher than the rest of the year. On the coast, all weekends have higher prices. If you can, travel at another time.

I LIVE HERE

YEAR-ROUND WILDLIFE

Tiffany Crist-Studley is a science teacher and self-proclaimed nature nerd based in the Bay Area.

Every season is wildlife season along California's coast. You can always see large porpoises, harbor seals and California sea lions, and we have an overabundance of creatures like elephant seals. It's common to see whales in the water at any time during the year, but there are different seasons for different varieties of whales. You'll see mule deer along the roadside and coyotes on grassy hills at dawn and dusk. Keep your eyes open, you'll see creatures around you – always!

Healdsberg (p220)

FROM LEFT: KARA JADE QUAN-MONTGOMERY/SHUTTERSTOCK, FUJIFUJISAKISAKI/SHUTTERSTOCK

FALL FOLIAGE

Fall is a sweet time to visit wine country: vineyards turn amber and temperatures hover around the mid-80s (high 20s°C) in Napa (p170) in September and October. Bring a jacket for cool evenings.

Weather through the Year: San Francisco

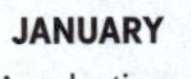

JANUARY	FEBRUARY	MARCH	APRIL	MAY	JUNE
Avg daytime max: **57°F** (14°C)	Avg daytime max: **58°F** (14°C)	Avg daytime max: **61°F** (16°C)	Avg daytime max: **63°F** (17°C)	Avg daytime max: **66°F** (19°C)	Avg daytime max: **71°F** (19°C)
Days of rainfall: 8	Days of rainfall: 7	Days of rainfall: 6	Days of rainfall: 4	Days of rainfall: 2	Days of rainfall: 1

FIRE WATCH

Keep an eye on real-time wildfire information using a reliable app like **Watch Duty** *(watchduty.org)* if you're traveling between June and November. For hyper-local air-quality data, look at **Purple Air** *(purpleair.com)*; wildfire smoke can sting eyes and provoke wheezes from many miles away.

The Big Festivals & Parades

California celebrates **LGBTQ+ pride** (p524) for the entire month of June, with costume parades, film fests and street parties. **SF Pride** (p69) sets the global parade standard with over a million people, tons of glitter and ounces of bikinis. **June and November**

Mexican-American foods, traditional song and dance, tours of landmark architecture – Spanish California culture comes to the fore during the loud, skirt-twirling **Old Spanish Days** fiesta (p351) in Santa Barbara. **early August**

Outside Lands (p109) bring three days of play to Golden Gate Park with music and comedy plus gourmet food, beer and wine. **August**

Old-school jazz cats, cross-cultural sensations and fusion rebels all line up to play the West Coast's legendary Monterey Jazz Festival, held on the Central Coast over a long weekend. **September**

Local & Quirkier Festivals

The **Hunky Jesus** contest (p92) in San Francisco's Dolores Park is both contest and fundraiser, and it's exactly as naughty as it sounds. **Easter**

Fans of the drama series flood Mendocino Village for tours, tea receptions and trivia at the **Murder, She Wrote Festival** (p239); '80s glasses are optional. **May**

Hot rods and hot action fete the classic film at **Salute to American Graffiti** in Petaluma (p201) . **May**

Sway to the sounds of bluegrass, big band, Americana and more with over two dozen live concerts at **Mendocino Music Festival** (p239). **July**

Ranch 'n' wine town Paso Robles has another claim to fame: the Polish-Californian composer **Ignacy Paderewski** (1860–1941), whose music is celebrated at an eponymous festival (p321) in his honor. **Late October to early November**

I LIVE HERE

SPRING FLOWERS

Dana Sundblad is director of development at the Botanical Garden in San Luis Obispo. *@slobotanical*

Superblooms are definitely down to luck. If you have a very wet January and February, March through May tends to be very bloomy. The best places to see the superblooms on the Central Coast are Carrizo Plain (pictured) and Montaña de Oro. Carrizo Plain is beautiful and you can see vast expanses of wildflowers. Go at off times: a lot of people track the superbloom and go at the same time, on weekends.

Superblooms

COASTAL FOG

Especially in Northern California, summer is marked by coastal fog that doesn't always burn off. So San Francisco can be socked in and chilly when just inland in Oakland it's a sunny 75°F (24°C). September is the best month for the North Coast.

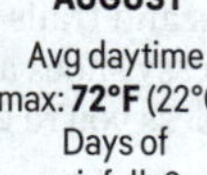

JULY	AUGUST	SEPTEMBER	OCTOBER	NOVEMBER	DECEMBER
Avg daytime max: **71°F** (22°C)	Avg daytime max: **72°F** (22°C)	Avg daytime max: **74°F** (23°C)	Avg daytime max: **70°F** (21°C)	Avg daytime max: **63°F** (17°C)	Avg daytime max: **57°F** (14°C)
Days of rainfall: 0	Days of rainfall: 0	Days of rainfall: 0	Days of rainfall: 2	Days of rainfall: 5	Days of rainfall: 7

FROM LEFT: UVL/SHUTTERSTOCK, AMAZON

Julia Pfeiffer Burns State Park (p309)

GET PREPARED FOR COASTAL CALIFORNIA

Useful things to load in your bag, your ears and your brain.

Clothes

Casual layers California is a laid-back, anything-goes kind of place, especially when it comes to fashion. LA is more fashion-conscious and San Francisco more relaxed or iconoclastic; most other cities are quite informal. Beware the changeable weather: layer up with sweaters, wraps or light jackets.

Hiking cover-ups Travelers who've only ever seen California on TV may get a shock along the coast, where marine fog reprimands anyone in shorts all morning and rolls back in the afternoon to make you wish you'd worn sweat-proof sunscreen. Wear long sleeves for sun-exposed outdoor activities (and long pants when hiking in tick-filled forests).

Comfortable shoes Walking shoes are essential for cities and trails alike. Even on nights out, dressy shoes and heels are not necessary unless you're going to a club with a dress code.

Local Languages

Stoked for a hella rad vacay, brah? Language goes way beyond California slang. Many locals are multilingual – more than 200 different languages are spoken here. The top five are English, Spanish, Chinese, Tagalog and Vietnamese. Around 45% of state residents speak a language other than English at home, twice the national average.

READ

Where I Was From (Joan Didion; 2003) California-born essayist shatters palm-fringed fantasies.

If They Come in the Morning (Angela Davis; 1971) Chronicles of the Black Power movement collected by one of its leading figures.

The Grapes of Wrath (John Steinbeck; 1939) Award-winning novel of Dust Bowl migration to California's Central Valley.

The Big Sleep (Raymond Chandler; 1939) Iconic Philip Marlowe mystery set in Los Angeles sets the bar for gumshoes.

Manners

Californians are casual by nature, but a few (unspoken) rules still apply.

Attitude Smiles go a long way here. Be friendly, even in a disagreement.

Greetings Shaking hands when meeting is a bit formal, but it's expected for business dealings and by some older adults.

Bargaining Haggling over the prices of goods usually isn't appropriate, except at outdoor markets and with sidewalk vendors.

Smoking Don't light up indoors (it's illegal) or anywhere else you don't see others doing it. Some restaurants have patios or sidewalk tables where smoking is tolerated (ask first or look around for ashtrays), but don't expect your neighbors to be happy about secondhand smoke.

Cannabis While people aged 21 and older can buy cannabis, smoking or consuming marijuana in public or on federal land (such as national parks and monuments) is illegal.

Eating out Californian restaurant etiquette tends to be informal. Only a handful of restaurants require more than a dressy shirt, slacks and shoes that aren't flip-flops. At other places, T-shirts, shorts and sandals are fine.

Tipping (p516) At restaurants, 18% to 25% is expected anywhere you receive table service. Counter service can still rate 10%, though it's not obligatory. Locals decide based on the preparation required (barista-made coffee may warrant a tip, a bottle of soda less so).

Driving It is illegal to drive under the influence of anything (alcohol, marijuana) or to carry open containers. When wine tasting, have a designated driver and keep any open bottles in the trunk.

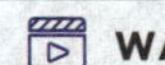

WATCH

PICTORIAL PRESS LTD/ALAMY

Vertigo (Alfred Hitchcock; 1958) The famous noir thriller set in San Francisco, starring James Stewart and Kim Novak.

LA Confidential (Curtis Hanson; 1997) Neo-noir tale of corruption and murder in 1950s LA.

Boyz n the Hood (John Singleton; 1991) Groundbreaking coming-of-age story set in LA's South Central.

Milk (Gus Van Sant; 2008) The biopic of Harvey Milk, the first openly gay man to hold a major US political office.

La La Land (Damien Chazelle; 2016; pictured) The highs, lows and what-ifs of striving in LA; a musical romance served sparkling but bittersweet.

LISTEN

American Beauty (Grateful Dead; 1970) Here's your road trip soundtrack: soulful folk-rock that sounds like sunshine and counterculture defiance.

All Eyez on Me (2Pac; 1996) Tupac Shakur's last album features the song 'California Love' and West Coast stars like Dr Dre and Snoop Dogg.

I've Got a Tiger by the Tail (Buck Owens; 1965) The Bakersfield Sound put the 'western' in country and western, along with performers like Merle Haggard.

Live at Winterland 1978 (Avengers; 1978) Gloriously raw and super-catchy punk rock recorded live as this legendary Bay Area punk band supported the Sex Pistols.

MUSTARD_ASSETS/SHUTTERSTOCK

Burrito

THE FOOD SCENE

California cuisine is a team effort that changes with every season – and it has changed the way the world eats.

As you graze the Golden State, you'll often want to compliment the chef – and they will pass it on to the staff, local farmers, fishers, winemakers and artisanal food producers who make their menu possible. 'Let the ingredients speak for themselves!' is the rallying cry of California cuisine. Most types of America's fruit and vegetables are grown here and you get the pick of the crop year-round. With fruit, vegetables, meat and seafood this fresh, heavy sauces and fussy garnishes aren't required to make meals memorable.

California cooking also reflects the contributions of some of the world's most celebrated food cultures. The state's deep Mexican and Latin American heritage means burritos regularly outshine burgers. And California has some of the best Asian cuisine available outside Asia. The California stew is also peppered with Mediterranean traditions – where the climate and soil are similar to California's – and Afro-Caribbean and southern soul cooking. Thus fusion is not a fad but second nature in California, where international flair blends beautifully with seasonal, local ingredients.

Global Soul Food

California belonged to Mexico before it became a US state in 1850, and around 40% of the population today is Latinx. It's no surprise, then, that Mexican classics remain go-to comfort foods, and upscale restaurants add novel twists to staple tamales and tacos. This blending of local produce

Best California Dishes

CALIFORNIA BURRITO
Mega-meal bursting out of a giant flour tortilla.

DUNGENESS CRAB
November-to-June favorite, eaten whole and in sandwiches.

SALMON
Appearing on menus statewide, freshly caught and prepared in myriad ways.

ARTICHOKES
Giant and delicious in springtime from farms around Castroville.

and international cuisines defines California's great culinary advantage: an experimental attitude toward food.

Even in its Wild West days when gold-rush miners and Chinese workers lived side by side, necessity and proximity meant everyone ate adventurously and cross-culturally, pairing whiskey and wine with tamales and Chinese noodles. Check out Tanya Holland's *California Soul: Recipes from a Culinary Journey West.*

Unbeatable Brunches

Weekend brunch is pure delight: you can savor farm-to-table food with splashes of champagne, surrounded by locals basking in their weekend downtime. Restaurants in California dominate US-wide brunch rankings and the combination of sunny patios and abundant local produce makes coastal cities like LA, San Francisco and San Diego leaders of the pack. Expect to put your name down and wait for a spot; join the crowd of folks outside wearing shades to conceal last night's excess. Ready to order? You can't go wrong with avocado toast, ricotta or yogurt pancakes, and *chilaquiles* (spicy eggs on tortillas).

Food Trucks

If fine dining isn't your style, local food truck fleets are standing by across the state. Food trucks serve up everything from *tacos al pastor* (marinated pork) or Indian curry-and-naan wraps to Chinese buns packed with roast duck and fresh mango. Come prepared with cash and sunblock: some trucks don't accept plastic cards, and lines can be long at peak hours. You'll often find batches of food trucks grouped together – sometimes in organized food parks – or single purveyors in habitual spots, like a supermarket parking lot. Search for 'food truck' and your location on Google Maps and check dedicated food websites such as

ROBERT HOLMES/GETTY IMAGES

Ice cream stand, Gilroy Garlic Festival (p290)

FOOD & WINE FESTIVALS

San Francisco Restaurant Week *(sfrestaurantweek.com)* Snap up sweet deals on special menus from top chefs.

Wine & Food Affair (p223) Tour over 100 Sonoma County wineries in November; a specialty dish is paired with their vintages.

California Avocado Festival *(carpinteriaca.gov/visitor-info/california-avocado-festival/)* Guacamole for days in Santa Barbara County in early October.

Sonoma Harvest Fair (p209) In October, get your spittoon ready for the country's biggest wine-tasting festival.

Paso Wine Fest (p321) A fiesta of good grapes and fine living at this mid-May event in Paso Robles.

Gilroy Garlic Festival (p290) Guzzle enough garlic to fend off a legion of vampires at this merry-making event.

Gravenstein Apple Fair (p205) Tuck into pies galore in Sonoma County in mid-August.

FORAGED FOOD
From wild chanterelles found beneath California oaks to hillside miner's lettuce.

OYSTERS
From Hog Island Kumamoto in Tomales Bay to Grassy Bar in Morro Bay.

CIOPPINO
Iconic San Francisco fish stew in a rich tomato broth.

CALIFORNIA ROLL
Sushi roll invented in 1960s LA using crab, avocado and cucumber.

BEST FARMERS MARKETS

San Luis Obispo's Farmers Market (p326) Thursday nights are filled with late-night eats and musical revelry.

Healdsburg Saturday Farmers Market (p223) A bounty of local produce in the heart of wine country, plus cooking demos and live music.

Santa Monica Farmers Markets (p423) A superabundance of local fruit, flowers and vegetables every Wednesday, plus a low-key local market scene on Saturday.

Santa Barbara Certified Farmers Market (p350) Brimming with local flowers, herbs and crunchy-fresh veggies every Saturday.

Ferry Plaza Farmers Market (p64) Step outside the gourmet-food-filled SF Ferry Building for the thrice-weekly market with more than 100 vendors.

Fort Mason Center Farmers Market (p49) Fifty farm stands and ready-made food vendors every Sunday, plus a Friday night market with food trucks.

eater.com. For mouthwatering reviews of legendary Cal-Mex street food, check out LA Taco *(lataco.com)*.

Wines & Cocktails

California's traditions of wine, beer and snazzy cocktails are continually reinvented by creative winemakers and micro-distillers – and, for the morning after, specialty coffee roasters come in mighty handy.

Strong drinks explain a lot about California. Mission vineyards first planted in the 18th century gave Californians a taste for wine. The mid-19th-century gold rush also played a role. Thirsty prospectors brought a rush on the bar, and by 1850 San Francisco had 500 saloons selling hooch to prospectors who'd struck it rich – or didn't.

After riding out the scourge of parasitic phylloxera, which destroyed vines and many wine-makers' livelihoods, Californian wine was primed for the big time – until Prohibition, that is. Broken-hearted wine makers were forced to heave their vines from the soil (or pretend they were creating 'sacramental wine'). Meanwhile rum-runners made a killing smuggling alcohol from 'Rum Row' on the coast to speakeasies across California and beyond.

ASHLEY SPINALE/SHUTTERSTOCK

Peppers, Fort Mason Center Farmers Market (p49)

When Prohibition was finally repealed in 1933, it unbottled California's pent-up wine-making creativity. The variety of grapes and wine production techniques exploded, resulting in the drops California is known for today, like chardonnay, cabernet sauvignon, merlot and pinot noir. The Prohibition era had also cultivated a decadently illicit bar culture – and fruity cocktail recipes to cover up the metallic taste of bathtub hooch – which you can still enjoy by ordering a 'Bee's Knees' cocktail at one of many 19th-century saloons across the state.

VEGAN & VEGETARIAN

Whether you credit California's environmentalism and local vegetables – or high-profile LA vegans – the Golden State is a satisfying destination for vegetarian and vegan diners. Unless you stumble into specialty restaurants that focus on steak or seafood, you won't have to hunt far for meat-free options. Entirely plant-based choices are increasing, too – especially in LA, SF and along the North Coast. Many options showcase California's produce while others lean into Mexican, Vietnamese, Indian and other veg-friendly cuisines. Locate vegetarian and vegan restaurants and health-food stores at *happycow.net*.

Specialties

Food Truck Hits

Dim sum Chinese small plates and dumplings.
Kalbi Korean flavor-bursting beef short ribs, marinated and grilled.
Jollof rice Spicy West African rice.
Cuitlacoche Corn smut, a sort of mold – a delicacy the world over.
Korean tacos Grilled, marinated beef and spicy pickled kimchi.
Pho Vietnamese noodle soup.
Grilled fish tacos Ideally hauled-from-the-pier fresh.
Birria Meat stew from Jalisco, usually using goat.
Sweet treats Including churros (sweet Mexican fried dough) or fresh-fruit hand pies.

Superb Seafood

Scoma's (p123) Pier-to-plate crab cakes, shrimp Louie salad and *cioppino* at an SF institution.
Fog Harbor Fish House (p56) Sustainable seafood classics simply prepared, from Dungeness crab to petrale sole.
Phil's Fish Market (p299) Slurp-worthy *cioppino* and saucy Sicilian salmon at a local legend near Monterey.
Spud Point Crab Company (p212) Head to Bodega Bay for crab sandwiches and outstanding chowder right on the water.
Marshall Store (p130) Fresh oysters from a family farm. Slurp au naturel with a twist of lemon or guzzle 'em grilled.
Jack's Seafood (p260) Bay views amplify the experience of just-harvested oysters and halibut burgers on Eureka's boardwalk.

Jollof rice

MEALS OF A LIFETIME

Benu (p66) Splash out on brilliant wine-paired tasting menus that look like minimalist art in San Francisco.
SingleThread (p222) Be dazzled at this celebrated restaurant in Healdsburg where food masquerades as nature.
San Ho Won (p97) Decadent Korean flavors meet California produce at this minimalist dining room in San Francisco.
Chez Panisse (p142) Where it all started – worship at the temple of Alice Waters in Berkeley.
Mister Jiu's (p69) Wonderfully innovative Chinese cuisine and a charming banquet-hall ambience in SF.
Providence (p384) Seafood washes elegantly ashore with flavors from Asia and the Med on beautiful LA plates.
Harbor House Inn (p241) A double Michelin-starred restaurant in the tiny town of Elk featuring hyper-local fare from nearby farms and shores.

THE YEAR IN FOOD

SPRING

When the sun comes out, farmers markets fill city streets with salad makings, fish-taco (pictured) trucks flock to California beaches and lines bend around the block for organic artisanal ice cream studded with just-picked berries.

SUMMER

Beach barbecues are better with wild coho salmon, corn on the cob (pictured) fresh salsa made with heirloom tomatoes and grilled peaches topped with edible lavender flowers.

FALL

Experience your first crush at harvest in wine country, get lost in corn mazes and pumpkin patches (pictured), and give thanks for California's bounty of fresh-fruit pies.

WINTER

Make the most of long winter nights with Dungeness crab (pictured), oysters and sand dabs. Celebrate Lunar New Year with lucky mandarins, and let mezcal-spiked craft cocktails warm you.

TOP: LOSANGELA/SHUTTERSTOCK; FROM LEFT: ADAM CALAITZIS/SHUTTERSTOCK, WWW.EDDIE-HERNANDEZ.COM/SHUTTERSTOCK, BTEIMAGES/SHUTTERSTOCK, ZIGZAG MOUNTAIN ART/SHUTTERSTOCK

FROM LEFT: OLIVERDELAHAYE/SHUTTERSTOCK, COREY JENKINS/GETTY IMAGES

Surfers, Santa Cruz (p284)

THE OUTDOORS

Surfing and beach-hopping are only part of the story. From hiking among wildflowers in spring to witnessing whale migrations in winter, California's coast has exhilarating activities all year round.

California's coast is wild, from its wave-slapped beaches to mountainous parks. Pick your lane: level walking trails and wheelchair-accessible whale-watching tours are ideal for mixed-ability groups, oceanside cycling trails are delightful for families, and there are enough scree-scrambling hikes to set even adrenaline junkies' pulses thundering. Wildlife will accompany every escapade. In the space of a day you can spot seals and sea lions on a cliffside hike, kayak beneath squadrons of seabirds and spy on silvery sardine shoals through a snorkeling mask.

Swimming & Surfing

If your California dream vacation means bronzing on the beach and paddling in the Pacific, head directly to Southern California. With miles of wide, sandy beaches between Santa Barbara and San Diego, you can be living the dream at least six months of the year. Ocean temperatures are tolerable by May or June, peaking in July and August. The rest of the year, use a wetsuit.

Central and northern California beaches are blustery and dramatic, with high swells crashing into rocky bluffs – they're better for walking and wildlife-watching than casual swimming. Their reliable, often colossal, waves are chased by highly experienced surfers, who head to the offshore break Mavericks near Half Moon Bay for waves that crest as high as 25ft.

If you've never set foot on a board, California's your chance. Surfing is an obsession

Adrenaline Rushes

BRACING SURF
Ride the wild and often icy swell in **Point Arena** (p242) and **Fort Bragg** (p242).

WATCHING WHALES
Spot gray, blue, humpback and sperm whales from viewpoints like the **Pigeon Point Light Station** (p161) or on a thrilling boat tour from **Monterey** (p296) or **Santa Cruz** (p289).

KITEBOARDING & WINDSURFING
Let the wind lift you at **Crissy Field** (p53) in San Francisco or **Mission Bay** (p492) in San Diego.

FAMILY ADVENTURES

Race the kids by scrambling up sand dunes and careening down in sleds at **LA's beaches** (p423).

Stroll 100ft high above the forest floor on the tree-slung bridges at **Sequoia Park Zoo's Sky Walk** (p261) – enjoy the sweet birdsong!

Kayak with otters and dive-bombing seabirds in **Moss Landing** (p292) or in the sheltered harbor of **Santa Barbara** (p348).

Compete with the kids at a group surf lesson in the gentle waves around **Santa Barbara** (p348) or **Huntington Beach** (p462).

Take the gang cycling along the seal-speckled shoreline of **Monterey** (p294) and watch for distant dolphins and whales.

Saddle up and join a horse-riding tour through flower-sprinkled meadows at the Ventura River Preserve near **Ojai** (p370).

up and down the coast, particularly in Santa Cruz, Orange County and San Diego, which happen to be great places to learn.

Easy Strolls & Epic Hikes

This coast was made for walking, whether you prefer ambling along a pier at sunset or hoofing it uphill for the reward of a dreamy panorama of the fog-drenched horizon. It's a choose-your-own-adventure playground where there's no need to commit to mammoth hiking trails: coastal reserves and parks almost always have a level loop trail or scenic lookout that's less than a mile from the trailhead. Some destinations, like Big Sur (p306), are ideal for 'drive and hike' trips where you drive along the coast from one short lookout trail to another.

More ambitious trails are abundant. Walk among the world's tallest trees in Redwood National & State Parks (p266) or tackle a section of the California Coastal Trail *(californiacoastaltrail.org)*, a network of public trails weaving along California's coast.

ACTION AREAS

For the best outdoor spots and routes, see the map on p38.

Mountain biking, San Luis Obispo (p326)

Cycling & Mountain Biking

Coastal California has outstanding cycling terrain including leisurely spins along beach boardwalks, adrenaline-fueled mountain rides and multiday road-cycling tours. Even heavily trafficked urban areas may have good cycling routes, especially in SoCal, like the scenic route along LA's beachside South Bay Bicycle Trail. Northern and central coast cities like San Francisco and Santa Cruz have bike-share schemes for urban pedaling and scenic routes like 17-Mile Drive (p298) are even better on two wheels.

The cycling season runs year-round in most coastal areas, although fog may rob you of views in winter and during 'May gray' and 'June gloom.' Avoid the North Coast and the mountains during winter (too much rain and snow at higher elevations) and inland SoCal in summer (too dang hot).

DIVING & SNORKELING
Along the coast, rocky reefs and kelp beds teem with sea creatures like those at **Channel Islands National Park** (p368).

KAYAKING & CANOEING
Paddle Sonoma County's meandering **Russian River** (p215) as it flows by vineyards and redwoods out to the ocean.

MOUNTAINOUS HIKES
Scale Bay Area peaks like **Mt Tam** (p127) and **Mt Diablo** (p139), or hit the trails in hilly **Big Sur** (p306).

CAVING
Scramble through talus caves and along craggy ridges in dramatic **Pinnacles National Park** (p305).

ACTION AREAS

Where to find Coastal California's best outdoor activities.

Walking/Hiking

1. Marin Headlands (p124)
2. Big Sur (p306)
3. Redwood National & State Parks (p266)
4. Lost Coast Trail (p254)
5. Pinnacles National Park (p305)
6. Point Reyes National Seashore (p128)
7. Lake Calavera Preserve (p500)

Animals/Wildlife

1. Monterey Bay (p298)
2. Santa Barbara Channel (p368)
3. Año Nuevo State Park (p161)
4. Point Lobos State Natural Reserve (p302)
5. Arcata Marsh & Wildlife Sanctuary (p365)
6. San Simeon (p315)

Surfing
1 La Jolla (p494)
2 Santa Cruz (p288)
3 Malibu (p423)
4 Newport Beach (p458)
5 Carpinteria (p353)
Cycling
1 Napa Valley (p175)
2 Golden Gate Bridge (p56)
3 Santa Barbara (p351)
4 Pacific Grove (p298)
5 Mt Tamalpais State Park (p127)
Snorkelling/Diving
1 La Jolla (p494)
2 Crystal Cove State Conservation Area (p461)
3 Monterey Bay (p298)
4 Channel Islands National Park (p369)
5 Point Lobos State Natural Reserve (p302)
0 200 km
0 100 miles
N
Santa Cruz
Monterey
Big Sur
Diablo Range
Fresno
Kings Canyon National Park
Sequoia National Park
Mt Williamson (14,380ft)
Mt Whitney (14,505ft)
Death Valley
Death Valley National Park
NEVADA
ARIZONA
Paso Robles
Cambria
Cayucos
Morro Bay
San Luis Obispo
Bakersfield
Mojave
Mojave National Preserve
Barstow
Needles
Santa Barbara
CHANNEL ISLANDS
Channel Islands National Park
Malibu
Santa Monica
Pasadena
Los Angeles
Newport Beach
Laguna Beach
Palm Springs
Indio
Blythe
Salton Sea
Imperial Valley
Colorado Desert
CATALINA ISLAND
SAN CLEMENTE ISLAND
PACIFIC OCEAN
Oceanside
La Jolla
San Diego
Tijuana
Mexicali
Yuma
MEXICO

COASTAL CALIFORNIA

THE GUIDE

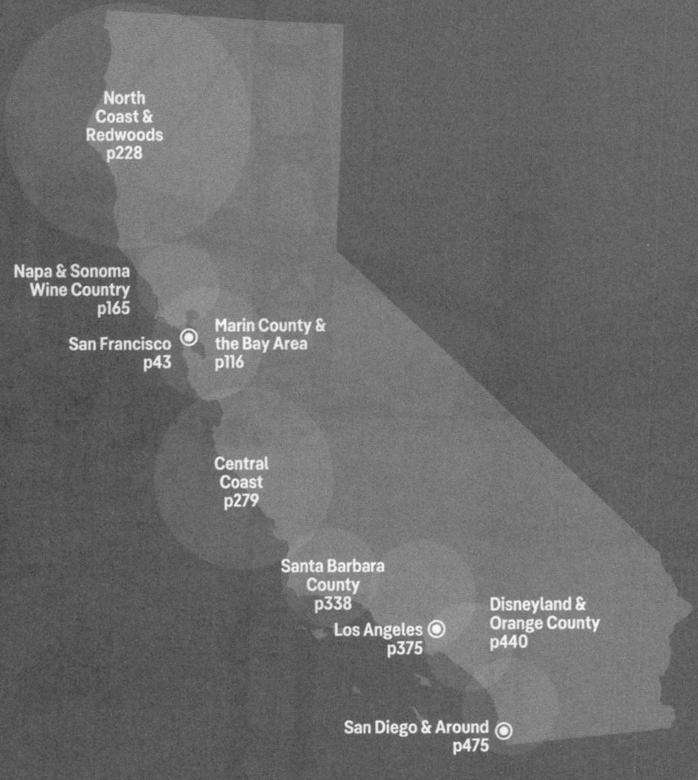

Chapters in this section are organised by hubs and their surrounding areas. We see the hub as your base in the destination, where you'll find unique experiences, local insights, insider tips and expert recommendations. It's also your gateway to the surrounding area, where you'll see what and how much you can do from there.

Muir Woods National Monument (p126)
GILBERTO MESQUITA/SHUTTERSTOCK

For places to stay in San Francisco, see p114

CANADASTOCK/SHUTTERSTOCK

Above: Golden Gate Bridge (p56); Right: the Castro (p101)

THE MAIN AREAS

PRESIDIO, MARINA & FISHERMAN'S WHARF
Beyond the iconic bridge, expect the unexpected. p48

DOWNTOWN, CIVIC CENTER & SOMA
Big buildings, big changes. p58

CHINATOWN & NORTH BEACH
Come for dinner, stay for stories. p67

NOB HILL & RUSSIAN HILL
Views from such great heights. p75

JAPANTOWN, FILLMORE & PACIFIC HEIGHTS
Postcard-perfect Victorians, waving kitties, music legends. p79

Researched by
Alison Bing

San Francisco

CALLING ALL FREE SPIRITS HOME

No matter what's going on in the world, know that flowers are blooming year-round along alleyways named after radical poets – if San Francisco didn't exist, you'd have to make it up.

Adventurous food, outrageous entertainment, impossible ideas: your time in San Francisco may seem like a wild dream, except that it's been this way from the start. Oysters and tamales topped the menu in this Mexico-run Ohlone settlement in 1848 – but a year and some gold nuggets later, Champagne and chow mein were served by the bucketload. Gold found in nearby Sierra foothills turned a sleepy 800-person village into a port city of 100,000 freewheeling prospectors, con artists, political dissidents, hard workers and big dreamers from across the globe.

Fast-forward through 175 years, and you'll find San Francisco in another boom/bust cycle – yet its free spirits endure. The city and its grand ambitions came crashing down in the 1906 earthquake and fire – but theater troupes and opera divas performed for free amid the ruins, bringing the city back to its feet and establishing SF's enduring tradition of free public shows. During WWII, soldiers accused of insubordination and homosexuality were dismissed in San Francisco, as though that would teach them a lesson. Instead the gay rights movement took root and SF's counterculture bloomed, inspiring West Coast jazz and Beat poetry. The Central Intelligence Agency tested LSD on local volunteers, who slipped it into punch at SF's 1966 Trips Festival – and the psychedelic '60s took off. The Summer of Love brought free food, love and music to the Haight. The Castro became a symbol of gay liberation, electing Harvey Milk as California's first out gay official. Amid incalculable losses from HIV/AIDS in the 1980 and '90s, San Franciscans wiped their tears and got to work, setting global standards for pandemic prevention and compassionate care.

As in the early days, free spirits from around the globe fit right in here – as the world's first sanctuary city since 1989, San Francisco welcomes all. This is the place to entertain wild ideas. Here, in the proving grounds for the internet, organic cuisine, free speech, biotech, LGBTQ+ rights and self-driving cars, nothing is impossible. So come on in: you're just in time for San Francisco's next act, and it's your turn on stage.

EDDIE-HERNANDEZ.COM/SHUTTERSTOCK

THE HAIGHT & HAYES VALLEY
San Francisco's hippie hotspot. **p85**

MISSION, DOGPATCH & POTRERO
Sunshine, murals, books & flavors galore. **p92**

THE CASTRO
Welcome to the gayborhood! **p101**

GOLDEN GATE PARK & THE AVENUES
SF's wild stretch of imagination. **p105**

Find Your Way

Walking and strutting are the preferred modes of transport in this 7x7-mile city – but there are hills to consider. Vintage cable cars summit the steep slopes between downtown and the northern waterfront, and streetcars and buses connect downtown to neighborhoods and beaches.

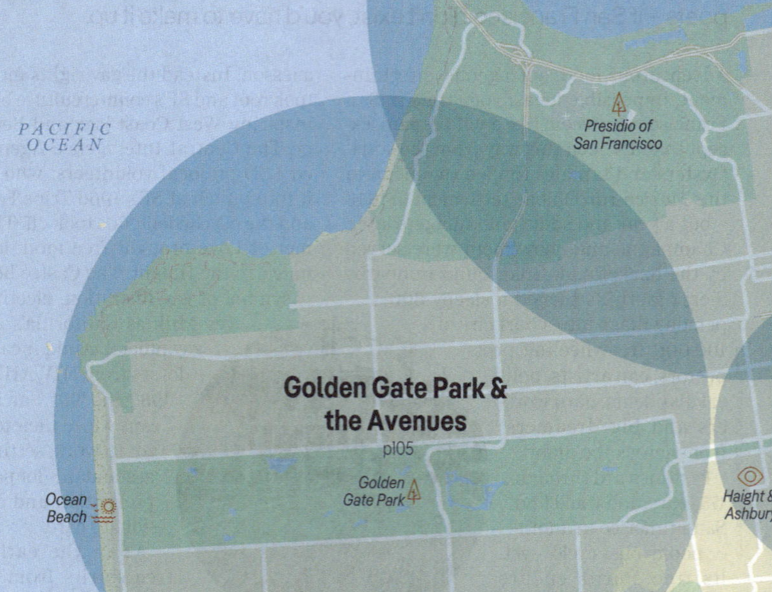

FROM THE AIRPORT

Bay Area Rapid Transit trains get you downtown in 30 minutes *(BART; bart.gov; fare $11.15)*, departing from SFO's International Terminal. Rideshare services including Lyft and Uber depart from Level 5 of the domestic parking garage (*$40–60*). Taxis depart outside baggage claim (*$55–65*).

RIDESHARE & ROBOTAXIS

SF-invented rideshare services Lyft and Uber are widely used – expect waits and/or premium pricing during peak-use times. Robotaxi service is now available in SF from Waymo *(waymo.com)*, aka Google's self-driving car fleet. To try it, download the Waymo One app.

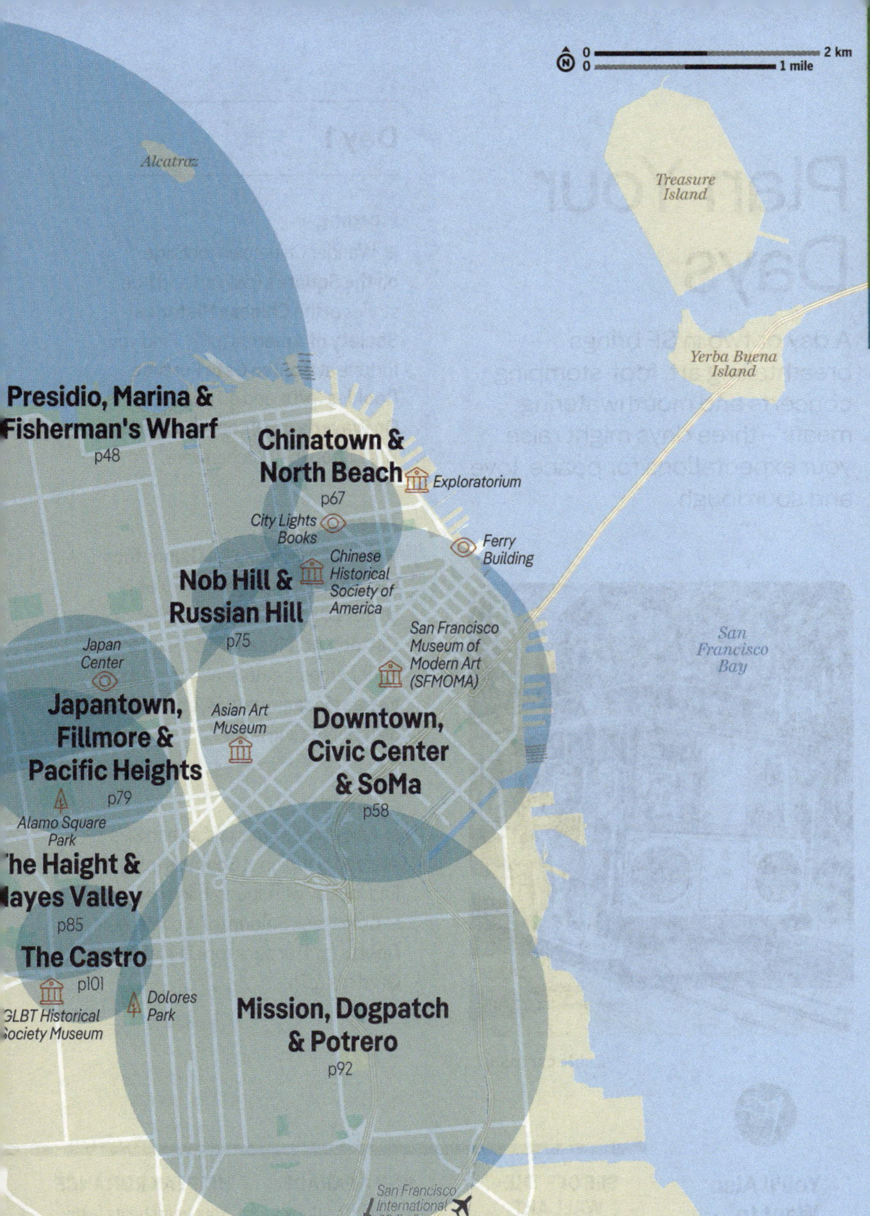

0 2 km
0 1 mile

Alcatraz
Treasure Island
Yerba Buena Island
San Francisco Bay

Presidio, Marina & Fisherman's Wharf
p48

Chinatown & North Beach
p67

Exploratorium
City Lights Books
Ferry Building
Chinese Historical Society of America

Nob Hill & Russian Hill
p75

San Francisco Museum of Modern Art (SFMOMA)
Japan Center

Japantown, Fillmore & Pacific Heights
p79

Asian Art Museum

Downtown, Civic Center & SoMa
p58

Alamo Square Park

The Haight & Hayes Valley
p85

The Castro
p101

GLBT Historical Society Museum
Dolores Park

Mission, Dogpatch & Potrero
p92

San Francisco International (10.5mi)

CABLE CARS & MUNI

San Francisco cable cars are total joyrides – grab the wooden bench or hang onto creaking leather straps and brace for downhill slides. Single rides cost $9, or get a Muni Visitor Passport *(sfmta.com; 1-/3-/4-day pass $15/35/47)*. Muni bus, streetcar and metro fares are $3/2.85 *(cash/Clipper card)*.

WALK

Limber up: San Francisco has 40+ hills to summit, with stairway hikes leading to vista points and Golden Gate Bridge views. The Bay waterfront is flat and scenic from Dogpatch to Crissy Field, and Golden Gate Park stretches over 50 blocks to Ocean Beach.

Plan Your Days

A day or two in SF brings breathtaking art, foot-stomping concerts and mouthwatering meals – three days might raise your expectations for peace, love and sourdough.

SERGII FIGURNYI/SHUTTERSTOCK

Cable car (p58)

Day 1

Morning

● Wander Chinatown for **Edge on the Square**'s (p69) art and true stories at the **Chinese Historical Society of America** (p69). Find your fortune at **Golden Gate Fortune Cookies** (p70), and go gourmet with **On Waverly** (p70) cookbooks and **Wok Shop** (p71) kitchenware.

Afternoon

● Sample dumplings at **Osmanthus Dim Sum Lounge** (p69), then cable car to Fisherman's Wharf to meet **Cartoon Art Museum** (p54) comic-book heroes, battle Space Invaders at **Musée Mécanique** (p54) and see **Pier 39** (p55) sea lions.

Evening

● Enjoy waterfront sunsets and SF's seafood cioppino at **Scoma's** (p55). End the day with spur-rattling cocktails at **Comstock Saloon** (p71), comedy at **Cobb's** (p74) or punk rock at **Mabuhay Gardens** (p71).

You'll Also Want to ...

Indulge your curiosity and follow your bliss where it leads. When you find inspiration, act on it: be part of the art, parade, romance, flavor, drama, culture and future.

SEE OFF-THE-WALL ART

Art explodes on mural-covered Mission streets – and you complete the art at **Asian Art Museum's** (p63) immersive installations, **Edge on the Square**'s (p69) participatory shows and **Minnesota Street Project** (p99) gallery openings.

JOIN A PARADE

San Francisco throws extravagant parades to celebrate people being exactly who they are – proud of their immigrant roots, chosen families and civil rights achievements – from **Chinese New Year** (p71) parades to month-long **Pride** celebrations.

HIT PEAK ROMANCE

Your heart beats faster, your knees go weak, your palms get sweaty – either this is true love or you're climbing one of San Francisco's 40-odd hills. Pause to admire the scenery from **garden-lined stairways** (p78) to the sparkling bay.

Day 2

● Get experimental at the **Exploratorium** (p57), where hands-on exhibits dare you to stop time, sculpt fog and dive headfirst into total darkness in the Tactile Dome.

Afternoon

● Go gourmet by the bay at SF's local food showcase: the **Ferry Building** (p64). Explore cutting-edge, multimedia art at **SFMOMA** (p59), or glimpse global art treasures at the **Asian Art Museum** (p63).

Evening

● Get the star-chef treatment with **Benu**'s (p66) multicourse feasts or **Rich Table**'s (p91) seasonal sensations. Cheer for virtuosos at world-renowned **SFJAZZ** (p90), **San Francisco Opera** (p62) or **San Francisco Symphony** (p62). Afterward, head to SoMa clubs to see where the night leads.

Day 3

Morning

● Stroll **Golden Gate Park** (p108), where wonders never cease at the **de Young Museum** (p109). Hang out with penguins at the **California Academy of Sciences** (p109) or beachcomb along **Ocean Beach** (p113).

Afternoon

● Enjoy reinvented Chinese American classics at **Mamahuhu** (p111), then head to the Mission for murals and galleries, disco-naps in **Dolores Park** (p92) and Calle 24's bookstores and **cafes** (p98).

Evening

● Get the definitive Mission burrito at **La Taqueria** (p96). Don't miss showtime at **Chan National Queer Arts Center** (p93), **Roxie Cinema** (p97) or **Oasis** (p66). Follow rainbow-lit sidewalks to Castro clubs or toast to new friends at legendary Mission bars.

FOLLOW YOUR TASTEBUDS

With 46 global cuisines packed into 46 square miles, San Francisco is like a greatest-hits compilation with no skips. SF holds the most Michelin stars of any US city; you might bump into the next great chef at the **Ferry Building** (p64).

HIT A DRAG SHOW

SF drag is outlandishly original at **Oasis** (p66), too wild for TV at **The Stud** (p66) and completely unpredictable at **Aunt Charlie's** (p65). Drag royals keep winning hearts and civil rights victories with false lashes and true courage.

GLIMPSE THE FUTURE

You can see ahead of the curve at **Gray Area** (p93) cyberpunk fests, **Cartoon Art Museum** (p54) sci-fi comic shows and **SFMOMA** (p59)'s futuristic installation art – and join **Exploratorium** (p57) experiments in progress.

DIVE INTO UNDERGROUND CULTURE

Some best discoveries are misleadingly named – ahem, **Free Gold Watch** (p89) and **House of Seiko** (p99) – and smartphones are discouraged at hotspots like **Faight Collective** (p90) and **Noc Noc** (p90).

Presidio, Marina & Fisherman's Wharf

BEYOND THE ICONIC BRIDGE, EXPECT THE UNEXPECTED

GETTING AROUND

The best way to see Fisherman's Wharf and Presidio nature trails is at your own pace, stopping for entertainment and photos. SF's northern waterfront is flat but vast, so walking shoes and buses are handy. Muni buses connect the Wharf, Marina and Presidio with points beyond, Golden Gate Transit crosses the bridge and Presidio GO shuttles cover Presidio parks. Download maps and schedules – especially if you're headed to the Presidio, where cell signal is variable. You can also cover the waterfront on rental bikes – but book ahead on weekends.

Make a grand entrance to San Francisco through the Golden Gate Bridge and follow the waterfront to nature hikes, immersive art, comic-book heroes and a WWII submarine. For centuries, Golden Gate Strait was the main entrance to San Francisco for new arrivals – note the shipwrecks dotting its shores. Luckily, the Golden Gate Bridge now offers easier entry and spectacular views besides. Enter the Presidio military base that's now a coastal preserve to spot only-in-SF sights: rare shorebirds on a former airstrip, priceless sculptures hidden in the woods and goosebumps galore on the clothing-optional end of blustery Baker Beach. To the west, the Marina has chic boutiques on a former cow pasture, deco date-night restaurants built atop old fairgrounds and a waterfront fort creatively repurposed for art. At Fisherman's Wharf, you'll meet local characters: lazy sea lions, legendary cartoonists, pinball wizards, scientific geniuses and actual fisherfolk.

R&R in the Presidio

Go play in an ex-army outpost

Since the Presidio has retired from military duty, civilians can throw strikes at the post's bowling alley, **Presidio Bowl** *(presidiobowl.com; per lane weekdays/weekends from $55/75; shoe rental $7.50)*, or bounce around **House of Air** *(houseofair.com; per hour adult/child $20/28)*, a hangar lined with trampolines. The former PX (provisions warehouse) is a **Sports Basement** *(sportsbasement.com)* stocking bikes and sporting equipment to rent, buy or trade. Presidio's **Outpost Playground** is wildly popular for nature-themed play structures and nearby food trucks.

LYNN FRIEDMAN/SHUTTERSTOCK

Fort Mason Center

Make Art, Not War, at Fort Mason

Find artistic inspiration in military storehouses

During WWII, **Fort Mason Center** shipped out 23 million tons of supplies - now it supplies creative inspiration to 1.4 million visitors annually. Dockside nonprofit **SF Camerawork** *(sfcamerawork.org; free)* has showcased next-wave photographers since 1974, while **Haines Gallery** *(hainesgallery.com; free)* represents leading global contemporary artists like Ai Weiwei, and **Arion Press** *(arionpress.com; free)* showcases letterpress art-book collaborations. Dockside Herbst Pavilion's arsenal of events includes **FOG Design+Art** *(fogfair.com; admission $35-40)* in winter, **San Francisco Art Fair** in spring, and **Renegade Craft Fair** and **West Coast Craft Fair** *(westcoastcraft.com; free)* in both summer and fall. Capture inspiration with art and craft supplies from well-stocked **Flax Art & Design**. It also hosts a weekly **farmers market** *(fortmason.org/event/fort-mason-center-farmers-market/)*.

Showtime in Waterfront Warehouses

Watch talents launch in Fort Mason

Pushing boundaries since 1967, **Magic Theatre** *(magictheatre.org; tickets $35-75)* stages breakthrough works like *Jerry Garcia in the Lower Mission,* plus freeform jazz services for

continued on p54

TOP TIP

Plan shoes and outfits strategically - coastal weather shifts suddenly and distances are further than they seem on maps. Dress in layers: windbreaker for Golden Gate Bridge hikes, cozy sweater for panoramic Presidio picnics and nice (but washable) shirt for seafood feasts at the Wharf or Marina.

EATING IN THE PRESIDIO & MARINA: DREAM DINNER DATES

Dalida: *Top Chef* powerhouse Laura Ozyilmaz brings Med flavors to the Bay, like stuffed mussels and Yemeni lamb stew. *11.30-2pm & 5-9pm Fri-Wed, 11am-2pm Thu* $$

Atelier Crenn: Global superstar chef Dominique Crenn creates edible art inspired by SF's seafaring legends and her own Sonoma farmstead. *5-9pm Tue-Sat* $$$

A16: How romantic: James Beard Award–winning wood-fired pizzas, house-cured salami and Italian wine. *5-9pm Mon-Thu, noon-9.30pm Fri-Sun* $$

Greens: Women chefs commandeer Fort Mason's mess hall, inventing flavor-bomb vegetarian dishes with organic ingredients since 1979. *11.30am-2.30pm & 5-9pm Tue-Sun* $$

PRESIDIO, MARINA & FISHERMAN'S WHARF

Golden Gate
San Francisco Bay
Golden Gate Bridge
Crissy Field
PACIFIC OCEAN
US Hwy 101
Lincoln Blvd
Long Ave
Old Mason St
Presidio Pkwy
Presidio Pet Cemetery
San Francisco National Military Cemetery
Ralston Ave
Kobbe Ave
State Hwy 1
Presidio of San Francisco
PRESIDIO
MAIN POST
Infantry Tce
Girard Rd
Edie Rd
Lombard St
Macarthur Ave
Arguello Blvd
Washington Blvd
Portola St
Presidio Blvd
Park Blvd
Presidio Golf Course
Pacific Ave
Jackson St

HIGHLIGHTS

1 Crissy Field
2 Golden Gate Bridge
3 Presidio of San Francisco

SIGHTS

4 Aquarium of the Bay
5 Arion Press
6 Baker Beach
7 Cartoon Art Museum
8 East Beach
9 FOG Design+Art
10 Fort Mason Center
11 Fort Point
12 Haines Gallery
13 Inspiration Point
14 Military Intelligence Service Historic Learning Center
15 Pier 39
16 Presidio Officers' Club
17 Renegade Craft Fair
18 San Francisco Art Fair
19 San Francisco Carousel
20 SF Camerawork
21 Spire
22 Tunnel Tops
23 West Coast Craft

ACTIVITIES

24 Adventure Cat
25 Batteries to Bluffs Trail
26 Ecology Trail
27 House of Air
28 Musée Mécanique
29 Oceanic Society Expeditions
30 Outpost Playground
31 Presidio Bowl
32 Red & White Fleet
33 Sports Basement

SLEEPING

34 Argonaut Hotel
35 HI San Francisco

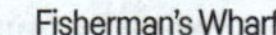

Fisherman's Wharf
36 Hotel del Sol
37 Infinity Hotel
38 Inn at the Presidio
39 Kimpton Alton
40 Lodge at the Presidio
41 Marina Motel
42 Union Street Inn

EATING
43 A16
see 39 Abacá
44 Atelier Crenn
45 Codmother Fish & Chips
46 Dalida
47 Eagle Cafe
48 Fisherman's Wharf Crab Stands
49 Fog Harbor Fish House
50 Greens
51 Palette Tea House
52 Presidio Pop Up
53 Scoma's
54 Surisan
55 Warming Hut

DRINKING & NIGHTLIFE
see 11 Round House Café

ENTERTAINMENT
56 BATS Improv
57 Magic Theatre

SHOPPING
58 Flax Art & Design

INFORMATION
59 Golden Gate Bridge Welcome Center
60 Presidio Visitors Center

OLEG PODZOROV/SHUTTERSTOCK

Baker Beach

TOP EXPERIENCE

The Presidio

Spies, Yoda, Andy Goldsworthy sculptures, Walt Disney drawings: SF's best-kept secrets are revealed along Presidio hiking paths. This retired army base is now a panoramic public park packed with attractions – including sweeping Golden Gate Bridge views previously only seen by top brass and passing commuters.

DON'T MISS

- Tunnel Tops
- Crissy Field
- Fort Point
- Baker Beach
- Andy Goldworthy's *Spire*
- Batteries to Bluffs Trail
- Military Intelligence Service Historic Learning Center

Back to Nature

'Presidio' means fort in Spanish – but in San Francisco, it's a playground. It started in 1776 as a Spanish military post built by conscripted Ohlone people, and was officially retired from military duty in 1996. To the obvious delight of shorebirds, puppies and people, the **Presidio of San Francisco** is now a national park. To allow wildlife to thrive in the park, commuter traffic was rerouted underground – revealing glorious views clear across the bay from driftwood-shaped picnic benches at **Tunnel Tops** park, with the nature-themed **Outpost Playground** downhill.

PRACTICALITIES

Scan this QR code for more information on opening times and entrance passes.

On hot days, race the crowds to **Baker Beach**, the sandy Presidio cove with spectacular views of the Golden Gate framed by wind-sculpted pines – plus nude sunbathing behind the rocks on the clothing-optional, gay-friendly, no-photography-allowed north end. Picnickers and sand-castle architects stick to the sandy south end, near the parking.

Happy Trails

Hiking adventures begin at the **Presidio Visitors Center**, well-supplied with trail maps. For a moderately challenging, inspirational 1.4-mile hike, follow the **Ecology Trail** through redwood groves and spring wildflower meadows to **Inspiration Point** for bird's-eye bay views, then push onward to reach the Presidio's artistic pinnacle: Andy Goldsworthy's **Spire**, made from reclaimed cypress trees. Adventurous hikers take on the 2.7-mile **Batteries to Bluffs Trail**, heading uphill above Baker Beach to splendid Golden Gate Bridge vistas.

Follow San Franciscan regulars to **Crissy Field** to stroll, jog, bike, skate or roll along scenic, flat, wheelchair-accessible paths. The strip where military planes once landed is now a reclaimed tidal marsh, where birders perch on strategically positioned benches. Puppies chase kite-fliers across Crissy Field's grassy lawn, and windsurfers skim bay waters along **East Beach**. Pick up the Bay Trail to reach **Fort Point** (1.6 miles from East Beach) and head over the **Golden Gate Bridge** (p56), or stop at certified-green cafe **Warming Hut** to browse California field guides and warm up with fair-trade coffee.

Military Secrets Revealed

Over two centuries, the Presidio stood armed and ready for invasions that never arrived. At an eye-watering cost of more than $100 million in today's terms, **Fort Point** *(free; 10am-5pm Fri-Sun)* mounted 102 cannons to fight the US Civil War – but Confederate ships never made it this far. **Battery Bluff** guns weren't fired in WWI, and Cold War Nike nuclear missile operations in **Battery Caulfield** were quietly suspended in 1974.

The **Presidio Officers' Club** was long off-limits to civilians – today it houses the **Heritage Gallery** *(free; 11am-4pm Fri-Sun)*, which showcases the Presidio's history as ancestral Ohlone homeland for over 10,000 years and its 250 years of military service for Spain, Mexico and the US. The Presidio's top-secret WWII spycraft school is now the **Military Intelligence Service Historic Learning Center** *(njahs.org/building-640; adult/child $10/free; noon-5pm Sat & Sun)*. Japanese American soldiers lived and trained in this drafty bunkhouse as code-breakers and spies for high-risk WWII intelligence missions, while their families were incarcerated as supposed 'enemy aliens' in accordance with US Executive Order 9066. Fascinating exhibits show how the Japanese American 442nd regiment became the most decorated unit in US history.

GOLDSWORTHY'S NATURAL WONDERS

Above Inspiration Point, you'll spot a natural yet artful formation: **Spire**, Andy Goldsworthy's contemporary sculpture created from 37 reclaimed Presidio cypress trunks. *Spire* was intended to disintegrate, but after it was damaged by fire, San Franciscans volunteered to reinforce it. Follow Lover's Lane Trail past the zig-zagging **Wood Line** and duck into the Officer's Club to view Goldsworthy's **Earth Wall**.

TOP TIPS

- Forgot to pack a picnic? No problem: **Presidio Pop Up** food trucks line the Parade Grounds from 9am to 3pm (to 4.30pm on weekends).
- If you'd rather catch your own lunch, try your luck under the Golden Gate Bridge on Torpedo Wharf. No license is required for fishing here; check posted catch limits. Watch and learn from local anglers, who catch sole and sniggle eels here in season.
- Presidio park rangers tell incredible true stories at 4pm **Tunnel Tops Campfire Talks** *(free)*, introducing legendary locals whose footsteps you're walking in – including indigenous healers, Buffalo Soldiers and Cold War spies.

ROSIE THE RIVETER & FRIENDS

During WWII, women and men came to the SF Bay to serve as shipbuilders. You may recall the poster of muscle-flaunting Rosie the Riveter proclaiming 'We Can Do It' – the model was Bay Area naval worker Naomi Parker Fraley. Bay Area shipbuilders worked long hours to turn the tides of WWII, building an entire ship every day for the duration of the war. Nearly half of all US military cargo ships were built here, plus one in five warships. By the 1950s, Bay Area women were staffing a new local industry: silicon-chip manufacturing.

continued from p49
St John Coltrane Church. **Bay Area Theater Sports**, aka **BATS Improv** *(improv.org; tickets adult/student $25/20)* hosts raucous improvised comedy in a range of styles: madcap musicals, SF rom-coms, B-movie sci-fi. Feeling brave? Book improv workshops online.

Game on at Musée Mécanique

Play vintage games at SF's Wild West arcade

Pier 45's massive boatshed can scarcely contain this collection of 300+ vintage mechanical amusements. For a buck at **Musée Mécanique** *(museemecanique.com; entry free)*, you can battle Space Invaders, get your fortune told by robotic wizards, peep at belly dancers through a vintage Mutoscope or get hypnotized by a Ferris wheel made of toothpicks.

Meet Superheroes at the Cartoon Art Museum

Get up close and personal with comic legends

Funded by Bay Area cartoon legend Charles M Schultz of *Peanuts* fame, the **Cartoon Art Museum** *(cartoonart.org;*

EATING AT THE WHARF: BRUNCH

Abacá: Friends become family over Filipino soul food, like fried chicken and pandan waffles. *7-9am & 5-9pm Mon, Tue, Thu & Fri, 8am-1.30pm & 5-9pm Sat & Sun* **$$**

Palette Tea House: Swanky dim sum – Wagyu potstickers, lobster dumplings – with tea or cocktails. *11.30am-7.30pm Sun-Thu, to 8pm Fri & Sat* **$$**

Eagle Cafe: Brunch with SF perks: crab Benedicts, sourdough French toast and eagle's-eye views over Pier 39. *8am-3pm* **$$**

Surisan: Warm up with Cal-Korean specials – savory *pajun* pancakes with shrimp and bacon, matcha mojitos. *9am-2pm & 5-9pm* **$**

JOSEPH CHRISTOPHER OROPEL/GETTY IMAGES

Pier 39

adult/child $10/4) showcases cartoon classics, including Batman covers, Calvin & Hobbes strips, Edward Gorey's Goth monsters and Trina Robbins' trailblazing feminist comics. At events, mingle with comic legends and local Pixar animators.

Family Fun on Pier 39

Choose your own bayside adventure

Sea lions took over **Pier 39** yacht docks in 1990 and have been making a public display of themselves ever since. Up to 2100 of them lounge here daily *(pier39.com; free)*. Families flock to see them, and for the amusement-park atmosphere without prohibitive entry fees – the antique **San Francisco Carousel** is $6 per ride *(10am-8pm)*. At not-for-profit, Smithsonian-affiliated **Aquarium of the Bay** *(aquariumofthebay.org; adult/child $28/20)*, visit 24,000 aquatic creatures in their habitats – walk through shark tanks, get mesmerized by jellies and join a fish-feeding frenzy.

BEST WAYS TO SAIL AWAY

When the fog lifts and sun shines, only one thing tops waterfront strolls: boating on the bay.

Oceanic Society: Naturalist-led Pacific whale-watching expeditions during migration seasons *(oceanicsociety.org; 7½hr; $300 per person)*.

Adventure Cat: Skim across the bay with the wind in your hair on catamaran trips, including 'Sail and Jail' getaways to/from Alcatraz *(adventurecat.com; 90min cruise adult/child $75/35, Sail and Jail $125)*.

Red & White Fleet: SF's original sunset bay cruises since 1892 – ring boxes keep popping. New triple-decker boats offer full bars and snacks *(redandwhite.com; 1hr cruise adult/child $39/29, 2hr sunset cruise $58/38)*.

EATING IN THE MARINA: PRIME PICNICS

Scoma's: Fishing boats docked out front supply 'pier-to-plate' Cal-Italian classics, from Dungeness crab cakes to SF's definitive cioppio (seafood stew). *noon-9pm* $$$

Codmother Fish & Chips: Crisp, fried-to-order Pacific cod with garlic fries at outdoor picnic tables. *11.30am-6pm Sun-Thu, to 7pm Fri & Sat* $

Fisherman's Wharf Crab Stands: Steaming cauldrons of Dungeness crab at Pier 45 sidewalk stands are ready for feasts. *11.30am-9pm, winter through spring* $

Fog Harbor Fish House: Bay views frame sustainable local favorites like Petrale sole, Pacific cod and Dungeness crab – simply prepared, so flavors shine through. *11am-9pm* $$

TOP EXPERIENCE

Golden Gate Bridge

No other bridge puts on a show like this. Morning mists lift to reveal the Golden Gate Bridge, glowing orange-red against blue skies. Give yourself a couple hours to walk the 1.7-mile span, with time for photo-ops. Stick around for the late-afternoon grand finale: as fog swallows commuter traffic, art deco towers float above the clouds. Magic.

BENJAMINHEATH/LONELY PLANET

TOP TIPS

- Watch acrobatic fog feats over coffee at **Round House Café**, the 1938 diner built by bridge engineer Alfred Finnila.
- If you get cold or tired walking across the bridge, catch any **Golden Gate Transit** bus back from the northern toll plaza.

PRACTICALITIES

- goldengate.org
- Vehicle toll: northbound free, southbound $9.50
- Welcome Center 9am-6pm daily

Iconic Design

It's hard to picture San Francisco without its iconic art deco suspension bridge, but the US War Department almost nixed this design in favor of a chunky concrete bridge with caution-yellow stripes. Local architects Gertrude Comfort Morrow and Irving Morrow realized that ships may pass in the night, but San Franciscans would have to live with the bridge every day. Working with engineer Joseph B Strauss, the Morrows submitted a counter-proposal to harmonize with the natural environment: a sleek suspension bridge painted a signature shade known as International Orange. Even though the War Department owned the land on either side, the City of San Francisco gave the ingenious orange bridge design the green light.

Death-Defying Feats

Stop by the **Golden Gate Bridge Welcome Center** to witness precarious construction work in progress, captured in jaw-dropping vintage photos – riveters balanced atop swaying cables 80 stories high, while divers plunged 110ft underwater with only a rubber hose for air. Take a moment to admire the bridge's signature color, still touched up by a daredevil crew of 34 painters suspended from the 764ft suspension towers.

TOP EXPERIENCE

Exploratorium

Can you stop time, sculpt fog or make sand sing? At San Francisco's living laboratory of science and human perception, you'll discover superhuman abilities you never knew you had – and emerge from the hands-on exhibits with a renewed sense of wonder.

GILBERTO MESQUITA/SHUTTERSTOCK

Mind-Expanding Experiences

Is there a science to skateboarding? How big is your blind spot? Can plankton make art? You have questions about life's mysteries, and the **Exploratorium** helps you find answers. MacArthur Genius–winning designers create 700+ hands-on exhibits to engage all the senses: try static-electricity hairdos, send whispered messages to strangers and dance with your own rainbow shadows in a light-refraction room.

The Tactile Dome

Slip off your shoes and step inside the mysterious geodesic **Tactile Dome**, and suddenly you're enveloped in total darkness. You'll have to rely on your sense of touch to guide you through an elaborate labyrinth – and emerge exhilarated, with hands tingling. Advance reservations and separate ticket required.

A Showcase for Experimental Thinking

The Exploratorium's mind-bending science exhibits are inspired by founder Frank Oppenheimer, a physicist who worked on the atom bomb with his brother Robert – but was blacklisted during the McCarthy era and barred from scientific research. He dedicated the rest of his life to promoting science in the public interest, teaching public high school and founding the Exploratorium in 1969. Today the Exploratorium covers Pier 15, including **Fog Bridge** and other free outdoor exhibits.

TOP TIPS

- At **After Dark Thursdays**, 18+ crowds bond over glow-in-the-dark mad-scientist cocktails, technology-assisted sing-alongs and special exhibits. Book ahead.
- The Exploratorium's scenic waterfront **Seaglass Restaurant** serves sit-down, locally sourced meals. It's closed on Monday.

PRACTICALITIES

- exploratorium.edu
- Entry adult/youth $40/30, after dark $23, Tactile Dome $16
- 10am-5pm Mon-Sat, noon-5pm Sun, after dark 6-10pm Thu

Downtown, Civic Center & SoMa

BIG BUILDINGS, BIG CHANGES

TOP TIP

Cable cars are a fun way to get around downtown – unless you get stuck waiting in line at the cable-car turnaround at Powell and Market Sts. Queue for Powell-Mason and Powell-Hyde cars before noon or hop the lesser traveled California St line near the Embarcadero.

Luring San Franciscans downtown after work takes a dazzling museum show, a killer cocktail, fabulous food or a kinky club – and there's plenty to choose from here. After 150 years of entertaining through earthquakes and pandemics, downtown arts venues have something for everyone, including immersive museums, iconic drag and Grammy-winning symphonies. Downtown is a huge swath of eastern San Francisco that encompasses subneighborhoods of Union Square, Civic Center and the Tenderloin, South of Market (SoMa), the Financial District (FiDi) and parts of Mission Bay. Civic Center is a zoning conundrum, with great performances and Asian art treasures on one side of City Hall and dive bars and transitional housing on the other. SoMa's high-tech landscape is fickle – Twitter/X has literally left the building here, but new AI startups keep cropping up in vacant spaces. When work's done, SoMa is where everyone gets down and dirty on the dance floor.

Ride All Three Cable-Car Lines

Max out your day pass

San Francisco's cable cars were invented in 1873 and designated a National Landmark in 1964. Part of the city's Muni system *(sfmta.com; cable car per ride/day pass $9/15),* SF's three cable-car lines complete 254,000 passenger trips per

continued on p62

GETTING AROUND

To see sights north of Union Square, hop a cable car. Powell-Hyde and Powell-Mason lines link downtown with Chinatown, North Beach and the Wharf; the California St line runs east–west to Van Ness Ave. Muni metro travels swiftly under Market St, while historic F-Market streetcars ambles between the Castro and Fisherman's Wharf above ground. The N line links downtown to the Haight, Castro and Golden Gate Park; the T links Dogpatch and Caltrain to Chinatown. East–west Muni buses 2, 5, 6, 7, 21, 31 and 38 connect downtown and SoMa with western neighborhoods; north–south lines 14, 19, 27, 30 and 45 connect to the Wharf or Mission.

TOP EXPERIENCE

San Francisco Museum of Modern Art

Boggle your mind and refresh your eyes at SFMOMA, where boundary-pushing modern and contemporary masterworks sprawl over seven floors of galleries. See the world-class 3rd-floor photography collection, meditate in Agnes Martin's secluded shrine behind 4th-floor abstract paintings, get an eyeful of Warhol's pop art on the 5th floor and immerse yourself in 7th-floor cutting-edge contemporary installations.

EGROY/SHUTTERSTOCK

TOP TIPS

- During SFMOMA opening hours, lobby and atrium art installations and 2nd-floor Bay Area art shows are free to visit without a ticket.
- Pick up limited-edition exhibition tees, catalogs and jewelry at ground-floor **Museum Store** *(11am-5pm Fri-Tue, noon-8pm Thu).*

PRACTICALITIES

- sfmoma.org
- Adult/senior/student/youth $30/$25/$23/free free first Thu, ground floor always free
- 10am-5pm Fri-Tue, noon-8pm Thu

1900 to Now: SFMOMA's Collection

Rotating experimental works and masterpieces from its massive collection, SFMOMA encourages viewers to constantly re-examine the contradictions and interpretations of some of the greatest works of our time. Head to the 2nd floor to see how SFMOMA began, with colorful works from Frida Kahlo, Paul Klee and Henri Matisse, and ponder Diego Rivera's radical worker portraits and Georgia O'Keefe's interpretations of nature and the feminine. Recent immersive installations include the disorienting mirrored infinity rooms of Yayoi Kusama, Olafur Eliasson's dazzling social-media sensation *One-Way Colour Tunnel* and Kara Walker's Octavia Butler–inspired lobby installation of robotic black figures transforming trauma.

The Living Wall & Sculpture Garden

Take a breather mid-visit with a quick outdoor detour. On the 3rd floor is the 30-foot-high Living Wall – the largest of its kind in the US, containing more than 19,000 plants. On the rooftop patio of Cafe 5 (5th floor) is a sunny sculpture garden, featuring major modernist works framed by skyscrapers.

DOWNTOWN, CIVIC CENTER & SOMA

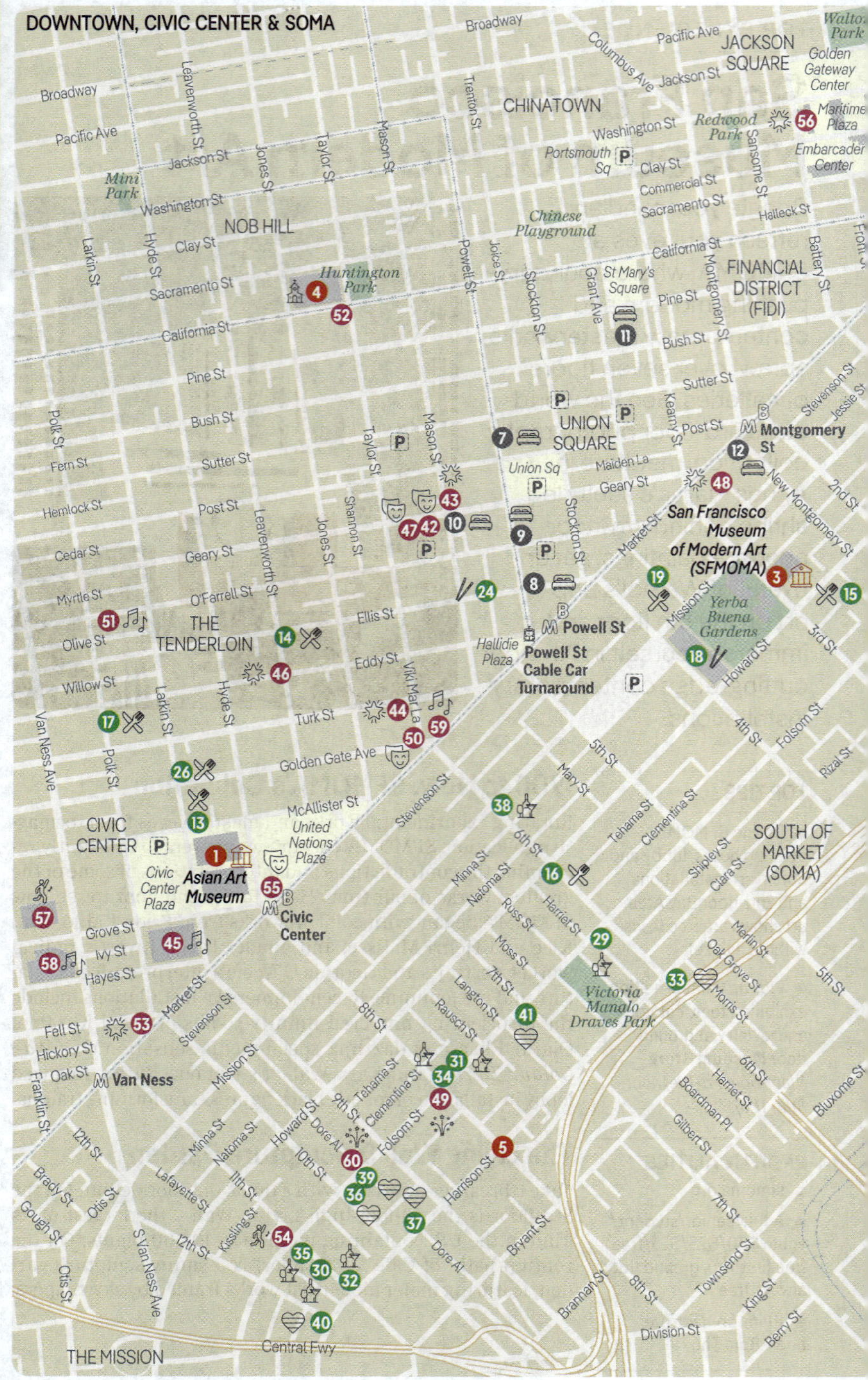

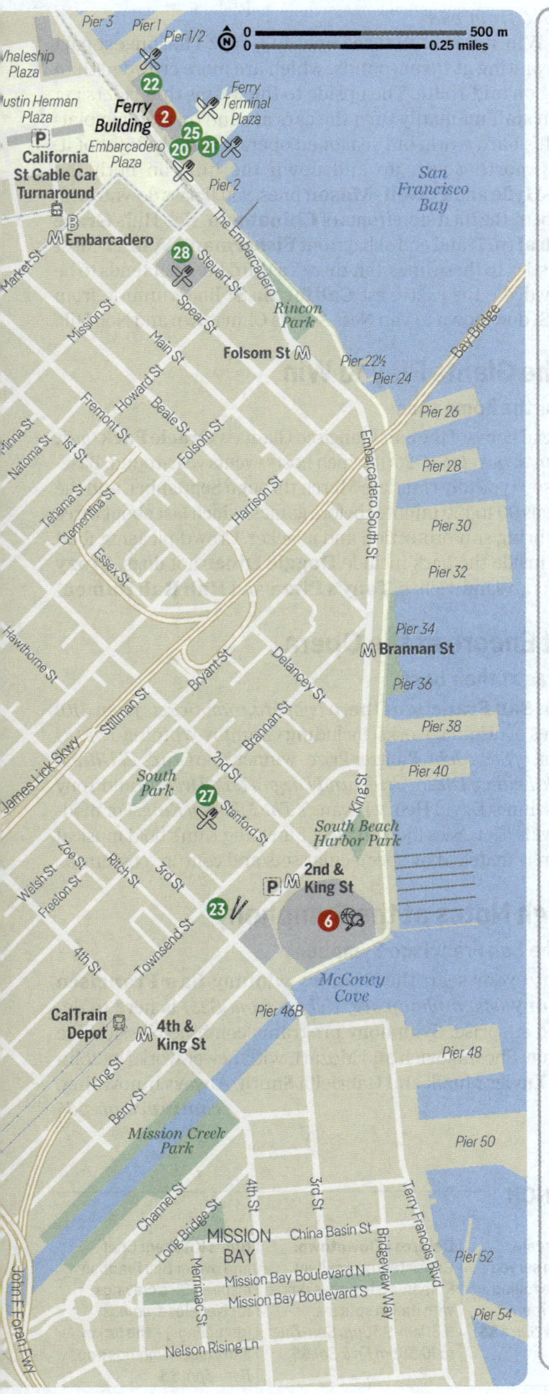

HIGHLIGHTS

1 Asian Art Museum
2 Ferry Building
3 San Francisco Museum of Modern Art (SFMOMA)

SIGHTS

4 Grace Cathedral
5 Leather & LGBTQ Cultural District
6 Oracle Park

SLEEPING

7 Beacon Grand
8 citizenM San Francisco Union Square
9 HI San Francisco Downtown
10 Hotel Nikko
11 Orchard Garden Hotel
12 Palace Hotel

EATING

13 ¡Chao Pescao!
see 2 Acme Bread Company
14 Azalina's
15 Benu
16 Bini's Kitchen
17 Brenda's French Soul Food
18 Dabao Singapore
19 Delarosa Downtown
20 Far West Fungi
21 Ferry Plaza Farmers Market
22 Hog Island Oyster Company
see 22 Humphry Slocombe
23 Kaiyō Restaurant
24 Kin Khao
25 Lunette
see 22 Ocean Malasada Company
26 Outta Sight Pizza
see 22 Peaches Patties
27 Rooh
28 Yank Sing

DRINKING & NIGHTLIFE

29 1015 Folsom
30 Butter
31 Cat Club
32 DNA Lounge
33 EndUp
34 F8
35 Halcyon
36 Hole in the Wall
37 Lone Star Saloon
38 Monarch
39 Powerhouse
see 2 Red Bay Coffee (Ferry Building)
40 SF Eagle
41 The Stud

ENTERTAINMENT

42 American Conservatory Theater
43 August Hall
44 Aunt Charlie's Lounge
45 Bill Graham Civic Auditorium
46 Black Cat
47 Curran Theatre
48 Dawn Club
49 Folsom Street Fair
50 Golden Gate Theatre
51 Great American Music Hall
52 Masonic Auditorium
53 Mr Tipple's Recording Studio
54 Oasis
55 Orpheum Theatre
56 Punch Line
57 San Francisco Ballet
see 57 San Francisco Opera
58 San Francisco Symphony
59 Warfield
60 Up Your Alley Fair

BARGAIN TICKETS

In San Francisco, world-class entertainment isn't just for tycoons. The San Francisco Symphony offers $25 terrace seats, where you can sit right behind the musicians and see the conductor's expressions. At the San Francisco Opera, rush tickets are available for as low as $28 from 11am to midnight the day before the performance, or until sold out – register to be notified when they're available. There are also 200 standing-room tickets ($10; cash only) for mainstage opera performances, which are for the rear orchestra or rear balcony. Tickets go on sale the day of each performance, starting at 10am.

continued from p58
month. Why not ride all three lines in a day? The longest part may be waiting at turnarounds, which are more crowded than hopping on mid-route. The upside to the wait is that riders get to watch staff manually turn the cars around on wooden platforms. It's hard work, but seasoned operators make light of it.

Riding north–south up and down the hills on both the **Powell-Hyde** and **Powell-Mason** lines, you'll pass downtown's skyscrapers, the tiled storefronts of **Chinatown**, Nob Hill's **Grace Cathedral** (p77) and end at bayfront **Fisherman's Wharf**. Most visitors stick to these lines, but there's a third line that tends to be less crowded – the east-west **California St** line, running from Market St downtown to Van Ness Ave via Chinatown and Nob Hill.

See the Giants Play to Win

Root for the home team

The official home of the San Francisco Giants is **Oracle Park** *(mlb.com/giants; tickets $16-200)*, which hosts events year-round. Baseball season typically runs late March through September, and the park opens 90 to 120 minutes before games, which last about three hours – bring sun protection and a jacket. Crowd-pleasing food options inside the park include **Doggie Diner** hot dogs, **Crazy Crab'z** crab sandwiches, **Tony's Pizza** and **Rah Rah Ramen**.

Shout Encore at the Opera

See divas at their best

Cheer for **San Francisco Opera** *(sfopera.com; tickets from $10)* premieres of original works, including Grammy-winning *The (R) Evolution of Steve Jobs*, Pulitzer Prize–winner Nilo Cruz's *El Último Sueño de Frida y Diego (Frida and Diego's Last Dream)* and Tony Award–winner David Henry Hwang's *The Monkey King*. For modern revivals of classics like *Carmen*, Eun Sung Kim's bold musical direction is matched by spectacular sets and couture costumes.

Hit High Notes at the Symphony

Enjoy the San Francisco Symphony

Hold onto your seat: the Grammy-winning **San Francisco Symphony** *(sfsymphony.org; tickets from $25)* is here to delight and surprise. Symphony programs combine classics like Beethoven, Shostakovich and Mozart, with newer works by John Adams, Xavier Muzik and Gabriella Smith. Always innovating,
continued on p65

EATING DOWNTOWN: LUNCH

Dabao Singapore: Emily Lim's Singapore-style hawker stall serves favorites like seafood laksa (spicy noodles). *11am-3.30pm Tue-Thu, to 7pm Fri-Sun* $

Yank Sing: Upscale, classic dim sum served steaming from a rolling cart. *11am-3pm Tue-Fri, from 10am Sat & Sun* $$$

Delarosa Downtown: Consistently excellent Roman-style pizzas pair with Italian spritzes. *11.30am-9.30pm Sun-Thu, to 10.30pm Fri & Sat* $$

Bini's Kitchen: Chef and owner Bini Pradhan inspired SF's cravings for Nepalese *momos* (dumplings) – the turkey and chicken *momos* pop. *11am-3pm* $$

TOP EXPERIENCE

Asian Art Museum

Travel across Asia without ever leaving San Francisco at the Asian Art Museum, surrounded by 18,000 artworks spanning 6000 years. Ground-floor galleries showcase contemporary artists from across the Asian diaspora, and new works interact with timeless masterpieces in upper-floor permanent collections.

ERIC BRODER VAN DYKE/SHUTTERSTOCK

Permanent Collection

Explore one of the most comprehensive collections of Asian art outside Asia from the top floor down, loosely following the path of Buddhism throughout Asia. Start with third-floor collections spanning Persian ceramics, Sikh paintings, South Indian temple sculpture, Javanese shadow puppets, Tibetan mandalas and the museum's beloved unofficial mascot: a 3000-year-old Chinese bronze rhinoceros. The second floor covers 6000-year-old Japanese earthenware, prized Korean moon jars, Chinese scrolls and a minimalist contemporary alcove for meditation.

East West Bank Art Terrace

Second-floor East West Bank Art Terrace is the largest rooftop art terrace in the US (7500 sq ft), featuring large-scale sculptures like Thai artist Pinaree Sanpitak's *Breast Stupa Topiary*, evoking Buddhist domes and the female form. Outdoor 2nd-floor Sun Family Art Terrace Cafe serves weekend afternoon snacks, wine and beer.

Special Exhibits

Ground-floor galleries feature traveling exhibits and special shows focusing on Asian American and Pacific Islander artists from across the Asian diaspora. Recent shows include Taiwanese video artist Yuan Goang-Ming's *Everyday War*, an immersive exhibit about pervasive violence in pop culture, and Sparsh Ahuja's and Sam Dalrymple's *Project Dastaan*, a collection of personal narratives about the impact of the 1947 partition of India and Pakistan.

TOP TIPS

- First-floor Asian Box cafe offers fast-casual, Vietnamese-inspired, locally sourced fare.
- Check the event calendar for upcoming artist talks, concerts and cookbook release parties.
- The Cha May Ching Museum Boutique has museum-exclusive prints, gifts and a kids section.

PRACTICALITIES

- asianart.org
- Adult/senior/student/child $20/17/14/free free first Sun
- 10am-5pm Fri-Mon, 1pm-8pm Thu

TOP EXPERIENCE

Ferry Building

The 1898 Ferry Building is now San Francisco's locavore landmark, featuring the Bay Area's standout restaurants and artisanal food purveyors. Score extra treats on Ferry Plaza Farmers Market days year-round – especially on Saturday, when the farmers market has more than 100 vendors.

BENJAMINHEATH/LONELY PLANET

Bakery, Ferry Building

TOP TIPS

- Bring sunscreen and patience: lines for popular vendors can be a 10- to 30-minute wait.
- Cash is the preferred payment method for many farmers market vendors. ATMs are inside the Ferry Building.

PRACTICALITIES

- ferrybuilding marketplace.com
- 7am-8pm
- Farmers market 10am-2pm Tue & Thu, 8am-2pm Sat

Ferry Building Marketplace

The Ferry Building's stately 240ft-tall clock tower was overshadowed by a freeway overpass until it was damaged in the 1989 Loma Prieta earthquake – and San Franciscans realized the bayfront views they'd been missing. After a four-year restoration, the building was relaunched as SF's monument to food: the Ferry Building Marketplace, showcasing SF's bounty of local, artisanal food. While vendors change, local staples like **Humphry Slocombe** ice cream, **Acme Bread Company** and **Far West Fungi** have held steady. Stop for breakfast at **Ocean Malasada Company** and **Red Bay Coffee**, lunch at **Peaches Patties**, happy hour at **Hog Island Oyster Company** and Cambodian dinners at **Lunette**.

Ferry Plaza Farmers Market

In addition to ready-made food inside the Marketplace, the **Ferry Plaza Farmers Market** run by nonprofit Foodwise takes place outside of the building three times a week – adding even more must-try foods to the checklist. Up to 25 vendors line up in the front of the building on Tuesday and Thursday. California's bounty is showcased at the Saturday market, hosting more than 100 vendors at booths that wrap around the front and south sides, attracting up to 25,000 visitors weekly.

continued from p62
the Symphony celebrates Día de los Muertos with Latin American orchestras, collaborates with music legends like Metallica and performs live with screenings of films like *Black Panther*.

Get Mesmerized by the Ballet

See prima ballerinas twirl

San Francisco Ballet *(sfballet.org)* is the country's oldest ballet company, founded in 1933 and still looking sharp in more than 100 shows annually at Civic Center's War Memorial Opera House. The season runs from December through May, with a vast repertoire that ranges from modern originals to the holiday classic *The Nutcracker*, which premiered here in 1944. Score rush tickets 48 hours ahead of showtime online *($35–79)* or $10 standing-room tickets at the box office, which opens four hours before curtain.

Catch Live Shows in the Theater District

See breakthrough acts in historic venues

Curtains are rising across San Francisco's **Theater District**. Touring smash-hit musicals like *Wicked* and *Mean Girls* play the historic **Curran**, **Golden Gate** and **Orpheum** theaters (ticketing & calendars at *broadwaysf.com*). **American Conservatory Theater** *(ACT; act-sf.org)* launches original works by major playwrights, from Tony Kushner's *Angels in America* to Kristina Wong's Pulitzer Prize–nominated *Sweatshop Overlord*. For laughs, hit **Punch Line** *(punchlinecomedyclub.com)*, which launched comedians from Robin Williams to Ali Wong. Music headliners play the baroque former bordello **Great American Music Hall** *(gamh.com)*, grand **Bill Graham Civic Auditorium** *(billgrahamcivic.com)*, rock-legendary **Warfield** *(thewarfieldtheatre.com)*, mid-century-mod **Masonic Auditorium** *(sfmasonic.com)*, and Prohibition-era speakeasy **August Hall** *(augusthallsf.com)*. SF's West Coast cool creds are restored at SF jazz clubs **Black Cat** *(blackcatsf.com)*, **Mr Tipple's Recording Studio** *(mrtipplessf.com)* and 1946-vintage **Dawn Club** *(dawnclub.com)*. Think you've seen it all? Not until you've hit an **Aunt Charlie's** drag show *(auntcharlieslounge.com)*.

Clubbing in SoMa

Hit SF's weekend nightlife hub

Dance parties rage in the club zone around 11th and Folsom Sts, usually going to midnight or 1am on weeknights, and 2am or

WHY I LOVE THE TENDERLOIN

Eric Ehler is chef and owner of Outta Sight Pizza. *(@intheweedz)*

As a local foodie, chef and art lover, I've been visiting and working in the Tenderloin for years. What drew me in was the eclectic urban feel that makes you feel like you're in a city – great restaurants, galleries and people. It's home to folks that are SF's heart and soul, keeping the city going from behind the scenes. Today, the focal point is the UN Plaza, where a world-class skate park is now located. You can watch a local skate like they're in the X-Games, and then go to the farmer's market. Truly a special experience. Truly San Francisco.

EATING IN CIVIC CENTER: DINNERTIME

¡Chao Pescao!: Colorful Cuban-Colombian restaurant serving deep-fried empanadas and signature salty-sour Tajín-fried chicken. *11.30am-8.30pm Tue-Sat* $$

Brenda's French Soul Food: Comforting, rich gumbo and ube beignets by queer Filipina Creole chef Brenda Buenviaje. *8am-8pm Wed-Mon, to 3pm Tue* $$

Azalina's: The breakout food star of the former Twitter building offers Malaysian fine dining, with an affordable $89 five-course tasting menu. *5-10pm Wed-Sat* $$$

Outta Sight Pizza: Grab a slice or commit to a 'hella mortadella' pie or mega-meatball sandwich on ciabatta with craft beer or wine. *11am-9pm* $

THE TENDER LEATHER HEART OF SF

SoMa's Leather and LGBTQ Cultural District has been a hub for leather culture since the 1960s, when local bars boosted business by opening for gay Sunday 'tea dances.' By the 1970s, SoMa had dozens of gay bars, bookstores, restaurants, bath houses and other LGBTQ+ spaces. When the AIDS epidemic hit, SoMa venues adopted safe sex protocols that set global standards for prevention. Today, the district includes legacy LGBTQ+ businesses and new venues that keep queer culture alive and evolving. Since 1984, Folsom Street Fair has been advocating for LGBTQ+ liberation and supporting the AIDS Emergency Fund. The District remains resilient – San Francisco wouldn't be San Francisco without it.

LET GO MEDIA/SHUTTERSTOCK

Orpheum Theatre (p65)

later on weekends. **Cat Club** is urban-legendary for New Wave nights, **Butter** serves rock anthems with soda-pop cocktails, and **DNA Lounge** hosts 18+ dance parties, from goth Death Guild to Latin house. After-hours **EndUp** has hosted gay Sunday tea dances since 1973, and **Halcyon** bumps to techno til dawn. **F8** ranges from hip-hop to dubstep, **Monarch** features multiple DJs with different vibes, and **1015 Folsom** packs out for EDM DJs and hip-hop across five dance floors.

Play in the Leather & LGBTQ Cultural District

Come out to LGBTQ+ bars and clubs

Come out to play in SoMa's **Leather & LGBTQ Cultural District**, SF's legendary queer and kink party hub and home to September's half-million-strong leather street party: **Folsom Street Fair**. At summer spinoff **Up Your Alley Fair**, the sun shines where it usually doesn't in Dore Alley. Both fairs are 18+; request consent and play safe with handy resources, including mpox-vax booths.

For kicks between fairs, drag club **Oasis** mounts outrageous shows and co-op **The Stud** hosts raucous events. **Lone Star Saloon** makes manly men warm and fuzzy at bear happy hour, **Hole in the Wall** draws gay bikers, shirtless gym queens throng **Powerhouse**, and wearing less is more at **SF Eagle**'s all-you-can-drink beer busts.

EATING DOWNTOWN: DESTINATION DINING

Kin Khao: Stellar Californian Thai cuisine with seasonal flair, such as slow-cooked local rabbit in green curry. *11.30am-2pm & 5.30-9pm Tue-Sun* **$$$**

Kaiyō Restaurant: Go for Nikkei (Japanese Peruvian) cuisine like matcha fettuccine, plus miso pisco cocktails. *5-10pm Mon-Thu, to 11pm Fri & Sat, to 9pm Sun* **$$**

Rooh: 'Progressive Indian' with seasonal ingredients, including saucy chili garlic crab and dahi puri semolina puffs with avocado. *5-9.30pm Sun-Thu, to 10pm Fri & Sat* **$$**

Benu: Chef Corey Lee's acclaimed contemporary Californian Asian cuisine is a multicourse celebration of the land and ocean that connect us. *5.30-9.30pm Tue-Sat* **$$$**

Chinatown & North Beach

COME FOR DINNER, STAY FOR STORIES

Grant St connects San Francisco's historic Chinese and Italian neighborhoods. Over 175 years, these neighbors have swapped epic stories of immigrant ingenuity, radical ideas, daring art and resilience against all odds.

Under Chinatown's pagoda roofs, you'll find noodles, rare teas, temples and Chinese orchestras, just like in the Gold Rush days – but you'll also find the future, with cutting-edge contemporary art, trend-setting restaurants and a packed calendar of cultural events. Wild parrots in North Beach tree-tops mimic the chatter at local bohemian bars and Italian cafes, serving enough espresso to fuel the next major poetry movement at free speech landmark City Lights.

Whether you're craving Peking duck, pizza or Peking duck pizza, you're definitely in the right place – stick around afterward for breakthrough comedy, raucous punk shows, Cantonese opera and West Coast cool jazz.

GETTING AROUND

Walking is the best way to see scenic Chinatown and North Beach. From downtown or Fisherman's Wharf, take the Powell-Mason or the Powell-Hyde cable car line to Chinatown and North Beach. The California St cable car passes through the southern end of Chinatown. The T metro line links Chinatown and North Beach to downtown and Dogpatch. Key bus routes are 1, 12, 30, 39 and 45.

TOP TIP

There's public parking underneath Portsmouth Sq *(to/after 5pm $4/8 per hour; per day $38)* and at Good Luck Parking Garage *(sfmta.com; $5/hr)*.

Time-Travel at the Chinese Historical Society of America

Follow epic tales inside a living landmark

Picture what it was like to be Chinese in America during California's Gold Rush, the Chinese exclusion era (1870–1943)

EATING IN CHINATOWN: CLASSIC DIM SUM

Good Mong Kok: Chinatown's busiest counter, where shrimp dumplings, pork siu mai and other classics are offered in takeout boxes. *7am-6pm* $

Hang Ah Tea Room: Century-old menus adorn Chinatown's original dim sum hotspot, serving purse dumplings, pillowy pork buns and custard bao. *10.30am-8pm* $$

Dim Sum Bistro: Don't let unconvincing food photos and bargain prices deter you from high-quality takeout, including tender shrimp and chive dumplings. *8am-3pm* $

Today Food: Witness dumpling mastery: dough rolled until translucent, loaded with veggies, shrimp and chicken, pinched and pan-fried or steamed to enjoy. *8am-8pm* $

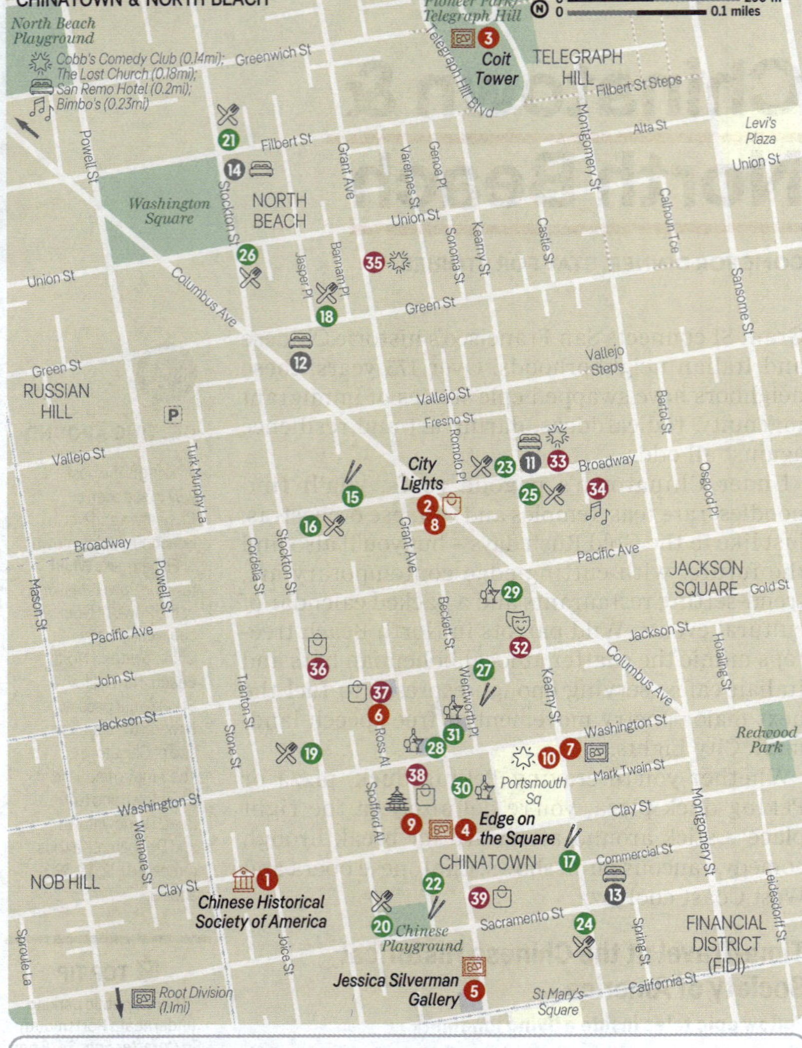

HIGHLIGHTS
1 Chinese Historical Society of America
2 City Lights
3 Coit Tower
4 Edge on the Square
5 Jessica Silverman Gallery

SIGHTS
6 41 Ross Alley
7 Chinese Culture Center
8 Jack Kerouac Alley
9 Tin How Temple

ACTIVITIES
10 Chinatown Alleyway Tours

SLEEPING
11 Green Tortoise Hostel
12 Hotel Bohème
13 Pacific Tradewinds Hostel
14 Washington Square Inn

EATING
15 China Live
16 Dim Sum Bistro
17 Four Kings
18 Golden Boy
19 Good Mong Kok
20 Hang Ah Tea Room
21 Liguria Bakery
22 Mister Jiu's
23 Osmanthus Dim Sum Lounge
24 Today Food
25 Tommaso's
26 Tony's Pizza Napoletana
27 Z & Y

DRINKING & NIGHTLIFE
28 Buddha Lounge
29 Comstock Saloon
30 Empress at Boon Lounge
31 Li Po

ENTERTAINMENT
32 Great Star Theater
33 Keys Jazz Bistro
34 Mabuhay Gardens
35 Savoy Tivoli

SHOPPING
36 Dong Hing Supermarket
37 Golden Gate Fortune Cookies
38 On Waverly
39 Wok Shop

and SF's hippie heyday at the **Chinese Historical Society of America** *(chsa.org; adult/student/child $12/10/5),* built as Chinatown's YWCA by Hearst Castle architect Julia Morgan. Exhibits in this 1932 landmark spotlight Chinese American culture, from WWII Chinatown nightclub posters to Bruce Lee's martial arts costumes and philosophy library.

Change Your Outlook in Chinatown Galleries

Glimpse the future in the making

Up the block from historic Portsmouth Square is **Edge on the Square** *(edgeonthesquare.org; free),* Chinatown's cutting-edge cultural hub and arts center. Drop in for fresh takes on current topics with impactful shows like 'All Eyes On Us: Invention & Ingenuity During Artistic Diasporas.' No one is a stranger or spectator here – the art invites you to leave your mark, and music and dance pull you into the groove. Edge events blend art, community and joy, from Chinatown Pride celebrations to live chef demos exploring Asian American identity through food.

Atop the pedestrian bridge spanning Kearny St, a mosaic sun graces the steps to the **Chinese Culture Center** *(cccsf.us; free).* This landmark art center on the Hilton's 3rd floor has expanded artistic horizons since 1965, sparking conversations through bold collaborations with contemporary Chinese artists from the mainland and across the diaspora.

Visit the Center's satellite gallery at **41 Ross Alley** *(41ross.org; free),* and gain deeper understanding of the local art scene on the Center's **Chinatown History and Art Walking Tours** *(1½ to two hours; four-person minimum; $45 per person).*

Between international art fairs, contemporary art stars converge at the **Jessica Silverman Gallery** *(jessicasilverman gallery.com; free).* Beyond frosted glass doors lie stunning parallel universes, featuring Ruby Tut's cosmic gardeners, Judy Chicago's world-birthing quilts and David Huffman's history-repairing Traumanauts.

Go Gourmet in Chinatown

Collect secret ingredients, tools and tips

Stockton St is a gourmet dream, lined with dim-sum takeout joints like **Good Mong Kok** (p67) and grocers like **Dong Hing Supermarket** selling gourmet condiments. If you've scored

CHINATOWN'S CONTEMPORARY ARTS SCENE

Candace Huey is head curator at **Edge on the Square** and co-chair of SFMOMA's SECA prize council.

At Edge on the Square, we celebrate Chinatown as an immigrant gateway and a touchstone for Asian American experience. Our programs are free and family-friendly, and expand what it means to be American. The Chinese Historical Society of America bridges past and present, and the **Center for Asian American Media Film Festival** launches new voices. Great Star Theater (p74) introduces younger audiences to Cantonese opera, and On Waverly (p70) curates Asian American authors and artists. Independent nonprofits like Southern Exposure (p99), Gray Area (p93) and Root Division give artists space to explore.

EATING IN CHINATOWN: FAMILY-STYLE FEASTS

Mister Jiu's: Brandon Jew's acclaimed Californian Chinese banquets feature lamb with plum sauce and roast Sonoma duck. *5-9pm Tue & Wed, to 10pm Thu-Sat* **$$$**

Z & Y: Spicy banquets guaranteed to make faces shine: Sichuan pork dumplings, flaming cauliflower and chili-oil-poached fish. *11.30am-3pm & 4.30-9pm Wed-Sun* **$$**

Osmanthus Dim Sum Lounge: Gourmet rule-breaker adds brandy to blistered beans, spinach to shitake dumplings and *pu-erh* tea to Old Fashioneds. *10.30am-8pm* **$$**

China Live: George Chen showcases modern Chinese dishes including kumquat-glazed Peking duck, plus top-notch tea and cocktails. *noon-9pm Mon-Fri, 4-9pm Sat & Sun* **$$**

TOP EXPERIENCE

Chinatown Alleyways

Chinatown's 41 historic alleyways have seen it all since 1849: gold rushes and revolution, incense and opium, fire and icy receptions. Local and national exclusion laws restricting Chinese immigration, employment and housing lasted for 73 years – but the community held its ground. Today, Chinatown's alleyways are cultural touchstones and places of possibility, through art, mutual aid and shared celebrations.

ADELE HEIDENREICH/SHUTTERSTOCK

TOP TIPS

- Teenage historians guide epic two-hour nonprofit **Chinatown Alleyway Tours** *(chinatownalleywaytours.org; adult/student/child $50/20/10)*, covering Sun Yat-sen's revolutionary plotting at 36 Spofford Alley to martial-artist Bruce Lee breaking down racial barriers.
- Respect people's privacy in their homes and workplaces when taking photographs.

PRACTICALITIES

- Free
- Between Grant Ave, Stockton St, California St & Broadway

Waverly Place

Through earthquakes, world wars and Prohibition gunfights, Waverly Place changed the culture around it. You'll spot the flag-festooned balcony of **Tin How Temple** *(9.30am-3pm Fri-Wed)*, where prayers have been offered since 1852 – even after the 1906 earthquake and fire, when altars were still smoldering. To pay your respects, follow sandalwood-incense aromas upstairs. Entry is free but offerings customary; no photography inside. Readers may remember Waverly as the namesake of one of the narrators in Amy Tan's novel *The Joy Luck Club*, and find new favorites at **On Waverly** *(onwaverly.com)*, which showcases Asian American authors and artists.

Ross Alley

You might recognize colorful **Ross Alley** from its cameos in ho-hum Hollywood blockbusters – *The Karate Kid Part II, The Pursuit of Happyness* – and its star turns in indie gems like *Who Is Michael Jang?* and *Chan Is Missing*. Stop by the Chinese Culture Center's contemporary art shows at **41 Ross** *(41ross.org; free)*, then seek your fortune at **Golden Gate Fortune Cookies** *(goldengatefortunecookies.com)*, where cookies are stamped from vintage presses, just as they were in 1909, when fortune cookies were invented in San Francisco.

reservations at wildly popular **Four Kings** *(itsfourkings.com; book 29 days in advance)*, you can savor ingeniously reinvented Chinatown classics, like Sichuan peppercorn-spiked mapo spaghetti.

At **China Live** (p69; *chinalivesf.com*), browse the gourmet shop while you wait for chef George Chen's modern Chinese feasts. Get equipped to make five-star meals at the **Wok Shop** *(wokshop.com)*, where owner Tane Chan jokes that she's sold 'woks for all walks of life' since the 1970s.

Celebrate Lunar New Year

Welcome spring with celebrations

Chinatown celebrates Lunar New Year for a month, with **night markets** *(bechinatown.weebly.com)* along lantern-lit Grant Ave. Stock up on lucky bamboo, red envelopes and miniature mandarin trees. Chase the 200ft dragon, legions of lion dancers and fierce tiny-tot martial artists at the **Chinese New Year Parade** *(chineseparade.com)*.

By the end of the night, everyone's happy and hoarse from exchanging best wishes for prosperity: *Gung hay fat choy!* (Cantonese) or *Gōng xǐ fā cái!* (Mandarin).

Rock Out in North Beach

Catch live shows at iconic underground venues

You're right on time for the revival of legendary North Beach clubs. **Bimbo's** *(bimbos365club.com)* is an iconic 1931 speakeasy known for danceable indie bands (Zap Mama, Dandy Warhols) and marquee talent (Adele, Van Morrison, Lizzo).

Keys Jazz Bistro *(keysjazzbistro.com)* features rotating residencies by international jazz talents and raucous classics by SF's Jazz Mafia. Punk's not dead at **Mabuhay Gardens** – the 1970s Filipino supperclub that took a chance on loud local acts, including the Dead Kennedys and an unsigned Metallica.

At quaint, mural-lined 1907 **Savoy Tivoli** *(savoytivoli.com)*, the tiny stage that survived earth-shaking shows by the Ramones, Muddy Waters and SF drag phenomenon Beach Blanket Babylon, is reinforced – ready when you are.

GRANT AVENUE'S BRILLIANT NEON

Grant Avenue became America's brightest street 100 years ago, as part of Chinatown's brilliant redesign. After the 1906 earthquake, developers schemed to push Chinatown outside SF, on the pretext that this thoroughfare was a red-light strip – never mind that white landlords profited. Savvy Chinatown leaders led by Look Tin Eli lobbied to rename shady DuPont St 'Grant Avenue,' and consulted architects to design its modern, pagoda-roofed Chinatown deco style. Dim lanterns were replaced with dazzling neon and dragon-wrapped street lamps. The image overhaul worked like a charm: photographers, partiers and celebrities flocked here, establishing neon-lit **Li Po** and **Buddha Lounge** as signature SF attractions.

DRINKING IN CHINATOWN: ICONIC BARS

Li Po: Enter the 1937 faux-grotto doorway for baiju-spiked mai tais under the Buddha. Brusque bartenders, cellar bathrooms, random dance-offs. *2pm-1.30am*

Comstock Saloon: Authentic Wild West saloon, complete with the trough where cowboys once relieved themselves. Cocktails remain potent. *4pm-midnight Tue-Sat*

Buddha Lounge: The vintage neon Buddha promises dangerously enlightening nights, featuring an eclectic jukebox. *1pm-2am*

Empress at Boon Lounge: Chinatown's 1966 landmark is crowned by this swanky octagonal lounge, featuring top-shelf cocktails and Cantonese bites. *5-10pm Mon-Sat*

TOP EXPERIENCE

Coit Tower

The exclamation mark atop Telegraph Hill is Coit Tower, dedicated to SF first responders by firefighting millionaire Lillie Hitchcock Coit, who raised eyebrows in the 1860s for smoking cigars, gambling, drinking and wearing men's gear like other firefighters. The 1930s lobby murals celebrating workers were initially denounced as communist, but are now landmarked.

RIGUCCI/SHUTTERSTOCK

TOP TIPS

- For a parrot's-eye panoramic view of San Francisco, take the creaky 1930s elevator to the tower's open-air **viewing platform**.
- For a challenge, hike up 13 flights of stairs to the Viewing Platform.

PRACTICALITIES

- sfrecpark.org
- Elevator adult/student/child $10/7/3
- Mural tour from $5
- 10am-6pm Apr-Oct, to 5pm Nov-Mar

Secret Treasures in the Stairwell

Book a tour up the narrow 2nd-floor **stairwell,** where recently revealed murals were hidden for 80 years. The seven murals show San Francisco in the 1930s – the showstopper is Jane Berlandina's strikingly modern egg-tempera mural *Home Life*, showing San Franciscans baking pies and kicking back.

Lobby Murals

Publicly funded **1930s lobby murals** show what daily life was like here during the Depression: San Franciscans organized dockworkers' unions, lined up at soup kitchens, partied despite Prohibition and read books – including Marxist manifestos – in Chinese, Italian and English. When they were completed in 1934, the artworks were so controversial that the opening of the tower was delayed by censors. Authorities called the 26 artists that painted them communists and demanded that radical elements be removed. The artists refused, and in a last-minute compromise, park employees painted over a hammer-and-sickle symbol in a union logo. Public opinion overruled the censors: San Franciscans embraced the murals as symbols of the city's openness. In 2012 voters passed a measure to preserve them as historic landmarks, and today the murals are freshly restored – and as bold as ever.

TOP EXPERIENCE

City Lights

Free spirits and free speech have found refuge at City Lights since 1957. Words were dangerous business back in the '50s, when library books were often banned, Hollywood screenwriters were blacklisted and comedians got arrested for swearing in North Beach nightclubs – but poet Lawrence Ferlinghetti founded City Lights Books anyway.

BENJAMINHEATH/LONELY PLANET

'A Kind of Library Where Books Are Sold'

As Ferlinghetti's hand-lettered sign says, idle browsing is highly encouraged. Wax poetic in the upstairs Poetry Room, load up on 'zines on the mezzanine and entertain radical ideas downstairs in the Pedagogies of Resistance section. On the main floor, City Lights publications include titles by Angela Davis, Diane di Prima and Noam Chomsky, proving the point on another of Ferlinghetti's signs: 'Printer's Ink Is the Greater Explosive.'

Poetry Room

City Lights' affordable Pocket Poets series brought poetry to the people, sparking the Beat poetry movement. Number four was Allen Ginsberg's epic *Howl and Other Poems* (1956), an instant sensation that got Ferlinghetti and City Lights manager Shigeyoshi Murao arrested for publishing poetry with homoerotic content. They fought charges of publishing obscenity not on technicalities but on artistic merits, and won a landmark free speech victory. Celebrate your freedom to read freely in the upstairs Poetry Room overlooking **Jack Kerouac Alley**, in the designated **Poet's Chair** with your choice of 60 Pocket Poets books – including *Howl*, available in 24 languages.

TOP TIP

- Duck into Jack Kerouac alley, a poetry-paved shortcut between Chinatown and North Beach.
- Visit Kerouac's favorite haunts: City Lights, neighboring Vesuvio and a stool by the golden Buddha at Li Po (p71) – he was a true believer in literature, Buddhism and beer.

PRACTICALITIES

- citylights.com
- 10am-10pm daily
- Free

THE OTHER BROADWAY

When San Franciscans reminisce about Broadway shows, they're not talking about Disney musicals. North Beach's Broadway strip has seen it all since the 1930s: the nation's first openly lesbian bar (Mona's, 1936), dedicated drag venue (Finocchio's, 1936), uncensored comedy acts (Jazz Workshop, 1961), topless strip club (Condor Club, 1964), and unionized strip club (Lusty Lady, 1997). Some shows here actually changed history: Carol Doda was arrested for going topless but won her case, and Lenny Bruce was arrested and acquitted of obscenity charges. SF Broadway shows continue to push buttons and boundaries, honoring almost a century of fearless performers.

JON BILOUS/ALAMY

Great Star Theater

Catch North Beach Comedy

See bold, breakthrough standup acts

Comedy and drag acts have packed North Beach clubs since the 1930s – comedian Lenny Bruce got arrested here for cursing in 1961 and won a landmark free speech victory. Today **Bimbo's** (p71) and **Cobb's Comedy Club** keep launching and relaunching careers – John Oliver, Mo Amer, Michelle Wolf – at cozy showcases with a two-drink minimum *(18+; tickets from $25)*. At tiny nonprofit **The Lost Church** *(thelostchurch.org)* and Chinatown's **Great Star Theater**, comics work up material for **SF Sketchfest** *(sfsketchfest.com)* – you saw it here first.

EATING IN NORTH BEACH: PIZZA AND FOCACCIA

Liguria Bakery: Bleary-eyed rockers and Italian grandmothers queue by 8am for cinnamon-raisin focaccia hot from the 100-year-old oven. Takeout only. *7am-noon Tue-Sat* $

Tony's Pizza Napoletana: Pizza-slinger champ Tony Gemignani ends coastal rivalries with Jersey tomato pies and Cal-Italia pizza. *noon-9.30pm Mon-Thu, to 11pm Fri-Sun* $$

Golden Boy: Punks have politely queued since 1978 for the Sodini's focaccia-crust pizza – try clam-and-garlic slices. Takeout only. *11.30am-9pm Sun-Thu, to 11pm Fri-Sat* $

Tommaso's: Charming North Beach since 1935 with wood-fired brick-oven Neapolitan pizza, cozy booths and communal tables. *5-10.30pm Tue-Sat, 4-9.30pm Sun* $$

Nob Hill & Russian Hill

VIEWS FROM SUCH GREAT HEIGHTS

Summit San Francisco's twin downtown hills and you'll discover everyone's heads are in the clouds up here – billionaires and penniless poets, rock stars and rock-star chefs, urban hikers and spiritual seekers. There's no getting around these peaks if you really want to see the city – Nob Hill stands between downtown and Chinatown, and Russian Hill rises between North Beach and Fisherman's Wharf. But first you have to get here: hop a cable car or brave a stairway hike. Towering above Union Sq, 'Snob Hill' has stunning views from grand hotels and Grace Cathedral. To its west is Russian Hill, with boutiques, restaurants and bars along Polk Gulch – San Francisco's historic 'gayborhood' before the Castro. Consider permission granted to follow your bliss – hop off a cable car, head to tiki bar happy hour, hear a cathedral organ recital or just watch the Bay Bridge lights twinkle. Your peak San Francisco experience awaits.

GETTING AROUND

The Powell-Hyde cable car line serves Russian and Nob Hills; Powell-Mason serves Nob Hill; and California runs from downtown through Chinatown and over Nob Hill to Van Ness Ave. Don't drive here if you can avoid it – the gradients from 24 to 31.5% are not good for your brakes or your blood pressure.

See How Cable Cars Work

Look behind the scenes at the Cable Car Museum

Hop off the Powell-Hyde or Powell-Mason cable car at Powell and Washington to see steampunk technology at work inside the **Cable Car Museum** *(cablecarmuseum.org; free)*. Check out a vintage car from inventor Andrew Hallidie's original 1873 fleet, then head downstairs to see the heart of the operation: eight giant spinning sheaves (grooved wheels) that propel the cable, guiding the cars along their routes.

TOP TIP

Find a west-facing bench at George Sterling Park to watch late-afternoon fog tumble over the Golden Gate Bridge. Alternatively, climb Filbert St to Vallejo Street Steps to see the Oakland hills glitter with sunsets.

DRINKING ON NOB HILL: CLASSIC BARS

Tonga Room: Tonight's weather forecast: foggy with 100% chance of typhoons every 20 minutes inside this 1943 tiki bar. *5-10pm Wed & Thu, to 11pm Fri & Sat*

Stookey's Club Moderne: Step up to the 1930s chrome-edged bar, where white-jacketed bartenders shake Corpse Reviver cocktails in time with jazz combos. *5pm-2am*

Top of the Mark: Toast sunsets with martinis at the sky-high 1939 piano lounge atop Mark Hopkins Hotel. *4-11 Sun-Thu, 3pm-12.30am Fri & Sat*

Summer Place: Inside windowless rock walls, happy hour unfolds nightly with seasonal cocktails and neighborly vibes. *2pm-2am Mon-Fri, from noon Sat & Sun*

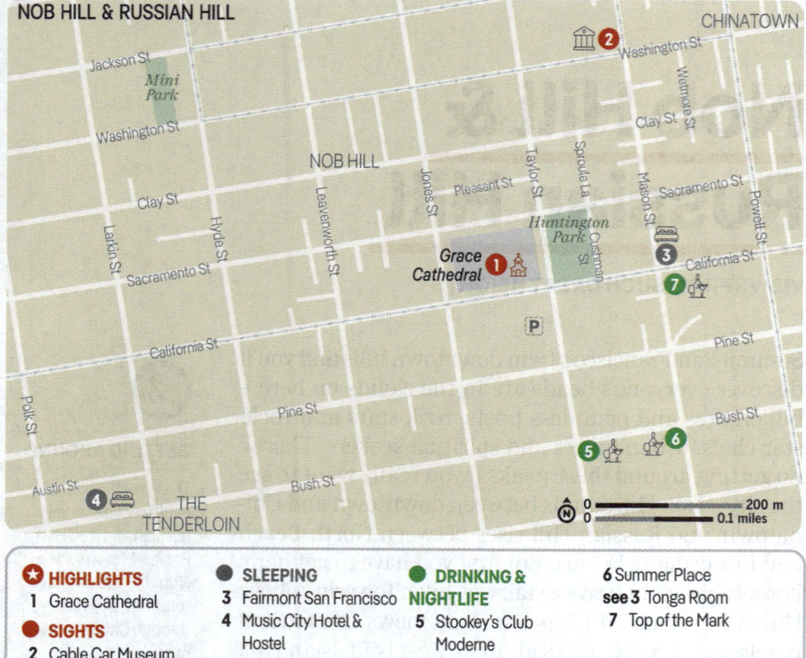

BACKGROUND

The Rise, Fall, and Rise of SF Cable Cars

Carnival rides can't compare to cable cars, San Francisco's vintage 1873 public transit. The idea came to inventor Andrew Hallidie after witnessing a horse carriage struggle uphill – and come crashing downhill. Such accidents were considered inevitable, but Hallidie knew better. If hemp-and-metal cable could haul ore out of California mines, it could transport San Franciscans uphill. Skeptical city planners granted Hallidie three months to launch his 'wire-rope railway.' Four hours after the deadline, Hallidie completed a downhill test-run. His cable car was a non-runaway success: by the 1890s, 53 miles of track crisscrossed SF.

But as other cities modernized, San Francisco's wooden trolleys seemed quaint. In 1947, SF's mayor pushed to replace cable cars with buses, which he claimed were cheaper – not factoring in the costs of bus-exhaust pollution. But loyal rider Friedel Klussmann did the math: cable cars brought in more tourism dollars than they cost in upkeep. The mayor demanded a public vote – and lost to 'the Cable Car Lady' by a landslide.

Today, you can catch a cable car at Friedel Klussmann Memorial Turnaround. Novices slide into strangers' laps – no seat belts here – while regulars leap onto running boards, grab poles, and enjoy the ride. Women weren't allowed to ride running boards until 1965, when 19-year-old Mona Hutchins was arrested for breaking this bogus rule – and won her case for women to enjoy San Francisco to the fullest.

TOP EXPERIENCE

Grace Cathedral

San Francisco's Gothic hilltop cathedral took 40 years to complete, with stained glass windows celebrating science, art works honoring interfaith achievements and murals commemorating the 1906 earthquake and 1945 UN charter signing in SF. Locals light candles beneath Beniamino Bufano's smiling statue of the city's patron saint and in the Interfaith AIDS Memorial Chapel, featuring Keith Haring's bronze altarpiece.

DALTON JOHNSON/SHUTTERSTOCK

Science in Stained Glass

Among the 68 stained-glass windows lining the Cathedral are a dozen 'Human Endeavor' panes celebrating scientific achievements and social progress – look for Albert Einstein amid swirling nuclear particles, activist and Nobel Peace Prize–laureate Jane Addams and Supreme Court Justice Thurgood Marshall.

Interfaith AIDS Memorial Chapel & Keith Haring's Last Work

To the right of the entry. Grace's Interfaith AIDS Memorial Chapel features a bronze angel of compassion altarpiece by artist-activist Keith Haring – his final work before his 1990 death from AIDS. On the opposite wall hangs a section of the AIDS Memorial Quilt; beneath it is a Book of Remembrance.

Labyrinths & Events

People of all faiths wander indoor and outdoor inlaid-stone labyrinths, meant to guide restless souls through three spiritual stages: releasing, receiving and returning. Check the website for events, including spectacular choral performances (don't miss Bach's *Magnificat* at Easter) plus inclusive weekly spiritual events, such as Thursday Choral Evensong, yoga with live music ($20 to $30), sound baths and candlelit meditation services.

TOP TIPS

- There's no charge to enter if you're praying, attending services or lighting a candle.
- Sightseeing visits include a self-guided audio tour.

PRACTICALITIES

- gracecathedral.org
- Adult/senior & youth/child $12/10/free
- 10am-5pm Mon-Sat, from 1pm Sun

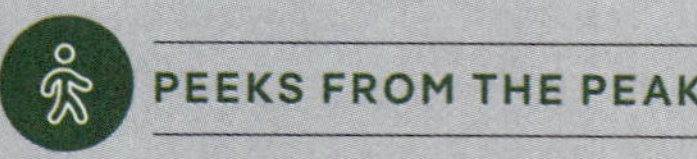

PEEKS FROM THE PEAKS

Climb stairways to staggering views along Vallejo steps, and wax poetic at Ina Coolbirth and George Sterling hilltop parks.

START	END	LENGTH
Vallejo Steps	Lombard Financial Center (Chase Bank)	from 2 miles; 1½ to 2½ hrs

Reach staggering heights with spectacular views along 1 **Vallejo Street Steps** leading from North Beach toward hilltop 2 **Ina Coolbrith Park**, named for California's first Poet Laureate. Pause to admire Bay views from the bench at Poet's Corner and you too may wax poetic.

Take the scenic route via steep stairs, past gravity-defying wooden cottages down to 3 **Macondray Lane** – so charming, it looks like something from a novel. And it is: Armistead Maupin used this shady, hidden byway as the model for Barbary Lane in his *Tales of the City* series. Stop for an ice-cream break at 4 **Swensen's** on Hyde and Union before you ascend Hyde toward Filbert St – San Francisco's steepest street, with a 31.5% grade and stellar views of North Beach churches and Coit Tower. One more block north on Hyde is 5 **George Sterling Park**, where you'll find sweeping views toward the Golden Gate Bridge, overlooking the town poet George Sterling called 'the cool grey city of love.'

Finally, head downhill and west along Lombard St to mosaic-wrapped 6 **Lombard Financial Center**, where California modernist Millard Sheets designed facade mosaics highlighting San Francisco history. During bank hours, head inside to admire floor-to-ceiling artwork by Sheets' studio.

Ina Coolbrith was a bohemian poet, editor and mentor – as well as the niece of Mormon prophet Joseph Smith.

Residents of **Macondray Lane** have green thumbs and a sense of humor. Recent garden sculptures include a family of stuffed jeans.

Japantown, Fillmore & Pacific Heights

POSTCARD-PERFECT VICTORIANS, WAVING KITTIES, MUSIC LEGENDS

The downhill sweep of Fillmore St leads from scenic hilltop parks and chic boutiques in Pacific Heights, through cultural and culinary TikTok hotspots in Japantown to buzzworthy restaurants and legendary music venues in the Fillmore – then uphill to Alamo Square's iconic Postcard Row. Don't let the quaint Victorians fool you: this neighborhood totally rocks. Japanese Americans have called this area home for over a century, and today Japantown is where J-pop stars and cosplay influencers shoot music videos in Peace Plaza. The Fillmore has been a nightlife hub since the jazzy 1930s and turned totally trippy in the psychedelic 1960s. Music legends still play live shows here. Hilltop Pacific Heights is ringed with mansions, many owned or once owned by powerful women – including nude model turned museum founder Alma Spreckels, 19th-century Black billionaire and Underground Railroad pioneer Mary Ellen Pleasant and former US House Speaker Nancy Pelosi.

TOP TIP

Every San Franciscan has a favorite Victorian. Find yours around Alamo Sq (from Golden Gate to Fell St, between Divisadero and Webster) and between Japantown's Sutter St and Jackson St in Pacific Heights. Multicolor 'Painted Lady' Victorians are irresistible photo-ops – but respect residents' privacy when taking photos.

Relax in Japantown Spas

Glow up and mellow out

Salt-scrub in the steam room, soak in the hot pool, take a cold plunge, reheat in the sauna, rinse and repeat at **Kabuki Springs & Spa** *(kabukisprings.com)*, Japantown's communal bathhouse. Men and women alternate days (cisgender and

continued on p82

GETTING AROUND

The 38 Geary bus will pick you up downtown and drop you right at Geary and Fillmore. Otherwise, you can hop the California cable-car line west to Van Ness Ave. From there, walk to Pacific Heights along Victorian-lined Sacramento St (one block north of California), detouring through lovely hilltop Lafayette Park. Then window-shop your way south along Fillmore St. At Post St, swing east to reach the Japan Center, or west to Pierce St, then walk south to Alamo Sq. Bus 22 helps you conquer neighborhood hills.

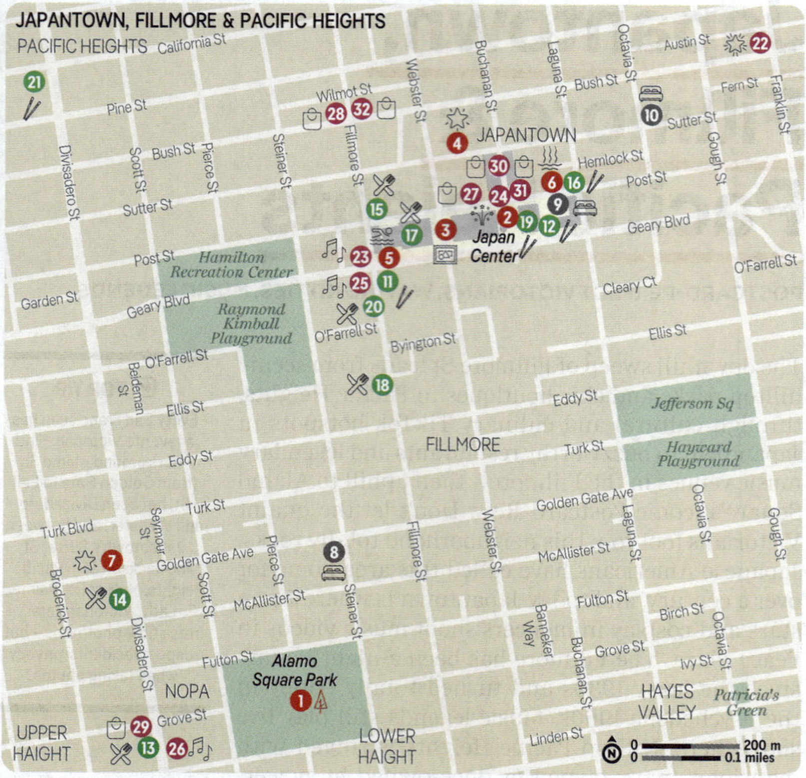

JAPANTOWN, FILLMORE & PACIFIC HEIGHTS

HIGHLIGHTS
1 Alamo Square Park
2 Japan Center

SIGHTS
3 Tokaido Arts

ACTIVITIES
4 Japanese Cultural & Community Center of Northern California (JCCCNC)
5 Kabuki Springs & Spa
6 Pearl Spa
7 Westside Cuts & Style

SLEEPING
8 Chateau Tivoli
9 Hotel Kabuki
10 Queen Anne Hotel

EATING
11 Aji Kiji
12 An Japanese Restaurant
13 Bar Crudo
14 Brenda's Meat & Three
15 Copra
16 Daeho Kalbijjim
17 Jina Bakes
see 17 Marufuku Ramen
18 Minnie Bell's Soul Movement
see 9 Nari
19 Sasa
20 State Bird Provisions
21 Tataki
see 17 Yakitori Edomasa

ENTERTAINMENT
22 Audium
23 Boom Boom Room
24 Cherry Blossom Festival
see 17 Festa
25 Fillmore Auditorium
26 Independent

SHOPPING
27 Baby the Stars Shine Bright
28 Crossroads Trading
29 Fibers of Being
see 25 In the Black
see 17 Kinokuniya Books
see 27 New People
30 Paper Tree
31 Soko Hardware
32 Zuri

EATING IN JAPANTOWN & FILLMORE: CROSS-CULTURAL FOOD

Brenda's Meat & Three: Only superheroes can finish chef/owner Brenda Buenviaje's shrimp and grits, let alone the fluffy biscuits – but it's fun trying. *8am-9pm* $

Daeho Kalbijjim: Go early or late for sizzling platters of *kalbijjim* beef topped with cheese and torched tableside. *11am-2.30pm & 4.30-9pm Mon-Fri, 10.30am-9pm Sat & Sun* $$

Minnie Bell's Soul Movement: Sip bubbly with Fernay McPherson's rosemary-infused fried chicken. *4-9pm Tue-Thu, 11am-2pm & 4-10pm Fri & Sat* $$

Yakitori Edomasa: Grilling since 1924, Edomasa makes yakitori skewers to order, from flavor-bomb chicken thighs to shitake mushrooms. *11am-2.30pm & 5-9.30pm Tue-Sun* $

TOP EXPERIENCE

Japan Center

Time travel to 1968 as you cross Japan Center's indoor wooden bridges, with *maneki-neko* (cat figurines) waving welcome from restaurant entryways. Hard to believe, but this kawaii-cute mall started with a knock-down fight. After WWII, 1500 Japantown residents returned from incarceration camps were again uprooted to build a mall. But residents and businesses rallied, converting the mall into a community hub.

KIT LEONG/SHUTTERSTOCK

East Mall, Japan Center

From Manga to Ukiyo-e

Entire afternoons disappear at **Kinokuniya Books**, between stunning art books (Daido Moriyama photography), tempting cookbooks (bento box lunches) and toys (smiling sushi plushies) – plus manga comics and Tokyo street-fashion mags. Across the hall, Kinokuniya's office and school supplies promise to make work and studying more fun – slow down with sloth-themed to-do lists and reward homework with panda-donut stickers. On Japan Center's indoor pedestrian bridge, stop at **Tokaido Arts** *(tokaidoarts.com; free)* to see a major collection of original *ukiyo-e* (Japanese woodblock prints) in mint condition – including Hokusai's sublime views of Mt Fuji, still vibrant over 200 years later.

All-Ages Entertainment

Vampire kittens and Alice in Wonderland characters occasionally roam the halls of the Japan Center, queuing politely for anime-themed photo booths and arcade games. Cosplay costumes could signal a festival, anime event or pop-up art mart – or just a typical Japan Center Saturday. Follow sounds of familiar tunes into **Festa** karaoke lounge *(festalounge.com; age 21+)*, where you too can rock the miniature stage for $2 per song plus liquid courage from yuzu shochu cocktails.

TOP TIPS

- West Mall has boutiques, arcades and sweet treats. Across Peace Plaza, the East Mall has date-night dining and cultural events.
- Top dining options include **Sasa** (p83), **Marufuku Ramen**, **Jina Bakes**, **Yakitori Edomasa** (p80) and **An Japanese Resturant** (p83).

PRACTICALITIES

- sfjapantown.org
- 8.30am-10pm
- Free

SHARP STYLES & BIG NIGHTS

Nate Thorner *(@natethebarber)* owns the barbershop **Westside Cuts & Style.** My pops started this barbershop with a partner named Jordan. Originally they called it Hair Jordans. Pops told me don't rush – you'll find a clientele because you take your time to make it right and tight. People with notoriety come through. I accompanied my counterpart Brandon to cut hair at Chase Center for a Warriors player. People come here for consistency, a good cut and fade, and because it feels like home. Historically, this was a thriving African American neighborhood, and I'm doing my little part to keep that alive. Next door, Effin Relax makes natural products. I also like Brenda's Meat & Three (p80), Bar Crudo and Minnie Bell's (p80).

SHEILA FITZGERALD/SHUTTERSTOCK

Cherry Blossom Festival

continued from p79

transgender alike) and bathing suits are required on all-gender Monday and Tuesday. Bath access is $49, or $20 with shiatsu massage (from $135). Women-only, clothing-free Korean **Pearl Spa** *(pearlspasf.com)* offers access to a cedar sauna, hot tub, cool pool, warming clay-ball pit and pink salt room with treatments, including seaweed massages ($200 for 90 minutes).

Discover Hidden Talents

Learn Japanese art forms from seasoned pros

Japantown has inspiration to spare: nonprofit **Japanese Cultural & Community Center of Northern California** *(JCCCNC; jcccnc.org)* runs affordable workshops with acclaimed local artisans, chefs, artists and performers. Get hands-on experience in person and online with *kaiseki* (seasonal meal) cooking, ikebana flower-arranging, *washi ningyo* (paper dolls), *doburoku* (home-brew sake) and *magewappa* (woodcraft). Check the calendar for upcoming events, including dance and taiko drumming workshops and performances from **GenRyu Arts** *(genryuarts.org)*.

Endless possibilities unfold at **Paper Tree** *(paper-tree.com)*, the paper-craft emporium behind Ruth Asawa's bronze *Origami Fountains* on pedestrian Osaka Way. Paper Tree has inspired origami since 1968, filling display cases with astounding paper creations: cocoon dresses, minuscule frogs and vast coral reefs. Beginners can fold their own Death Star with *Star Wars* kits, while decoupage pros freestyle with *washi* (handmade paper).

EATING: DATE-WORTHY SHARED PLATES

Nari: Day-Glo flavors make Pim Techamuanvivit's Thai-California dishes as mind-blowing as Fillmore shows, including cured *kampachi* with pear and chili jam. *5.30-9pm* **$$**

Copra: Feast on edible art with regional Indian flavors and SF flair: Kerala shrimp mango curry and puffy passionfruit poori. *5-10pm daily, 11.30am-2pm Sat & Sun* **$$**

State Bird Provisions: Mini-plates pack mega-flavors, including savory ricotta-sourdough pancakes and quail nested in slow-cooked onions. *5.30-10pm* **$$**

Bar Crudo: Pair craft beer with local oysters and porcini-crusted black cod – plus happy-hour seafood chowder (to 6.30pm). *5-9pm Mon-Sat* **$$**

Japantown keeps a busy schedule of festivals and creative workshops year-round – between the **Nihonmachi Street Fair** *(nihonmachistreetfair.org)* and **Cherry Blossom Festival**, GenRyu also organizes art programs to celebrate Hina Matsuri (Girls' Day), Keiro no Hi (Respect for the Aged) and Midori no Hi (Greenery Day). Since 1925, four generations of the Ashizawa family have made it their mission to source ikebana, bonsai, tea-ceremony and Zen rock-garden supplies at **Soko Hardware** *(sokohardware.com)*, so you can take the inspiration home.

Catch Music Legends Live

Hear SF's eclectic soundtrack at its source

Music legends keep rocking neighborhood venues here – '30s blues, '50s jazz, '60s rock, '70s punk, '90s hip-hop and current headliners. **Boom Boom Room** *(boomboomroom.com)* packs its 1930s checkered-linoleum floor with R&B and funk. Lines down the block signal showtime at the legendary **Fillmore Auditorium** *(thefillmore.com)*, where Jimi Hendrix, Janis Joplin, Aretha Franklin and the Grateful Dead rocked – upstairs is lined with '60s psychedelic posters, and free posters are still distributed after sold-out shows. Bragging rights are earned at small yet mighty **Independent** *(theindependentsf.com)*, featuring indie dreamers (Magnetic Fields, Death Cab for Cutie), music legends (George Clinton, Metallica) and alterna-stars (Superchunk, Tokimonsta). Dig the vibes at **Audium** *(audium.org; tickets adult/student $30/20)*, a 1967 sound sculpture emitting meditative, 90-minute 'room compositions.'

Signature Style

Try on global trends and SF styles

Upgrade travel wardrobes with **Zuri** *(shopzuri.com)* tunics, ethically made in Kenya in joyous prints: chickens, pretzels, fireworks. **New People** *(newpeopleworld.com)* brings Tokyo style to SF, with Lolita Goth mini-pinafores at **Baby the Stars Shine Bright** *(shop.baby-aatp.com)* and mod graphic shifts at **Sou Sou** *(sousouus.com)*. **Fibers of Being** *(shopfibersofbeing.com)* offers modern styles for all genders – SF rodeo tees, nonbinary bling – and gently-worn looks sell for less at **Crossroads** *(crossroadstrading.com)*. Complete your look with sharp cuts from **Westside Cuts & Style** *(instagram.com/westsidecutsandstyle)* and accessories from **In the Black** *(intheblackshop.com)*, Fillmore's Black design showcase.

JAPANESE ARTS & CULTURE

Sensei Melody Takata is the founder of **GenRyu Arts** and renowned taiko drummer, shamisen player and arts educator.

I first came to San Francisco with my taiko group. Now I'm raising my two kids and teaching and performing in Japantown. The **Cherry Blossom Festival** is Japantown's biggest event, **Nihonmachi Street Fair** is going strong after 50 years and **Japan Day** *(japanweeksf.com)* is a mini-Cherry Blossom Festival. There are arts events and workshops year-round at the JCCCNC, Japan Center popups and weekly free Paper Tree origami classes. We're staging shows in the Julia Morgan-designed **Issei Women's Building**, built by and for the Japantown community, where US civil rights leaders worked. Bringing those stories forward is an honor and joy.

EATING IN JAPANTOWN & FILLMORE: SUSHI

Sasa: Enjoy *kaiseki* (a seasonally inspired menu) or order *kanpachi nigiri* and creamy scallop-salmon '49er rolls. *5.30-9pm Mon, noon-2pm & 5.30-9pm Tue-Sun* **$$$**

Tataki: Satiny, sustainable seafood cut with gem-like precision lures sushi savants to this cozy spot for neighborly happy hours (to 6.30pm). *4.30-8.30pm* **$$**

Aji Kiji: Impress picnic dates by preordering Aji's jewel-box bento – sashimi, nigiri and maki with a fish-shaped container of soy sauce. *11am-4pm Tue-Sat* **$$**

An Japanese Restaurant: Reserve via text for a sushi speakeasy, serving 20 lucky diners 8-course *omakase* ($135) or Pacific seafood a la carte. *5.30-9.30pm Tue-Sat* **$$$**

TOP EXPERIENCE

Alamo Square

These graceful 'Painted Lady' Victorian mansions have housed bordellos, jazz speakeasies and hippie communes, and survived elegantly intact – including east-end Postcard Row and the northwest-corner Westerfeld mansion, once home to SF's biggest hippie commune. Earthquakes and fire couldn't destroy these Victorians, yet redevelopment almost did, until neighbors banded together to save this historic district.

GAGLIARDIPHOTOGRAPHY/SHUTTERSTOCK

'Painted Lady' Victorian mansions

TOP TIPS

- On sunny days, claim a hilltop picnic table framed by gabled Victorian rooflines and wind-sculpted pines.
- 'Dog-o'clock' occurs around sunset, when pups frolic freely on Alamo's grassy west side.
- At the hilltop playground, kids climb up and slide down Victorian playhouses.

PRACTICALITIES

- sfrecpark.org
- Free
- 5am-midnight

Meet the Painted Ladies

When prospectors struck it rich in the Gold Rush, they upgraded from downtown tenements to pastel 'Painted Lady' Victorian flats around **Alamo Square Park**, embellished to the eaves with gilded woodwork and look-at-me bay windows. Since Alamo Square's Painted Ladies were built on bedrock, many survived the 1906 earthquake – until 1950s developers began demolishing this diverse, historic neighborhood to clear the way for luxury high-rise condos. Some 38 blocks of affordable Victorian homes and small businesses were destroyed before public outcry stopped the destruction in a landmark win. Today you'll spot fresh 6-10 color schemes inspired by SF's 1970s Colorist Movement, when San Franciscans restored many Painted Ladies to their full glory.

Westerfield House

On Alamo Square's northwestern corner stands **Westerfeld House**, a gilded Stick Italianate Victorian with a spooky watchtower. This 28-room mansion was built by candy baron William Westerfeld in 1889, and survived subsequent incarnations as a jazz speakeasy and a legendary 50-person hippie commune. Filmmaker Kenneth Anger filmed satanic rituals in the tower with Church of Satan founder Anton LaVey, involving one grumpy lion coaxed up four flights of stairs.

The Haight & Hayes Valley

SAN FRANCISCO'S HIPPIE HOTSPOT

Hippie idealism thrives in the Haight with street musicians, anarchist comic books and psychedelic murals splashed on every available surface. In the 1960s, thousands of young people from across the country flocked to the corner of Haight and Ashbury, drawn by psychedelic bands, revolutionary politics and free-love communes – a moment seen through a more critical eye in Joan Didion's 1967 essay 'Slouching Toward Bethlehem.' Counterculture kids called themselves freaks and flower children; *San Francisco Chronicle* columnist Herb Caen dubbed them 'hippies.' The Upper Haight has hung onto its roots: hippies reminisce about glory days while trailed by their embarrassed teenage relations, and new-age practitioners load up on chakra-cleansing crystals. Down in the Lower Haight there are mellower vibes on designated slow streets, where dog walkers wrangle their herds and cyclists and skaters zig-zag around steep hills. Next door in Hayes Valley, Zen monks and jazz legends drift past some of the city's best restaurants.

TOP TIP

You'll need more than fair-trade coffee or local microbrews to power through Haight St sightseeing. Veer off the main drag to Divisadero for affordable brunch and lunch spots, or head to Hayes Valley for critically acclaimed dining (reserve ahead) and shows at SFJAZZ Center.

Observe the Time at Haight & Ashbury

It's always 4:20 here

In 1967's Summer of Love, the San Francisco fog was laced with pot, incense and burning military draft cards, and at the

continued on p88

GETTING AROUND

Walking is the best way to explore the area's bookstores, boutiques and Victorians – start in the Upper Haight, then walk downhill to the Lower Haight and hit Hayes Valley in time for dinner. Bus lines 6 and 7 travel along Haight St, connecting downtown to Golden Gate Park. Line 22 links the Lower Haight to the Mission and the Marina, while the 43 connects the Upper Haight to the Marina. At the Van Ness Muni metro stop one block east of Hayes Valley, you can hop the N line, which stops near the Lower and Upper Haight and heads onward to Ocean Beach.

THE HAIGHT & HAYES VALLEY

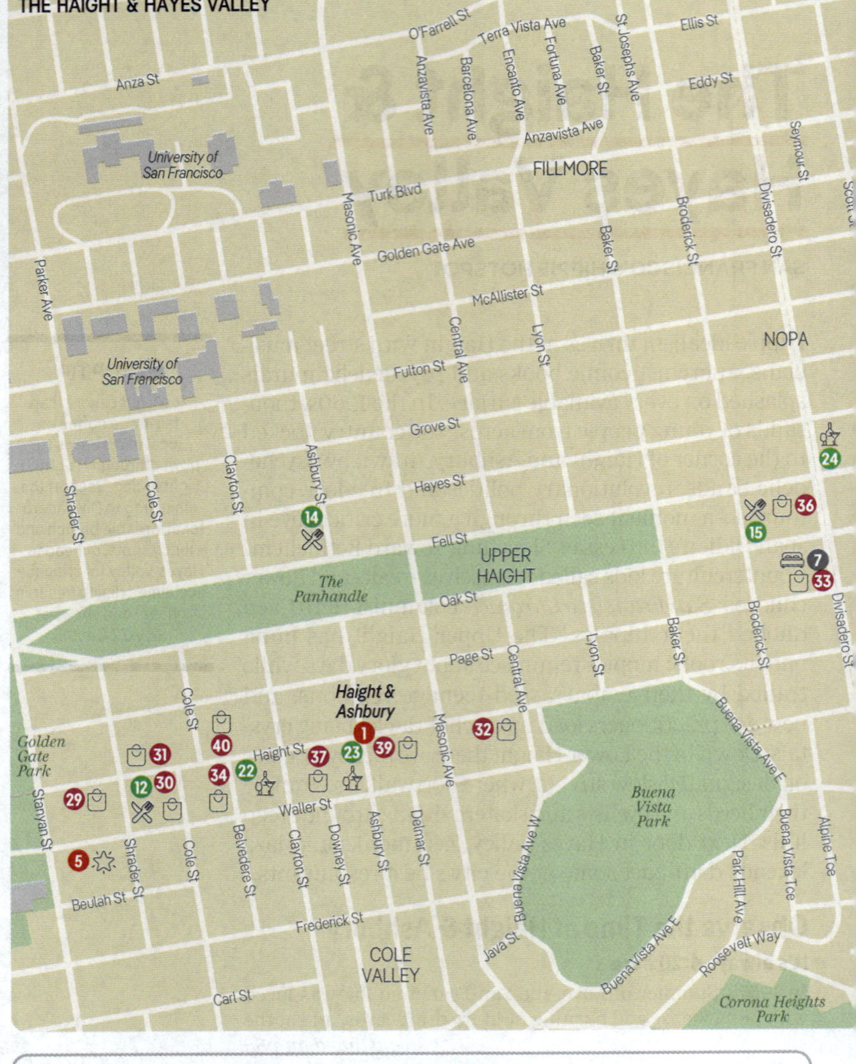

HIGHLIGHTS
1 Haight & Ashbury
2 Haight Street Art Center

SIGHTS
3 San Francisco Zen Center

ACTIVITIES
4 Church of 8 Wheels
5 Free Gold Watch

SLEEPING
6 Hayes Valley Inn
7 Metro Hotel
8 Parsonage

EATING
9 a Mano
10 Doppio Zero
11 DragonEats
12 Escape from New York Pizza
13 Gioia Pizzeria
14 Karma Cafe
15 Nopalito
16 Om Sabor
17 Otra
18 Rad Radish
19 Rich Table
20 Robin

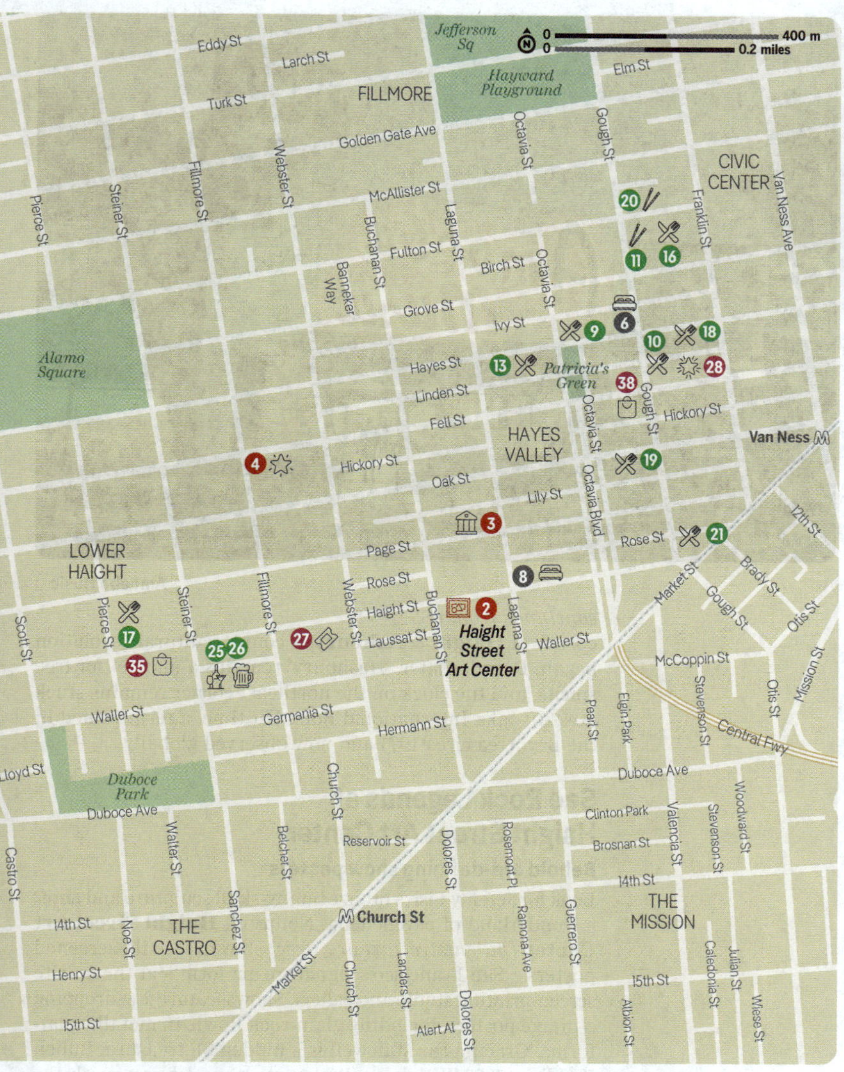

- **21** Zuni Cafe

DRINKING & NIGHTLIFE

- **see 30** Alembic
- **22** Aub Zam Zam
- **23** Club Deluxe
- **24** Madrone Art Bar
- **25** Noc Noc
- **26** Toronado

ENTERTAINMENT

- **27** Faight Collective
- **28** SFJAZZ

SHOPPING

- **29** Amoeba Music
- **30** Booksmith
- **31** Borderlands Books
- **32** Bound Together
- **33** Comix Experience
- **34** Decades of Fashion
- **35** Fuzz & Sway
- **36** Gamescape
- **37** Held Over
- **38** Isotope
- **39** Relic Vintage
- **40** Wasteland

GRANT HENDERSON/ALAMY

Amoeba Music

continued from p85
corner of **Haight & Ashbury**, a countercultural revolution began. Decades later, 'Hashbury' remains a magnet for free spirits, and the clock on the northeast corner remains stuck at 4:20 – aka International Bong Hit time, a term coined in the Bay Area circa 1971 and now observed globally.

See Rock Legends at Haight Street Art Center

Behold era-defining show posters

Look for Jeremy Fish's bronze bunny-skull sculpture and enter a wonderland of psychedelia. Nonprofit **Haight Street Art Center** *(haightstreetart.org; free)* showcases silk-screened posters – San Francisco's signature art form – at the on-site screen-printing studio and gallery. Shows feature jaw-dropping vintage posters, including glam-rock Bowie in metallic platforms. Gracing the stairwell is a hidden SF treasure: Ruben Kaddish's 1937 WPA fresco *Dissertation on Alchemy,* surely the trippiest mural ever commissioned by the US government. The center is open from noon to 6pm, Thursday through Sunday.

EATING IN HAIGHT & HAYES VALLEY: VEGAN & VEGETARIAN

Rad Radish: Plant-based menu that satisfies munchies, from Pineapple Express Impossible burgers to chili crisp cauliflower. *9am-8.30pm Sun-Fri, to 9.30pm Sat* **$**

Om Sabor: Creative, ecofriendly meat-free spins on nostalgic favorites inside the audiophile cocktail lounge Phonobar. *5-10pm Wed-Sat, 5-9pm Tue* **$**

DragonEats: Tofu banh mi will give you something to roar about at this casual, veggie-friendly Vietnamese deli. *11am-6pm Mon-Sat, to 5pm Sun* **$**

Otra: Start off strong with spicy salsa macha on black beans, followed by sweet potato tacos from this vegetarian-friendly menu. *5-10pm* **$$**

Complete Collections at Amoeba Music

Shop deep cuts and certified bops

Enticements are hardly necessary to lure fans to the West Coast's most eclectic collection of new and used music and video, but **Amoeba Music** *(amoeba.com)* offers listening stations, free zines with uncannily accurate staff reviews and runs a foundation that's saved one million acres of rainforest. This cavernous former bowling alley holds upwards of 100,000 vinyl records, CDs and cassettes covering obscure jazz to mainstream hip-hop. It also hosts Live at Amoeba free concerts.

Hit High Scores at Free Gold Watch

Retro pinball galore

You've hit the jackpot: inside a working screen-printing shop, **Free Gold Watch** *(freegoldwatch.com)* arcade is crammed with 50+ vintage pinball games. Most cost a buck or less to play, including Elvis, Godzilla and SF-favorite Dirty Harry; don't miss Secret Juju Gallery's rare 1970s games. Power up with arcade staples – pizza, hotdogs, nachos – plus craft beers and cocktails.

Go on a Vintage Shopping Spree

Wander through wardrobes of the past

Rock a new/old style from **Wasteland** *(shopwasteland.com)*, a converted-cinema vintage superstore with a wall of prized vintage concert tees. Or check out **Decades of Fashion** *(decadesoffashionsf.com)*, a wearable museum featuring Gilded Age opera gloves and *Dynasty*-era power blazers. **Relic Vintage** *(relicvintagesf.com)* is an elegant haberdashery of pinstriped suits and poodle skirts, while 1970s Western wear from **Held Over** *(@heldovervintage)* demands to go line-dancing. The vintage party keeps grooving at **Fuzz & Sway** *(@fuzznswayshop)*, a motherlode of mod dresses and funky maxi-skirts.

Get on a Roll at Church of 8 Wheels

Believe in the power of 'rolligion'

At the **Church of 8 Wheels** *(churchof8wheels.com; skate rental $5)*, worship begins with '80s music blaring from the pulpit and congregants skating backward under a disco ball. This church-turned-roller rink offers family-friendly skate sessions

HAIGHT HANGOUTS

Becka Robbins is the founder of nonprofit **Books Not Bans** *(@booksnotbans)*, sending LGBTQ+ literature to communities facing book bans. Here are her favorite reading spots in the Haight.

Aub Zam Zam
Bring a booklight and read in the bar, 'cuz books are awesome and so are Zam Zam's martinis. The jukebox provides the perfect background music.

Karma Cafe
She's giving macrame. Ditch the stressy laptop crowd and pull up with a book at this cute hippie joint. The coffee is fine, but the smoothies are where it's at.

Club Deluxe
This place is my paradise, perfect for a solitary outing with a book. Listen to the best local bands while enjoying a good read.

EATING IN THE HAIGHT & HAYES VALLEY: PIZZA

Escape from New York Pizza: Pair a slice of pesto with roasted garlic and potato with a vintage shopping spree. *10am-10pm Sun-Thu, 10am-2am Fri & Sat* $

Gioia Pizzeria: The name means joy in Italian, and that's what it delivers with seasonal toppings and housemade cannoli. *11am-10pm* $

Doppio Zero: Classic Neapolitan pizzas hot from a wood-fired oven – try the namesake. *11.30am-10pm Mon-Thu, to 11pm Fri & Sat, to 9.30pm Sun* $$

a Mano: Basic but not boring pizzas and show-stealing pastas, including handmade rigatoni. *11.30am-9.30pm Mon-Thu, to 10.30pm Fri & Sat, to 9pm Sun* $$

BEST PLACES TO GEEK OUT

Isotope: At this comic-book lounge, flip through superhero serials and eye the toilet seats signed by famous illustrators, then head upstairs to relax on comfy leather sofas with local graphic novelists, some of whom lead workshops here. Holds signings and free comic-book days. *(facebook.com/isotopecomics)*

Gamescape: Since 1985, the city's tabletop gaming headquarters has featured game supplies designed by local cooperatives. Stick around for indie board-game nights and card tournaments. *(gamescapesf.com)*

Comix Experience: Comic-book deep cuts, signed first editions and kid-friendly graphic novels all find their home in this tiny neighborhood shop. Join the club to get the best graphic novel of the month at your doorstep. *(comixexperience.com)*

at 5pm to 6.30pm on Friday, 2.30pm to 6.30pm on Saturday, and 6pm to 7.30pm Sunday and Tuesday. Afterward, anyone 18 and up can get their skate groove on at goth nights, silent discos and soul roll Sundays.

Leave Plans to Faight Collective

See what Faight has in store for you

Looking for an affordable yoga studio? Radically free craft workshop? Comedy show? Place to get a DIY thigh tat? At the crossroads of Fillmore and Haight, **Faight Collective** *(thefaight.com)* is a maker gallery upstairs and unpredictable events space downstairs, featuring yoga, open mics, live music and something called 'collective envisioning.'

Stomp for More at SFJAZZ

Find bliss at SF's premier jazz venue

Jazz legends and singular talents from Argentina to Yemen are showcased at **SFJAZZ** *(sfjazz.org)*, America's largest jazz center. Enjoy brilliant sound in Miner Auditorium, where the stage is regularly stormed by soul icon Mavis Staples, punk poet Laurie Anderson and Tony-winning dancer Savion Glover. All seats have drink holders and clear stage views. Hear fresh takes on classic jazz albums and poets riffing with combos in the downstairs Joe Henderson Lab.

Browse Book Nooks

Read, drink, repeat

Booksmith *(booksmith.com)* co-owns adjoining **Alembic** bar *(alembicsf.com)* – fair warning in case you wake up tomorrow amid piles of signed San Francisco novels. Explore literature's outer realms at **Borderlands Books** *(borderlands-books.com)*, dedicated to science fiction, fantasy, mystery and horror. Since 1976, volunteer-run anarchist book collective **Bound Together** *(boundtogether.org)* has supplied free thinkers with organic-permaculture manuals, social history and radical comics, while coordinating SF's annual Anarchist Book Fair and running the Prisoners' Literature Project – they make us tools of the state look like slackers.

DRINKING IN THE HAIGHT: EPIC NIGHTS

Noc Noc: Who's there? Trance DJs, anarchist hackers and Burning Man founders, that's who. Post-apocalyptic cave rave. *5pm-1am Sun-Thu, to 2am Fri & Sat*

Aub Zam Zam (p89): Persian arches, *1001 Nights* murals, 1930s jazz on the jukebox and top-shelf cocktails at low-shelf prices. *3pm-2am Mon-Fri, 1pm-2am Sat & Sun*

Madrone Art Bar: Bump into art installations on Motown Mondays, Saturday global disco and Prince/Michael Jackson parties. *4pm-2am Mon-Sat, 3pm-1.30am Sun*

Toronado: Glory hallelujah, beer-lovers: your prayers are answered. Genuflect before the chalkboard altar that lists 40-plus beers on tap. *11.30am-2am*

KEVIN HUTCHINSON/FLICKR/CC BY 2.0 ©

San Francisco Zen Center

Breathe in, Breathe Out

Meditate at the Zen Center

Since 1969, the Julia Morgan–designed **San Francisco Zen Center** *(sfzc.org)* has been home to one of the largest Buddhist communities outside of Asia. Watch sunlight fill the Zendo during free morning zazen *(5:25am daily)*, and check out events: half-day garden meditations, workshops blending breath work with beatboxing and Trans Sangha, meditation by and for the trans community *(7pm every other Thursday)*.

KEEPING PEACE & LOVE ALIVE IN THE HAIGHT

Ever since America's youth fled to the Upper Haight in the 1960s as a place to fit in, panhandling has been part of the scene, from buskers to teens scrounging for bus fare – no judgment, no obligation. Back in the '60s, Haight hippies and Black Panthers distributed free food around the Bay, and while you're in town, you can keep those neighborly good vibes flowing. You could pack grocery bags on Saturday at historic Haight Ashbury Food Program *(thefoodprogram.org)*, serve hot meals or make care packages at Glide's homeless service center *(glide.org)* or donate to local nonprofits – all thoughtful gestures to repay San Francisco hospitality, and ensure everyone has a chance to feel at home here.

EATING IN THE HAIGHT AND HAYES VALLEY: MEMORABLE MEALS

Rich Table: Impossible cravings begin with mind-bending dishes: porcini doughnuts, Dungeness crab latkes, sea-urchin cacio e pepe. *5-10.30pm Tue-Sat* $$$

Zuni Cafe: Turning menu staples into gourmet go-tos since 1979, like Caesar salad with house-cured anchovies. *5-9.30pm Tue-Sun, 11am-3pm Fri-Sun* $$$

Robin: Trust the chef's choice. There's no menu, but decadent ingredients like Wagyu beef and caviar are sure to please. *5-9.30pm Wed-Sun* $$$

Nopalito: Fresh, organic ingredients in colorful Mexican dishes that warm even the foggiest of days. *11.30am-9pm Sun-Tue & Thu-Sat, 4.30-9pm Wed* $$

Mission, Dogpatch & Potrero

SUNSHINE, MURALS, BOOKS & FLAVORS GALORE

GETTING AROUND

The Mission is flat and walkable, though you may want to hop a bus to Dogpatch. The 48 runs east–west from Dogpatch via the Mission to Ocean Beach, and the 22 connects Dogpatch, the Mission, Haight, Fillmore and Pacific Heights. The BART runs from downtown: hop off at 24th St or 16th St – the latter station is sketchy, but close to the bustling Valencia and 16th hub. The 14 bus connects Mission to downtown and the Embarcadero, and the 49 travels Van Ness Ave to the Wharf. Both stop near mural-lined Calle 24.

☑ TOP TIP

You'll feel at ease walking this area by day, but keep your street smarts sharp walking alone at night – especially around the 16th St BART station and around deserted Dogpatch warehouses.

Enjoy the district's sunny microclimates with a burrito in one hand and a book in the other, surrounded by a local crowd of filmmakers, grocers, techies, skaters and novelists. Wrapped in murals and sunshine, the Mission welcomes you to hang out at bookstores, art spaces and taquerias – especially along Calle 24 (24th St), SF's designated Latino Cultural District. The Mission is also a magnet for lesbians, Asian Americans and Arab Americans – all are welcome and celebrated in multicultural Mission arts, food and festivals. There's nightlife for everyone here: lesbian bars, historic saloons, cinemas and experimental theater. Valencia St is hipster central, but don't be too quick to scoff: try their excellent coffee, baked goods, vintage shops and maker spaces. Waterfront Dogpatch is creatively repurposing rusty industrial docks into parks, arts and music venues, and Potrero throws down at punk shows and art openings.

See SF's Sunny Side at Dolores Park

Loll the day away

Welcome to San Francisco's sunny side, home to street ball and Mayan-pyramid playgrounds, taco picnics and semi-professional tanning. At **Dolores Park** *(sfrecpark.org; free)*, grassy slopes are dedicated to lolling, while lowlands host soccer, Frisbee, political protests and other local sports. Good weather brings major events, including Easter's **Hunky Jesus** drag contest *(thesisters.org; free)*, free summer movie nights and fall performances by the **San Francisco Mime Troupe** *(sfmt.org; free)*.

Join Mission Cultural Festivals

Celebrate life to the fullest

No place celebrates life quite like the Mission. SF is far from Rio, but you'd never know it during **Carnaval** *(carnaval sanfrancisco.org; free)*, when everyone shakes their tail

DAVID TRAN PHOTO/SHUTTERSTOCK

Carnaval

feathers in the Mission streets. For **Día de los Muertos** *(dayofthedeadsf.org; free)*, brass bands, lowriders and dancing skeletons honor the dead along Calle 24, community altars line **Potrero del Sol/La Raza Skate Park** *(sfrecpark.org)* and **Mission Cultural Center for Latino Arts** *(MCCLA; missionculturalcenter.org)* hosts art shows and epic mole tastings. Flor y Canto (Flower and Song) and Paseo Poetico fill Mission streets with poetry and the joy of living.

Showtime in the Mission

Hang onto the edge of your seat

Brace for impact: at Mission performance spaces like **ODC Theater** *(odc.dance)*, risky, raw dance performances leave audiences gasping. **Gray Area** *(grayarea.org; events sliding scale $0-50)* blurs boundaries between art and science, culture and technology with mind-expanding programs – immersive electronica shows, 3D art workshops, psychedelic cyberpunk festivals – in historic Grand Theater. **Chan National Queer Arts Center** *(sfgmc.org)* hosts SF's Gay Men's Chorus – as seen in the award-winning documentary *Gay Chorus Deep South* – plus boundary-pushing Q-lab theater and raucous

continued on p96

DRINKING IN THE MISSION: ICONIC BARS

Trick Dog: Each new menu captures an SF obsession, proof the bar often called America's best never runs out of tricks. *4pm-midnight Sun-Thu, to 2am Fri & Sat*

Royal Cuckoo Organ Lounge: DJ jams on an organ among lucha-libre-masked customers. *6pm-midnight Mon, 4pm-2am Tue-Thu, from 3pm Fri-Sun*

Pop's Bar: Approach the 1937 bar for cocktails named after lowrider cars that kick into overdrive when DJs spin. *6am-2am*

Zeitgeist: At this biker beer garden, you've got two seconds to choose a craft beer from 64 on tap – tough but fair. *2-11pm Mon-Wed, to midnight Thu, to 1am Fri & Sat, noon-9.30pm Sun*

HIGHLIGHTS
1 826 Valencia
2 Balmy Alley
3 Clarion Alley
4 Creativity Explored
5 Dolores Park
6 Mission Cultural Center for Latino Arts
7 Women's Building

SIGHTS
8 500 Capp St
9 House of Seiko
10 Incline Gallery
11 Jack Fischer Gallery
12 Southern Exposure

ACTIVITIES
13 Potrero del Sol/La Raza Skatepark
14 Precita Eyes Mission Mural Tours

EATING
15 Burma Love
16 Donaji
17 Farmhouse Kitchen Thai Cuisine
18 Flour + Water
19 Freekeh
20 Komaaj Mazze & Wine Bar
21 La Corneta Taqueria
22 La Palma Mexicatessen
23 La Taqueria
24 Old Jerusalem
25 Pancho Villa
26 Reem's
27 San Ho Won
28 Shizen
29 Taqueria El Farolito
30 Udupi Palace

DRINKING & NIGHTLIFE
31 Casements Bar
32 El Rio
33 Jolene's
34 Mother
35 Pop's Bar
36 Royal Cuckoo Organ Lounge
37 Trick Dog
38 Zeitgeist

ENTERTAINMENT
39 Alamo Drafthouse Cinema
40 Bissap Baobab
41 Brava Theater
42 Brick & Mortar

43 Carnaval
44 Chan National Queer Arts Center
45 Chapel
see 39 Foreign Cinema
46 Gray Area
47 Hunky Jesus Contest
48 ODC Theater
49 Red Poppy Art House
50 Roxie Cinema
51 Marsh

SHOPPING
52 Adobe Books & Arts Coop
53 Dog Eared Books
54 Double Down
55 Medicine for Nightmares
56 Mission Comics & Art
57 Needles & Pens
58 Sour Cherry Comics

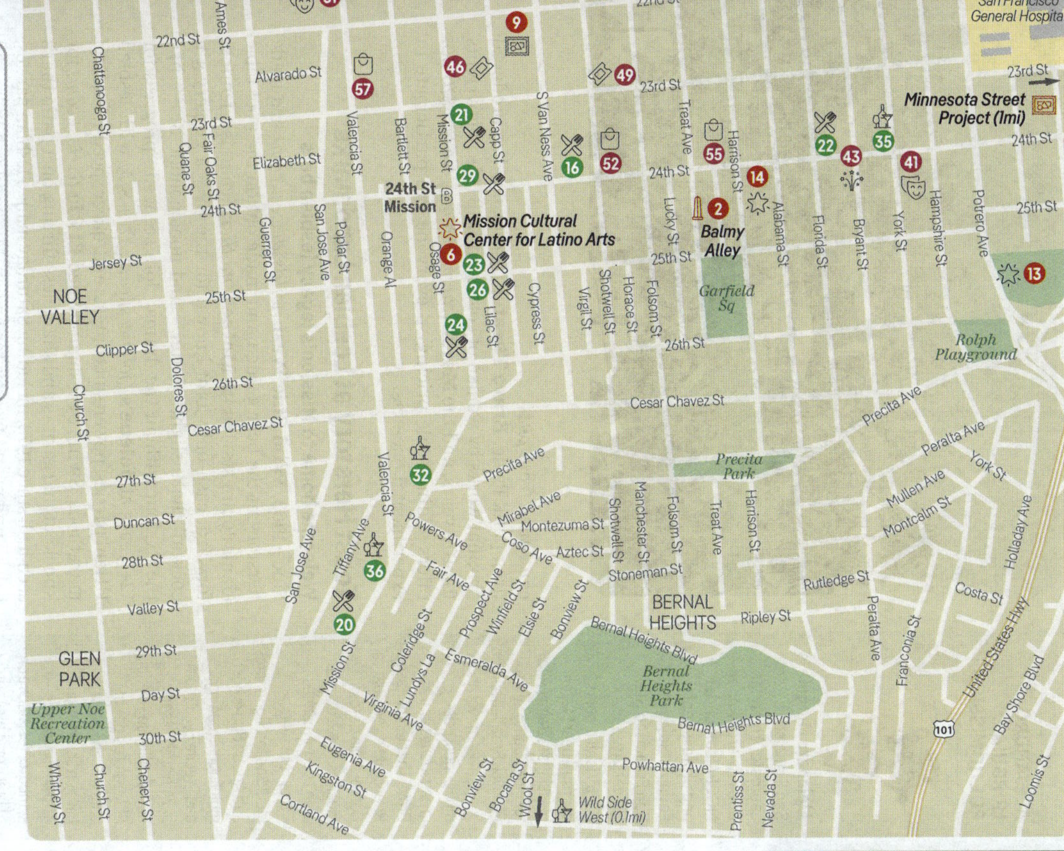

ALEJANDRO MURGUÍA'S POETIC MISSION

Alejandro Murguía is San Francisco's Poet Laureate, American Book Award winner, MCCLA cofounder and professor of Latino Studies at San Francisco State University.

Poetry is all around us. You'll hear Mayan blessings in Balmy Alley for Flor y Canto Literary Festival, Brazilian samba songs at Carnaval and multilingual poetry in *panaderías* and at Brava Theater for Paseo Poético. Mission Cultural Center's Dia de los Muertos Aztec dances aren't performances – they're prayers. Medicine for Nightmares and Adobe Books host multilingual readings, and Precita Eyes' mural at 24th and Folsom honors Alfonso Texidor, *El Tecalote's* poetry editor. Juana Alicia's Mission library mural is a flowering cactus – a symbol of resistance on a library built by Andrew Carnegie. What could be more poetic?

continued from p93
drag punk Pride. **Brava Theater** *(brava.org)* has produced original works by women of color and LGBTQ+ playwrights for 40+ years, and the **Marsh** *(themarsh.org; tickets $10-50)* offers sliding-scale pricing so everyone can participate in experimental one-acts.

Toast Herstory at Lesbian Landmarks

Welcome home to Mission's legacy lesbian bars

Since 1962, **Wild Side West** *(wildsidewest.com)* has made herstory in the beer garden and made out on the pool table (Janis Joplin started it). **Mother** *(mothersf.com)* is a femme-forward, cash-only joint known for the Ex – a gingery gin cocktail that's slightly bitter – and nonalcoholic BFF – like the Ex, 'but without the drama.' Join scenes in progress for 12+ years at **Jolene's** *(jolenessf.com; free-$15)* with lesbian UHaul parties, power-suit contests and 'queer speed-friending' marathons. Swing by lesbian-owned **El Rio** *(elriosf.com)* for knockout margaritas and shameless flirting on a patio that's seen it all since 1978, including Saturday mango lesbian parties, salsa Sunday and free oyster Friday. Mission Irish pubs and lesbian bars have historically attracted different clienteles – but Irish lesbian-owned **Casements Bar** brings everyone to

EATING IN THE MISSION: CLASSIC BURRITOS

La Taqueria: Miguel Jara's burrito has hardly changed since 1972: grilled meats, slow-cooked beans, flour tortillas and housemade salsa. *11am-8:45pm Wed-Sun* $

La Corneta Taqueria: Roving mariachis serenade Mission families gathered in this mural-lined taqueria for extra-special burritos with plump prawns. *10am-9pm* $

Pancho Villa: Meal-sized 'baby burritos' are not to be confused with 'regular,' which is the size of a baby. Slather with salsas at the condiment bar. *10am-10pm* $

Taqueria El Farolito: Follow late-night lines to this no-frills, cash-only taqueria for meat-packed, forearm-sized burritos. *10am-1:45am Sun-Thu, to 2:45am Fri & Sat* $

JEJIM/GETTY IMAGES

Dolores Park (p92)

the mural-lined patio for Guinness, 50+ Irish whiskeys and California-fresh pub grub.

See Something New in Old Mission Cinemas

Catch eye-opening Mission movies

The Mission's 1909 **Roxie Cinema** *(roxie.com)* is a neighborhood nonprofit with an international reputation for year-round film festivals, including Center for Asian American Media's **CAAMFest** *(caamfest.com; May)*, LGBTQ+ **Frameline Film Fest** *(frameline.org; June)*, **Jewish Film Festival** *(jfi.org; July)* and **Arab Film Festival** *(arabfilminstitute.org; November)*. **Alamo Drafthouse Cinema** *(drafthouse.com)* screens blockbusters and cult revivals in a 1932 movie palace, while serving movie-themed cocktails, mocktails, beer, burgers and all-day brunch. At **Foreign Cinema** *(foreigncinema.com)*, timeless films accompany chef Gayle Pirie's seasonal, sustainable California cuisine.

Load Up on Comics & Zines

Spend action-packed afternoons in the Mission

Heads will roll and fists will fly inside **Mission:Comics & Art** *(missioncomicsandart.com)*, featuring indie comics *(Snotgirl,*

BRAVA FOR NEW MURALS

Under Brava Theater's towering vintage marquee, a glorious new mural features two women breathing life into this historic 1926 deco theater. Brava has been staging new works by women and queer playwrights here for more than 40 years – from V-day monologist Eve Ensler to Culture Clash comedy – and now hosts more than 200 events annually. The colorful wraparound mural by Agana and her crew covers the entire three-story Brava building, with larger-than-life female figures invoking creative spirits, plus a gentle reminder to 'smash the patriarchy' over the ticket booth.

EATING IN THE MISSION: SPECIAL OCCASIONS

San Ho Won: Minimalist bistro serving maximalist Korean flavors – *jebi churi* filet packs more flavor than an entire steakhouse. *5-9.30pm Thu-Sun, to 10pm Fri & Sat* **$$$**

Flour + Water: Rustic yet elegant Italian dishes, from classic mortadella-stuffed tortellini to creative duck and butternut garganelli. *5-9.30pm* **$$**

Farmhouse Kitchen: Farm-to-table Thai, with turmeric-laced Sonoma fried chicken and Make a Wish cocktails in genie's lamps. *11.30am-2pm & 5-8.30pm Sun-Thu, 4.30-9.30pm Fri & Sat* **$$**

Donaji: Celebrate with deep Oaxacan flavors and organic Californian ingredients in red mole–braised short ribs and churro s'mores. *5-10pm Wed & Thu, to 10.30pm Fri & Sat* **$**

MISSION SCHOOL COOL

In the '90s, skate culture, underground comics and graffiti met in Mission alleys – and the art world hasn't been the same since. Art critic Glen Helfand dubbed the movement 'Mission School,' including artists who drew outside the lines of fine arts' programs like SF graffiti/mural/zine/skate artists Margaret Kilgallen, Barry McGee, Ruby Neri and Chris Johanson. SF's indie art spaces invited Mission School artists indoors, launching the 'Beautiful Losers' group show – outsider slang from Leonard Cohen's 1966 counterculture novel – with a 2008 documentary that made Mission School artists mainstays at museum shows and art fairs. What's next? Find out in Mission alleys.

SABRINA DALBESIO/LONELY PLANET

Red Poppy Art House

Head Lopper) alongside marquee titles *(Walking Dead, Star Wars)*. **Sour Cherry Comics** *(sourcherrycomics.com)* earns fan followings for its vast queer comics selections, community fundraisers and DIY zines. Entertain new ideas at zine newsstand **Needles & Pens** *(needles-pens.com)*, from *Crap Hound* collages to Finn Cunningham's *Mental Health Cookbook*. **Dog Eared Books** *(dogearedbooks.com)* picks include graphic novels and zines, including Jordan Karnes' *It Hasn't Stopped Being California Here*. **Double Down** zine emerged from SF's women and nonbinary street-skater scene, and its HQ stocks back issues and inspiration galore.

Dream on in Mission Bookstores

Get lit in the Mission

Stranger-than-fiction events unfold during October's **Litquake** *(litquake.org)*, America's biggest, most outlandish literary festival, with authors spilling secrets over drinks at the legendary **Lit Crawl**. **Adobe Books & Arts Coop** *(adobebooks.com)* delivers wall-to-wall inspiration – limited-edition art books, rare cookbooks, well-thumbed poetry – plus zine launch parties and art openings. **Medicine for Nightmares** *(medicinefornightmares.com)* showcases bilingual books in front, art shows and community events in back. When you're running

EATING IN THE MISSION: VEGETARIAN & VEGAN

Shizen: No boring cucumber rolls here. Enjoy eggplant nigiri and mushroom and tempura asparagus rolls with gochujang aioli. *5-9pm Sun-Thu, 4-9.30pm Fri & Sat* **$$**

La Palma Mexicatessen: Handmade tamales, *huaraches* (stuffed masa) and pupusas (tortilla pockets) with vegan, vegetarian or meat fillings. *8am-5pm Wed-Mon* **$**

Udupi Palace: Hot dates call for a 2ft-long paper *dosa* (lentil-flour pancake) and satisfying *idli* (fluffy lentil-rice cake) with coconut chutney. *noon-8.30pm* **$**

Burma Love: Flavors here hug your tongue, then deliver a swift kick – get fermented tea-leaf salad, caramelized eggplant and top-notch cocktails. *11.30am-3pm & 5-10pm* **$$**

low on pirate supplies and fresh ideas, nonprofit **826 Valencia** *(826valencia.org)* stocks spyglasses and McSweeney's publications to support youth writing workshops.

Explore the Mission's Alternative Art Spaces

See breakthrough art in unusual spaces

Be the first to glimpse artworks destined for museum retrospectives, international art fairs and Marc Jacobs handbags, all by local artists with developmental disabilities at nonprofit **Creativity Explored** *(creativityexplored.org)*, and join the creative fray at **Imaginate Saturdays** *(noon-3pm; free; all ages welcome)*. Lose track of time in the repurposed watch-repair shop that's now **House of Seiko** gallery *(houseofseiko.info; free)*, and ramp up your art collection at **Incline Gallery** *(inclinegallerysf.com; free)*, an ex-mortuary ramp where bodies were once transported. Art ties the room together at nonprofit **Southern Exposure** *(soex.org; donations welcome)*, from fundraising drawing rallies to Resist and Rejoice art parties. At nonprofit **500 Capp St** *(500cappstreet.org; free Sat visits)*, the Mission home of late sculptor David Ireland overflows with experimental installations.

Look Ahead at Minnesota Street Projects

See gallery shows that launch art movements

An old factory showcases new talents at nonprofit **Minnesota Street Project** *(minnesotastreetproject.com)*. Shows here are free and fearless, from meticulously crafted dreamscapes at **Eleanor Harwood Gallery** *(eleanorharwood.com)* to **Jack Fischer Gallery**'s multimedia think-pieces *(jackfischer gallery.com)*. **Casemore Gallery** *(casemoregallery.com)* features renowned photographers – Jim Jocoy's club-kid portraits, Todd Hido's eerie suburban subdivisions – and **Anglim/Trimble** *(anglimtrimble.com)* launches Bay Area art movements, from Beat assemblage to Bay Area conceptualists. Galleries stay open until 8pm for First Saturday artist talks and workshops.

Cheer on the Warriors

Catch a game at the Chase Center

The Bay Area's frequent NBA champions (four times since 2014) play basketball to win at San Francisco's new **Chase Center** *(chasecenter.com)*. Between seasons, the Chase Center hosts marquee pop and comedy headliners.

BEST MISSION MUSIC VENUES

Chapel: Musical prayers are answered in a 1914 California arts-and-crafts landmark with heavenly acoustics for folkYEAH! indie artists and performance -art mayhem.

Brick & Mortar: Break out of radio ruts and playlist loops with outlandish bands rocking the mortar loose, from breakthrough Popscene shows to NPR Tiny Desk artist showcases.

Bissap Baobab: Come for shareable Senegalese food, stick around for live acts and DJs after 9pm – bachata, Cuban jazz, Afrobeats, flamenco and jam sessions.

Red Poppy Art House: A snug Mission storefront doubles as a concert hall for international artists-in-residence, from Armenian duduk virtuosos to Argentine tango quartets.

EATING IN THE MISSION: BEST MEZZE

Komaaj Mazze & Wine Bar: Brilliant flavors rarely found outside northern Iran like pomegranate-glazed smoked trout. *5.30-9pm Tue-Thu, noon-3pm & 5.30-10pm Fri-Sun* $$

Reem's: Acclaimed chef Reem Assil serves sensational, sustainable Palestinian Californian comfort food. *11am-3pm & 5-9pm Tue-Sat* $

Freekeh: Share classic dips and tangy *musakhan* (chicken or mushrooms rolled into lavash) with arak limonada. *5.30-9pm Tue-Sun, 10am-2.30pm Sat & Sun* $

Old Jerusalem: Bond over generous portions of Palestinian and Syrian classics, including shawarma and *mansaf* (lamb pilaf)). *11am-10pm Wed-Mon* $

TOP EXPERIENCE

Mission Murals

Frida Kahlo and Diego Rivera have no idea what they started. Since the Mexican power couple came to SF for a working honeymoon in the 1930s, they've inspired generations of muralists to create 500-plus Mission murals – a splendid show of political dissent, community pride and street-art bravado. Today, multistory murals cover Calle 24, SF's Latino Cultural District.

JOHN LANDER/ALAMY

Clarion Alley

TOP TIPS

- Outdoor murals are free for all to enjoy – but if you're posting a pic on social media, kindly credit the muralist.
- Muralists lead weekend **Precita Eyes walking tours** that last just under two hours. Proceeds fund mural upkeep and new commissions.

PRACTICALITIES

- Buses 12, 14, 48 and 49 stop at Calle 24
- BART 24th St Mission stop is blocks from Balmy Alley.

Balmy Alley

Inspired by Mexican artists Frida Kahlo and Diego Rivera, Mujeres Muralistas (Women Muralists) began painting garage doors here in 1973, turning a neglected backstreet into a neighborhood landmark. Today **Balmy Alley** murals are maintained by nonprofit **Precita Eyes** *(precitaeyes.org; mural tours adult/youth $25/10)*, including early Frida Kahlo homages, a 1985 memorial for El Salvador activist Archbishop Óscar Romero and Lucía González Ippolito's homage to 'Women of the Resistance.'

Clarion Alley

Most graffiti artists shun broad daylight – but not in **Clarion Alley,** SF's street-art showcase maintained by neighbors and Clarion Alley Collective. Over 900 murals have been created by Clarion artists since 1992, but few survive the tests of time and tagging – survivors include Megan Wilson's daisy-covered *Tax the Rich* and Jet Martinez' glimpse of Clarion Alley inside a forest spirit.

Women's Building

America's first women-owned-and-operated community center has housed 150 women's organizations since 1979 – and the 1994 *Maestrapeace* mural celebrates the **Women's Building** as a herstory landmark. Mission muralistas worked with 100 volunteers to cover the building with goddesses and women trailblazers.

The Castro

WELCOME TO THE GAYBORHOOD!

Rainbow flags gaily wave hello at the world's premier LGBTQ+ culture destination, spiritual home to club kids, career activists, leather daddies and drag stars alike. San Francisco's Castro district became a global queer hub in the 1970s, when Castro businessman Harvey Milk became California's first openly gay elected official. Along Market and Castro Sts, Rainbow Honor Walk sidewalk plaques honor Milk and 67 other LGBTQ+ heroes – including civil rights leader James Baldwin, Nobel Laureate Jane Addams and local icons including trans activist Lou Sullivan and SF's Absolute Empress José Sarria. Castro nightlife is legendary, but when the sun comes out, the neighborhood really shines – being out in broad daylight is a freedom this community fought for and thoroughly enjoys, especially on weekends when everyone's out and about at Castro cafes, stores and community venues. The little neighborhood under the giant rainbow flag remains a global symbol of freedom.

TOP TIP

The F streetcar stops at Jane Warner Plaza, named for the pioneering lesbian officer who patrolled the Castro. On sunny days, rainbow-themed seating and bizarre public art make for prime people-watching, – including glimpses of Castro nudists, legally obliged to cover up with strategically placed socks.

Showtime at Castro Theatre

Organ overtures at a deco-fabulous theater

The towering neon marquee blinks welcome to the C-A-S-T-R-O at the **Castro Theatre** *(castrotheatre.com)*, architect Timothy Pflueger's 1922 Spanish-Moorish-Asian fantasy cinema. Showtime starts when the mighty organ rises – and no, that's not a euphemism. The 'Mighty Wurlitzer' pipe organ emerges

GETTING AROUND

Strutting is the preferred method of travel in the Castro. Historic F line streetcars run to the Castro from Fisherman's Wharf, covering Market St through downtown. Trouble is, they sometimes get stuck in traffic and you can wait for what feels like forever. If the service is slow, take underground-metro K, L or M trains, which move (much) faster beneath Market St – same ticket, same price. J trains travel from downtown along Church St to 18th St and beyond. The 24 connects the Castro to bustling Divisadero St, and the 33 goes to the Haight and the Mission.

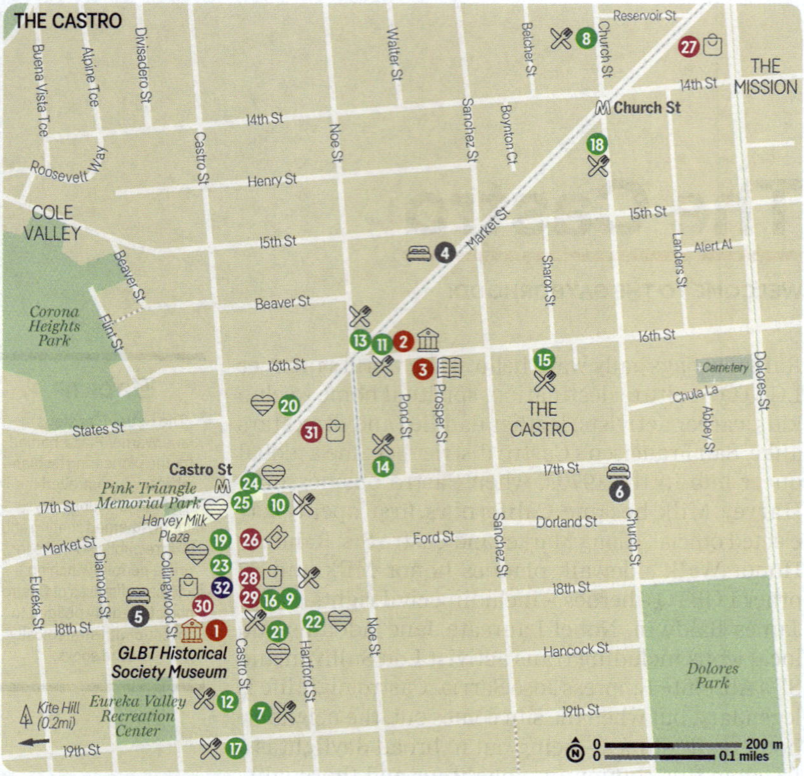

THE CASTRO

HIGHLIGHTS
1 GLBT Historical Society Museum

SIGHTS
2 Photo Booth Museum by Photomatica

ACTIVITIES
3 Eureka Valley Library

SLEEPING
4 Beck's Motor Lodge
5 Hotel Castro
6 Parker Guest House

EATING
7 Anchor Oyster Bar
8 Beit Rima
9 Blind Butcher
10 Cafe de Casa
11 Dinosaurs Sandwiches
12 Fable
13 Fisch & Flore
14 Frances
15 Gai Chicken Rice
16 Poesia Cafe
17 Spike's Coffees and Teas
18 Thoroughbread & Pastry

DRINKING & NIGHTLIFE
19 440 Castro
20 Beaux
21 Midnight Sun
22 Moby Dick
23 QBar
24 The Cafe
25 Twin Peaks Tavern

ENTERTAINMENT
26 Castro Theatre

SHOPPING
27 Apothecarium
28 Cliff's Variety
29 Fabulosa Books
30 Local Take
31 Stag & Manor

INFORMATION
32 Strut

EATING IN THE CASTRO: BUDGET PICKS

Dinosaurs Sandwiches: Monster banh mi sandwiches stomp hunger with Vietnamese fixings, topped with jalapeños, mayo and pickled carrots. *10am-7pm* **$**

Gai Chicken Rice: The solution to cold snaps and tentative tummies is Hainan-style poached chicken with rice, soup and cucumber salad. *11am-9pm* **$**

Beit Rima: Palestinian comfort food: braised lamb, *shakshuka* and lemony hummus that makes you pucker up. *11am-9pm Sun & Tue-Thu, to 9.30pm Fri & Sat* **$**

Fisch & Flore: Enjoy fresh seafood and watch the entire gay world go by from the sun-drenched corner patio. *2-9pm Wed & Thu, 11am-10pm Fri-Sun* **$$**

from the orchestra pit to play show tunes, leading crowd sing-alongs to Judy Garland's anthem 'San Francisco' before all-star drag revues, A-list queer comedy and premieres for LGBTQ+ Frameline Film Festival.

Pay Respects at GLBT Historical Society Museum

Know your queer history

America's first queer history museum showcases a century of San Francisco LGBTQ+ ephemera – including Harvey Milk's campaign literature and Keith Haring's posters urging SF to 'Act Up Fight AIDS' – alongside exhibits highlighting queer culture throughout history. **GLBT Historical Society Museum** *(glbthistory.org; entry $10)* has collected community history since 1985, capturing deep struggles and sheer queer joy that make visits bonding experiences for the LGBTQ+ community and allies alike. The shop features books researched here, historic posters – yes, SF's 1970 Gay-In was an actual event – and fridge magnets quoting Harvey Milk: 'You gotta give 'em hope.' Indeed.

Read the Rainbow at Fabulosa Books

Oh so Fabulosa!

Fabulosa means 'fabulous' in Polari, 19th-century gay theater slang – and the selection at **Fabulosa Books** *(fabulosa books.com)* is as fabulously colorful as the Castro's rainbow crosswalks, with categories ranging from Lesbians!! to Gender-Funky Sci-Fi. Dig through bins of vintage ephemera, browse forgotten literary masterpieces and don't miss author readings packed with local characters. Nonprofit Books Not Bans operates out of the (literal) closet in the back, sending LGBTQ+ books to communities where access is restricted.

Strut Your Stuff

Life-saving care and life-affirming art

In the 1980s and '90s, the AIDS epidemic devastated the Castro – but amid incalculable loss, the community founded life-saving San Francisco AIDS Foundation, the nonprofit behind **Strut** *(sfaf.org)*. This landmark community center offers free and low-cost health services, including PrEP and PEP, health screenings, walk-in counseling, substance-abuse treatment and support groups. ID required; privacy assured. Strut's event calendar includes gallery shows, open mics and Beyond Binary art afternoons.

PANORAMAS & POSES IN THE CASTRO

Panda Dulce is a founding queen of Drag Story Hour. Here are her recs for family-friendly afternoons in the Castro.

Walk up Kite Hill: At this rocky **overlook**, you can follow Market St to where the wharf kisses the Bay.

Strike a pose: I love to take visitors of all ages to the **Photo Booth Museum**. Snap some old school, four-shot strips in retro photo booths.

Be regaled with a drag story hour: Join us at the **Eureka Valley Library**, where drag artists perform fun read-alouds for kids. Remember to ask permission to take a photo or selfie. Cash tips are customary and appreciated.

EATING IN THE CASTRO: COZY CAFES

Poesia Cafe: Traditional focaccia and espresso drinks in a snug indoor-outdoor space. *8am-6pm Sun, to 5pm Mon, 7.30am-5pm Tue-Thu, to 6pm Fri & Sat*

Cafe de Casa: Dark roast coffee and colorful Brazilian fare to match the Castro's rainbow spirit. *8am-6pm Mon-Sat, to 5pm Sun*

Thoroughbread & Pastry: Chocolate bread, olive *fougasse* and sourdough sandwiches from SF Baking Institute founder Michel Suas. *8am-4pm Wed-Fri, to 5pm Sat & Sun*

Spike's Coffees and Teas: Cute bulldogs scowl from to-go cups at this fiercely independent coffee spot. *7am-5pm Mon-Fri, from 7.30am Sat & Sun*

BEST SHOPPING FOR HIM & HOME

Apothecarium: Consult experts at America's best-designed marijuana dispensary, according to *Architectural Digest*, then appreciate the local art and designer couches. *(apothecarium.com)*

Cliff's Variety: DIY maestros at the 1936 general store with gasp-worthy window displays won't raise an eyebrow at your need for silver body paint and a jar of rubber nuns.

Local Take: Take in the local scenery with Castro Theatre marquee prints, F streetcar T-shirts or belt buckles featuring vintage Muni maps. *(localtakesf.com)*

Stag & Manor: Dashing decor lets you take the Castro home: brass lanterns wink welcome at guests, and fair-trade throw pillows show dates how thoughtful yet laid-back you are. *(stagandmanor.com)*

GIMAS/SHUTTERSTOCK

Castro Theatre (p101)

Toast Freedom in Historic Gay Bars

Brace for stiff drinks and drag numbers

The vintage rainbow neon arrow points the way to a local landmark: originally opened in 1935, **Twin Peaks Tavern** became the world's first gay bar with windows open to the street in 1971. You can call anyone Ishmael at **Moby Dick** so long as you're buying. Its sign has been a Castro photo-op since 1977, and the commemorative mural outside is fab. The most happening bar on Castro St is **440 Castro** *(the440.com)* – a magnet for bearded dudes, especially on 2-for-1 Wednesday and Friday. 'Servicing the Castro for over 50 years' is no small claim to fame – and **Midnight Sun** *(midnightsunsf.com)* lives up to its motto daily with good vibes and strong drinks (2-for-1 until 9pm daily).

Dance the Night Away

Hit the rainbow dance floor

With a Harvey Milk mural and rainbow light-up dance floor, **The Cafe** *(cafesf.com)* is the obvious place to throw your own coming-out party, with the likes of Latinx Picante Thursday and lesbian Sugar Saturday; check the calendar. Club kids shimmy and shout over remixes on the dance floor at **QBar** *(qbar-sf.com)*, while smokers flirt on the patio. The candy store of Castro clubs, **Beaux** *(beauxsf.com)* serves every flavor: Pan Dulce Wednesday, go-go Manimal Friday, Big Top Sunday featuring *Rupaul's Drag Race* stars and monthly sapphic dance party LesBeaux.

EATING IN THE CASTRO: HOT DINNER DATES

Frances: Menus showcase handmade pastas, juicy steaks, local wines and lumberjack date cake to satisfy your discerning lumberjack date. *5:15-9:15pm Tue-Sat* $$$

Anchor Oyster Bar: Since 1977, Castro's port of call for sustainably sourced local oysters and cioppino (seafood stew). *2-8pm Thu-Mon* $$$

Blind Butcher: Intimate seating, moody lighting, standout steaks and decadent vegetarian dishes make this a date-night go-to. *5-10pm daily, 11am-3pm Sat & Sun* $$

Fable: Snag a garden table and sip on California wines paired with local halibut or bougie burgers. *11am-9pm Mon-Fri, 10am-10pm Sat, 10am-9pm Sun* $$

Golden Gate Park & the Avenues

SF'S WILD STRETCH OF IMAGINATION

Bison roam, penguins waddle, hippies drum and surfers rip along San Francisco's most outlandish stretch of scenery. Paved paths and off-road trails criss-cross the 50-block-long Golden Gate Park, good for both mellow strolls and epic hikes. Along the residential avenues that cover 50-odd (occasionally very odd) blocks from Stanyan St to Ocean Beach, you'll find Korean BBQ, Gaelic jam sessions, French pastries and Hong Kong movie matinees. This is one chill global village, where hard-core surfers and gourmet adventurers hang out and chow down together. South of Golden Gate Park are candy-colored Sunset District homes, mom-and-pop restaurants on Irving St and surf hangouts around Judah and 45th. North of the park are indie boutiques and cinemas, plus some of SF's best bakeries, bars and affordable dining.

GETTING AROUND

The N line streetcar runs from downtown through the Sunset to Ocean Beach. Buses 1, 31 and 38 run from downtown through the Richmond, while 7 and 6 head from downtown through the Haight to the Sunset. Buses 5 and 21 skirt the northern edge of Golden Gate Park, while north–south buses 28, 29 and 44 cut across the park. Bus 2 covers Clement St, 33 connects to the Haight, Castro and Mission.

Catch the Stern Grove Festival

See headliners for free in SF's urban dell

America's oldest free music festival has rocked the Sunset's shaggy redwood and eucalyptus grove every summer since 1938 – recent headliners include Sleater-Kinney, Diana Ross, Tegan & Sara, Janelle Monáe, X and SF's own Michael Franti. **Stern Grove Festival** *(sterngrove.org)* tickets are available by online lottery: they're released six weeks before shows, and winners have 72 hours to claim them before they're given away to other lucky fans.

TOP TIP

Opera divas, indie acts, bluegrass greats and hip-hop heavies take turns rocking SF gratis, from the often wintry days of June through golden October afternoons. Most concerts are held in Sharon Meadow or at the Polo Fields on weekends; for upcoming events, consult *golden-gate-park.com*.

Explore the Sunset Surf Scene

Stay dry or get wet with Sunset surfers

Dip your toes into SF surf culture at **Mollusk** *(mollusksurfshop.com),* where legendary shapers (surfboard makers) create limited-edition boards, and surfer-artists show in the back gallery. Surfers browse wetsuits, *Surfer's Journal* back issues

continued on p110

HIGHLIGHTS
1 California Academy of Sciences
2 de Young Museum
3 Golden Gate Park
4 Lands End
5 Legion of Honor
6 Ocean Beach

SIGHTS
7 Breast Cancer Memorial Garden
8 Buffalo Paddock
9 Conservatory of Flowers
10 Japanese Tea Garden
11 Lands End Lookout
12 Lincoln Park
13 National AIDS Memorial Grove
see 1 Osher Rainforest Dome
14 San Francisco Botanical Garden
15 Sunset Dunes
16 Sutro Baths
17 Sutro Heights Park

ACTIVITIES
18 Aqua Surf Shop
19 Coastal Trail
20 Lincoln Park Golf Course
21 Out There Watercolors
22 Sharon Art Studio
see 1 Steinhart Aquarium

EATING
23 Aziza
24 Bettola
25 Chapeau
26 Dragon Beaux
27 Han Il Kwan
28 Hook Fish Co
29 Mamahuhu
30 Manna
31 Mini Potstickers
see 24 Taqueria Los Mayas
32 Thanh Long
33 The Laundromat

DRINKING & NIGHTLIFE
34 Beach Chalet

ENTERTAINMENT
35 Hardly Strictly Bluegrass
36 Outside Lands

SHOPPING
37 Case for Making
38 Mollusk

PUNG/SHUTTERSTOCK

Conservatory of Flowers

TOP EXPERIENCE

Golden Gate Park

When San Franciscans refer to 'the park,' there's only one that gets the definite article: Golden Gate Park. Everything SF holds dear is here: free spirits and free music, butterfly domes and underground art, tiny penguins and hushed redwood groves, tenacious bonsai and massive bison. Landmark venues celebrating nature, music, art and science are dotted across the park's 1017 acres.

DON'T MISS

- de Young Museum
- San Francisco Botanical Garden
- California Academy of Sciences
- Conservatory of Flowers
- National AIDS Memorial Grove
- Hardly Strictly Bluegrass Festival

Natural Wonders

SF's mile-wide and 3-mile-long wild streak starts with the **Conservatory of Flowers** *(gggp.org;,adult/youth & senior/child $17/7/3)*, a restored 1878 greenhouse full of orchids, lilies and carnivorous plants – check the online schedule for holiday light shows and art events. Combined tickets *(adult/youth & senior/child $33/21/9)* offer same-day admission to the Japanese Tea Garden and 55-acre **San Francisco Botanical Garden**, which covers a world of vegetation from South African savanna to New Zealand cloud forest. Plants here are serenaded by professional musicians at **Flower Piano** *(gggp.org/flowerpiano)*.

PRACTICALITIES

- sfrecpark.org • 24hr • free

At the park's wild western edge, bison have roamed the **Buffalo Paddock** since 1889. Blue butterflies alight on your shoulders in the **Osher Rainforest Dome**, starfish wave hello in **Steinhart Aquarium** and penguins waddle their way through the **California Academy of Sciences** *(calacademy.org; adult/child from $49/45)*, championing weird, wild science since 1853. Night owls party at **NightLife events** *($25; 6-10pm Thu; ages 21+)*, featuring themed cocktails and Planetarium shows. Kids may not technically sleep during Academy Sleepovers, but they might jump-start science careers.

Art in the Park

The park's all-star art attraction is the **de Young Museum** *(famsf.org; adult/youth $20/free)*. Main-floor exhibits range from Inuit carvings to California prison photography; upstairs features Oceanic carvings and the textile collection; and blockbuster basement retrospectives range from surrealist Frida Kahlo to photographer Ansel Adams. For park panoramas, take the elevator up to the top of the 144ft **observation tower** – or cloudwatch in James Turrell's Skyspace installation, hidden under the Osher Sculpture Garden. Access is free to the tower and store; ticket includes free same-day entry to the Legion of Honor (p110). City-supported nonprofit **Sharon Art Studio** offers workshops to create your own masterpieces *(1-3 day workshops $150-350; ages 18+)*, and **Out There Watercolors** runs outdoor painting expeditions *(outtherewatercolors.com; $120 per hour, up to 4 people, ages 12+)*.

Park Music Events

Golden Gate Park has hosted epic festivals ever since the 1967 Human Be-In urged free spirits to 'tune in, turn on, drop out.' Dig the vibes year-round at free **Music Concourse** shows, weekend **Hippie Hill** drum circles and the free annual **420 Festival** *(420hippiehill.com)*, named after International Bong Hit Time (4:20pm). Mega-festivals are held around the **Polo Fields** – notably **Hardly Strictly Bluegrass** *(hardlystrictly bluegrass.com; free)*, held the first weekend in October, and alt-Coachella fest **Outside Lands** *(sfoutsidelands.com)*, held the first weekend in August.

Meditative Moments

Since 1894, the 5-acre **Japanese Tea Garden** *(gggp.org; adult/youth & senior/child $15/7/3; first hour free)* has blushed pink with cherry blossoms in spring and turned flaming red with maple leaves in fall. Don't miss the meditative Zen Garden and Tea House fortune cookies (introduced right here). For peaceful reflection ringed by redwoods and paving-stone tributes, step into the **National AIDS Memorial Grove** – founded in 1991 to commemorate millions of lives lost to the AIDS epidemic. At **Breast Cancer Memorial Garden** *(sfrecpark.org)* off Conservatory Dr, the secluded hilltop is ringed with benches and flowers.

PARK ORIGINS

Golden Gate Park was considered impossible when first backed by San Franciscan voters in 1866. New York's Central Park architect Frederick Law Olmsted balked at transforming 1017 acres of dunes into parkland, so plans fell to civil engineer William Hammond Hall. He insisted that instead of planned casinos, racetracks and a plaster igloo village, Golden Gate Park should showcase – here's a radical idea – nature.

TOP TIPS

- John F Kennedy Dr is pedestrian-only starting at 9th Ave – a weekend hotspot with roller disco and free Lindy Hop dance lessons.
- Pick up bicycle rentals inside the park at Parkwide Bike and Surrey (*parkwide.com; rentals from $22.50/2hrs*).
- When the weather's behaving, pedal boats and rowboats are available daily at the restored 1946 Stow Lake Boathouse (*row/pedal boats $26/32.50*).
- Kids flock to the park's historic children's playground to ride the vintage 1912 carousel (*adult/child $2.50/1*), scoot down 1970s concrete slides and scale the new climbing wall.

WHAT HAPPENED TO SUTRO BATHS?

It's hard to imagine from these ruins, but Victorian dandies and working stiffs once converged here for bracing baths in woolen rental swimsuits. Millionaire Adolph Sutro built hot and cold indoor pools in 1896 to accommodate 10,000 bathers – but in 1897, bath bouncers denied Black San Franciscan John Harris access. He promptly sued Sutro and won a landmark case for desegregating community facilities. The baths went bust in 1952, and in 1964 developers began razing them to build high-rise condos amid a public outcry. An arsonist burned what was left of the bath buildings in 1966, possibly for the insurance money. But even in ruins, the baths remain iconic, providing a fitting backdrop for 1971's comedy classic *Harold & Maude*.

(continued from p105)
and *Surfing Guide to California*, while kooks (newbies) try on Mollusk's 'kelp bed cruiser, wave peruser' T-shirts. Ready to hit the waves? Most SF surfers get their start in protected coves, like East Beach at Crissy Field (p53). Check out rental surf gear and surf lessons offered at **Aqua Surf Shop** *(aquasurfshop.com; lessons $120 to $150; rental per day bodyboard/wetsuit $10/15, surfboard $25-35).*

Mingle with Masterpieces at the Legion of Honor

Look inside the city's monumental treasure box

A museum as eccentric and illuminating as San Francisco itself, the **Legion of Honor** *(famsf.org; adult/child $20/free)* showcases eclectic art treasures: Monet water lilies and John Cage soundscapes upstairs, ancient cuneiform tablets and Enrique Chagoya's border-crossing Mayan codex downstairs. Each year, the Legion invites provocative contemporary artists to engage

EATING IN THE SUNSET: MEGA-FLAVOR MEALS

Thanh Long: Classic crab – roasted, tamarind or 'drunken' – with garlic noodles and warm An family welcomes. *4.30-8pm Sun, Wed & Thu, to 9pm Fri & Sat* $$

Hook Fish Co: Join surfers at weathered wooden tables for fresh, sustainable Pacific seafood in tacos or burritos, atop salads, or in fish and chips. *11.30am-9pm* $

Mini Potstickers: Dumpling experts pack mini-dumplings with Wagyu beef and flavor-bomb veggies. *10.30am-3pm & 5-8.30pm Mon-Fri, 10.30am-8.30pm Sat & Sun* $

Manna: Home-style Korean cooking, including *kalbi* (BBQ short ribs) and *dol-sot bibimbap* (sizzling stone pot rice); parties of four max. *11am-9.30pm Tue-Sun* $

VENTU PHOTO/SHUTTERSTOCK

Golden Gate Bridge viewed from Lands End

with the priceless permanent collection – Wangetchi Mutu positioned her bronze *Shavasana* sculptures of two Black women in the long shadow of Rodin's *The Thinker*. Blockbuster shows range from Guo Pei's fantasy couture to Picasso's sketchbooks, alongside selections from the **Achenbach Collection's** 90,000 works on paper. Entry to the downstairs **museum cafe** and store is free, and museum entry is free after 4.30pm. Tickets cover free same-day entry to the de Young Museum (p109).

THANKS, BIG ALMA

Legions of art fans owe thanks to 'Big Alma' de Bretteville Spreckels, the SF sculptor's model who changed the art world. In 1902, she publicly sued the gold miner 'personal defloweration' and 'breach of promise' – and won. Then Big Alma volunteered to model for Union Sq's Goddess of Victory monument, towering triumphantly with a cast-in-bronze wardrobe malfunction. The statue-selection-committee chair was sugar baron Adolph Spreckels, who became Big Alma's 'sugar daddy' and left her his fortune. Big Alma raised funds to rebuild post-earthquake SF, investigated working conditions for women for the US Department of Labor and donated the Legion and Maritime Museum to her beloved San Francisco.

Hike to Lands End

Wander along the edge of the continent

Looking out from **Lands End** *(nps.gov/goga)* at the wild, endless Pacific, you'll realize that ancient mapmakers had a point – if ever there were a place for mermaids, monsters and magic, this is it. Trails through this rugged landscape reward you with glimpses of shipwrecks, sea lions and the Golden Gate Bridge. At low tide, follow the steep path past the ruins of **Sutro Baths** and through the sea-cave tunnel to sublime Pacific panoramas.

EATING IN THE RICHMOND: DELIGHTFUL DINNERS

Aziza: Cal-Moroccan plates arrive with fragrant fanfare: wild salmon tagine, lamb *shakshuka* and chicken confit bastilla. *5-9.30pm Wed-Sun, 10.30am-2pm Sat & Sun* $$$

Mamahuhu: Fresh takes on nostalgic Chinese American classics: sustainable beef and broccoli, sweet-and-sour cauliflower, shiitake-mushroom mapo tofu. *11.30am-9pm* $

Chapeau: Head to this family-owned French bistro for well-priced tasting menus ($50-92) that feature classics like onion soup and duck cassoulet. *5-9pm Wed-Sun* $$$

The Laundromat: The only thing you'll clean at Laundromat is your plate – memorable square pizzas come loaded with tasty toppings. *8am-2pm & 5-9pm Wed-Sun* $

MELANIE HOBSON/SHUTTERSTOCK

Sutro Baths (p111)

Above the baths, you'll find the **Lands End Lookout** visitor center and **Sutro Heights Park** public gardens, built in 1885 and splendidly restored with native plants. From the Lookout, the **Coastal Trail** winds along Lands End bluffs, offering end-of-the-world views and low-tide sightings of coastal shipwrecks along the way to **Lincoln Park** *(sfrecpark.org)*. America's legendary coast-to-coast Lincoln Hwy officially ends at this 100-acre park, which served as San Francisco's cemetery until 1909. At Lincoln Park, you can duck into the Legion of Honor (p110) or descend the gloriously tiled Lincoln Park Steps (near 32nd Ave). If you've got energy to burn, push onward through the Presidio to reach the Golden Gate Bridge – or book in advance for a round at scenic **Lincoln Park Golf Course** *(lincolnparkgolfcourse.com; weekday/weekend $54/61)*.

EATING IN THE RICHMOND: LUNCH

Taqueria Los Mayas: *Panuchos* (bean-filled tortillas) come piled with Yucatecan *cochinita pibil* (tangy barbecued pork) and housemade salsas. *11am-9pm* $

Dragon Beaux: Hong Kong meets Vegas at Geary Blvd's decadent Cantonese dim sum restaurant. *11am-3pm & 5-9pm Mon-Fri, from 10am Sat & Sun* $$

Bettola: Your friendly neighborhood *tavola calda* (hot table) dishes lasagna, prosciutto-loaded white pizza and brined rotisserie chicken. *11am-9pm* $

Han Il Kwan: Join surfers and grandmas for epic lunches: sizzling meats and stone bowls brimming with bibimbap. *11am-8pm Sun & Mon, to 9pm Thu-Sat* $

TOP EXPERIENCE

Ocean Beach & Sunset Dunes

At this blustery, atmospheric city beach, the sun sets over the Pacific – though fog banks may swallow it first. Standing on this serene stretch of golden sand with your back to the city, you can watch the Pacific ebb and flow as it always does, with only a few brave surfers to remind you what century you're in.

MARLEYPUG/SHUTTERSTOCK

Ocean Beach

San Francisco's 3.5-mile **beach** is not like most California scenes in Hollywood movies – this moody, misty setting is better suited to meditative solo walks or bonding with friends. This was the original site of Burning Man; bonfires are allowed in artist-designed fire pits from March to October until 9.30pm. Swimmers, beware riptides; beachcombers, mind sneaker waves. Face the Pacific and spot brave surfers, passing ships and sea lions bobbing in the waves.

Sunset Dunes

At the southern end of Ocean Beach is a new 50-acre waterfront park called **Sunset Dunes**. By popular vote in 2024, San Francisco converted a section of highway to park trails for joggers, cyclists, skaters and walkers to enjoy. Stick to paths in areas undergoing habitat restoration and keep dogs on leash to protect wildlife. The dunes offer shelter for birdwatching – including skittish snowy plover shorebirds in winter – plus picnics and outdoor painting expeditions with **Out There Watercolors** (p109). To paint the sunset, pick up art supplies at nearby **Case for Making** *(caseformaking.com)*, where artisans make pigments specifically to capture subtle Pacific hues.

TOP TIPS

- Take a break at the **Beach Chalet** *(beachchalet.com)*, with splendid 1930s frescoes.
- Break out your favorite costume for **Bay to Breakers** *(baytobreakers.com)*, a truly fun 7.5-mile run from the Embarcadero to Ocean Beach. Joggers dressed as salmon run upstream.

PRACTICALITIES

- parksconservancy.org
- 24hr; parking lot closes at 10pm
- Free

Places We Love to Stay

$** Budget **$$** Midrange **$$$ Top End

Presidio, Marina & Fisherman's Wharf

MAP p50

HI San Francisco Fisherman's Wharf $ Get million-dollar waterfront views in an ex-army barracks that's now SF's top hostel. Choose private rooms or dorms (some co-ed), all with shared bathrooms and a communal kitchen offering free breakfasts.

Marina Motel $ Stay at a sitcom-set vintage 1939 motel with kitschy-cute rooms with kitchenettes – scuffed but well-maintained, with murals and free parking off busy Lombard St.

Hotel del Sol $$ With splashy beach-ball color schemes, palm-lined courtyard and heated outdoor pool, the Marina's mid-century motor lodge is SF's top choice for families.

Lodge at the Presidio $$ The officers' post turned ecolodge has dashingly handsome guestrooms with pillowtop beds, historic photos and commanding views – request a room overlooking the Golden Gate Bridge.

Infinity Hotel $$ Smartly contemporary yet snugly comfortable, the Infinity on Lombard St offers unexpected perks: bonus bidets, steam showers and roof-deck views from here to infinity.

Argonaut Hotel $$$ Built as a cannery in 1908, Fisherman's Wharf's top hotel remains a waterfront character, with exposed-brick walls, century-old beams and nautical decor in snug guest rooms.

Inn at the Presidio $$$ The Presidio's former officers' quarters now welcome civilians as a national-park lodge, with oversize rooms featuring pillowtop beds, suites with gas fireplaces and hiking trailheads out back.

Kimpton Alton $$$ The Wharf's hip hangout has sleek modern guestrooms big enough to use in-room yoga mats, record players and workstations so you can pretend to work remotely.

Union Street Inn $$$ Live like a Victorian socialite at this grand B&B with six antique-filled guestrooms, afternoon tea in lush gardens and generous breakfasts in the parlor.

Downtown, Civic Center & SoMa

MAP p60

citizenM San Francisco Union Square $ An elevator operator guides you to the colorful modern lobby at this Dutch boutique chain; rooms are small, iPad-controlled, clean, hip and affordable – plus there's a rooftop deck.

HI San Francisco Downtown $ In a restored historic building near the Tenderloin, hostel rooms are safe and clean, nonsqueaky bunks have personal power points and the shared lounge and kitchen are sociable.

Orchard Garden Hotel $$ SF's first LEED-certified green hotel is surprisingly affordable and conveniently located just outside Chinatown, with a gym, a rooftop deck and optional breakfast at the sustainable Roots restaurant.

Hotel Nikko $$ Convenient Union Sq hotel with friendly staff and quiet, decent-sized rooms with luxurious high thread-count linens. On-site restaurant Anzu offers a Japanese breakfast included in room rate.

Palace Hotel $$$ The 1906 landmark Palace remains a monument to turn-of-the-century grandeur, with Maxfield Parrish paintings in the bar, teatime in the marble Garden Court and a vast pool.

Beacon Grand $$$ Right off Union Sq, the Beacon offers magnificent welcomes in its Spanish-Moroccan lobby and smallish rooms with business-class amenities and proper beds – plus dynamite cocktails at Starlite rooftop bar.

Chinatown & North Beach

MAP p68

San Remo Hotel $ Built in 1906, this North Beach boarding house offers cheerful Italian grandma-styled rooms with eclectic antique furnishings and shared bathrooms. Remodeled rooms have private baths, but lack space and character. No elevator.

Pacific Tradewinds Hostel $ San Francisco's smartest all-dorm hostel has a fully equipped kitchen (free coffee, tea and PB&J sandwiches), spotless showers, sturdy bunk beds, laundry (free sock wash), luggage storage, no lockout time and, best of all, fun staff. No elevator.

Green Tortoise Hostel $ North Beach's hostel encourages bonding with pool, ping-pong, games, co-working stations and weekly live music shows in the sunny ballroom. Perks include a sauna, free breakfast, good wi-fi, on-site laundry and communal kitchen. Dorm rooms have generous lockers.

Hotel Bohème $$ The quintessential North Beach inn has smallish rooms named after Beat writers with wrought-iron beds, original artwork and small bathrooms. Some rooms face noisy Columbus Ave and there's no elevator – but novels practically write themselves here.

Washington Square Inn $$ Facing sunny Washington Sq, this 1910 inn offers snug retro-mod guestrooms, some with a bathroom across the hall. But this is a charming location, with a sociable front room for coffee. No elevator or on-site staff; entry via digital key system.

Nob Hill & Russian Hill

MAP p76

Music City Hotel & Hostel $ This Lower Nob Hill (aka 'Tendernob') music-themed hostel has decor dedicated to Green Day and the Beatles. It's committed to the cause with a live music venue attached to the lobby.

Fairmont San Francisco $$$ Magnificent marble lobby, opulent mosaic penthouse suite – plus San Francisco eccentricity, including the tiki Tonga Room and the circus-mural Cirque Bar. Guest rooms have business-class comfort. For historic appeal, reserve in the original 1906 building; for jaw-dropping views, go for the tower.

Japantown, Fillmore & Pacific Heights

MAP p80

Queen Anne Hotel $$ Once a girls' boarding school, this grand 1890 pink Victorian mansion is period-perfect: carved wood beds, antique vanities, tasseled curtains. Rooms are comfy, though the wallpaper is too close for comfort in some. Includes continental breakfast, afternoon tea and sherry.

Chateau Tivoli $$ The source of neighborhood gossip since 1892, this gorgeous Painted Lady mansion hosted Isadora Duncan, Mark Twain and (rumor has it) the ghost of a Victorian opera diva. Antique-filled rooms, most with ensuite baths and no TV; 3-course breakfast included.

Hotel Kabuki $$$ Japanese mid-century modern meets 1960s SF in cleverly updated decor: Noguchi tables flank shibori tie-dyed bedheads, trippy collages adorn slate-gray walls. Helpful concierges, meditation garden, well-equipped fitness center and best of all: dinner on-site at Nari.

The Haight & Hayes Valley

p86

Hayes Valley Inn $ Like a European pension, this reasonable find has simple rooms: two with bunks, two with singles and the turret rooms fit three. All share bathrooms, a napping dog in the parlor and welcoming staff. No elevator.

Metro Hotel $$ Hip Divisadero St is lined with boutiques and restaurants, and Metro Hotel is in a prime position. Rooms are cheerful and clean, and quirky art enlivens newly refreshed rooms. No elevator.

Parsonage $$$ At this 1883 Italianate Victorian, with original Carrara-marble fireplaces, rose-brass chandeliers and period furnishings, antique-adorned rooms are named after San Francisco's grand dames. Architect Julia Morgan gets the best views. Two-night minimum.

The Castro

MAP p94

Beck's Motor Lodge $$ This mid-century motel is looking sharp, young for its age and even a tad upscale. A gay go-to, rooms here book out early for Pride and Folsom Street Fair.

Hotel Castro $$ Stay out late and wake up inspired in the Castro, amid stunning photo-mosaics of Harvey Milk and Sylvia Rivera at this smart boutique hotel. Enjoy signature cocktails in the downstairs lounge and sunsets on the rooftop terrace.

Parker Guest House $$ Make your gay getaway in grand style at this Edwardian estate. Guestrooms feature stately beds and generous closets for coming out of, and continental breakfasts, wine and sherry are included.

JAMES KIRKIKIS/SHUTTERSTOCK

Fairmont San Francisco

Researched by
Ryan Ver Berkmoes

Marin County & Bay Area

WHERE THE COAST MEETS THE BAY

From wild walks by the Pacific to the magnificence of Hwy 1, from redwood splendor to bounteous tables, the greater Bay Area endlessly beguiles.

The San Francisco Bay Area encompasses a bonanza of natural vistas and wildlife. Cross the Golden Gate Bridge into Marin County and visit wizened ancient redwoods body-blocking the sun, and herds of elephant seals chilling on the sands of Point Reyes. Gray whales blow spray off the filigreed coast, while hawks prowl the skies over the wild sands and shaggy hills of the Marin Headlands.

In the East Bay, Oakland is the diverse, radically proud place San Francisco once was. Berkeley sparked the locavore food movement that spread worldwide and, together with its long-standing university, continues to be at the forefront of environmental and left-leaning political causes. North, you'll find gritty bayside towns and national park sites recalling nearly forgotten chapters of history.

Academic and urbane Stanford University is the soul of Palo Alto, which in turn is the heart of Silicon Valley, the land of start-up legends and louche billionaires. Travel the world without leaving San Jose, the low-key powerhouse anchor to the valley's fortunes.

Meandering along endlessly beautiful coast south of San Francisco, Hwy 1 traces 70 miles of undeveloped coastline south to Santa Cruz. Spot whales offshore, and seals and sea otters close in. Lose count of the sandy cove beaches and ribbons of dunes amid wetlands and redwoods. Pause for an hour or a day in Half Moon Bay, Pescadero or a bend in the road.

ANATOLIY LUKICH/SHUTTERSTOCK

THE MAIN AREAS

For places to stay in Marin County & Bay Area, see p162

JASON TODD/GETTY IMAGES

Left: elk, Point Reyes National Seashore (p128); Above: Muir Woods (p126)

PALO ALTO
Silicon Valley's well-heeled center.
p148

SAN JOSE
Vibrant and multicultural.
p153

HALF MOON BAY
Top stop on Hwy 1.
p156

Find Your Way

The Bay Area surrounds the San Francisco Bay, which breaks up this large region into individual areas. The coasts are more unified in their raw beauty and intrigue.

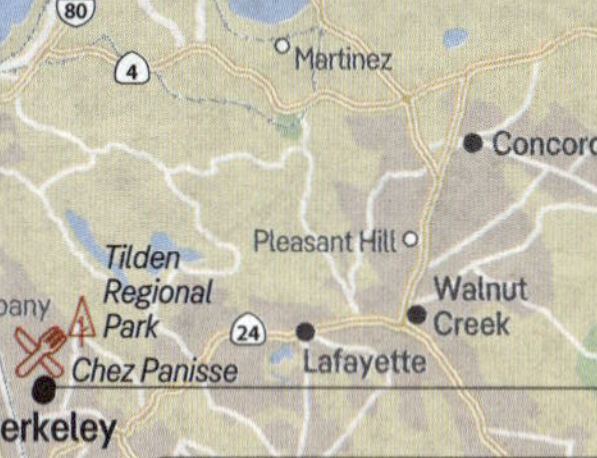

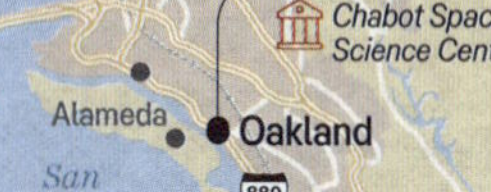

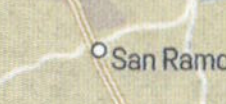
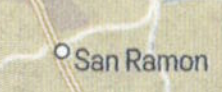

Point Reyes, p128

A beautiful national seashore with miles of wave-tossed beaches, some teeming with enormous elephant seals. A must stop before continuing on Hwy 1.

Sausalito, p122

Reachable by ferry, a town right on the bay with bohemian roots, and gateway to the Marin Headlands and Muir Woods and beyond.

Berkeley, p140

The famous university town is a delight to explore on foot, from the campus to the surrounding neighborhoods. Head north for intriguing national park sites.

Oakland, p132

The big city across the bay from San Francisco offers intriguing, walkable and contrasting neighborhoods, with some of the region's best eating.

Half Moon Bay, p156

The anchor of the sensational segment of Hwy 1 between San Francisco and Santa Cruz. Be overawed by myriad wonders north and south.

Palo Alto, p148

The heart of Silicon Valley has an enticing downtown and the genteel charms of Stanford University. Further afield are beautiful open spaces.

San Jose, p153

The state's third-largest city is a web of international neighborhoods with Mexican, Vietnamese, Japanese and other cultures. It's near top Silicon Valley sights.

CAR

The ideal way to explore the Bay Area. Hwy 1 north and south of the Golden Gate is best experienced with the freedom of your own wheels. A car is less necessary in the main cities of the East Bay and Peninsula.

TRAIN

The Bay Area is well-connected by train. BART has fast services from San Mateo via San Francisco to all the major points in the East Bay. Caltrain is another winner, knitting together the Peninsula from SF to San Jose, via Palo Alto.

FERRY

An expanding network of ferries connects the cities around the bay in fast and scenic style. It's *the* way to visit Sausalito and a fine way to reach Larkspur and the Smart train north. Oakland and Alameda are also easily reached.

Plan Your Time

Marin County and the Bay Area is a region where you can spend your time savoring just one place, or you can indulge your every peripatetic urge.

LUUUSI/SHUTTERSTOCK

Tennessee Beach (p126)

If You Only Do One Thing

- Head to Marin County. If coming from San Francisco, you can take the ferry to **Sausalito** (p122) and have lunch. Afterward, walk back to SF via **Fort Baker** (p123) and across the Golden Gate Bridge, with its incredible views of the Bay Area and massive ships passing below. Or, go deeper into the county and take the shuttle bus to **Muir Woods National Monument** (p126) to feel the otherworldly presence of the magnificent stand of old-growth redwoods.

- If in a car, stop at the **Marin Headlands** (p124) for the superb views, then follow Hwy 1 north through beach towns like **Stinson Beach** (p126). Finish at **Point Reyes National Seashore** (p128), which combines beaches with raw nature, including massive elephant seals in season.

Seasonal Highlights

Winter may bring rain, but Bay Area temperatures inspire envy. Spring and fall are beautiful, while summer ranges from chilly on the coast to blazing inland.

JANUARY

Winter storms (in non-drought years) mean driftwood on the beaches, pounding surf and salmon running in some redwood-forest streams. Pack your rain gear.

MARCH

With spring, hillsides trade tawny brown for impossibly bright green speckled with orange California poppies. Driving two-lane backroads amongst the rolling hills, you'll swear the vivid virescence makes your eyes hurt.

MAY

One of the best months to visit the Bay Area. The weather is warm and the inland areas have not yet reached temperatures that suck in the fog. Visitor numbers are manageable.

Three Days to Travel Around

- After don't-miss Marin County, add in the essential East Bay. **Oakland** (p132) and **Berkeley** (p140) abut and, with their utterly different personalities, will give you days and days of diverse activities and eating.

- In Oakland, stop by the **Oakland Museum of California** (p134) for an enlightened look at the state. Walk around **Lake Merritt** (p136), and stop by **Jack London Sq** (p135) for a drink where the man himself once did homework and later drank.

- In Berkeley, walk the **Cal campus** (p140), soaking up the atmosphere, and enjoy some superb meals. Then pop north to Richmond for the eye-opening exhibits of societal change at the **Rosie the Riveter WWII Home Front National Historic Park** (p146).

If You Have More Time

- Get your vehicle and cruise Hwy 1, south from **Pacifica** (p159). In fact, you may wish to do this if you only have one day. The 70 miles to **Santa Cruz** (p284) along this fabled road make up one of the world's most beautiful drives. Stop off at any beach that catches your eye, but know that to see them all would require a month or more. There are coves like **Gray Whale Cove State Beach** (p159) and wide-open expanses like **Gazos Creek State Beach** (p161). See the tiny tidepool creatures that live in the rocks at **Fitzgerald Marine Reserve** (p159).

- Stop for lunch at **Half Moon Bay** (p156) or **Pescadero** (p160) and circle back to SF, or continue to Santa Cruz and beyond.

JUNE

Watch for **county fairs** to start being held around the region with their bodacious foods, cheesy thrill rides, barnyard animals, familiar stage acts and fireworks.

AUGUST

If visiting from afar, pack warm clothes! The sight of visitors in shorts and t-shirts shivering while trying to enjoy the splendors of Hwy 1 on a foggy day has entertained residents for decades.

OCTOBER

How big is your pumpkin? The famous **Half Moon Bay Art & Pumpkin Festival** (p158) celebrates the Halloween icon while neighboring fields are dotted with enormous numbers of the seasonal orange icons.

DECEMBER

Colder temps bring crisply clear skies so you can appreciate the mountains surrounding Silicon Valley and along the coast. If you're lucky, the tops of Mt Tamalpais and Mt Diablo will get dusted with snow.

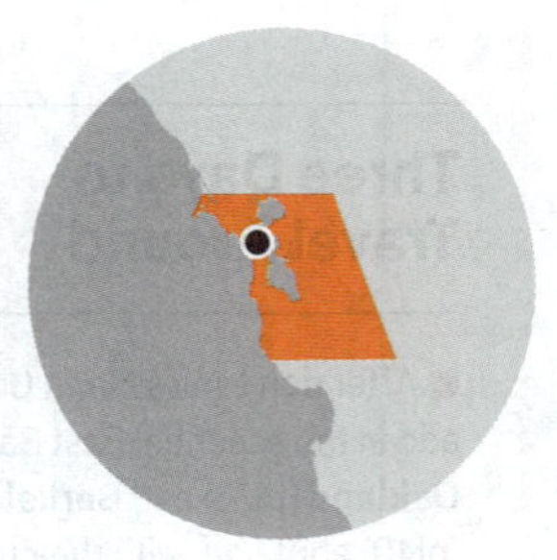

Sausalito

VIEWS | VILLAGE | FERRY RIDES

GETTING AROUND

Golden Gate Ferry *(goldengate.org; adult/child $14/7)* links regularly with San Francisco's Ferry Building. Blue & Gold Fleet ferries sail from Pier 41 in the Fisherman's Wharf area for a similar price. These 30-minute rides afford fabulous bay views. Golden Gate Transit buses frequently cross the Golden Gate Bridge to/from San Francisco and also further north to San Rafael and Sonoma County. Marin Transit offers public bus service as far as Bolinas and Point Reyes.

Perfectly arranged on a sheltered harbor on the bay, Sausalito is undeniably lovely. Named for the tiny willows that once populated the banks of its creeks, it's famous for its colorful houseboats bobbing in the bay. Much of the well-heeled downtown has uninterrupted views of San Francisco and Angel Island.

A major tourist hub, Sausalito is jam-packed with souvenir shops and fair-to-middling boutiques. It's the first town you'll encounter after crossing the Golden Gate Bridge from San Francisco.

Sausalito began as a busy lumber port with a racy waterfront. Dramatic changes came in WWII when Sausalito became the site of Marinship, a vast shipbuilding yard just north of the center. After the war a new Bohemian period began, with hundreds of residents living on houseboats. Today the town defines genteel.

Interactive Bay Exhibit

The whole bay in miniature

One of the coolest things in this beautiful town, fascinating to both kids and adults, is the Army Corps of Engineers' **Bay Model Visitor Center** *(spn.usace.army.mil/Missions/Recreation/Bay-Model-Visitor-Center; free)*. Housed in one of the old Marinship warehouses, it's a 1.5-acre hydraulic model of San Francisco Bay and the delta region that shows how the whole bay works.

TOP TIP

Parking can be a pain – if you're just visiting town and/or hiking locally, take the ferry from San Francisco. If you're combining a visit to Sausalito with the nearby Marin Headlands and Point Reyes, a car is essential – prepare for parking challenges.

Walking Sausalito & the Golden Gate Bridge

San Francisco's best day-trip walk

One of the Bay Area's best walks begins and ends in San Francisco (p43) and features some of the region's best scenery.

Catch a mid-morning ferry to Sausalito, enjoying the views of Alcatraz and Angel Island. Stroll the town and get refreshments and a picnic. Follow East Rd south along the beautiful shoreline until you reach Fort Baker. Walk under the **Golden Gate Bridge** and curve up the access road until you reach the popular viewpoint.

Cross the bridge on the eastern walkway (the west side is for cyclists). Dress warmly! It's 1.7 miles across. It's 5 miles from

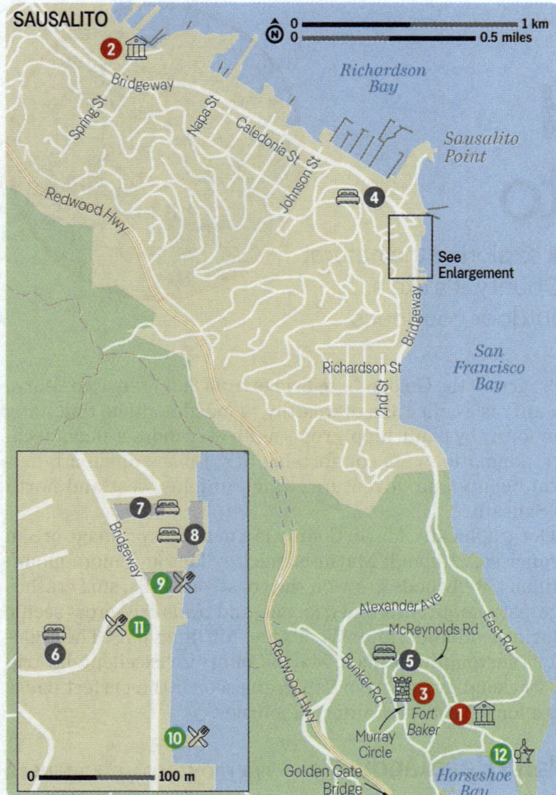

SIGHTS
1 Bay Area Discovery Museum
2 Bay Model Visitor Center
3 Fort Baker

SLEEPING
4 Casa Madrona Hotel & Spa
5 Cavallo Point
6 Gables Inn Sausalito
7 Hotel Sausalito & Suites
8 Inn Above Tide

EATING
9 Barrel House Tavern
10 Scoma's
11 Venice Gourmet Delicatessen & Pizzeria

DRINKING & NIGHTLIFE
12 Travis Marina

Sausalito to the San Francisco side of the bridge, where you can stroll onwards to the Presidio and the Marina.

Enticing Fort, Seafront & Museum

Explore Fort Baker

Below the north tower of the Golden Gate Bridge, surprisingly uncrowded **Fort Baker** *(nps.gov/goga; free)* hides in plain sight. Stroll Horseshoe Bay, watch the winter-time crab fishers, and get a snack or lunch from one of several good outlets.

A highlight is the **Bay Area Discovery Museum** *(bayareadiscoverymuseum.org; $20)*, a child-centric, indoor-outdoor facility.

HISTORIC FORT BAKER

Fort Baker helped guard the entrance to the San Francisco Bay. The army tried to stem its perennial problem of desertion by making the facilities here better than average with porches, large windows and even indoor toilets!

Today trails extend along the coast and you can even spend the night in former officers' quarters at the luxe **Cavallo Point Lodge** (p162).

EATING & DRINKING IN SAUSALITO: OUR PICKS

Scoma's: Old-school classics such as cioppino (a piquant seafood stew) and Crab Louie salads served on a pier. Fresh seafood line-up changes daily. *11.30am-9.30pm* $$$

Venice Gourmet Delicatessen & Pizzeria: In the center, build a picnic with Italian sandwiches, prepared foods and baked goods or a crispy pizza. *9am-5pm* $

Barrel House Tavern: Waterfront tavern serves California cuisine like local cheeses and charcuterie fare. Good list of regional beer, wine and spirits. Book. *11am-9pm* $$

Travis Marina: Fort Baker's near-secret bar welcomes everyone with incredible bay and bridge views. Regular live music. *4-8pm Fri, noon-8pm Sat, noon-6pm Sun*

Beyond Sausalito

Spend a day or a week exploring the natural wonderland of Marin County. It's like a concentrate of fresh outdoor goodness.

Places

GETTING AROUND

Ferries from San Francisco serve Tiburon and Larkspur. The latter connects with the Smart train, which runs north to San Rafael and on to Santa Rosa via Petaluma.

Golden Gate Transit and Marin Transit operate local bus services along the Hwy 101 corridor. Marin Transit also serves Stinson Beach, Bolinas and Point Reyes via connections from Sausalito.

Just across the Golden Gate Bridge from San Francisco, Marin County is a collection of wealthy, wooded hamlets that hang tenuously by haute hippie roots as an ever-more-affluent tech-era population gets comfortable. It's a place of superb natural beauty and adventure, which unfolds west and north of Sausalito.

Geographically, Marin County is a near mirror image of San Francisco, although Marin is much wilder and more mountainous. Redwoods grow on the coast-side hills, surf crashes against remote cliffs and beaches, and trails crisscross scenic Marin Headlands, Muir Woods and Mt Tamalpais. These glorious surroundings make Marin County an excellent day trip or weekend escape from San Francisco, or the perfect pause on a longer coastal California journey.

Marin Headlands

TIME FROM SAUSALITO: **10 MINS**

Awesome views, hikes & animal sanctuary

The cliffs and hillsides of the **Marin Headlands**, a mere 15 minutes by car from Sausalito, rise majestically at the north end of the Golden Gate Bridge, their rugged beauty all the more striking given the fact that they're only a few miles from San Francisco's urban core. A smattering of forts and bunkers are left over from a century of US military occupation. It's no mystery why this is one of the Bay Area's most popular hiking and cycling destinations: as the trails wind through the near-pristine headlands, they afford stunning views of the sea, the bridge and San Francisco, and lead to isolated beaches and secluded picnic spots.

The historical **Point Bonita Lighthouse** *(nps.gov/goga/pobo; free)* is a breathtaking half-mile walk from Field Rd parking area. Harbor seals haul out seasonally on nearby rocks.

At the western end of Bunker Rd sits spectacular **Rodeo Beach** *(parksconservancy.org/parks/rodeo-beach)*, partly protected from wind by high cliffs. All along the coastline you'll find cool old battery sites – abandoned concrete bunkers dug into the ground with fabulous views. Start at **Battery Townsley** *(free)*, a half-mile walk or bike ride up from the Fort Cronkhite parking lot. The **Coastal Trail** leads to **Muir Beach**. The headlands are also laced with superb mountain-biking trails. The **Julian Trail** is a rewarding 12-mile dirt loop.

MICHAEL VI/SHUTTERSTOCK

Memorial plaque, Angel Island Immigration Station

Above Rodeo Beach, the **Marine Mammal Center** *(marine mammalcenter.org; free)* rehabilitates injured, sick and orphaned sea mammals before returning them to the wild. Reserve a slot in advance and you can see adult seals and pups being cared for from an observation deck.

Angel Island

TIME FROM SAUSALITO: **15MIN**

Once notorious oasis in the bay

In the middle of San Francisco Bay, **Angel Island** was a hunting and fishing ground for the Miwok people. In the early 20th century, it was nicknamed the 'Ellis Island of the West' as it had a US Immigration Station that was used to screen and detain Chinese immigrants as part of the racist Chinese Exclusion Act. Later, the island served as a military base, a WWII Japanese internment camp and an anti-aircraft missile site. Besides the **Immigration Station** *(aiisf.org; adult/child $5/3)*, there are forts and bunkers with thought-provoking displays amid the natural beauty.

History aside, Angel Island is a natural wonderland. You can hike the 5-mile perimeter trail with its all-star views of the Bay Area, or to the summit of 788ft Mt Livermore. Alternatively, enjoy a picnic in a protected cove or beach, looking out at the seemingly close yet distant urban grid. On most days crowds are few, even though access is easy by ferry from San Francisco, Sausalito and Tiburon. Bikes can be rented near the daytime cafe by the ferry dock.

BEST STATE PARKS IN MARIN COUNTY

China Camp State Park: Just northeast of San Rafael, this park preserves a Chinese shrimp-fishing village from the beginning of the 19th century. Fishers and their families were able to live here away from the rampant racism found across California. *friends ofchinacamp.org; parking $5*

Olompali State Historic Park: Marin County was once among the homes of the Coastal Miwok people. The park preserves the site of a village that was inhabited from about 6000 BCE until 1850. Reach it from Hwy 101 in Novato. *olompali.org; parking $8*

Samuel P Taylor State Park: In the coastal hills along Sir Francis Drake Blvd, this large preserve has groves of redwoods and streams that fill with spawning salmon in winter. *parks.ca.gov*

EATING BEYOND SAUSALITO: OUR PICKS

Village Sake: World-class Japanese food in Fairfax; the *izakaya* (pub-style fare and tapas-like small dishes) are paired with craft beers and sake. *5-8pm Wed-Sun* **$$$**

Madcap: West of San Rafael in San Anselmo is this outpost for beautifully crafted Californian fare. Ever-changing Asian-accented menu. *5-8.30pm Tue-Sat* **$$$**

Parkside Cafe: On Stinson Beach, the snack bar serves soft-serve ice cream, the restaurant aims higher with seafood platters garnished with caviar. *7.30am-9pm* **$$**

Pelican Inn: Oh-so-quaint pub takes you from Muir Beach to the Cornish Coast. Trad high-end pub fare. Beef Wellington is ideal on a foggy day. *11am-10pm* **$$**

BEST BEACHES

Tennessee Beach: Many say the 1.8-mile hike to this secluded cove is their favorite ever, given the stark Pacific scenery of jagged rocks, sheer hills and raw, natural scenery.

Muir Beach: A quiet hamlet with a pretty gray-sand beach. Hike here from the headlands or Muir Woods.

Stinson Beach: The wide, blond sand buzzes on warm, sunny weekends. The town has a handful of eateries and lots of vacation rentals.

Bolinas: This surfer's hangout got on the map for being off the map: road signs to the town often vanish in the night.

Steep Ravine Beach: The name says it: park along Hwy 1 and hike down a challenging trail for nearly a mile to an often deserted, rocky beach.

BRET J UNGER/SHUTTERSTOCK

Cathedral Grove, Muir Woods

Camping on Angel Island mixes serene isolation with an evening light show around the bay.

Golden Gate Ferry operates up to four ferries daily to Angel Island from San Francisco's Ferry Building from April to October *(goldengate.org; round-trip adult/child $31/16; 30 minutes)*. There's a reduced schedule November to March. Buy tickets before boarding.

Angel Island–Tiburon Ferry operates ferry service to the island from downtown Tiburon from May to September *(angelislandferry.com; round-trip adult/child $18/15; 15 minutes)*. Schedules vary by the day; book online in advance.

Muir Woods

TIME FROM SAUSALITO: **30 MINS**

Small hikes to big trees

Wander among an ancient stand of the world's tallest trees in 550-plus-acre **Muir Woods National Monument** *(nps.gov/muwo; adult/child $15/free)*, a 30-minute drive from Sausalito. Only by luck did this stand of old-growth coast redwoods *(Sequoia sempervirens)* survive the massive clear-cutting of the 19th and 20th centuries.

The shortest hiking option is the 1-mile **Main Trail Loop**, a gentle walk alongside Redwood Creek to the 1000-year-old trees at **Cathedral Grove**; it returns via **Bohemian Grove**, where the tallest tree in the park stands more than 258ft high and where you can see how coast redwoods have evolved to

EATING BEYOND SAUSALITO: BEST CASUAL DINING

Pupuseria Blankita: El Salvadorean restaurant serves sublime handmade *pupusas* (corn cakes) with fillings from cheese to veggie to grilled steak. *10am-8pm* $

Sam's Anchor Cafe: Decades-old waterfront cafe in Tiburon known for vintage cocktails and excellent brunch and lunch fare. *noon-10pm* $$

Kitchen Sunnyside: New-age socialists mix with tech billionaires for elevated comfort food in Mill Valley. Best seats are on the sidewalk. *8.30am-2.30pm* $$

Sunday Marin Farmers Market: In a region of excellent farmers markets, one of the best. Vast array of produce and prepared foods; dozens of food trucks. *8am-1pm Sun* $

survive regular forest fires. More bracing is the 2-mile hike up to the top of the aptly named Cardiac Hill to reach the **Dipsea Trail**, which climbs over the coastal range and down to Stinson Beach.

You can also walk down into Muir Woods by taking trails from the Panoramic Hwy, such as the **Bootjack Trail** from the Bootjack picnic area, or from Mt Tamalpais' Pantoll Station campground, along the **Ben Johnson Trail**.

Note that visitors to Muir Woods must reserve and pay in advance for parking at the park, or weekend shuttle transportation from the Larkspur Landing Ferry Terminal. Check online *(gomuirwoods.com)* for details and current conditions.

Try to come midweek, early in the morning or late in the afternoon, when tour buses are less common. Even at busy times, a short hike will get you out of the densest crowds and onto trails with huge trees and stunning vistas. A woodsy cafe serves local and organic food and hot drinks. Note: in 2025, the Trump Administration ordered the removal of signage highlighting the important roles played by Indigenous people and women in saving Muir Woods.

Mt Tamalpais

TIME FROM SAUSALITO: **45 MINS**

Hike Marin's peak

Looming over Marin County and a 45-minute drive from Sausalito, majestic **Mt Tamalpais** (Mt Tam; 2572ft) holds more than 60 miles of hiking and biking trails, lakes, streams, waterfalls and an impressive array of wildlife – from plentiful newts and hawks to rare foxes and mountain lions. Wind your way through meadows, oaks and madrone trees to breathtaking vistas over the San Francisco Bay, Pacific Ocean, towns, cities and forested hills rolling into the distance.

Mt Tamalpais State Park *(parks.ca.gov; free)* encompasses about 10 sq miles of parklands and more than 60 miles of trails. Don't miss the summit of **East Peak**. Panoramic Hwy climbs from Hwy 1 through the park, then winds downhill to Stinson Beach.

San Rafael

TIME FROM SAUSALITO: **15 MINS**

Frank Lloyd Wright's architectural masterpiece

The oldest and largest town in Marin, **San Rafael**, a quick 15-minute drive north of Sausalito, is slightly less upscale than most of its neighbors but doesn't lack atmosphere in its strollable downtown.

Just north, the region's premier architectural sight is the eye-catching **Marin County Civic Center** *(marincounty.gov; free)*, the flamboyant masterpiece by Frank Lloyd Wright (1867–1959), who didn't live to see its 1962 completion. Wright designed the horizontal hillside buildings to flow with the natural beauty of the county's landscape, with sky-blue roofs, sand-colored walls and a gold tower pointing to the heavens. Self-guided tours are fascinating, but check for the regular free guided tours.

In utter contrast to the south, **San Quentin State Prison** is the notorious hulking mass best viewed from the Larkspur ferry.

BEST SHOPS

Bolinas People's Store: Small co-op grocery store near the beach. Serves fair-trade coffee and sells organic foods, camping supplies and other goods.

Nicasio Valley Cheese Company: Sample the soft cheeses at one of Marin County's most renowned cheesemaking shops in rural Nicasio.

Book Passage: One of the Bay Area's best bookstores in Corte Madera. Hosts big-name author appearances.

Depot Bookstore & Cafe: Bohemian Mill Valley has its own great bookstore in an old train station that was once served by a logging railroad.

Sustainable Exchange: Get locally made, fair-trade products from cosmetics to housewares in San Rafael. Ten minutes browsing can easily turn into an hour.

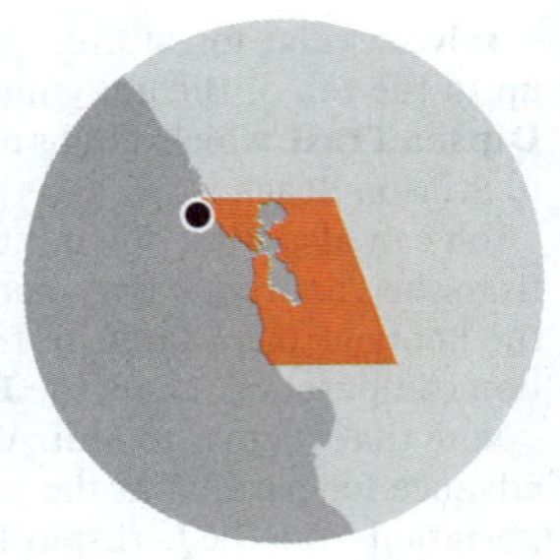

Point Reyes

RUGGED NATURE | WILDLIFE | OUTDOOR ADVENTURE

GETTING AROUND

Barring bad traffic, you can reach the entrance to the national seashore in about 1½ hours from San Francisco. From here to the furthest reaches of the park can take another 45 minutes of driving. Marin Transit runs public buses as far as Inverness via Olema, the park's Bear Valley Visitor Center and Point Reyes Station from San Rafael. Roads are narrow, so cycling can be challenging on the main roads.

TOP TIP

A mile west of Olema, the **Bear Valley Visitor Center** *(nps.gov/pore; 9.30am-5pm)* has maps, information and worthwhile exhibits. It's a vital first stop to find out about wildlife-spotting conditions, including beach closures and mandatory shuttle buses to busy areas. The Earthquake Trail details the San Andreas Fault, which runs close by.

Windswept Point Reyes peninsula is a rough-hewn beauty that has always lured marine mammals and migratory birds; it's also the site of scores of shipwrecks. In 1579, Sir Francis Drake landed here to repair his ship, the *Golden Hind*. During his five-week stay, he mounted a brass plaque near the shore claiming this land for England. In 1595, the first of many ships lost in these waters went down. Despite modern navigation, the dangerous waters here continue to claim boats and bits of cargo from catastrophes over the decades still wash up on shore.

Point Reyes National Seashore protects 100 sq miles of pristine ocean beaches and coastal wilderness. It has phenomenal outdoor opportunities. Hikes take you to remote corners where you can spot huge animals, from elks to elephant seals, and walk wave-tossed beaches where your footprints will be the only human evidence amid driftwood, seashells and shorebird scratchings.

Hit the Beaches

Point Reyes' world-class coast

Virtually every strip of sand is a long drive from anywhere at Point Reyes, but every one is worth the effort. **Limantour Beach** is a great all-around beach with an array of wilderness hikes and stunning sunsets. **Drakes Beach** is backed by white sandstone cliffs and is arguably the most gorgeous of the main beaches. There's also the seasonal **Kenneth C Patrick Visitor Center**, which offers information, especially in elephant-seal mating season. West-facing **Point Reyes Beach** offers 11 miles of solitude. On many days the sky turns an iridescent vermilion at sunset. Bring a blanket and enjoy the show.

Trails, Seabirds & Elk Reserve

Hike the Point Reyes wilderness

Alluring trails crisscross Point Reyes over hillsides and along the shoreline. For views, the **Inverness Ridge Trail** heads for around 3 miles up to **Point Reyes Hill** (1339ft), affording

HIGHLIGHTS
1 Point Reyes National Seashore

SIGHTS
2 Abbotts Lagoon
3 Alan Sieroty Beach
4 Drakes Beach
5 Limantour Beach
6 Pierce Point Ranch
7 Pierce Point Rd
8 Point Reyes Beach
9 Point Reyes Hill
10 Tomales Point
11 Tule Elk Reserve

ACTIVITIES
12 Blue Waters Kayaking
13 Bolinas Ridge Trail
14 Inverness Ridge Trail
15 Tomales Bay Trail
16 Tomales Point Trail

SLEEPING
17 Cottages at Point Reyes Seashore
18 Dancing Coyote Beach Cottages
19 Motel Inverness
20 Nick's Cove
21 Tomales Bay Resort & Marina
22 Tomales Hotel

EATING
23 Bovine Bakery
24 Cafe Reyes
25 Saltwater Oyster Depot
26 Tap Room
27 Toby's Coffee Bar

SHOPPING
28 Point Reyes Books

INFORMATION
29 Bear Valley Visitor Center
see 4 Kenneth Patrick Center

spectacular vistas of the entire national seashore. Savor the raw beauty of the beaches extending off to the horizon.

For wildlife, **Pierce Point Rd** continues to the huge windswept sand dunes at **Abbotts Lagoon**, full of peeping killdeer and other shorebirds. At the end of the road is historical **Pierce Point Ranch**, the trailhead for the 9.4-mile round-trip **Tomales Point Trail** through the **Tule Elk Reserve**. The many elk are an amazing sight, standing with their big horns against the backdrop of **Tomales Point**. The herd is one of the last in the lower 48 states of the US. You may or may not see herds of dairy cows, depending on the results of a controversial 2025 agreement to remove them to allow the elk more freedom.

EATING NEAR POINT REYES: OUR PICKS

Saltwater Oyster Depot: Chef-run bistro in Inverness with a sophisticated local seafood menu. Seasonal offerings feature the famous oysters. *5-8pm Fri-Mon* $$

Tap Room: Inverness spot for sandwiches, burgers and noodle bowls alongside microbrews and top regional wines. A convivial mix of residents and visitors. *4-9pm Mon-Sat* $$

Bovine Bakery: The place to get breakfast and/or a picnic near the entrance to the peninsula. Organic treats, sandwiches, breads and good coffee. *7am-4pm* $

Cafe Reyes: Enjoy wood-fired pizza inside, on the patio or to go at this Point Reyes Station favorite. Great range of toppings. *noon-8pm* $$

Beyond Point Reyes

The beauty and bounty of nature extend beyond Point Reyes to the little towns situated on Hwy 1 wending north along the coast.

GETTING AROUND

You'll need your own wheels to get around the region beyond Point Reyes. This stretch of Hwy 1 is among the most popular, so expect to travel slowly.

Your best views will be on the left heading north. Do everyone a favor, especially long-suffering locals, and use the many pullouts to let speedier drivers pass. It's easy to get caught up in the incredible scenery and have cars pile up behind you, but having more than five cars stacked up behind you is a moving violation in California traffic law.

If you have a timetable for your journey along Hwy 1 continuing on from Point Reyes, toss it out the window. There are many alluring little villages where you can sample the products of the bay, plus the dairies and ranches that thrive in the rolling green hills. Plan on stopping often.

Point Reyes Station is the gateway to the north. Pause at Point Reyes Books, where the staff curate regional titles, many written by local authors. From here, Hwy 1 hugs Tomales Bay, where you can see the famous oyster farms. Cafes and restaurants serving the same dot the road which continues inland to the village of Tomales, from where you can detour to hidden Dillon Beach.

Marshall

TIME FROM POINT REYES: **15 MINS**

Oh, shucks!

Fresh oysters from **Tomales Bay** are a much-loved local specialty. From south to north, the following three waterfront restaurants are all right on Hwy 1 in and around barely there Marshall, 15 to 20 minutes' drive north of Point Reyes Station. On weekends, they get crowded and you might find a band playing. Sitting on an open deck with a local microbrew (there are many, although Stumptown is always great) and some tasty freshly shucked oysters is sublime.

The relaxed **Marshall Store** *(11am-3pm)* has a fine deck perfect for slurping down BBQ or raw local oysters, sourced from the restaurant's own farm. Smoked-seafood plates are also good, as is anything made with crab in season (winter, if available).

Hog Island Oyster Company is a minor oyster empire in Marshall. It has several outlets, including a **retail shack** *(9am-5pm)* selling fresh local shellfish and seafood plus picnic supplies, a much-loved reservation-only outdoor **oyster bar** *(11am-4pm Fri-Mon)* and a full-service restaurant to the south, **Tony's Seafood** *(11.30am-4pm Tue-Thu, to 7.30pm Fri & Sun)*.

Dive deep – not literally! – into the oyster experience on a Hog Island Oyster Company **Farm Tour** *(hogislandoysters.com; $48-180)* where you'll see how they're farmed, harvested and shucked. Book tours (75 minutes to three hours) in advance.

ANDREW MONTGOMERY/LONELY PLANET

Oysters, Marshall Store

At vintage 1930s **Nick's Cove** *(11am-7pm)*, perched over Tomales Bay, trophy heads are mounted on knotty-pine walls and there's a roaring fireplace. The seafood dishes – including the local oysters – are impeccable. It's a sprawling place, with a pier out into the bay and **rooms** (p162).

Dillon Beach

TIME FROM POINT REYES: **45 MINS**

Surf, sand & views

Dillon Beach is one of the most worthwhile detours you'll make off Hwy 1 in Marin County. The 19th-century village of Tomales, where the Dillon Beach road begins, offers plenty of reasons to stop for its excellent cafes.

Once you're fueled up on good eats and coffee, make the 4-mile jaunt west to the sand. The drive passes outcrops of weirdly sinuous boulders as you get ever-greater glimpses of the Pacific. In peak summer season, you might notice that flocks of rental cars in your rearview mirror have thinned.

Once down at the sand, you will find plenty of parking and a relaxed, welcoming attitude. Firewood is sold at the park entrance so you can have a bonfire on the wide, flat beach. An immediate highlight is the view of Tomales Point at Point Reyes National Seashore directly across the water. Walk south for empty stretches and dunes.

BEST OUTDOOR ADVENTURES AROUND POINT REYES

Bolinas Ridge Trail: An undulating 10.5-mile route for hikers or cyclists, has great views, and starts about 1 mile east of Olema.

Alan Sieroty Beach: On a tiny peninsula on Tomales Bay, this beach is sheltered and faces south. Families like the calm waters.

Blue Waters Kayaking: Offers various guided tours of Tomales Bay; otherwise, you can rent kayaks to explore the bay on your own. *bluewaterskayaking.com; tours from $115*

Tomales Bay Trail: A great all-around loop trail that takes in the best of local scenery (in spring, the viridian grasses hurt your eyes).

Food & Farm Tours: Explore the bounty of West Marin County, from organic dairies to produce farms to cheese producers. *foodandfarmtours.com; tours from $250*

EATING AROUND POINT REYES: QUICK EATS

Toby's Coffee Bar: Snack bar in a Point Reyes Station feed store perfectly captures the local vibe. Excellent coffee drinks and snacks. *6.30am-5pm* $

Route One Bakery & Kitchen: Superb flat-pan pizza by the slice draws residents from afar to Tomales. Bakery items, sandwiches and coffee also reward. *7.30am-2pm* $$

Out the Door: The fresh fish tacos will have you lining up for more at this takeout spot in Tomales. Options change daily. *noon-6pm Fri-Mon* $

Coastal Kitchen: On a bluff above Dillon Beach, casual eats served on a deck with brilliant sunset views. Longer summer hours. *noon-7pm* $$

Oakland

STATE MUSEUM | WORLD FOOD | WORLD-CLASS ARCHITECTURE

GETTING AROUND

Oakland is well-connected. Amtrak serves Sacramento, the Central Valley and San Jose. BART serves the East Bay, Oakland's airport, San Francisco and SFO. AC Transit runs a dense network of bus routes, and San Francisco Bay Ferry links Jack London Sq to San Francisco's Ferry Building *(25 minutes)*.

TOP TIP

Broadway is the backbone of downtown Oakland, running north from touristy Jack London Sq. The genteel Rockridge neighborhood lies west of Broadway along College Ave, near the Berkeley border. Downtown, Telegraph Ave branches off Broadway and heads north to Berkeley via the vibrant Temescal neighborhood (between 40th and 51st Sts).

Oakland is where the Bay Area's diverse, artsy and radical folks have enshrined a free-thinking way of life. Oaklanders are fiercely proud that their home retains the mixed ethnic tableau and unapologetic left-wing politics San Francisco once enshrined, and they know this backdrop is threatened by million-dollar residential homes, already present even in formerly middle-class neighborhoods.

Oakland is full of historical buildings and colorful businesses. With such easy access from San Francisco via BART or ferry, it's worth spending part of a day exploring here on foot or by bike.

Oakland's eateries are among the Bay Area's best, most innovative and most affordable, due to the cultural diversity and the fact that up-and-coming chefs can more readily start a business here. The city abounds with favorites in walkable neighborhoods. Uptown, Temescal and Rockridge attract culinary trendspotters. Oakland's busiest and hippest bars are in the Uptown district, often just a short stumble from BART.

The City's Heart

Downtown Oakland & Chinatown

Pedestrianized **City Center**, between Broadway and Clay St, 12th and 14th Sts, forms the heart of downtown Oakland. Enjoy a free noontime concert. Nearby **Oakland City Hall** is a beautifully refurbished 1914 beaux-arts masterpiece. Walking the streets, look for old gems such as the 1914 **Cathedral Building**, a Gothic Revival wonder on a triangular plot. It was a setting for Boots Riley's 2018 sublime dark comedy *Sorry to Bother You*.

Old Oakland, west of Broadway between 8th and 10th Sts, is lined with restored historical buildings dating from the late 19th century. The area has a lively restaurant and after-work scene. Stop in at happening **Oeste** *(5-10pm)* for a

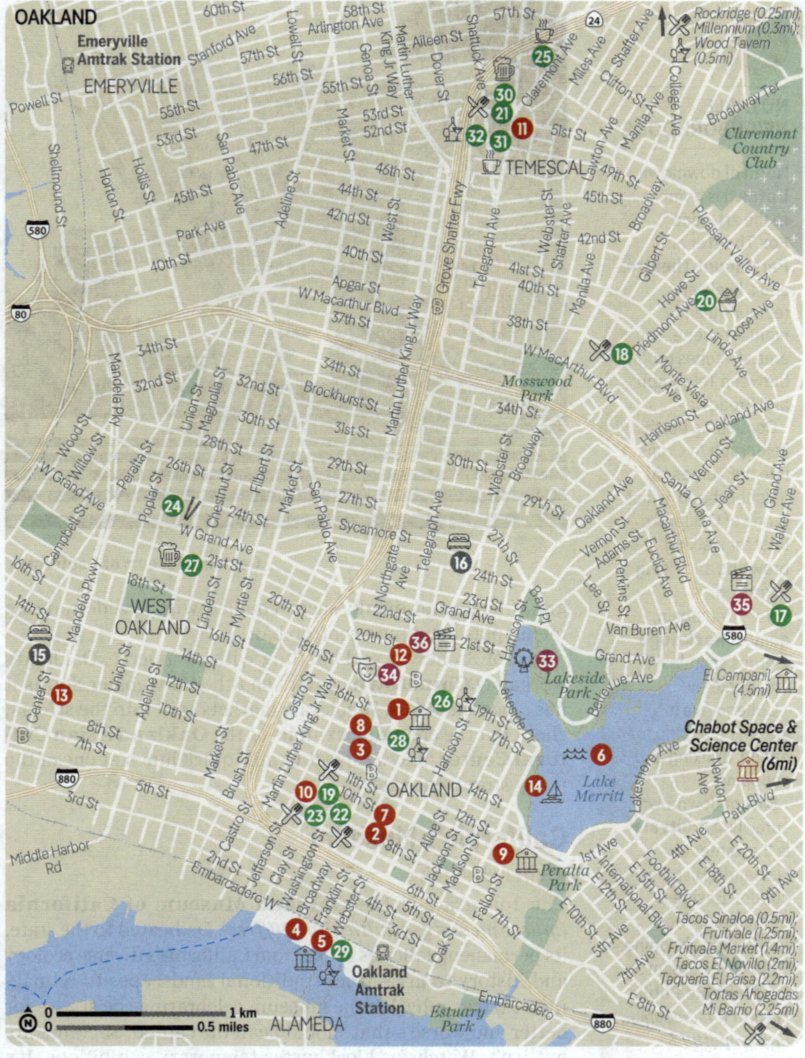

● **SIGHTS**
1 Cathedral Building
2 Chinatown
3 City Center
4 Jack London Square
5 Jack London's Cabin
6 Lake Merritt
7 Oakland Asian Cultural Center
8 Oakland City Hall
9 Oakland Museum of California
10 Old Oakland
11 Temescal
12 Uptown
13 West Oakland

● **ACTIVITIES**
see 4 California Canoe & Kayak
14 Dolce Vita Gondola

● **SLEEPING**
15 B-Love's Guest House
16 Kissel Uptown Oakland

● **EATING**
17 Arizmendi Bakery
18 Commis
19 Cook and Her Farmer
20 Fentons Creamery
21 FOB Kitchen
22 Horn Barbecue
see 4 Jack London Square Farmers Market
23 Oeste
24 Soba Ichi

● **DRINKING & NIGHTLIFE**
25 Alem's Coffee
26 Bar 355
27 Ghost Town Brewing
28 Golden Bull Bar
29 Heinold's First & Last Chance Saloon
30 Kingfish Pub & Cafe
31 North Light
32 Snail Bar

● **ENTERTAINMENT**
33 Children's Fairyland
34 Fox Theater
35 Grand Lake Theatre
36 Paramount Theatre

NOTABLE NEIGHBORHOODS

North of downtown, **Uptown** is home to the art-deco **Fox Theater** and **Paramount Theatre**, and a lively arts, restaurant and nightlife scene. The area stretches roughly between Telegraph and Broadway.

Continuing north, Telegraph Ave runs into the **Temescal** neighborhood, which is one of Oakland's best for walking, browsing and being surprised.

North yet again, genteel **Rockridge** merges seamlessly into Berkeley.

College Ave is another fine strip for eating, drinking and shopping.

East of downtown, sprawling **Fruitvale** is the center of Oakland's Hispanic culture. Besides tremendous food, there is top shopping. Grab an ice cream at the **Fruitvale Public Market** *(unitycouncil.org/property/public-market; 10am-7pm).*

NICOLASMCCOMBER/GETTY IMAGES

Oakland Museum of California

great music-and-drinks scene coupled with a wide-ranging menu, plus a hopping rooftop bar.

East of Broadway and bustling with commerce, Oakland's workaday **Chinatown** centers on 8th and Webster Sts, as it has since the 1850s. Wholesale markets spill into the streets; check out the changing exhibits at the **Oakland Asian Cultural Center** *(oacc.cc; free).* Grab a quick lunch at one of the many storefront cafes.

California's Museum

Right In Oakland

The top draw is the **Oakland Museum of California** *(museumca.org; adult/child $19/free).* Dedicated to the state, its permanent galleries range from California's diverse ecology and history to art – from traditional landscapes to reimagined cartography. It's the museum celebrating the state – for better and worse – that should be in the capital, Sacramento, but isn't. Watch for blockbuster temporary exhibitions. It's open 11am to 5pm Wednesday to Sunday.

EATING IN OAKLAND: CASUAL DINING

Horn Barbecue: Oakland's own celebrity chef, Matt Horn, serves the masses his renowned brisket, pulled pork and sausage. Finish with banana pudding. *noon-9pm* $$

Fentons Creamery: Everyone wants a scoop of luscious ice cream at this old-school Piedmont Ave parlor. Also has old-fashioned lunches and snacks. *11am-10pm* $

Arizmendi Bakery: Great for breakfast or lunch near Lake Merritt. Bakery co-op not for the weak-willed: vegetarian pizza, chewy breads and gigantic scones. *8am-8pm* $

Cook and Her Farmer: Grab a stool or a table at this oyster joint and wine bar inside Swan's Market in Old Oakland. *11am-8pm* $$

A Square with a Past & a View

Waterfront Jack London Sq

The waterfront where writer and adventurer Jack London caroused in the 1890s now bears his name. **Jack London Sq** offers great opportunities for kayaking around the harbor or strolling the docks, especially when the **Farmers Market** *(11am-4pm Sun)* takes over. Contemporary redevelopment has added generic urban condos, plus popular restaurants and bars. **California Canoe & Kayak** *(calkayak.com)* rents kayaks and stand-up paddleboards (SUP). Book ahead for a tour ($59) along the waterfront.

On the edge of the square, **Jack London's Cabin** is reconstructed in part using the logs from his original 1898 cabin in the Yukon territory of Canada, and the historical wooden hovel allows visitors a peek inside life during the gold-rush era. Seemingly more popular is a statue of a wolf (or maybe a sled dog, or is it *The Call of the Wild's* Buck?), which kids love to pose with.

Stop by nearby **Heinold's First & Last Chance Saloon** *(11am-8pm)*, an 1883 bar constructed from wood scavenged from an old whaling ship and, yes, a favorite of London's. (There's a photo of him as a student 'studying' there at age 10 in 1886.) Keeled to a severe slant during the 1906 earthquake, the building's tilt might make you feel self-conscious about stumbling before you even order (avoid the tilt by drinking at the inviting outdoor tables).

The International Blvd Taco Hunt

Sublime Mexican food

Running southwest from Oakland's center, International Blvd lives up to its name. It's the crucible for a world of Bay Area cultures. One of the most famous is its extraordinary Mexican and Central American fare, which you can enjoy at restaurants, sidewalk and alley tents and busy taco trucks.

When Michelin called the exquisite little **Taquería El Paisa** *(9am-9pm)* a 'temple of tacos,' International Blvd had reached a superlative level of recognition. And the hype is not unjustified, the tacos are excellent: simple, fresh and garnished with *nopales* (cactus).

Given that new choices open regularly, your best option is to make your own discoveries on the stretch roughly between 20th and 50th Aves. Here are a couple of options to start.

Tortas Ahogadas Mi Barrio *(9am-6pm)* celebrates Jalisco-style food, which includes tacos dorados. Savor the fiery salsa.

OAKLAND'S HIDDEN LANDMARK

Somewhat hidden away near the hills of East Oakland is a landmark structure that is rarely visited, yet has proved to be one of the most influential buildings of the 20th century.

The initially unremarkable, 72-ft **El Campanil** was built as the bell tower for the former Mills College. Designed by the incomparable Julia Morgan (p144), it was constructed with reinforced concrete, a then-radical choice by the groundbreaking architect.

Two years after completion, the devastating 1906 earthquake destroyed thousands of Bay Area buildings, including many by Morgan's critics. However, the El Campanil was untouched. In the decades since, it's been a model for the use of reinforced concrete in buildings worldwide and continues to bring Morgan acclaim as one of the great structural engineers.

EATING IN OAKLAND: OUR PICKS

Millennium: Beloved for vegan surprises like pumpkin tamales and parsnip *okonomiyaki* (Japanese savory pancakes). Opt for the tasting menu. *5-9pm* **$$**

Commis: Chef James Syhabout's paean to innovative dining, on Piedmont Ave. Reserve a counter seat for the kitchen show. Menus are fixed-price. *5-10pm Tue-Sat* **$$$**

FOB Kitchen: Janice Dulce's Filipino restaurant in Temescal. Order anything with pork plus the garlic rice. Cocktails and a popular weekend brunch. *11am-9pm* **$$**

Soba Ichi: Long waits for a table are spent in a West Oakland garden – if the handmade soba noodles don't sell out first. *5-9pm Wed-Sun* **$$**

WEST OAKLAND

Battered by the 1989 earthquake, bedeviled by homeless encampments, surrounded by freeways, suburbanites and a busy container port, **West Oakland** embodies every non-gentrified aspect of the city's history. It's here that the Black Panther Party began its uncompromising campaign for African American rights. Its free lunch programs for school kids are still revered today. A few decades earlier, CL Dellums led the railway porters union as it fought both for better wages and also for the civil rights of people across the US. Throughout West Oakland vibrant murals celebrate the area's heritage and culture. Experience the past and present on the **Black Liberation Walking Tour** *(blwt.org)*, an occasional event that tells the neighborhood's stories.

The **Tacos El Novillo** food truck *(8am-11.30pm)* is first among many and gives you too many choices: taco or burrito? Which of the many meats? (The carnitas – seasoned pulled pork – gets raves...)

Another winning truck, **Tacos Sinaloa** *(9am-1am)*, assembles plates of tacos with artistic care, right down to the slices of radish. Seafood options are popular and the burritos will see you through a long journey.

Lovely Lake Merritt

Find fun day and night

Follow Grand Ave east of Broadway from the center and you'll run into the serene shores of **Lake Merritt**, one of Oakland's treasures. An urban respite, the lake is a popular place to stroll or go running (a 3.2-mile paved path circles the water), with bonsai and botanical gardens, a bird sanctuary, green spaces, a boathouse and gondola rides with **Dolce Vita Gondola** *(dolcevitagondola.com; $135)*.

Grand Ave (north of the water) and Lakeshore Ave (east of the lake) are pedestrian-friendly streets with intriguing shops, restaurants, cafes and bars. Look for the landmark 1926 **Grand Lake Theatre** *(renaissancerialto.com)* on the lake's northern edge. It's home to the wildly popular annual

DRINKING IN OAKLAND: OUR PICKS

Ghost Town Brewing: Goth meets industrial-cool at a West Oakland brewery known for its IPAs. Lots of seating indoors, plenty outside for when the fog clears. *3-10pm*

Wood Tavern: Top California wines in Rockridge, plus locally sourced, casual food. Grab a stool at the bar or a table with friends. *11.30am-9pm Tue-Sun*

Bar 355: Classy cocktail bar near Lake Merritt. Order an old-fashioned or a sidecar; alternatively, the bartenders know how to make anything classic. *4pm-2am Mon-Sat*

Golden Bull Bar: Beloved smallish venue downtown that packs in 150 people for wide-ranging local bands, from techno to punk and beyond. *4pm-midnight Wed-Sun*

THOMAS WINZ/GETTY IMAGES

Gondolas, Lake Merritt

Noir City Film Festival *(noircity.com)*, hosted by TCM's Eddie Muller, celebrating film noir movies.

A Playground of Fantasies

Everyone loves children's fairyland

Kids of all ages love Lake Merritt's **Children's Fairyland** *(fairyland.org; adult/child $19/17)*, a 10-acre attraction that dates from 1950 and hasn't changed much since – we say that with love! With its little Aesop theater and Peter Rabbit's garden, it ticks all the nostalgia boxes for a sweeter, simpler time that probably didn't exist. The park's oldest ride is a beautifully restored, *Alice in Wonderland*–themed carousel dubbed the **Wonder-Go-Round**.

Explore the Cosmos

To infinity and beyond

Stargazers go gaga over the **Chabot Space & Science Center** *(10am-5pm Fri-Sun; adult/child $24/19)*, a kid-oriented science and technology center in the Oakland Hills with loads of exhibits on subjects from space travel to galactic phenomena, as well as cool planetarium shows. It's the official visitor center for the South Bay's NASA Ames Research Center. Check out gear that will be used on future space missions.

TEAM BETRAYAL

As recently as 2019, Oakland had three major league sports teams playing at its aging multipurpose sports complex, the **Oakland Coliseum**. Today, it has none.

First to go was the NFL's Oakland Raiders, which decamped to Las Vegas in 2019. Despite having rabid fans, no agreement on building the team a new stadium could be reached.

The NBA's Golden State Warriors were next, although they didn't go far. A grand new sports palace, the Chase Center, lured them across the bay to San Francisco.

Finally, baseball's Oakland A's left in 2024 for Las Vegas via Sacramento. Fans and the city felt betrayed by a team that had demanded a new stadium and then when the conditions were met, left anyway.

DRINKING IN TEMESCAL: OUR PICKS

Alem's Coffee: East African cafe on Temescal's edge; the outdoor patio is a popular community gathering place in the morning. Good hot chocolate. *7am-7pm*

Snail Bar: Natural and organic wines are just some of the uncommon treats; small-plate pairings change weekly. *5-10pm Wed-Sun*

North Light: Cocktail bar with a bookstore; albums – many for sale – provide tunes. Creative booze mix, vegan treats and patio tables. *4pm-midnight*

Kingfish Pub & Cafe: Beloved dive bar with cheap beer in what was once a bait shop. Play shuffleboard on the back patio. *3pm-midnight*

Beyond Oakland

The East Bay is not all Oakland and Berkeley. Natural and cultural attractions range from the bay to the peaks.

Places

GETTING AROUND

Alameda is reached by buses from Oakland and two ferry lines from San Francisco. BART heads south down the East Bay as does Amtrak and AC Transit buses. Emeryville is the end point for Amtrak's long-distance *California Zephyr* train.

Mostly, however, for experiences further afield such as Mt Diablo, having your own wheels will be a great help.

A lower cost of living (compared to SF), a creative arts scene, offbeat shopping, woodsy parks and better weather are just some of the attractions that lure people to the East Bay.

Alameda is an actual island, thanks to a narrow channel separating it from Oakland. Its surrounding waterfront has sensational bay views and attractions to fill an afternoon. Elsewhere, the string of towns heading south to Fremont and its vast Tesla factory defines no-nonsense.

Near the base of the soaring alabaster Bay Bridge, Emeryville was once the home of thriving Ohlone villages, which featured towering shell mounds built from bay oyster and clam shells. Today it's mostly known for Pixar Animation Studios (not open for visitors).

Alameda

TIME FROM OAKLAND: **10 MINS**

Base Spirits

The west end of Alameda, only 10 minutes by car from Oakland, was once a major naval air station. Long closed, the former base is slowly being transformed into a new neighborhood. Most significantly, several vast old hangars near the USS *Hornet* have been repurposed as Spirits Alley, prosaically known as Monarch St.

Top draws include **St George Spirits** *(stgeorgespirits.com; tastings from $19)*, the alley's anchor, which makes gin, vodka and whiskey. **Gold Bar Distillery** *(goldbarwhiskey.com; classes from $49)* offers classes in making cocktails from its high-end whiskeys.

Floating veteran of war & space

When they splashed down after their lunar landing, the Apollo 11 astronauts were lifted aboard the **USS Hornet Sea, Air & Space Museum** *(uss-hornet.org; adult/child $25/10)*, a Cold War–era aircraft carrier that began life in WWII. It's now docked amidst the old naval base. On a self-guided tour of this immense warship, you'll see an array of historic aircraft on display in the hangar deck and up top on the wind-blown flight deck. The Hornet's role in the Apollo moon-landing missions is fully covered.

JCHANGCC/SHUTTERSTOCK

USS *Hornet*

Mt Diablo

TIME FROM OAKLAND: 1 HR

The East Bay's tallest point

Collecting a light dusting of snowflakes on the coldest days of winter, **Mt Diablo** (3849ft) is more than 1200ft higher than Mt Tamalpais in Marin County. On a clear day (early on a winter morning is a good bet) the views from Diablo's summit are vast and sweeping. To the west you can see over the bay and out to the Farallon Islands; to the east you can look out over the Central Valley to the Sierra Nevada.

The peak is contained within **Mt Diablo State Park** *(parks.ca.gov; vehicle entrance $10)*, which offers rock climbing, stargazing, wildflowers in springtime and the tarantula mating season in the fall. It's threaded by more than 170 miles of hiking trails good for every taste and ability. Birdwatchers may spot hundreds of species, including peregrine falcons and other raptors.

The park's highlight is literally at the top of the peak, where the beautiful and historic **Summit Museum Visitor Center** *(free)* dates from 1942. It features a lookout tower and displays about the park's natural and cultural history. There's even an aviation beacon dating to WWII. Easily reached by car – and by numerous hiking trails – the summit gets crowded on weekends. Find some peace on the Mary Bowerman Loop, an easy 0.8-mi loop trail around the summit that mixes natural beauty with sweeping views.

The park is in Contra Costa County, 14 miles east of Oakland. It's most easily accessed off I-680 at Danville or Walnut Creek.

EAST BAY RAP & HIP HOP

Since the 1980s, West Coast rap and hip-hop have spoken truth. LA has often been in the forefront, but Oakland and the East Bay have been right there too. The son of a Black Panther leader, Tupac Shakur combined party songs and hard truths learned on Oakland's streets until his death in 1996.

The breakout artist in the 1990's was Oakland native MC Hammer, with his landmark album *Please Hammer Don't Hurt 'Em*. Reacting against the increasing commercialization of hip-hop, the Bay Area scene produced underground 'hyphy' (short for hyperactive) artists such as E-40 and Mistah F.A.B. More recently, East Bay groups like Blackalicious, The Coup, Michael Franti & Spearhead, and Kamaiyah are known for their political commentary.

EATING & DRINKING IN THE EAST BAY AREA: OUR PICKS

Los Carnalitos Restaurant: Buried in a Hayward strip mall with uncommon choices such as *cochinita* (slow-roasted pork). *9am-9pm Mon-Sat* $

Domenico's Italian Deli: We dare you to navigate the myriad sandwich options at this Alameda fave toppings, cheeses, breads, spreads... they're all superb. *11am-5pm Mon-Sat* $

Spinning Bones: Creative bistro with Pacific flavors. Roasted meats, seasonal vegetables and offbeat sandwiches. Special bento menu for kids. *11.30am-8pm* $$

Forbidden Island Tiki Lounge: In Alameda, one of the Bay Area's most infamous tiki bars serves every rum-soaked cliché imaginable. Potent mai tais. *4pm-midnight*

Berkeley

CULTURED & LEARNED | GARDENS | ARCHITECTURE

GETTING AROUND

Berkeley is well served with three BART stations; the Downtown Berkeley stop is convenient to most sights and campus. AC Transit buses cover the main roads and provide links across the East Bay. There's limited ferry service to San Francisco.

Berkeley is synonymous with protest, activism and left-wing politics. Here, 'woke' is an essential attribute, not an aspersion.

But beyond those tropes is a busy, attractive city, a blend of yuppie and hippie and student, all existing side by side with great regional restaurants, twee toy stores, Latin American groceries, high-end organic food halls and the misty green campus of the University of California, Berkeley (aka 'Cal'). It's easy to stereotype 'Bezerkeley' for some of its recycle-or-else PC crankiness and occasional overbearing self-righteousness. But some of that attitude is justified: at the end of the day Berkeley has, more often than not, been on the right side of environmental and political issues that have defined the rest of the nation.

Green spaces in the hills and on the flats of the bay, plus enticing neighborhoods, make Berkeley a good day trip or stop from anywhere in the Bay Area.

TOP TIP

Telegraph and Shattuck Aves are packed with cafes, cheap restaurants and bookstores. Berkeley's Little India runs along University Ave. College Ave in Elmwood near Rockridge is lined with shops and bakeries. The popular Gourmet Ghetto stretches along Shattuck Ave north of University Ave. Further northwest, Solano Ave boasts offbeat shops.

UC Berkeley Campus

Go Bears!

The Berkeley campus of the **University of California** (called 'Cal' by both students and locals; *berkeley.edu*) is the oldest university in the state. Founded in 1866, the first students arrived in 1873. Today, Cal has more than 40,000 students, over 1500 professors and more Nobel laureates than you could point a particle accelerator at.

From groovy **Telegraph Ave**, enter the campus via **Sproul Plaza** and **Sather Gate**, a center for people-watching, soapbox oration and pseudotribal drumming. Just wandering the campus is a delight – on a sunny afternoon, you may be tempted to join in some Frisbee throwing.

Stop by the **Koret Visitor Center**, off Piedmont Ave in Memorial Stadium where Cal's Golden Bears play football, for information or to join a guided tour. The website has an array of downloadable self-guided tours and maps.

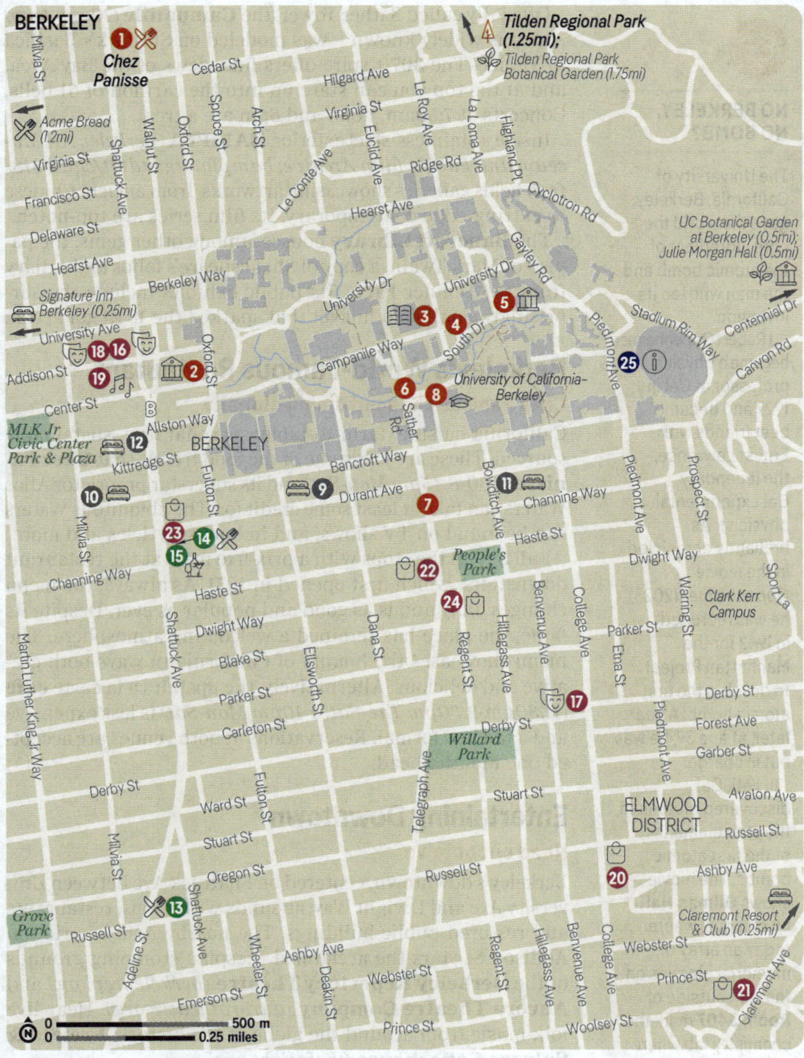

HIGHLIGHTS
1 Chez Panisse

SIGHTS
2 BAMPFA
3 Bancroft Library
4 Campanile
5 Gilman Hall
6 Sather Gate
7 Telegraph Avenue
8 University of California – Berkeley

SLEEPING
9 Berkeley City Club
10 Downtown Berkeley Inn
11 Graduate Berkeley
12 Hotel Shattuck Plaza

EATING
13 Berkeley Bowl Marketplace
14 La Note

DRINKING & NIGHTLIFE
15 Cornerstone

ENTERTAINMENT
16 Aurora Theatre Company
17 Berkeley Playhouse
18 Berkeley Repertory Theatre
19 Freight & Salvage Coffeehouse

SHOPPING
20 Book Society
21 Dark Carnival Imaginative Fiction Bookstore
22 Moe's Books
23 Pegasus Books
24 Sleepy Cat Books

INFORMATION
25 Koret Visitor Center

NO BERKELEY, NO BOMB?

The University of California, Berkeley, gave the world the core ingredient of the atomic bomb and the man who led its invention.

J Robert Oppenheimer became a physics professor at Cal in 1927 and became best friends with Ernest Lawrence, the legendary Cal experimental physicist. As brilliantly chronicled in the movie *Oppenheimer* (2023), he was recruited in 1942 for the Manhattan Project to develop the first atomic bomb. A year later, at age 39, he was put in charge.

In 1941, Cal discovered plutonium, the core element of the first atomic bombs. The movie shows **Gilman Hall** on campus, where today an array of memorial plaques on the wall outside of **Room 3407** mark the chemistry lab where this occurred.

Officially called Sather Tower, the **Campanile** *(10am-4pm)* – as it is widely known – was modeled on St Mark's Basilica in Venice. The 307ft spire offers fine views of the Bay Area, and at the top you can stare up into the carillon of 61 bells. Concerts at 7:50am, noon and 6pm are a treat.

Inside a stainless-steel exterior, **BAMPFA** *(Berkeley Art Museum and Pacific Film Archive; bampfa.org; adult/child $18/free)* holds galleries showcasing artworks, from ancient Chinese to cutting-edge contemporary. Its film series are top-notch.

The **Bancroft Library** houses, among other gems, the papers of Mark Twain, a copy of Shakespeare's folios and a diary from the Donner Party. Its public exhibits include the surprisingly small gold nugget that sparked the 1849 gold rush.

Berkeley's World-Famous Restaurant

Chez Panisse changed dining globally

California cuisine, farm-to-table, seasonal fare, sustainably sourced. These are just some of the food trends that **Chez Panisse** *(5.30-8:45pm Mon-Sat)* and its superstar proprietor Alice Waters can take at least some credit for. The ubiquitous Waters can be found on TV shows, and in books, articles and more.

Pull out all the stops with a prix-fixe meal at the restaurant downstairs, which first opened in 1971. As always, the menu changes daily and is as good and popular as ever. Despite its fame, the place has retained a welcoming atmosphere. The menu showcases the bounty of California in ways both creative and delicious. Alternatively, the upstairs a la carte **cafe** *(11.30am-2.30pm Tue-Sat, 5-10pm Mon-Sat)* is less expensive and a tad less formal. Reservations at both venues are accepted one month ahead.

Entertaining Downtown

Head out of town

Berkeley's downtown, centered on Shattuck Ave between University Ave and Dwight Way, abounds with shops, restaurants and restored public buildings. The nearby Arts District on Addison St stars the acclaimed thespian stomping grounds of the **Berkeley Repertory Theatre** *(berkeleyrep.org)* and **Aurora Theatre Company** *(auroratheatre.org)*. Hear live folk music from around the globe at the historic **Freight & Salvage Coffeehouse** *(thefreight.org)*.

Beauty in Berkeley's Hills

Revel in Cal's Botanical Garden

Nature begins in the hills right at the east end of campus. With 34 acres and more than 10,000 types of plants, the **UC Botanical Garden at Berkeley** *(botanicalgarden.berkeley.edu; adult/child $18/8)* has one of the most varied collections in the country. Flora from every continent except Antarctica is lovingly tended here, with special emphasis on Mediterranean species that grow in California. You'll also find areas devoted to the Americas, the Mediterranean and southern Africa.

GADO IMAGES/GETTY IMAGES

Chez Panisse

Stretch your legs on the nearby fire trail that loops around surrounding Strawberry Canyon, offering great views of town and the off-limits Lawrence Berkeley National Laboratory. Find the trailhead on the east side of Centennial Dr just southwest of the botanical garden.

The Smartest Posie Patch

Wander Tilden Park Botanical Garden

Further up from Cal's garden, 2079-acre **Tilden Regional Park** *(ebparks.org/parks/tilden; free)* is Berkeley's best park and has its own notable garden.

The wonderfully wild-looking **Botanical Garden** celebrates native California plants and has an excellent visitor center. Here, you'll find volunteers eager to explain the myriad species being grown. Many of these knowledgeable people are retirees from Cal with a lifetime of experience both teaching and

EATING & DRINKING IN BERKELEY: CASUAL DINING

Berkeley Bowl Marketplace: Vast indie supermarket with foods from the Bay Area and the world; huge produce department with rare varieties. *9am-8pm* $

Acme Bread: One of the region's best bakeries, beloved for its take on classic sourdough bread. Memorable snacks like the ham and cheese croissant. *8am-4pm* $

La Note: Casual cafe with a strong French accent. Popular at breakfast (goat cheese is an option), lunch brings salads and sandwiches. Sunny garden. *8am-2pm* $$

Cornerstone: Welcoming bar with regular live music. Seating inside and outside, 50 tap beers (many unusual) and tasty comfort food. *11.30am-midnight*

BERKELEY'S BEST BOOKSTORES

Moe's Books: New and used books in a vast store south of campus. Renowned for its knowledgeable staff, enjoy browsing across four floors.

Dark Carnival Imaginative Fiction Bookstore: One of the oldest science-fiction, fantasy and horror bookstores west of the Mississippi. It's all controlled chaos; lose yourself in the stacks.

Pegasus Books: Right on the Shattuck Ave commercial strip, Pegasus has great staff recommendations and daily specials on new and used titles.

Book Society: Browsing for books in this cozy, comfy space is all the better given the machines in back that dispense wine by the glass.

Sleepy Cat Books: You'll find the namesake felines dozing away as you browse the carefully curated selection of offbeat fiction and hard-to-find nonfiction.

PAUL CHINN/THE SAN FRANCISCO CHRONICLE VIA GETTY IMAGES

Swimming pool, Berkeley City Club

researching horticulture, so you can expect any question you conjure up to result in detailed and well-informed answers!

Whiteboards list daily events, which can include tours, lectures and other informative activities.

Elsewhere, Tilden Park has nearly 40 miles of hiking and multiuse trails of varying difficulty, from paved paths to hilly scrambles, including part of the magnificent Bay Area Ridge Trail.

Berkeley's Landmark Architect

See Julia Morgan's creations

Julia Morgan's ties with Cal began when she became the first woman to graduate from the civil engineering program. She is best known as William Randolph Hearst's favorite architect and the designer of Hearst Castle (p316), but over her prolific career she designed more than 700 buildings, including some noteworthy Berkeley creations. (One of her Oakland buildings changed engineering practices worldwide, p135.)

Julia Morgan Hall (1911) was originally a meeting place for female students (who, like Morgan, a Cal alum, were a small minority over 100 years ago). Now relocated to the UC Botanical Garden, it exemplifies her low-slung designs clad in redwood. At the southwest corner of campus, the **Berkeley City Club** (1929) picks up many of Hearst Castle's Moorish and Romanesque design elements. It's now a hotel (p162).

The **Berkeley Playhouse** (1910) on College Ave is typically understated and makes beautiful use of redwood. It was built as the St John's Presbyterian Church and is on the National Register of Historic Places.

Beyond Berkeley

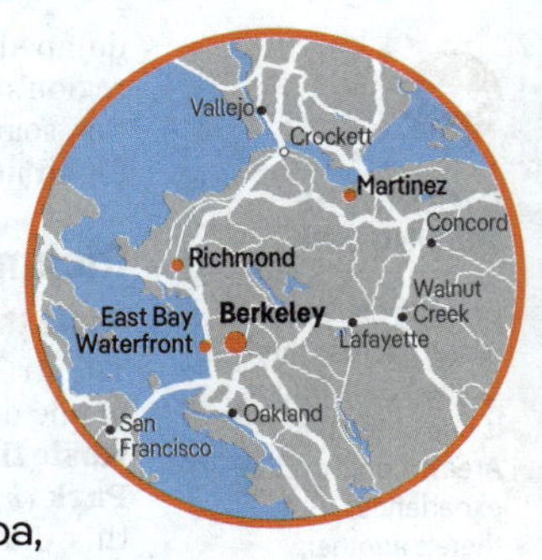

Follow the bay to visit sights, far from the tourist glitz of San Francisco, Marin and Napa, which are nonetheless uniquely compelling.

Many of the most interesting sights and activities beyond Berkeley as you head north and east around the bay toward the Sacramento Delta are close to the water. This includes three national parks that each cover a significant aspect of American life: the wholesale societal changes brought by WWII, the emergence of an appreciation for America's natural splendor and a little-visited memorial to an avoidable and shocking wartime tragedy.

Along the bay, trails, parks and open places provide diverse ways to get outside in the fresh breezes off the water. You can walk, hike, fly a kite, paddle a kayak, sail a boat, learn to ride an SUP or revel in the funkiest of al fresco art.

Places

GETTING AROUND

Richmond is well served by BART and Amtrak. AC Transit buses provide local coverage in Alameda County. Further east, services become more sparse and having your own wheels is the most practical way to tour around.

When driving East Bay freeways such as the I-80, be aware that they become heavily congested during morning and evening rush hours.

East Bay Waterfront

TIME FROM BERKELEY: **10-20 MINS**

Action & art at the shore

Looking west from the East Bay Shore, the San Francisco Bay makes a beautiful backdrop for a photo – even when it's not sunset – what with Alcatraz, the city skyline and the distant Golden Gate Bridge.

A string of parks and public spaces from Emeryville through Albany offers plenty of options for enjoying the view, playing in the bay breezes and getting out on the water.

Berkeley Recreation & Wellbeing Adventures *(recwell.berkeley.edu/wellness-offerings/adventures)* is run by UC Berkeley at the **Berkeley Marina**. Open to non-students, it organizes sailing, windsurfing, SUP and kayaking classes and gear rental. Reservations are a must through the website.

Go fly a kite at **Cesar Chavez Park** at the north end of the Berkeley Marina. With nearly 20 acres of flat, unobstructed waterfront and near-constant breezes, this is an ideal venue for sending your own creation aloft. Finding the right kite is easy, thanks to **Highline Kites** *(highlinekites.com)*, which sets up shop in a truck at the north end of the park every weekend *(1.30-6.30pm)*. Prices start at under $15 and the colorful choices are vast.

Discover community-made outdoor art, nearly 200 species of birds and wild, windy walks at the **Albany Bulb**, a legacy landfill that juts out into the bay and dates back over 100 years to a time when communities (and a dynamite factory!)

CYCLING THE MISSING LINK

Cruising on two wheels across the Golden Gate Bridge is one of the Bay Area's iconic cycling experiences. But there's another, longer, bridge that you can ride across. No, sadly, it's not the Bay Bridge, but rather, the unheralded, unloved **Richmond–San Rafael Bridge** in the North Bay. One entire lane on the upper deck of the span has been walled off for bikes, which has been a real boon for exploring the region.

Using combinations of BART and the San Francisco–Larkspur Golden Gate ferry, you can create huge circle rides of various lengths from the East Bay and San Francisco. The 5.5-mile bridge affords grand views of Marin, Alameda and Contra Costa Counties and the bay while you ride.

dumped their garbage in the water. Today it offers one of the region's most offbeat walks, a 1.8mi looping stroll past castles, soaring figures, abstract shapes and more, all made from found junk and flotsam.

Richmond

TIME FROM BERKELEY: **20 MINS**

Rosie the Riveter's home

The struggle for civil rights and women's equality is the focus of one of the East Bay's most significant historical sites, the **Rosie the Riveter WWII Home Front National Historic Park** *(nps.gov/rori; free)*. Located on the bay in Richmond, this illuminating museum is part of what remains of four adjoining Kaiser shipyards built during WWII.

Thousands of workers toiled here in shifts around the clock. To meet the insatiable need for labor, scores of women were brought into the workforce, along with a huge number of African Americans, who had faced discrimination in California. They achieved the remarkable feat of building nearly 750 freighters and warships during WWII using mass-production techniques.

Displays cover the huge societal changes spawned by the shipyards and the challenges the workers faced in finding housing and basic life balance. Then, when the war ended, the shipyards closed and jobs disappeared, other than a few at the pollution-belching refineries on the bay – which remain in operation. Richmond is still depressed decades later.

Look for the large freighter, the **SS Red Oak Victory** *(redoakvictory.us; $15-25)*, docked across from the visitor center. It's one of the last surviving ships to be built here and is open 10am to 3pm Sunday.

Martinez

TIME FROM BERKELEY: **30-45 MINS**

John Muir's home

Naturalist John Muir's former residence is part of the **John Muir National Historic Site** *(nps.gov/jomu; free)*. It sits in a pastoral patch of farmland in bustling, modern Martinez, far up the bay, near the beginning of the Sacrament–-San Joaquin Delta.

Though Muir wrote of sauntering the Sierra Nevada with a sack of tea and bread, it may be a shock for those familiar with the iconic Sierra Club founder's ascetic weather-beaten appearance that this house (built by his father-in-law in 1883) is a model of Victorian Italianate refinement, with a tower cupola and a daintily upholstered parlor.

EATNG & DRINKING BEYOND BERKELEY: OUR PICKS

Seabreeze: Casual choice near the Berkeley Marina with a few terrace tables. Fish sandwiches, fries and clam chowder are all made to go. *9am-6pm* **$$**

Kaleidoscope Coffee: In compact Point Richmond, the charming neighborhood west of the national historic site, serves great coffee and snacks. *7am-7pm* **$**

Bull Valley Roadhouse: Port Costa roadhouse dating to 1897, with classic American fare and potent cocktails. Ambitious menu with casual options. *noon-9pm Wed-Sun* **$$**

States Coffee: House-roasted coffee served in the heart of Martinez; good snacks and baked goods. Plot out your day on the lovely patio. *7am-4pm* **$**

EWY MEDIA/SHUTTERSTOCK

Rosie the Riveter WWII Home Front National Historic Park

Muir's 'scribble den' has been left as it was during his life, with crumpled papers overflowing from wire wastebaskets and dried-bread balls – his preferred snack – resting on the mantelpiece.

Acres of the family's fruit orchards still stand, and visitors can enjoy seasonal samples. The grounds include the 1849 **Martinez Adobe**, part of the ranch on which the house was built, and oak-speckled hiking trails on nearby **Mt Wanda** (660ft), named for one of Muir's daughters.

A little-known & moving memorial

On July 17, 1944, 320 sailors and civilians were killed when ammunition being loaded onto a freighter exploded at the Port Chicago military base, east of Martinez.

The disaster was heard and felt in Oakland, 30 miles away and beyond. The ship being loaded vanished. Despite the disaster's scope, it's little known today. Most of those killed were African American sailors, working under horrific conditions. During WWII the US military was still segregated and African Americans were given the worst jobs.

Today, the **Port Chicago Naval Magazine National Memorial** *(nps.gov/poch; free)* is a simple and poignant monument at the blast site. It receives few visitors as the location is an active military base, and visits require advance reservations.

THE EAST BAY'S LESSER-KNOWN SIGHTS

Crockett: One of the historic towns dotting the bayshore has an appealing dash of vintage charm.

Benecia: Across the narrow Carquinez Strait, this city was once the state's capital (1853–54) as recalled at the **Benicia Capitol State Historic Park** *(adult/child $3/2).*

Port Costa: Hidden by barren hills, this 19th-century waterfront hamlet has popular weekend roadhouses next to train tracks.

Eugene O'Neill National Historic Site: Hidden in the San Ramon Valley, the Nobel-winning playwright of *The Iceman Cometh* lived here from 1937. *nps.gov/euon; free*

Niles Canyon Railway: Old steam and diesel trains follow a scenic route between Niles and Sunol. *ncry.org; adult/child from $25/15*

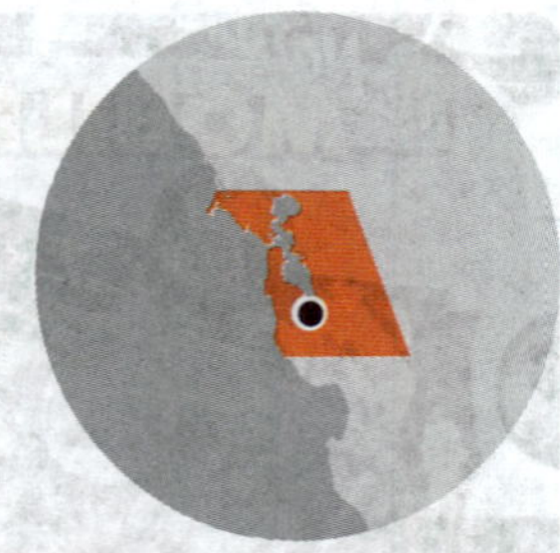

Palo Alto

AFFLUENT NEIGHBORHOODS | UNIVERSITY TOURS | HIKING

GETTING AROUND

Speedy and newly electrified Caltrain commuter trains serve San Francisco (50 minutes) and San Jose (25 minutes). VTA buses connect Palo Alto with the rest of Silicon Valley, including San Jose. Stanford University has a free public shuttle service for the campus and the immediate area.

☑ TOP TIP

Stanford University presents a self-consciously rural appearance and adjoins a namesake luxury shopping center. Both are west of the busy Caltrain tracks. Downtown is a walkable delight. Past pricey neighborhoods and Hwy 101, East Palo Alto is a separate city, which enjoys little affluence.

Palo Alto is Silicon Valley's ritziest city. Even a modest bungalow here may cost over $2 million, while upscale boutiques, bistros and spas crowd downtown streets.

It's also the mythical heart of Silicon Valley. Bill Hewlett and David Packard got their start here in their legendary garage (you can see it at 367 Addison Ave). Steve Jobs lived and died here. Larry Page and Sergey Brin were students at Stanford University when they started Google. The list goes on. But it's not all lightness and joy. Palo Alto was the home of convicted fraudsters Elizabeth Holmes and Sam Bankman-Fried, while the ethics of the billionaire venture capitalists on Sand Hill Rd and tech oligarchs are ever more questioned.

Sprawled across nearly 13 sq miles just west of downtown, Stanford University lays claim to the city's soul. Built by Leland Stanford, one of the original 'robber barons,' it grew to become a prestigious, wealthy and conservative institution.

Exploring Stanford

Touring art and architecture

Stanford University *(stanford.edu)* is one of America's top universities academically and among the most expensive. The faux California Mission Revival–style campus is a genteel place to stroll, with public artwork and murals. (Note: the rivalry with publicly funded UC Berkeley is intense.) Having been built on the site of the Stanford family's horse farm, the university maintains the humble-brag nickname The Farm.

Stop by the **Stanford Visitor Center** *(visit.stanford.edu)* off Galvez St for self-guided tour info and maps. Many cover the multitudes of public art around campus. Download the Stanford Mobile app which has walking tours.

Auguste Rodin's *Burghers of Calais* bronze sculpture marks the entrance to the **Main Quad** (begun 1887), an open plaza where the original 12 campus buildings – a mix of Romanesque

SIGHTS
1 Cantor Arts Center
2 Hoover Tower
3 Main Quad
4 Memorial Church
5 Stanford University
6 Wunderlich County Park

ACTIVITIES
7 Baylands Observation Deck and Boardwalk
8 Stanford Dish Loop
9 Windy Hill Preserve

SLEEPING
10 Coronet Motel
11 Dinah's Garden Hotel
12 Leland Hotel Palo Alto
13 Nobu Epiphany
14 Rosewood Sand Hill

EATING
15 Camper
16 Palo Alto Creamery
17 Tamarine Restaurant & Gallery

DRINKING & NIGHTLIFE
18 Vino Locale

INFORMATION
19 Stanford Visitor Center

and Mission Revival styles – are joined by the **Memorial Church** (1903). The church is noted for its beautiful mosaic-tiled frontage, stained-glass windows and five organs with more than 8000 pipes.

A campus landmark to the east of the Main Quad, the 285ft-high **Hoover Tower** *(hoover.org/library-archives/visit/hoover-tower; $8)* is part of the conservative Hoover Institution, a Stanford-affiliated public policy research center. An elevator-accessed observation platform on the 14th floor offers sweeping Bay Area views.

BEST HIKES NEAR PALO ALTO

Stanford Dish Loop: The hilly 3.7-mile paved path is popular with runners, walkers and science nerds who want to see the 150ft-diameter radio telescope ('the Dish').

Baylands Observation Deck and Boardwalk: A hub for hiking trails that follow the bay shoreline through parks and wildlife-filled estuaries.

San Andreas Fault Trail: Learn all about earthquake geology on this gentle 1.5-mile self-guided path inside the **Los Trancos Open Space Preserve**.

Wunderlich County Park: Untouched peninsula nature: trails follow hillsides, gulches and streams under shady redwoods and oaks.

Windy Hill Preserve: For more outdoor options, head west into the Santa Cruz Mountains. Start at this grass-covered hilltop where trails radiate into the redwoods.

PANDORA PICTURES/SHUTTERSTOCK

Stanford University (p148)

Think Rodin

Stanford's masterpiece of a museum

Fronted by Ionic columns, the **Cantor Arts Center** *(museum.stanford.edu; free)* includes works from ancient civilizations to contemporary art, spanning the globe. The museum is renowned for its Rodin collection of over 200 works displayed both inside and out in a garden. Of course there's a de rigueur *The Thinker*. Rotating shows are eclectic in scope and include well-curated photography exhibitions.

EATING & DRINKING IN PALO ALTO: OUR PICKS

Camper: In Palo Alto's symbiotic twin Menlo Park, classic NorCal seasonal menu of locally sourced food prepared creatively. *10am-1pm Sat & Sun, 5-8:45pm Mon-Sat* **$$$**

Tamarine Restaurant & Gallery: Exquisite Vietnamese food served in artful surrounds. Cocktails pair with small and large plates. *11.30am-2.30pm & 5-9pm* **$$$**

Palo Alto Creamery: A downtown institution, sparkling chrome-and-red-booths and a look from 1923; famous for breakfasts, milkshakes and pies. *8am-9pm* **$$**

Vino Locale: Wine bar in a Victorian house with an inviting terrace. Unpretentious by local standards, the focus is on regional foods and tasty bites. *3-9pm*

Beyond Palo Alto

Roam the land where billionaires are spawned and enjoy your own tech fantasy. Divert to bay and mountain pleasures.

South of San Francisco, squeezed tightly between the bay and the coastal foothills, a long swath of cities, towns and suburbia runs down to San Jose. Dotted inside this area are famous names such as Silicon Valley, Menlo Park and Mountain View.

You won't find Silicon Valley on any map: it's a nickname coined in the 1970s. As silicon chips form the basis of modern computers, and the Santa Clara Valley – stretching from Palo Alto through Sunnyvale and Cupertino to San Jose – is thought of as the birthplace of the tech revolution, the region is dubbed 'Silicon Valley.' It's hard to imagine that through the 1960s it was still a region of apricot, Bing cherry and walnut orchards.

GETTING AROUND

Silicon Valley's streets and freeways are often traffic-clogged with frustrated Lamborghini drivers (and others). Caltrain efficiently links city and town centers between San Francisco and San Jose. VTA provides fill-in bus and light-rail services. However, your own wheels are best for visiting this sprawling area. Choose your freeway: Hwy 101 is the spine of Silicon Valley, while the I-280 is the less congested, scenic alternative.

Silicon Valley

TIME FROM PALO ALTO: **20-45 MINS** 

Tech's got a history

The vast and well-funded **Computer History Museum** *(computerhistory.org; adult/child $20/free)* in Mountain View has themed exhibits drawn from its 100,000-item collection. Displays cover the range of technology and, depending on your interest, can easily absorb half a day. Artifacts range from the abacus to iPhone prototypes. Docents are often industry luminaries who've got time to kill now that their IPOs have vested.

The storied chipmaker Intel – one of the reasons Silicon Valley got its name – runs the reinvigorated **Intel Museum** *(intel.com; 9am-5pm)* in Santa Clara, which covers the use of silicon in producing microchips, several decades of nearly unbelievable innovation in chip production and – not surprisingly – Intel's involvement, plus you can see how chips are made.

Visiting tech icons

Apple occupies a chunk of its longtime corporate home of Cupertino. Its **Visitor Center** *(apple.com/retail/appleparkvisitorcenter; 10am-7pm)* has an Apple Store, a sleek cafe and a rooftop deck that allows a glimpse of the company's infamous 'flying saucer' headquarters. The basement bathroom corridors are eerily reminiscent of the Apple TV+ series *Severance*, about an evil corporation dedicated to mind control.

Google, in Mountain View, finally has a public facility called the **Google Visitor Experience** *(visit.withgoogle.com; 9am-7pm)* and, like Google, it's huge. There's a store, but there's also bayside trails, public art, games, displays, cafes and much more. You can easily spend a couple of hours here.

Meta's headquarters is an agglomeration of office buildings surrounded by parking lots near the Dumbarton Bridge across from East Palo Alto. Nothing is open to the public. The one visitor-friendly location is the **Meta Store** *(meta.com; 11am-6pm Mon-Sat)*, hidden away in Burlingame. Here you can try out the company's latest virtual-reality gizmos and, yes, buy a T-shirt.

Valley towns worth a look

Cities and towns line the peninsula south from San Francisco, flowing seamlessly from one to the next. The more notable names include the following:

San Mateo has good bayshore parks, such as the **Coyote Point Recreation Area** *(parks.smcgov.org/coyote-point-recreation-area)*.

Atherton is the wealthiest zip code in the USA, with old-money families that predate Silicon Valley. Vast mansions are cloistered between high hedges and fences.

Woodside has good casual-chic roadside cafes on Hwy 84 and is the gateway to the magnificent open lands of the Santa Cruz Mountains along Skyline Blvd.

Saratoga and **Los Gatos** are rarified neighbors. Each has an atmospheric town center ready-made for strolling – a local rarity.

SILICON VALLEY TIMELINE

Since the 1950s Silicon Valley has spawned thousands of companies thanks to its ecosystem of talented people, many universities, and venture capitalists and others ready with funding.

1950s: Major corporations like Hewlett-Packard, Lockheed and Xerox set up in the Santa Clara Valley. Tech companies form to serve them, making early semiconductors.

1957: The birth of Fairchild Semiconductor is a foundational moment, spawning legends like Intel.

1960: Researchers discover the remarkable properties of silicon in chips.

1969: The earliest form of the internet includes Stanford.

1970s: Apple, Atari and Oracle are founded.

1980s: Adobe, Cisco and Sun Microsystems are founded.

1990s: Google, Netflix, Netscape, PayPal and Yahoo are founded.

2000s: Facebook, Twitter and Uber are founded.

EATING & DRINKING IN SILICON VALLEY: OUR PICKS

Buck's Restaurant of Woodside: Legendary meeting place for tech entrepreneurs and VCs, who discuss funding over upscale diner fare at picnic tables. *8am-9pm* **$$**

DH Noodles: Lanzhou-style Chinese specialities (hand-pulled noodles and rich beef broth), reflecting the region's Muslim influence. Near Cupertino. *11am-9pm* **$$**

Dolce Spazio Dessert Cafe: House-made gelato in sexy flavors like 'Oreogasmic.' Not the place for fruity sorbets; also cakes and shakes. In Los Gatos. *noon-10pm* **$**

Das Bierhauz: Tech-fave in Mountain View; a beer garden serving German classics and over a dozen Old World beers on tap in big steins. *11am-10pm* **$$**

San Jose

HISTORY PARK | MUSEUMS | DIVERSE CUISINES

Though culturally diverse and rich in history, San Jose – carpeted with Silicon Valley's suburbia – has always been in San Francisco's shadow. Founded in 1777 as El Pueblo de San José de Guadalupe, San Jose is California's oldest Spanish civilian settlement. Its downtown is fairly modest for a city that's California's third-most populated (after LA and San Diego). It does bustle with 20-something partiers on weekends, in part thanks to its large namesake state university.

Industrial parks, high-tech computer firms, surprisingly leafy neighborhoods and strip malls are sprawled across the city's landscape. Underneath all this is fertile land where some of the world's most bounteous orchards grew as recently as the 1960s.

This West Coast multiethnic melting pot has excellent restaurants scattered throughout. While specific sights are few, the city is a good pit stop on the way to Santa Cruz, Monterey or north to San Francisco.

GETTING AROUND

San Jose is a transportation hub. Its busy airport has international and domestic flights and is a good alternative to San Francisco's. Caltrain offers excellent service up the peninsula to San Francisco. Amtrak regional trains serve Oakland, Sacramento and the Central Valley. Amtrak's wonderful long-distance *Coast Starlight* runs north to Seattle and south to LA. VTA runs bus and light-rail service across the South Bay.

Oddball Sight

Touring one lady's obsession

San Jose's top attraction is also the strangest: **Winchester Mystery House** *(winchestermysteryhouse.com; adult/child from $46/23)* is a ridiculous yet fascinating and elaborate Victorian mansion filled with 160 mostly non-utilitarian rooms with dead-end hallways and a staircase that runs up to a ceiling. It was the obsession of Sarah Winchester, who seemingly couldn't live without constant hammering. Guided tours cover the basics and previously little-seen corners.

TOP TIP

Drive 9 miles northwest of downtown San Jose to the tiny old village of **Alviso** in the estuary at the south end of the bay. This is big-sky country and there are hikes galore on the trails of the **Don Edwards San Francisco Bay National Wildlife Refuge** *(fws.gov/refuge/don-edwards-san-francisco-bay)*.

Architecture Tour

Walk into the past

Historical buildings from all over San Jose have been brought together in **History Park** *(historysanjose.org; free)*, an

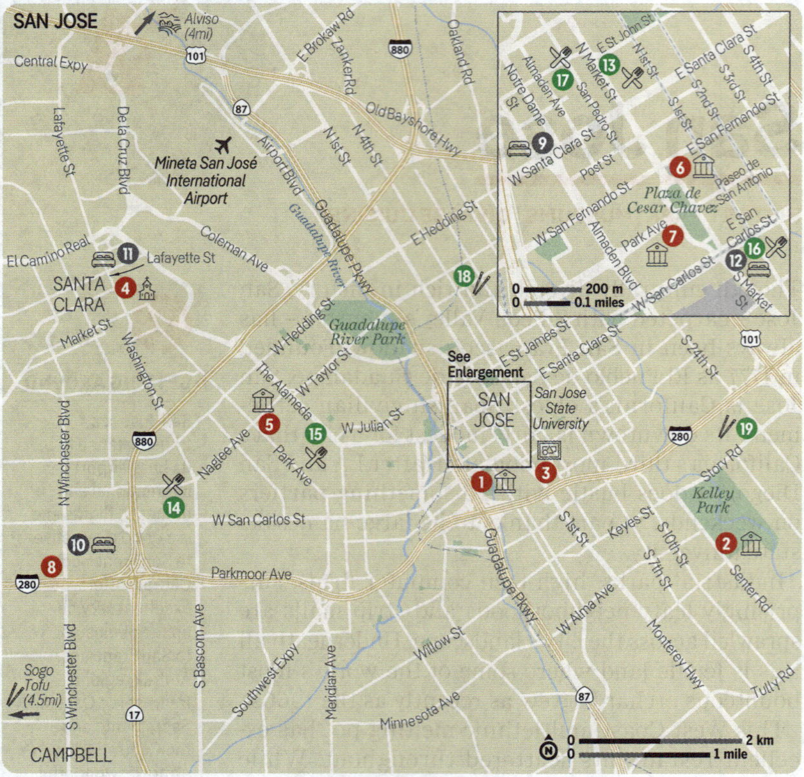

SIGHTS
1 Children's Discovery Museum
2 History Park
3 MACLA
4 Mission Santa Clara de Asís
5 Rosicrucian Egyptian Museum
6 San Jose Museum of Art
7 Tech Interactive
8 Winchester Mystery House

SLEEPING
9 Hotel De Anza
10 Hotel Valencia
11 Kasa University-Airport Santa Clara
12 Westin San Jose

EATING
13 Back A Yard Caribbean Grill
14 Falafel's Drive In
15 Luna Mexican Kitchen
16 Original Joe's
17 San Pedro Square Market
18 Shuei-Do Manju Shop
19 Vịt Đông Quê

EATING IN SAN JOSE: OUR PICKS

Original Joe's: Downtown institution serving casual meals including sublime burgers. Comfy booths and a full bar. *4-10pm* **$$**

Back A Yard Caribbean Grill: The sauces and marinades are all made in-house. Fab jerk chicken and curried goat. *11am-8pm Tue-Sun* **$$**

San Pedro Square Market: Travel the world at this vibrant food hall. Choices include Italian, Peruvian, Korean and, yes, American. *11am-10pm* **$$**

Falafel's Drive In: A beloved San Jose institution for nearly 60 years; pitas brim with crunchy, herby falafel and creamy tahini. *10am-8pm* **$**

CREATISTA/SHUTTERSTOCK

Winchester Mystery House (p153)

immersive open-air museum that recreates the 19th century in the valley. The centerpiece is a scaled-down replica of the 1881 **Electric Light Tower**. Other buildings include the 1880 **Pacific Hotel**, which houses an old-timey ice-cream parlor and rotating art exhibits, and **migrant houses**, which show the spartan living conditions of farmworkers. Park exhibits highlight Chinese, Portuguese and other early communities. Galleries in various buildings have worthwhile special exhibitions.

Santa Clara has tech companies surrounding its namesake university, which is home to the 1777 **Mission Santa Clara de Asís** *(scu.edu/missionchurch; free)*.

SAN JOSE'S BEST MUSEUMS

Tech Interactive: An excellent technology museum that examines subjects from robotics to biofeedback, genetics to virtual reality. *thetech.org; adult/child $36/28*

San Jose Museum of Art: Permanent collection of 20th-century works plus imaginative changing exhibits. *sjmusart.org; adult/child $20/free*

MACLA: Gallery highlights Latino artists; one of the Bay Area's best community arts spaces, with live music, theater and thought-provoking visual-arts exhibits. *maclaarte.org; free*

Rosicrucian Egyptian Museum: Extensive collection includes statues, household items and mummies. *egyptianmuseum.org; adult/child $15/10*

Children's Discovery Museum: Yet another science museum, this one with hands-on displays for kids. *cdm.org; $18*

EATING IN SAN JOSE: OUR PICKS

Shuei-Do Manju Shop: Japanese pastries, candy and shaved ice; beloved for its house-made mochi (rice-based pastries). *10am-4pm Thu-Sun* $

Luna Mexican Kitchen: Brings a farm-to-table ethos to sophisticated Mexican fare. The bar goes beyond the margarita cliches. *9am-9pm* $$

Vịt Đồng Quê: Simple storefront stars in the Little Saigon neighborhood with its duck dishes and piquant accompaniments. *10am-7pm Wed-Mon* $$

Sogo Tofu: Long-running strip-mall stalwart offers picnic-worthy meals made with its own organic Taiwanese-style tofu. *8am-5pm* $

Half Moon Bay

SURFING | COASTAL WALKS | PUMPKINS

GETTING AROUND

SamTrans provides useful local bus services. Route 294 runs on the frequently traffic-clogged Hwy 92 over to the peninsula and the Hillsdale Caltrain station. Route 117 runs north along Hwy 1 to Pacifica. On weekends, especially in summer, Hwy 1 through Half Moon Bay gets jammed with traffic.

TOP TIP

Mavericks is the intense surf break that became world famous thanks to videos beginning in the 1990s – waves here can top 60ft after storms. A surf competition was held here sporadically until 2016. To glimpse the distant action, take binoculars and hike around **Pillar Point** west of the namesake harbor.

Home to a long coastline, mild albeit foggy weather (bring layers!) and Mavericks, one of the biggest and gnarliest surf breaks on the planet, Half Moon Bay and neighboring Miramar and El Granada are prime real estate.

The Ohlone people lived here for thousands of years before Spanish missionaries colonized the land in the late 1700s; it was developed as a beach resort in the early 1900s and was a destination for smuggled booze from Canadian ships offshore during Prohibition. Today, it's the main coastal town between San Francisco (29 miles north) and Santa Cruz (49 miles south) and makes an ideal Hwy 1 pit stop.

Although the shallowness of the bay means it should be called Quarter Moon Bay, the long stretches of sandy beach and coastal bluffs attract surfers, hikers and active-minded weekenders. The small downtown is architecturally historic and good for a stroll.

Fun on the Coast

Lazing, hiking and kayaking

Crescent-shaped and over 4 miles long, **Half Moon Bay State Beach** *(parks.ca.gov)* is a beautiful ribbon of sand along the Pacific. Much of it is nearly untrodden and it's easy to leave other visitors behind as you walk along the sandstone cliffs and dunes.

The 7.2-mi **Coastside Trail** runs the length of Half Moon Bay from the bluff above Manhattan Beach north to Pillar Point Harbor. Look for driftwood after storms and watch for whales offshore.

When the bay is calm, get out and cruise on the water with **Half Moon Bay Kayak Co** *(hmbkayak.com; from $30hr)*, which rents kayaks and SUP sets.

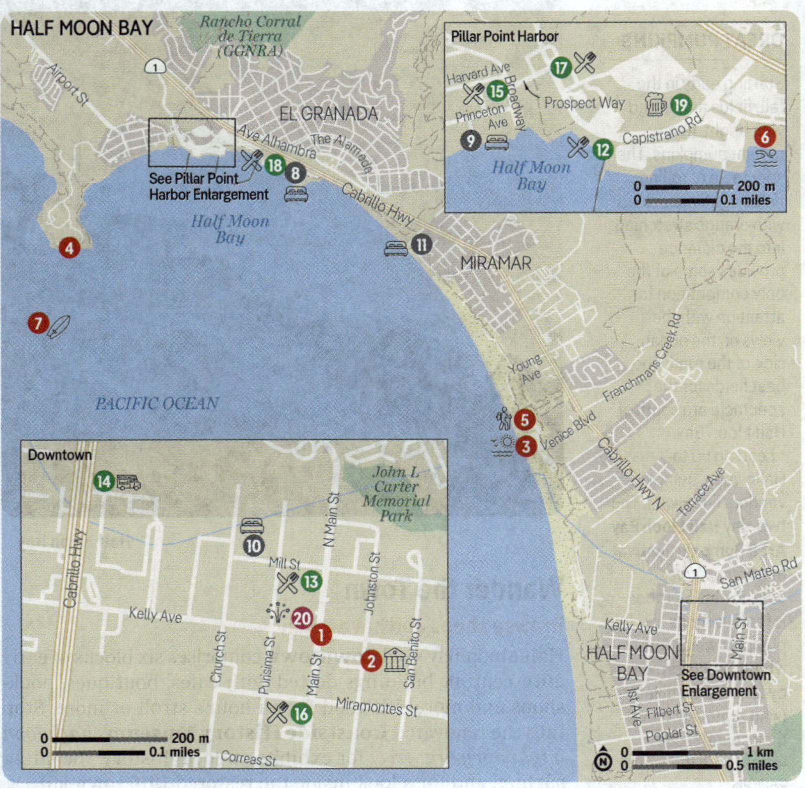

SIGHTS

1 Downtown Half Moon Bay
2 Half Moon Bay Coastside History Museum
3 Half Moon Bay State Beach
4 Pillar Point

ACTIVITIES

5 Coastside Trail
6 Half Moon Bay Kayak Co
7 Mavericks

SLEEPING

8 Beach House Half Moon Bay
9 Inn at Mavericks
10 Mill Rose Inn
11 Oceanfront Beach Villa

EATING

12 Barbara's Fishtrap
13 Ciya Mediterranean Cuisine
14 Dad's Luncheonette
15 Jettywave Distillery
16 Moonside Bakery & Cafe
17 Old Princeton Landing Public House & Grill
18 Sam's Chowder House

DRINKING & NIGHTLIFE

19 Hop Dogma Brewing Co

ENTERTAINMENT

20 Half Moon Bay Art & Pumpkin Festival

GREAT PUMPKINS

Starting early in the fall, fields are dotted with bright, nearly radiant pumpkins. The spectacle of rolling fields tightly speckled with orange stretching into the distance provides some of the only competition for attention with the views on the ocean side of the road. The best fields for the spectacle are south of Half Moon Bay.

Leading up to Halloween, pumpkin vendors line Hwy 1. The two-day **Half Moon Bay Art & Pumpkin Festival** *(hmbpumpkinfest.com)* in mid-October is famous for its pumpkin weigh-off, where beasts grown by fanatical cultivators (who zealously guard their secrets) can weigh more than 2500lb.

OXANA MILITSINA/SHUTTERSTOCK

Half Moon Bay

Wander the Town

Browse shops and have lunch

Half Moon Bay's old **downtown** comprises six blocks of early 20th-century buildings dotted with cafes, boutiques, bookshops and more. It's good for an hour's stroll or more. Stop into the renovated **Coastside History Museum** *(halfmoonbayhistory.org; free)* for exhibits on local history, including surfing, and for a look inside the restored 1919 town jail.

EATING & DRINKING IN HALF MOON BAY: OUR PICKS

Jettywave Distillery: One of many fine choices near Pillar Point Harbor, serves locally caught seafood with Med and Thai accents. *noon-8pm Fri-Sun* **$$**

Barbara's Fishtrap: At Pillar Point Harbor serving clam chowder and Bay Area standards. *11am-8.30pm* **$$**

Sam's Chowder House: Causes Hwy 1 traffic backups on weekends. Famous for its namesake clam concoction. *11am-8.30pm* **$$**

Hop Dogma Brewing Co: Top NorCal brewery serves hop-forward beers like Nintai, a Japanese-style rice lager, and West Coast IPAs. *2-8pm*

Old Princeton Landing Public House & Grill: Half Moon Bay's top venue for live music; all-day bar with elevated bar chow. *9am-11pm* **$$**

Ciya Mediterranean Cuisine: Uses local ingredients and produce for dishes that capture flavors from around the Eastern Med. *11am-9pm* **$$**

Moonside Bakery & Cafe: Makes a fine croissant; top-end diner for breakfast and lunch; baked treats stretch around the storefront. *7.30am-3.30pm* **$**

Dad's Luncheonette: Old caboose on Hwy 1 near downtown; serves creative hamburgers. Red wine by the can. *11am-4pm Thu-Sun* **$**

Beyond Half Moon Bay

One of California's highlights, the famous drive on Hwy 1 south from San Francisco is one of the state's unmissable pleasures.

Places

The 70-mile stretch of the Pacific Coast Hwy (Hwy 1) from San Francisco to Santa Cruz is one of California's most bewitching oceanside jaunts. Outside of Half Moon Bay, it's a sinuous ribbon of road, passing beach after beach. From Pacifica to the end of San Mateo County is 41 miles; just enjoying this stretch can easily fill an entire day, even before you reach Davenport and the splendors of Santa Cruz County. Besides the easily accessed beaches alongside Hwy 1, there are countless others hidden from view. If you see a string of vehicles with surfboard racks parked roadside, you'll find a trail across the fields leading to some impossibly lovely cove reached by an often perilous cliffside trail.

Pacifica

TIME FROM HALF MOON BAY: **30 MINS**

Wild pleasures & promises

The lazy beach town of Pacifica, just 15 miles south of downtown San Francisco and 20 minutes by car north of Half Moon Bay, signals the end of the city's urban sprawl and the start of the wild Pacific coastline. Pacifica's real appeal is as the gateway to the spectacular run south on Hwy 1.

Pacifica State Beach *(parks.ca.gov; free)* is long, scenic and gets pounded by surfable waves. Gear rental is available nearby at **Nor-Cal Surf Shop** *(norcalsurfshop.com)*.

Immediately south of Pacifica is the **Devil's Slide**, a gorgeous coastal cliff area now bypassed by a tunnel. Hikers and cyclists cruise along the **Devil's Slide Trail**, a 1.3-mile section of the old road. Parking areas perch above the sheer, filigreed cliffs, with waves crashing below and pelicans flying overhead.

Montara & Moss Beach

TIME FROM HALF MOON BAY: **15 MINS**

Life in the tidepools

The villages of **Montara** and **Moss Beach** punctuate a stretch of coast interwoven by cliffs and sand. Just north, **Gray Whale Cove State Beach** is one of the coast's many popular clothing-optional beaches. At Moss Beach, the fabulous **Fitzgerald Marine Reserve** *(fitzgeraldreserve.org; free)* protects tide pools teeming with sea life such as colorful starfish, crabs and urchins. A small visitor center provides an introduction to the wealth of

GETTING AROUND

SamTrans bus route 117 runs from Half Moon Bay to Pacifica. From there, buses connect to BART stations. Route 294 runs on the frequently traffic-clogged Hwy 92 to the peninsula and the Hillsdale Caltrain station.

On weekends, especially in summer, Hwy 1 through Half Moon Bay gets thick with tourist traffic. Further south, you'll need your own vehicle to follow the coast to Santa Cruz County. Experienced cyclists brave the narrow shoulders of Hwy 1 from Pacifica to Santa Cruz.

BEST SIGHTS INLAND FROM HWY 1

Skyline Blvd (AKA Hwy 35): Follows the ridge of the Santa Cruz Mountains, for vistas from the ocean to the San Francisco Bay. Passes many parks and trailheads.

Hwy 84: Runs for 20 curvaceous miles between Hwy 1 and Woodside, through open spaces, redwoods and the tiny one-bar hamlet of La Honda.

Sky Londa: Big-tree-shaded crossroads of Hwys 35 and 84; buzzes with hikers and outdoor enthusiasts comparing notes at the cafe.

Butano State Park: Witness nature's recovery from the 2020 wildfires in a serene park webbed with hiking trails. *parks.ca.gov; free*

Portola Redwoods State Park: Some 2800 acres of redwood-carpeted clefts and hillsides, riven by creeks and waterfalls along mossy banks. *parks.ca.gov; per vehicle $10*

life along the coast. The best time to visit the tidepools is near low tide, the website gives the daily tide schedule. And don't overlook the harbor seals and the trail leading into the old cypress forest.

Pescadero

TIME FROM HALF MOON BAY: **25 MINS**

Rural charm, toats & good food

A foggy speck of coastal crossroads between Half Moon Bay and Santa Cruz, 19th-century Pescadero is 2 miles inland from Hwy 1 and the coast with its orgy of scenery. It's a place of old buildings and old-fashioned farms that seems far removed from Silicon Valley, just over the hills that are emerald-green in spring and parched to burlap-brown the rest of the year.

On weekends the tiny downtown strains its seams with long-distance cyclists panting for carbs and day-trippers dive-bombing in for lunch at favored stops like **Duarte's Tavern**.

Year-round attractions include **Harley Farms Goat Dairy** *(harleyfarms.com; tours from $60)*, where you can get close to the cloven-hoofed sources of the delicious soft cheese that's for sale along with other deli items. Farm tours include kids (the goat kind) which kids (the human kind) love – as do older human kids. You can also taste wines from the local **Sante Arcangeli Family Wines** *(santewinery.com)*, known for its pinot noirs and chardonnays.

Out at the sea-breeze-scented coast, the wild Pacific beaches are populated by seals and pelicans. The state parks offer a cornucopia of tide-pool rocks, coves and inland forests of redwood canopies interspersed with fields of bushy artichokes.

Beaches, tidepools & wetlands

Pescadero State Beach *(parks.ca.gov; parking $8)* features a long strand (keep an eye out for seals) backed by dunes and interrupted by rocky tide pools. Stop to explore the marine-life-rich coastal tide pools on rocky outcroppings. On stormy days, the parking area facing the turbulent Pacific is a fine place for a picnic.

Pescadero Marsh Natural Preserve is on the inland side of Hwy 1, at the turn for Pescadero. The main **Pescadero Marsh Trail** winds through these verdant wetlands. Look for blue herons, deer, raccoons, foxes and, sniff, skunks.

Bean Hollow State Beach *(parks.ca.gov; free)* is another beguiling mix of sand and rocks. The eroded sandstone cliffs here have shapes that Antoni Gaudí would've been envious of, pockmarked by groovy honeycombed formations called tafoni. The park's highlight is **Pebble Beach**, where the shore is awash with bite-sized eye candy of agate, jade and carnelian.

WHERE TO EAT IN PESCADERO

Duarte's Tavern: Always thronged by happy masses feasting on crab cioppino, cream of artichoke soup and olallieberry pie. Reserve. *11am-3pm Wed-Mon* **$$**

Arcangeli Grocery Co: Prime purveyor of picnics, famed for hot-from-the-oven stuffed artichoke-herb bread, which some enjoy more than others. *11am-5pm Wed-Mon* **$**

Downtown Local: Spot that Tonka truck you forgot at the beach in this cafe jammed with memorabilia while you wait for your coffee. *8am-5pm* **$**

Mercado & Taqueria De Amigos: Classic line-up of well-made Mexican food served from an old corner gas station. Enjoy at the picnic tables or on a picnic. *9am-8pm* **$**

Pigeon Point

TIME FROM HALF MOON BAY: **30 MINS**

Unmissable beacon

Occupying a small outcrop, the 115ft-high **Pigeon Point Light Station** (1872) is one of the West Coast's tallest lighthouses. It's part of the **Pigeon Point Light Station State Historic Park** *(parks.ca.gov; free)*, which includes one of this coast's rare places to stay, the **HI Pigeon Point Lighthouse** (p163) hostel.

After years of work, the lighthouse once again stands proud with a nearly new exterior. Besides the fresh paint, it has new stainless-steel details. Visits to the interior should be allowed again sometime after 2026. In the meantime, the lighthouse remains active with an automated LED beacon. Walk the trails along the bluff and look out for gray whales in winter.

Stroll your own ribbon of sand

South of the lighthouse, **Gazos Creek State Beach** is nearly 1.5 miles-long. Untrodden sand, blustery wind and ceaseless waves are the norm. Note how the devastating 2020 fires in the Santa Cruz Mountains came right down to Hwy 1 and crossed over to the ocean's edge. Across Hwy 1, get a snack, lunch, a fresh beer and a tank of gas at **Highway 1 Brewing Co** *(noon-5pm Fri-Sun)*, one of the few oases on this stretch of the Pacific Coast Hwy.

Año Nuevo State Park

TIME FROM HALF MOON BAY: **35 MINS**

Witness elephant seals on the beach

Año Nuevo State Park *(parks.ca.gov; parking $10)* is home base for one of the world's largest mainland breeding colonies of northern elephant seals. More raucous than a full-moon beach rave, up to 10,000 boisterous elephant seals party down year-round on the dunes of **Año Nuevo Point**, their squeals and barks reaching fever pitch during the winter pupping season.

During the mating and birthing time from December to the end of March (peak season), visitors are only permitted access to the reserve on heavily booked guided tours. Tour bookings can be made 56 days in advance *(reservecalifornia.com; $11)*.

The rest of the year, free visitor permits from the entrance station are required; arrive before 3.30pm April to November. From the ranger station, it's a 3- to 4-mile round-trip hike on sand to whichever beach the seals are on that day; allow two to three hours. Dogs are not allowed. Amidst all the focus on the elephant seals, it's easy to forget that Año Nuevo itself is a beautiful and untouched coastal area with scores of birds.

WHY IS IT SO FOGGY?

When the summer sun's rays warm the air over the chilly Pacific, fog forms and hovers offshore, where prevailing winds drive it onshore, where it often burns off within a mile or two. Meanwhile, the state's interior, the Central Valley, which is ringed by mountains like a giant bathtub, gets scorching. The main break in the mountains is at the bay; as the inland warm air rises, it sucks in foggy air that flows around the Bay Area.

In July, it's not uncommon for noncoastal areas to top 100°F (38°C), while the coast barely reaches 70°F (21°C). It's why you see so many shivering tourists on Hwy 1, who thought it was 'summer.'

EATING & DRINKING ALONG HWY 1: OUR PICKS

Sage Bakehouse: Cool roadside bakery with a large deck offering ocean glimpses in Montara. Savory pies in the Brit tradition. Many teas plus coffee. *7am-6pm* $

El Gran Amigo: This Montara outfit has been slinging prized 'supershrimp' burritos, carne-asada tacos, and combo plates for decades. Good salsa. *10.30am-9pm* $

Moss Beach Distillery: Overlooking the cove where bootleggers used to unload Prohibition liquor; heated ocean-view deck. Steaks, seafood, cocktails. *noon-7.30pm* $$

Pie Ranch: Near the Santa Cruz County line, a wooden-barn wonderland of prepared foods made with house-grown produce and berries. Don't miss. *11am-5pm* $

Places We Love to Stay

$ Budget $$ Midrange $$$ Top End

Sausalito

MAP p123

Gables Inn Sausalito $$ Tranquil, stylish and peaceful. The inn includes a historical 1869 home and has 13 rooms, four cottages and three apartments, some with grand views.

Hotel Sausalito & Suites $$ Near the ferry dock, this stolid 1915 hotel has loads of period charm. Rooms enjoy partial bay views.

Inn Above Tide $$$ Posh and spacious rooms and suites – most with private deck and fireplace – that levitate over the water near the ferry terminal. Huge views.

Casa Madrona Hotel & Spa $$$ Classic Sausalito hotel with modern amenities. The property is divided into a 12-room, 'hillside' mansion and a collection of 'harborside' cottages, all with bay views.

Cavallo Point $$$ Spread over 45 scenic acres of landmark Fort Baker, luxe rooms in officers' quarters or contemporary, stylish 'green' accommodations with exquisite bay views.

Marin County Beaches

Pelican Inn $$ Twee English cottage in Muir Beach with cozy rooms and a popular pub. Close to the beach and Muir Woods.

Sandpiper Lodging at the Beach $$ A quick stroll to Stinson Beach; rooms and cabins are comfy and cute, all with a gas fireplace and kitchenette; in a lush garden.

Smiley's $$ Seven rooms in separate buildings behind this Bolinas bar (with good, casual food) that dates to 1851. Rooms are modern, with bright, contemporary decor.

Waters Edge Hotel $$$ A large deck extends over the bay in Tiburon; tasteful rooms have an elegant minimalism, with romantic water views.

Inverness

MAP p129

Cottages at Point Reyes Seashore $$ Tucked into the woods, family-friendly with kitchenette rooms. Activities include tennis, hot tub, croquet, and horseshoes. Also, a saltwater pool and private nature trail.

Motel Inverness $$ Appealing motel with fine service. Not many rooms with views, but the property is on gorgeous wetlands. Common area has seasonal roaring fire.

Tomales Bay Resort & Marina $$ Basic bayside marina motel with 36 great-value rooms and an unheated pool. Chat with fishers on the docks and see how they're bitin'.

Dancing Coyote Beach Cottages $$$ Serene modern cottages on Tomales Bay with skylights and decks with views in all directions. Full kitchens and fireplaces.

Marshall

MAP p129

Tomales Hotel $$ In the heart of town, vintage wooden hotel reopened in 2022 with nine modern rooms. Wide porches run around two floors.

Nick's Cove $$$ Fronting a peaceful cove at Marshall, waterfront vacation cottages variously feature wood-burning fireplaces, deep soaking tubs and private decks.

Oakland

MAP p133

B-Love's Guest House $ Artist Traci 'B-Love' Bartlow rents out rooms in her West Oakland house which includes a garden. Shared bathroom with Bartlow's photography on the walls.

Kissel Uptown Oakland $$$ A hip boutique hotel in Uptown. Large, comfortable and modern rooms across six floors. Close to nightlife.

Berkeley

MAP p141

Downtown Berkeley Inn $ Near downtown, budget motel has good-sized rooms with minimal frills offering a balance of budget and proximity to Berkeley's main drag.

Graduate Berkeley $$ Only a block from campus, seven-story 1928 hotel plays up its ties to the university. Collegiate-inspired details throughout.

Hotel Shattuck Plaza $$ A 100-year-old downtown jewel with red Italian glass lighting, flocked Victorian-style wallpaper – and a peace sign tiled into the floor.

Signature Inn Berkeley $$ Reimagined motel-style inn a few blocks south of Berkeley's main drag and university. Good-sized rooms with a dash of style; plenty of parking.

Berkeley City Club $$$ Designed by Julia Morgan (p135), refurbished 1929 historical landmark building has lush and serene Italianate courtyards. Some rooms have great Bay views.

Claremont Resort & Club $$$ The East Bay's glamorous white 1915 landmark with elegant restaurants, a fitness center, swimming pools, tennis courts and a full-service spa.

Richmond

Hotel Mac & Suites $$ In the appealing enclave of Point Richmond, a vintage three-story brick hotel combined with a modern wing. Comfortable rooms with relaxed style.

East Brother Light Station Bed & Breakfast $$$ One of many tiny islands dotting the bay, this one is unique for having an 1873 lighthouse and a B&B. Incredible views; access by boat from Richmond.

Palo Alto

MAP p149

Coronet Motel $ Tidy, family-owned, two-story motel in an incredible location near Stanford. Contemporary rooms, kitchenette suites and a small outdoor pool.

Dinah's Garden Hotel $ South of the university campus and downtown, has great rates, oversized rooms, balconies, garden-filled grounds and an outdoor pool.

Leland Hotel Palo Alto $$ Upscale motel-style inn that keeps prices low by limiting staff. Rooms have many extras like cookies; the location is near nightlife.

Nobu Epiphany $$$ In an elegant highrise, sleek downtown boutique hotel has its own tech concierge. Light, airy rooms have myriad luxuries.

Rosewood Sand Hill $$$ Storied low-rise hotel sprawls over a hillside. Massive designer-style rooms with distant views. Off famous Sand Hill Rd. Thursday is billionaires' singles night in the bar.

San Jose

MAP p154

Hotel De Anza $$ Opened during the Jazz Age, this downtown high-rise is an art deco beauty that pays homage to the property's history.

Kasa University-Airport Santa Clara $$ Close to Santa Clara University, contemporary hotel with a huge roof deck that includes a pool, sweeping Silicon Valley views and more.

Hotel Valencia $$$ Boutique hotel in the Santana Row shopping complex near Winchester Mystery House. Outdoor pool and hot tub create a stylish oasis of contemporary design.

Westin San Jose $$$ Better known by its old name, the Sainte Claire, this atmospheric 1926 landmark has a drop-dead gorgeous lobby with stretched-leather ceilings.

Montara & Around

HI Point Montara Lighthouse Hostel $ On a site dating to 1875, the current lighthouse was moved here in 1928. Fab views, kitchen and firepit plus private rooms and dorms.

Ocean View Inn $$ Modest-sized, modern inn across from cliffs overlooking the ocean. Rooms have contemporary decor and there are big views from the deck.

Half Moon Bay

MAP p157

Oceanfront Beach Villa $$ Modern complex on Miramar Beach away from Hwy 1. Most rooms have ocean views; sleep to the sounds of surf.

Mill Rose Inn $$ Right near the center of Half Moon Bay on a large plot with private gardens filled with flowers.

Inn at Mavericks $$$ Oceanfront luxury, spacious rooms with gas fireplaces and private decks or patios. Close to Pillar Point Harbor.

Beach House Half Moon Bay $$$ Overlooking the bay from the bluffs near Pillar Point Harbor, loft-style suites with wood-burning fireplaces; outdoor heated pool.

Pescadero & Around

HI Pigeon Point Lighthouse $ One of the few places to stay on this stretch of coast is also the most coveted. Book well ahead; don't miss the hot tub.

Costanoa $$ Coastal resort with tent bungalows, rooms in woodsy lodges and cabins with porches. Many activities.

Pescadero Creek Inn $$ Private two-room cottage and spotless Victorian rooms in a restored century-old farmhouse with a tranquil creekside garden.

AURORA ANGELES/SHUTTERSTOCK

Inn Above Tide

For places to stay in Napa & Sonoma Wine Country, see p226

LATYPOVA/GETTY IMAGES

Above: Hot-air balloons over the Napa Valley (p170); Right: Bodega Head Trail (p212)

THE MAIN AREAS

NAPA
Wine epicenter. **p170**

ST HELENA
Quaint northern Napa Valley hub. **p182**

SONOMA
History-rich wine-valley town. **p190**

PETALUMA
Retro downtown with gastronomic flair. **p199**

Researched by
Alexis Averbuck

Napa & Sonoma Wine Country

WHERE VINEYARDS, REDWOODS AND OCEAN MEET

California's premier wine valleys celebrate its vineyards, rolling hills, redwoods and unspoiled coast with fantastic food, wine and cool communities.

In a single day in Napa Valley, you can wallow in volcanic mud in Calistoga, learn how to make roux in St Helena and spend a wild night among giraffes on a Wine Country safari. That's after tasting some of the world's best vintages. Here, organic family wineries dare to make wines besides classic cabernets, while bicyclists commuting between former stagecoach stops wave hello to sous-chefs weeding organic kitchen gardens.

Head west to Sonoma County to wander thousand-year-old redwoods, pop a bottle of bubbly in Healdsburg and meet the talent behind farm-to-spliff dispensaries in Sebastopol. The region remains a magnet for free spirits. Adventure author Jack London attracted like-minded bohemians to Sonoma Valley while romantics and rebels roamed the Russian River Valley, establishing Guerneville as a pioneering LGBTQ+ resort.

Emerging at the coast, fishing towns like Bodega Bay bring in the Pacific's bounty, and trails wind across windswept bluffs. Your heart will soar with untrammeled views of waves crashing along the shore – most of the land out here is protected.

Good living seems to come naturally here, but people work hard to make that possible. Napa and Sonoma have faced fire, earthquakes, droughts and floods. But after each disaster, the people in America's fanciest farmland rebound. Raise a toast to Napa and Sonoma: living proof that with exceptional dedication and a splash of liquid courage, California dreams really do come true.

VENTU PHOTO/SHUTTERSTOCK

SEBASTOPOL
Artsy bohemian hangout. **p203**

RUSSIAN RIVER VALLEY
Wine, redwood and river playground. **p215**

HEALDSBURG
Laid-back chic, wine, art and food. **p220**

Find Your Way

Napa and Sonoma counties and their myriad smaller valleys are surprisingly vast. They're easiest seen with your own wheels, but transit.511.org is a helpful resource to see the interlocking transit networks, mostly geared toward residents.

Russian River Valley, p215
Glide in a canoe, kayak or inner tube down the lazy summer river, or cruise valley wineries to the fantastic Sonoma Coast.

Sebastopol, p203
Get to know local winemakers, bakers, distillers, musicians, gardeners and budtenders in California's most prolifically creative farm town.

Petaluma, p199
Vibe on classic Americana along an exquisitely preserved riverfront downtown loaded with breweries and dining options.

Healdsburg, p220

Wine-taste and boutique-browse your way around the plaza before cycling to nearby vineyards or debating the merits of all the dinner restaurants.

St Helena, p182

This charming town is a treat in its own right, with a historic center, but it's also a hub for northern Napa Valley vineyards.

Sonoma, p190

Stroll beneath palm trees along the adobe-lined plaza into California's past. Then seek sustenance at myriad restaurants and tasting rooms.

Napa, p170

Wine and dine like a rock star, with California's most prized reds, world-acclaimed chefs' tasting menus, and restorative brunches at five-star resorts.

CAR

Hitting the road is the best way to explore sprawling Wine Country. This way you can discover its secluded valleys and cool-cat towns, and tour the wineries scattered across the countryside. Don't drive buzzed, though – book a tour or a rideshare instead.

TRAIN

Sonoma-Marin Area Rail Transit (SMART) offers rail services in Sonoma and Marin counties from the Sonoma County Airport to downtown San Rafael. The Napa Valley Wine Train takes you from downtown Napa to St Helena and back in tourist coaches.

BICYCLE

Wine Country is a dream for cyclists. For many, the highlight of a California trip is the sun-dappled, winery-lined roads and trails linking valley wineries. They're scenic, mostly flat, and easy for beginners. Some of the regional parks also offer adrenaline-pumping mountain biking.

Plan Your Time

Go with the flow in Wine Country: stroll small towns or cycle to sun-drenched vineyards before a siesta and a meal that defines 'farm-to-table.' Or venture towards the coast for riverfront redwoods and rugged ocean-scapes.

PEREZOO/SHUTTERSTOCK

Table Rock, Robert Louis Stevenson State Park (p189)

Short on Time

● If you're an oenophile new to the region, head to **Napa** (p170). Start at town tasting rooms like **Gamling & McDuck** (p172) before roaming out to vineyards in **Carneros** (p178), where vines meet marshland and the Bay beyond. Pick your poison: high-end art at **Donum Estate** (p180) or **Hess Persson Estates** (p179) or relaxed family vineyards at **Robledo** (p195) and **Ceja** (p178). Prebook a cooking class at **Culinary Institute of America** (p185).

● North up the valley, the tastings continue. Shop for a **picnic** (p184) then walk it off in **Bothe-Napa Valley State Park** (p188) or **Robert Louis Stevenson State Park** (p189). Dine extremely well in **St Helena** (p185) then wash all your cares away with a **hot-springs soak** (p188).

Seasonal Highlights

Make summer reservations in Napa and Sonoma Valleys and on the coast. Hotel rates also jump during September and October's grape-crushing.

MARCH

Cinephiles delight in the **Sonoma Valley Film Festival** (p195), running for over 20 years. Vineyards are sprouting after their winter pruning and temperatures are mild during **Wine Road Barrel Tasting** (p209) in Sonoma County.

MAY

Napa's three-day **BottleRock** (p175) festival of music, food and wine is followed by **La Onda** (p175) music festival. **Women's Weekend** (p216) rolls into Guerneville and **Healdsburg Wine & Food Experience** (p223) celebrates local makers.

JUNE

Healdsburg Jazz Festival (p223) kicks off at venues across town, while **Art at the Source** (p193) open-studio visits allow you to visit artists' ateliers throughout Sonoma County.

Three Days to Explore

- Continue your Wine Country adventure with a look inside the adobe mission on **Sonoma's plaza** (p190). Then meander along the valley's vine-lined roads, stopping frequently for tastings at spots like **Gundlach-Bundschu Winery** (p194). Explore **Bartholomew Estate** (p195), an oak-dotted winery and preserve, then channel *The Call of the Wild* at **Jack London State Historic Park** (p196).

- Get a teeny taste of western Sonoma County, which makes Napa and Sonoma look uptight by comparison. Grab lunch in Santa Rosa at **Mitote Food Park** (p209) before making a beeline for **Sebastopol** (p203). Tour **organic farms** (p205) or take a walk from beach to bluff in **Sonoma Coast State Park** (p212) before kicking back with oysters and chilled wine at **Rocker Oysterfeller's** (p213) or **Fishetarian** (p212) in **Bodega Bay**.

If You Have More Time

- Raft up in the **Russian River Valley** (p215) where you can combine **a float on the river** (p217) with mescal cocktails at **El Barrio** (p218) in Guerneville or seafood on the coast at **Café Aquatica** (p219) or **River's End** (p219) in Jenner. Time your trip for Occidental's **Thursday Farmers Market** (p211) and dance outside at dusk or hit up the **great local breweries** (p210).

- Wine-taste your way up **Westside Rd** (p219) to **Healdsburg** (p220). If it's a Tuesday or Saturday morning, its abundant **farmers market** (p223) is a must for wares well beyond food, or on Tuesday afternoon, plan to picnic at a **free summer concert** (p223) on the plaza. If you love to cycle, peddle the wine roads of the **Dry Creek Valley** (p223) or along **West County trails** (p207).

JULY

Fourth of July celebrations light up across Napa and Sonoma counties, and peak season for floating the Russian River brings the **Monte Rio Variety Show** (p219), with unannounced celebrity guests, such as Conan O'Brien.

AUGUST

High summer brings the booming **Sonoma County Fair** (p209) to Santa Rosa. Guerneville's **Lazy Bear Week** (p216) and Sebastopol's **Gravenstein Apple Fair** (p205) light up western Sonoma County.

OCTOBER

During the grape harvest (or 'crush'), America's biggest wine competition, **Sonoma Harvest Fair** (p209), pairs well with the **Sonoma County Art Trails** (p193) open-studio tours across the county.

NOVEMBER

During **Wine & Food Affair** (p223) let your taste buds be your guide to 100 Sonoma County wineries offering a featured dish and wine pairing. **Napa Valley Film Festival** (p175) kicks off in Napa.

Napa

WORLD-FAMOUS WINES | ART COLLECTIONS | TOP CUISINE

TOP TIP

Wine tasting in Napa Valley is a pricey undertaking. Some tasting fees are waived with a set bottle purchase. To save, consider more reasonably priced Russian River, Healdsburg and Alexander Valley wineries (p225); they also sometimes accept walk-ins. Many wineries will ship for you, or get Bodega Shipping Co *(bodegashippingco.com)* to do it.

Your first stop in Napa may be the only one you need for a dream Wine Country getaway. With laid-back downtown tasting rooms, historic music halls featuring major musicians and Oxbow Public Market offering affordable gourmet fare, downtown Napa is where Napans come to relax.

Napa's riverbank parks are part of the town's sustainable 'living river' design to manage seasonal floods. And its lush hillsides kick off the steady carpet of wineries running straight up the valley.

It's hard to believe that in 2014 this was the epicenter of an earthquake that registered 6.0 on the Richter scale, causing $1 billion in damage. While Napa was rebuilding, the 2017, 2019 and 2020 fires hit – and when winter rains finally came, so did Napa River floods. Yet, through it all, Napa kept rebuilding – steadily and thoughtfully – and the city remains the sweet spot where wine flows and conversation meanders, just like the Napa River.

Historic Streets & Tasting Rooms

Sample wines in the central city

Napa's buzzy **1st St** is lined with indie wine-tasting rooms in historic storefronts and casual bistros packing California-grown flavor into globe-trotting menus.

GETTING AROUND

Downtown Napa is centrally located in Napa Valley, between scenic Silverado Trail to the east and busy St Helena Hwy/Hwy 29 to the west. The multiuse **Napa Valley Vine Trail** *(vinetrail.org)* connects downtown Napa to Yountville, St Helena to Calistoga and American Canyon to Vallejo. **Vine** *(vinetransit.com)* bus C gets you around downtown Napa; bus 10 gets you from downtown Napa to St Helena and Calistoga. Bus 11 links downtown Napa to the Vallejo Ferry Terminal, where ferries run to San Francisco. Express bus 29 connects Napa to El Cerrito del Norte BART station. You can pay *(adult/child $2/1.25)* with cash (no change given) or with a Bay Area transit Clipper card.

HIGHLIGHTS
1 Culinary Institute of America at Copia
2 Napa Valley Welcome Center
3 Oxbow Public Market

SIGHTS
4 Brown Downtown
5 Covert Estate
6 Hendry
7 Krupp Brothers Downtown Tasting Room
8 Matthiasson Winery
9 Napa Valley Opera House
10 Palmaz
11 Skyline Wilderness Park

ACTIVITIES
12 Napa Valley Balloons
13 Napa Valley Gondola
14 Napa Valley Vine Trail
15 Napa Valley Wine Train

SLEEPING
16 Archer
17 Blackbird Inn
18 Elm House Inn
19 Hotel Indigo Napa Valley
20 Milliken Creek Inn
21 Napa Winery Inn

EATING
22 Bear
23 Bistro Don Giovanni
24 Compline
25 Contimo Provisions
26 Dutch Door
27 El Muchacho Alegre
28 Kenzo
29 Winston's

DRINKING & NIGHTLIFE
30 Gamling & McDuck
31 Rebel Vinters
32 Trade Brewing
33 Vintner's Collective

ENTERTAINMENT
see 9 Blue Note Napa
see 34 BottleRock Music Festival
34 La Onda
35 Uptown Theatre

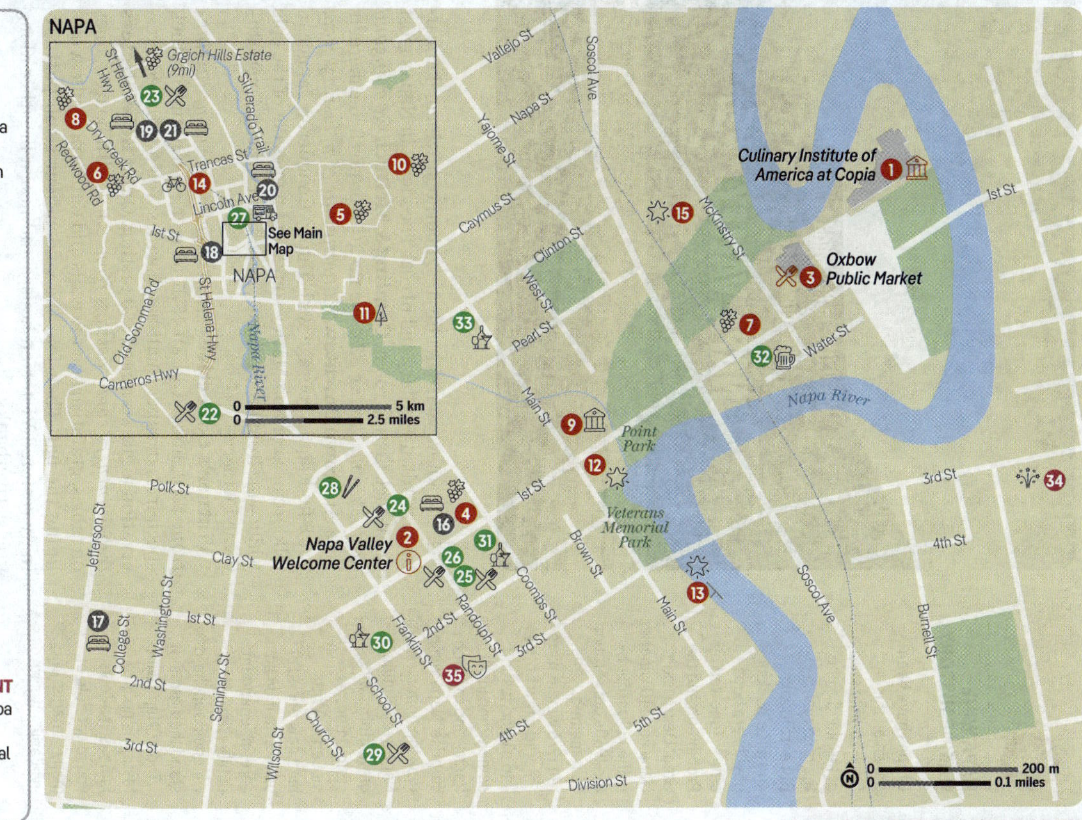

NAPA WINE-MAKING HISTORY

Grapes have been grown on this 5-by-35-mile strip of farmland since the gold rush. But earthquakes and juice-sucking phylloxera bugs struck, followed by Prohibition and the Great Depression. Napa had 140 wineries in the 1890s, but by the 1960s only around 25 remained.

In 1976 winemakers entered a few bottles into a blind tasting competition in Paris – and to much surprise, Napa wines took top honors. As Napa's reputation grew, global wine conglomerates moved in. With land now priced at up to $1 million an acre, independent, family-owned wineries work hard to stand their ground.

Today, Napa wine tasting is not just famous, it allows you to get hold of many vintages only available on-site.

Get to know your friendly neighborhood winemaker/cartoonist Adam McClary and his cat Theodosia in Napa's most punk-rock tasting room, **Gamling & McDuck** *(gamlingandmcduck.com; tasting $35)*. No neckties or rarefied cabernets here. At **Brown Downtown** *(brownestate.com; tastings from $50)*, find liquid courage with Duppy Conqueror, Jamaican folklore hero of Bob Marley songs and namesake of the epic white wine from Brown Estate, Napa's first African American-owned winery.

Vintner's Collective *(vintnerscollective.com; tastings from $50)*, housed in an 1875 former saloon and brothel, specializes in super small-batch wines. You don't need a reservation for its standard $50 tasting. Or hit **Rebel Vinters** *(rebelvintners.com; tastings from $30)*, with board games on tables, graffiti art on the walls and California indie wines lining the bar. Then join the golden-hour stroll past lovingly restored Victorian houses and take a breather along grassy riverbanks.

EATING IN NAPA: EASY BITES

Winston's: Start the day with amazing baked goods and stick-to-your-ribs breakfast sandwiches with a happy brunching crowd. *7am-2pm* $

Contimo Provisions: Midday is prime for outstanding sandwiches... but it also makes killer biscuit sandwiches for breakfast. *8am-3pm Tue-Sat* $

Dutch Door: Beloved casual takeout joint featuring all-organic food, from fried chicken to kale bowls. *11.30am-3pm Wed & Thu, to 6pm Fri & Sat* $

El Muchacho Alegre: If tacos are your jam, head for this taco truck parked at 751 Jackson St in an out-of-the-way residential neighborhood. *10am-8pm Mon-Sat* $

PGIAM/GETTY IMAGES

Napa Valley Wine Train

Napa by Train or Gondola

Kick back, take it all in

Chug along in the **Napa Valley Wine Train** *(winetrain.com; ticket incl dining from $223)* from downtown Napa to St Helena and back in a plush vintage dining car, with meal service included and optional winery stops...if you choose one, make it historic **Grgich Hills Estate** *(p187; grgich.com)*, which aims to produce wines sustainably through regenerative farming practices. Trains depart from Napa Valley Wine Train Depot on McKinstry St near 1st St.

If floating is more your speed, glide downstream with **Napa Valley Gondola** *(napavalleygondola.com; from $175)* on a private gondola, watching the sun set over the city. Your gondolier can serenade you in Italian, but the scenery and wine on offer are totally California, dude. On this single-oared boat you and up to five friends can hang out with ducks, spot herons and otters, and see how ecologists are restoring Napa River.

WINE-TASTE LIKE A PRO

Swirl, sniff and swish. Swirl your wine in the glass to release aromas, then have a good sniff to excite your salivary glands. Take a small sip and swish it around your mouth so all your taste buds get in on the action.

Sip and spit. If you love what you're tasting, you'll want to try plenty – and that means pacing yourself. It's fair game to spit out your last sip, or even pour leftovers into the spittoon (aka 'chuck bucket').

Remember to eat. Some wineries serve bites; otherwise snack in between.

Consider joining wine clubs carefully. Your pourer may suggest joining their wine club (to buy discounted bottles annually). Don't feel pressured, especially if you're tipsy and fuzzy on the details.

EATING IN NAPA: FINE DINING

Kenzo: Napa Michelin-starred Japanese magic paired with top wine and sake in chic minimalist harmony. Book ahead. *5.30-8.30pm Wed-Sun* **$$$**

Compline: This cozy, unpretentious bistro/wine bar offers a short, seasonal menu of hearty dishes. *5-11pm Wed & Thu, 11.30am-11pm Fri-Sun* **$$$**

Bistro Don Giovanni: With copper pans, garden fountains and black-vested waiters, the Don ladles on Italian charm. Weekends get packed and loud. *11.30am-9pm* **$$$**

Bear: Stanly Ranch's creative Californian fare spans Asian-dressed oysters to delicate handmade pastas. *7am-10pm* **$$$**

TIPS FOR NAPA ON A BUDGET

Free wine-tasting passes: Once you reserve your accommodations, call the concierge to ask what wine-tasting passes they have available.

Wining & dining downtown: Downtown Napa has the broadest, best selection of affordable dining options in Napa Valley, or head to **Oxbow** to see what's cooking. Downtown Napa tasting rooms offer a choice of wine by the glass or reasonably priced tasting flights. Restaurants will let you bring your own wine with minimal/no corkage.

Free sights & entertainment: CIA at Copia offers free museum shows, demos, tastings and other events daily. You might luck into free music at Oxbow – especially on Locals' Night *(Tuesday 5-8pm)*.

BRUCE YUANYUE BI/GETTY IMAGES

Oxbow Public Market

Food Markets & Cooking Classes

Daytime grazing in gourmet style

Deliciousness abounds in Napa. But why commit to just one dining establishment when you could graze at a dozen of Napa's finest? At **Oxbow Public Market** *(oxbowpublicmarket.com)*, assemble the meal of your California dreams with all-star dishes – perhaps Hog Island Oyster Co oysters mignonette and Eiko's *hamachi* sushi bonbons with Fieldwork Brewing Company farmhouse ale, followed by Ritual Coffee espresso. Or if it's breakfast time, don't miss Model Bakery's treats.

Also in the Oxbow area, downtown Napa's **Culinary Institute of America at Copia** *(ciaatcopia.com; classes from $85)* offers drop-in cooking or wine classes, demos, documentaries and star-chef panels too spicy for TV. Hit the free Chuck Williams Culinary Arts Museum upstairs, buy Marketplace gadgets and signed cookbooks downstairs, or have a meal at the Grove.

If you'd like to throw in a little wine and beer tasting while you're in the Oxbow area, **Krupp Brothers Downtown Tasting Room** *(kruppbrothers.com; tastings from $45)* and **Trade Brewing** *(tradebrewing.com)* are just across the street from each other.

DRINKING IN NAPA: WINERIES NEAR DOWNTOWN

Palmaz: Julio and Amalia Palmaz produce Napa's most buzzworthy wines on its 600-acre hillside estate. *by appointment*

Matthiasson Winery: This sustainable winery, a short drive on Napa's western low slopes, makes a citrusy rosé of syrah and robust Napa white blend. *by appointment*

Hendry: Joyful wine aficionados make this low-key winery a fave. Fees waived with equivalent purchase. Four estate hiking tours per year. *by appointment*

Covert Estate: Part of the Coombsville appellation using sustainable methods to make Bordeaux-style cabernet franc, cabernet sauvignon, syrahs. *by appointment*

Live Local Music & Festivals

Grooving and movies

Hitting high notes since 1880, the opulent **Napa Valley Opera House** has survived earthquakes and fires to find its second wind, and is making a late-breaking career shift into jazz. The **Blue Note Napa** *(bluenotenapa.com)* calendar features weekend global jazz talent and midweek locals' nights – and the drinks menu here puts other clubs to shame, with cult wines and house-brewed craft beer. With restored 1937 art deco swagger and excellent sound, tiny **Uptown Theatre** *(uptowntheatrenapa.com)* hosts big names in music and comedy.

FOR GASTRONOMES

You really can't beat California for food and wine. To learn more about the state's **food scene**, see p32.

Plan to be in Napa in May for breakout-hit three-day music, food and wine festival **BottleRock** *(bottlerocknapavalley.com)*, where huge lineups include marquee names such as Janelle Monáe, Green Day and Ice Cube. The same group also puts on the festival **La Onda** *(laondafest.com)* for two days at the end of May, featuring primarily Spanish-language musical genres.

Or celebrate the silver screen at November's **Napa Valley Film Festival** *(napavalleyfilmfest.org)*, where movies about food and wine are obvious crowd-pleasers, but the roster includes documentaries and narrative films as well.

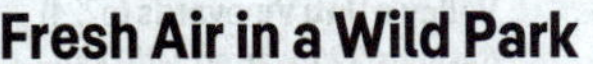

Fresh Air in a Wild Park

Hiking Skyline Wilderness Park

Feeling like stretching your legs and getting a good look at the Napa views? Head to **Skyline Wilderness Park** *(skylinepark.org)*. The park blooms with springtime wildflowers and California perennials in its Martha Walker Native Plant Habitat. Check it out then hit over 25 miles of hiking and mountain-biking trails, an archery range or disc-golf course. You're allowed to picnic with wine – so pick up supplies in town before you come. You can also camp with either tents or RVs. Be sure to reserve ahead during events like the BottleRock festival.

HELP ME PICK:

Napa & Sonoma Valley Wineries

California wine country is famous. But with 1000 wineries to choose from across Napa and Sonoma counties, where do you even begin? To make your next favorite wine easier to find, we're giving you a few places to start. Sustainably produced wines are a hallmark of the region. Learn more on p173.

Where to sip if you love...

Vineyard Walks & Inspiring Views

Many wineries set in the vineyards (as opposed to city-based tasting rooms) offer vineyard tours and walks for an increased price. Some of our favorite views and walks in the Napa Valley are at **Chappellet Winery** (p186), **Cuvaison Winery** (p178) and **Pride Mountain Vineyards** (p187). And don't forget art-forward **Hess Persson Estates** (p179) and **Donum Estate** (p180).

Food Pairings

Food and wine pairings are a common part of high-end tastings. Servings are usually super small, and range from simple charcuterie to gourmet.

Napa Valley's **Brasswood** *(brasswood.com; tastings from $20)* is beloved for its excellent on-site **restaurant** (p184). At **VJB Cellars** *(vjbcellars.com; tastings from $30)* in Sonoma Valley, taste prized Italian wines like robust white friulano and aleatico rosé while lunching in its **gourmet deli** (p198).

Other foodie moments include Windsor's **Bricoleur Vineyards** *(bricoleurvineyards.com; tastings from $40)* where you can splash out on a multicourse extravaganza of pairings. **Mayo Family Winery Reserve Room** (p198) also offers small plates; and food and wine pairings feature at **Flowers** (p219), **Idlewild** (p222) and **Davis Estates** *(davisestates.com; tastings from $100)*, to name but a few.

Tasting on a Budget

In the **Napa Valley** we like **Bennett Lane Winery** (p187) *(tastings from $35)*, **Nichelini Family Winery** (p186) *(tastings $30, occasional flashback Friday with $15 tastings)* and Brasswood *(tastings from $20)*. In **Sonoma Valley** try **Kunde** (p198) *(tastings from $25)* and **Gundlach-Bundschu** (p194) *(tastings from $25)*. Around **Sebastopol** visit **Balletto** (p206) *(tastings from $20)*, **Freeman** (p206) *(tastings from $35)*, **Iron Horse** (p206) *(tastings from $35)*, **Martinelli** (p207) *(tastings from $25)* and **Hanna** (p225) *(Russian River location tastings $30)*. **Russian River Valley** includes **Porter Creek** (p219) *(tastings $30)*, **Porter-Bass** (p219) *(tastings $25, waived with purchase)* and **Korbel** *(tastings from $15)*. **Dry Creek Valley's Unti Vineyards** (p224) *(tastings $25, waived with bottle purchase)* and **Emmitt-Scorsone Wines** (p224) *(tastings $25)* pair well with **Alexander Valley's Soda Rock Winery** (p225) *(tastings from $25)*. Remember: tasting rooms often have lower rates than wineries.

Sparkling Wines

If you're looking for a bit of bubbly, hone right in on Carneros' **Domaine Carneros** and **Artesa** or Napa's excellent **Schramsberg** (p189). Further west in Russian River, **Iron Horse Vineyards** (p206) and **Equality Vines** (p217) are tops, while **Korbel** is a widely distributed mega-producer.

HOW TO...

Book Ahead Almost all of the wineries in Napa and Sonoma are reservation-based, so book ahead.

Walk-Ins Some accept walk-ins when they have an open spot. Check first online on **Tock** *(exploretock.com)*.

Napa Valley Welcome Center *(visitnapavalley.com)* occasionally have wine-tasting passes (ask at your hotel, too).

Telephoning The old-fashioned method still works and is worth trying at the last minute – you might get lucky!

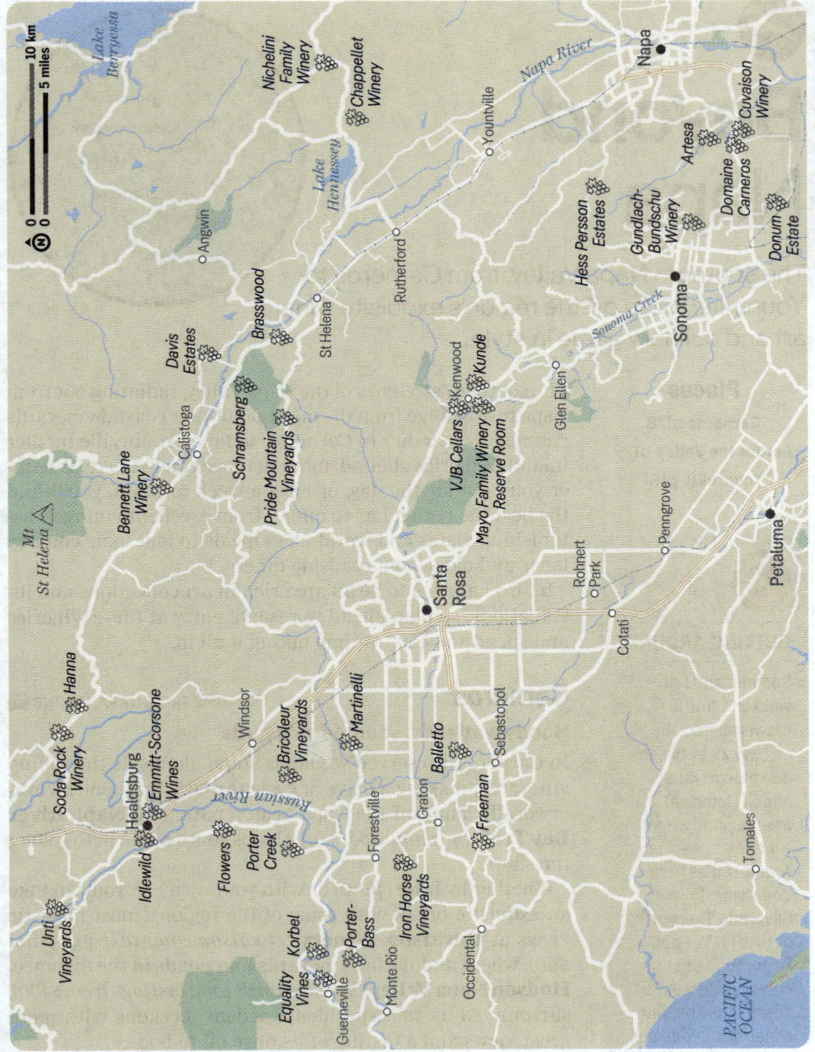

DIY or guided tour?

If you don't have a designated driver, book a ride with Designated Drivers Napa Sonoma. Guided tours can make everything friction-free, but add to the cost. Often you pay for the tour itself, as well as all the tasting fees, food, a fuel fee and a tip for the driver/guide.

Platypus Wine Tours *(platypustours.com)* specializes in backroad vineyards, historic wineries and family-owned operations.

Active Wine Adventures *(activewine adventures.com)*, covering Napa and Sonoma, works up your appetite for gourmet food, wine and craft beer, with your choice of adventures.

Laces and Limos *(lacesandlimos.com)* offer slow, scenic routes around Napa Valley in chauffeured tuk-tuk (auto-rickshaw).

You can also go vineyard-hopping by bicycle...try Getaway Adventures/Wine Country Bikes *(getawayadventures.com)*, Sonoma Adventures *(sonoma-adventures.com)* and Backroads *(backroads.com)* for Napa and Sonoma bike tours.

Beyond Napa

The southern Napa Valley, from Carneros to Yountville, kicks off the region's exquisite wine, art and culinary game in style.

Places

GETTING AROUND

Summer and fall weekend traffic crawls, especially on Hwy 29 between downtown Napa and St Helena at around 5pm, when wineries close. For scenic drives from Yountville, follow Silverado Trail north, or take Mt Veeder Rd through pristine countryside west of Yountville. The Vine *(vinetransit.com)* bus 10 doesn't stop in Yountville proper, but across Hwy 29 at the Veterans' Home.

The southern stretches of the Napa Valley, radiating out from Napa town, range from the moist pinot-noir coastal vineyards rimmed by marshes in Carneros, to fancy Yountville further inland. Wineries abound, more than we can list here. Whether you're in for the day, or have a week to roam, you'll find the best the region has to offer – from excellent vintages, astonishing vistas and world-class meals to lonesome country lanes and old-school roadside diners.

It also happens to be an area rich in art collections and installations, so plan ahead to reserve entry at these wineries and spend some extra time taking it all in.

Carneros

TIME FROM NAPA: **15 MINS**

Moody wetlands, vaunted vineyards

In Carneros, preserved wetlands stand alongside the rolling vineyards, making a drive or cycle through this zone an otherworldly jaunt off the Napa beaten path. The **Napa River Bay Trail** *(napaoutdoors.org)* loops south of Carneros along the shore.

Whether by **bike** (p180) or with your own car, you can take an exquisite break with some of the region's most majestic views at **Cuvaison Winery** *(cuvaison.com; tastings from $60)*, where undulating vineyards join ponds in the distance. **Hudson Napa Valley** *(hudsonranch.com; tastings from $100)*, surrounded by vast succulent gardens, beckons with more great views and a tasting of its olive oil to boot.

Low-key **McKenzie-Mueller Winery** *(mckenziemueller.com; tastings $35)* is tucked into the heart of Carneros' vineyards. The romance started in the vineyards at **Ceja** *(cejavineyards.com; tastings from $40)*...Amelia Morán met Pedro Ceja in 1967, when they were both picking grapes for Mondavi in Napa. Marriage, kids and decades of trailblazing later, Amelia is the first Mexican-American woman winery president – and that vineyard romance is captured in Ceja's signature pinot noir, aged chardonnay and Vino de Casa, a satiny blend of Italian arneis and chardonnay. You can taste their wines at their tasting room on the outskirts of Sonoma.

LEONARD ZHUKOVSKY/SHUTTERSTOCK

Cellar, Hess Persson Estates

NAPA CREATIVITY

Carolyn Ellis, a Napa artist, calls out her favorite places to experience art. *carolynellis.com*

Hess Art Collection (p179): World-class modern art, with an amazing drive up Mt Veeder Rd through vineyards with views.

Di Rosa Center for Contemporary Art: Sculpture garden, galleries and picnic grounds with 1600 artworks.

R+D Kitchen, Yountville: Best burger, chocolate sundae and cocktails.

Napa Lighted Art Festival: Transforms Napa into a mini Burning Man, with large-scale light projections and sculptures. *donapa.com; late Jan to late Feb*

Donum Estate Art Collection (p180): Hands-down best sculpture garden in the valley.

Across the Valley

TIME FROM NAPA: **15 MINS**

Art collections paired with wine

Climb a winding country road 20 minutes' drive west of Napa up beyond vineyards through oak forests to an ivy-covered hilltop stone winery at **Hess Persson Estates** *(hesspersonestates.com; tastings from $85 incl museum, museum walk with director $110)*. Here, wine tastings can be paired with California's finest private contemporary-art collection. Thought-provoking installation art starts with Leopoldo Maler's 1974 burning typewriter – an homage to his uncle, a newspaper editor killed by Argentina's junta. Other highlights include Anselm Kiefer's sculpture of lead shingles from Cologne Cathedral, and Andy Goldsworthy's giant ball of manzanita branches.

Scrap-metal sheep dotting the hillside hint that something unusual is afoot on 217 acres of Carneros countryside at **di Rosa Center for Contemporary Art** *(dirosaart.org; adult/child $25/5)*. This groundbreaking collection was the personal passion of free-spirited reporter-turned-grape-farmer Rene di Rosa, who hung hyperrealist Robert Bechtle paintings on the ceiling and installed spooky Tony Oursler videos in his cellar. Today the gatehouse gallery showcases Viola Frey's monumental 1970s ceramic sculpture, David Best's art cars and visiting California artists, while inspiration overflows into the Sculpture Meadow.

EATING & DRINKING IN CARNEROS: OUR PICKS

Angelo's Wine Country Deli: Look for the cow on the roof roadside for fat sandwiches with smoked meats. *9.30am-4.30pm Wed-Mon* $

Boon Fly Café: Leisurely weekend brunches with killer eggs Benedict with jalapeño hollandaise, handmade doughnuts and excellent burgers. *7am-9pm* $$

Lou's Luncheonette: Fried chicken, and po'boys, hush puppies, burgers and milkshakes. At a simple whitewashed diner with a patio. *8am-3pm Wed-Sun* $

Kivelstadt Cellars & WineGarten: Wrap up with live music at this easygoing wine garden. There's a playground for kids, too. *11am-5pm Thu-Mon* $$

HOW DO I BECOME A CALIFORNIA WINE AFICIONADO?

Pour yourself a nice glass and settle in with one of these top wine books: Jon Bonné's *The New California Wine: A Guide to the Producers and Wines Behind a Revolution in Taste* (2013), Jane Lopes' *Vignette: Stories of Life and Wine in 100 Bottles* (2019), Julia Harding and Jancis Robinson's *The Oxford Companion to Wine* (2015), and Eric Asimov's *How to Love Wine: A Memoir and Manifesto* (2012).

Also, during crush (autumn harvest), when vine leaves turn brilliant colors and you can smell fermenting fruit on the breeze, farmers throw big parties with vineyard workers. To score party invitations, join your favorite winery's wine club. No one wants to miss the good times – reserve ahead and budget accordingly.

Craving some Ai Weiwei with your chardonnay or pinot? The extraordinary contemporary-art collection at nearby **Donum Estate** *(thedonumestate.com; tastings from $75)* is surrounded by lavender fields, vineyards and an organic farm. Take the tour, glass of chardonnay in hand, roaming Yayoi Kusama's polka-dotted pumpkin, Gao Weigang's brass-tube maze and Keith Haring's embracing figures.

If you're an architecture buff, head north to **Quixote Winery** *(quixotewinery.com; tastings from $50)* – that gold-leafed onion dome sprouting from the grassy knoll is the work of Austrian eco-architect Friedensreich Hundertwasser, whose signature crayon-colored ceramic pillars frame broken-tile mosaic walls.

Cycling Napa Valley

What better way to cruise the vineyards than by bike? The **Napa Valley Wine Trail** *(vinetrail.org)* connects vineyards, wineries, downtown Napa and Yountville via 12.5 miles of walking and cycling paths. The trail is just a piece of an ambitious 47-mile stretch that will eventually connect the Vallejo Ferry Terminal to Calistoga. For now, to bike onward to Calistoga, take tree-lined Silverado Trail instead of hot, traffic-heavy Hwy 29.

You can rent a bike or book a tour at **Napa Valley Bike Tours** *(napavalleybiketours.com; bicycle/e-bike rental per day $54/94, tours from $150)* or **Calistoga Bikeshop** *(calistoga bikeshop.com; bicycle/e-bike rental per day from $50/93, tours from $170)*. Other biking guides cover parts of the Napa Valley, too, and give a range of tours. We like Getaway Adventures/Wine Country Bikes (p177), based in Calistoga and Healdsburg.

Lovely picnic spots

While a picnic in the vineyards is bucket-list material, strict zoning laws make it tricky to find places to picnic legally in Napa.

JAMIE PHAM/ALAMY

Cuvaison Winery (p178)

If you're heading to a winery, call ahead to see if picnicking is allowed (it's customary to buy a bottle of your host's wine if it is). If you don't finish your wine, stash it in the trunk – California law forbids driving with an uncorked bottle in the car.

Here's a short list of prime picnic spots, in south-north order across Napa Valley: Skyline Wilderness Park (p175), Gundlach-Bundschu Winery (p194) or Bartholomew Estate Winery (p195), Pride Mountain Vineyards (p187), Bothe-Napa Valley State Park (p188) and Old Faithful Geyser (p188).

Yountville

TIME FROM NAPA: **25 MINS**

Play with the culinary all-stars

Planets and Michelin stars are mysteriously aligned over **Yountville**, a tiny Western stagecoach stop 25 minutes' drive north of Napa that's been transformed into a global dining destination. It sounds like an urban legend – until you take a stroll down Yountville's quiet, tree-lined Washington St.

Say hey to interns weeding **French Laundry herb gardens** and trainee sommeliers grabbing lunch at the **Tacos Garcia** truck. You've just met the talents behind a thousand meals of a lifetime each week – and you can probably buy them a beer later. **French Laundry** *(thomaskeller.com)* itself dazzles through nine opulent courses (if you can get a reservation), but you can also grab takeout at **Bouchon Bakery** *(bouchonbakery.com)* – just wait in the hefty line.

For a bit of wine tasting, head across the valley floor to a batch of excellent wineries: **Antinori Napa Valley** *(antinorinapavalley.com)*, **Shafer Vineyards** *(shafervineyards.com)* and **Regusci Winery** *(regusciwinery.com)*.

CARNEROS, WHAT'S IN A NAME?

This stretch of bayfront lowlands spanning both Napa and Sonoma counties is 15 minutes' drive south of Napa. Historically it was shared by Patwin people to the east and Coastal Miwok to the west. Mexican shepherds named it Los Carneros ('The Rams') back in the 1830s – and until recently, sheep had the run of the place. In the 1960s, savvy farmers reckoned that thin-skinned pinot-noir grapes might actually prefer the foggy, damp microclimates that made woolly sheep feel right at home.

Carneros is an American Viticultural Area (AVA) spanning Napa and Sonoma counties. Though online addresses indicate one county or another, the sights are all in the same vicinity.

FOR WINE LOVERS

California's broad array of wine regions mean you find top tipples all across the state. Check out **Paso Robles' wineries** (p318) for more top cabs or **Santa Ynez Valley** (p354) near Santa Barbara, and pretend you're in the movie *Sideways*.

St Helena

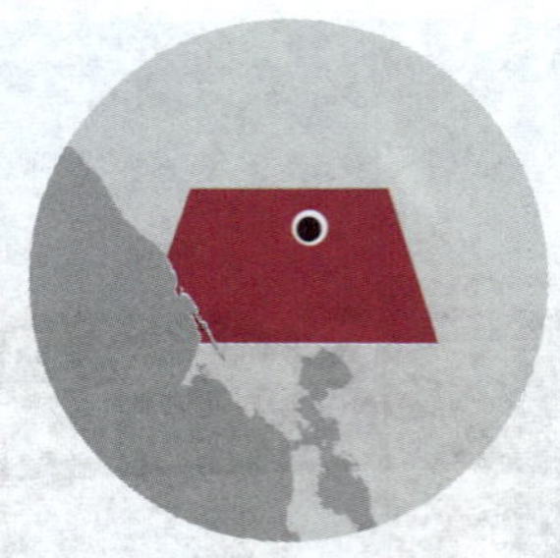

WINE AND CUISINE | EXHILARATING WALKS | RICH HISTORY

GETTING AROUND

Parking in downtown St Helena is next to impossible on summer weekends. Tip: look behind the visitor center. Napa Vine *(vinetransit.com)* connects St Helena to downtown Napa and Calistoga on bus 10, and provides transit around town on the St Helena Shuttle for $1. To schedule a pickup, call 707-963-3007 or access its website or Ride the Vine app during operating hours.

TOP TIP

St Helena is loaded with fabulous restaurants and nearby wineries where you'll need reservations. If you haven't booked, you can shop for a picnic (p184). **St Helena Welcome Center** *(sthelena.com)* has information and lodging assistance, and can help with winery booking.

Even people with places to go and wine to drink can't resist a closer look at St Helena (pronounced ha-LEE-na). One or two blocks down Main St, cars suddenly swerve to the curb so that passengers can photograph this road that looks exactly like a Western movie set. But this scene is the real deal: three blocks of Main St are a designated National Historic District, covering 160 years of California history – including the 1913 Cameo Cinema, one of the oldest movie theaters still in operation in America.

Today Main St is lined with restaurants, gourmet shops and tasting rooms. Further up the street, the 1889 Greystone Cellars château is home to the Culinary Institute of America. If you're thirsty, you're in luck: there's more than an acre of wine grapes per resident in St Helena.

Stroll Through Wine-Making History

Visit a mill and winery from St Helena's past

Stroll the historic downtown of St Helena and you may wonder, what's the story behind this pretty little town? Well, this area was Native Wappo land until it was taken by Spain, and became a territory of Mexico – more specifically, the property of Maria Ygnacia Soberanes, the niece of Mexican commander General Vallejo. The matriarch of a family of savvy businesswomen.

Doña Maria sold off parcels of land that had potential as vineyards, but saved the best for her daughters, giving Isadora the Bale grist mill – still grinding flour today – and prime vineyards to Caroline. See history in action at the mill, now in **Bale Grist Mill State Historic Park** *(parks.ca.gov)*, where you can watch the original French buhr millstones grind flour on the weekends, and take home bags of just-ground cornmeal for a donation. In October, join the **Old Mill Days** *(napavalleystateparks.org; admission $5)* living-history festival.

Romance and business converged again when Caroline married German winemaker Charles Krug. Together they were pioneers in planting vineyards and they founded Napa's first

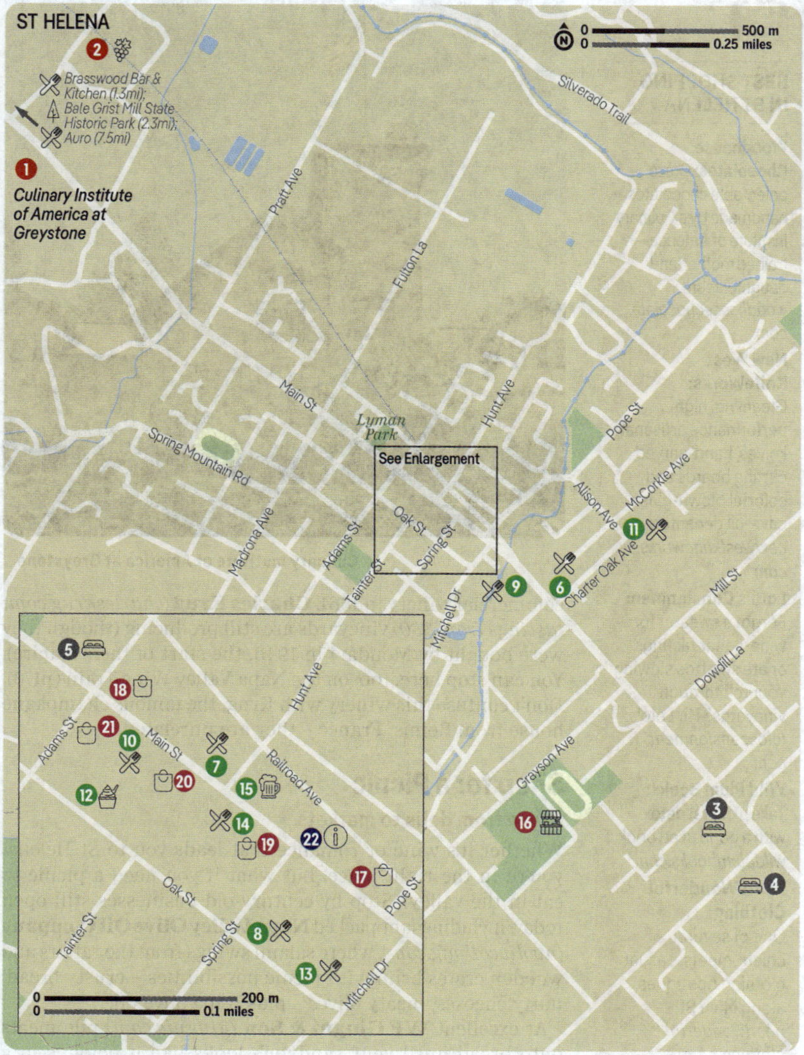

ST HELENA

Brasswood Bar & Kitchen (1.3mi); Bale Grist Mill State Historic Park (2.3mi); Auro (7.5mi)

1 Culinary Institute of America at Greystone

Silverado Trail
Pratt Ave
Fulton La
Main St
Lyman Park
Hunt Ave
Pope St
Spring Mountain Rd
See Enlargement
Madrona Ave
Adams St
Oak St
Spring St
Tainter St
Alison Ave
McCorkle Ave
Charter Oak Ave
Mitchell Dr
Mill St
Dowdell La
Grayson Ave
Railroad Ave

0 — 500 m
0 — 0.25 miles

0 — 200 m
0 — 0.1 miles

HIGHLIGHTS
1 Culinary Institute of America at Greystone

SIGHTS
2 Charles Krug

SLEEPING
3 El Bonita Motel
4 Harvest Inn
5 Wydown Hotel

EATING
6 Charter Oak
7 Cook St Helena
see 1 Gatehouse Restaurant
8 Goose & Gander
9 Gott's Roadside
10 Model Bakery
11 Napa Valley Olive Oil Company
12 Roman Holiday
13 Sunshine Foods
14 WF Giugni & Son

DRINKING & NIGHTLIFE
15 Erosion Tap House

SHOPPING
16 Farmers Market
17 Lolo's Consignment
18 New West KnifeWorks
19 Pearl Wonderful Clothing
20 Wild Plum Books
21 Woodhouse Chocolates

INFORMATION
22 St Helena Welcome Center

BEST SHOPPING IN ST HELENA

Woodhouse Chocolates: Graze delectable chocolates handmade by a Culinary Institute of America–trained mother-and-daughter team. *woodhousechocolate.com*

New West KnifeWorks: Gleaming, high-performance artisanal knives, hand-carved cutting boards and colorful blown-glass olive-oil decanters. *newwestknifeworks.com*

Lolo's Consignmen: Forgot a sweater for wine-cellar tastings, or are stilettos slowing your roll through vineyards? Hit Lolo's. *lolosconsignment.com*

Wild Plum Books: Take a digital detox with a good used book. *wildplumbooks.com*

Pearl Wonderful Clothing: One of several chichi-meets-casual clothing boutiques along Main St. *pearlwonderfulclothing.com*

ROSANGELA PERRY/SHUTTERSTOCK

Culinary Institute of America at Greystone

commercial winery in 1861. **Charles Krug** *(charleskrug.com; tastings from $50)* vineyards are still producing (though they were bought by Mondavi in 1943, the start of their empire). You can stop here, too, on the Napa Valley Wine Train (p173). Don't confuse this winery with Krug, the famous champagne house from Reims, France – they are unrelated.

Shop for a Picnic

Graze from delis to markets

Whether it's wine or romance that leads you to St Helena, you're in the right place, but what if you need a picnic to eat in the valley? Stop by century-old businesses still open today, including jam-packed **Napa Valley Olive Oil Company** *(nvoliveoilmfg.com)*, where salami swings from the rafters and wooden crates brim with picnic possibilities – crusty bread, nutty cheeses, meaty olives – plus Napa olive oil.

At excellent **WF Giugni & Son** *(giugnis.com)* pile meats onto bread until your sandwich looks like it belongs in a comic strip, then drizzle with 'Giugni juice' (red-wine-vinegar

EATING IN NORTHERN NAPA VALLEY: LUXURY LIVING

Auro: Exquisite 7-course tastings menus in pure California elegance, paired with wine to match. A meal of a lifetime. *5-9pm Wed-Sat* $$$

Brasswood Bar + Kitchen: Fresh mozzarella, handmade pastas and pizzas paired with the winery's cab sauvignons and malbecs. *11.30am-9pm* $$$

Charter Oak: Enjoy a romantic dinner in an 1878 sherry distillery. Each dish showcases signature seasonal ingredients, often from this farm. *11.30am-8.30pm* $$$

Goose & Gander: Step inside this arts-and-crafts cottage to discover a swanky clubhouse bistro. Slip downstairs to the basement speakeasy. *4.30-10pm* $$$

dressing). You can also hit **Sunshine Foods**, the town's best grocery store, which has a delicious deli. Grab a pint of top gelato at **Roman Holiday** *(romanholidaygelato.com)*.

If you're in town on a Friday morning, fill your bag at St Helena's **Farmers Market** *(sthelenafarmersmkt.org)* at Crane Park, half a mile south of downtown. Since 1986, farmers and friends have converged around pristine local produce, ready-to-eat homemade treats, flowers, crafts and live music. Look for demos with star chefs in the tent and kids' programs under the redwood trees.

POWERFUL FEMALE CALIFORNIOS

To learn more about Mexican land grants, Californios and early matriarchs, visit **Ávila Adobe** (p394), the oldest standing residence in Los Angeles, home to Francisca Ávila de Rimpau.

Cooking & Wine-Tasting Classes

Celebrate food and wine at the CIA

Final exams never tasted as good as the ones served at the renowned **Culinary Institute of America at Greystone** *(CIA; ciachef.edu/california)* inside an 1889 stone château. Taste A-students' work at the **Gatehouse Restaurant** and bakery–cafe, and educate your palate at weekend wine-tasting classes and cooking demonstrations. Get in on the action with hands-on one-day classes and load up on gourmet-school supplies in the gadget- and cookbook-filled shop. For more classes and demos, visit the **CIA at Copia in downtown Napa** (p174).

Float over Napa Valley

Ballooning and flying in Wine Country

If you think Wine Country scenery is breathtaking, wait until you see it from 3000ft up in the air. The biplane and balloon rides here have limited capacity, so book ahead and prepare yourself for a once-in-a-lifetime, adrenaline-rush experience.

Napa Valley's signature hot-air-balloon flights leave early, at around 6am or 7am, when the air is coolest and mists are rising from the vineyards. Many offer a champagne toast or brunch on landing. Call **Balloons Above the Valley** *(balloonrides.com)*, **Napa Valley Balloons** *(napavalleyballoons.com)* or **Aloft** *(nvaloft.com)*, Napa's most established ballooning outfit.

Vintage Aircraft Co *(vintageaircraft.com)* flies over Sonoma in old-school biplanes with an expert pilot who'll do loop the loops on request.

DOÑA MARIA'S LOVE STORY

When Maria Ygnacia Soberanes fell for English Protestant Dr Edward Turner Bale, it caused an uproar. Dr Bale became a Mexican citizen and converted to Catholicism, winning over the Vallejo family – and co-ownership of Maria's 28 sq miles of land.

The couple had six children together by 1849, when the news arrived: gold had been discovered in California. Dr Bale headed for the hills during the gold rush, but this time he was out of luck. He died within months, leaving Doña Maria with kids, mining debts and a legal fight to own her own land as a woman – back then this wasn't allowed under US law.

EATING & DRINKING IN ST HELENA: OUR PICKS

Model Bakery: Get renowned fluffy cornmeal-dusted English muffins, breads and baked goods, but be prepared for long lines on weekends. *6am-4pm* $

Gott's Roadside: Hit this retro burger joint, and sprawl on the lawn and feast on grass-fed beef burgers oozing with Point Reyes blue cheese. *11am-9pm* $

Cook St Helena: Small space, small menu and big flavors are signatures of this local-favorite bistro for earthy Cal-Italian cooking. *11.30am-8.30pm Mon-Fri* $$

Erosion Tap House: Beer on tap and wine, but save room for the ice-cream flight. *3-8pm Mon & Wed, from noon Thu-Sun* $

Beyond St Helena

Vaunted vineyards and spritzing hot springs carpet the northern end of the Napa Valley, radiating out from St Helena.

Places

Today when wine aficionados look at this green valley around Oakville and Rutherford, they see red – thanks in no small part to Robert Mondavi, the visionary vintner who knew back in the 1960s that Napa was capable of more than jug wine. His marketing savvy launched Napa's premium reds to cult status. Meanwhile up the road, trailblazing winemaker Mike Grgich made history in 1976 with the first Napa chardonnay to win over French judges in international wine competitions. Further north, Calistoga bubbles with mineral hot springs, and the hills around this part of Napa Valley are studded with excellent wineries – more than you can explore on one trip.

The Northern Valley

TIME FROM ST HELENA: **20 MINS**

Wonderful wineries & lone lakes

Pick your geographical zone around St Helena and wineries abound. Here's our quick-and-dirty guide to the regions.

Cruise 10 minutes from St Helena to the eastern hills for a spectacular drive along Sage Canyon Rd by **Lake Hennessey** (where you can stop and fish for a bit) to reach oak-topped Pritchard Hill and the thrilling **Chappellet Winery** *(chappellet.com; tastings from $125)*. Magnificent views vie for your attention as you taste in the barrel-filled vaulted redwood winery itself. Pair it with the much humbler **Nichelini Family Winery** *(nicheliniwinery.com; tastings $30)*, perched on a dramatic ravine. It was founded in 1890 and has been in the same family ever since. Some summers it runs a flashback Friday with $15 tastings, and it accepts walk-ins any day. You can continue along to **Lake Berryessa** for more water sports and picnic spots.

On the other side of Lake Hennessy, and also family-owned, **Amizetta Vineyards** *(amizetta.com; tastings $100)* has sweeping views back toward the lake and books up – plan ahead to survey the panorama during a personalized wine-tasting experience.

On the valley floor, pop into 100%-organically-farmed **Ghost Block Estates** *(ghostblockwine.com; tastings from $55)* or nearby **Frog's Leap** *(frogsleap.com; tastings from $45)*, where you can follow vineyard cats through enchanted gardens, and drink in the views from the loft of an 1884 barn. Across the

GETTING AROUND

Downtown Calistoga is flat, easy and charming to walk/bike around. Napa Vine bus 10 gets you from Calistoga to St Helena and downtown Napa. Vine operates a Calistoga Shuttle, providing door-to-door service within city limits. To schedule a pickup, call 707-963-4229 or access its app or website during operating hours.

Find biking information and rentals at **Calistoga Bikeshop** (p180) *(calistogabikeshop.com)*.

JOHN S LANDER/LIGHTROCKET VIA GETTY IMAGES

Indian Springs (p188)

way, **Round Pond** *(roundpond.com; tastings from $40)* also offers fantastic food upgrades on a vineyard-view stone patio and its olive-oil tastings, too.

Go west, high into the Spring Mountain District (AVA; American Viticultural Area) and smack on the county boundary, to reach family-owned **Pride Mountain Vineyards** *(pridewines.com; tastings from $50)*. Winemaker Matt Ward's sustainable-farming vineyard team shares credit for its cult-status cabernet and merlot. Along a valley just north, in the misty pine trees near Bothe-Napa Valley State Park (p188) **Stony Hill** *(stonyhillvineyard.com; tastings from $85)*, is one of the oldest wineries in the region, and one of the first producers of chardonnay in the US.

North of Calistoga, seek out **Bennett Lane Winery** *(bennettlane.com; tastings from $35)* for its sustainable farming practices and fab cabernets.

Oakville & Rutherford

TIME FROM ST HELENA: **10 MINS**

Laid-back life in the valley

Sprawling winery complexes along Hwy 29 dominate the landscape with gilded signs and gated entrances – including **Robert Mondavi** *(robertmondaviwinery.com; tastings from $60)* and **Grgich Hills Estate** *(grgich.com; tastings from $60)*, a stop on the **Napa Valley Wine Train** (p173). Grgich Hills won the Great Wine Capitals Sustainable Wine Tourism Practices award in 2024.

You'll recognize the hamlets of **Oakville** and **Rutherford** when you hit the historic 1881 **Oakville Grocery** *(oakvillegrocery.com)*, 10 minutes' drive south of St Helena. Turn off Hwy 29 onto cross-valley roads, and you'll find the excellent **La Luna Taqueria & Market** *(lalunamarket.com)*, where the wine-fridge sign says 'Tacos y vinos' – accept the invitation.

BEST WINERIES TO WALK OR BIKE TO FROM ST HELENA

Cliff Family Winery *(cliffamily.com)*: Sustainably produced wines, food truck and community spirit.

Spring Mountain Vineyard *(springmountainvineyard.com)*: A good winery to pair with **Fantesca Estate & Winery**, just up the road.

Sinegal Estate *(sinegalestate.com)*: Dating to 1879, with lush gardens and a pond, featuring cabernet sauvignon and franc, pinot noir and sauvignon blanc.

Tres Sabores *(tressabores.com)*: Sauvignon blanc named a *New York Times* top 10 pick and a collectors' favorite rare rosé.

Joseph Phelps *(josephphelps.com)*: Here's the secret to Phelps' iconic red-blend Insignia, made with each season's best grapes since 1974: there are no rules.

ROBERT LOUIS STEVENSON IN THE NAPA VALLEY

Honeymoons in Napa Valley are often epic – but the 1880 honeymoon of Robert Louis Stevenson and Fanny Osbourne was epically awful. Robert was sick and they were broke, so they wound up squatting in an abandoned bunkhouse at extinct volcanic cone Mt St Helena's Silverado Mine, now part of Robert Louis Stevenson State Park.

There are details at St Helena's **Robert Louis Stevenson Museum** *(stevensonmuseum.org; donations welcome)* of how this honeymoon trip inspired Stevenson's travel memoir *The Silverado Squatters*, making his reputation for harrowing adventure stories that eventually included *Treasure Island* and *Strange Case of Dr Jekyll and Mr Hyde*.

Offbeat organic wineries abut low-key high-end hotels hidden in the heart of Napa Valley, such as **Rancho Caymus** *(ranchocaymusinn.com)*, built by pioneering vintner Mary Tilden Morton; and **Auberge du Soleil** *(aubergedusoleil.com)* with its vaunted restaurant, a prime spot for champagne-soaked proposals.

Bothe-Napa Valley State Park

TIME FROM ST HELENA: **5 MINS**

Hike, swim & camp

If you're looking for a fine place for a picnic, look no further – with redwoods for shade in summer, wild orchids in spring, bright leaves in fall and soft moss carpets in winter, **Bothe-Napa Valley State Park** *(napaoutdoors.org/parks; per car $10)* is fantastic year-round.

About 8000 years ago, Native Koliholmanok people inhabited this area, and past the park entrance you'll find a Native American plant garden, as well as trailheads for the Redwood Trail (1.5 miles one-way) and Ritchey Trail (4 miles one-way), passing the ruined 1880s homestead of firefighting philanthropist Lillie Hancock Coit, benefactor of Coit Tower (p72) in San Francisco.

Cool off in summer at the outdoor **swimming pool** near the Ritchey Creek campground (p226) and day-use picnic area. You can also stay over in cool yurts and cabins.

Calistoga

TIME FROM ST HELENA: **15–25 MINS**

Hot springs & champagne

With soothing natural hot springs, bubbling volcanic mud pools and a dramatically spurting geyser, Nilektsonoma (Calistoga), 15 minutes' drive north of St Helena, was renowned across Talahalusi (Napa Valley) by the Indigenous Wappo (Brave) people for some 8000 years. Then in 1859 a braggart named Samuel Brannan came along and claimed to have discovered the place. The town's odd name comes from Brannan, believing it would develop like the New York spa town, Saratoga. Apparently Sam liked his drink, and at the founding ceremony tripped on his tongue, proclaiming it the 'Cali-stoga' of 'Sara-fornia.' The name stuck.

By 1873 Brannan had lost a fortune promoting **Calistoga** as California's signature spa resort. But look around Calistoga today and you might think he'd pulled it off.

At **Indian Springs** *(indianspringscalistoga.com)* guests can glide from mud baths to an Olympic-sized outdoor spring-fed pool then move on to **Sam's Social Club** *(samssocialclub.com)* for bubbly bathrobed happy hours. Across the street, the 1952 spa-motel **Dr Wilkinson's** *(drwilkinson.com)* offers de-stress sessions in mineral-water pools, extra-squishy mud baths and 'beer brew' (hops-infused mineral baths).

Most spa treatments are adults-only, but **Old Faithful Geyser** *(oldfaithfulgeyser.com; adult/child $15/9)* keeps tykes entertained, as do mineral hot-springs pools at 1947 **Calistoga Motor Lodge & Spa** *(calistogamotorlodge.com)* and best-value **Roman Spa Hot Springs** *(romanspahotsprings.com)*.

For more adult bubbly, explore the historic sparkling-wine caves at Green Certified **Schramsberg** *(schramsberg.com; tastings from $65)* and glimpse the traditional French champagne riddling and racking methods before sampling the *tête de cuvées* (best of the vintage). Don't-miss wineries include **Vincent Arroyo** *(vincentarroyo.com; tastings $30)* and **Olabisi** *(olabisiwines.com; tastings $40)* for exclusive small-batch wines.

Wildlife safaris & petrified trees

Kids ready for some extra thrills? Really splash out and spice it up over the hill at **Safari West** *(safariwest.com; from adult/child $110/45)*. They'll be ecstatic on a jeep trip among giraffes, zebras and flamingos, plus overnight glamping. For the general safaris you must be four years old, but some of the private ones don't have age limitations.

En route, swing into the **Petrified Forest** *(petrifiedforest.org; adult/child $14/6)*, where three million years ago a volcanic eruption at Mt St Helena blew down the stand of redwoods, now petrified.

Robert Louis Stevenson State Park

TIME FROM ST HELENA: 1 HR

Hike & bike tough ascents

The extinct volcanic cone of **Mt St Helena** marks a dramatic end to Napa Valley, and you can explore it at **Robert Louis Stevenson State Park** *(napaoutdoors.org; free)*. It's a strenuous 5-mile climb to the peak's 4343ft summit, but what a view – 200 miles on a clear day.

For a shorter hike with views over valley vineyards, take **Table Rock Trail** (2.2 miles one-way) from the parking-area trailhead.

Super-fit hikers can also tackle the nearby **Oat Hill Mine Trail**. It's one of Northern California's most technically challenging trails – 8.3 miles (one-way) with an elevation change of 1500ft along an 1893 stagecoach route – and draws hardcore mountain bikers and hikers. For shorter but still challenging day hikes, turn back midway at Holm homestead's stone ruins. This trailhead's at the intersection of Hwy 29 and Silverado Trail.

Check conditions and seasonal closures before setting out, as the park gets snow in winter. There's no water (so bring your own), restrooms, trash collection (pack yours out) or camping.

THE DIRTY LOWDOWN

Calistoga mud isn't just wet dirt: it's a blend of volcanic ash, peat and hot mineral spring water. If you're wondering why some baths cost more, it might be the silkier mud with higher volcanic ash content... or maybe it's the marketing.

Mud-bath packages take one to 1½ hours, combining semi-submergence in warm mud, hot mineral-water soaking and a steam bath or blanket-wrap. Variations include thin, painted-on clay-mud wraps (called 'fango' baths, good for those uncomfortable sitting in mud), herbal wraps and seaweed baths. Check for midweek deals from lodging sites and the **Calistoga Visitors Center** *(visitcalistoga.com)*. Reservations are essential, so book ahead, especially for summer weekends.

EATING & DRINKING IN CALISTOGA: OUR PICKS

Bella Bakery: Your friendly neighborhood top-notch bakery and coffee bar, with perfect quiche and chocolate-layer cake. *6am-2pm Mon-Sat, from 7am Sun* $

Lovina: Garden lunches here are a dream – and inspiration for chef Leticia Martinez, who composes produce into California sensations. *5-9pm nightly, 10am-2pm Sat & Sun* $$

Buster's Southern BBQ: Napa Valley's favorite back-to-basics barbecue stop, with sunny outdoor tables. *10am-8pm, to 7pm Sun* $

Solbar: Chill out at luxe Solage resort with creative cocktails in the lounge or on the patio. *7am-9pm Sun-Thu, to 9.30pm Fri & Sat* $$$

Sonoma

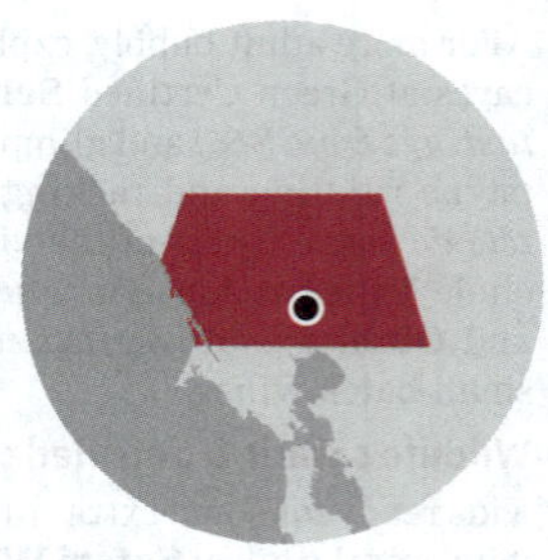

MISSION HISTORY | ART AND SHOPS | DELICIOUS WINES

TOP TIP

There are lots of historic inns and romantic cottages suitable for a midrange budget, but those counting pennies will have better luck in Santa Rosa or Petaluma. Off-season rates plummet. Reserve ahead and ask about parking, as some inns don't have lots. **Sonoma Valley Visitors Bureau** *(sonomavalley.com)* offers loads of local information.

Enchanting downtown Sonoma seems a world apart from mundane everyday life. Stroll streets lined with long-standing trees and Victorian houses, and you'll find heritage inns, indie boutiques and some 30 tasting rooms. A bicycle ride away are more parks, historic sites, sensational family-owned restaurants and (how did you guess?) wineries.

Native Americans originally converged here at the village of Huichi to trade goods and songs. Many died in outbreaks of measles and smallpox that arrived with the friars of Mission Solano. When Mexico secularized California's missions and the lands were officially returned to Native Americans, those land deeds were not honored. Instead, Sonoma's mission vineyards were claimed by settlers.

On one particularly drunken night in 1846, a band of settlers took over the Sonoma barracks and proclaimed a breakaway Bear Flag Republic. Not a shot was fired, and after a confusing month US forces claimed Sonoma as US territory.

Plaza Ringed by Monuments

Amble through California history

The city of Sonoma's pride and joy is the **plaza** – the largest town square in all of California, it's surrounded by local

GETTING AROUND

Sonoma Hwy (Hwy 12) is lined with wineries and runs up the valley from Sonoma town, past Glen Ellen, through Kenwood to Santa Rosa, then on to western Sonoma County. From Napa you can get a rideshare to downtown Sonoma, where many sights, wine-tasting rooms and restaurants are within walking or cycling distance (there is no bus service between the two towns). Public transportation is not convenient, so it's best to have your own wheels to explore the valley and its wineries. In a pinch, Sonoma County *(sctransit.com)* bus 32 is the local free shuttle, and infrequent buses 30 and 34 (also serving Petaluma) go up the valley to Santa Rosa. Bus 40 goes southwest to Petaluma on weekdays only.

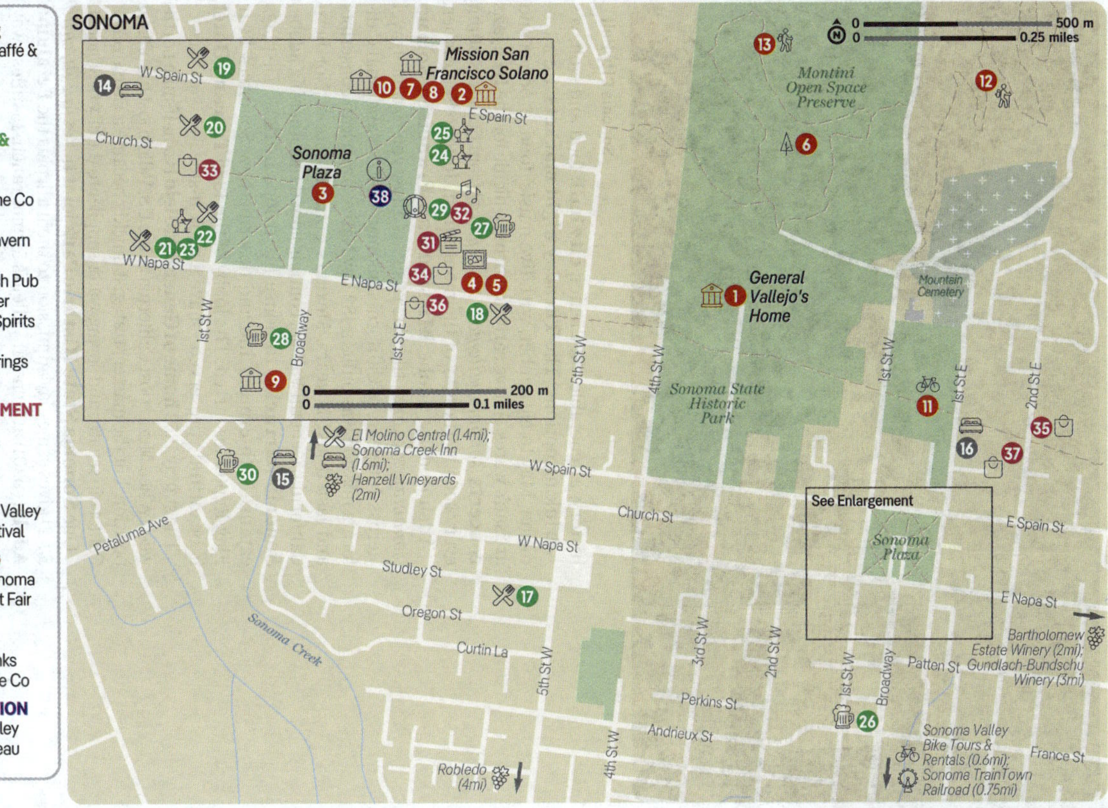

HIGHLIGHTS
1 General Vallejo's Home
2 Mission San Francisco Solano
3 Sonoma Plaza

SIGHTS
4 Arts Guild of Sonoma
5 La Haye Art Center
6 Montini Open Space Preserve
7 Sonoma Barracks
8 Sonoma State Historic Park
9 Sonoma Valley Museum of Art
10 Toscano Hotel

ACTIVITIES
11 Sonoma City Trail
12 Sonoma Overlook Trail
13 Valley of the Moon Trail

SLEEPING
14 An Inn 2 Remember
15 Cinnamon Bear Creekside Inn
16 Cottage Inn & Spa

EATING
see 5 Cafe La Haye
17 Delicious Dish
18 Enclos
19 Girl & the Fig
20 Sunflower Caffé & Wine Bar
21 Tasca Tasca
22 Valley

DRINKING & NIGHTLIFE
23 Beacon
24 Bedrock Wine Co
25 Capo Isetta
26 Hopmonk Tavern Sonoma
27 Murphy's Irish Pub
28 Pomme Cider
29 Prohibition Spirits Distillery
30 Sonoma Springs Brewing Co

ENTERTAINMENT
31 Sebastiani Theatre
32 Sonoma Speakeasy
see 31 Sonoma Valley Film Festival

SHOPPING
33 Chateau Sonoma
34 Global Heart Fair Trade
35 Patch
36 Tiddle E Winks
37 Vella Cheese Co

INFORMATION
38 Sonoma Valley Visitors Bureau

KIT LEONG/SHUTTERSTOCK

Sonoma City Hall

history, a venerable old theater, **city hall**, food and – oh, yes – drinking options. The **Tuesday night markets** are a tradition, May to November, with live music, food, produce and artisan's wares. Arrive early and bring a picnic for the **free jazz concerts** *(sonomavalleyjazzsociety.org)* from 6pm to 8.30pm every second Tuesday of the month from June to September.

Anchored by adobe **Mission San Francisco Solano** *(sonomaparks.org)*, the plaza's sights allow you to time-travel across 200 years of California history. The 21st and final California mission was built in 1823 by Native American conscripts and lasted just 11 years. Mexico's Comandante of Northern California, General Vallejo, commissioned the other big adobe, **Sonoma Barracks**, to house his troops in 1834. Displays capture 19th-century life and describe how Sonoma's Bear Flag Republic started. The lobby of the 1886 **Toscano Hotel** is beautifully preserved – have a peek inside.

The stately 1852 **home of General Vallejo** is a half-mile northwest. When Mexico lost California to the US, Vallejo lost his official position, but the master strategist quickly became a US citizen, a California senator and spring-water supplier to the city of Sonoma.

One **Sonoma State Historic Park** joint ticket *(adult/child $3/2)* gives same-day admission to them all, plus the **Petaluma Adobe** (p201) at General Vallejo's former ranch, 15 miles away.

EATING IN SONOMA TOWN: THE HIGH LIFE

Enclos: This 30-seat temple of California cuisine sources produce from organic Stone Edge Farm & Winery. Global flavors. *5-9pm Wed-Sat* **$$$**

Cafe La Haye: Warm feelings are mutual between farmers, chefs and visitors at cozy La Haye. Produce is sourced within 60 miles. *5.30-9pm Tue-Sat* **$$$**

Girl & the Fig: Celebrated bistro with hearty feasts of rustic French fare and large space for eating alfresco. *11.30am-9pm Mon-Thu, from 10am Sat & Sun* **$$$**

Tasca Tasca: Sea, garden, land: choose your next culinary adventure and this inspired tapas bar will take you there. *11.30am-9pm* **$$**

Pair Local Art & Libations

Creativity for all the senses

Sonoma remains staunchly independent-minded and proud of its creativity, which is on display at **Sonoma Valley Museum of Art** *(svma.org; adult/child/family $10/free/15)* and the **Arts Guild of Sonoma** *(artsguildofsonoma.org; admission free)*. Make an appointment to visit collective **La Haye Art Center** *(lahayeartcenter.com; admission free)* in a converted foundry where you can tour its gallery and meet the artists – sculptor, potter and painters – in their studios.

In June join **Art at the Source** *(artatthesource.org; free)* and in October **Sonoma County Art Trails** *(sonomacounty arttrails.org; free)*, each are two-week events that give you a chance to travel from studio to studio, learning about local artists. The maps of the ateliers are available year-round and are a good resource for art lovers.

Book ahead at **Bedrock Wine Co** *(bedrockwineco.com; tastings from $45)* to pair your art with wines in a historic saltbox cottage hung with tintype portraits and antique Sonoma maps. Morgan Twain-Peterson and Chris Cottrell are reviving California's old vine-field blends with grapes sourced from tiny NorCal ('Northern California') blocks, including classic zinfandels and obscure varietals like Alicante Bouschet.

Or, compare quaffs at **Pomme Cider** *(pommecidershop.com; flight of ciders $21)*, with its convivial cascades of cider on tap.

Shopping in Sonoma Town

Unusual souvenirs and tasty treats

Sonoma is lavish in its boutiques and eclectic shops. Step back in time at **Tiddle E Winks** *(tiddleewinks.com)*, a retro 1950s variety store packed with nostalgic fun for all ages: windup toys, classic board games and penny candy.

French whimsy meets California quirk at **Chateau Sonoma** *(chateausonoma.com)*, Sarah Anderson's curiosity cabinet of a shop. Visit **Global Heart Fair Trade** *(globalheartfairtrade.com)* for unique handmade gifts, festive clothing and jewelry, recyclable decorations and artisan chocolates in support of a worthwhile cause: all sales ensure living wages for makers.

Right in downtown Sonoma, pick up heirloom tomatoes and more, from May to November, at the **Patch**, California's oldest community-run urban farm, beloved by neighbors and protected from developers for at least 150 years. Across the street, **Vella Cheese Co** *(vellacheese.com)* has been making

TOUGH HISTORY

Miwok, Pomo, Wintun and Wappo people thrived in this fertile region for about 10,000 years before they began trading with Russian trappers and Spanish ranchers some 300 years ago, and were subsequently wiped out by disease and genocide.

Over the centuries, Sonoma County's rich agricultural lands (from dairies to apple orchards), terraced vineyards and pristine forests have been hit with earthquakes, wildfires, floods and droughts.

Nonetheless, modern and pioneering conservation initiatives have successfully protected west Sonoma County's ancient redwoods, which were once heavily logged to build San Francisco, and the California Coastal Commission preserves its raw, rocky coastline.

EATING IN SONOMA TOWN: RELAXED & DELICIOUS

Valley: This welcoming wine bar dishes up creative, seasonal offerings...California comfort food at its best. *9am-3pm & 5-9pm Thu-Mon* $$

El Molino Central: Sustainably homegrown ingredients and Sonoma's Mexican culinary traditions at this 1930s roadside mainstay. *11am-8pm Mon-Thu, from 9am Fri-Sun* $

Delicious Dish: Succulent burgers, fresh-catch fish sandwiches and salads with fries at a field-side diner with a patio. *10.30am-6.30pm Mon-Thu, to 2.30pm Fri* $

Sunflower Caffé & Wine Bar: The big back garden at this local hangout is a great spot for breakfast, a no-fuss lunch or afternoon wine. *8am-3pm* $$

BEST HIKES & BIKES NEAR SONOMA

Montini Open Space Preserve: Trails wind above Sonoma, with their rolling grassland and oak woodlands. Trailheads at 1st St W and 4th St W in Sonoma lead to two overlooks, and the trail from 4th St is ADA-accessible. *overlookmontini.org*

Valley of the Moon Trail: This Montini trail connects to beautiful, volunteer-maintained **Sonoma Overlook Trail**: It's 3 miles of spectacular hiking through oaks, bay trees and native wildflowers.

Sonoma City Trail: Downtown Sonoma is small, flat and perfect for biking with this 1.5-mile trail. *sonomacity.org*

Sonoma Valley Bike Tours & Rentals: Rents bikes, e-bikes and tandem bikes. Rentals include helmets and – crucially – a winery map. Also guided rides. *sonomavalleybike tours.com*

spaghetti Western for almost 100 years – its two-year-aged dry jack is meant for shaving atop rustic dishes.

Kids Cut Loose on Trains & Rides

Live it up at the Sonoma TrainTown Railroad

All aboard! At **Sonoma TrainTown Railroad** *(traintown.com)* kids ride the rails *($9.75)* in miniature boxcars, while adults squeeze in and try not to bang into anything on the 1.25-mile, 20-minute loop through narrow tunnels and shrunken towns. Toddlers pose in engineer caps on the carousel, and older kids squeal on vintage 1968 rides, including the Mine Train coaster and Ferris wheel *($4.25 per ride)*.

Vineyards near Sonoma Town

Family-friendly wineries

Several Sonoma wineries were damaged by fires in 2017 and 2019. They've regrouped and replanted with more climate-resilient grape varietals and new fire-preventing measures. The inspired vintages they're producing are proudly featured on Sonoma menus.

California's oldest family-run winery, **Gundlach-Bundschu** *(gunbun.com; tastings from $25, incl tour from $80)*, looks like a castle, and everyone gets a royal welcome at the bar. Six generations of Bundschus have kept the delightful dry gewürztraminer flowing since 1858. Bike down a country lane past farmstead donkeys for a tour of the 1800-barrel cave and a picnic by the pond. Concerts regularly rock Gun-Bun's redwood barn and outdoor amphitheater.

Sonoma's most idyllic winery, **Hanzell Vineyards** *(hanzell.com; tasting & tour $90)*, has views to die for over Sonoma all

KENT SORENSEN/SHUTTERSTOCK

Gundlach-Bundschu winery

the way to San Francisco Bay. Take your seat in the historic stone barn for exceptional organically produced chardonnays and pinot noirs.

Sprawling **Bartholomew Estate Winery** *(bartholomewestate.com; tastings from $45)* was established in 1857 at the birth of California's wine industry under Hungarian count Ágoston Haraszthy, and now its certified-organic vineyards produce sauvignon blanc, cabernet sauvignon and zinfandel. Picnics are allowed in the estate's sun-dappled private park (free and open to visitors); there's a 3-mile trail through vineyards, oaks, madrones and redwoods. Pass the pond to reach an overlook with sweeping vistas. You can also go riding on horseback with **Sonoma Valley Trail Rides** *(sonomavalleytrailrides.com; ride & tasting $160)*.

Robledo *(robledofamilywinery.com; tastings from $40)* winery was built from the ground up by Reynoldo Robledo, who started in the industry as a farm worker in 1968 and became Sonoma's go-to vineyard expert. His kids run the winery now, and welcome you to estate tastings at the hand-carved bar.

For wineries, restaurants and lodging in Carneros further south, see p178.

BEST LIVE MUSIC & ENTERTAINMENT

Hopmonk Tavern Sonoma: An 1888 farmhouse comes roaring back to life as a booming tavern and year-round beer garden, serving a dozen Hopmonk microbrews plus guest beers. Stick around for live music Friday through Sunday, and brace for the unexpected at Wednesday open mics. *hopmonk.com*

Sonoma Speakeasy: Live music, karaoke, mixologists and good vibes. *sonomaspeakeasy.com*

Murphy's Irish Pub: Both a pub and a music venue. *sonomapub.com*

Sebastiani Theatre: Sonoma plaza's community-run, 1934 Mission Revival cinema hosts global indie art-house films, director-led screenings, and in March the **Sonoma Valley Film Festival** *(sonomafilmfest.org)*. *sebastianitheatre.com*

DRINKING IN SONOMA: FROM COCKTAILS TO WINE BARS

Prohibition Spirits Distillery: Versions of Italian aperitifs, elderflower gins, brandy distilled from prickly pear. *11am-6pm Sun-Thu, to 7pm Fri, 10am-7pm Sat*

Capo Isetta: Smack on the plaza, this welcoming wine bar spreads the good life with mellow tunes, excellent wines and friendly staff. *noon-9pm*

Beacon: Loud, busy speakeasy vibes rise on crowded weekends. Classic cocktails and inventive mixology are the orders of the day. *5-11pm*

Sonoma Springs Brewing Co: One of two brewpubs to the west of the plaza. Makes a range of IPAs and German-style beers. *3-9pm Mon-Fri, from 1pm Sat & Sun*

Beyond Sonoma

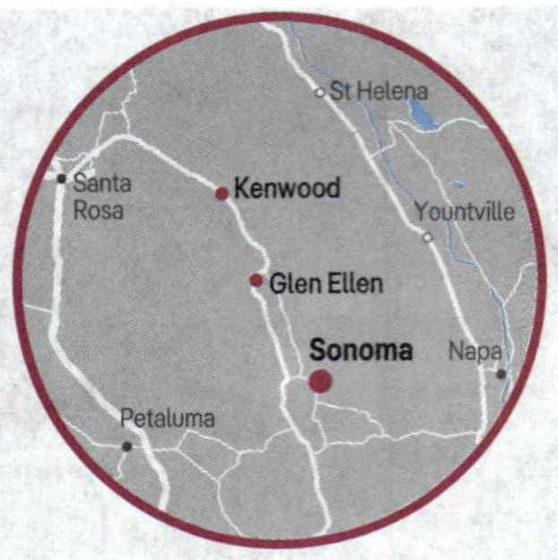

Century-old vines and charming settlements that are both fun-loving and down-to-earth fill the Sonoma Valley.

GETTING AROUND

Sonoma Valley has around 40 wineries. To go vineyard hopping, you'll realistically want a car or bicycle. Glen Ellen is a nice bike ride from Sonoma – 7 miles on quiet country roads. Kenwood is another 5 miles north. Or book Designated Drivers Napa Sonoma *(ddnapasonoma.com)*. Infrequent Sonoma County Transit *(sctransit.com)* bus 34 goes north from Sonoma to Santa Rosa and 30 goes to Santa Rosa (also looping in Petaluma)

The rhythm of Sonoma Valley is an easy groove to fall into, following tracks worn over thousands of years. Here you're tracing the steps of Miwok, Pomo and Wintun people who converged in this lush valley to feast, relax and swap stories. They called this place the Valley of the Moon, and the mystical name has stuck locally. Heading up the valley from Sonoma, the tiny, quaint 19th-century resort town of Glen Ellen is full of surprises: acclaimed restaurants, recycled art masterpieces, rare Japanese maples, wilderness horseback rides, stiff martinis and luxury cottage hideaways. Further north, the batch of vineyards known as Kenwood lures you with wine-pairing feasts and hikes up Sugarloaf to appreciate where you've been.

Glen Ellen

TIME FROM SONOMA: **15–25 MINS**

Creative haunts

A 20-minute drive north of the town of Sonoma, tiny **Glen Ellen** (population 1200) is a jumble of little cottages behind white picket fences along a poplar-lined creek. Back in 1905 it was a swinging resort town with natural hot springs that lured California's rich and renowned, including the world's most famous author at the time, Jack London.

The town has remained a magnet for trailblazing writers and artists, including gonzo journalist Hunter S Thompson and food writer MFK Fisher – you can tour her **Last House** on the wildflower-laden **Bouverie Preserve** *(egret.org; suggested $20 donation)*. You must reserve.

Get the call of the wild at Jack London's ranch

Even a novelist can farm land as fertile as Sonoma's, as you'll see 25 minutes' drive north of Sonoma town at **Jack London State Historic Park** *(jacklondonpark.com; per car $10)*, where the adventure author of *The Call of the Wild* and his wife, editor and fellow writer Charmian Kittredge London built Beauty Ranch as their writing retreat and pioneering organic farm. At the **museum,** insightful displays cover Jack's death-defying travels and his controversial ideas, including socialism and Darwinism. Don't miss Jack's rejection letters in the downstairs bookstore. From the museum, it's a hilly half-mile walk to the ruins of their Wolf House, passing **Jack's grave site** along the way.

DREAMART123/SHUTTERSTOCK

Jack London State Historic Park

Wineries and farms

You're in the heart of Sonoma, one of the world's most prestigious pinot-noir regions, and **Talisman Wines** *(talismanwine.com; tastings from $45)* has award-winning vintages to prove it. Founder/winemaker team Scott and Marta Rich collaborate with legendary pinot growers from Carneros to the Sonoma coast. Pixar animator John Lasseter's **Lasseter Family Winery** *(lasseterfamilywinery.com; tastings from $60)* specializes in organic wines in the Rhône and Bordeaux traditions.

At the southern end of Glen Ellen, **Oak Hill Farm** covers 25 acres with organic flowers and produce, framed by lovely oaks and manzanita trees. Buy from the farm's **Red Barn Store** on Saturdays, April to December.

Soak in hot springs

Jump into Sonoma tradition at **Morton's Warm Springs** *(mortonswarmsprings.com; admission $23)*, 3.5 miles north of Glen Ellen. Geothermal springs have attracted families here for 10,000 years, and today, 108°F (42°C) mineral springwater fills two pools at this local-favorite, vintage-1950s day resort. Come for the afternoon – there's an organic cafe, BBQ, lawns and volleyball. To keep water pristine, wait 15 minutes after applying sunscreen, and shower before entering the pools. Reserve – it usually books out on weekends.

BEST WILDERNESS PARKS & GARDENS IN SONOMA VALLEY

Sugarloaf Ridge State Park: Explore around 25 miles of fantastic hiking and biking trails. There's **camping** (p226). *sugarloafpark.org*

Sonoma Valley Regional Park: Oak woodlands with trails, includes ADA-accessible 1.2-mile Valley of the Moon trail. Picnic areas and dog park. *parks.sonomacounty.ca.gov*

Sonoma Botanical Garden: World-renowned 25-acre botanical garden specializing in flora of Asia. *sonomabg.org*

Hood Mountain Regional Park: Wilderness trails for hiking, biking, horseback riding crisscross 3600 acres, including **Mt Hood**. Hike-in camping 2 miles into the park. *parks.sonomacounty.ca.gov*

EATING IN GLEN ELLEN: OUR PICKS

Les Pascals Patisserie: Flaky, butter-glossed croissants, baguettes, savory quiches, tarts. *6am-4.30pm Mon, Tue, Thu & Fri; from 7am Sat & Sun* $

Mill at Glen Ellen: South of town, this beloved venue crafts casual fare that can be adapted to vegans and vegetarians. *11.30am-7.30pm Wed-Sun* $$

Glen Ellen Star: *Food & Wine* star chef Ari Weiswasser and Erinn Benziger-Weiswasser (from Benziger Winery) keep food excellent and mood relaxed. *5-9pm* $$$

Wine Country Chocolates: When chocolate, wine and ice cream are all you need... be an aficionado of daily ganache selections. *11am-4pm Thu-Sat* $

BEST WINE COUNTRY COOKING CLASSES

Culinary Institute of America at St Helena and Napa: Wine and food classes.

Epicurean Connection, Sonoma: Cheese- and butter-making with pros. *theepicureanconnection.com*

Sonoma Food Tour, Sonoma: Culinary and wine tours. *sonomafoodtour.com*

Parker Hill Provisions, Healdsburg: Lisal Moran teaches baking, pasta and art. *parkerhillprovisions.com*

Central Milling, Petaluma: Bread, baby, bread. Galettes, croissants, baguettes, oh my! *centralmilling.com*

Sonoma Family Meal, Petaluma: This nonprofit's programs combat food insecurity and offering job training for residents. *sonomafamilymeal.org*

STEVE PROEHL/GETTY IMAGES

Kunde winery

If you're looking for a swishier spring, glide 5.5 miles south of Glen Ellen to the area called **Boyes Hot Springs**. There, you'll indulge yourself at **Fairmont Spa at Sonoma Mission Inn** *(fairmont.com; day use from $99)* a classic Spanish Mission-style resort updated with elemental modern twists: flower-shaped pools, stone firepits, heated terra-cotta floors.

Kenwood

TIME FROM SONOMA: **25 MINS**

Northern Sonoma Valley wineries

Rolling grass- and vine-covered hills rise from Sonoma Valley. Its 40-odd wineries get less attention than Napa's, but many are equally good. If you love zinfandel, syrah and pinot noir, you're in for a treat. A few **Kenwood area** landmarks (there is no town per se, rather a collection of vineyards 25 minutes' drive north of Sonoma town) have stood the test of time – including the little 1860s red schoolhouse, now **Muscardini Cellars** *(muscardinicellars.com; tastings from $35)* tasting room. It's also home to **B Wise** tasting room *(bwisevineyards.com; tastings $30, cave tastings $100)*, which welcomes walk-ins; or book ahead to taste in its Moon Mountain cave.

Friendly **Kunde** winery *(kunde.com; tastings from $25)*, on a historic ranch of vast vineyards, offers mountaintop tastings with impressive valley views and guided hikes (reserve). Or just stop by for a tasting (a rarity, in reservation-required Wine Country). Also visit VJB Cellars (p176) for Italian varietals and food.

EATING IN KENWOOD: OUR PICKS

Mayo Family Winery & Reserve Room: Wining and dining: tasting paired with seven small plates. *by appointment 10.30am-6.30pm Thu-Mon* $$$

Salt & Stone: French food craving from Sonoma's Bordeaux-style wines? Stop for a bistro meal on a sunny patio. *11am-9pm Thu-Tue, 2.30-9pm Wed* $$

Golden Bear Station: High concept, beautifully presented comfort food, from homemade pastas and pizzas to pork chops in a Cali-mod room. *5-9pm Wed-Sun* $$$

La Cucina at VJB: For authentic Italian sandwiches and salads, order at the counter of VJB's Italian-varietal winery. Homemade sauce, pesto, mozzarella. *10am-4pm* $

Petaluma

VINTAGE VIBE | FOODIE ENCLAVE | FRESH FARMLAND

The historic town of Petaluma, just a short drive south of Santa Rosa and west of downtown Sonoma, is Sonoma County's sleeper hit. One of California's oldest cities, built around a river and served by rail, it used to be a conduit for the northern counties' abundance on its way south to the burgeoning Bay Area, and the region was renowned for its chicken farms and dairies.

Now Petaluma grabs attention for its walkable, quaint downtown, packed with dining venues, taprooms and wine bars, and its foggy and wind-whipped wine appellation, dubbed 'the Petaluma Gap.' The region's chardonnays, pinot noirs and syrahs have earned a reputation for their elegance and complexity. It's also home to two of the Bay Area's premier breweries.

Petaluma is a fine place to while away the day, exploring the food-and-drink havens of the city's old brick-building downtown center, then party into the night.

TOP TIP

The word Sonoma describes a town, a valley and a much bigger county, so always check *where,* when someone says 'we're in Sonoma.'

Get to Know a Bay Area Boomtown

Cruising the Petaluma strip

Petaluma was established in 1858 and its charming downtown area (packed with unique iron-front architecture that survived the 1906 earthquake) and lovingly preserved Victorian houses are on the National Register of Historic Places. Learn more at the free **Petaluma Historical Library &**

GETTING AROUND

Reach Petaluma from San Francisco via Golden Gate Transit *(goldengate.org)* bus or from the Larkspur Ferry on SMART rail *(sonomamarintrain.org)*, which continues north to Santa Rosa and its airport. Groome Transportation *(groometransportation.com)* buses serve Oakland Airport and SFO.

Getting around by car is easiest, and parking spots abound outside of the walkable town center. Within town, you can also ride Petaluma Transit *(transit.cityofpetaluma.net)* buses. Infrequent Sonoma County Transit *(sctransit.com)* bus 30 and 49 link to Sonoma. Buses 44 and 48 head north to Santa Rosa.

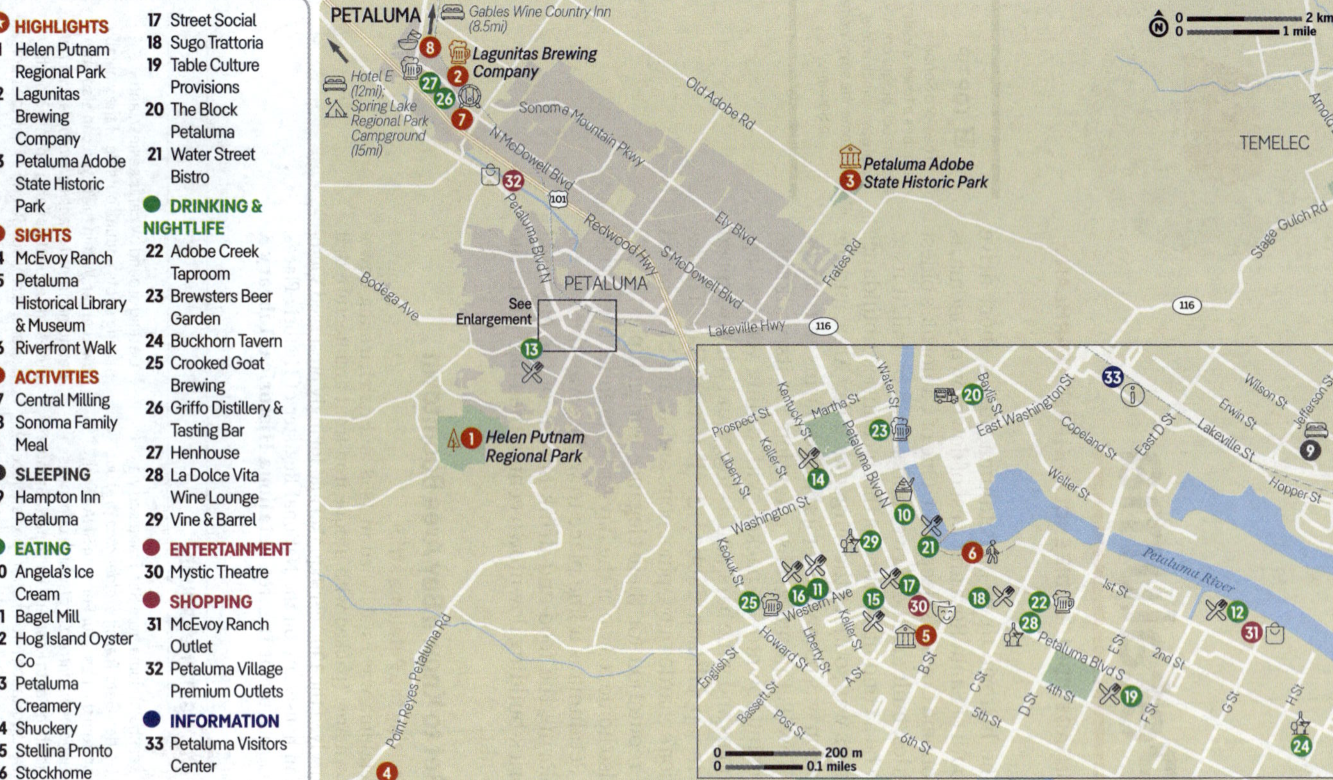
HIGHLIGHTS
1 Helen Putnam Regional Park
2 Lagunitas Brewing Company
3 Petaluma Adobe State Historic Park
SIGHTS
4 McEvoy Ranch
5 Petaluma Historical Library & Museum
6 Riverfront Walk
ACTIVITIES
7 Central Milling
8 Sonoma Family Meal
SLEEPING
9 Hampton Inn Petaluma
EATING
10 Angela's Ice Cream
11 Bagel Mill
12 Hog Island Oyster Co
13 Petaluma Creamery
14 Shuckery
15 Stellina Pronto
16 Stockhome
17 Street Social
18 Sugo Trattoria
19 Table Culture Provisions
20 The Block Petaluma
21 Water Street Bistro
DRINKING & NIGHTLIFE
22 Adobe Creek Taproom
23 Brewsters Beer Garden
24 Buckhorn Tavern
25 Crooked Goat Brewing
26 Griffo Distillery & Tasting Bar
27 Henhouse
28 La Dolce Vita Wine Lounge
29 Vine & Barrel
ENTERTAINMENT
30 Mystic Theatre
SHOPPING
31 McEvoy Ranch Outlet
32 Petaluma Village Premium Outlets
INFORMATION
33 Petaluma Visitors Center
PETALUMA
Gables Wine Country Inn (8.5mi)
Lagunitas Brewing Company
Hotel E (12mi); Spring Lake Regional Park Campground (15mi)
0 2 km
0 1 mile
Old Adobe Rd
Sonoma Mountain Pkwy
N McDowell Blvd
Petaluma Blvd N
Petaluma Adobe State Historic Park
TEMELEC
Arnold Dr
Stage Gulch Rd
Ely Blvd
Redwood Hwy
S McDowell Blvd
Frates Rd
PETALUMA
See Enlargement
Bodega Ave
Lakeville Hwy
116
101
Helen Putnam Regional Park
Point Reyes Petaluma Rd
Water St
Baylis St
East Washington St
Copeland St
East D St
Lakeville St
Wilson St
Erwin St
Jefferson St
Hopper St
Weller St
Prospect St
Kentucky St
Martha St
Petaluma Blvd N
Keller St
Liberty St
Washington St
Keokuk St
Western Ave
Howard St
English St
Bassett St
Post St
A St
B St
C St
D St
E St
F St
G St
H St
1st St
2nd St
4th St
5th St
6th St
Petaluma Blvd S
Petaluma River
0 200 m
0 0.1 miles

Museum *(petalumamuseum.com)*, housed in a spectacular neoclassical building and providing a bounty of local information and weekly walking tours between May and October.

Strolling the **riverfront walk** is a treat, though kayaks have replaced the paddleboats and steamers of yore. George Lucas' seminal, Academy Award–nominated film *American Graffiti* (1973) was primarily filmed here. The annual May festival **Salute to American Graffiti** *(americangraffiti.net)* sees 400 classic cars cruising the strip and you can watch the movie on a big screen.

Go further back in the past just 4 miles northeast of town at the historic Rancho de Petaluma, where General Vallejo planted the area's first grapevines. The 1830s residence stands today as the **Petaluma Adobe State Historic Park** *(petalumaadobe.com; adult/child $3/2 ticket includes* Sonoma State Historic Park; p192).

Sample Farm-Fresh Goodies

Petaluma's olive oil, cheese and ice cream

All the abundant farms, rolling hills and grazing cows you see in the distance produce top food and dairy. Taste olive oil southwest of town at **McEvoy Ranch** *(mcevoyranch.com; tastings from $35)*. You can also have lunch or take a ranch tour *(from $55)*. It has an **outlet** downtown with up to 40% savings on olive oils and its line of lotions and soaps.

Pop into **Petaluma Creamery** *(springhillcheese.com)* for organic local cheeses and ice cream. There's also great ice cream at **Angela's Ice Cream** *(angelasicecream.com)*, which also has other branches around the region. If you'd like to get out onto a dairy farm, check with **Petaluma Visitors Center** *(visitpetaluma.com)* to find out which rural dairies and creameries are open to the public. Shoppers looking beyond food, will also love the **Petaluma Village Premium Outlets** *(premiumoutlets.com)* north of town, and myriad art and antique shops in town.

Eating Your Way Through Petaluma

California cornucopia

Start out at one of the town's many bakeries or cafes, like **Stellina Pronto** *(stellinapronto.com)* for Italian sweet or savory pastries, or learn why sourdough is queen at The **Bagel Mill** *(thebagelmill.com)*.

Lunch at **Water Street Bistro** *(waterstreetbistropetaluma.com)*, where excellent French fare meets riverfront views. The crab chowder is to die for. Keep the seafood theme going at the

BEST PETALUMA SPOTS FOR MICROBREWS

Lagunitas Brewing Company *(lagunitas.com)*: One of the US' top breweries, a pioneer of microbrewing beloved for its IPAs and imperial stout.

Henhouse *(henhousebrewing.com)*: Palace of Brewing with a Santa Rosa location, too. Focuses on fresh brews and community experience.

Crooked Goat Brewing *(crookedgoatbrewing.com)*: Taproom for Sebastopol brewery: great line of sours, lagers, West Coast IPAs.

Adobe Creek Taproom *(adobecreekbrewing.com)*: Outpost of Novato brewery, with IPAs, lagers and stouts.

Brewsters Beer Garden *(brewsters-beergarden.com)*: Listen to live music, drink beer and eat snacks at picnic tables.

DRINKING IN PETALUMA: TOP WATERING HOLES

La Dolce Vita Wine Lounge: Settle into the golden, romantic light for myriad wines with small plates and pizzas. *3-9pm Tue-Thu, to 10pm Fri & Sat*

Vine & Barrel: Talkative owner serves wines and tapas at a wooden bar in this wine shop. *noon-5pm Sun & Wed, to 9pm Thu, to 11pm Fri & Sat*

Griffo Distillery & Tasting Bar: Stock up on spirits and quaff cocktails, sometimes with live music. *9am-5pm Mon-Wed, to 9pm Thu, 2-7pm Fri-Sun*

Buckhorn Tavern: Sidle up to the bar at Petaluma's old-school landmark bar, complete with a pool table and occasional karaoke. *10am-1am*

WELCOME TO FLATBACK

The word Petaluma comes from the Miwok words *pe'ta* (flat) and *lu'ma* (back), referring to the gentle openness of the valley behind the hill. Mexico's Comandante of Northern California, Mariano Guadalupe Vallejo, then used it for his giant Rancho Petaluma, granted to him in 1834.

In the 1830s, Mexico had won a war against Spain, and got stuck with an unwanted prize: Spain's missions in California. Mexico decreed that the land should revert to native control – but the memo was somehow mislaid by Comandante Vallejo. Settlers, including Vallejo, snapped up extensive mission lands, including ranches and vineyards. The nearby town of Vallejo, 27 miles southeast of Petaluma, retains the Comandante's name.

DENISTANGNEYJR/GETTY IMAGES

Petaluma waterfront

Shuckery *(theshuckeryca.com)*...oysters of course, paired with wine or sangria. Compare and contrast the bivalves at **Hog Island Oyster Co**'s *(hogislandoysters.com)* cool hole-in-the wall on the riverfront.

You can really mix it up at **Stockhome** *(stockhomerestaurant.com)* for Swedish-Mediterranean delights. In the evening, go classic at **Sugo Trattoria** *(sugotrattoria.com)*, or embrace a real date-night treat with the always inventive tasting menus at **Table Culture Provisions** *(tcprovision.com)*. Nip into the 100-year-old Lan Mart Building to discover what's on the menu at **Street Social** *(streetsocial.social)*, where wildly creative dishes change constantly.

For a more casual night, slide into **The Block** *(theblockpetaluma.com)*, for a rotating lineup of food trucks, including a permanent pizzeria. Gather around one of the firepits and grab a local microbrew, too.

Want to dig deeper? Take one of the cooking classes (p198) in the area.

Walk for Photo Ops of Rolling Hills

Sweeping views form Helen Putnam Regional Park

Roam the hills just outside of Petaluma at **Helen Putnam Regional Park** *(parks.sonomacounty.ca.gov; parking per car $7)* to get fantastic views of the town and the rolling hills, emerald in winter and spring, and sere beige in summer – a great spot for pics. The park is dog friendly, too.

FOR FILM BUFFS

California is the USA's moviemaking capital (**Hollywood**; p380) and a favorite for filming locations, with Petaluma standing in for **Modesto** (p201) in *American Graffiti*, Hitchcock's *The Birds* in **Bodega** (p212) and the **Griffith Observatory** (p396) featuring in *Rebel Without a Cause*, to name a few.

Catch a Play or Movie

Be a culture vulture

Petaluma has a top North Bay venue: the 1911 **Mystic Theatre** *(mystictheatre.com)*, originally built for vaudeville but now hosting live music and occasional film screenings. For theatre-lovers the **Cinnabar Theater** *(cinnabartheater.org)* company stages plays in two different venues.

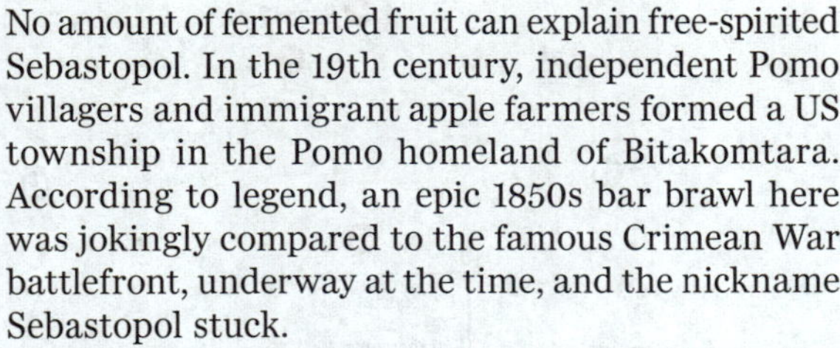

Sebastopol

WEST COUNTY HUB | ART | ECLECTIC CUISINE

No amount of fermented fruit can explain free-spirited Sebastopol. In the 19th century, independent Pomo villagers and immigrant apple farmers formed a US township in the Pomo homeland of Bitakomtara. According to legend, an epic 1850s bar brawl here was jokingly compared to the famous Crimean War battlefront, underway at the time, and the nickname Sebastopol stuck.

While the rest of Wine Country started growing grapes, Sebastopol kept growing heirloom apples, vegetables and wildflowers developed by local horticulture hero Luther Burbank. Back-to-the-land hippies brought fresh ideas to western Sonoma County, including organic farming, home beekeeping and marijuana cultivation. Now even the traffic medians are pesticide free, and the entire town is a nuclear-free zone. Anywhere you go, you can't miss the local characters, some more famous than others. Tom Waits lives on the outskirts, and Grateful Dead drummer Mickey Hart occasionally jams. Sebastopol just keeps bringing legends to life.

GETTING AROUND

Central Sebastopol is best walked or biked, and trails radiate through the countryside. Cyclists can take the paved Joe Rodota Trail to Santa Rosa and then the SMART train south (Petaluma or Larkspur Landing's Bay Ferry to San Francisco). Sonoma County Transit *(sctransit.com)* buses include a free local shuttle (Route 24). Central Sebastopol is a great walking town.

TOP TIP

Sebastopol Area Chamber of Commerce & Visitors Center *(sebastopol.org)* has maps and information. Buy *Sebastopol Walks* by Richard Nichols for town walks and country rides and rambles on the Joe Rodota Trail, through bird-watchers' paradise wetland **Laguna de Santa Rosa** – its learning center *(lagunafoundation.org)* hosts exhibits and activities – and beyond.

Fantastical Sculptures, Local Creativity & Vintage Wares

Art for art's sake

A cow rides a tractor, a rocket blasts off the lawn and a dinosaur grabs a red convertible for lunch: it's all happening on **Florence Ave**, in dozens of sculptures by **Patrick Amiot** *(patrickamiot.com)* which are painted by Brigitte Laurent and made for neighbors' yards from recycled junk. You'll spot plenty more throughout the county, and you can order pieces at their **Big Times Art Studio**.

Skip the airport souvenirs and opt for art instead...around the corner at **Sebastopol Center for the Arts** *(sebarts.org; admission free)*, see the world from the perspective of Sonoma County's boundary-pushing artists, working in media from

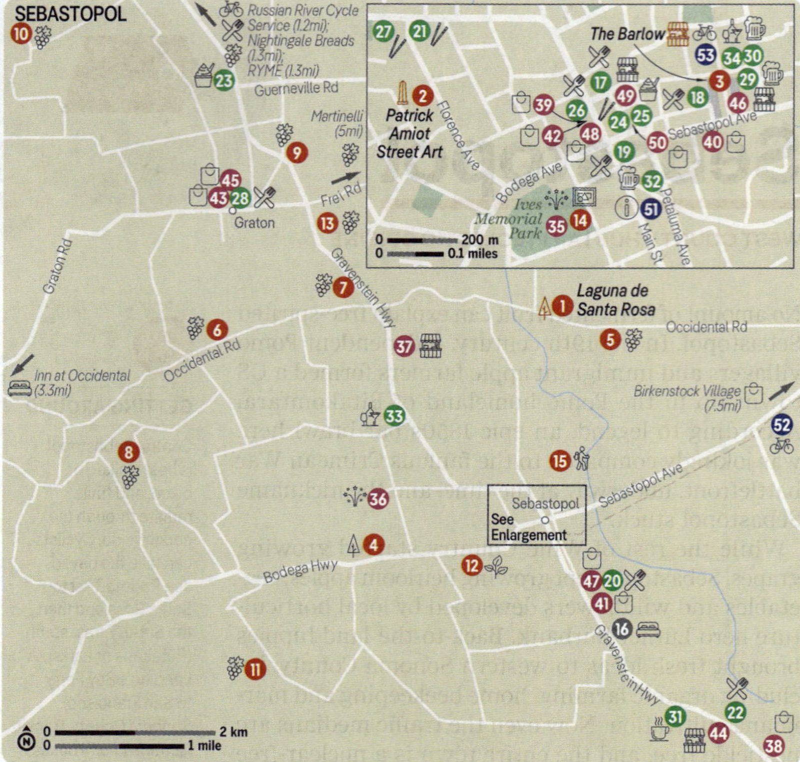

HIGHLIGHTS
1 Laguna de Santa Rosa
2 Patrick Amiot Street Art
3 The Barlow

SIGHTS
4 Atascadero Creek Ecological Reserve
5 Balletto
6 Char Vale
7 Emeritus
8 Freeman
9 Furthermore Wines
10 Iron Horse Vineyards
11 Littorai
12 Luther Burbank's Gold Ridge Experiment Farm
13 Merry Edwards
14 Sebastopol Center for the Arts

ACTIVITIES
15 West County Regional Trail

SLEEPING
16 Fairfield Inn & Suites

EATING
17 Cozy Plum
18 Fern Bar
19 Goldfinch
20 Incas Peruvian Cuisine
21 Khom Loi
22 La Bodega Kitchen
23 Mom's Apple Pie
24 Ramen Gaijin
25 Screamin' Mimi's
26 Sebastopol Cookie Co
27 Sushi Tozai
28 Willow Wood Market Cafe

DRINKING & NIGHTLIFE
29 Crooked Goat Brewing
30 Golden State Cider Taproom
31 Hardcore Espresso
32 Hopmonk Tavern
33 Horse & Plow
34 Region

ENTERTAINMENT
35 Apple Blossom Festival
36 Gravenstein Apple Fair

SHOPPING
37 Andy's Produce
38 Antique Society
39 Artisana
40 Attico
41 Beekind
42 Copperfield's Books
43 Graton Gallery
44 Midgley's Country Flea Market
45 Mr Ryder & Co Art & Antiques
46 Sebastopol Community Market
47 Solful
48 Sumbody
49 Sunday Organic Farmers Market
50 Toyworks

INFORMATION
51 Sebastopol Area Chamber of Commerce & Visitors Center

TRANSPORTATION
52 Joe Rodota Trail
53 Revel Cycles

fiber arts to glass and plain ol' paint (used to glorious effect). It organizes excellent open-studio weekends countywide, with **Sonoma County Art Trails** *(sonomacountyarttrails.org)*, in October, and **Art at the Source** *(artatthesource.org)*, in June.

Charming central Sebastopol is also dotted with creative shops, from **Artisana** *(artisanafunctionalart.com)* with hand-hewn housewares and jewelry; **BeeKind** *(beekind.com)* for all things bee-based; and **Toyworks** *(sonomatoyworks.com)*, any tot's dreamscape. At **Sumbody** *(sumbody.com)*, mushrooms, goats' milk and chocolate are ingredients in ecofriendly, small-batch bath products. Feed your head at independent **Copperfield's Books** *(copperfieldsbooks.com)*.

Browse antique and vintage stores like **Attico** *(attico store.com)* and macro-collective **Antique Society** *(instagram .com/antiquesociety.sebastopol)*, and on Sundays search for treasures at sprawling **Midgley's Country Flea Market** *(mfleamarket.com)*.

In the hamlet of **Graton**, 4 miles to the north, swing by **Graton Gallery** *(gratongallery.net)* and **Mr Ryder & Co Art & Antiques** *(facebook.com/MrRyderAntiques)* next door to round it all out.

Apples, Daisies & Good Times

Hearty horticulture and hard cider

Sebastopol had a reputation for boozy shenanigans long before Sonoma County's wine industry took off, because the heirloom-apple orchards that thrived here weren't originally intended for roadside bakery **Mom's Apple Pie** *(momsapplepieusa.com)*. They were used to make hard cider – a tradition upheld today at **Hopmonk Tavern** *(hopmonk.com)* and **Horse & Plow** *(horse andplow.com)* tasting room, and celebrated twice annually at the **Apple Blossom Festival** *(appleblossomfest.com)* in April and **Gravenstein Apple Fair** *(gravensteinapplefair.com)* in August.

The old apple cannery on the edge of Sebastopol was repurposed into **The Barlow** *(thebarlow.net)*, home to Sebastopol's upstart makers, including **Golden State Cider Taproom** *(drinkgoldenstate.com)*, celebrated **Crooked Goat Brewing** *(crookedgoatbrewing.com)*, **Region** *(drinkregion.com)* tasting room, as well as several wineries.

About 150 years ago, horticulturalist Luther Burbank cultivated fruit trees and daisies (like popular Shasta daisies, the 1901 hybrid of flowers from three continents) at **Luther Burbank's Gold Ridge Experiment Farm** *(wschs.org/farm; admission free)*, which is open to the public. You can also reserve to taste namesake Gold Ridge Farms' organic apple and olive-oil products.

Get to Know West County Winemakers

Pinots, chardonnays and more

In the 1970s, while chef Alice Waters established California cuisine, **Merry Edwards** *(merryedwards.com; tastings from $45)* was championing California wine from her vineyard – becoming the first woman in Napa's Winemakers' Hall of Fame while

BEST WAYS TO GO LOCAL

Sonoma County Farm Trails: Family-friendly farms, pick-your-own orchards, some of the best organic plant nurseries. *farmtrails.org*

Sunday Organic Farmers Market: Live music in town square with vats of organic kombucha, small-batch elderberry syrup and dried maitake-mushroom jerky. *sebastopol farmersmarket.org*

Sebastopol Community Market & **Andy's Produce:** Admire the fruits of West County's labor at these food markets. *cmnaturalfoods.com; andysproduce.com*

Solful *(solful.com)*: Meet Your Pot Farmer events at Sebastopol's cannabis dispensary.

Birkenstock Village: Santa Rosa's family-owned shoe store. *birkenstock village.com*

HOMEGROWN BOUNTY

Nicholas Izzarelli, Sebastopol native and owner-operator of **Goldfinch** tells us his favorite ways to eat local. *goldfinchsebastopol.com*

Check out a farmers market or winery (**Iron Horse** is my go-to), and meet incredibly talented and hardworking people showcasing what this county has to offer. As for restaurants, I LOVE **Terrapin Creek** (p212) in Bodega Bay. Every dish is thoughtful, delicious and perfectly executed. **Khom Loi** offers locally sourced dishes with amazing Thai street-food flavors. On the coast, stop by **Hog Island Oyster Co** or **The Marshall Store** for the freshest seafood, beautiful scenery and chill Sonoma County vibes.

putting California pinots on the map. Just north on Hwy 116 at **Furthermore Wines** *(furthermorewines.com; tastings from $35)*, start with pinot, break for *bocce* and live music, then return to the urgent matter of pinot, or better yet, its mysterious rosé of pinot noir.

Redwoods encircle **Freeman** vineyards *(freemanwinery.com; tastings $40)*, trapping mists that winemaker/founder Akiko Freeman captures in cool-climate pinots and chardonnays. Vineyards are actually a minority crop on **Littorai** *(littorai.com; tastings from $70)*, a 30-acre biodynamic estate, where bees, birds and beneficial insects create an integrated ecosystem.

Roll along pastoral Green Valley Rd – surrounded by rolling farmland, apple orchards and vineyards, plus the occasional Shetland pony – to raise a toast at **Iron Horse Vineyards** *(ironhorsevineyards.com; tastings from $35)* with sparkling wines that have been served at White House inaugurations.

Sebastopol is ringed by vineyards, so you can just keep going, with **Emeritus** *(emeritusvineyards.com; tastings from $40)*, **Balletto** *(ballettovineyards.com; tastings from $20)* and **Char Vale** *(charvalewinery.com; tastings from $28)* and if space is available, walk-ins are welcome.

EATING IN SEBASTOPOL: OUR PICKS

Goldfinch: Delectable locally sourced fare with killer cocktails and golden atmosphere. *11.30am-8.30pm Wed-Sun, from 5pm Mon & Tue* $$$

Ramen Gaijin: Upbeat mood fueled by (spicy!) pork-belly ramen, (tasty!) short ribs and cocktails (fun!). Book ahead. *noon-9pm Tue-Sat* $$

Fern Bar: Come for '70s atmosphere, with stained-glass and amber lighting – stay for shared plates. *4-9pm Mon-Thu, 11am-10pm Fri-Sun* $$

La Bodega Kitchen: Inspired vegan and vegetarian food paired with wine from the adjoining wine store. *4-9pm Thu-Mon* $$

Incas Peruvian Cuisine: Savory dishes, from chicken stew to braised lamb shank. *11.30am-9pm Mon-Sat, noon-8pm Sun* $$

Sushi Tozai: Enjoy the catch off the Pacific coast with delicious sushi. Cheerful family-run spot. *5-9pm Tue-Sun* $$

Cozy Plum: Delicious vegan wraps, bowls, burgers, sandwiches and tacos. Large portions and quick service. *11am-8pm* $$

Willow Wood Market Cafe: In Graton: comfort food, champagne cocktails. *9am-8pm Mon-Sat, to 3pm Sun* $$

DIANE N ENNIS/SHUTTERSTOCK

Sebastopol vineyard

Cycle West County Trails

Peddle through orchards and vineyards

What better way to experience the scenery than to peddle the region's bike trails through vineyards, orchards and wetlands? The mostly paved 5.5-mile **West County Regional Trail** *(parks.sonomacounty.ca.gov)* is protected from cars most of the way, and links Sebastopol, Graton and Forestville with farm and pasture views, and a nice elevated boardwalk north of Graton that passes through the **Atascadero Creek Ecological Reserve** *(wildlife.ca.gov; free)*. Look online for multiple access points. This track connects to rails-to-trails greenway **Joe Rodota Trail** *(parks.sonomacounty.ca.gov)* to Santa Rosa.

Rent bikes and e-bikes in Sebastopol at **Revel Cycles** *(revelcycles.com; 2 hours bike/e-bike $40/60)* or in Forestville at **Russian River Cycle Service** *(russianrivercycles.com; half-/full-day rental from $35/45)*, at the head of the trail.

FORESTVILLE'S BEST STOPS

The main drag of little **Forestville**, between Sebastopol and the Russian River, is lined with old-timey storefronts.

Nightingale Breads: The aroma of Jessie Frost's organic breads changes traffic patterns. Stop for a bite. *nightingalebreads.com*

RYME: Beloved tasting room *(tastings $35)*: a low-key, more affordable way to sample local wines. *rymecellars.com*

Martinelli: Quaint red barn on River Rd where the family-owned winery *(tastings from $25)* has been bucking convention since 1887, when a young Tuscan winemaker eloped to California to grow grapes on notoriously steep, rocky Jackass Hill. Award-winning zinfandels, pinots and muscat. *martinelliwinery.com*

EATING & DRINKING IN SEBASTOPOL: INDIE FOODS & SWEET TREATS

The Barlow (p205): Two-acre village of indie food producers, ice creamers, artists, winemakers, coffee roasters and distillers. *hours and prices vary*

Screamin' Mimi's: Luscious homemade ice cream served by the ounce. Choose from a seasonal lineup of flavors. *11am-9.30pm Sun-Thu, to 10pm Fri & Sat* $

Sebastopol Cookie Co: Indie bakery making restorative triple-chocolate cookies, snickerdoodles and more. *8.30am-5pm Tue-Sat, 9am-3pm Sun* $

Hardcore Espresso: Shambolic spot with quirky art around gardens and patios and crammed inside, plus top coffee and baked goods. *5.30am-5.30pm* $

Beyond Sebastopol

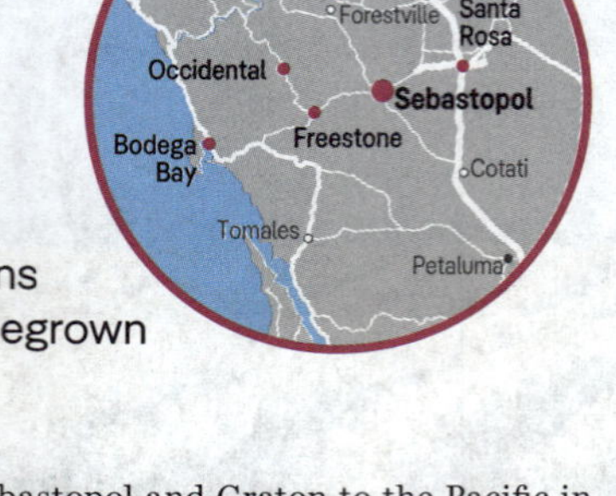

Trace valleys through forested mountains out to the Pacific Coast, reveling in homegrown fare and easygoing settlements.

Hills undulate from Sebastopol and Graton to the Pacific in the west and up to the Russian River in the north, the valleys golden in summer. In winter and spring, rain-greened pastures rise to the redwood- and oak-topped hills. Vineyards carve up the acreage, as do historic communes and quintessential Northern California hamlets.

World-class wineries, a nationally famous day spa, and excellent creameries, bakeries and restaurants spice up the mix. So too do heartfelt gatherings like Occidental's farmers market, where live music fills the night sky as folks from the hills around come down and say hi.

This is a region in which to kick back, drop out and see what happens.

Santa Rosa

TIME FROM SEBASTOPOL: **20 MINS**

Get to know the downtown

Wine Country's biggest city, **Santa Rosa** *(visitsantarosa.com)* is modern-day Americana, with cottage rose gardens, hikers trekking **Trione-Annadel State Park** *(parks.ca.gov; admission free)* and life booming in the culturally Latinx **Roseland** neighborhood.

GETTING AROUND

A vehicle is the easiest way to get around outside of Sebastopol and Santa Rosa – buses, while they do run in the countryside, are infrequent. Seasoned cyclists ply country lanes – be alert whether you're on two wheels or four. Sonoma County Transit *(sctransit.com)* buses radiate out from Santa Rosa. Santa Rosa City Bus *(srcitybus.org)* runs an extensive network of local buses in that city (using a Bay Area–wide Clipper Card). **Santa Rosa Transit Mall** is a regional hub. Golden Gate Transit *(goldengate.org)* buses run between San Francisco and Santa Rosa. Mendocino Transit *(mendocinotransit.org)* bus 95 goes from Santa Rosa to Bodega Bay and up the coast to Pt Arena. Bus 65 goes north to Windsor and beyond. SMART train *(sonomamarintrain.org)* goes between Sonoma County Airport in the north, via Santa Rosa and Petaluma, south to Larkspur and the SF Ferry system.

Groome Transportation *(groometransportation.com)* buses shuttle between Sonoma County Airport, Santa Rosa, and San Francisco and Oakland airports.

JANE TYSKA/MEDIANEWS GROUP/THE MERCURY NEWS VIA GETTY IMAGES

Russian River Brewing Co

The main heart and shopping stretch is **4th St** along central **Old Courthouse Sq**. The city makes international news each year when **Russian River Brewing Co** *(russianriverbrewing.com)* releases its brilliantly bitter double IPA Pliny the Elder, which prompts campouts at the door, and remains a place of pilgrimage for craft-beer lovers year-round.

Walk 4th St to reemerge across the freeway at historic **Railroad Sq** and take in the tree-shaded, mural-lined streets of the **South A Street Art District**, stopping and smelling the flowers – many are fragrant varietals; like the Santa Rosa, plum developed for delight, utility and sustainability just up the street at **Luther Burbank Home & Gardens** *(lutherburbank.org; grounds free, tour adult/child $12/free)*. This is where pioneering horticulturist Luther Burbank (1849–1926) cultivated 800 hybrid plant species over 50 years.

To learn more, take a trip through Sonoma County's past, present and future in the **Museum of Sonoma County** *(museumsc.org; 11am-5pm Wed-Sun)* in side-by-side history and art museums.

Take an international food tour

Santa Rosa is a world tour in excellent eats – from homemade dim sum at **Hang Ah** *(hangahdimsum.com)* to Ethiopian at **Abyssinia** *(my-abyssinia.com)*, French pâtisserie and bread at **Goguette** *(goguettebread.com)* and **Pascaline** *(pascalinebistro.com)*, a favorite local hangout for delicate pastries and bistro-style brunch.

Santa Rosa is awash with good Mexican restaurants, especially around the Roseland area on Sebastopol Rd. Sample widely at **Mitote Food Park** *(mitotefoodpark.com)*, where taco trucks actually make specialties from all over Mexico alongside a bar. Markets like **Lola's** *(lolasmarkets.com)* also have great taqueria counters.

Across the street, **O Sushi** *(santarosaosushi.com)* is one of our favorites for Japanese. Or try **Sushi Rosa** *(sushirosa.com)* by Old Courthouse Sq.

SONOMA COUNTY'S FAIRS

Sonoma County Fair: Monster truck rallies, the NorCal BrewFest, Elvis Impersonation Contest, World Championship Grape Stomp, a Hall of Flowers, a petting zoo: this is a 10-day festival of Americana. Concerts are free with admission. In August. *sonomacountyfair.com*

Sonoma Harvest Fair: America's biggest and arguably toughest wine competition – 1000 wines judged blind, by winemakers, sommeliers and critics – see if you agree with Double Gold winners, feast on award-winning food. In October. *harvestfair.org*

Wine Road Barrel Tasting: In March, wineries from Alexander Valley to Russian River throw open wine-cave doors to sample from the barrel. *wineroad.com*

BEST SANTA ROSA BREWERIES

Russian River Brewing Co: World-famous releases of IPA Pliny the Elder. Sip triple-IPA Pliny the Younger with pizza. *russianriverbrewing.com*

Cooperage Brewing Company: Barrel-aged sours, stouts and more. *cooperagebrewing.com*

Iron Ox Brewing Company: IPAs, spiked seltzers and sodas and hop water, beer cocktails, food truck. *ironoxbeer.com*

Shady Oak Brewing: Family-owned, making sour ales and IPAs, often with wild yeast and regional ingredients. *shadyoakbrewing.com*

Henhouse Brewing: Tap-masters explain the brews; another location in Petaluma. *henhousebrewing.com*

Barley & Bine Beer Cafe: Windsor's brewpub has 38 taps of Cali goodness. *barleybinebeercafe.com*

DAVIDGREITZER/GETTY IMAGES

Wild Flour Bread bakery

'Good grief, Charlie Brown!'

Beloved worldwide, the *Peanuts* comic strip was drawn in Santa Rosa by cartoonist Charles M Schulz. If you fly into **Charles M Schulz Sonoma County Airport**, you can take your pic with Snoopy in the terminal. Keep an eye out for giant fiberglass statues all over the city, part of the **Peanuts on Parade** celebration of the characters.

The wonderful-for-all-ages **Charles M Schulz Museum** *(schulzmuseum.org; adult/child $12/5)* follows the journey of Snoopy, Charlie Brown, Lucy and the gang from their 1950 introduction to last laughs in 2000. Downstairs are original Schulz drawings. Upstairs are artists' tributes to *Peanuts*, plus an exacting recreation of Schulz' art studio: markers on a reclaimed-wood desk and a video of Schulz drawing – a fluid poem in ink. Schulz was originally from Minnesota, and so built an **ice rink** *(snoopyshomeice.com)* on-site, too. Check the website for public skating hours and prices.

Freestone

TIME FROM SEBASTOPOL: **15 MINS**

Escape to a unique day spa

From the instant you turn onto **Bohemian Hwy** at Freestone, you're in for a wild ride. Freestone is a former stagecoach stop with a current population of 32, yet the road is

EATING & DRINKING IN SANTA ROSA: SNACKS, CAFES & BARS

Bird & the Bottle: When you're not sure what you're craving, try a little bit of everything... from grilled lamb meatballs to duck confit tacos. *11.30am-9pm* $$$

Criminal Baking Co: Join the line for triple-cheese knishes, deep-dish quiches, quinoa salad bowls, and toasted-rye chocolate-chip cookies. *7.30am-3pm* $

Espressioso's Coffee: Conveniently located on 4th St with ethically sourced coffee roasted by the owners and spot-on coffee drinks. *6am-6pm Tue-Sun* $

Willi's Wine Bar: Grab a spot on the heated patio or sociable bar for wine-tasting, comparing Sonoma and international wines, and pair with tapas. *11.30am-9pm* $$$

lined with cars. People arrive from far and wide to nibble on planet-sized sticky buns at **Wild Flour Bread** *(wildflourbread.com)* and get buried up to their necks in cedar chips – a Japanese tradition – at **Osmosis Day Spa** *(osmosis.com)*. The spa ritual here begins with organic tea in the bonsai garden, then proceeds to a redwood tub full of soft, fermenting cedar and rice bran – the woodsy aroma and dry-enzyme action will warm you to the bone. Up until recently, it's been the only cedar bath in North America (the other is in Lake Tahoe), and attracts celebs and hippies alike.

FOR ART LOVERS

In addition to reveling in the *Peanuts* museum or local winery Paradise Ridge, where outdoor sculptures thrill on a gorgeous hillside, experience more art at **San Francisco's downtown museums** (p59).

Occidental

TIME FROM SEBASTOPOL: **20–30 MINS**

Farmers market party and offbeat treats

Occidental (population 1126) is the surprising mountaintop lumber town that time forgot and trees reconquered – with help from visionary ecologists and back-to-the-land hippies. The power of countercultural thinking is celebrated when partying breaks out mid-May to October at the Thursday **Occidental Community Farmers Market** *(occidentalcommunity farmersmarket.com)*. Crafts, flowers, cheese, organic produce, mushrooms and giant pans of Pacific seafood paella fill the street, and musicians light up the evening as friends and family mingle. Grab great draft brews at **Altamont General Store** *(altamontgeneralstore.com)* and sit curbside and watch the world go by, or combine family-style epic ravioli with local vintages at the **Union Hotel** *(unionhoteloccidental.com)*.

Drop by **Bohème Wines Cellar Door** *(bohemewines.com)* for wine tasting. At **Hinterland & Neon Raspberry** *(neonraspberry.com)* everything is recycled, organic and/or women-made with punk attitude.

Check the schedule at **Occidental Center For the Arts** *(occidentalcenterforthearts.org)* to keep it all going.

Soar through the trees

North of Occidental, get your adrenaline going on a zipline through the redwoods at **Sonoma Zipline Adventures** *(sonomacanopytours.com; zipline from $109)*. Afterwards you can wind down the hill to reach the Russian River at Monte Rio.

Cruise from redwoods to the wide-open ocean

Sonoma County's most memorable drive may not be through the grapes (though Westside Rd is a contender; see p219), but along these 10 miles of winding byway from Occidental to the ocean. It's best in the late morning, when fog lifts and sun filters through the trees.

First, reach the ridgeline on **Coleman Valley Rd**, head left onto Joy Rd and right onto Fitzpatrick Lane to find a hidden glory: the **Grove of the Old Trees** *(landpaths.org)*. Picnic or stroll the easy 1-mile loop trail.

Back on Coleman Valley Rd, pass gnarled oaks and craggy rocks to ascend 1000ft, until the vast blue Pacific unfurls

BEST SONOMA COAST STATE PARK WALKS

Bodega Head: This 265ft promontory is great for whale-watching (sometimes docents dot the trail for explanations).

Pomo Canyon Red Hill Trail: One of Greater Bay Area's premier trails from Pomo Canyon up over coastal hills to Shell Beach (6.5 miles walked as a loop).

Shell Beach: Boardwalk and trail lead to a stretch perfect for tide-pooling and beachcombing.

Kortum Trail: This 3.75-mile trail connects **Wright's Beach** to **Blind Beach** just south of Goat Rock Beach.

Goat Rock Beach: Walk to the harbor seals lazing at mouth of the Russian River. Rock archway offshore.

Salmon Creek Beach: Situated around a lagoon; 2 miles of hiking, good waves for surfing.

at your feet. The road ends at coastal Hwy 1, where you can explore Sonoma Coast State Park and eat oysters in serene **Valley Ford**.

Bodega Bay

TIME FROM SEBASTOPOL: **30 MINS**

Sonoma Coast State Park

Stretching 16 miles north from **Bodega Head** to **Vista Trail**, four miles north of Jenner, the glorious **Sonoma Coast State Park** *(parks.ca.gov)* is actually a series of beaches separated by beautiful rocky headlands. Some are tiny, hidden in little coves, while others stretch wide. Most are connected by hiking trails winding along the bluffs. Bring your camera – the views are stunning, with rock outcrops, mini islands, inlets and crashing waves.

During summer, morning fog generally burns off by midday. Exploring this area makes an excellent daylong adventure, but facilities are minimal, so bring water, food and sun protection, as well as a charged cell phone (though signal is spotty), in case of emergency. Surf is often too treacherous to wade through, so keep a close eye on children.

EATING IN BODEGA BAY: SEAFOOD FORWARD

Spud Point Crab Company: Crab shack serving salty-sweet crab sandwiches and real clam chowder (which wins local culinary prizes). *hours vary* $$

Terrapin Creek Cafe & Restaurant: Elegant restaurant repping the slow-food movement. Locally sourced dishes lean seafood. *4.30-8.30pm Thu-Mon* $$$

Fishetarian: This always-reliable fish market and deli features a deck near the water and a seafood menu (from oysters and ceviche to fish sandwiches). *11am-8pm* $$

Gourmet Au Bay: Head to the spacious deck to enjoy a salty breeze with your snacks at this sophisticated wine bar. *noon-6pm Thu-Sun, to 3pm Mon* $$

VENTU PHOTO/SHUTTERSTOCK

Bodega Bay

THE BIRDS

Bodega Bay is a pearl in a string of sleepy fishing towns that line the North Coast and was the setting of Alfred Hitchcock's terrifying 1963 avian horror flick *The Birds*. Although special effects radically altered the actual layout of the town, you still get a good feel for the supposed site of the farm owned by Mitch Brenner (played by Rod Taylor). The once-cozy **Tides Wharf & Restaurant**, where much havoc occurs, is still there but is now a restaurant complex. Venture 5 miles inland to the tiny town of **Bodega** and you'll find two icons from the film: **Potter Schoolhouse** and **St Teresa of Avila Church**. Both stand just as they did in the movie – a crow overhead may make the hair rise on your neck.

Fishing, whale-watching & marine life

Bodega Bay's downtown, houses, restaurants, hotels and shops, along busy Hwy 1, is not made for strolling. But on the west side, a peninsula resembling a crooked finger juts out to sea at Bodega Head, forming the entrance to **Bodega Harbor**, one of the North Bay's premier fishing and crabbing spots. This is your chance to get out and try your hand at catching ling cod, rock cod, king salmon and Dungeness crab. We like **Reel Magic Sport Fishing Charters** *(reelmagicsportfishing charters.net)* and **Bodega Bay Sportfishing Center** *(bodegabaysportfishing.com)*. You can also go whale-watching from here with **Bodega Bay Whale Charters** *(bodegabay whalecharters.com)*.

Celebrate it all at **Bodega Bay Fishermen's Festival** *(bbfishfest.org)* in May.

If you want to get into the water, easygoing one-stop-shop **Bodega Bay Surf Shack** *(bodegabaysurf.com)* has all kinds of equipment rentals, including SUPs and kayaks, lessons and good local information. It also rents bikes for landlubbers.

Also on the peninsula, **Bodega Marine Laboratory & Reserve** *(marinescience.ucdavis.edu)*, run by UC Davis, has docent-led tours on Friday afternoons (reserve).

EATING AROUND OCCIDENTAL: OUR PICKS

Hazel (Occidental): Join a fabulous dinner party – wine flows and *oohs!* erupt as dishes arrive bubbling from wood-fired ovens. *5-9pm Tue-Sun* $$$

Howard Station Cafe (Occidental): Since the 1870s, Howard's has restored travelers and ranchers with reliable, generous, comforting brunches. *7.30am-2pm* $

Rocker's Roadhouse (Valley Ford): Oyster and New Orleans-style cooking. Also has a spot in Bodega Bay (Rocker Oysterfeller's). *11am-8pm, from 10am Sun* $$

Farmhouse Inn (Forestville): The region's Michelin-starred River Rd gourmet landmark, with refined, locally raised organics. *5.30-8.30pm Thu-Mon* $$$

CRUISING THE SONOMA COUNTY COAST TO MENDOCINO

Celebrate an uninterrupted stretch of coastal highway that skirts rocky shores, secluded coves and wind-sculpted beaches.

START	END	LENGTH
Bodega Bay	Mendocino	110 miles; 5 hrs

Start alongside the fishing fleets of ❶ **Bodega Bay**, cruising through the wild Pacific coast scenery of Sonoma County State Park (p212) until you reach the seal colony at the mouth of the Russian River at Goat Rock in ❷ **Jenner**. Continuing north, stretch your legs again at **Jenner Headlands Preserve** or continue straight to ❸ **Fort Ross State Historic Park**, a reconstruction of a 19th-century Russian fur-trading fort.

From there, the road twists past the free ❹ **Kruse Rhododendron State Natural Reserve** rhododendron groves. One of the best reasons to spend the night around these parts is ❺ **Salt Point State Park**, a 6000-acre stunner with sandstone cliffs dropping into a kelp-strewn sea and hiking trails crisscrossing windswept prairies and wooded hills.

Weather-beaten but ritzy private community ❻ **Sea Ranch** lines an ocean bluff with five beaches open to the public. Next up, ❼ **Gualala** is a hub for weekend getaways, with its **arts center**. Another half-hour up the coast, climb ❽ **Point Arena Lighthouse**, which has guarded the windy point since 1908. Slip a little further north to ❾ **Elk**, a hamlet famous for clifftop views of towering rock formations. Overnight in ❿ **Mendocino**.

Look for the unique, redwood swirl of **Sea Ranch Chapel**. You can pop in from dawn to dusk.

At Sea Ranch, **Stengel Beach** has a large, free parking lot and a short cypress-lined trail to a wooden staircase to the beach.

The road plunges down a canyon to **Russian Gulch State Beach**, a windswept arc of creamy sand, then switchbacks up to the bluff-top.

Russian River Valley

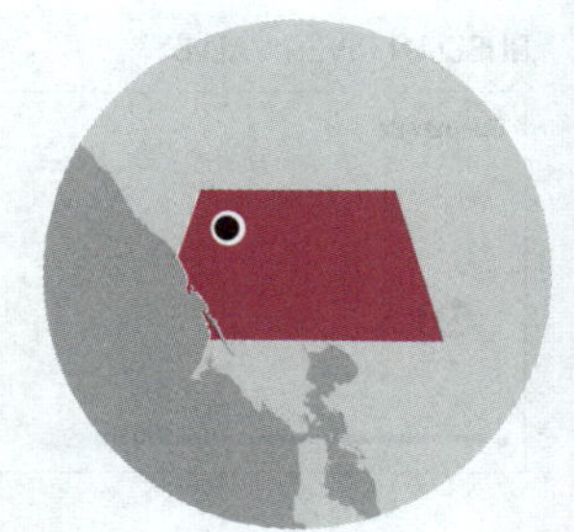

RIVER FLOATS | MISTY WINES | REDWOOD FORESTS

The Russian River has long been a good-time summer-weekend destination for Northern Californians who come to canoe, hike redwood forests, BBQ, taste wine and live life at a lazy pace.

Though the source of the Russian River is north in Ukiah, and the valley begins outside of Healdsburg, when locals talk about hitting 'The River,' they mean the wide stretch starting around lively Guerneville, winding past mellow Monte Rio and Duncans Mills, and flowing into the Pacific at Jenner. For thousands of years, Indigenous Pomo people called this river on the east side of their homelands the Ashokawna ('eastern water'). But once Russians established Fort Ross as a trading post for bear pelts, it became known as the Russian River.

Lately, Russian River Valley vineyards have taken their place among California's important wine appellations, especially for cold-weather grapes like pinot noir. Easy days floating on the river call for toasts, ably supplied by local wineries and Sonoma County microbreweries.

TOP TIP

Get top-tier year-round guided birding tours throughout the region with Teresa and Miles Tuffli whose website *(imbirdingrightnow.com)* is a font of info on the abundant birds of the river. For fishing info and supplies, visit **King's Sport & Tackle** *(kingsrussianriver.com)*. The **Russian River Visitor Center** *(russianriver.com)* provides additional insights in Guerneville.

Happening Town with LGBTQ+ Flair

Playing in Guerneville

The Russian River's biggest vacation spot, **Guerneville** (pronounced *GURN*-vill) only has about 4700 residents, but almost doubles in size on hot summer weekends, when folks come from

GETTING AROUND

West County's winding roads get confusing and there's limited cell-phone service – carry a proper map or download your maps for offline use. The couple of Sonoma County Transit *(sctransit.com)* buses that serve the area (lines 20 from Santa Rosa to Sebastopol, Forestville and the Russian River area as far as Monte Rio; and 28 from Guerneville to Occidental) are very infrequent. On summer weekends and holidays, to avoid parking nightmares take the **Regional Parks River Shuttle** *(parks.sonomacounty.ca.gov; all-day ticket adult/child $5/free)* from El Molino High School in Forestville; it can drop you at Steelhead Beach and pick you up at Sunset Beach if you float down the river (p217).

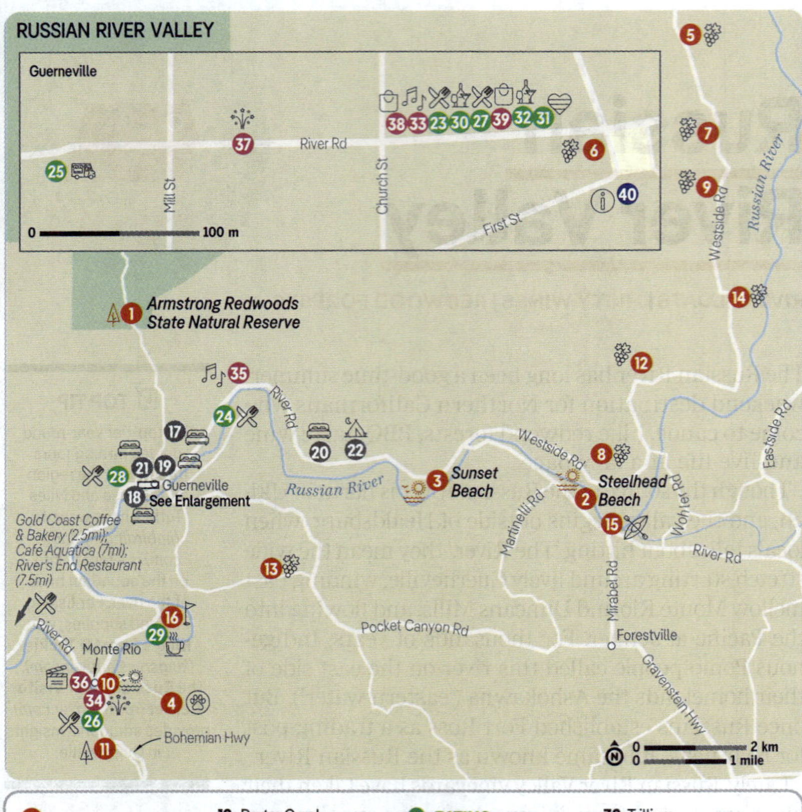

HIGHLIGHTS
1 Armstrong Redwoods State Natural Reserve
2 Steelhead Beach
3 Sunset Beach

SIGHTS
4 Bohemian Grove
5 De La Montanya
6 Equality Vines
7 Flowers
8 Gary Farrell
9 MacRostie
10 Monte Rio Beach
11 Monte Rio Redwoods Regional Park & Open Space Preserve
12 Porter Creek
13 Porter-Bass
14 Rochioli Winery

ACTIVITIES
15 Burke's Canoe Trips
see 26 Creekside Park Skate Park
16 Northwood Golf Club

SLEEPING
17 Boon Hotel + Spa
18 Dawn Ranch
19 Highlands Resort
20 Mine + Farm
21 R3 Hotel
22 Schoolhouse Canyon Campground

EATING
23 Boon Eat + Drink
24 Farmhand
25 Guerneville Taco Truck
26 Lightwave Coffee & Kitchen
see 16 Northwood Restaurant
27 Piknik Town Market
28 Saucy Mama's

DRINKING & NIGHTLIFE
29 Bia Cafe
30 El Barrio
31 Rainbow Cattle Company
32 Trillium

ENTERTAINMENT
33 Main Street Bistro
34 Monte Rio Variety Show
35 Rio Nido Roadhouse
36 Rio Theatre
37 Russian River Pride

SHOPPING
38 Guerneville Bank Club
39 King's Sport & Tackle

INFORMATION
40 Russian River Chamber of Commerce & Visitors Center

all over to hike redwoods, float the river and hammer cocktails poolside. For decades it has been one of the Bay Area's most gay-flavored getaways, and welcomes you to let your hair down and be yourself.

This town is a good time had by all since the 1870s, and it hasn't lost its honky-tonk reputation yet. Just ask burly gay partiers in town in late July and early August for **Lazy Bear Week** *(lazybearweek.org)*, sun-worshiping lesbians in May on

Women's Weekend *(womensweekendrussianriver.com)* and assorted San Francisco scenesters along for the ride. **Russian River Pride** *(russianriverpride.org)* kicks off in September.

Downtown Guerneville is a year-round destination, though, with cafes, indie-maker boutiques, fun casual dining and straight-friendly gay bars like **Rainbow Cattle Company** *(queersteer.com)*, the Guerneville go-to for decades. For a most sedate experience, try wine tasting for a cause at **Equality Vines** *(equalityvines.com; tastings $35)* where proceeds from the wines go toward organizations committed to equality for all.

Gay resorts (which are also typically straight-friendly) include Highlands Resort (p227) and R3 (p227), while the historic Fife's Resort is now Dawn Ranch (p227).

Floating or Paddling Down the River

Goof off with river otters

During summer and fall the absolute best thing to do on the Russian River is to float down it, on a tube or whatever inflatable you can find, with some friends and a flask in hand, passing posing herons. It'll cost you nothing (other than the price of your floaty).

Guerneville's **Johnson's Beach** *(johnsonsbeach.com; parking $10, tube/kayak/canoe rental per day $10/55/65)* is the epicenter of inner tubes, paddleboat rentals and beach concessions, with a campground and cabins to boot. There's also good river access east of Guerneville at **Sunset Beach** *(sonoma-county.org; day-use $12)*, plus sandy beaches and swimming holes downstream toward **Monte Rio Beach** *(mrrpd.org; canoe rental hr/½-day/day $30/45/65)*. You can also do a more organized float with **Burke's Canoe Trips** *(burkescanoetrips.com; canoe rental incl shuttle $95)*.

On summer weekends and holidays, **Regional Parks River Shuttle** *(parks.sonomacounty.ca.gov; day ticket adult/child $5/free)* runs from El Molino High School in Forestville and can drop you at **Steelhead Beach** and pick you up at Sunset Beach. Plan for at least four to five hours – the river is slow-moving – you'll have to do more paddling than you expect, and pack supplies (like drinking water). For picnic supplies, **Guerneville Bank Club** *(guernevillebankclub.com)* and **Piknik Town Market** *(pikniktownmarket.com)* make everything from avocado sandwiches to homemade ice cream. The small farmers market meets on Wednesday afternoons, and there's a Safeway in Guerneville.

In winter, the river can flood during heavy rains, and beach vendors close. But it's a fine time for watching osprey and blue heron ply the moody river mists from the shore.

WHY I LOVE SONOMA COUNTY

Alexis Averbuck, Lonely Planet writer

The final stretch of the Russian River winds by tiny Duncans Mills as the valley broadens out, edged by meadows. Then the terrain rolls into soft coastal hills that change color depending on the season, but there're always grazing cows enjoying the ocean breeze. The view opens wider still at the river's mouth, seals bouncing on the broad beach. It is perfect for a sunset cocktail at River's End restaurant with sheer cliffs and torquing rock towers stretching to either side and the Pacific sparkling in front. I also love to drive the Sonoma coast here, and throw in crab sandwiches at Bodega Bay's Spud Point Crab Company, or have a date night with my peachy husband at Terrapin Creek.

EATING IN GUERNEVILLE: OUR PICKS

Boon Eat + Drink: Tiny, always-packed bistro. Homegrown ingredients for hyperlocal flavor from the chef-owner's Boon Hotel. *4-8pm Wed-Sun* $$

Saucy Mama's: Po'boys, ribs, chicken and catfish at this welcoming southern soul-food place with lashings of sides, at California prices. *4-8pm Wed-Sun* $$

Guerneville Taco Truck: Lines queue for fantastic burritos, quesadillas and tacos. Spice lovers add diablo salsa and jalapeños. *11.30am-9pm* $

Farmhand: Kick back on the river-view deck with fat deli sandwiches or breakfasts (biscuits and gravy...avocado toast) made on the spot. *9am-4pm Fri-Wed* $

FROM 'STUMPTOWN' TO QUEER RESORT

Between the 1840s and 1870s, prospectors stripped the Russian River's redwoods, shipping them to San Francisco to build houses. Guerneville was nicknamed 'Stumptown' for the giant stumps that studded the landscape.

Nature made a comeback, and by the early 1900s there was a new boom: nature tourism. The railroads prospectors used to haul supplies were converted to hauling tourists, who came for cool summers. And a pioneering LGBTQ+ summer resort scene blossomed in Guerneville, still thriving today.

Meanwhile around neighboring Monte Rio, captains of industry, famous performers and US presidents frolicked nude at the secret, 2700-acre, all-male **Bohemian Grove** *(bohemianclub.com)*.

LEANNA RATHKELLY/GETTY IMAGES

Armstrong Redwoods State Natural Reserve

Old-Growth Redwoods

Walk in ancient groves

The oldest tree in Guerneville's magnificent 805-acre **Armstrong Redwoods State Natural Reserve** *(parks.ca.gov; per car $10)* is a true survivor: 309ft high, 1400 years old and named for a lumber baron. Colonel James Armstrong bought these woodlands in 1874 to log, but changed his mind when he saw the old-growth redwoods. Follow the well-maintained, wheelchair-accessible loop trail to take it in.

Famous Redwood Golf Course

Puttin' around in Northwood

Golfers should head to the bucket-list **Northwood Golf Club** *(northwoodgolf.com)*, a gorgeous vintage 1920s Alister MacKenzie–designed nine-hole course in the redwoods. It used to be the course for Bohemian Grove, which was connected by a walking bridge across the river. Now it's open to all. Just beside the course, the **Northwood Restaurant** *(northwoodbistro.com)* serves fabulous breakfasts and Bloody Marys, plus there's a patio beneath the redwoods and occasional live music and karaoke. Neighboring **Bia Cafe** *(facebook.com/BiaNorthwood)* rustles up delish breakfast sandwiches and espresso drinks.

DRINKING IN GUERNEVILLE: COCKTAILS, WINE & MUSIC

El Barrio: Kick back with Guerneville's best craft cocktails: classic mezcal margaritas, seasonal specials or Bloody Marias *4-9pm Wed-Sat, 11am-3pm Sun*

Trillium: Sip wine, beer and cider by the glass or in flights paired with fresh oysters, small plates and tasting boards. *1-9pm Fri & Sat, 5-7.30pm Sun-Tue*

Rio Nido Roadhouse: Bands rock the poolside stage at this kid-friendly roadhouse restaurant, 4 miles east of Guerneville. *noon-9pm Mon-Fri, from 10am Sat & Sun*

Main Street Bistro: Live music is the reason to come here for drinks. Food is pricey for what you get and service uneven. *3-11pm Mon-Thu, noon-midnight Fri-Sun*

Good Times with the Kids

From skate parks to flicks and festivals in Monte Rio

If you're looking for something to do with the kids on land, if you have bikes or skateboards with you, bounce over to **Monte Rio**, where they can hit the **Creekside Park Skate Park** *(mrrpd.org; free)* next to excellent **Lightwave Coffee & Kitchen**. You can also stretch your legs in the 2023-opened 515-acre **Monte Rio Redwoods Regional Park & Open Space Preserve** *(parks.sonomacounty.ca.gov; parking $7)*.

Check the schedule at the **Rio Theatre** *(monteriotheater.com)* to take them for a movie in a repurposed Quonset hut. And if you happen to be in town in June for RioFest *(friendsofmonterio.org)* and July for **Monte Rio Variety Show** *(monterioshow.org)*, they're both super kid-friendly.

Wine Tasting in the Russian River Valley

Idyllic wine road and a hidden winery

The Russian River Valley has become one of California's most distinctive and important wine appellations, and the highest concentration is along **Westside Rd**, between Guerneville and Healdsburg. Take this world-class country drive through redwood hills, sun-drenched vineyards and mossy oaks, even if you aren't a wine taster.

MacRostie *(macrostiewinery.com; tastings from $45)* is tops for gorgeous views and pinots regularly racking up high points from critics. At **Flowers**, *(flowerswinery.com; tastings from $75)* foodie bites and wine pair perfectly, like chardonnay and fennel-pollen-sprinkled *gougères*, and ridge-top pinot noir with black nori.

Step inside the 1930s toolshed at **Porter Creek** *(portercreek vineyards.com; tastings $30)* for sensational, sustainable pinot noir, syrah, viognier and chardonnay – casual wine tasting at its best.

Room for more? Hit the **Gary Farrell** *(garyfarrellwines.com; tastings from $55)*, **De La Montanya** *(dlmwine.com; tastings $30)* and **Rochioli** *(rochioliwinery.com; tastings $25)* vineyards.

One of the region's best hidden wineries is in the hills near Monte Rio: **Porter-Bass** *(porter-bass.com; tastings $25, waived with purchase)*, where mists swirl around redwoods and biodynamic vines yield outstanding vino, poured for you at a wood-plank bar under a walnut tree by the vintner herself, Sue Bass.

RUSSIAN RIVER VALLEY WINES

Nighttime coastal fog drifts up the Russian River Valley, then usually clears by midday. Pinot noir does beautifully here, as does chardonnay, which also grows in hotter regions, but prefers the longer 'hang time' of cooler climes.

Today there are 70-odd wineries spread across 15,000 acres, listed in the handy Russian River Wine Road map (*wineroad.com*). The highest concentration of wineries is along gorgeous Westside Rd, between Guerneville and Healdsburg. Prices are generally far more reasonable than over in Napa Valley.

Guerneville, Monte Rio, Healdsburg and Occidental are the most sensible bases for wine tasting in the Russian River Valley.

EATING IN MONTE RIO & DOWNRIVER: OUR PICKS

Lightwave Coffee & Kitchen: Fresh Mediterranean fare at a relaxed cafe with great coffee alongside the skate park in Monte Rio. *9am-3pm Wed-Mon* $$

Gold Coast Coffee & Bakery: Stop in Duncans Mills for pastries like gooey butterhorns or thin-crust pizza, plus occasional live local music. *7am-6pm* $

Café Aquatica: Jenner's waterfront cafe makes for lazy days sitting at the river-ocean confluence, coffee or crab roll in hand. *8am-4pm* $

River's End: Spectacular ocean views, old-school fully stocked bar and seasonal menus of local fare. Perfect date night. *5-9pm Fri-Tue* $$$

Healdsburg

CULINARY HOTSPOT | CHIC WINE-TASTING | CHEERFUL PLAZA

TOP TIP

Events take place across Alexander, Dry Creek and Russian River Valleys (check *wineroad.com*). **Healdsburg Chamber of Commerce** *(healdsburg.com)* and **Healdsburg Museum** *(healdsburgmuseum.org)*, covering Sonoma County life, offer a wealth of information.

Today Healdsburg has it all – looks, style, taste, plenty of money – but its history is a real-life telenovela. It began with forbidden romance, when rebellious SoCal ('Southern California') teenager Josefa Carrillo fell for wisecracking Massachusetts-born sea captain Henry Fitch. Josefa and Henry planned to homestead a 75-sq-mile ranch on leased Wappo land, but Henry died of pneumonia in 1849, leaving Josefa widowed at age 39, with 11 kids and a not-yet-working ranch. An uninvited guest named Harmon Heald squatted on the property until the US government auctioned it off to bidders, including Heald.

When the dust finally settled in 'Heald's-burg' in the 1860s, a Victorian village flourished around the town's sun-dappled square and ranchlands were planted, with farms and vineyards.

Nowadays Healdsburg is a gourmet magnet, with farm-inspired bistros and tasting rooms for nearby wineries. Or jump north to Alexander Valley and small-town Geyserville and Cloverdale, where country living embraces you in a sense of quiet escape.

GETTING AROUND

The center is easily walkable, and different walking paths crisscross town. Sonoma County Transit *(sctransit.com)* route 67 shuttles around Healdsburg, and bus 60 connects to Santa Rosa and Cloverdale. Some hotels offer shuttles from Sonoma County airport.

Parking *(ci.healdsburg.ca.us/872/Parking)* is easier and cheap or free once you get out of the plaza zone. Since 1976, **Spoke Folk Cyclery** *(spokefolk.com)* has been getting visitors to vineyards on rental bikes. Cycle along vineyard-lined West Dry Creek Rd or **Westside Rd** (p219), where California sunshine and valley mists produce wonderfully nuanced wines. Download bike maps from Spoke Folk or at *ci.healdsburg.ca.us*.

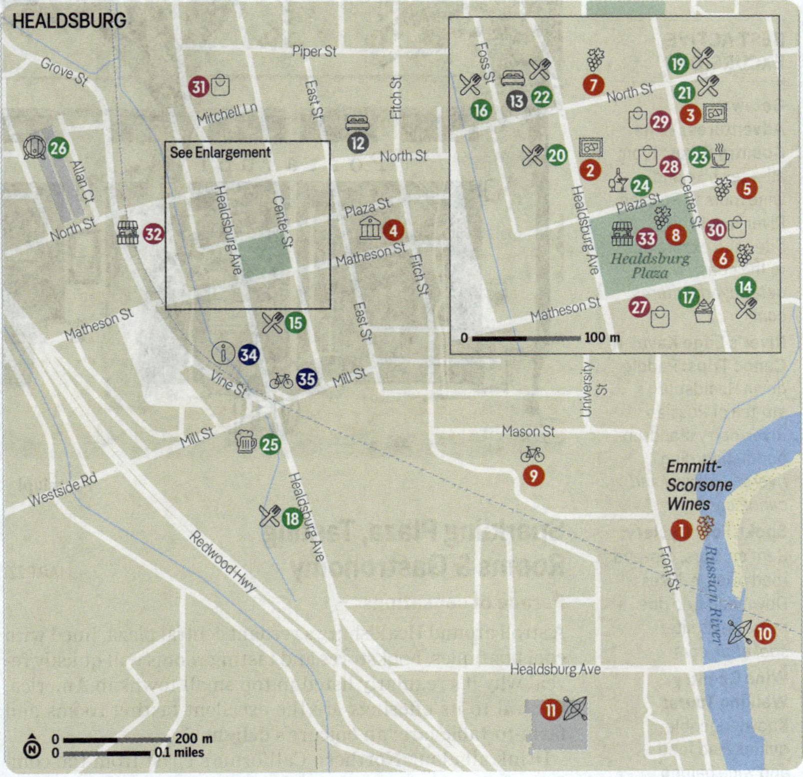

HIGHLIGHTS
1 Emmitt-Scorsone Wines

SIGHTS
2 Erickson Fine Art
3 Healdsburg Center For the Arts
4 Healdsburg Museum
5 Idlewild
6 Lioco
7 Portalupi
see 30 Upstairs Gallery
8 Wine Country Walking Tours

ACTIVITIES
9 Getaway Adventures/ Wine Country Bikes
10 River's Edge Kayak & Canoe Trips
11 Russian River Adventures

SLEEPING
12 Camellia Inn
13 Hotel les Mars

EATING
14 Acorn Cafe
15 Barndiva
16 Little Saint
17 Noble Folk Ice Cream & Pie Bar
18 Quail & Condor
19 SingleThread
20 Troubadour Bread & Bistro
21 Valette
22 Willi's Seafood & Raw Bar

DRINKING & NIGHTLIFE
23 Black Oak Coffee Roasters
24 Duke's Spirited Cocktails
25 Elephant in the Room
26 Young & Yonder

SHOPPING
27 Copperfield's Books
28 Gallery Lulo
29 Jam Jar
30 Levin & Co
31 Modern Antiquarium
32 Saturday Farmers Market
33 Tuesday Farmers Market on the Plaza

INFORMATION
34 Healdsburg Chamber of Commerce

TRANSPORTATION
35 Spoke Folk Cyclery

BEST ACTIVE EXCURSIONS

Getaway Adventures/Wine Country Bikes: From all-ages bike and wine tours to Russian River kayak/bike rides and excursions to the coast/Napa. *getawayadventures.com*

River's Edge Kayak & Canoe Trips: Paddle down Healdsburg's stretch of Russian River, or try stand-up paddleboarding. *riversedgekayakandcanoe.com*

Spoke Folk Cyclery: Rent cruisers, top-end road bikes, e-bikes. Download free ride maps on its site. *spokefolk.com*

Wine Country Walking Tours: Knowledgeable guides lead food and wine pairing tours through some of Healdsburg's best tasting rooms. *winecountrywalkingtours.com*

Russian River Adventures: Paddle on the river/e-bike the vineyards. *russianriveradventures.com*

DANIEL LANE NELSON/SHUTTERSTOCK

Portalupi

Sparkling Plaza, Tasting Rooms & Gastronomy

MAP P221

Parade of sensations

A stroll around Healdsburg's verdant central plaza, lined with cool boutiques, bookstores and tasting rooms will quickly reveal why it's regularly listed in top small towns in America. Central to its offerings are the excellent tasting rooms and farm-to-table fare: an epicure's delight.

Drink all along Northern California's coast from the comfort of your lounge seat at **Lioco** *(liocowine.com; tastings from $30)*, specialist in coastal chardonnays and pinot noirs. At **Idlewild** *(idlewildwines.com; tastings $30)* especially fascinating Piedmontese wines are quietly made by fourth-generation winemaker Sam Bilbro. Also of Italian origin, the wines at **Portalupi** *(portalupiwine.com; tastings from $20)* include unexpected sparkling barbera. The most difficult problem with eating in Healdsburg is choosing where to go. You can splash out on a gastronomic temple like **SingleThread** *(singlethreadfarms.com)*, where edible Sonoma landscape is the first of 11 sensational seasonal courses, ranging from vineyard 'cover crop' grains to forest-floor-foraged morel dashi – a tour de force of nature.

'Healdsburg-inspired' aptly describes Dustin and Aaron, the locally born brothers behind **Valette** *(valettehealdsburg.com)*, and the meals they share with friends and strangers alike. You might spot Dustin at Healdsburg Farmers Market, hauling a wagonful of produce destined for his menus.

Little Saint *(littlesainthealdsburg.com)*, with a delicious plant-based menu, lights up on its free music Thursdays. Any day, slurp ocean-fresh oysters with crisp white wines at **Willi's Seafood & Raw Bar** *(willisseafood.net)*. And what's not to love about **Noble Folk Ice Cream & Pie Bar** *(thenoblefolk.com)*? A dessert dream beyond ice cream – lemon-lavender cupcakes, brownie cubes and raspberry brown-butter macarons are tastier than they'll look on your social media.

Remarkable Produce & Live Music Market Days

MAP P221

Tuesday and Saturday certified farmers markets

On sunny Tuesdays from May to September, the **farmers market** *(healdsburgfarmersmarket.org)* on the Plaza begins with warm hellos from Sonoma County farmers and rolls into inspiring cooking demos and live music, plus seasonal events. Graze regional delicacies, such as Dry Creek peaches, steaming hot samosas, bean-to-bar chocolate, award-winning cheeses and organic Preston olive oil. You can also shop for unique handmade gifts. On Saturdays *(8.30am to 9pm, from April to December)* the **market** sets up in the West Plaza Parking Lot at North and Vine streets, one block west of the Plaza.

Browse Art, Antiques & More

MAP P221

Galleries, shops and bookstores

Healdsburg's center is dotted with crafty shops packed with creative wares and contemporary art galleries, such as **Healdsburg Center For the Arts** *(healdsburgcenterforthearts.org)*, **Erickson Fine Art** *(ericksonfineartgallery.com)*, **Jam Jar** *(jamjargoods.com)* and **Gallery Lulo** *(gallerylulo.com)*.

You probably guessed that Sonoma County barns are full of eccentric collectibles – and here's proof. Thirty local vendors share their obsessions...1930s kitchen canisters, space-themed barware...in 6700 sq ft of warehouse space at **Modern Antiquarium**.

Upstairs Gallery *(upstairsartgallery.net)* sits above family-owned old-school bookstore **Levin & Co** *(levinbooks.com)*. The sign of a healthy creative community? A whole second indie books store: **Copperfield's Books** *(copperfieldsbooks.com)*.

Crushing on Rural Wineries

MAP P224

Dry Creek Valley escape

Hemmed in by 2000ft-high mountains, **Dry Creek Valley** is relatively warm, ideal for sauvignon blanc and zinfandel,

BEST ENTERTAINMENT & FESTIVALS

Tuesdays in the Plaza Concerts: In summer, join **free Tuesday concerts**; food vendors from 5pm, music 6–8pm. *healdsburg.gov*

Farmers Market Concerts: Check website for what's playing at Tuesday's market. *healdsburg farmersmarket.org*

Healdsburg Jazz Festival: In June, jazz venues include wine-tasting courtyard **Bacchus Landing** *(bacchuslanding.com)*. *healdsburgjazz.org*

Healdsburg Wine & Food Experience: In May, revel in local/ international wine and farm-to-table food. *healdsburgwineand food.com*

Wine & Food Affair: In November, 100 Sonoma County wineries offer a featured dish and wine pairing. *wineroad.com*

EATING & DRINKING IN HEALDSBURG: COOL BAKERIES & CAFES

MAP P221

Quail & Condor: Bakers from SingleThread make superb French-style pastries and bread, a perennial favorite. *8am-3pm Wed-Mon* $

Acorn Cafe: Stop in for coffee and breakfast or gourmet sandwiches, end up people-watching on the Plaza patio. *8am-3pm Mon-Fri, to 5pm Sat & Sun* $$

Troubadour Bread & Bistro: Classic boulangerie: sandwiches by day, pricey bistro with a set menu by night. *7am-4.30pm Tue-Sat, 8am-3pm Sun* $$$

Black Oak Coffee Roasters: Power up before wine tasting with fair-trade, house-roasted coffee made by those who know how. *7am-5pm* $

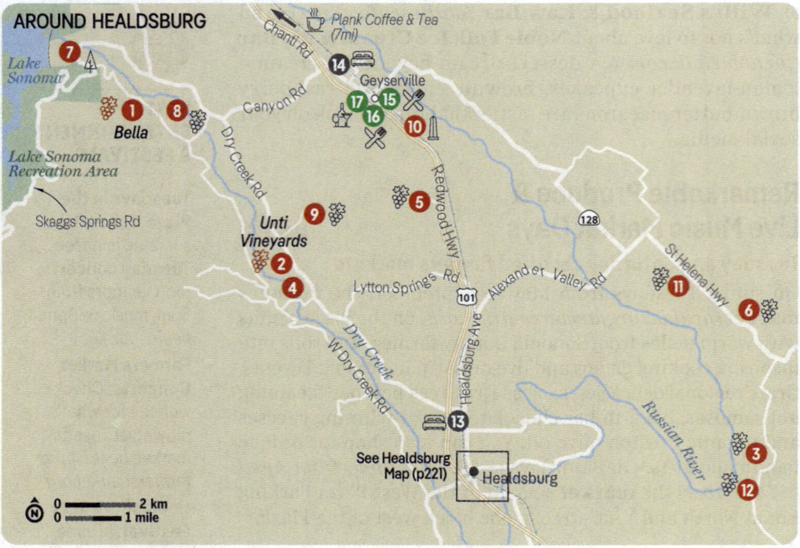

AROUND HEALDSBURG

HIGHLIGHTS
1 Bella
2 Unti Vineyards

SIGHTS
3 Carpenter Wine
4 Dry Creek Valley
5 Francis Ford Coppola Winery
6 Hanna
7 Lake Sonoma Recreation Area
8 Preston Farm & Winery
9 Reeve Wines
10 Sculpture Trail
11 Soda Rock Winery
12 Sutro Wine

SLEEPING
13 Best Western Dry Creek
14 Geyserville Inn

EATING
15 Cyrus
16 Diavola Pizza

DRINKING & NIGHTLIFE
17 Geyserville Gun Club

and in some places cabernet sauvignon. Roll down the valley's undulating country lane – one of Sonoma County's great back roads, ideal for cycling.

The caves at **Bella** *(www.bellawinery.com; tastings from $35)* are as pretty as the name suggests and are impressively hardworking, turning grapes from 105-year-old estate vines into prize zinfandels and syrah. From the tasting-room window at **Unti Vineyards** *(untivineyards.com; tastings $25, waived with bottle purchase)*, rolling vineyards look like sun-drenched Tuscan hills – and that's exactly what you'll taste in your wineglass: organically farmed Mediterranean noble grapes that thrive in these conditions. Dry Creek's best find is **Emmitt-Scorsone Wines** *(emmitt*

DRINKING IN HEALDSBURG: OUR PICKS

MAP P221

Elephant in the Room: Music takes center stage five nights a week at this rollicking pub, walkable to the center. Cover charge on weekends. *1pm-midnight*

Barndiva: Swing in for a predinner cocktail at the bar here, with original concoctions like the Guava Hermosa featuring hibiscus-infused tequila. *5-9pm Thu-Mon*

Young & Yonder: This hip distillery is turning some heads with its takes on absinthe, gin, vodka and bourbon. *2-7pm Fri, noon-7pm Sat, noon-5pm Sun*

Duke's Spirited Cocktails: Creative craft cocktails – once the drink kicks in, so does the dance floor. *4pm-11pm Mon-Thu, 2pm-2am Fri, noon-2am Sat & Sun*

scorsone.com; tastings $25), hidden on a back road, and it does its tastings in town. Upstart cult wine labels Judge Palmer and Domenica Amato are made here as well, you can picnic on-site, and walk-ins are welcome for some weekend hours.

Patio tastings at **Reeve Wines** *(reevewines.com; tastings $50)* let you admire the vineyards and sheep pastures as you sip poetry-inducing rosé of pinot noir and alluring single-vineyard sangiovese. **Preston Farm & Winery** *(prestonvineyards.com; tastings $35)* grows heirloom produce and raises livestock to support an integrated ecosystem – sheep handle weeding, and artichokes and radishes help with pest control. The farm store sells produce and olive oil, while the bar pours citrusy sauvignon blancs.

Geyserville's Wild West Vibes & Pools

MAP P224

Laid-back life and Coppola Winery

As Hwy 101 begins its long journey north from Healdsburg, the valley widens, with pastures and vineyards carpeting the way. Twelve minutes' drive north of Healdsburg, welcome to **Geyserville**, population 830. But where are the geysers? Wander the town's old wooden boardwalk, and you'll find Wild West character and a **sculpture trail**, but no sign of the geothermal wonders that initially attracted visitors in 1847. The hot springs are located underground, and produce 20% of California's renewable energy. To get into hot water, reserve a spot at the vast hilltop swimming pools at the **Francis Ford Coppola Winery** *(francisfordcoppolawinery.com; tastings from $35)*.

Boating, Fishing, Hiking & Biking

MAP P224

The pleasures of Lake Sonoma

A teal lake and wilderness preserve amid golden Sonoma foothills 20 minutes' drive north of Healdsburg, scenic **Lake Sonoma** is the heart of **Lake Sonoma Recreation Area** *(spn.usace.army.mil/Missions/Recreation/Lake-Sonoma)*. In 1983, the US Army Corps of Engineers built Warm Springs Dam for practical purposes, including flood control and irrigation – and the result was this sporting jackpot, with a lake for boating and fishing, miles of trails for hiking and biking, a hillside archery range and a fish hatchery that's helped restore Sonoma's once-endangered steelhead.

BEST ALEXANDER VALLEY WINERIES

Soda Rock Winery: Follow Hwy 128 to this tasting room for excellent California zinfandel. Walk-ins welcome. Down the road, Chalk Hill AVA vineyards flourish at indie, women-run wineries. *sodarockwinery.com*

Carpenter: Try velvety pinots under a sheltering oak with cofounder/sommelier Laura Carpenter Hawkes introducing natural wines with distinct personalities. *carpenterwine.com*

Sutro: Hike the vineyard with fifth-generation winemaker Alice Sutro for chardonnay and cabernets. *sutrowine.com*

Hanna: Taste sunny, rustic, estate-grown chardonnay, zinfandel and cabernet. Also has a vineyard near Sebastopol with tastings. *hannawinery.com*

EATING & DRINKING IN GEYSERVILLE: OUR PICKS

MAP P221, 224

Cyrus: Who would expect this remote restaurant to have a Michelin star? Exquisite Sonoma County fusion in a modern glass room. *5-9pm Thu-Sun* **$$$**

Diavola Pizza: A contender for California's most perfectly crispy thin-crust, wood-fired pizza, with house-cured salumi and sausage. *11.30am-9pm* **$$**

Plank Coffee & Tea: House-roasted espresso drinks and an impressive 50 loose-leaf teas, plus homemade quiche and baked treats. *7am-2pm* **$**

Geyserville Gun Club: Cocktails and beers on tap meet sake and live music... delish food, too, at this small-town bar. *5-9.30pm Sun-Fri, to 11pm Sat* **$$**

Places We Love to Stay

$** Budget **$$** Midrange **$$$ Top End

Napa

MAP p171

Elm House Inn $$ Tidy rooms with generic furnishings in soft pastels a 15-minute walk to downtown. Hot tub.

Napa Winery Inn $$ Request a remodeled room at this good-value hotel north of downtown.

Hotel Indigo Napa Valley $$ Reasonable value, basic 2-story hotel on the suburban strip north of Napa.

Blackbird Inn $$$ Relax in a ruggedly handsome 1902 California Craftsman cottage with eight plush rooms.

Archer $$$ Live like a vintner who's just won Double Gold at downtown Napa's most happening hotel.

Milliken Creek Inn $$$ Understatedly elegant small-inn charm with boutique-hotel service and Napa indulgence.

Yountville

Maison Fleurie $$$ Rooms at this ivy-covered country inn are in a century-old home and carriage house, decorated in French-provincial style.

Petit Logis $$$ Wake to the aroma of croissants from next-door Bouchon Bakery.

Poetry Inn $$$ Contemporary inn with staggering views over Stag's Leap vineyards. Recite sonnets on your balcony.

North Block Hotel $$$ Both sup and stay over at trendy North Block in the village center.

St Helena

MAP p183

El Bonita Motel $$ Free up funds for vintage wines by staying at this affordable vintage motel.

Wydown Hotel $$$ Historic inn redone by a contemporary art collector, with smart rooms and savvy staff.

Harvest Inn $$$ Get in touch with nature at this wooded wine estate, with Tudor-timbered lodges, stone-pillared bungalows, and cedar-shingled cabins.

Calistoga

Bothe-Napa Valley State Park Ritchey Creek Campground $ Wake up in the redwoods, canvas-sided yurt or restored historic cabin.

Aurora Park Cottages $$ This quiet row of sunny yellow immaculate cottages sits back from Calistoga's main road amid trees and flower gardens.

Wine Way Inn $$ This small B&B, set in a 1910-era arts-and-crafts-style house close to the road, has friendly owners.

Meadowlark Country House $$$ Ranch on 20 lush acres with clothing-optional wellness area: hot tub, sauna and pool.

Brannan Cottage Inn $$$ Stay in the iconic 1862 gingerbread cottage of Samuel Brannan, the hustler/entrepreneur who founded Calistoga.

Sonoma Town

MAP p191

Sonoma Creek Inn $ Quirky 16-room motel with retro-Americana decor, including vintage California travel posters and postcard lamps.

Cinnamon Bear Creekside Inn $$ Decent value proposition close enough to the plaza that you could walk.

An Inn 2 Remember $$ Steps from the plaza, this vintage 1910 charmer offers warm welcomes and comfortable lodgings.

Cottage Inn & Spa $$$ Private patios for morning pastries, with a tinkling fountain and on-site spa. What's not to love?

Sonoma Valley

Sugarloaf Ridge State Park Camping $ Lovely hilltop campground near Kenwood, with 48 drive-in sites, clean coin-operated showers.

Glen Ellen Inn & Martini Bar $$ Have a stiff martini then hit the sheets at these welcoming cottages and inn.

Jack London Lodge $$ Sprawl in a spacious, well-kept room with big comfy beds at this mod motel with a pool and hot tub.

Beltane Ranch $$$ African American millionaire civil-rights pioneer Mary Ellen Pleasant built this beautiful ranch in 1892.

Olea Hotel $$$ Relax in impeccable luxury in the oak-blanketed hills of Glen Ellen.

Petaluma to Santa Rosa

MAP p200

Hotel E $ Beaux-arts beauty with signature clocktower on Santa Rosa's Old Courthouse Sq.

Spring Lake Regional Park Campground $ Santa Rosa's 72-acre reservoir, 10 miles of hiking trails, and campsites in the shade of oaks.

Hampton Inn Petaluma $ This boutique-style offering in the gorgeous 1892 Petaluma silk mill is the hippest Hampton Inn you'll ever see.

Gables Wine Country Inn $$$ Friendly Victorian-home B&B draped in antique luxury, with brilliant breakfasts and a verdant spread.

Sebastopol & Occidental

MAP p204

Fairfield Inn & Suites $ Modern farmhouse styling makes this Sebastopol Marriott (the only hotel in town) better than typical chains.

Inn at Occidental $$ Escape the ordinary at this 16-room Victorian inn with heirloom quilts for getting cozy in the redwoods.

Bodega Bay & Coast

Wright's Beach Campground $ Best of the Sonoma Coast State Park, because sites one to 10 are right on the beach. Book well ahead.

Salt Point State Park Campgrounds $ Two campgrounds, convenient for tide-pooling, have sites with cold water. Inland Woodside is protected by Monterey pines.

Bodega Dunes Campground $ The largest campground in the Sonoma Coast State Park with close to 100 sites in high dunes.

Bodega Harbor Inn $ Half a block inland from Hwy 1, this modest, agreeable blue-and-white shingled motel is the town's most economical option.

River's End Inn $$$ Ocean-view cottages have no cell service but do have wi-fi. Many come with fireplaces, decks and breathtaking views.

Timber Cove Resort $$$ Dramatic '60s-modern bluff-top inn refurbished into a luxury lodge. Tinkling piano and crackling fireplace fill the a vast lobby.

Sea Ranch Beach Rentals $$$ Rents out vacation homes exclusively at the Sea Ranch development.

Russian River Valley

MAP p216

Schoolhouse Canyon Campground $ Redwood grove two miles east of Guerneville with well-tended campsites across the road from the river.

Highlands Resort $$ Mellow out in the redwoods at Guerneville's most relaxed LGBTQ+ and straight-friendly resort. Adults only.

R3 Hotel $$ Ground zero for party-all-day LGBTQ+ crowd, Triple R (as it's known) has standard motel-style rooms surrounding a happening bar and pool deck.

Mine + Farm $$$ Modern B&B in a 1906 farmhouse next to Korbel Vineyards and near Sunset Beach.

Boon Hotel + Spa $$$ Sleek retreat, walking/biking distance to Guerneville and Armstrong Woods; 14 spacious rooms feature fireplaces.

Dawn Ranch $$$ Riverside century-old whitewashed cottages let you drift off to the shushing wind in the trees.

Healdsburg & Geyserville

MAP p221

Best Western Dry Creek $ This generic motel has good service and a hot tub. Price is the reason to stay.

Geyserville Inn $ Amid Alexander Valley vineyards walking distance from Geyserville. Request a deluxe room with balcony or fireplace. Pool and hot tub.

Hotel les Mars $$$ Spacious guest rooms have four-poster beds you might find hard to leave, until breakfast arrives at your door.

Camellia Inn $$$ Cheery pink 1871 mansion, with camellia-filled gardens, sociable parlors and upbeat, helpful innkeepers.

JAMES KIRKIKIS/SHUTTERSTOCK

El Bonita Motel

Researched by
Amelia Mularz

North Coast & Redwoods

PEEK BEHIND THE REDWOOD CURTAIN

On California's northernmost coast, curiosity is rewarded with unspoiled beaches, old-world architecture and the world's tallest trees.

Wild is the word that constantly springs to mind when visiting the North Coast. The beaches – hundreds of miles of dune-dotted and driftwood-strewn sand – are notably untamed. Fern- and moss-covered canyons require that visitors play by their rules if they want to have a look (like wading through a creek, as is the case at Fern Canyon in Prairie Creek Redwoods State Park). The forests, often referred to as 'the redwood curtain' because the trees grow so tall and dense, will bring out your wildest urges to hike further, to ascend higher (like taking a canopy-grazing gondola ride at the Trees of Mystery in Klamath) and see more. Then there's the wildlife: the Roosevelt elk you'll catch casually grazing, the elephant seals lazing by a Lost Coast lighthouse and the roughly 330 species of birds that touch down at Arcata Marsh and Wildlife Sanctuary.

Locals here are pretty wild, too. In Eureka, they've preserved a town's worth of Victorian-era architecture and simultaneously pushed the drive-thru experience into the 21st century, offering a way to get your morning java and a joint on the go. But the wildest part of this region is how often you'll find yourself blissfully alone. It's common to pause at one of the state's most awe-inspiring lookout points and realize you have it all to yourself. In those moments you're likely to think, 'Wow, now *that's* wild.'

PANAS WIWATPANACHAT/SHUTTERSTOCK

THE MAIN AREAS

For places to stay in North Coast & Redwoods, see p276

PAOLO TRALLI/SHUTTERSTOCK

Left: Wooden sculpture, Trees of Mystery (p269); Above: Humboldt Redwoods State Park (p256)

Find Your Way

Because the region has hundreds of miles of coastline, tens of thousands of acres of redwoods and vast swaths of vineyards, you could close your eyes, point to any spot on the map and find breathtaking beauty.

Redwood National & State Parks, p266
Up and down Hwy 101 you'll find parks filled with neck-craning trees, untamed beaches and prairie wilderness, plus a few roadside attractions.

Eureka, p259
Offering the closest thing to 'city life' in the region, Eureka has street art, superb seafood restaurants and outdoor adventure.

AIR
For Mendocino and Clear Lake, the Charles M Schulz–Sonoma County Airport in Santa Rosa is the closest option for flights. The Lost Coast, Eureka and Redwood National and State Parks are best serviced by California Redwood Coast–Humboldt County Airport (aka Arcata–Eureka Airport) in McKinleyville.

OREGON
CALIFORNIA
Smith River National Recreation Area
199
96
Crescent City
Siskiyou Wilderness
Klamath River
Marble Mountain Wilderness
Klamath
101
Prairie Creek Redwoods State Park
Redwood National & State Parks
Orick
96
Redwood National Park
Dunsmuir
Coffee Creek
Trinidad
Hoopa
Trinity Center
Shasta-Trinity National Forest
McKinleyville
Trinity Alps Wilderness
Manila
Arcata
Trinity Lake
Shasta Lake
5
Samoa
Arcata Bay
299
Eureka
Humboldt Bay
Weaverville
Whiskeytown-Shasta-Trinity National Recreation Area
299
Whiskeytown Lake
Fortuna
Ferndale
101
Hayfork
Redding
Scotia
36
3
211
Shasta-Trinity National Forest
Platina
Humboldt Redwoods State Park
Weott
Petrolia
36
Six Rivers National Forest
Honeydew
Red Bluff

The Lost Coast, p251

Go where even the roads don't travel on this rugged coastline that's a dream for hikers and backpackers.

Mendocino, p234

This historic seaside village, dotted with distinctive water towers, is an ideal base for coastal strolls with a side of gallery hopping.

Clear Lake, p246

Small towns, wineries and a dormant volcano surround the largest natural lake in California.

BUS

Those willing to piece together bus travel through the region will face a time-consuming headache, but connections are possible to most towns. Companies include Greyhound, the Mendocino Transit Authority, the Redwood Transit System and Redwood Coast Transit.

CAR

You'll almost certainly need a car to explore this region. Those headed to the far north should take Hwy 101, the faster inland route, then cut over to the coast. Hwy 1 hugs the coast, then cuts inland and joins Hwy 101 at Leggett.

Trail
Shelter Cove
Leggett
Covelo
Yolla Bolly-Middle Eel Wilderness
Paskenta
Mendocino National Forest
Black Butte Lake
Westport
Eel River
Fort Bragg
Jackson Demonstration State Forest
Caspar
Willits
Snow Mountain Wilderness
Lake Pillsbury
Mendocino
Albion
Upper Lake
Nice
Lucerne
Ukiah
Elk
Philo
Lakeport
Clear Lake
Boonville
Manchester
Hopland
Kelseyville
Clearlake
Point Arena
Anchor Bay
Cloverdale
Gualala
Sea Ranch
Lake Berryessa
Sacramento
PACIFIC OCEAN
20
101
1
175
29

Plan Your Time

Whatever your time constraints, the North Coast is your oyster. Here's how to make the most of your time hiking, paddling, sipping, and oohing and aahing.

GEARTOOTH PRODUCTIONS/SHUTTERSTOCK

Beach, Lost Coast Trail (p254)

You've Got a Weekend

- If you've only got a weekend, hightail it to **Mendocino** (p234), which puts the region's best foot forward. Drive up Hwy 101 and cut through **Anderson Valley** (p244), where travelers can sip excellent wine. Stroll the gorgeous bluff along the **Mendocino Headlands Trail** (p234), dine at one of the many exquisite restaurants and stay in a historic **water tower** (p237).

- The next day, paddle a redwood canoe up **Big River** (p237) and check out the local **art galleries** (p238). Take the long way home on scenic roads, stopping for secluded coves, quiet coastal parks and the majestic **Point Arena Lighthouse** (p242).

Seasonal Highlights

Spring is lovely on the North Coast, as weather warms and wildflowers start to pop. Coastal fog dominates in summertime, harvest is big in the fall and winter is quiet and cozy.

JANUARY

Prime time to spot migrating whales, colonies of elephant seals, monarch butterflies in the trees and hundreds of bird species along the Pacific Flyway.

APRIL

The **Lost Coast** (p251) is covered in wildflowers, including California poppies, lupines and Douglas irises. Low tide, aka peak tidepooling time in **Shelter Cove** (p253) is conveniently midday.

MAY

It's festival season. The **Murder, She Wrote Festival** (p239) comes to Mendocino, the **Pinot Noir Festival** happens in Anderson Valley and the quirky **Kinetic Grand Championship** (p263) hits Eureka.

Your OOO Is Set

● With a week you have time to hike the entire **Lost Coast Trail** (p254), plus tack on a few days for additional exploring (or indulgent recovery). The trail takes two to four days, depending on direction and tidal timing, and includes coastal camping.

● If you're heading south, stick around the end point in **Shelter Cove** (p251) for a couple days and book an oceanfront room with a hot tub. Spend at least one afternoon inland driving the mighty **Avenue of the Giants** (p256), and consider a night in **Ferndale** (p258), California's quaintest town. Shop Ferndale's charming Main St and admire the town's butterfat palaces, perfectly preserved Victorian buildings.

You'll Be Sure to Write

● Eureka! You have discovered a way to escape daily life for over a week and you'll be rewarded with redwoods galore. Start in the town of **Eureka** (p259), easily accessed via the California Redwood Coast-Humboldt County Airport, and spend a couple days **kayaking** (p263) the historic harbor, taking in the **Victorian architecture** (p262) and popping over to Arcata to go **thrifting on the plaza** (p264).

● Head north to hunt for agates on the beach in **Sue-meg State Park** (p274), then check in at a B&B in Trinidad and hike the dramatic **headlands** (p272). Further north, you'll hit **Redwood National & State Parks** (p266), where you'll find days worth of hiking and plenty of opportunities to hang out with the world's tallest trees.

JULY

The **Mendocino Music Festival** (p239), the town's most exciting event of the year, takes place. **Fourth of July** is also a great time to visit, with a parade and lots of live jazz.

AUGUST

Cultural demonstrations, a 5K run, live music and good eats are all part of the fishy fun at the **Klamath Salmon Festival** (p268).

OCTOBER

The **wine regions** celebrate their harvest with food-and-wine shindigs, grape-stomping 'crush' parties and barrel tastings. Some events start in September.

NOVEMBER

In Fort Bragg, the Skunk transforms into the **Mushroom, Whisky and Wine Train** (p242). Rain and fog envelop the coast, and having a wood-burning stove becomes super cozy.

Mendocino

WILD BEACHES | RESTAURANTS | HISTORIC TOWN

GETTING AROUND

Mendocino Village is small and entirely walkable, and you can easily stroll to the Mendocino Headlands from town. But to get to other state parks and area attractions, you'll want a car. If you're flying in, Charles M Schulz–Sonoma County Airport in Santa Rosa is the closest; it's just over a two-hour drive. If you're comfortable going car-free, Mendocino Transit Authority does have a direct bus from the airport to Mendocino once a day.

TOP TIP

Many of the shops, galleries and restaurants in town close for a day or two midweek. Plan your hikes and outdoor activities for those days and save shopping and fine dining for weekends.

A number of North Coast cities have a logging past, but consider Mendocino the connoisseur's historic timber town. Transplants from New England founded the village and lumber mill in 1852, bringing with them architectural influences that can still be seen in the area's Victorian buildings. The logging industry thrived through the turn of the century, but when the mill closed in the 1930s both the town's population and economic stability took a hit. Things turned around with the establishment of the Mendocino Art Center in 1959, revitalizing the town and infusing it with the artistic charm that's now as much a part of its makeup as its logging past. Today, tourism is Mendocino's main industry, and though its population hovers only in the hundreds, nearly 2 million travelers make a pilgrimage each year to shop its exquisite art galleries, dine at its top-tier restaurants and marvel at the views from atop the Pacific-kissed bluffs.

Timber Town Time Machine

Step inside an 1860s house

To get up close and personal with life in a 19th-century logging town – as in peeping at the kinds of products kept in medicine cabinets during the era – head to the **Kelley House Museum** *(kelleyhousemuseum.org; suggested $5 donation)*. William Kelley, a businessman who once owned almost all the land that would become Mendocino, built this historic house in 1861. Today, visitors can wander its bedrooms and see period furnishings and personal effects.

A Diamond in the Bluff

Stroll an extraordinary oceanside trail

If hiking trails were judged by ocean views, the path at **Mendocino Headlands State Park** *(parks.ca.gov; free)* would score an uncontested 10/10. For over two miles in one direction,

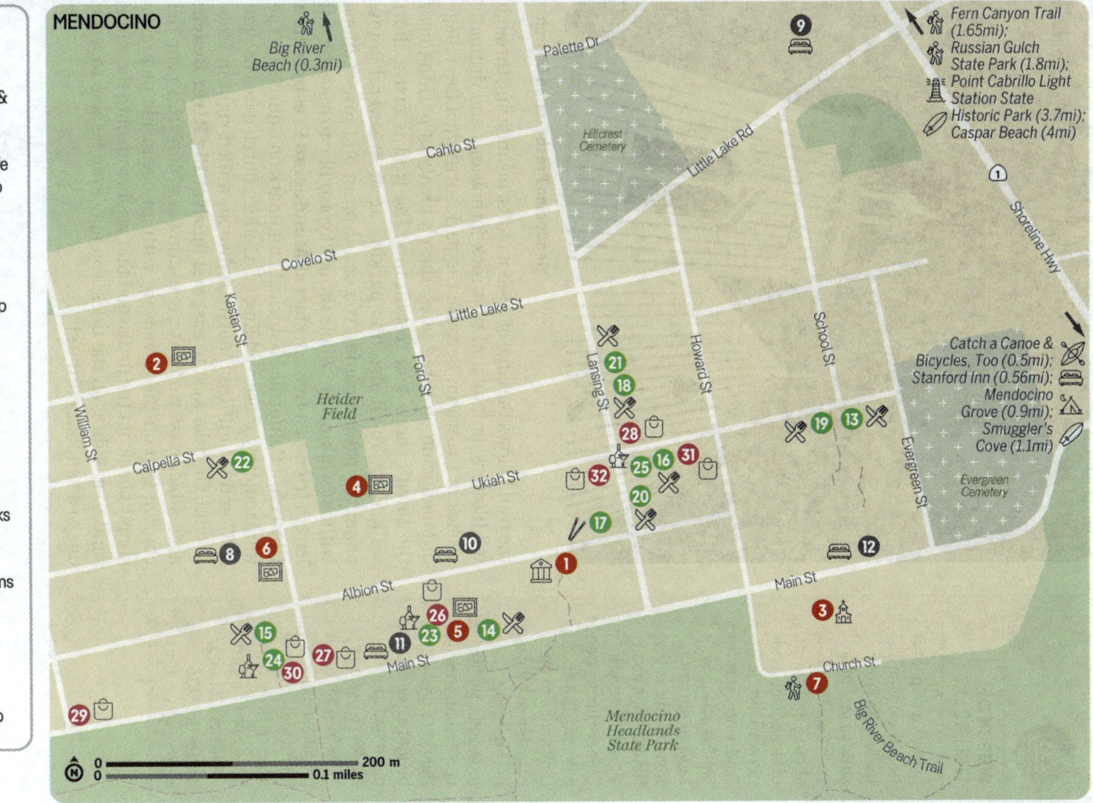

SIGHTS
1 Kelley House Museum
2 Mendocino Art Center
3 Mendocino Presbyterian Church
4 Partners Gallery
5 Prentice Gallery
6 The Highlight Gallery

ACTIVITIES
7 Mendocino Headlands State Park

SLEEPING
8 JD House
9 Joshua Grindle Inn
10 MacCallum House
11 Mendocino Hotel and Garden Suites
12 Sweetwater Inn & Spa

EATING
13 Café Beaujolais
14 Flow Restaurant & Lounge
15 Fog Eater Cafe
16 Frankie's
17 Gnar Bar
18 GoodLife Cafe & Bakery
19 Luna Trattoria
20 Mendocino Cafe
21 Patterson's Pub
22 Trillium Cafe

DRINKING & NIGHTLIFE
23 Dick's Place
24 Fog Bottle Shop and Wine Bar
25 MendoVino

SHOPPING
26 Astoria Home Decor & Gifts
27 Gallery Bookshop & Bullwinkle's Children's Books
28 Mendocino Gems
29 Mendocino Jams & Preserves
30 Out of This World
31 Slug Sister Vintage
32 The Study Club

WRECK OF THE FROLIC

In 1850, a ship retired from the opium trade – the *Frolic* – struck a reef near Point Cabrillo (p238), about 3 miles north of Mendocino, and ran aground. Jerome Ford, who came from San Francisco to salvage the cargo, was too late as the Native Pomo had already recovered the Chinese luxury goods onboard. But Ford took notice of the coast's real treasure: the enormous redwoods. He teamed up with entrepreneur Henry Meiggs, who bought a sawmill and had it transported to Big River. During the mill's 50-year run, it produced a billion board feet of timber, which was used to build San Francisco – and then rebuild it after the 1906 earthquake.

MICHAEL VI/SHUTTERSTOCK

Mendocino Presbyterian Church

the trail follows the edge of 70-foot bluffs, meandering through wildflowers on land and past rock formations and dramatic arches in the water. Because the park surrounds the village of Mendocino on three sides, there's plenty of parking near the town's shops and restaurants; the trail is just a short walk away. You'll also find parking areas at several points along the path, meaning you can drop in on those sections without walking the whole thing. If you'd like to hike the full length from east to west, start at **Mendocino Presbyterian Church**, a California Historical Landmark on Church St. The immaculately preserved English Gothic church dates back to 1867 and is built from native redwood, milled right in Mendocino. Or, hike west to east and finish at **Big River Beach**, accessible by way of a staircase down a bluff trail near the church. Cap off the adventure with an oceanside picnic, or simply check out the driftwood that washes up onto the white sand. Depending on the tides, you may even be able to wade out to a sandbar off the shore.

EATING IN MENDOCINO: OUR PICKS

GoodLife Cafe & Bakery: Start the day with a blackberry danish or biscuits smothered in sausage gravy – this really is the good life. *7.30am-2pm* $

Mendocino Cafe: The eclectic menu at this lunch and dinner spot includes a Thai burrito, Indian masala curry and locally caught rockfish. *11am-4pm & 5-9pm* $$

Trillium Cafe: Stop by for fine dining focused on organic seasonal ingredients or order a picnic basket to go. *11.30am-2:15pm & 5-8.30pm Fri-Tue* $$$

Fog Eater Cafe: This cozy vegetarian spot serves southern-inspired recipes for dinner and a full brunch menu on Sundays. *4-8pm Wed-Sat, 10am-2pm Sun* $$

Water (Tower) World

Get to know the town's signature structures

Take one look around Mendocino Village and you'll see why it earned the nickname 'town of water towers.' While about 30 of these elevated tanks still remain, the town once had over 100 of them. Built in the late 19th century, the water towers collected and stored rainwater for year-round use, as the town didn't have a central water system. Get to know a number of these structures on a two-hour water-tower walking tour hosted by a docent from the Kelley House Museum (p234). To step inside one – and simultaneously browse for retro clothes – head to **Slug Sister Vintage** *(slugsistervintage.com)*, located inside a charmingly petite tower. Or you can have a meal at **Flow Restaurant & Lounge** *(mendocinoflow.com)*, which requires climbing the water-tower stairs to reach its 2nd-floor entrance. It's highly recommended for its ocean views.

Finally, if it's R&R in a reservoir that you're after, book an overnight stay. **Joshua Grindle Inn** *(joshuagrindlemendocino.com)*, **Sweetwater Inn & Spa** *(sweetwaterspa.com)*, **MacCallum House** *(maccallumhouse.com)* and **JD House** *(innsofmendocino.com)* all have rooms located in water towers.

Big Adventure on Big River

Paddle a redwood outrigger

Catch a Canoe & Bicycles, Too *(catchacanoe.com)*, located on the Big River at **Stanford Inn** *(stanfordinn.com)*, isn't your average boat-rental business. Sure, they have basic kayaks to borrow, but they really specialize in locally made redwood outriggers. These water craft – which draw inspiration from the redwood vessels made by Native tribes – are steadier and easier to steer (thanks to a foot-controlled rudder system) than common canoes. Rent one for three hours *(adult/child $60/30 per person)* or the whole day *(adult/child $90/45 per person)*. Outriggers can accommodate two to six people, and one design, the Canine Cruiser, is even geared toward pups who want to join for an afternoon of paddling. Additionally, a Catalina Catamaran Canoe fits up to 10 people, with two connected, side-by-side vessels, so you can bring your whole party to the river.

MENDOCINO'S BEST SHOPS

Gallery Bookshop & Bullwinkle's Children's Books: Snag a bestseller, an outdoor guide or a title from a California small press.

The Study Club: Embrace your coastal fantasy life with high-end knitwear, homegoods and beauty products.

Out of This World: Birders, astronomy buffs and science geeks head directly to this binocular, telescope and science-toy shop.

Astoria Home Decor & Gifts: Follow the brick path to this charming boutique stocked with floral fragrances, candles and locally made charcuterie boards.

Mendocino Jams & Preserves: Here's your chance to slip something sweet into your suitcase, like a jar of small-batch wild blackberry jam.

EATING IN MENDOCINO: OUR PICKS

Frankie's: For a casual bite, family-owned Frankie's is the place for falafel, salads and pizza (gluten-free options available). Ice cream too. *11am-8pm Tue-Sun* **$**

Gnar Bar: Get grab-and-go poke, sushi rolls and dumplings at this convenient corner spot. You can even order online. *11am-6pm Wed-Mon* **$$**

Luna Trattoria: Northern Italian cuisine meets the North Coast at this dinner spot with outdoor seating in a charming garden. *5-9pm Tue-Sun* **$$$**

Café Beaujolais: Set in an 1893 Victorian farmhouse, the Café serves French-California dinners and Sunday brunch. *5-9pm Wed-Sat, 9.30am-12.30pm Sun* **$$$**

MURDER, SHE WROTE

Fans of the TV show, which ran for 12 seasons from 1984 to 1996, may spot some familiar sights in Mendocino, which often served as the real-life backdrop for the show's fictional (and crime-riddled) town known as Cabot Cove, Maine. Angela Lansbury, who played the show's protagonist, the mystery writer and amateur sleuth Jessica Fletcher, said that it was more cost effective to shoot in Mendocino rather than in rural Maine.

Blair House, an 1888 Victorian inn on Little Lake St that still welcomes overnight guests, served as the exterior of Fletcher's home. Lansbury also filmed various outdoor scenes around town, including cycling on Ukiah St and chatting with another character on a bluff at Mendocino Headlands State Park.

A Hub for the Arts

Go gallery hopping

Make a pilgrimage to the place that turned this lumber town into an artist enclave: the **Mendocino Art Center** *(mendocinoartcenter.org)*. Visitors are welcome to drop in and wander its gallery, filled with works from local artists, for free from Thursday through Sunday. Don't miss the gift shop, where ceramics, jewelry and T-shirts are for sale. If you'd like to get in on the crafting action, check out the center's calendar for workshops that take place on a single day or over a weekend. Past classes have included throwing large pots on the wheel, punch-needle rug hooking for beginners and screen printing with natural dyes.

If you still haven't scratched your artistic itch, stop by some of the other galleries in town. **The Highlight Gallery** *(thehighlightgallery.com)* has two stories of paintings, ceramics, jewelry and handcrafted wood furniture, while **Mendocino Gems** *(mendocinogems.com)* focuses entirely on jewelry, representing local artisans in addition to featuring their own creations made from precious metals and stones. The smaller yet superbly curated collection at **Partners Gallery** *(partnersgallery.com)* is usually centered around a theme that changes monthly. And speaking of small, if you have limited space in your suitcase but would love to bring home original art to commemorate your time on the coast, **Prentice Gallery** *(prenticefineart.com)* has an impressive array of miniature acrylic-on-canvas paintings.

A Legendary Lens

Take a stroll to Point Cabrillo Light Station

Watch for whales, step inside a historical home, and learn about a lighthouse that's been guiding ships since 1909. It's all at the **Point Cabrillo Light Station State Historic Park** *(pointcabrillo.org; suggested $5 donation)*. The adventure begins on the half-mile stroll from the parking lot to the lighthouse (handicapped parking is available closer to the Light Station in front of the residences). The paved path is lined with whale trivia to get you hyped for the plumes of mist you might see offshore, especially between December and April. Eventually, you'll pass a residence on your right that once served as housing for first assistant lighthouse keepers. Today, it's a museum *(11am-4pm)* with interiors restored to their 1930s glory, so head in for a self-guided tour. You'll also pass

DRINKING IN MENDOCINO: OUR PICKS

Fog Bottle Shop and Wine Bar: A sister spot to Fog Eater Cafe, this cozy cantina offers wine flights, bottles to go and nibbles. *noon-7pm Wed-Sun*

Dick's Place: For nearly a century, this beloved dive bar has toasted tourists and locals alike – just be sure to have cash on hand. *11.30am-2am*

Patterson's Pub: Here's an Irish-style watering hole with almost as many beers on tap as there are water towers in Mendocino. *11am-11pm*

MendoVino: Sample Anderson Valley pinot noirs, sauvignon blancs and chardonnays without leaving town. Flights, glasses and bottles available. *11am-5pm*

LUCKY-PHOTOGRAPHER/SHUTTERSTOCK

Point Cabrillo Light Station

the homes for the head lightkeeper and the second assistant lightkeeper plus a couple cottages – all of these are available for overnight stays from $158 per night. Past the residences is the Marine Science Exhibit, a kid-friendly pitstop with aquariums of tiny marine organisms. Next, you'll reach the lighthouse, which triples as a museum and gift shop. After you've learned about the point's original keepers – the Native Pomo people – head out to the trails along the bluffs and keep your eyes peeled for marine wildlife.

Walk Among Waterfalls

Check out Russian Gulch State Park

The **Fern Canyon Trail** in **Russian Gulch State Park** *(parks.ca.gov; per vehicle $8)*, about three miles north of Mendocino Village, offers a scenic payoff for a relatively low lift from your hiking boots. Follow a flat, 2-mile trail along Russian Gulch Creek until you reach a fork in the road. Head left and it's only about three-quarters of a mile to a 36-foot waterfall. Feeling ambitious? Take the right fork, which is the Falls Loop Trail, and you'll get an additional 1.6 miles of lush forest hiking and eventually end up at the same waterfall.

TOP MENDOCINO FESTIVALS

Mendocino Whale Festival: Come for the whales, stay for the wine. During peak migration in early March, tastings give wildlife watchers another reason to visit.

Murder, She Wrote Festival: Each May, devotees of the TV series converge on Mendocino for walking tours, tea receptions and trivia.

Mendocino Film Festival: Usually spanning a weekend in late May and early June, this event celebrates cinema with dozens of screenings plus live music.

Fourth of July: Independence Day includes a parade plus live jazz on the lawn at the Mendocino Art Center.

Mendocino Music Festival: In July, catch the sounds of bluegrass, big band and Americana with concerts on the coast.

Beyond Mendocino

Tiny towns and big flavor, including plenty of wine, can be found within minutes of Mendocino.

Places

GETTING AROUND

Exploring the area around Mendocino means driving both north and south on Hwy 1, where cell service is limited and rideshare services are even more scarce. You'll need a car. Give yourself plenty of time to reach your destination, as construction can turn stretches of the highway into a one-lane road. There's a good chance you'll stop along the way to take in the coastal views.

As you pull away from Mendocino, you might think you're leaving all the action behind, but you'd be mistaken. Within a few minutes you'll hit Little River, home to the lush Van Damme State Park, followed by art-filled and Michelin-celebrated Elk just a bit further south. North of Mendocino, Fort Bragg is a fun day trip for families, especially little ones obsessed with trains, as well as for anyone who wants to feast their eyes on the astoundingly beautiful Mendocino Coast Botanical Gardens. Inland, there's Anderson Valley, a cool-climate wine appellation known for its award-winning pinot noir and chardonnay. If you're flying out of Sonoma County Airport in Santa Rosa, a stop in Anderson Valley makes sense. You'll pass a number of the area's wineries right on Hwy 29, which is on your way.

Little River

TIME FROM MENDOCINO: **10 MINS**

A Pygmy Forest for all

One of the most accessible hiking trails in Mendocino County is also one of its most unique. The **Pygmy Forest Trail** at **Van Damme State Park** *(parks.ca.gov; per vehicle $10)* is a quarter-mile loop built on a wheelchair-accessible boardwalk over swampy surroundings. You'll see dwarf manzanita, rhododendron, bishop pine and Mendocino cypress, among other petite plants. The area's nutrient-starved soil is the reason for their stunted growth. To head directly to the Pygmy Forest Trail, don't enter through the park's main entrance. Instead, head south on Hwy 1 and take the first left onto Little River Airport Road. In about three miles, you'll see a sign for the parking lot on your left.

For a longer hike, head through the park's main entrance to the **Fern Canyon Trail**, a 5.6-mile round-trip route. Grab a brochure from a box at the beginning of the trail for a self-guided tour that introduces area flora and fauna along the first mile of the path. Afterward, head across Hwy 1 to the exceptionally scenic **Van Damme Beach**, where there's parking, bathrooms and oceanfront lounging.

R ALAN MEYER/SHUTTERSTOCK

Pygmy Forest Trail

Elk

TIME FROM MENDOCINO: 30 MINS

Michelin-starred dining

In the tiny coastal town of Elk, where the population doesn't even top 300, you can get a meal at a Michelin-starred restaurant. The 20-seat ocean-view restaurant at the **Harbor House Inn** *(theharborhouseinn.com)*, helmed by chef Matthew Kammerer, has earned an impressive two Michelin stars. The lunch and dinner tasting menus change daily, but always focus on hyperlocal ingredients. Make a reservation well in advance, as a table here is one of the hottest for over a hundred miles.

Manchester

TIME FROM MENDOCINO: 45 MINS

Go horseback riding on the beach

The only thing better than a stroll on a wild Mendocino beach is a horseback ride on a wild Mendocino beach. **Ross Ranch** *(rossranch.biz; rides $70 per person)* leads tours on Manchester Beach and makes the logistics a breeze. Owner Tobi Ross will likely be your guide and is quick to respond to reservation requests. She'll lead you on a 90-minute ride on an unspoiled beach and even volunteer to snap photos of your group on your trusty steeds.

BEST SHOPS BEYOND MENDOCINO

Matson Mercantile: Located inside the early 1900s Elk Garage, this general store has hardware and cute gifts.

Artists' Collective in Elk: Creators from around the coast sell their art here, including paintings, photography, jewelry and pottery.

Lost Coast Found: Locally made pottery, antique home goods and a good selection of vintage clothing. In Fort Bragg.

Lunar Tide: Forgot your healing crystals at home? Grab some quartz and citrine in Fort Bragg, plus a mystical bath bomb.

The Bookstore: Fort Bragg spot for used books and vinyl. Stop in and snag your next beach read.

EATING BEYOND MENDOCINO: OUR PICKS

Little River Inn (p276)**:** Dinner is open to the public at this classic coastal resort. Afterward, grab a nightcap at the ocean-view Whale Watch Bar. *5-8pm* **$$$**

Jumbo's Win Win: This Philo burger joint with soft serve ice cream is the place to be after a day of Anderson Valley wine tasting. *11am-7:45pm* **$**

The Elk Store: Hit up this retro-style general store for all your picnicking needs, including hot and cold deli sandwiches. *11am-5pm Wed-Mon* **$**

The Wharf Restaurant: Watch ships come and go as you dig into pan-seared scallops and fish tacos at this Fort Bragg favorite. *noon-8pm Thu-Tue* **$$$**

TOP SURF SPOTS AROUND MENDOCINO

To rent gear, swing by **Lost Surf Shack** in downtown Fort Bragg.

Smuggler's Cove: Right in Mendocino, just south of the village, Smuggler's Cove has intermediate waves in the winter.

Caspar Beach: Beginners can surf at this beach just 10 minutes north of Mendocino Village. Wear a wetsuit.

Virgin Creek: This Fort Bragg beach is suitable for beginners, and on bigger days can be fun for more experienced surfers.

Point Arena Pier: About 35 miles south of Mendocino Village, this spot is best suited for experienced surfers.

Cooks Beach: Good spot for beginners, but it's over an hour from Mendocino to Gualala.

Point Arena

TIME FROM MENDOCINO: 1 HR

A classic beacon you can climb

Point Arena Lighthouse *(pointarenalighthouse.com)* is one of the tallest towers in California, and you can climb all 115 feet. Tours *($5, plus a $5 site fee)* include entry to the tower, a brief chat about its history and access to its outer platform (a great place to look for whales). The nearby museum doubles as a gift shop.

Fort Bragg

TIME FROM MENDOCINO: 20 MINS

Botanicals, bluffs & brew

Spread across 47 acres, **Mendocino Coast Botanical Gardens** *(gardenbythesea.org; adult/senior/child $23/18/8)* is home to a variety of themed gardens (including rose, succulent, magnolias and camellias), four miles of trails, oceanfront vistas and a whale-watching cottage. Feeling inspired by all the botanicals? The gift shop sells gardening gear as well as seeds gathered from the property. **Rhody's Garden Café**, near the garden's entrance, serves coffee, lunch and ice cream (orange cream float!) with a flower-filled view.

Riding retro rails

All aboard for some family-friendly fun. The **Skunk Train** *(skunktrain.com; rides from $50)* dates back to 1885 and gets its name from the stinky fumes these rail cruisers used to emit. But don't worry, the fumes are now substantially reduced. Today, this classic train takes passengers on scenic rides through the redwoods. The 90-minute **Pudding Creek Express**, which includes a stop halfway through the journey so that you can stretch your legs and enjoy a snack under the trees, is perfect for youngsters. Adult passengers can add on a wine package and get a bottle of the train's own Skunk Train Red Cuvée. Keep an eye on the calendar for special events. In November, for example, the Skunk becomes the **Mushroom, Whisky and Wine Train**. Passengers get a lesson from local foragers, in addition to sampling tasty morsels and sips.

A treasure-covered beach

Treasure? Or trash? Well, it's like they say, one person's trash is another's treasure. Starting in the early 1900s, Fort Bragg residents tossed untold amounts of detritus off a bluff and into the surf, expecting it would simply disappear. Instead, the refuse returned to them as sea glass. To this day, you can find these colorful fragments at **Glass Beach**, a popular beachcombing destination. After hunting, head to the nearby **Sea Glass Museum** to get a better understanding of your haul. The exhibit cases include descriptions of what objects may have created each color of sea glass.

JUSTINEMT17/SHUTTERSTOCK

Mendocino Coast Botanical Gardens

HELP ME PICK:

Anderson Valley Tasting Rooms

Napa and Sonoma may get all the attention in California, but that's what makes Anderson Valley even cooler. This under-the-radar gem, on the tail end of a picturesque drive through the redwoods if you're coming from Mendocino, is filled with friendly tasting rooms. In all, it only stretches for about 15 miles along Hwy 128, but the region's 30+ wineries – with notable varietals including pinot noir and chardonnay – are sure to dazzle wine dabblers and experts alike.

Where to sip if you...

Want to be Spontaneous

Navarro Winery No reservations needed at this casual yet widely respected winery. The tasting room has two indoor counters and an outdoor picnic area draped with sweet-smelling wisteria blooms.

Husch Vineyards Reservations are only required for groups of six or more at this tasting room set in a converted pony barn from the late 1800s. The oldest winery in Anderson Valley, Husch is family owned and produces 22 different wines.

SARAHSTIERCH/FLICKR/CC BY 1.0 UNIVERSAL ©

Wine bottle, Goldeneye winery

Have Kids in Wow

Meyer Family Cellars Not only are kids allowed here, they'll find some fun on the property's playground while the adults sip pinot noir with notes of pomegranate and blackberry. For older kids, there's an onsite disc golf course.

Foursight Wines In addition to wine tastings, Foursight also offers kid-friendly tours of their lavender field and native plants pollinator garden. Guests can even pick a bundle of lavender to take home.

Are Feeling Hungry

Pennyroyal Farm This sister property to Navarro Winery is a vineyard, creamery and veggie-growing farm. As such, tasting-room guests can purchase small-batch cheeses and farm fare in addition to sampling the wine.

Goldeneye Tasting options here include a seasonal snack, a cheese plate, cheese and charcuterie pairings, or caviar. Be sure to make a reservation – you'll find a link on Goldeneye's website.

Want Something Other Than Wine

The Madrones In addition to two wine tasting rooms, this Mediterranean-style compound also has an apothecary fitting for the Emerald Triangle (the name for the area's cannabis-producing region). Pick up locally grown cannabis and keep an eye out for themed weekends during the spring and summer with farm tours and music.

Gowan's Heirloom Ciders For 150 years Gowan's has been growing apples, and you can sample the fruits of their labor (literally) with a visit to their cider-tasting orchard. Try the cider slushie on a hot day.

Anderson Valley Brewing Company The brewery's Boonville home is a 30-acre kid- and dog-friendly fun zone known as Beer Park. Take your pick from 20 beers on tap, play disc golf and occasionally catch live music.

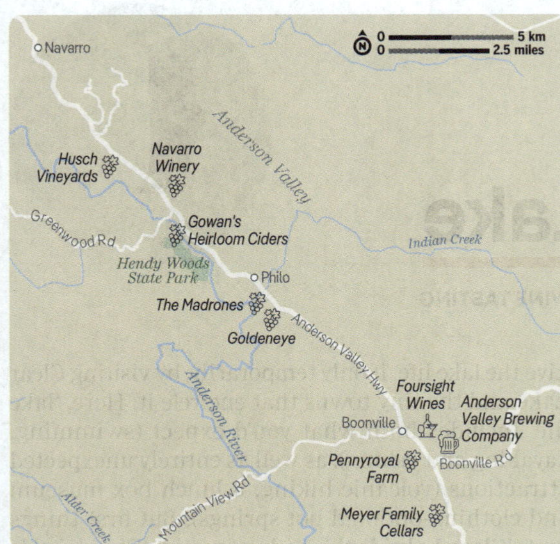

HOW TO

When to go Most tasting rooms are open 11am to 5pm. The Anderson Valley Pinot Noir Festival is held in May; harvest season (Aug-Oct) is another prime time.

Book in advance Check to see if your winery of choice requires reservations, especially for groups of six or more. During harvest months, book well in advance.

Budget Basic tastings run between $10 and $45 per person. You'll pay more for food pairings.

Top tip Buy a bottle to take home, as many wineries here have limited distribution and you likely won't find them elsewhere.

DIY or guided tour?

Having trusted transportation is the most crucial consideration for a day of tasting. If you have a designated driver in the group, the good news is that many of the wineries are located one after another on Hwy 128, so it's not difficult to find them. Coming from Mendocino, you'll hit the area's wine towns in this order: Philo, Boonville and then Yorkville. Plan your tastings accordingly.

If everyone in your party wants to partake in the pinot extravaganza, book a car service. Uber is not readily available for spur-of-the-moment pickups and the wineries aren't walkable from one to the next. Tour Mendocino *(tourmendocino.com)* offers a fully customizable, private all-day experience for up to eight guests *($695 for the van and driver, plus $40 per person)*. The day includes refreshments and lunch as well as visits to three wineries of your choice. They also have a multi-group tour *($175 per person)* with visits to three wineries, all chosen by Tour Mendocino, plus lunch. Another option is Mendo Insider Tours *(mendoinsidertours.com)*, a local transportation company that'll help you craft the wine day of your dreams. They have cars for smaller groups as well as a Sprinter van for parties of six or more. Plus, their knowledgeable chauffeurs can give you tasting-room recommendations along the way.

Wine bottles, Navarro Winery

MICHAEL DEFREITAS NORTH AMERICA/ALAMY

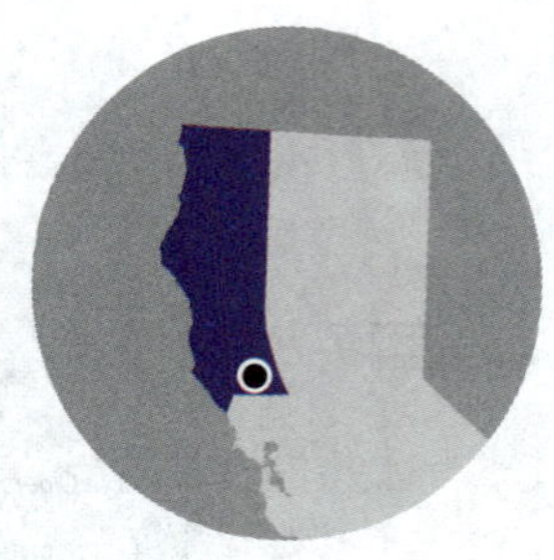

Clear Lake

FISHING | VOLCANOS | WINE TASTING

GETTING AROUND

Having your own vehicle is definitely the way to go. But Lake Transit operates weekday routes between Clearlake and Calistoga. Buses serve Ukiah from Lakeport. Since piecing together routes and times can be difficult, it's best to phone ahead *(707-263-3334)*.

Live the lake life, if only temporarily, by visiting Clear Lake and the tiny towns that encircle it. Here, 'lake life' includes both what you'd expect (swimming, kayaking and fishing), as well as entirely unexpected attractions (volcanic hiking, a lunch box museum and clothing-optional hot springs). But first things first: 'Clear Lake' is the body of water; 'Clearlake' is a town on its southeastern side. The body of water has 100 miles of shoreline and 68 sq miles of surface area. It's actually the largest naturally occurring freshwater lake entirely in California (Lake Tahoe is bigger but straddles Nevada). It's also considered the oldest lake in North America, and dates back 1 to 2 million years, according to geologists. With a 4300ft dormant volcano lording over it and an under-the-radar reputation, Clear Lake is both geographically stunning and easy on the budget.

TOP TIP

When vacationing here in summertime, ask around about the algae situation. Avoid drinking water that has come from the lake and be careful about when and where you (and your pets) go swimming.

Hiking Trails & History

Experience Clear Lake State Park

Dip your toe into Clear Lake, both metaphorically and literally, at **Clear Lake State Park** *(parks.ca.gov; per vehicle $8)*, which has a sampling of what makes the area great. Swim, fish, hike and bike, and get a feel for the lake's Indigenous history by following the moderate half-mile **Indian Nature Trail**, which gives an overview of how the Pomo people used the area's resources. The trail passes through what was once a Pomo village.

Summit a Volcano

Hike Mount Konocti

The fact that Mount Konocti (4305ft) is a dormant volcano is actually only part of what makes it so intriguing. If you follow the Wright Peak Summit Trail – a 6-mile out-and-back route – you'll also spot an off-the-grid early 1900s cabin as well as the wreckage from a tragic 1970 plane crash. The hike begins

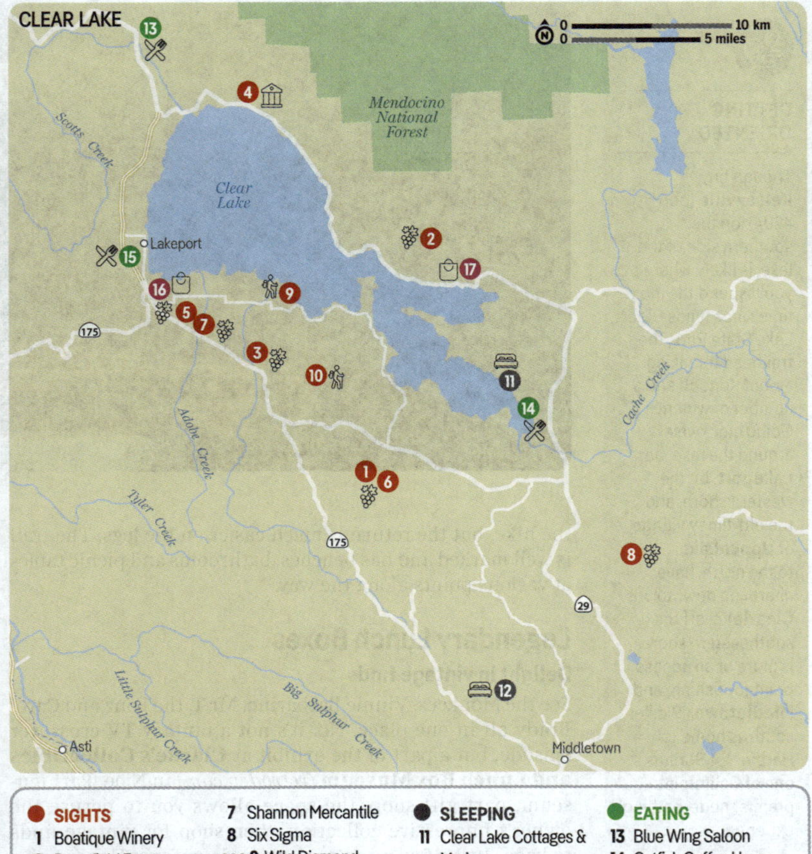

SIGHTS
1 Boatique Winery
2 Brassfield Estate Winery
3 Chacewater Winery & Olive Mill
4 Clarke's Collectibles and Lunch Box Museum
5 Kaz Winery
6 Laujor Estate Winery
7 Shannon Mercantile
8 Six Sigma
see 8 Wild Diamond Vineyards

ACTIVITIES
9 Clear Lake State Park
see 9 Indian Nature Trail
10 Mount Konocti County Park

SLEEPING
11 Clear Lake Cottages & Marina
12 Harbin Hot Springs
see 9 Kelsey Creek Campground
see 3 Suites on Main
see 13 Tallman Hotel

EATING
13 Blue Wing Saloon
14 Catfish Coffee House
15 Park Place Restaurant
see 3 Saw Shop Public House

SHOPPING
16 Clearlake Outdoors
17 Limit Out
see 13 Oliveira's Antiques

at the **Mount Konocti County Park** trailhead *(518 Konocti Rd, Kelseyville)*, where you'll find plenty of parking plus bathrooms. From there, it's a steep climb to the top, gaining 1800ft of elevation. You'll pass Downen Cabin, where the intrepid and peace-seeking Mary Downen lived solo in the early 1900s, about two miles into the hike. The mangled pieces of the white-and-turquoise Navion A aircraft, visible just to the right of the trail, lie scattered just before the peak's summit. At the top, you'll find multiple picnic tables and near-360° views. Of course, you'll get an eyeful of Clear Lake below, and on a clear day you can also spot Mount Lassen and Mount Diablo in the distance. At this point, you're only halfway done with

GETTING ORIENTED

Though tiny, **Kelseyville** (pop 4204), on the southern side of the lake, is likely where you'll spend the most time since it has Clear Lake State Park, the trailhead for hiking Mount Konocti and a number of wineries. Going clockwise around the lake, both **Lakeport**, on the western shore, and the old-timey village of **Upper Lake**, to the north, have charming downtowns. **Clearlake**, off the southeastern shore, is more of an access point for fishing, and **Middletown**, 19 miles south, is home to Harbin Hot Springs, one of California's premier nude-bathing experiences.

the hike, but the return is much easier on the legs. The trail is well marked and has benches, bathrooms and picnic tables at various points along the way.

Legendary Lunch Boxes

Delight in vintage finds

See the Monkees, Vinnie Barbarino, Mr T, the Fonz and Carol Brady all in one place. No, it's not a fantasy TV crossover episode, but a part of the exhibit at **Clarke's Collectibles and Lunch Box Museum** *(retrodeb.com)* in Nice. Part museum, part gift shop, the space allows you to peruse the owner's impressive collection, then shop for vintage finds to keep. Just a few minutes away in downtown Upper Lake, the vintage fun continues at **Oliveira's Antiques**, which has a collection of vintage Western accessories, including hats and jewelry.

An Angler's Paradise

Cast for bass on Clear Lake

Called the bass capital of the West, Clear Lake lures sport fishers from across the country. Largemouth bass make up two-thirds of the fish caught on Clear Lake – crappie, bluegill,

EATING AROUND CLEAR LAKE: OUR PICKS

Saw Shop Public House: Laid-back Kelseyville restaurant with farm-to-table cuisine and delicious cocktails in Mason jars. *noon-8pm Tue-Sat, from 11am Sun* $$

Park Place Restaurant: Lakeport's premier dining venue has classic Italian and American dishes and killer lake views. *11am-7pm Sun-Thu, to 8pm Fri & Sat* $$

Blue Wing Saloon: Cozy up on the heated veranda with casual American fare and live music at this Upper Lake restaurant in the Tallman Hotel. *hours vary* $$

Catfish Coffee House: With a drive-thru window, this is the spot to grab coffee and bagels in Clearlake. *5.30am-6pm Mon-Fri, 6am-6pm Sat, 6.30am-6pm Sun* $

LORI A JONES/SHUTTERSTOCK

Mount Konocti County Park (p246)

carp and catfish make up the remaining third. To get in on the angling action, base yourself at the **Clear Lake Cottages & Marina** *(clearlakecottagesandmarina.com)* in the town of Clearlake. The property has a private launch as well as boat rentals for overnight guests. Book waterfront cottage #27 and you can even fish from your private balcony. Free public boat launches can also be found at various points around the lake. Lakeport, for example, has ramped access on 1st, 3rd and 5th Sts. Also in Lakeport, bait and tackle shop **Clearlake Outdoors** *(clearlakeoutdoors.com)* is a go-to spot for bait and tackle, and **Limit Out** *(limitoutbaitshop.com)* has you covered on the opposite side of the lake, in Clearlake Oaks.

Hippie Hot Springs

Strip down and heat up

Harbin Hot Springs *(harbin.org)* is the oldest hot springs in California, and visiting these clothing-optional baths is practically a rite of passage. There's a youthful, no-frills vibe, and it's also decidedly hippie-dippie (don't be surprised when the bare-chested lady next to you starts chanting mantras). If you're comfortable in the buff, it can be a revelatory experience. The heart and soul of the 1700-acre retreat center is the spring-fed pool area, with eight baths of varying temperatures, plus a sauna and sundeck offering sweeping valley views. Lodging is in creekside caravans, domes or hilltop cottages. Budget travelers can also pitch a tent or sleep in the car and pay for 24-hour access. Day use *($50; not required for overnight guests)* gives you up to six hours to explore the facilities and dine at the organic (and mostly vegetarian) **Dancing Bear Cafe**. All visitors 18 and over, including both overnight and day-use guests, are required to become a member; membership starts at $15 per month.

KELSEYVILLE PEAR FESTIVAL

Held on the last Saturday in September, Lake County's largest one-day event is a real hoot and a showcase of the region's agricultural heritage, including the almighty pear. Think parades, live music and dancing on three stages, a giant decorative pear, a pie-eating contest, a scarecrow contest and plenty of street vendors. There are special exhibits all over town, from a tractor and engine show to a display on the history of Kelseyville farming within the Pear Pavilion. The event has grown from just 1500 attendees in 1993 to more than 10,000 in recent years. The festival's highly appropriate slogan? 'Catch the small-town magic.'

SIP & STAY

If an entire day of wine tasting isn't enough, why not sleep at a winery too? **Boatique** and **Chacewater** have short-term rentals on their property, and **Laujor** has one just above its tasting room. For an even better experience, check out **Bed & Barrel at Stonehouse Cellars** *(stonehousecellars.com)*. Set on 145 acres of secluded countryside, this winery rents a room and a suite within a luxury home, as well as a stylish and cozy three-bedroom ranch. All guests have access to vineyard hiking trails, a pool, a hot tub and a large patio with a BBQ grill. And breakfast is made with farm-fresh local ingredients.

A Wine Country Less Traveled

You're not in Napa anymore

There are some 30 wineries around Clear Lake. All are incredibly welcoming and they typically waive tasting fees if you purchase a bottle. Start your tasting adventure at **Six Sigma** *(sixsigmaranch.com)*, a historic ranch and winery spread across more than 4000 acres in Lower Lake, where you can sip on a full-bodied cab or an earthy tempranillo in the tasting room, mountain bike the ranch's trails and take the excellent vineyard tour in a converted military vehicle. From there, continue south to the nearby **Wild Diamond Vineyards** *(wilddiamond.com)* and its hilltop tasting village, a collection of tables under shade canopies and a refurbished shipping container. The best part: you can sip astoundingly good reds while looking down on Napa (literally).

Hop onto Hwy 29 and start driving toward Kelseyville, where many of the wineries are concentrated. At **Laujor Estate Winery** *(laujorestate.com)*, do the classic tasting and soak up the impressive views from an outdoor fire pit. Then, head over to **Boatique Winery** *(boatiquewines.com)* for more Red Hills AVA sampling, as well as an outstanding view of Mt Konocti and a prized collection of antique wooden boats. Continue on to Kelseyville proper, where **Chacewater Winery & Olive Mill** *(chacewaterwine.com)* offers tastings of organic wine and olive oil. Bring your favorite bottle to the picnic area out back where you can play horseshoes or bocce ball in front of the olive groves.

If you've got even more time, head over to the **Shannon Mercantile** *(shannonfamilyofwines.com)*, a buzzy tasting room with 12 wines on tap, plus picnic areas and cornhole. There's also cult favorite **Kaz Winery** *(kazwinery.com)*, where they're all about blends. Whatever is in the organic vineyards goes into the wine – and they're blended at crush, not during fermentation. Or make a trip across the lake to **Brassfield Estate Winery** *(brassfieldestate.com)*, a stunning Tuscan-style winery in the unique High Valley appellation, surrounded by magnificent gardens.

A Lake County winery

TERRY W RYDER/SHUTTERSTOCK

The Lost Coast

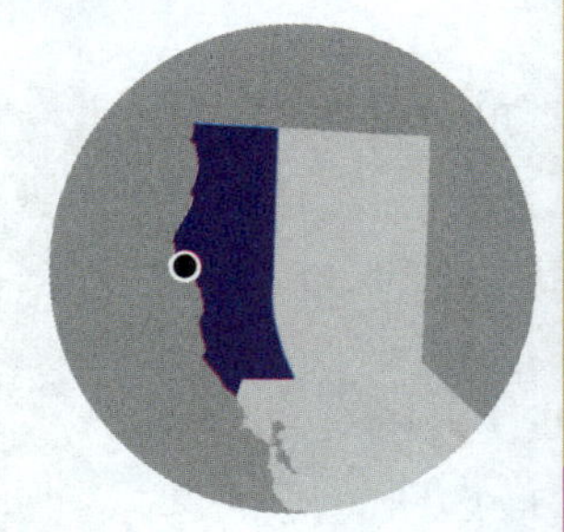

EPIC HIKES | REMOTE BEACHES | TIDEPOOLS

Even in the country's most populated state, you can still find delightful solitude on a wild beach – and the Lost Coast is the place for it. The longest stretch of undeveloped coastline in California is a superlative backpacking destination and a glimpse into California's past, with foggy, windswept coves and rugged 4000ft peaks that plunge into a frothy sea. The coast became 'lost' when the state's highway system deemed the region unruly in the mid-20th century and bypassed it. There is one sizable and difficult-to-reach community: Shelter Cove, perched on a south-facing bluff surrounded by the King Range National Conservation Area. Some folks arrive via the airstrip, while others brave the narrow, curvy road. Once you get there, you'll be rewarded with oceanfront accommodations and endless opportunities to unplug, even if you don't want to bust out your hiking boots.

GETTING AROUND

There's no public transportation on the Lost Coast, but you can book a shuttle service to pick you up from the end of the Lost Coast Trail if you make the multiday journey. We recommend Lost Coast Adventure Tours *(lostcoastadventures.com; per person $98)*, which operates daily shuttles from Shelter Cove to Mattole Beach.

Picnicking with Panoramic Views

Enjoy a DIY outdoor meal

On your way into Shelter Cove, stop off at the **Shelter Cove General Store** *(sheltercovegeneralstore.com)* to grab sandwich supplies, snacks, locally brewed beer or a bottle of wine. Next door, the **Shelter Cove Gift Shop** is one of the few places in town to grab a souvenir or sweatshirt. Take your supplies to either **Abalone Point** or **Seal Rock** for a Pacific-view picnic. Both spots sit on a bluff overlooking the ocean and have picnic tables.

TOP TIP

Visit with the mindset of taking it easy (other than when you're hiking the trails, of course). Shelter Cove is not a bustling city, and restaurant kitchens in town close as early as 7pm. Kicking back and enjoying the natural splendor is the area's big draw.

Urchins & Abalone Galore

Tidepooling in Shelter Cove

Probably the most fascinating (and free!) Lost Coast activity is discovering the diverse and wonderfully weird creatures living in the tidepools. Anemone, urchin, crabs and bright sea stars are all easily visible; these are some of the best pools on the North Coast.

HIGHLIGHTS
1 Lost Coast Trail

SIGHTS
2 Abalone Point
3 Cape Mendocino Lighthouse
see 3 Mal Coombs Park
4 Punta Gorda Lighthouse
5 Seal Rock
6 Shelter Cove Beach

ACTIVITIES
7 Black Sands Beach
8 Deadman's
9 Lost Coast Adventure Tours
10 Mattole Beach Trailhead
11 Shelter Cove Boat Ramp

SLEEPING
12 Inn of the Lost Coast
see 10 Mattole Campground
see 18 Needle Rock Campground
see 17 Tides Inn
13 Usal Beach Campground

EATING
14 Gyppo Ale Mill
15 Mario's Marina Bar
see 9 Mi Mochima
16 Shelter Cove General Store
17 Surf Point Coffee House

SHOPPING
see 16 Shelter Cove Gift Shop

INFORMATION
18 Needle Rock Visitor Center

Start your tidepooling adventure by parking at **Mal Coombs Park**, where you can't miss the **Cape Mendocino Lighthouse** *(capemendocinolighthouse.org; free)*. Originally located about 60 miles north of here, the lighthouse was moved in 1998 for preservation purposes. Today, it's maintained by the Cape Mendocino Lighthouse Preservation Society, who open it to the public as a museum each summer, from Memorial Day to Labor Day.

After giving the historic lighthouse a look, head down the set of stairs to the beach. At low tide, the area looks otherworldly, with exposed rugged black rocks. You may find treasures in the sand, like pieces of petrified wood or dried urchin shells, but climb the rock formations (always keeping an eye on the tide, of course, and peer into the puddles where there's an entire world of living aquatic critters.

Catch a Gnarly Wave

Surfing Shelter Cove

Intermediate surfers looking to ride the swell should give Shelter Cove's most popular wave a go. Set in the town's namesake cove, **Deadman's** is known for long lefts and rights, with the rights being a bit slower. Spring and fall usually provide the best conditions (summer waves tend to be small) since it's southwest facing. And because the coastline here is crescent shaped, the swell ranges anywhere from triple-overhead at Point Delgada to chest-high at the **Shelter Cove Boat Ramp** *(sheltercovefishingpreservation.wordpress.com)*.

Bring your own board and wetsuit (there aren't rentals in town) and prepare for a decent amount of effort to reach Deadman's. You'll have to park at the boat launch and walk over half a mile, passing **Shelter Cove Beach** (the only swimmable beach in town) on your way. Once you get there, be mindful of changing tides, as Deadman's Beach has rocky abutments on either end. Be mindful of the locals too – surf sites have described the vibes as 'intimidating.'

WHY I LOVE THE LOST COAST

Amelia Mularz, Lonely Planet writer

'Hey! Over here!' shouted a local who had joined my mission to spot a sea star in the wild. My excitement nearly sent me tumbling into a frothy puddle of seawater and sea anemone. 'I can't believe this is your first,' she said. 'It's truly a momentous occasion,' I replied, laughing. What I'd intended to be a 10-minute stop at the tidepools below the Mal Coombs Park bluffs in Shelter Cove had turned into a three-hour odyssey. Bounding between black rocks and crouching to peer into entire galaxies of marine life had unleashed a childlike joy that I hadn't felt in years. The Lost Coast is exactly that kind of place: where stopovers become highlights and nature discoveries are somehow deeply personal.

EATING IN SHELTER COVE: OUR PICKS

Surf Point Coffee House: Coffee, housemade pastries and wines to pair with lunch at this bistro with breathtaking views. *7.30am-4pm Fri-Wed, to 4.30pm Thu* $

Mi Mochima: From out of nowhere comes delicious and authentic Venezuelan cuisine: empanadas, arepas and *patacón* sandwiches. *hours vary* $$

Gyppo Ale Mill: California's most remote brewery serves its own lagers, pilsners and blondes. Burgers and wings, too. *5-9pm Mon-Thu, from noon Fri-Sun* $$

Mario's Marina Bar: This local hangout has an ever-changing global menu, killer ocean views from its patio and frequent live music. *hours vary* $$

RON KARPEL/SHUTTERSTOCK

Lost Coast Trail, Punta Gorda Lighthouse in distance

TOP EXPERIENCE

The Lost Coast Trail

The best way to see the Lost Coast is to hike. And while the 24.6-mile Lost Coast Trail between Mattole Beach and Black Sands Beach is a bucket list adventure, it's not for everyone. It requires multiple days, a permit and a shuttle ride back to your car. The good news: there are day hikes along the Lost Coast Trail, too.

DON'T MISS

- Mattole Beach
- Punta Gorda Lighthouse
- Black Sands Beach
- Sinkyone Wilderness State Park
- Bear Harbor

Mattole Beach to Black Sands Beach

This is the whole shebang: the full 24.6-mile Lost Coast adventure. Technically, the Lost Coast Trail extends even further south into Sinkyone State Park (we've included day hikes in that area), but the classic, multiday backpacking experience is this northern section through the King Range National Conservation Area. Because the trail can be dangerous at times, with impassable sections at high tide, going with a group or hiring a private guide is highly recommended. **Lost Coast Adventure Tours** *(lostcoastadventures.com; guided tours from $900)* is a popular and well-respected pick. They offer

PRACTICALITIES

- Day-hiking doesn't require a permit, but overnight trips do. Reserve online at *recreation.gov*.
- Fees: $6 per permit reservation, plus $12 per person area fee.

both north-to-south hikes (five days, four nights) and south-to-north trips (four days, three nights). They provide meals, bear canisters (required for all hikers) and shuttles. If you prefer to go it alone, you can still book a shuttle with Lost Coast Adventure Tours to get you back to your car.

Mattole Beach to Punta Gorda Lighthouse (Day Hike)

No need to pack a sleeping bag for this one. A day hike that starts at the same point as the long-haul trek, this out-and-back route is 6 miles total, traversing sand and coastal shrubbery, with the now-defunct **Punta Gorda Lighthouse** as a turnaround point. From Ferndale, it's about a 75-minute drive along winding, remote roads to the **Mattole Beach Trailhead**. There, you'll find a campground, parking and public bathrooms. Pack a picnic lunch to enjoy at the lighthouse, where you're also likely to see large groups of elephant seals lazing on the sand below.

Black Sands Beach to Gitchell Creek (Day Hike)

If you're staying in Shelter Cove and want to stretch your legs along charcoal-colored sand, this is a convenient choice. Just minutes from the main part of town, **Black Sands Beach** is the southern point of the multiday hike. There's a parking lot and bathrooms near the trailhead, then it's a 7.4-mile out-and-back trek. You'll walk Black Sands for about two miles before passing **Horse Mountain Creek**, at which point the terrain becomes a bit more rocky and trickier to navigate. At your turnaround point, **Gitchell Creek**, you're likely to see overnight campers, as the next 4.5-mile stretch just beyond that becomes impassable at high tide.

Needle Rock to Whale Gulch (Day Hike)

Within Sinkyone State Park, **Needle Rock Visitor Center** *(parking $8)* gives you even more access to coastal hiking. From the visitor center, you can head south to Bear Harbor, or take this 4.6-mile route north. You'll travel grassy sections (with a couple spur trails that lead down to the water), and pass **Jones Beach** before reaching **Whale Gulch**. Wildlife abounds.

Needle Rock to Bear Harbor (Day Hike)

While much of the southern section of the Lost Coast Trail includes forest, this out-and-back 6.2-mile hike, leaving from Needle Rock Visitor Center and heading south, has plenty of ocean views. Tides, though, aren't a concern, as the trail is inland enough that you won't have to battle soaked pathways. The turnaround point, **Bear Harbor**, was once the western terminus of the Bear Harbor Railroad, built in the 1890s. You can still spot rusted rails in the area today.

PUNTA GORDA LIGHTHOUSE HISTORY

Now simply a rest stop for hikers, Punta Gorda Lighthouse was once a functioning beacon for boats. It was first lit on January 15, 1912, and proved difficult to access from the beginning. Lightkeepers had to travel 11 miles by horseback to reach the nearest town, Petrolia, for supplies. In 1951, the Coast Guard abandoned the lighthouse, opting instead for an offshore lighted buoy to warn ships.

TOP TIPS

- Lost Coast Adventure Tour's owner, Blu Graham, offers the following top tips.
- This is one of the most physically demanding coastal hikes in the country, with rugged terrain, deep sand and unpredictable footing.
- Take the weather seriously. Severe storms on the Lost Coast can bring pummeling wind, rain and surf conditions.
- Plan your tidal windows with plenty of buffer time. Don't cut it close; factors to consider include swell size, wind and storm surge.
- Make all arrangements before you arrive. This includes shuttle rides, food, supplies and accommodations. Services are limited here.

Beyond The Lost Coast

Find your way back to civilization and solid footing via an impossibly quaint town or soothing swimming hole.

Places

GETTING AROUND

After traversing the tricky roads along the Lost Coast, you'll be happy to see good ol' Hwy 101 again. A head's up that there's no public transportation around Ferndale, and you also need your own wheels to explore Humboldt Redwoods State Park. Bring a bicycle and you can ride the entire length of the Avenue of the Giants.

If you need extra motivation to get through the full 24.6-mile Lost Coast Trail, let it be this: the nearby settlement of Butterfat City. Technically, that's just a nickname for Ferndale (it's a reference to the town's dairy heyday), but the sentiment remains. Emerge from the coastal wilderness and you'll be treated to good meals and old-school hospitality. Because of its proximity – and the butterfat – Ferndale is the ideal base for exploring the northern portion of the Lost Coast. But if you're heading south, a stop at Standish-Hickey State Recreation Area, near Leggett, and a splash in a swimming hole might be in order. Or, hightail it to the world-famous Avenue of the Giants for even more hiking.

Standish-Hickey State Recreation Area

TIME FROM SHELTER COVE: 1¼ HR

Cool off in a swimming hole

For little more than the price of a fancy coffee drink, you can access one of California's best swimming holes: a dream if you're visiting in the summer. Park in the **Standish-Hickey State Recreation Area** *(parks.ca.gov; per vehicle $8)* and hike about half a mile to the **South Fork of the Eel River**. It's even better if you work up a sweat – that water can be ice cold!

Humboldt Redwoods State Park

TIME FROM SHELTER COVE: 1 HR

Explore the avenue of the giants

Tree huggers, take note: the sprawling redwood groves within **Humboldt Redwoods State Park** *(parks.ca.gov; free)* rival – and some say surpass – those in Redwood National Park, which is a long drive further north. The quickest, easiest way to enjoy the park is to exit Hwy 101 when you see the **Avenue of the Giants** sign and take the smaller, two-lane alternative to the interstate; it's an incredible 32-mile stretch and there are plenty of great stops along the way.

If you're coming from the south, **Stephens Grove** is the first pull-out with truly impressive redwoods, which have

YAYA ERNST/SHUTTERSTOCK

Humboldt Redwoods State Park

grown up tall thanks to the nutrient-dense alluvial flat, or flood plain, on which they stand. Parking is easy and there's a short 0.7-mile hike – the **Governor William D Stephens Loop Trail** – that serves as a perfect introduction to the park. If you're interested in a longer hike within lesser-explored territory, drive another 6 miles north to the **Children's Forest**. This is another alluvial flat, and there's rarely anyone here, particularly if the seasonal bridge isn't up over the South Fork of the Eel River. The hike begins at the **Williams Grove Day-Use Area** *(per vehicle $8)*, from which it's a half-mile to the river. After the crossing, the mile-long loop trail brings hikers into a grove that endured a large wildfire in 2003. After about a decade, the resilient forest regained its beauty, and the only evidence of the fire was a burned-up park sign.

Another 10 miles north you'll find **Founders Grove**, the most-visited area of the park thanks to its convenient location beside the Hwy 101 off-ramp. Unless you're dead set on doing the easiest and most popular thing, skip it and instead visit the nearby but lesser-explored **Rockefeller Grove**. Here you can contemplate nature in peace or jump on the **Bull Creek Flats Trail**, a 10-mile hike around what's been called 'the world's tallest forest.'

STORIES OF BIGFOOT

What's with all the Bigfoot stuff?

No doubt you'll notice odes to the hair-covered cryptid all along the Avenue of the Giants. He's been spotted, allegedly, within Humboldt Redwoods State Park. He's also been spotted in Redwoods National Park and Eureka, and cynics might say it's all too convenient for the area gift shops, but maybe the guy just gets around.

Probably the most famous California sighting happened in the town of Willow Creek, also in Humboldt County, but a good 2-hour drive north of the Avenue of the Giants. It's now home to a Bigfoot museum. Closer to these parts, you'll find a dedicated gift shop in Garberville, called Legend of Bigfoot. But Bigfoot tees and plushies also abound on the Avenue itself.

EATING BEYOND THE LOST COAST: OUR PICKS

The Peg House: The burgers, BBQ oysters and blackberry sundaes are standouts, but everything's amazing at this roadside gem in Leggett. *7.30am-7pm* $

Benbow Inn Restaurant: Here's the place to indulge in a fancy meal served in an elegant Garberville dining room. Start with martinis at the bar. *hours vary* $$$

Chimney Tree Grill: Feast on local grass-fed beef burgers, fresh-baked pies and soft-serve ice cream in Phillipsville, on the Avenue of the Giants. *11am-8pm* $

Avenue Cafe: Located on the Avenue of the Giants in Miranda, this cafe cooks up Bigfoot-inspired sandwiches, burgers and pizzas. *11am-8pm* $$

WELCOME TO BUTTERFAT CITY

Ferndale earned the nickname Butterfat City thanks to its history in the dairy biz. In the late 19th century, Danish dairymen brought their trade to town and formed neighborhood creamery cooperatives.

By 1890, there were already 11 creameries in the Ferndale area, and their butter was considered the best in the state. Around this time the town took on another nickname, Cream City.

With the city's creameries making a killing, especially by demanding high prices down in San Francisco, Ferndale prospered and ornate Victorian architecture sprang up all over town. These well-to-do buildings – like the Gingerbread Mansion, which is now a B&B – became known as butterfat palaces.

ADELE HEIDENREICH/SHUTTERSTOCK

The Farmer's Daughter

Ferndale

TIME FROM MATTOLE BEACH: 1¼ HR

Shopping in a Victorian town

Even if you can resist the charm of Ferndale's B&Bs, spending an afternoon here is highly recommended. The town's **Main St** has one-off boutiques and great spots for a casual bite. Fun fact: famed restaurateur Guy Fieri grew up here, so you know the food is good. Plus, Ferndale probably has the most charming public bathroom in the region (a noble distinction). The exterior has Victorian-style decor to match much of the historic architecture in town.

Start off energized by popping into **Main Street Coffee Co** for a Mexican mocha or latte, then head next door to **Sunshine and Fog**, which isn't just the forecast for the day but also a women's boutique. Next, cross the street to the **Ferndale Arts Gallery** *(ferndalearts.com)* to appreciate the area's homegrown creativity. On the next block, **The Farmer's Daughter** specializes in homewares, especially kitchen items like strawberry-print juice glasses and floral tea towels. **The Blacksmith Shop** *(ferndaleblacksmith.com)* celebrates old-school craft with metal arts, including stunning jewelry forged from old coins. And speaking of old school, **Golden Gait Mercantile** *(goldengaitmercantile.com)* has the feel of a retro general store, with candy displayed in barrels, and they even have a small museum onsite that's an ode to general stores of yesteryear. Across the street, **Humboldt's Hometown Store** *(humboldtshometownstore.com)* has gifts from around the county and plenty of Guy Fieri merch.

EATING IN FERNDALE: OUR PICKS

Ferndale Meat Company: Grab sandwiches and chips from this deli counter on your way to Mattole Beach and the Lost Coast Trail. *8am-5pm Mon-Sat* $

VI Restaurant and Tavern: Make like the wealthy dairymen of yesteryear and dine in a Victorian mansion. Ribeye and pork chops are on the menu. *8am-9pm* $$$

Tuyas: Treat all your senses with Mexican cuisine, Spanish wine and art made by locals. *11.30am-8pm Sun-Thu, to 9pm Fri & Sat* $$

The Red Front Store: Ice cream tastes better when you enjoy it on a cow-print bench set along old-timey Main Street. *7am-9pm Mon-Fri, 8am-8pm Sat & Sun* $

Eureka

STREET ART | VICTORIAN ARCHITECTURE | HISTORIC HARBOR

"I have found it!' That's the meaning of the Greek word *eureka*, and what the mathematician Archimedes reportedly shouted after he came to understand the principle of buoyancy as he sank into his bath. It's also California's official state motto and the name of Humboldt County's capital – both fitting applications. In the city of Eureka, you're likely to find plenty of moments of joyful discovery. One of the biggest draws here is the perfectly preserved Victorian architecture that's concentrated in the city's charming Old Town district. Take a brief break from land and hop in a kayak for a tour of Humboldt Bay, where you're likely to make a number of historical discoveries (plus reconfirm the principle of buoyancy). Back on solid turf, you just might discover your new favorite seafood restaurant, as Eureka has plenty of delectable dining options with fish-focused menus.

GETTING AROUND

The Redwood Transit System operates buses between Eureka and cities to the north and south, making stops up and down Hwy 101. For local transportation, the Eureka Transit Service operates buses Monday to Saturday. Both options are $2 per ride.

Humboldt History Lesson

Visit the Clarke Historical Museum

Set in an early 1900s bank, the **Clarke Historical Museum** *(clarkemuseum.org; $10 suggested donation)* covers Humboldt County's past, including the area's Native American cultures, the gold rush, farming traditions and the lumber industry. Peeking into a re-created Victorian-era bedroom is especially fun, as is seeing the museum's 400-pound 'man-eating clam' display. Allot extra time to browse the gift shop, which includes vintage finds.

TOP TIP

For up-to-date happenings around town, check the Lost Coast Outpost *(lostcoastoutpost.com)*. They'll let you know about that night's karaoke event, comedy show or concerts, and also post details of traffic hazards and expected weather conditions.

Not-So-Run-of-the-Mill Millworks

Get hands-on with historic craftsmanship

Part museum, part professional woodworking studio, part center for learning traditional crafts – there's nothing quite like the **Blue Ox Historic Village** *(blueoxhistoricvillage.com; self-guided tour adult/child $15/11; guided tour adult/child $30/15)*. Featured on the Magnolia Network TV show *The*

EUREKA

SIGHTS
1 Clarke Historical Museum
2 Historic Eagle House
3 Morris Graves Museum of Art
4 Romano Gabriel Wooden Sculpture Garden

ACTIVITIES
5 Humboats Kayak Adventures
6 Humboldt Cannabis Tours

SLEEPING
7 Carter House Inns
see 2 Inn at 2nd & C
8 The Pinc

EATING
9 Café Marina & Woodley's Bar
see 2 Gallagher's Restaurant and Pub
10 Jack's Seafood
11 Living the Dream Ice Cream
12 Los Bagels

DRINKING & NIGHTLIFE
13 Lost Coast Brewery & Cafe
see 2 Phatsy Kline's Parlour Lounge
14 The Shanty
15 The Speakeasy

ENTERTAINMENT
16 Kinetic Grand Championship

SHOPPING
17 Dick Taylor Craft Chocolate
18 Eureka Books
see 20 Land of Lovely
see 18 Many Hands Gallery
19 Patricks Candy
20 The Humboldt Mercantile
see 18 The Little Shop of Hers

EATING IN EUREKA: OUR PICKS

Jack's Seafood: Fresh oysters, clam chowder and halibut burgers complement the bay views at this spot right on the boardwalk. *11.30am-8pm* **$$**

Los Bagels: Try a banana slug-shaped bagel at this totally unique bakery that combines the Jewish deli tradition with Mexican flavors. *7am-3pm* **$**

Gallagher's Restaurant and Pub: The place for seafarers or anyone who fancies fish & chips with a pint. *11am-8.30pm Tue-Fri, 11.30am-8.30pm Sat, 11am-4pm Sun* **$$**

Café Marina & Woodley's Bar: Located on Woodley Island, Café Marina is a go-to for a post-paddle sandwich or plate of grilled prawns. *8.30am-8pm* **$$**

Craftsman, this outpost dedicated to old-school arts has a massive collection of Victorian-era woodworking machinery (still used today), a print shop, craftsman's apothecary (for mixing stains, varnishes, paints and glues) and textile atelier. And that's only what's inside the main building. Outside, guests can explore a skid camp – complete with a bunk house, cook shack and theater – and imagine what it was like to live in the area as a logger in the early 1900s. Keep walking the grounds and you'll also come upon working blacksmithing and ceramics studios, plus meet a horse or two.

If you're happy wandering the property at your own pace, stop by anytime between 9am and 3.30pm from Monday to Friday for a self-guided tour. You're still likely to catch a professional craftsman in action even if you stop by unannounced. Or you can reserve a 90-minute guided tour with either Viviana or Eric Hollenbeck, the founders, who will show you around. For the ultimate experience, book a Blue Ox class *(adult/child from $120/90)*, such as blacksmithing, ceramics or stained-glass making.

Hiking 100 Feet High

Stroll the redwood canopy

At the **Redwood Sky Walk** *(redwoodskywalk.com)* inside Eureka's **Sequoia Park Zoo** *(redwoodzoo.org; adult/child $25/13)*, you can climb up into a redwood grove and explore the ancient giants from 100 feet above the forest floor. The elevated trail is the longest of its kind in the western United States, and the construction of its ascent ramp, launch deck, accessible main loop, nine viewing platforms and optional hanging bridge were all designed by 'en-tree-preneurs.'

Upon entering the zoo, wander past the flamingos on your left and the river otters on your right, and soon you'll reach the ascent ramp, which zigzags at a gentle incline up to the launch deck. From there, the fully accessible main walkways and platforms offer a rare glimpse into a mesmerizing ecosystem: curious barn owls perch in the canopy; gnarled, oversized burls protrude from massive trunks; and from above, you can peer over swirling patches of ferns and bushy red huckleberry.

For the most intrepid visitors, there's the 'adventure leg,' a series of Costa Rica–style hanging bridges that complete the Sky Walk loop. Take your time, watch your footing and relax as you become part of the life in the redwood canopy. If you're feeling hungry afterward, the zoo has an onsite restaurant, the **Evergreen Eatery**, serving sandwiches, pizza and kid-friendly finger foods.

EUREKA'S BEST SHOPS

The Humboldt Mercantile: Snag redwoods tees, hemp hand soap and local hot sauce at this souvenir hotspot.

Many Hands Gallery: Like visiting a few dozen artists' studios in one fell swoop; the gallery stocks ceramics, jewelry and pretty leather journals.

Land of Lovely: Consider a visit here your personal invitation to luxuriate and pick up a new robe, bath soaks and botanical candles.

Eureka Books: Browse new, used and rare books, then have the Zoltar machine in front read your fortune.

The Little Shop of Hers: Find an expertly curated collection of vintage clothes and accessories for both him and her.

EATING IN EUREKA: BEST SWEET TREATS

Dick Taylor Craft Chocolate: Stop by the pretty factory and tasting room for this craft chocolatier based in Eureka. *8am-6pm Mon-Sat, noon-4pm Sun* $

Living the Dream Ice Cream: Cones, shakes and sammiches are all on offer at this perfect spot by the Eureka Boardwalk. *noon-9pm Mon-Thu, to 10pm Fri & Sat* $

Patricks Candy: Since 1941, Patricks has been tempting locals with their creams, chews and nuts – see the saltwater taffy being made. *10am-5.30pm Mon-Fri* $

Ramone's Bakery & Cafe: They roast their own organic coffee and bake decadent desserts, like chocolate silk tarts and cream puffs. *7.30am-5pm Mon-Sat* $

EUREKA'S HISTORIC ARCHITECTURE

This loop will satisfy both your architectural appetite and your actual appetite, as it's bookended by beloved restaurants.

START	END	LENGTH
Los Bagels	Café Waterfront	1½ miles; 2 hrs

Grab coffee to go at 1 **Los Bagels** (p260), located in an 1877 Italianate building, then head west on 2nd St until you hit the historic 2 **Eagle House**, originally a hotel, on the corner of 2nd and C Sts.

Looping around, take a left on C St and another left on 3 **Opera Alley**, where you can enjoy a series of street art murals. At E St, take in the 1911 Classical Revival building that houses the 4 **Clarke Historical Museum** (p259) on your right. Continue on Opera Alley to see a pretty 5 **purple Victorian** on your left before the intersection with L St. 6 **Carter House** (p277) is on the corner of L and 3rd Sts; returning to 2nd St, make a right to reach M St, where you'll see 7 **The Pink Lady** and 8 **Carson Mansion**.

Return west on 2nd St. On your right, at 525, you'll pass the former 9 **Vance Hotel**, an Italianate-style building from 1872, across from a unique purple-and-green building on your left. Now 10 **The Greene Lily** restaurant, the 1866 Classical Revival building was once the Oberon Saloon. At F St, stop in at 11 **Many Hands Gallery** (p261) and 12 **Eureka Books** (p261), both in historic buildings, then finish at 13 **Café Waterfront**, originally the Wave Saloon, for lunch.

Paddle Through Time

Kayak Humboldt Bay

Get a totally different perspective of Eureka and learn about its rich past on a kayak tour with **Humboats Kayak Adventures** *(humboatskayaking.com; adult/child from $55/45)*. The Humboldt Bay Kayak Eco-Tour includes a cruise to Tuluwat Island, the ancestral home of the Wiyot tribe, and a float past the city's Victorian-era waterfront, with commentary from your guide throughout. Or, go with the Sunset Kayak Tour, which also includes a bit of history but is more geared toward beginners. Single or double kayaks are available, and tours depart from the Woodley Island Marina.

When in Humboldt...

Marijuana tourism

Part of the Emerald Triangle (the cannabis-producing region of Northern California), Eureka has long had a reputation as a weed destination. Though the landscape has certainly changed (many locals say for the worse) with recreational legalization and higher regulatory fees, you can still have a unique Eureka experience. **GR Coffee & Cannabis** has a drive-thru window where you can get java and a joint. If you'd like to visit a working farm, **Humboldt Cannabis Tours** *(humcannabis.com; from $155)* will happily take you.

Murals & Museums

Appreciating Eureka's art

Walk a block in Eureka and you'll experience art in one form or another. The walls are covered in murals (many created by the legendary Duane Flatmo), utility boxes feature paintings and sidewalks are scrawled with poems. The city crackles with creativity and teems with people who love to harness it.

Wander over to the **Romano Gabriel Wooden Sculpture Garden** *(romanogabriel.com)* in Old Town for whimsical outsider art enclosed by aging glass. For 30 years, the wooden characters in Gabriel's front yard delighted locals. After he died in 1977, the city moved the collection here. For those seeking a more traditional setting, the **Morris Graves Museum of Art** *(humboldtarts.org; adult/child $5/free)* is a rotating showcase of works by artists from both the North Coast and around the world.

THE TRIATHALON OF THE ART WORLD

Visit in May and you might see moving sculptures taking to the streets of Eureka. The region's famous **Kinetic Grand Championship** takes place over Memorial Day weekend each year.

The three-day race is a battle of both engineering savoir-faire and artistic flair, as human-powered art vehicles – think five-wheeled bicycles, oversized tortoises and pedal-propelled bananas – traverse sand, street and even Humboldt Harbor. The race starts on the Arcata Plaza, moves to the Eureka waterfront and finishes on Main St in Ferndale, the setting of the event's very first race back in 1969.

DRINKING IN EUREKA: BEST FOR BEER AND COCKTAILS

The Shanty: Popular with hipsters for its pinball, pool and sweet back patio, this is the coolest bar in town. *noon-2am*

Lost Coast Brewery & Cafe: Head to their restaurant on 4th St for craft beers and burgers, or visit the brewery for a tour. *11.30am-9pm Wed-Sun*

Phatsy Kline's Parlour Lounge: Located inside the historic Eagle House, Phatsy's is the place for a fancy cocktail. *4-9pm Wed & Thu, to 11pm Fri & Sat*

The Speakeasy: Squeeze in with the locals at this New Orleans–inspired bar with live blues and a convivial atmosphere. *4-11pm Sun-Thu, to 2am Fri & Sat*

Beyond Eureka

Just outside the city, the hippie college town of Arcata has thrifting fun, good bites, coastal biking and extraordinary birdwatching.

GETTING AROUND

The Arcata and Mad River Transit System is the public bus option in town *($2 per ride)*. Because it's tied to the university, it's primarily a weekday service and only makes limited runs when CalPoly is on break. An even better way to get around town is to test out the Humboldt Bikeshare program, which allows you to reserve bikes through the free Movatic app. There's a sizable network of cycle lanes in Arcata.

Mere minutes to the north of Eureka is the region's most progressive town, Arcata, which earned the nickname Sixties by the Sea as a result of all the countercultural activity that happened here in the 1960s – and still continues to this day. Once called Union, the town played a large part in Northern California's gold rush, acting as a base for supplies. These days, the gold in Arcata might be considered its educational offerings – with the innovative and STEM-focused California State Polytechnic University in town – or its redwood forests and magical marsh. Arcata's grassy central square regularly swells with college students, campers and wanderers, and hosts a farmers market each Saturday that can't be missed.

Arcata

TIME FROM EUREKA: **10 MINS**

Thrifting in Arcata Plaza

An impressive selection of second-hand shops sits just off of Arcata's flower-filled plaza. **Miranda's Rescue Thrift Store** *(mirandasrescue.org)* has weekly sales, and **Vintage Avenger** is expertly curated. **Daydream** *(daydreamarcata.com)* has gently used hiking boots, and at **Eco-Groovy Deals** *(ecogroovydeals.com)* you can pick up a psychedelic tapestry in addition to new-to-you threads. If you're all set clothing-wise, head to **People's Records** *(peoplesrecordsarcata.com)* for vinyl and cassettes or **Tin Can Mailman** *(tincanbooks.com)* for used books.

Bike the Hammond Coastal Trail

If you'd like to give your hiking boots a rest and hop on two wheels, hit the **Hammond Coastal Trail**. The path, which is a mix of asphalt and gravel, runs 5.5 miles from the **Mad River Bridge** in Arcata to **Clam Beach** in McKinleyville. Along the way, you'll wind past coastal pastures, spot remnants of old railroad tracks, cruise within forested tunnels and enjoy views of both the Mad River and Pacific Ocean. Plus, there are convenient stops along the way for a bathroom or snack break. **Hiller Park**, about 1.5 miles in, has bathrooms and picnic tables, and **Murray Rd**, another mile north, has tables, too. If you didn't bring your own bike on the trip, you can rent one (either standard or electric) from **Wildtrail**

WATERSPIX/SHUTTERSTOCK

Lesser yellowlegs, Arcata Marsh & Wildlife Sanctuary

(wildtrailtours.com; standard bike per day from $69; e-bike half-/full-day $80/100), who will even deliver it for free within a 7-mile radius of Arcata. They also offer a two-hour **Hammond Trail Tour** *(standard/e-bike $107/129)*, if you prefer to ride with a guide.

Embark on a bird-watching adventure

The **Arcata Marsh & Wildlife Sanctuary** *(cityofarcata.org)* is an innovative combination: it's both a sustainable wastewater treatment facility and a celebrated birding park. Spread across 307 acres, the area includes freshwater marsh, salt marsh and roughly five miles of paths for walking or cycling. Birding is particularly great here because of its location along the Pacific Flyway – a major migratory route for birds that breed in California, Mexico and South America. If you want to get in on the feathered fun, volunteers lead free guided walks every Saturday, rain or shine, at 8.30am. Open to beginner bird-watchers as well as seasoned seekers, it's the perfect opportunity to get out on the marsh and mingle with nature-loving locals who never miss a week. Meet at the end of South I Street in Arcata (continue past the small parking area to a larger lot). If you see the wooden 'Audubon Nature Walks' sign, you're in the right place.

BIRDING AT ARCATA MARSH

Kathryn Wendel, president of the Redwood Region Audubon Society, gives a season-by-season birding guide.

Spring:
Look for neotropical migrants passing through, including western tanagers and warblers.

Summer:
It's breeding season. Watch for brightly colored orange-and black Bullock's orioles and yellow-breasted chats.

Fall:
From the marbled godwit to the red-necked phalarope, fall is the season for shorebirds, which come to fatten up for their long migration.

Winter:
Look out for waterfowl, including teal, northern shovelers and American wigeon. It's also a great time for raptors, like sharp-shinned hawks and merlins.

EATING & DRINKING IN ARCATA: OUR PICKS

Slice of Humboldt Pie: Expect everything from chicken pot pie to lemon raspberry pie, plus savory empanadas. *10am-9pm Tue-Thu, to 10pm Fri & Sat* $

Tomo Sushi: Located on the plaza within the historic Hotel Arcata, Tomo is the place for maki rolls and teriyaki. *4-8.30pm Mon-Sat* $$

Cafe Mokka: Order an espresso and cozy up next to the fire at Finnish Country Sauna and Tubs. *11am-11pm Sun-Thu, to midnight Fri & Sat* $

SALT: This low-lit, nautical-themed restaurant serves the coastal flavors of Italy alongside craft cocktails. *3.30-9pm Tue-Sun* $$$

Redwood National & State Parks

NATURAL WONDERS | HIKING | REVAMPED MOTELS

GETTING AROUND

A car is an absolute must since you'll be logging a lot of miles – plus traversing some pretty remote roads – as you bounce between parks and trails. Word to the wise: try to divide the parks into two sections: southern (Redwood National Park and Prairie Creek Redwoods State Park) and northern (Del Norte Coast Redwoods State Park and Jedediah Smith Redwoods State Park). Group activities accordingly so you don't burn through time (and gas) backtracking multiple times.

TOP TIP

Cell service is extremely spotty in this area, even when you're off the trails and making a pit stop in town. Download trail maps, driving directions and a good podcast or two for offline use.

Waterfalls, fern-covered canyons, rugged ocean coastline and, oh yes, the world's tallest trees...It's all part of the experience in this unique four-in-one park system. Located in the upper reaches of California's Pacific Coast, the area is maintained through a partnership between the National Park Service and California State Parks. That means that in addition to Redwood National Park, this northern natural wonderland also includes three state parks (from south to north): Prairie Creek Redwoods State Park, Del Norte Coast Redwoods State Park and Jedediah Smith Redwoods State Park. Because it's not your typical national or state park, there aren't gated entrances to the area (with two exceptions). Instead, the parks sit along a 50-mile driving route on Hwy 101. To experience them all, use Orick as your gateway town in the south, and Crescent City as the gateway or terminus in the north. Then all you have to do is make many, many stops in between.

Prairie & Redwoods from the Road

Take a scenic drive

Get warmed up for all the natural beauty you'll experience by taking in your surroundings on a picturesque drive. About two miles north of Orick, in **Redwood National Park** *(nps .gov/redw)*, **Bald Hills Road** is a winding jaunt over hills and alongside prairies, with an occasional lupine superbloom. The **Newton B Drury Scenic Parkway**, a 10-mile stretch in Prairie Redwoods State, is just as the name suggests – an extraordinarily scenic route through untouched ancient redwood forests. And **Howland Hill Road** is a 10-mile, unpaved stunner through the towering ancient redwoods of **Jedediah Smith Redwoods State Park** *(parks.ca.gov)*.

HIGHLIGHTS
1 Prairie Creek Redwoods State Park
2 Redwood National Park

SIGHTS
3 Bald Hills Road
4 Enderts Beach
5 Gold Bluffs Beach
6 Howland Hill Road
7 Jedediah Smith Redwoods State Park
8 Trees of Mystery

ACTIVITIES
see 7 Boy Scout Tree Trail
9 Fern Canyon Loop
10 Lady Bird Johnson Grove
11 Newton B Drury Scenic Parkway
12 Redwood Yurok Canoe Tour
13 Simpson-Reed & Peterson Loop
14 Stout Grove Loop
15 Trillium Falls Loop

SLEEPING
16 Elk Meadow Cabins
see 5 Gold Bluffs Beach Campground
see 21 Historic Requa Inn
see 14 Jedediah Smith Redwoods Campground
see 8 Motel Trees
see 20 Roosevelt Base Camp

EATING
17 Chart Room Restaurant
see 12 Country Club Bar & Grill
18 Hiouchi Cafe
19 Kin Khao Thai & Sushi Bar
see 20 Mojo Pizza
20 Orick Market
see 19 SeaQuake Brewing
21 The Historic Requa Inn

ENTERTAINMENT
see 12 Klamath Salmon Festival

INFORMATION
see 19 Crescent City Information Center
see 14 Hiouchi Visitor Center
see 14 Jedediah Smith Visitor Center
22 Prairie Creek Visitor Center
23 Thomas H Kuchel Visitor Center
see 12 Yurok Country Visitor Center

YOU'RE IN YUROK COUNTRY

With 6500 enrolled members, the Yurok Tribe (which means 'downriver people') is California's largest Native American group. Historically, they've been celebrated as expert basket weavers, canoe makers and fishers, and the traditions continue to this day. The tribe even hosts an annual **Klamath Salmon Festival** each August. In addition to supporting the tribe by hiring Yurok people as outdoor guides, consider purchasing their locally made handicrafts. You'll find dangly earrings made from pieces of abalone shell, and long beaded necklaces strung with pine nuts and tubular dentalium shells. Resembling miniature elephant tusks, these shells were once used as currency. One great place to shop is the **Yurok Country Visitor Center** in Klamath.

GERRY MATTHEWS/SHUTTERSTOCK

Paul Bunyan and Babe the Blue Ox statues, Trees of Mystery

Just Bluffing

Hit the beach

If you're looking for beaches within the parks, **Gold Bluffs Beach** fits the bill in the southern section. Drive right up and bring your pup (though keep him or her on a leash) and take in the tide. Part of **Prairie Creek Redwoods State Park** *(parks.ca.gov)*, this wild coastline got its name for the gold that was once discovered in the area. Gold Bluffs Beach is open for day use and also has an overnight campground. The area can get quite busy, as the start of the popular one-mile Fern Canyon Loop Trail (p270) is nearby. Note that an entry permit is required from May 15 through September 15; reserve online at redwoodparksconservancy.org/fern-canyon. Throughout the year, there's a fee of $12 per car to access the beach, unless you have a state or national park pass.

In the northern section of the parks, just south of Crescent City, **Enderts Beach** is the place to be. There's no entry fee and the drive from Hwy 101 is much shorter than to Gold Bluffs, but getting to the sand does require a half-mile hike.

EATING IN THE NORTHERN PARKS: OUR PICKS

Chart Room Restaurant: Up in Crescent City, this harborside spot has views of sea lions and top-notch chowder. *11am-7pm Wed, Thu & Sun, to 8pm Fri & Sat* $$

Kin Khao Thai & Sushi Bar: Traditional Thai dishes and maki rolls hit the spot at this Crescent City eatery. *hours vary* $$

SeaQuake Brewing: Pizzas, burgers and beer, of course, are all on tap at this Crescent City brewery. *11.30am-8pm Sun-Thu, to 9pm Fri & Sat* $$

Hiouchi Cafe: A breakfast and lunch spot in Hiouchi, near Jedediah Smith Redwoods State Park. The cafe will gladly pack you a meal to go. *7am-2pm* $

One important note: neither of these beaches are suitable for swimming, as currents are extremely strong. But Enderts does have the best tidepooling within the park's boundaries.

Family Fun in the Forest

Visit Trees of Mystery

Disneyland may have Mickey and Minnie, but **Trees of Mystery** *(treesofmystery.net; adult/child $30/15)*, something of a nature-focused amusement park, has Paul Bunyan, Babe the Blue Ox and the redwood tree itself. It's not technically part of the national or state park systems, but it does lie along the parks' corridor so you're likely to pass by as you drive through the town of Klamath – and a stop is highly recommended. The park itself is a nature trail with attractions along the way, including intriguingly shaped redwood trees, a series of aerial suspension bridges in the canopies and a gondola ride to a scenic lookout. At times it's cheesy, but it's also the delightful kind of roadside attraction that feels straight out of a different era. And in fact, Trees of Mystery has been family-owned and operated since 1946.

After completing the trail, browse souvenirs in the massive gift shop (they have a good selection of books on local history and hiking, in addition to Paul and Babe salt and pepper shakers) and wander through the attached museum. Called the **End of the Trail Collection**, the museum has free admission and is filled with Native American artifacts as well as jewelry for purchase. If you'd like to make a full weekend of the experience, there's a retro roadside motel across the street, **Motel Trees** (p277) *(moteltrees.com)*, and a restaurant called **Forest Cafe** *(forestcafe.net)*.

Ride a Redwood down the Klamath River

Take a Yurok canoe tour

If you're going to visit Yurok Country, experience it the traditional Yurok way – by floating the Klamath River in a handcrafted vessel. June through August, visitors can book a two-hour **Redwood Yurok Canoe Tour** *(visityurokcountry.com; adult/child $150/100)* and ride in one of three dugout redwood canoes, the traditional boats of the Yurok people, the Native Americans who have been living along the Klamath for centuries. Along the ride, your guide will introduce the river's history as well as its unique geography and wildlife.

MAGNIFICENT ROOSEVELT ELK

Roosevelt elk roam the coast and forestland, and encountering these majestic creatures is as cool as it is worrisome, particularly during the August to October mating season. Bulls can weigh up to 1000 pounds and do damage with their antlers and legs, while cows with calves can also become aggressive.

Human-elk conflict has been on the rise in Northern California, and scientists are making a concerted effort to study the elk in hopes of identifying solutions. Protect both yourself and the elk by staying at least 75 feet away. They can run at speeds of up to 40mph, which is considerably faster than Olympic sprinter Usain Bolt (28mph).

EATING IN THE SOUTHERN PARKS: OUR PICKS

Orick Market: Grab snacks, picnic supplies and marshmallows for your campfire at this convenience store located right off Hwy 101 in Orick. *10am-9pm* **$**

Mojo Pizza: In the same parking lot as Orick Market, this food truck serves wood-fired pizzas sure to satiate the hungriest hikers. *11am-7pm Mon-Sat, from noon Sun* **$**

The Historic Requa Inn: Scarf down a plate of pancakes with a side of Klamath River views. *8-10am Apr-Oct, 8.30-9.30am Nov-Mar* **$**

Country Club Bar & Grill: This Klamath eatery has everything you'd want from a roadside stop: burgers, beer and a jukebox. *noon-8pm Wed-Mon* **$$**

Redwood National & State Parks Hiking Trails

Trying to choose a hiking trail at a national or state park can be overwhelming, so imagine what happens when you combine four parks into one. To help you make sense of the options, we've selected six all-star trails that meet specific criteria. As a reminder, tackling the southern half of the park system before moving north (or vice versa) makes logistics easier, so we've noted in parenthesis where each trail lies.

Where to hike if you...

Want Something Quick

Fern Canyon Loop (south)
There's nothing quite like this Prairie Creek canyon trail, which follows a stream surrounded by towering fern-covered walls that once served as a backdrop for *Jurassic Park: The Lost World.* The loop is only a mile, though you should allot at least 30 minutes to drive the windy gravel road (Davison) from Hwy 101 to the trailhead parking lot. Tip: wear water shoes or bring a backup pair of sneakers. Your feet will get wet.

Simpson-Reed & Peterson Loop (north) Hike two trails in under an hour at Jedediah Smith Redwoods. Combining these two short loop trails creates a 0.8-mile hike through a redwood grove that's suitable for just about any ability level. You'll start on Simpson-Reed Trail and keep veering left to add on the Peterson Loop portion of the walk. Eventually, you'll return to the Simpson-Reed Trail to finish the hike.

CAVAN-IMAGES/SHUTTERSTOCK

Fern Canyon Loop

Have Kids in Tow

Lady Bird Johnson Grove (south) This 1.4-mile hike in Redwood National Park is the ideal length for little ones. There are a number of benches where you can stop for a rest. Or give your kids a history lesson: the trail gets its name from the former first lady Claudia Johnson, whose husband, President Lyndon B Johnson, signed the bill to create this park in 1968.

Stout Grove Loop (north)
First-time hikers will feel a major sense of accomplishment when they finish this 0.6-mile loop in Jedediah Smith Redwoods. The extraordinarily picturesque surroundings – redwoods soaring above a lush forest floor – will have them permanently hooked on the great outdoors.

Hope to See a Waterfall

Trillium Falls Loop (south)
At only 2.7 miles and with a trailhead that's right off Hwy 101, this Prairie Creek path also qualifies for the quick and kid-friendly categories. The scenic and soothing falls are located in the first half-mile of the walk, so you could do the hike as a short out-and-back.

Boy Scout Tree Trail (north)
You'll have to put in a little more work to see the falls along this trail in the Jedediah Smith Redwoods, but it's worth it. The total out-and-back distance is 5.6 miles; Fern Falls is the turnaround point. Your muscles will stay active, with intermittent climbs, occasional sets of stairs and a few bridge crossings.

STEPHEN MOEHLE/SHUTTERSTOCK

Trillium Falls

HOW TO

When to go Spring is a favorite time to visit, with wildflowers in bloom and smaller crowds than summer. However, summer has drier conditions.

Book in advance Some sites, like Tall Trees Trail and Gold Bluffs Beach (which includes the Trillium Falls Loop), require advance permits during summer.

Fees There's no general entry fee for Redwood National and State Parks, though some day-use areas, including Gold Bluffs Beach *($12)*, do have fees.

Top tip Be sure to have cash on hand, as Gold Bluffs Beach kiosk only accepts cash and checks.

Visitor centers and campgrounds

Multiple parks means multiple visitor centers – five in total – which is extra convenient for getting additional details from park experts when you're on the ground. All of the visitor centers have maps. **Thomas H Kuchel Visitor Center**, located in Orick, is the furthest south. Then comes **Prairie Creek Visitor Center** at the southern end of the Newton B Drury Scenic Parkway. The **Crescent City Information Center** is located at park headquarters, then comes **Jedediah Smith Visitor Center** and the **Hiouchi Visitor Center**, both in Hiouchi. The latter has exhibits about local Native art and culture.

Want to spend the night in the parks? Camping is the only way to do so, as you won't find any hotels within the parks' boundaries.

Take your pick between four developed campgrounds and seven designated backcountry options. The developed campgrounds, managed by the state parks, all have bathrooms, food storage lockers, firewood for sale and potable water, and two have year-round cell reception. Be sure to reserve your campsite in advance *(reservecalifornia.com)*, especially during the busy summer season. For the backcountry campgrounds, you'll need to request a free permit online anytime between 160 days and 24 hours in advance. These campgrounds still have some amenities, but they don't have drive-up access – instead, you have to hike to your site.

Beyond Redwood National & State Parks

Find more state parks, plus a charming town perched before a jaw-dropping headland and dramatic offshore rock islands.

Places

GETTING AROUND

As with the redwood parks area, you'll be spending the majority of your time cruising Hwy 101, so a car is definitely necessary. The good news: cell reception here is better than it is further north, so you should be okay with pulling up directions on your smartphone. If you need to gas up, do so around Trinidad.

Just south of Redwood National and State Parks, you'll find the perfect seaside village of Trinidad, a magical beach peppered with semi-precious pebbles in Sue-meg State Park, and the kayaking and bird-watching paradise that is Humboldt Lagoons State Park. While this area is big on beauty and adventure, it covers a relatively small stretch off of Hwy 101. From Trinidad in the south to Humboldt Lagoons in the north, the driving time is less than 20 minutes (and the lagoons are only about 25 minutes from Eureka/Arcata airport). That makes this area a nice stop-off either before or after you've explored the redwoods in the northernmost part of the state – though you'll still get to ogle more of the towering trees here.

Trinidad

TIME FROM ORICK: **20 MINS**

Take in Trinidad's coast

To get the lay of the land, head out on a hike at Trinidad Head, which soars 358ft above the Pacific Ocean. The **Trinidad Head Loop** is a scenic 1.4-mile stroll that offers views of partially submerged rock formations, wildflowers, an 1871 lighthouse and maybe even whales during migration season (December through April). The path is paved. For parking, follow Lighthouse Road down toward the ocean and **Trinidad State Beach** *(parks.ca.gov; free)*. Grab a spot in the lot on your right (Bay St, on the left, leads to the town's harbor and pier). The loop's trailhead is on the southern side of the parking lot up a series of steps.

After your hike, stroll over to the beach, which makes the perfect spot for a post-walk picnic. Or, grab breakfast or lunch at **Seascape Restaurant** *(seascapetrinidad.squarespace.com)* at the pier. It's open daily from 8am to 4pm, serving locally smoked salmon, bay oysters and microbrews from the area.

NAERADNUOVO/SHUTTERSTOCK

Trinidad State Beach

ALL ABOUT ABALONE

Primarily found in Pacific regions like California and Japan, these marine mollusks usually clamp tightly to rocky surfaces, feeding on algae that floats by. Their shells provide protection from predators, and the interior is the part that's prized for its iridescent kaleidoscope of colors.

Additionally, abalone meat, which is rich in protein, has long been savored in various cultures, including Japanese and Native American. In fact, up until recently, Californians on the North Coast still took part in recreational abalone diving. But because of declining populations, due to a combination of factors, including overfishing and climate change, abalone hunting has been on pause since 2017. Empty abalone shells, however, are fair game for beachcombers.

Shopping in Trinidad

Shopping in this tiny town isn't an all-day affair, but you'll find a few cute shops with totally unique souvenirs. Within minutes of rolling into town from the Hwy 101 exit, you'll come upon a group of stores on your right, just off of Main St. **Windandsea** *(windanseajewelry.com)* specializes in handcrafted jewelry, with earrings, cuffs and pendants made from abalone shells. They're also your go-to spot for stuffed banana slugs, glow-in-the-dark Trinidad tees and wind chimes. **Sea Around Us**, in a distinct building with weathered-wood shingles, is the place for crafters: get beads made from abalone, pine nuts and dentalia to string your own creation. The shop has been family-owned for three generations. Next, there's **Trinidad Trading Company** *(trinidadtrading.com)*, where you'll find hand-blown glass goods and Pacific Coast–inspired stationery. They also have locally made abalone baubles and wire-wrapped agate rings, which might make you feel better if you strike out at **Agate Beach** (p274).

Eating in Trinidad

Once you've worked up an appetite, **Trinidad Bay Eatery** *(trinidadeatery.com)* is the place to indulge in heaping portions of chowder (voted the best in Humboldt), served in sourdough bread bowls or with a side of garlic toast. Anything from their selection of melts or the seafood platter are solid choices, too. They're open for lunch and dinner, though you're likely to find long waits on weekend evenings in the summer.

For something casual and quick, **Headies Pizza & Pour** *(headiespizzatrinidad.com)* serves individual slices and full pies. Their menu constantly changes, so stop in to see what flavorful combinations they're sliding into the oven that day (gluten-free and vegan options available).

ALWAYS THERE

If you have an old map, you might notice a state park that seemingly no longer exists: Patrick's Point. That was the name of Sue-meg State Park until 2021, when the California State Park and Recreation Commission voted unanimously to change it.

The name Patrick's Point came into use after an Irish settler named Patrick Beegan spent time in the area briefly in the 1850s. He was accused of killing a Native American boy and fled, yet the name stuck. Nearly a century later, the name has reverted back to what the Yurok people have used since time immemorial – Sue-meg, which means 'always there.'

Sue-meg State Park

TIME FROM ORICK: **25 MINS**

A rockhounding haven

Anyone that appreciates a treasure hunt, both kids and adults included, will enjoy a visit to **Agate Beach**. This 2-mile stretch of sand gets its name for the semi-precious agate stones you may find scattered about. You'll find other types of pretty pebbles, too – including jade and jasper – all polished by the mighty Pacific. In addition to rockhounding, visitors can explore tidepools and keep their eyes peeled for whales and sea lions. To access the area, leave your car in the Agate Beach Campground lot and follow the designated trail down toward the water, winding past wildflowers and coastal shrubbery. It's only about a 0.3 mile-walk, but the trail descends 200 feet and is steep. Hold on to the hands of little ones and be sure to bring a bag or bucket for all your treasures.

Humboldt Lagoons State Park

TIME FROM ORICK: **10 MINS**

Lagoon hopping

The largest lagoon system in the US, **Humboldt Lagoons State Park** *(parks.ca.gov)* is home to four landlocked bodies of water. From south to north, they are: Big Lagoon, Dry Lagoon, Stone Lagoon and Freshwater Lagoon. If you'd like to take a dip, **Big Lagoon** has shallow spots where the water temperature is suitable for swimming in the summer. **Dry Lagoon**, as the name implies, isn't quite a bountiful body of water – it's more marshy than a lake. Decades ago, farmers drained it for growing crops, which didn't work out. Today, there's excellent bird-watching in the area.

If you're a diehard lagoon lover and want to spend the night, **Stone Lagoon** has a unique boat-in-only campground with six sites. To rent a kayak *(from $40)*, head to the Stone Lagoon Visitor Center, just off Hwy 101. You're also welcome to bring your own kayak and launch it near the visitor center. **Freshwater Lagoon** also has a boat launch on its northwest side. Swimming and fishing are popular activities here. If you'd like to angle for largemouth bass, catfish, cutthroat trout and stocked rainbow trout, be sure to get a California fishing license in advance.

VIVEK SEKAR/GETTY IMAGES

Humboldt Lagoons State Park

Places We Love to Stay

$ Budget $$ Midrange $$$ Top End

Mendocino

MAP p235

The Mendocino Hotel and Garden Suites $ Established in 1878, this character-filled place is a relic of the Old West.

Mendocino Grove $$ This glamping gem by the sea has safari-style tents and elegant bathhouses.

MacCallum House $$ A historic landmark, the main house has 19 unique rooms, some with claw-foot soaking tubs.

JD House $$ Enjoy breakfast delivered to your door at this hotel decked out in nautical style and surrounded by an English garden.

Stanford Inn $$$ A solarium-enclosed pool, organic gardens and a widely celebrated vegan restaurant are all part of the experience at this superlative resort.

Little River

Van Damme State Park Campground $ Three miles south of Mendocino, this campground gives you easy access to the Fern Canyon Trail and a scenic beach.

Little River Inn $$$ All rooms here have ocean views, and many also have fireplaces and hot tubs. There's also a golf course on the grounds.

Elk

Elk Cove Inn, Restaurant & Spa $$ A romantic escape set in a 19th-century Craftsman with ocean views, a rooftop deck and a beachfront gazebo.

Harbor House Inn (p241) **$$$** Home to a Michelin-starred restaurant, Harbor House also features traditional guest rooms in the main building and standalone cottages.

Anderson Valley

Hendy Woods State Park Campground $ Open to camping year round, Hendy Woods has 92 sites spread across two campgrounds, plus four cabins in Cabin Colony.

The Boonville Hotel and Restaurant $$ Take your pick between 17 unique rooms, then stay on the property for a multicourse meal with a regularly changing menu.

The Madrones (p244) **$$$** A destination for wine and cannabis, the Madrones is a Mediterranean compound with guest accommodations, two tasting rooms, an apothecary and restaurant.

Fort Bragg

Beachcomber Motel and Spa $$ Located near Glass Beach, Beachcomber has rooms with hot tubs and fireplaces, plus a large communal deck with grills.

Noyo Harbor Inn $$$ This luxury hotel is set in a historic Arts and Crafts mansion; rooms feature stunning woodwork.

Clear Lake

MAP p247

Kelsey Creek Campground $ Snag a lakeside site at this year-round campground inside Clear Lake State Park.

Harbin Hot Springs (p249) **$** Located in Middletown, this clothing-optional compound has camping, cottages and unique dome-style stays.

Clear Lake Cottages & Marina (p249) **$$** This is the ultimate retreat for fishing fans in the town of Clearlake, with boats to rent, a launch and guest cottages.

Tallman Hotel $$ Here's an elegant Upper Lake hotel featuring a shady garden, walled-in pool, brick patios and classy porches.

Suites on Main $$ A collection of bright, contemporary suites with full kitchens, the property has a backyard garden and views of downtown Kelseyville.

The Lost Coast

MAP p252

Mattole Campground $ At the northern point of the Lost Coast Trail, this campground is just steps from the beach and has 27 sites.

Usal Beach Campground $ Inside Sinkyone Wilderness State Park, this is a somewhat lawless Lost Coast campground that's accessed from the south via Hwy 1.

Needle Rock Campground $ Another option inside Sinkyone Wilderness State Park, with 10 basic sites and a cozy barn.

Tides Inn $$ Perched above Shelter Cove's tidepools, the squeaky-clean rooms here offer excellent views.

Inn of the Lost Coast $$$ Rooms have ocean-facing balconies and kitchenettes; one suite even has a hot tub and sauna.

Ferndale

Gingerbread Mansion $$ Stay in one of the most iconic Victorian mansions on the North Coast. The rooms are just as exciting as the inn's exterior.

Victorian Inn $$ Situated in an old bank on Ferndale's main drag, the Victorian has period-style wallpaper and funky antiques.

The Shaw House $$ Bring your whole crew for a stay at California's oldest B&B – the family suite has three beds, a fireplace and claw-foot tub.

Eureka

MAP p260

The Pinc $ Stay in Eureka's iconic Pink Lady mansion – some (more budget-friendly) rooms have shared bathrooms.

Inn at 2nd & C $$ This glorious historic hotel has been tastefully restored to combine Victorian-era decor with every possible modern amenity.

Carter House Inns $$ Choose a room in the Hotel Carter, Carter House, Carter Cottage or Bell Cottage and enjoy free wine on arrival.

Arcata

Hotel Arcata $ Anchoring the plaza, this renovated 1915 brick landmark has friendly staff and comfortable, old-world rooms.

Front Porch Inn $$ This boutique oasis has elaborate themed rooms and a magical outdoor bathhouse with private soaking tubs surrounded by moss- and fern-covered walls.

Redwood National and State Parks

MAP p267

Gold Bluffs Beach Campground $ Within Prairie Creek Redwoods State Park, sleep within easy reach of a secluded beach and Fern Canyon.

Jedediah Smith Redwoods Campground $ Stay in the main loop, outer loop or redwoods cabin area, with cabins that sleep up to six.

Motel Trees $ Kiddos will be excited about the views of the jumbo Paul Bunyan statue across the street at Trees of Mystery.

Roosevelt Base Camp $$ Fitting for a classic road trip, this amenity-filled stay (popcorn in your kitchenette and wood by the firepit) is in a refurbished 1950s motel.

Historic Requa Inn $$ Every room at this 100-year-old inn has a Klamath River view. One room is the town's former post office.

Elk Meadow Cabins $$$ These spotless and bright cabins have equipped kitchens and elk on the lawn. Bonus: they're sandwiched between two redwood parks.

Trinidad

Trinidad Bay Bed & Breakfast $$$ Hospitality is king at this B&B perched above Trinidad Bay. Gourmet breakfasts and cozy rooms with ocean views.

Lost Whale Inn $$$ High above the crashing waves north of Trinidad, this spacious, modern and light-filled B&B has stunning views.

Sue-meg State Park

Agate Beach Campground $ Calling all rockhounding fans: Sue-meg has a campground and cabin area at the entry point for Agate Beach.

Abalone Campground $ As Sue-meg's largest campground, Abalone is your best bet for finding a site during peak times.

MICHAEL VI/SHUTTERSTOCK

Carter House Inns

For places to stay in Central Coast, see p336

ANTIGONI ROUKA/SHUTTERSTOCK

Above: McWay Falls (p309); Right: surfing, Steamer Lane, Santa Cruz (p288)

THE MAIN AREAS

SANTA CRUZ
Rolling surf and quirky energy. **p284**

MONTEREY
Marine wildlife and oceanside amusements. **p294**

BIG SUR
Coastal road trips and forest hikes. **p306**

Researched by
Anita Isalska

Central Coast

WILD SHORES FOR WANDERING SOULS

With soul-stirring road trips, legendary surfing and free-and-easy attitudes, the Central Coast might just be California's sweet spot.

Along the coast from Santa Cruz to San Luis Obispo, savage landscapes are everywhere. Cliffs and sea stacks are smashed by the waves, redwood forests reach skyward and volcanic peaks defy all sense of time.

This natural drama feeds everyday life for Central Coasters. Wave-lashed Santa Cruz is best known for surfing, while sea life has defined Monterey Bay from its fishing past to its present-day marine conservation. The billowing sea fog drenches vineyards, helping create fantastic wine around San Luis Obispo, while the Salinas Valley nourishes vast fields of grain, grapes and garlic. The land fuels writers and artists, too: John Steinbeck, Henry Miller and Jack Kerouac all found inspiration here, while visionary architects like Julia Morgan and Hugh W Comstock made San Simeon and Carmel-by-the-Sea respective canvases.

DALTON JOHNSON/SHUTTERSTOCK

Spanish colonists rolled through in the late 18th century, founding mission settlements to convert Native Americans and establish a claim on the land. Churches, adobes and cemeteries bear witness to Native American cultural erasure and death from European-introduced diseases, and the Central Coast has some of the best-preserved relics of this era.

For sunny beaches, head further south. But for wind-buffeted hikes, white-knuckle road trips and a taste of the truly remote, there's the Central Coast. It's a sensory overload where the scent of sagebrush and salty sea air make you feel bracingly alive, while fog-diffused light adds an ethereal glow. Come awaken something in yourself.

CAMBRIA & CAYUCOS
Mellow beach towns with old-school charm. p312

PASO ROBLES
Wine country, art and fine dining. p317

SAN LUIS OBISPO
Youthful city amid beaches and peaks. p326

Find Your Way

You will find marine wildlife, wine country and hiking across the Central Coast; pick a hub (Santa Cruz, Monterey, San Luis Obispo) and day trip from there. Better yet, embrace total freedom by road-tripping.

Santa Cruz, p284
What you picture when you hear 'California surf culture': chill vibes, crashing waves and good-time nightlife, plus delightful hikes through forests and along fog-draped coast.

Monterey, p294
With a big, blue bay teeming with marine life, this is paradise for whale-watchers, kayakers and snorkelers. Don't miss the fantastic aquarium and historic Cannery Row.

Big Sur, p306
Life-changing ocean views on the ultimate California road trip. There are pristine forests and remote backcountry trails for hikers of all levels.

Boulder Creek
Henry Cowell Redwoods State Park
Santa Cruz Beach Boardwalk
Santa Cruz
Cowell's Beach
Aptos
Morgan Hill
Gilroy
Watsonville
San Luis Reservoir
Hollister
San Juan Bautista
Moss Landing
Monterey Bay
Cannery Row
Salinas
Monterey Bay Aquarium
Monterey
Carmel-by-the-Sea
Pinnacles National Park
Salinas River
Soledad
Los Padres National Forest
Big Sur
Pfeiffer Beach
Henry Miller Memorial Library
Julia Pfeiffer Burns State Park
Santa Lucia Range
Ventana Wilderness
King City
San Ardo
Lucia
Jolon

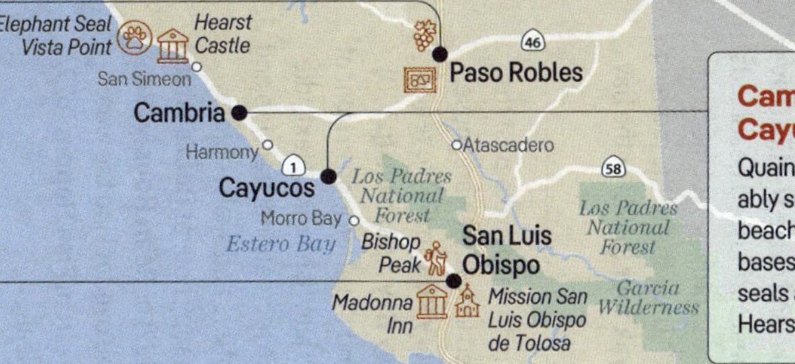

Paso Robles, p317

Best experienced through your taste buds, Paso's inland wine country beckons with gourmet restaurants and outstanding syrah.

Cambria & Cayucos, p312

Quaint, chic and enjoyably slow-paced, these beach towns are ideal bases to see elephant seals and extravagant Hearst Castle.

San Luis Obispo, p326

Life is sweet in this relaxing university town with beaches, vineyards and mountains all within 15 minutes' drive.

CAR

Driving is more than getting from A to B, it's pure freedom! There are thrilling views along the coast, while inland roads meander through ranches, vineyards and redwood forests. Driving gives you flexibility to explore national and state parks unimpeded, and detour to remote little towns.

TRAIN & BUS

Though it's not the most scenic part of the route, the *Coast Starlight* train connects the Bay Area (Oakland and San Jose) with Salinas (near Monterey), Paso Robles and San Luis Obispo. Smaller towns can often be reached by bus but schedules are patchy; plan ahead.

BICYCLE

Getting between major cities by bike isn't recommended, but there are many places perfect for pedaling. Santa Cruz has a bike-share scheme, Monterey has abundant rentals, and San Luis Obispo has urban and mountain bike trails. Cyclists will love scenic 17-Mile Drive (p298).

Plan Your Time

Short on time? Pick one base and theme, like Santa Cruz surfing, Monterey marine life or Paso Robles wineries. You can wing it when road-tripping, but book accommodations ahead in summer. No car? Stick to cities.

KROPICI/SHUTTERSTOCK

Santa Cruz Beach Boardwalk (p286)

If You Only Do One Thing

- Head straight to **Monterey** (p294) for history, wildlife and seaside diversions. In the morning, rent a bike and cycle **17-Mile Drive** (p298) past surf-kissed headlands and cypress groves. Not much of a cyclist? Then spend the morning on a **kayak tour** (p298) of the bay instead.

- Back in town, dawdle past the revamped industrial warehouses of **Cannery Row** (p296) to reach **Monterey Bay Aquarium** (p300) and spend the afternoon in front of hypnotic jellyfish tanks. Next, idle along the recreational trail, looking out for otters and seals, before hitting happy hour at **Hula's Island Grill** (p299) or **Pearl Hour** (p298). Then dine overlooking the water; the views from **Fish Hopper** (p297) are magical.

Seasonal Highlights

Weather stays mild from spring through fall (though the ocean's chilly!). Summer gets uncomfortably hot inland.

JANUARY & FEBRUARY

Sea fog, gray whale sightings and uncrowded parks. Witness the heavyweight drama of mating, fighting and newborn pups at the **elephant seal vista point** (p315) in San Simeon.

MARCH & APRIL

Montaña de Oro (p330) blazes with spring color and calla lilies bloom in **Big Sur** (p308). **Wine events** (p321) span March in Paso Robles.

MAY & JUNE

Warm but not yet scorching inland. By the coast, consistent waves are perfect for beginners; time for a **surfing lesson in Santa Cruz** (p284).

Three Days to Travel Around

- Devote day one to history, harbor seals and seaside fun in **Monterey** (p294). Spend day two road-tripping **Big Sur** (p306), stopping at scenic overlooks and rambling among giant redwoods at **Pfeiffer Big Sur State Park** (p309). Dine with inspiring blue views at **Nepenthe** (p310); you've earned it.

- If Hwy 1 is open all the way to **San Simeon** (p315), drive there on day three to meet **elephant seals** (p315) and take a tour of William Randolph Hearst's art-filled estat,. **Hearst Castle** (p316). Have dinner in understatedly chic **Cambria** (pick **Robin's**, p315) or merry **Cayucos** (**Lunada's**, p314) garden is magic). If the highway to San Simeon is closed, it's a long detour: you'll have just as good a time spending day three on a morning hike in staggeringly scenic **Point Lobos** (p302) then an afternoon in fancy **Carmel-by-the-Sea** (p302).

Greatest Hits in 10 Days

- Begin your road trip in **Santa Cruz** (p284): surf, see **redwoods** (p291), **kayak with otters** (p292) and defy gravity at the **Mystery Spot** (p289). On day three, hit **Monterey** (p294) and take a bike along **17-Mile Drive** (p298) before driving to **Big Sur** (p306).

- Spend day five hiking the forest trails in **Pfeiffer Big Sur State Park** (p309) or tough backcountry in the **Ventana Wilderness** (p310). On day six, drive to meet elephant seals in **San Simeon** (p315) and tour ostentatious **Hearst Castle** (p316). Revel in the long route via Salinas' **National Steinbeck Center** (p304) and the **River Road** (p304).

- On day seven, tour exceptional wineries in **Paso Robles** (p317). Finish in easygoing **San Luis Obispo** (p326) with day trips to a beaut spot like **Morro Bay** (p331).

JULY & AUGUST

Prime time to see **humpback whales** in Monterey Bay (p294). Vampires beware, you can smell late July's **Gilroy Garlic Festival** (p290) from miles away.

SEPTEMBER

Mild weather for camping in **Big Sur** (p306) and state parks, plus merriment at **Capitola Art & Wine Festival** (p284).

OCTOBER

Vineyards around Paso Robles glow scarlet and gold, and the city celebrates its most **famous composer** (p321). Waves get wild enough for pro surfers in **Santa Cruz** (p284).

NOVEMBER & DECEMBER

Monarch butterflies flutter down to **Pacific Grove** (p299) and **Santa Cruz** (p284), and migrating birds fill the skies at **Pinnacles** (p305) and **Elkhorn Slough** (p292).

Santa Cruz

BEACHES | SURF CULTURE | FOREST HIKES

GETTING AROUND

Santa Cruz is big: there's Westside (parks/surf spots), the boardwalk and downtown (seaside fun/nightlife), Seabright (restaurants/good-value hotels) and chic Capitola, 5 miles east. Exploring is easiest by car. Rideshares can spare you traffic and parking pain. Buses connect Front St with Seabright and Seacliff (No 1) and Capitola (No 2; 20 minutes' walk from beach); rides $2. Look for e-bike sharing docks all across town *(santacruz.bcycle.com; 30min trip $7)*.

TOP TIP

Standout events are the pre-1950s car festival **Woodies on the Wharf** *(santacruzwoodies.com; late Jun)* and street performances and local libations at **Capitola Art & Wine Festival** *(capitolaartandwine.com; Sep)*. The City of Santa Cruz site lists events *(cityofsantacruz.com/community/special-events)*.

Between Silicon Valley and Monterey, the city of Santa Cruz is where students, dropouts and tech royalty all compete for the best surf breaks. In 1885, a surfing demonstration by Hawaiian princes caused a sensation and Santa Cruz has been chasing thrills ever since.

The Beat Generation of the 1950s and '60s made other waves. By saying 'no' to social conformity (and 'yes' to psychedelics) they helped establish Santa Cruz as a refuge for artists and society opt-outs. Counterculture never went away, and there's an uneasy tension between big money and the desire to 'keep Santa Cruz weird.'

Marine mist hangs low, diffusing sunlight to mystical effect. It also helps sustain local vineyards and state parks, with fern-floored redwood forests tucked among the Santa Cruz Mountains. Hike deep into forests, scream your head off on the Giant Dipper or kick back with microbrews. There are no rules to time in Santa Cruz.

Surf's Up!

Learn to surf on Cowell's Beach

Even if your surfing experience goes no further than clinging to a bodyboard for dear life, that can all change in the gentle, predictable waves lapping **Cowell's Beach**. This sheltered cove on the west side of the Santa Cruz Wharf (p286) has excellent conditions, especially during the spring, for first-timers to finally stand up on a board.

Book a class with venerable **Richard Schmidt Surf School** *(richardschmidt.com)*, teaching first-timers and improvers since 1978 (all equipment included). You'll start by finding your balance on the beach, springing push-up style onto your board in a single (eventually elegant) motion, and learn how to assess the horizon for promising breaks.

Now prepare to fall over repeatedly. You'll paddle into the waves, spit out mouthfuls of saltwater and just maybe feel the

HIGHLIGHTS
1 Cowell's Beach
2 Santa Cruz Beach Boardwalk

SIGHTS
3 Capitola Beach
4 Natural Bridges State Beach
5 Pleasure Point Beach
6 Santa Cruz Wharf
7 Steamer Lane
8 The Hook
9 UCSC Arboretum & Botanic Garden
10 Venetian Court
11 West Cliff Drive

ACTIVITIES
12 Monarch Trail

SLEEPING
13 Hotel Paradox
14 Pacific Blue Inn

EATING
15 Abbott Square Market
16 Chocolat
17 Hanloh
18 Penny Ice Creamery

DRINKING & NIGHTLIFE
19 11th Hour
20 Blue Lagoon
see 3 Capitola Wine Bar
21 Humble Sea Brewing Company
22 Makai Island
23 Roxa Hammock Cafe
24 Venus Spirits
25 Verve Coffee Roasters
26 Vino by the Sea
27 Walnut Ave Cafe

STORM-TOSSED SANTA CRUZ WHARF

Jutting out into the Pacific from the southern end of the beach boardwalk, **Santa Cruz Wharf** morphed from a potato-shipping outpost in 1914 into a big cog in Monterey Bay's sardine-canning machine, until the industry collapsed in the 1950s. It found a new identity for vacationers, who continue to pile into its bars and restaurants, or just peer through the portholes at sea lions, which can grow up to 8ft long. It lost its crown as the longest pier on the West Coast when violent waves in December 2024 caused a 150ft section to collapse, though you can't keep this venerable wharf down: the remainder was up and running again just two weeks later.

head-rush of keeping your balance for a few glorious seconds as you ride the surf! Beware: walking on water is addictive, and the only cure is more surfing.

Beach Boardwalk Thrills

Get playful on roller coasters and a popular beach

Yelps of delight ring out from the Giant Dipper as it rattles along its tracks. Sugary air wafts from stalls selling funnel cakes and cumulonimbus-sized puffs of cotton candy. Families, groups of teens and wide-eyed visitors all pile onto the **Santa Cruz Beach Boardwalk** *(beachboardwalk.com; hours vary, check the website)*. Whether or not you go on any rides, this is a joyous place to bask in all the family-friendly fun.

Founded in 1907, this palace of amusements, sprawled along a wooden boardwalk lining Santa Cruz Beach, is the oldest of its kind in the US. Don't skip a spin on the **Looff Carousel** (1911), with its original 1894 pipe organ, and the wildly popular landmark **Giant Dipper** (1924) wooden roller coaster. Tip: get garlic fries *after* the fast-rotating **Cyclone** and 125ft **Double Shot**, not before.

Flop onto **Santa Cruz Beach** and, when the adrenaline has subsided, head to nearby **Santa Cruz Wharf** for a sundowner.

EATING IN SANTA CRUZ: OUR PICKS

Hanloh: Outstanding bar-restaurant with a short menu of well-spiced and slow-cooked Thai meals. Inside the Bad Animal bookstore. *5-9pm Wed-Sun* $$$

Abbott Square Market: Counter-serve choices galore: coffee, sushi, Venezuelan arepas and West African vegan stews. *8am-10pm Sun-Thu, to 11pm Fri & Sat* $

Chocolat: Eat more chocolate! Start with three types of mole, chocolate-BBQ pork and chocolate mezcal martinis. *noon-4pm Fri-Sun & 5-9pm Thu-Mon* $$

Penny Ice Creamery: Cult favorite for classic/outlandish flavors (blood-orange creamsicle, butter caramel). Yes to toasted marshmallow topping. *noon-11pm* $

DAVID A LITMAN/SHUTTERSTOCK

Santa Cruz Beach Boardwalk

Vino by the Sea *(vino-by-the-sea.com; 4pm-late Wed-Fri, from 2pm Sat & Sun)* has craft beers, local wines and ocean views, but we have a soft spot for kitsch tiki hut **Makai Island** *(makaisantacruz.com; 11am-9pm Mon-Fri, from 9am Sat & Sun)*, where the revolving bar gives you a changing view of the water while you contemplate a classic mai tai or whopping 'Scorpion Bowl.'

Strolling the boardwalk is free. Families and groups should buy passes online and in advance for the best deals on rides, otherwise there are kiosks on the boardwalk to buy last-minute or single-ride tickets (the boardwalk is cashless).

Heavenly Hummingbirds

Spy on pixie birds in an exotic arboretum

Shady groves, tropical flowers, the minty tang of eucalyptus on the air...there are many reasons to visit the **UCSC Arboretum & Botanic Garden** *(arboretum.ucsc.edu; adult/child $10/5; 9am-5pm)* but the chance of glimpsing hummingbirds tops our list.

Among 300 plant species at this diverse garden, managed by University of California, Santa Cruz, are nectar-rich blooms that attract two different kinds of hummingbird. For the

SANTA CRUZ IN HORROR MOVIES

After sunset, Santa Cruz seems altogether less salubrious. No wonder horror moviemakers love to use it as an ironically grisly setting. In *The Lost Boys* (1987), a bleached-blond Kiefer Sutherland played the leader of a vampire crew who dangle from the Trestle Bridge, get into fights at the Looff Carousel and race motorcycles along the boardwalk. Santa Cruz also starred in Jordan Peele's unsettling *Us* (2019), in which Adelaide (Lupita Nyong'o) meets her doppelgänger beneath the boardwalk. Even rainbow-bright Capitola (p289) has a creepy claim to fame: a still-unexplained attack by ferocious shearwater birds in 1961 is said to have provided inspiration for Alfred Hitchcock's *The Birds* (1963).

DRINKING IN SANTA CRUZ: BEST CAFES

Verve Coffee Roasters: Santa Cruz–born Cali chain with phenomenal espresso. Also in Westside and Pleasure Point (near Capitola). *7am-6pm*

Roxa Hammock Cafe: There's no better example of grungy local wellness culture than this gothic cafe serving mysteriously relaxing libations. *noon-9pm*

11th Hour: Third-wave coffee excellence: leafy minimalist interior, unbelievable espresso and enticing baked goods. Westside and downtown locations. *7am-5pm*

Walnut Ave Cafe: Nostalgic 1990s-era cafe–diner that's popular for coffees, Italian sodas and hangover brunches. *8am-3pm Mon-Fri, to 4pm Sat & Sun*

CHEAP THRILLS ON THE WESTSIDE

Not much cash to splash on activities and tours? The Westside has free options galore.

West Cliff Drive: Bracing sea views on a level walking trail from the wharf to Natural Bridges.

Natural Bridges State Beach: Bird-watching by the mighty sea stacks of a wave-lashed beach. Parking is $10, no fee if you walk in.

Monarch Trail: From mid-October to mid-February, monarch butterflies overwinter in the eucalyptus grove behind Natural Bridges.

Wilder Ranch State Park: More than 7000 wild acres with coast-hugging trails, cliffs and marshland.

Steamer Lane: Hold your breath watching surfers catch colossal waves from this cinematic vantage point.

LEGO 19861111/SHUTTERSTOCK

Humpback whale, Monterey Bay National Marine Sanctuary

best chance of witnessing these petite pollinators, go to the South Africa and Australia gardens early in the day or right at the end of the afternoon. They look otherworldly as they dive to drink from coral bells while their wings beat more than 60 times per second. Anna's hummingbirds are visible year-round; look for a telltale glint of cerise feathers (males) and iridescent green (females). From late February to May, ruby-throated Allen's hummingbirds join the nectar-sipping party. Look out for California quails scurrying between bushes, and red-tailed hawks and northern harriers wheeling above.

Buses 11 and 19 travel between Front St and the arboretum, or it's 15 minutes by rideshare.

Humpbacks, Dead Ahead!

Find out how whale breath smells

Surfers don't own these foamy waters. They're mere guests in the **Monterey Bay National Marine Sanctuary** *(montereybay.noaa.gov)*, which teems with whales and dolphins from Marin (p124) down to Cambria (p312). Different sea giants glide through the depths, depending on the season – and on clear days you can spot distant tails and whale spray from land. But the most thrilling encounters are on a wildlife cruise. Your boat will race to view graceful humpbacks plunging into

DRINKING IN SANTA CRUZ: OUR PICKS

Humble Sea Brewing Company: Classic and unconventional beers crafted at this breath-of-fresh-air brewery. *11am-9pm*

Venus Spirits: Stylish bar shaking up concoctions from house-made agave spirits and oak-aged gins. Classy snacks too. *5-9pm Mon-Thu, 4-9pm Fri, 11.30am-9pm Sat & Sun*

Blue Lagoon: Grungy in a good way, this dive bar/nightclub is the place for live music and messy antics. It gets raucous! *4pm-1.30am*

Capitola Wine Bar: Small spot pouring pinot, craft cider and local beer to the sound of string bands and jazz. *3-9pm Wed & Thu, noon-10pm Fri & Sat, 1-6pm Sun*

the deep. You'll cling to the railing to watch a pod of Pacific white-sided dolphins performing synchronized leaps. Whales sometimes get curious and surface close by, belching out a plume of rotten fish breath.

Santa Cruz Whale Watching *(santacruzwhalewatching.com; tour adult/child $66/48)* sends tour boats out into the bay, captained by immensely knowledgeable marine mammal enthusiasts. Slightly cheaper, shorter tours *(adult/child $50/33)* stay closer to shore and spy on sea lions, otters, seabirds and dolphins. They're great for kids but have longer odds for seeing whales. Boats are 56 to 60ft long and yes, there are toilets and a bar (though we'd advise buying their anti-nausea ginger candy before testing your stomach with anything else...these waters get choppy).

Gravity-Defying Photos

Take a tongue-in-cheek tour of the Mystery Spot

Some tourist traps are so charming that travelers smile and play along. The **Mystery Spot** *(mysteryspot.com; tour adult/under-3 $10/free; parking $5)* is one such place, a 150ft-diameter zone in the redwood forest north of Santa Cruz that's said to defy gravity. It's a wacky insight into American road-trip history: the 1940s and '50s were a boom-time for entrepreneurs building novel attractions to encourage drivers to come their way (and part with their cash).

Timed tours by warm and witty guides lead you up the painfully steep walkway where you'll be treated to various 'scientific' demonstrations. (Spoiler: they're visual illusions triggered by the tilted angles of the wooden cabin built on site. Or are they?!)

The Mystery Spot is popular, largely because of the trompe l'oeil photo opportunities. It's open 10am to 5pm Monday-Friday, to 9pm Saturday and Sunday. Reserve tickets ahead, especially on weekends and holidays (and bring cash if you're rocking up on the day). You'll need to drive or go by rideshare; ask staff to help you get a return ride.

Rainbow-Colored Capitola

Stroll into beachside nostalgia

Five miles east of Santa Cruz, Capitola's most photogenic corner is **Venetian Court**, signposted just after the bridge across Soquel Creek. These candy-colored 1920s beach condos, built in doll's-house-like Mediterranean Revival style, light up social-media feeds; be mindful that these are private residences as you pass through. Bus 2 from Front St in Santa Cruz gets you within 20 minutes' walk.

BEST BEACHES AROUND CAPITOLA

Capitola Beach: Family-friendly city beach in easy reach of Capitola's cafes and restaurants.

New Brighton State Beach: Sandy shores hemmed with tree-capped bluffs, with walking trails and a campground. Two miles east of Capitola.

Seacliff State Beach: Popular for swimming, strolling and sunsets. The sunken freighter, the SS *Palo Alto*, is off-limits. Three miles east.

Rio del Mar State Beach: Wide and sandy beach, far from the Capitola crowds. Four miles east.

The Hook: Overlooking Pleasure Point, a barely-there beach to launch a board into reliable breaks. Watch skilled surfers from The Hook parking lot.

Beyond Santa Cruz

If you think the city of Santa Cruz has kooky energy, get ready for beast-stalked forests, singular festivals and fending off sea otters.

Places

GETTING AROUND

It's cruisier by car but day trips are possible by public transportation. The No 35 bus *(scmtd.com)* travels between Santa Cruz and Felton. It's more of an expedition to reach Moss Landing (No 1 or 2 to Watsonville, followed by a southbound bus along Hwy 1, if you have abundant time). If you're traveling from the Bay Area, Caltrain commuter services connect San Jose Diridon station with Gilroy, but you have limited options from there.

The Santa Cruz Mountains, sharpened by the San Andreas Fault and topping out at 3786ft, form a spiky dividing line between the Bay Area and the Central Coast, heralding your arrival to a wilder space. This is where fog fills the valleys and old-growth redwoods form fairy-rings in temperate rainforests.

Santa Cruz' boardwalk and blond beaches gave it fame, but every town around here has its 'thing,' whether it's Bigfoot (Felton) or garlic (Gilroy). Plus the locals are pretty darn cute: sea otters are so numerous in Moss Landing that you'll struggle to keep your distance, while six different kinds of owl, plus hawks and hummingbirds, preen in the forests north and east of Santa Cruz.

Gilroy

TIME FROM SANTA CRUZ: 1 HR

Have a garlickin' good time

If you're driving between San Francisco and Santa Cruz or Monterey, that sweet, funky aroma means you're getting close to Garlic City.

Known as the 'Garlic King,' founding farmer Kiyoshi Hirasaki started a garlic boom in the 1920s. The cattle-ranching and timber town of Gilroy was soon producing more than half the USA's garlic. Gilroy celebrates this aromatic bulb in late July at the **Garlic Festival** *(gilroygarlicfestivalassociation.com)* with three days of garlic cook-offs, live music and pungent produce, but you can get your garlic fix at any time.

Start by admiring the **Garlic Mural** then hunt out a garlicky place to eat. **Garlic City Cafe** (closed Monday) is famous for doling out garlic soups and garlic fries, but we love the mouth-singeing garlic prawns at casual **Mariscos Puerto Vallarta**, three blocks south of downtown. If you're traveling with kids, **Gilroy Gardens** *(gilroygardens.org; admission $65)*, four miles west of downtown, has leafy grounds and fairground attractions. It's open 11am to 5pm, June to mid-August; and weekends from late August to May.

No time? Then load up on garlic oils and relishes (and maybe a scoop of garlic ice cream!) at **Garlic World** or the **Garlic Shoppe**; they're easy pullovers if you're driving north on Hwy 101.

AITOR GONZALEZ FRIAS/SHUTTERSTOCK

Santa Cruz Beach Train

Santa Cruz Mountains

TIME FROM SANTA CRUZ: **15 MINS**

Be awed by redwoods, old & new

A 40-acre grove rises high just 6 miles north of Santa Cruz in **Henry Cowell Redwoods State Park** *(parking $10)* and it's easily reached on the level 0.8-mile **Redwood Grove Loop Trail**. The park's tallest is the 282ft 'Giant;' look up to spot burls, the 'beauty spots' of redwoods, and down to see banana slugs.

More tranquil trails are 8 miles northeast of Santa Cruz in the **Forest of Nisene Marks State Park** *(parking $8)*, named after a farming family matriarch whose descendants donated 9700 acres of land to the parks system. These comparatively young trees show forest regeneration in action after rampant 19th-century logging. Steep, fern-fringed trails lead down to Aptos Creek. Keep an eye out for fossils scattered around the riverbed (but no souvenirs!).

Catch a steam train through the forest

A shrieking whistle pierces the silence and steam wisps above the treetops. In the 1870s, this train transported lumber but these days excited visitors fill the open-air carriages. The **Redwood Forest Train** *(roaringcamp.com; 10.30am daily; adult/child $42.35/26.45)* offers a 75-minute narrated journey, while the **Santa Cruz Beach Train** *(daily Jun–mid-Aug, Sat & Sun only Apr, May, late Aug; return adult/child $46.59/31.75)* chuff-chuffs to the Santa Cruz Beach Boardwalk (p286). Both depart from **Roaring Camp**, the recreated gold-mining village in Henry Cowell Redwoods State Park. Buy tickets online, it's very popular with families.

Sip fruits of the land at a hilly hideaway

We don't know which we appreciate more, hard cider or organic wine. Fortunately **Hallcrest Vineyards** *(hallcrestvineyards.com)* serves both at its idyllic tasting room west of Felton. Open

THE SASQUATCH OF SANTA CRUZ

Heard an unexplained whooping sound in the Santa Cruz Mountains? Bigfoot, an elusive apelike cryptid, is scoffed at by most scientists but many believers claim he stalks remote forests in North America. The town of Felton, 7 miles north of Santa Cruz, was Bigfoot ground zero for decades, thanks to a Bigfoot museum operated until 2024 by local enthusiast Michael Rugg. Though Rugg has retired and the museum is indefinitely on hiatus, stories of the 'Santa Cruz Sasquatch' are still murmured at local watering holes. Curious? Narrow in on recent sightings on the Bigfoot Field Researchers Organization website *(bfro.net)* or just grab a T-shirt or bumper sticker with a Bigfoot silhouette; they're on sale everywhere.

SLOUGH SAFETY & TIPS

Weather: Go early before the wind picks up. Sea fog burns off fast, so wear sunscreen even if it's cloudy.

Keeping your distance: Stay five kayak lengths away from marine mammals. If one of them pops up nearby, gently paddle backwards. Keep your vessel pointing away from them.

Wildlife seasons: Come in spring to see otter pups cuddling their mothers. Fall and winter are ideal to spot migrating birds.

Pets: Don't bring your dog; don't leave them in the car, either.

Warning: Under the Federal Marine Mammal Protection Act, you can be fined thousands of dollars or even risk jail time for bothering seals and otters.

noon to 5pm Thursday to Monday, and occupying a hilly retreat that dates back to the 1880s, Hillcrest was one of the first wineries in the Santa Cruz Mountains. Settle in at the outdoor deck for green views, tart ciders and tastings of chardonnay and pinot noir. Utterly relaxing.

Moss Landing

TIME FROM SANTA CRUZ: **30 MINS**

Evade sea otters in Elkhorn Slough

This coastal wetland is less about spotting wildlife, and more about wildlife spotting you. Southern sea otters, harbor seals and seabirds are so abundant in this biodiverse salt marsh that you'll find yourself frantically paddling away from them, just to keep your distance.

Rent a kayak or SUP from **Monterey Bay Kayaks** *(montereybaykayaks.com; half-day rental $48)* in **Moss Landing** (open 9am to 5pm). At first glance, the roaring highway and concrete stacks of a natural-gas power plant seem an unlikely setting for a marine preserve. But a short paddle under the highway bridge sends you into **Elkhorn Slough**. As your oar sweeps through sea grasses, and sends the occasional moon jellyfish into a spin, you'll notice curious faces pop up in the waters of this 7-mile tidal estuary. Seals and sea lions have been known to bob their heads above the surface, startling kayakers (who risk a stiff fine for getting too close). No inhabitant of the California coasts garners coos of delight quite like these playful creatures, and more than 125 sea otters have been counted in Elkhorn Slough.

Look up, too: pelicans dive-bomb the waters with torpedo-like precision, just one of 116 kinds of birds spotted in this biodiverse sanctuary, including peregrine falcons and other fly-by species traveling the Pacific flyway migratory route.

EATING & DRINKING AROUND SANTA CRUZ: OUR PICKS

White Raven: Charmingly rustic, this art-filled hippie haven in Felton has espresso and baked goodies. *6.30am-1.30pm Mon-Fri, from 7am Sat & Sun* $

Taqueria Vallarta: Generous tacos and burritos that demand two hands (and two stomachs) at this down-home Mexican spot in Felton. *9am-10.30pm* $

Cafe Motif: An airy, mosaic-floored Gilroy cafe whipping up Filipino brunches, buttermilk pancakes and cocktails. *8am-9pm Wed-Sat, to 6pm Sun-Tue* $$

Sea Harvest: The perfect finale to time on Elkhorn Slough: Baja rockfish tacos, fried calamari or prawns and chips on a waterfront deck. *10am-8pm* $

WALKING THROUGH THE CENTURIES IN SAN JUAN BAUTISTA

Between Gilroy and Salinas, this little town has an interesting history, from Catholic missionaries to Mexican influence. Take a walking tour of its centuries-old buildings.

START	END	LENGTH
Mission San Juan Bautista	Masonic Lodge	1.5 miles; 1 hr

Begin at the cacti-fringed cloisters of the **1 Mission San Juan Bautista**. Founded in 1797, it has the largest church of California's 21 original Spanish missions. Tucked away in a rose garden on the other side of 2nd St is the **2 Settler's Cabin**, a log hut typical of the 1830s...snug! Stroll southeast along 2nd St to pass the red-and-white **3 Plaza Hotel**, a former Spanish barracks; and **4 José Castro Adobe**, built by Alta California general and governor José Antonio Castro then bought by survivors of the Donner Party disaster. Turn right on Washington St and right again on 3rd St; you'll pass charming boutiques en route to the Greek Revival–style **5 Glad Tidings Church** (1863). Swing left and then turn right along 4th St for four garden-lined blocks, then turn left down Monterey Rd to see **6 Marentis House**, an elegantly Gothic buttercream-colored construction dating to 1873. You'll hear the faint roar of the highway as you turn right on Church St and approach the **7 cemetery**, where 19th-century tombs enjoy eternal views of San Benito County's green hills. Follow Church St east then turn right on 3rd St; after three blocks, hang left on San Jose St, passing Verutti Park. When you turn right on 2nd St, you'll see the grand old walls of the mission complex lining the way to your final stop, the striking blue-and-cream **8 Masonic Lodge** (completed in 1869).

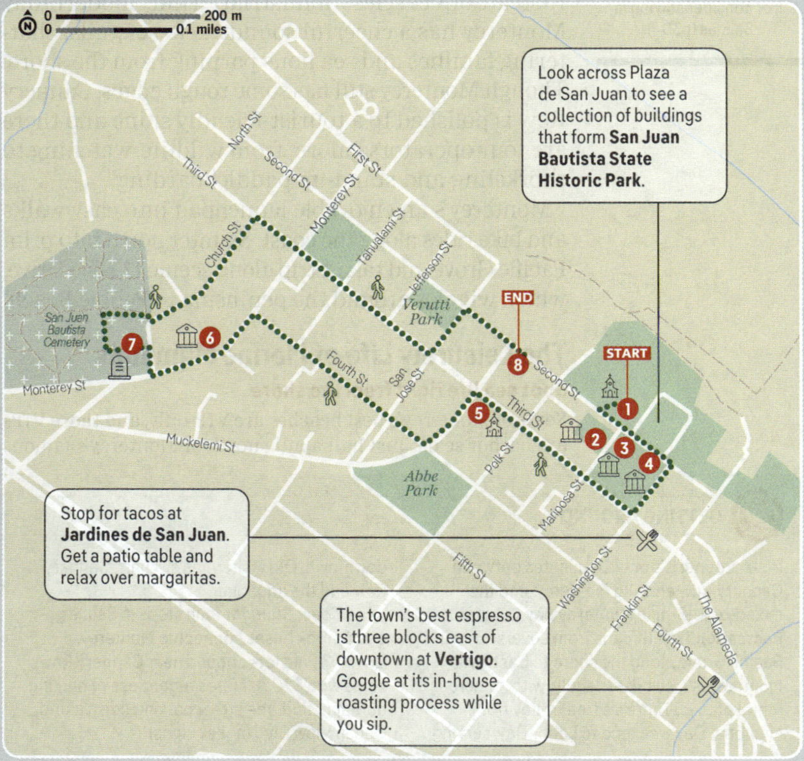

Monterey

AQUARIUM | SEASIDE CHARM | INDUSTRIAL HISTORY

TOP TIP

Good-value hotels exist near Cannery Row, if you don't mind street noise. Quieter B&Bs line Ocean View Blvd, which links Monterey with neighboring Pacific Grove. Weekend rates sting. Find budget chain hotels downtown off Munras Ave, or east off Hwy 1, or consider staying in Salinas (p304).

Basking on the northern shore of Monterey Peninsula, the city of Monterey is a tourism darling and a center for marine conservation. Thanks to its famous aquarium, sparkling waterfront and spruced-up factory buildings, it's one of Hwy 1's most popular stops.

Things have changed since literary titan John Steinbeck immortalized Monterey in *Cannery Row* (1945); you'll need to squint to picture the stinking fish canneries and steamy brothels described in the novel. Instead of ceaseless industrial grind, modern-day Monterey has a cheerful soundtrack: seagulls, chattering families and sea lions parping from the shore. Though Monterey still has some rough edges, Cannery Row is polished to a tourist-friendly shine and there are tour operators galore, from wildlife-watching to snorkeling and stand-up paddleboarding.

Monterey's an enjoyable launchpad into easy walks and bike rides along the coast. Saunter north into prim Pacific Grove and take a trip along scenic 17-Mile Drive, which wiggles around the peninsula to Pebble Beach.

The Leisurely Life of Marine Mammals

Spot sea life right from the shore

Some of Monterey's best beaches are VIP-only, and those VIPs are harbor seals. Just half a mile north of Monterey's famous

GETTING AROUND

Walk around! It's only 20 minutes between Cannery Row and Old Monterey, and the mixed-use, 18-mile **Monterey Bay Coastal Recreation Trail** threads from Lovers Point in Pacific Grove along the shore to Castroville. Monterey is also bike-friendly, with numerous rental places. There's a free trolley from Memorial Day weekend to Labor Day, serving downtown, Old Fisherman's Wharf, Cannery Row and the aquarium.

The *Coast Starlight* train stops in Salinas, and Amtrak buses connect to Monterey. Driving? Paid lots abound near Cannery Row, some with $20 flat fares regardless of parking duration; find free street parking north along Ocean View Blvd (check signs).

MONTEREY

HIGHLIGHTS
1 Cannery Row
2 Monterey Bay Aquarium

SIGHTS
3 17-Mile Drive
4 17-Mile Drive: Pacific Grove Gate
5 American Tin Cannery
6 Asilomar State Beach
7 Bird Rock
8 Cooper-Molera Adobe
9 Cypress Point Lookout
10 Lovers Point
11 Old Fisherman's Wharf
12 Old Monterey Jail
13 Pacific Biological Laboratories
14 Pacific Grove Monarch Sanctuary
15 Restless Sea
16 San Carlos Beach
17 Steinbeck Plaza
18 Wing Chong Company Grocery

ACTIVITIES
19 Adventures by the Sea
20 Aquarius Dive Shop
21 Big Sur Adventures
22 Harbor Seal Viewing Point
23 Mad Dogs & Englishmen
24 Monterey Bay Kayaks
25 Monterey Bay Whale Watch

SLEEPING
26 Jabberwock Inn
27 Martine Inn
28 Spindrift Inn

EATING
29 Ambrosia
30 Fish Hopper
31 Gallery Cafe
32 Happy Girl Kitchen
33 Hula's Island Grill
34 Passionfish
35 Revival Ice Cream
36 Whaling Station Steakhouse

DRINKING & NIGHTLIFE
37 Crown & Anchor
38 Pearl Hour
39 Sovino
40 Tidal Coffee

WHALE-WATCHING SEASON FOREVER

Much like humans, whales visit Monterey Bay all year round. Their migration seasons overlap, meaning you have a chance of seeing colossal marine mammals whenever you travel. You can see humpbacks from March through November but your best shot to see these mighty creatures slapping a fin is in July and August. Blue whales have a shorter season: your optimum chance of sighting the world's biggest mammal is from May to October. Winter has action, too: from December to around mid-May, gray whales glide through Monterey Bay, and you can see killer whales. There are numerous whale-watching tour operators, including **Monterey Bay Whale Watch** *(montereybay-whalewatch.com)*, and more options in Santa Cruz (p288).

aquarium is the **Harbor Seal Viewing Point** where plump seals loll on a protected arc of pristine white sand. Further south, spy on sea lions from the pier at **San Carlos Beach** and **Old Fisherman's Wharf**. Along the way you'll spy playful sea otters and sea lions that belly-flop from the rocks.

Historic Cannery Row

Amble from overfishing to ocean conservation

On **Cannery Row**, cacophonous fish factories have been replaced by a different kind of chaos: merry-making tourists! Formerly Ocean View Ave, the street was renamed in 1958 after author John Steinbeck captured this gritty neighborhood in his masterpiece *Cannery Row* (1945). Meandering along Cannery Row combines industrial history with the innocent pleasures of present-day Monterey. Make sure you idle through a souvenir store or slurp soft-serve along the way.

Start a block northwest of the aquarium at the 1926 **American Tin Cannery** (when we passed through, it was destined to transform into a hotel). This powerhouse factory was one of the big players on Cannery Row in the 1930s and '40s, when the pungent tang of fish was heavy in the air.

Factories operated day and night, processing 250,000 tons of sardines annually. The Norwegian founder of **Hovden Cannery** pioneered undersea pipes to vacuum tons of fish into his factory every minute. These innovations were so viciously efficient that fish numbers dwindled

SEA-OTTER SIGHTINGS

Sea otters are a frequent sight along the Central Coast, and one of the best places to see them is from a kayak on Elkhorn Slough in **Moss Landing** (p292), an estuary brimming with marine mammals.

JEJIM/SHUTTERSTOCK

Fish Hopper

and factories closed one after another; Hovden sealed its final tin in 1973. But cosmic balance has been restored: this site of voracious overfishing is now a bastion of ocean conservation, home to the aquarium (p300).

A few steps south and across the street is the former **Wing Chong Company Grocery** (1918). Monterey's fishing industry was developed in the 1850s by Chinese fishers who established themselves at Point Ahlones. Wing Chong was also the inspiration for a similarly named grocery in Steinbeck's *Cannery Row*.

Continue walking south along Cannery Row and note the **Pacific Biological Laboratories** building, where ecology pioneer Ed Ricketts, a close friend of John Steinbeck, preserved marine specimens (free public tours on the second Saturday of the month, except December). When you arrive at **Steinbeck Plaza**, contemplate the writer's own description of Cannery Row as 'a poem, a stink, a grating noise, a quality of light, a tone, a habit, a nostalgia, a dream.'

SECRETS OF THE DEEP

Yerlany Mendez, interpretive program specialist at **Monterey Bay Aquarium** (p300), explains her passion for marine conservation.

I've always wanted to explore the unknown. I wanted to go to space! The first time I came to Monterey Bay Aquarium, one of the volunteers told me how the ocean is the great unexplored – that led me to pursue marine science.

Part of my role is contributing to various DEIA initiatives, like bilingual programs in Spanish, English and even blended language. I get joy from children coming through and teaching their family the things we teach them. I dive in the Kelp Forest exhibit and feed all the animals, including sharks. But my favorite tank is called the Bottom Dwellers, with amazing sea slugs, sea stars, crabs and sponges.

EATING IN MONTEREY: ECOFRIENDLY EATS

Happy Girl Kitchen: An eco-conscious, one-stop shop for coffee, every-grain avocado toast and deli food, just two blocks from Ocean View Blvd. *7am-5pm* $

Passionfish: Sustainably harvested seafood and local ingredients, from tomato-truffle scallops to 12-hour lamb. Well-priced small-batch wine. *5-9pm* $$$

Fish Hopper: Dishing up sustainable fish since 1950, this place overhangs the bay for splendid views to accompany pasta, seared tuna or ribeye. *10.30am-9.30pm* $$$

Revival Ice Cream: Passionfruit-mango, and honeyed 'Bee's Knees' are among plant-based scoops. Dairy options. All organic. *noon-9pm Sun-Thu, to 10pm Fri & Sat* $

WRITERLY RETREAT

Looking for more literary history? Follow in Jack Kerouac's footsteps in **Big Sur** (p306). In his 1962 work *Big Sur*, Jack Duluoz (Kerouac's alter ego) finds comforting solitude in Bixby Canyon before loneliness and vice drive him back to San Francisco.

Monterey Bay's Watery Wonders

Snorkel and paddle among sea life

Your paddle snags on a tangle of bull kelp as you swish through the water. Harbor seals watch you warily before disappearing below the waterline. Monterey Bay looks very different from a kayak or stand-up paddleboard, with up-close sights and sensations you'd otherwise miss.

Set out in the morning, before ocean breezes set vessels swaying. You can launch right from Del Monte Beach by renting from **Monterey Bay Kayaks** *(montereybaykayaks.com; rentals per person from $40)* or join one of its 90-minute guided harbor tours *(per person from $60)* to spot seals, sea lions and otters without disturbing their natural behaviors.

Want to go deeper? **Aquarius Dive Shop** *(aquariusdivers.com/guided-tours)* lead one-hour snorkeling tours of the kelp forest *(from $150)* and guided dive tours *(1-/2- dive tour $80/100)* for certified divers. You can also rent a mask and snorkel *($10)* and DIY. It's eerily beautiful below the surface, where kelp flutters in the ocean currents, and sea stars wink from the rocks; reserve tours a week ahead.

Settlers, Sailors & Gold Rush Rebels

Take a walk around Old Monterey

Unpeel Monterey's tempestuous 19th-century history by mooching around Old Monterey, the neighborhood extending south from the Old Fisherman's Wharf. Built from granite in 1854, **Old Monterey Jail** *(free)* became the thick-walled temporary home of numerous Gold Rush–era gangsters and vigilantes. It's open 10am to 4pm, Thursday to Sunday. Three blocks east, find the 1827 **Cooper-Molera Adobe** *(coopermolera.org)*, the ornate home of a fur-trading merchant; open 10am to 2pm, Friday and Saturday.

The Prettiest Road from Pacific Grove

17-Mile Drive is best by bike

Cycling **17-Mile Drive** *(pebblebeach.com/17-mile-drive)* is a bracing, all-sensory alternative to traveling by car. It's accessible from sunrise to sunset; allow three to four hours (less on an e-bike, more if you want a leisurely lunch).

DRINKING IN MONTEREY: OUR PICKS

Pearl Hour: Original cocktails in a chandeliered setting with a rock 'n' roll soundtrack. Distinguished drinks, unpretentious clientele. *6pm-late Wed-Mon*

Sovino: We love this intimate wine bar for its California vino and woodsy interior. *3-9pm Mon, Tue & Thu; to 10pm Fri, 1-10pm Sat, to 8pm Sun*

Tidal Coffee: The richest espresso, the bluest views. Get a latte with locally roasted beans; enjoy the patio, burritos and cinnamon rolls. *6am-4pm*

Crown & Anchor: Convivial clone of a British pub. Admire anglophile curios hanging from the walls and sip a G&T. *4pm-late Mon-Fri, from noon Sat & Sun*

ALEXANDER DEMYANENKO/SHUTTERSTOCK

17-Mile Drive

Rent wheels in Monterey; **Adventures by the Sea** *(adventuresbythesea.com/cannery-row; half-day bike/e-bike $45/59)* has genuine service and the shared walking/cycling **Monterey Bay Coastal Recreation Trail** runs right from its doorstep. Follow the trail north past snoozing harbor seals and rocky **Lovers Point**. The car-free recreation trail ends here; pedal south and west to join Sunset Dr to reach the **Pacific Grove Gate** entrance to 17-Mile Drive. Drivers pay a fee *($12.25)* but cyclists are waved through like celebrities.

The '17-Mile Drive' signs direct you from champagne-colored beaches to rocky coves. Waves at the **Restless Sea** are almost hypnotic, while **Bird Rock** has armies of pelicans and barking sea lions. At the left-turn onto Spyglass Hill Rd, 3.5 miles past the entrance gate, you have two choices. Dedicated cycle lanes end here, so it's safer to turn onto Spyglass Hill Rd to Pebble Beach. If you're experienced at road cycling and can assertively share winding roads with cars, continue along 17-Mile Drive to the knotted groves at **Cypress Point Lookout**. Whichever route you take, Pebble Beach Golf Resort's **Gallery Cafe** welcomes sweaty cyclists for spicy egg skillets and protein smoothies...fuel for the journey back!

MONTEREY WITH KIDS

Big Sur Adventures: Guided e-bike tours of **17-Mile Drive** tailor-made for families.

Adventures By The Sea: Rents kayaks and stand-up paddleboards *(from $35)* for gliding through the kelpy bay.

Mad Dogs & Englishmen: Put the kids in a sidecar attached to a classy e-bike *(from $95)* and pedal the recreational trail.

Tidepooling: Myriad coves offer an eyeful of anemones; try **Lovers Point** and **Asilomar State Beach**.

Cannery Row: In the former fish-canning district, you're never far from candy and ice cream.

Pacific Grove Monarch Sanctuary: See masses of butterflies every year between mid-October and mid-March.

EATING IN & AROUND MONTEREY: MEMORABLE MEALS

Whaling Station Steakhouse: Old-school cool: prime rib, classic cocktails and white-glove service. The bar's super for solo diners. *4.30-8pm* **$$$**

Ambrosia: Authentic Indian food in a leafy garden or fountained dining room. Lunch buffets, à la carte in the evening. Popular! *11.30am-2:45pm & 4-9pm* **$$**

Hula's Island Grill: Coconut shrimp rolls, poke bowls, macadamia-dusted barramundi in a tiki bar. *4-9.30pm Mon-Wed, to 10pm Thu-Sat, to 9pm Sun* **$$**

Phil's Fish Market: Legendary Castroville seafood spot simmering up rich cioppino (seafood stew), complete with crab legs and scallops. Fifteen miles north. *10am-7pm* **$$**

TOP EXPERIENCE

Monterey Bay Aquarium

The aquarium overhanging Monterey Bay has a mission to educate the world about ocean conservation, and its sharks, rays and mesmerizing jellyfish tanks fascinate all age groups. Allow half a day: admire playful sea otters, spy on an octopus and go eye-to-eye with scowling wolf eels. You'll emerge with deep respect for our mighty but fragile oceans.

PHOTOCRITICAL/MONTEREY BAY AQUARIUM

Leopard shark, Kelp Forest tank

TOP TIPS

- Buy tickets online, in advance.
- Queues are long in the morning. Early afternoon, you'll likely waltz right in (though it'll be crowded inside).
- Check posted timings of 'Encounters,' live events like feeding times and meeting an albatross (note: they're extremely popular!)

PRACTICALITIES

- montereybayaquarium.org
- Admission adult/child $65/50
- 10am-5pm

Kelp Forest & Monterey Bay Habitats

Split across two floors, the 28ft **Kelp Forest** showcases the full height of these teeming native ecosystems. Golden ropes of kelp sway in the water as Pacific dogfish and sea bass glide past. The **African penguin enclosure** is nearby (2nd floor).

Touch Pool & Great Tide Pool

Ever heard the unbridled joy of a kid who has greeted a bat ray for the first time? The **Touch Pool** allows safe encounters with squishy shallow-water critters. Step outside through the thrilling wave-crash tunnel; 600 gallons of sea water are pumped through every 30 seconds, and you can take selfies with a backdrop of cascading foam. Views overlooking the **Great Tide Pool**, and across Monterey Bay, are dazzling.

Open Sea & Into the Deep Zones

A walkway leads to the **Open Sea Zone**. Tanks of sea nettle jellyfish unfurling their orange stingers are almost emblematic of the aquarium. Close by, the gigantic Open Sea Tank feels like a movie theater where the stars are tuna that zip past in a silvery flash. Downstairs in the **Into the Deep Zone**, jellyfish and siphonophores look like disco lights. Our favorite: lobed comb jellies that resemble little spaceships whirring through the deep. Don't miss the Japanese spider crabs, who always look ready for a fight.

Beyond Monterey

Head south to stick to the dramatic and dreamy coast, or go east for gritty towns and less-trodden trails.

Four miles south of downtown Monterey is Carmel-by-the-Sea. Once the stomping ground of literary trailblazers like Jack London and Sinclair Lewis, these days it feels like one big country club, where immaculately coiffed locals stroll by white-sand beaches. The wave-crashing drama of Point Lobos is just south, while Carmel Valley's wine country rolls east.

Bigger and more hectic is the city of Salinas, 17 miles northeast of Monterey via the hiking terrain of Fort Ord. Salinas has John Steinbeck's legacy and the River Road Wine Route among its draws. From here, Hwy 101 and Rte 25 take you to the west and east sides of vastly underrated Pinnacles National Park, its rock spindles forming a spectacular backdrop to hikes through shadowy canyons and oak forests.

Places

GETTING AROUND

This realm is made for travel on foot. Point Lobos, Pinnacles and Fort Ord have wondrous hikes, while Carmel-by-the-Sea is highly walkable. The trick is getting here. Cars still reign supreme but some day trips via public transit are more than possible. Buses connect Monterey with Carmel-by-the-Sea (No 5) and Salinas (No 20); find schedules on *mst.org*.

Fort Ord

TIME FROM MONTEREY: **20 TO 30 MINS** 

Roving through a former US Army base

Your feet sink into the sand as you follow the quarter-mile trail to the beach. The ocean is framed by dunes, and driftwood is artfully strewn on the sand. At **Fort Ord Dunes State Park**, 7 miles north of Monterey, millennia of wind and wave action created these sandy mounds. But their recent history is even more interesting: until 1994 the military kept watch here.

Fort Ord's transformation from rifle-operator range into coastal beauty spot is quite the glowup. Seven thousand rounds of spent ammunition were cleared after the land was donated to the Parks Program. The prickly carpet of greenery over the dunes is mostly ice plants, introduced to stabilize the dunes, though these hardy magenta-flowering weeds have proved destructive for other species.

On the other side of Hwy 1, 86 miles of inland cycling and hiking trails spider through the **Fort Ord National Monument**, another slice of formerly military land (now overseen by the Bureau of Land Management; *blm.gov*). Multiple trailheads branch from Inter-Garrison Rd and some along Rte 68 (respectively, the north and south fringes of the park).

CARMEL'S REAL-LIFE DOLLHOUSES

There's a reason Carmel-by-the-Sea looks like it was plucked from the pages of a fairy-tale. More than two dozen buildings have steep gabled roofs, undulating lines and craggy stone chimneys, the design hallmarks of self-taught architect Hugh W Comstock (1893–1950). Their whimsical appearance was inspired by Hugh's wife, Mayotta Browne Comstock, who operated a successful business selling 'Otsy-Totsy' dolls. Mayotta wanted to create a magical home for her rosy-cheeked ragdolls, and Hugh quickly went to work. First came the 'Hansel and Gretel Cottages,' then the 'Snow White Summer Palace.' The candy-colored houses remain some of the most coveted real estate in Carmel.

Point Lobos

TIME FROM MONTEREY: **15 MINS**

Hike a loop of craggy Point Lobos

Sheer cliffs, tide pools and pine groves: **Point Lobos State Natural Reserve** collects all the drama of California's Central Coast within a 550-acre peninsula. Chain together multiple short trails for a loop of the entire reserve; allow 4 to 5 hours. Bring binoculars, as many wildlife hot-spots are offshore in the distance.

Start among the moss-clung trees of the **South Plateau Trail**, then follow signs to the **Bird Island Trail**, which hugs the shore. You pass the jewel-like water of Gibson Beach before rounding the bend to **Bird Island**, where battalions of seabirds pose offshore, from gangs of cormorants to irritable pelicans. Along the **South Shore Trail** to **Sea Lion Cove** you hear marine mammals before you see their gray bodies from afar.

The number of hikers slims down along the **Cypress Grove Trail**. At the end of the **North Shore Trail**, cut things short by following the Whalers Knoll and Lace Lichen trails back to the entrance, or complete the loop by continuing to the **Whalers Cabin Museum**, with remnants of huts built by the first wave of Chinese migrants in the early 1850s.

The parking lot fills up by midmorning but parking highway-side avoids the fee (*$10*).

Carmel-by-the-Sea

TIME FROM MONTEREY: **10 MINS**

Tasting the good life

Absurdly picturesque Carmel-by-the-Sea is where designer poodles lead their owners to restaurants with 'yappy hours' and weekends are spent clinking mimosas. Start on the cypress-framed **beach**, then sashay along Ocean Ave. Tucked-away **Dawn's Dream Winery** *(dawnsdreamwinery.com)* is a casual spot to sip, while popular **De Tierra** *(detierra.com)* spills onto the street. Further east, the **Comstock Historical Hill District** has a fairy-tale atmosphere... pinch yourself!

Carmel Valley

TIME FROM MONTEREY: **30 MINS**

A wine-tasting wander

Pop a cork in Carmel Valley and you'll hit a winery. Vineyards benefit from the Santa Lucia Mountains' mild climate but many tasting rooms cherry-pick wines from across Monterey

EATING IN CARMEL-BY-THE-SEA: BEST BRUNCHES

Stationaery: Brunches from lobster rolls to shakshuka in a tucked-away venue. Mimosas, Bellinis, espresso martinis! *8am-3pm daily, 5.30-9pm Thu-Sat* $$$

La Bicyclette: Huevos rancheros and French toast join European tartines and prosecco at this popular spot. *8.30-10.30am Fri-Sun, 11am-9pm daily* $$$

Village Corner: Come for big skillets and hearty omelettes with lashings of Kir Royale (bubbly and cassis). *8am-4pm Sun-Wed, to 9pm Thu-Sat* $$

Grasing's: Crab avocado toast, eggs with chicken sausage. Also French flavors like sole meunière. *10.30am-3pm, 5-9.30pm Sat & Sun, noon-3pm & 5-9pm Mon-Fri* $$$

PHOTO BY CHRIS AXE/GETTY IMAGES

Bird Island, Point Lobos

County. They're clustered together in a small, walkable strip... no coin-toss to designate a driver! Tastings are $25 to $35.

Begin at **McIntyre Vineyards** *(mcintyrevineyards.com)*; from pinots to chardonnays, this is one to savor. Founder Steve McIntyre is one of the originators of the Sustainability in Practice (SIP) program. Open 11am to 5pm.

Five minutes walk east is **I. Brand & Family** *(ibrandwinery.com)*. Think of this place as a tireless wine detective hell-bent on seeking out the most intriguing independent drops, from zesty steel-barrel-aged albariño to smoky red grenache. We could spend hours in the rustic-chic tasting room. (Oh wait, we did...) Open 11am to 5pm, Thursday to Monday.

One block west is family-run **Joyce Winery** *(joycewineco.com)*. Sample its local wines (exceptional pinot noir), as well as sauvignon blanc, syrah and rosé from its vineyard further inland in Arroyo Seco. Mop it up with a cheese platter. Open noon to 5.30pm, Wednesday to Monday.

Next door, edgy artwork and animal prints make **Scratch** *(scratchwines.com)* feel like a saucy-but-classy '70s boudoir. Sparkling rosé is a jubilant finale. Open noon to 7pm Sunday to Thursday, and to 8pm Friday and Saturday.

WHAT IS SUSTAINABLE WINE-MAKING?

Byron Kosuge, winemaker at SIP-certified McIntyre Vineyards, shares what sustainable wine-making means to him.

A vineyard is a biome in which grapevines are part of the community, but not all of it. The other plants, critters and insects, they all have a contribution – down to fungi and microbes that fix nutrients in the soil. The more sensitive you are to the health of the land, the better the wine is going to be. Each patch of land has its own thing to say through the wine. The other part of sustainability, that is equally important, is taking care of the people who are growing the grapes. Making your vineyard the best place that it can be is all part of the equation.

EATING IN CARMEL VALLEY: BEST SPOTS TO SOP UP THE BOOZE

ROUX: Classic recipes from Spain, Italy and France, like gnocchi bolognese, paella and brandied shrimp. Completely satisfying. *5-8pm Wed-Mon* **$$$**

Carmel Valley Creamery Co: Out-of-town micro-dairy. Come for chèvre and poppyseed cheese, stay for espresso and pastries. *7.30am-5pm* **$**

Trailside Cafe: Filling pub food: grilled artichokes to myriad mac 'n' cheeses. Long tap list. *9am-8pm Mon-Wed, 4-8pm Thu, 9am-9pm Fri, 8am-9pm Sat, 8am-8pm Sun* **$$**

Corkscrew Cafe: In an elegantly vintage 1930s building, attentive service and wood-fired pizzas. Organic everything, outstanding wine list. *11.30am-7pm Wed-Mon* **$$**

WHY I LOVE SALINAS

Anita Isalska, Lonely Planet writer

Like all the most interesting people, Salinas takes a little getting to know. The first few times I visited, I was making a quick coffee stop on a drive to somewhere more glamorous (probably Monterey!). But between the earnest welcomes, great breweries and phenomenal Mexican food, Salinas worked its nonchalant magic. The city is laid-back, unshowy and a low-key gateway to some of the best pinot noir I've ever tasted. It's surrounded by farms and green hills that feel vibrantly alive. It doesn't hurt that Salinas is the home of writer John Steinbeck, whose reflections on travel – the hope, the vulnerability, the absurdity! – still ring so true.

JASON BUSA/SHUTTERSTOCK

Pinnacles National Park

Salinas

TIME FROM MONTEREY: **30 MINS**

See through the eyes of John Steinbeck

A tangle of traffic surrounded by farmland, Salinas is 'America's Salad Bowl.' See its miles of tilled soil and hum of industry from the perspective of its most famous son, John Steinbeck (1902–68), author of Pulitzer-winning *The Grapes of Wrath* (1939), *Of Mice and Men* (1937) and *Cannery Row* (1945).

At the **National Steinbeck Center** *(steinbeck.org; adult/child $15/7)*, Steinbeck's upbringing and creative works come to life through interactive exhibits and videos. Not a Steinbeck fan? Go anyway: his pin-sharp observations capture hard-scrabble life in California in profound (and often amusing) ways. Round off the experience with a light lunch at volunteer-run **Steinbeck House**, four blocks west.

Drive an unsung wine route

The **River Road Wine Trail** *(riverroadwinetrail.com)* follows the curves of the Salinas River. The drive is rewarding, with neat rows of vines, fields of cabbage and irrigation sprinklers cascading plumes of water into the air.

EATING & DRINKING IN SALINAS: OUR PICKS

Villa Azteca: Made from local ingredients, these Oaxacan specialties are beautifully plated. *11am-4pm & 5.30-9.30pm Tue-Fri, 3-9.30pm Sat, 10am-4pm Sun* $$

Beerded Bean: A small-batch coffee roastery, taphouse and community hub with live music. *6am-9pm Mon-Thu & Sat, to 11pm/later Fri, 8am-5pm Sun*

XL Public House: Outstanding craft beer selection. Come for sours, ciders and IPAs, stay for trivia and comedy. *5.30-10pm Tue-Thu, 5pm-midnight Fri & Sat*

Patria: Get your schnitzel, pizza or goulash on! Patria's super rustic, from European comfort food to cozy interior design. *11am-2pm Mon-Fri, 4-9pm Mon-Sat* $$$

Just 15 miles southeast of Salinas, family-run **Odonata Winery** (*odonatawines.com*), open 11am to 5pm, pours small-batch sparkling wine and French-oaked reds. Continue for 16 miles to **Wrath Wines** (*wrathwines.com*), where smoky, fruity and exceptionally smooth pinot noirs slosh into glasses. It's open 11am to 5pm, Friday to Monday.

Less than 3 miles east, see where local wine production began at the 1791 **Soledad Mission** (*soledadmission.com; by donation*). Inside is an old winepress dating back to vine cultivation by Spanish settlers. It's open 10am to 4pm, Tuesday to Sunday.

Pinnacles National Park

TIME FROM MONTEREY: **FROM 1¼ HR**

Light up the dark in a cave-speckled park

Carved out by ancient volcanoes, underexplored **Pinnacles National Park** draws climbers, hikers and bird-watchers to its craggy heights. Pick a side, there's no road connecting the two: western Pinnacles (accessed from Monterey, via Soledad on Hwy 101) is more spectacular but the east side is easier to reach if you're day-tripping from San Francisco (via Paicines, via Rte 25).

If you do one hike on the park's **west side**, make it the **Balconies Cliffs & Cave Trail** (2.4 miles), a two-hour loop with panoramic views and creepy talus caves. Bring a flashlight (better yet, a headlamp); the dim glow of your phone won't do. Set off from the Chaparral parking lot and plains of scrub unfurl before you. Tackle the trail clockwise: you'll follow ridges, hopscotch past lichen-spattered boulders, gaze at rocky cathedrals spearing the sky, then descend to a riverbed where things get noticeably cooler. Entering the cave, use your flashlight to continue on the trail. It's a narrow scramble (claustrophobes, turn around) but you'll emerge feeling reborn.

The **Prewett Loop** (0.9 miles), from the westside **ranger station**, is more accessible. After only a few steps along this level loop trail you see green hills and mountains rolling into the distance. Round the bend to overlook slopes alive with juniper trees and, in spring and summer, wildflowers.

On the **east side**, the **Moses Spring to Rim Trail** (2.2 miles round trip) generally takes 1½ hours (maximum 500ft elevation) and doesn't require scrambling on your knees; ideal for less sure-footed travelers to glimpse the park's boulder-formed caves. Keep an eye out for California red-legged frogs: this trail also leads to **Bear Gulch Reservoir**, one of several sites around California where conservation programs are bringing at-risk amphibians back from the brink.

Arrive early and ideally park by 9am; trailhead parking lots fill up fast from spring to fall, even on weekdays.

THE RETURN OF RED-LEGGED FROGS

Dr Katy Delaney monitors amphibians for the NPS.

California red-legged frogs are the biggest native frog in the western USA and California's state amphibian. They're listed as threatened, and urbanization, pollution and non-native fish are really bad for them. Hikers should stay on marked trails and out of streams.

Reintroducing frogs is messy. We harvest egg masses, put them in Tupperware on ice, and take them to new sites and care for them in the stream. Sometimes that's a long hike, with boulder-scrambling, rattlesnakes and ticks. We feed them for 2½ months and release them right there. Once they're adults, we go out at night with flashlights to do surveys, identifying them by eye-shine – it's the most fulfilling project.

Big Sur

ROAD TRIPS | HIKING | EPIC VIEWS

GETTING AROUND

Public transportation links have been suspended since 2020, so you need wheels to explore Big Sur – ideally a car but confident cyclists also sweat their way along this section of Hwy 1. Road closures are common, so check Hwy 1's conditions on *roads.dot.ca.gov* before a trip all the way from Carmel to Ragged Point.

Reaching some trailheads in the Ventana Wilderness requires a 4WD; do your research on *ventanawild.org*, ask locally about weather and driving conditions, and get the latest from the **ranger station** *(lpforest.org/big-sur-station).*

When you imagine the great California road trip, you're picturing the drive through Big Sur along Hwy 1. Between the Pacific Ocean and the Santa Lucia Mountains, this inspiring strip of coast extends roughly between Carmel-by-the-Sea and San Simeon.

Spanish settlers nicknamed Big Sur 'the big country to the south' *(el país grande del sur)*, and its high cliffs, long beaches and the forest-clad mountains of the Ventana Wilderness all have immense scale. There's a long tradition of wandering souls rekindling their artistic inspiration here, including writers Henry Miller, Jack Kerouac and Hunter S Thompson, and Big Sur's remoteness is still alluring.

Of Monterey County's five million annual visitors, many head straight to Big Sur – so don't be surprised that this ends-of-the-earth wilderness has booked-out venues and traffic choking the highway. Managing visitor numbers sustainably is an ongoing dilemma. Big Sur's residents rely on tourist income (it's the lion's share of the economy) but crowded highways and trails strain local life and damage natural spaces; tread lightly.

Quirky Literary Outpost

Tour a forested haven for artists and writers

A ramshackle open-air art gallery with freaky sculptures and paintings greets you outside the **Henry Miller Memorial Library**. Between Andrew Molera State Park (p309) and Julia Pfeiffer Burns State Park (p309), it's a bewitching introduction to Big Sur's literary history.

Don't be fooled by 'memorial' in the name. This is a living, breathing artistic outpost that welcomes flaneurs and book-browsers to its redwood-shaded grounds. Founded by novelist Henry Miller's dear friend, the painter Emil White,

HIGHLIGHTS
1 Henry Miller Memorial Library

SIGHTS
2 Bixby Bridge
3 Old Coast Road

ACTIVITIES
4 Pine Ridge Trail

SLEEPING
5 Fernwood Resort
6 Glen Oaks Big Sur
7 Post Ranch Inn

EATING
8 Big Sur River Inn
see 5 Fernwood Tavern
9 Nepenthe

DRINKING & NIGHTLIFE
10 Big Sur Taphouse

INFORMATION
11 Big Sur Station

it was a gallery before its conversion into a nonprofit-run arts center-turned-bookshop.

Shelves in the **bookstore** *(henrymiller.org)* are laden with authors who found inspiration in Big Sur. But this thoughtfully curated den has enough contemporary nonfiction and avant-garde poetry to detain any lover of the written word. Open 11am to 5pm, Wednesday to Sunday; check the website for live events.

Rattle Your Bones on the Old Coast Road

Lofty views and hair-raising bends

Your 4WD rocks from side to side as it climbs the uneven dirt road. Green valleys and the fearsome Pico Blanco (3694ft) are spread out in front of you. There aren't many roads less traveled in Big Sur, but the **Old Coast Road** is worth every pothole. The best time to go is a fresh spring day (dry summers kick up dust).

Accessible to skilled drivers with 4WDs, this 14-mile serpentine accesses Big Sur's lush inland. Roll down your windows to drink in its distinctive scent of sagebrush mixed with the sea breeze. You'll descend into the cooling shade of redwood

TOP TIP

Big Sur has no official boundaries, nor a downtown. It's remote: come with a full tank and plenty of snacks. Gas stations (near Big Sur River Inn and at Ragged Point) are eye-wateringly expensive. Local mini-marts are pricier than regular grocery stores.

ROAD TRIP

Big Sur Magic

Surreally beautiful, Hwy 1 from Point Lobos to Ragged Point dances along fearsome cliffs and through forest groves. Don't rush, a day is doable but stay overnight to marinate in Big Sur's magic. Download maps (there's no cell service) and research online: when we last cruised through, a section of road south of Lime Creek Bridge remained closed due to a rock slide.

1 Painters Point

This **clifflookout** is a breathtaking introduction to Big Sur. Prolong the views on a 1.5-mile return hike to inspiring Soberanes Point just south.

The Drive: This section gets hectic with distracted drivers. Watch the road!

2 Garrapata Beach

Stroll the trail above attractively rock-studded **Garrapata Beach**. It crosses a creek where white calla lilies bloom (mid-February to mid-April).

The Drive: Cross bridges and skirt headlands along the next four miles to Bixby Bridge. Only stop for photos if it's safe.

3 Bixby Bridge

This 1932 **bridge** clasps devilishly steep Bixby Canyon, looping 260ft over a golden beach. Castle Rock Viewpoint offers a picture-perfect vantage point.

The Drive: Ocean views are on show throughout this meandering 8-mile stretch to Andrew Molera State Park.

SALILBHATT/SHUTTERSTOCK

Keyhole Arch, Pfeiffer Beach

❹ Andrew Molera State Park

Meadows, beaches and bluffs make this **state park** a joy to explore. For views of rolling surf, take the Bluffs Trail (1.7 miles one way).

The Drive: The road nudges inland and the next 4.5 miles are lined with redwoods, a precursor to rambles in the state park.

❺ Big Sur Lodge

This **lodge** in **Pfeiffer Big Sur State Park** is a convivial place to grab coffee and baked goods before a heavenly forest hike; head high to Valley View (2 miles round-trip, 200ft elevation).

The Drive: After 1.5 miles, take a sharp right (Sycamore Canyon Rd) to Pfeiffer Beach.

❻ Pfeiffer Beach

This **beach** shimmers purplish when the light hits just right, the gift of manganese garnet from crumbling hills nearby. In winter you can catch sunset through Keyhole Arch...otherworldly.

The Drive: Rejoining Hwy 1, it twists and turns for 10 forested miles then follows a serpentine stretch with Pacific views.

❼ McWay Falls

Julia Pfeiffer Burns State Park is a beloved stop for 80ft **McWay Falls**, which cascades onto the beach. If the overlook trail is closed, viewpoints are signed from Hwy 1.

The Drive: If the road's open, 33 ocean-view miles extend to Ragged Point. In 2025, travelers had to turn around at Lime Creek, 4 miles south of McWay Falls.

❽ Ragged Point

At this **headland**, toothy cliffs drop to deep blue ocean. A short but steep walk descends to an ashen beach and unreliable Black Swift Waterfalls. Celebrate journey's end at Ragged Point's inn-restaurant.

forests before revving uphill to bird's-eye views of Bixby Bridge (p308). Don't block the road (ranchers and farmers rely on it), there are plenty of places to pull over to admire the forests, thickly carpeted with redwood sorrel and hand-shaped thimbleberry plants.

This was the original 19th-century access route to Big Sur, a nerve-testing journey for horse-drawn wagons. Even with a car, it's not for the meek: consider getting a guide with **Big Sur Adventures** *(bikebigsur.com)* so you can focus on the views.

SAFE & SENSITIVE TRAVEL

The fragile landscape and volume of travelers demands an extra degree of care, so drive and hike attentively. Resist the urge to park roadside on Hwy 1 when there isn't room; there's always another scenic lookout. Be cautious of other drivers parking and pulling out suddenly, especially around Bixby Bridge. Only drive dirt tracks like the Old Coast Road if you've done local research into access, road conditions and weather...and you have a 4WD and know how to handle it.

Stay on marked trails, regardless of potential photo ops. Otherwise you contribute to damaging soil erosion and habitat disturbance (and risk being scolded by locals). Don't ever light fires anywhere other than designated fire rings in camping areas.

Back to Nature in the Ventana Wilderness

Get ready to rough it

The call of the wild is deafening in the **Ventana Wilderness** *(ventanawild.org)*. Inland from Big Sur's glittering coast, its 375 mountainous square miles of hardy chaparral and old-growth redwoods are spiderwebbed with backcountry hiking trails.

Only the outdoors-iest may apply. Big Sur is an ever-shifting realm, where landslides, vegetation growth and weather conditions can turn easy trails into danger zones. Some trailheads are only accessible by dirt roads. Get the latest from rangers (and book overnight camping) at **Big Sur Station** *(lpforest.org/big-sur-station; parking $10)*, open 9am to 4pm.

From here, the popular but tough **Pine Ridge Trail** (22 miles) extends across forest, river crossings, campsites and considerable elevation gain. The reward: breathtaking valley views and meadow, spangled with flowers in spring.

EATING & DRINKING IN BIG SUR: OUR PICKS

Nepenthe: Ocean views are reason enough for steak frites and scallops at this local institution. Reserve ahead. Fab on-site gift shop. *11.30am-4.30pm & 5-10pm* $$$

Big Sur River Inn: Nourishing salads and knockout smoked ribs, but tables by the Big Sur River are the selling point of this efficient place. *8am-9pm* $$

Big Sur Taphouse: Need something hoppy to cool your hike-heated body? Get beers on tap in this casual pub or outdoor deck. *noon-9pm* $$

Fernwood Tavern: This welcoming spot has a cozy pub-restaurant with a woodsy deck to guzzle burgers, sandwiches, salads, pizzas and cocktails. *noon-10pm* $$

THE HIGHWAY OF LANDSLIDES

In spring 2025, Big Sur received a dubious distinction: the longest ever road closure in Hwy 1's history. When the highway first opened in 1937, it brought money, construction and a tourism boom...along with dynamite-blasted devastation to Big Sur's hills and cliffs. Ever since, the highway has been fickle. Landslides periodically rain down rocks and mud that completely block access and there are no easy detours: you really do have to turn right around. Repairs take years (three and counting, last time we visited) and grind to a halt when it rains or when new surface cracks are observed. For cut-off locals, the effect on businesses is tough. But road closures are also routine, all part of the challenges and mysteries of life in Big Sur.

Bixby Bridge (p308), Hwy 1

TRICE JACOBS/SHUTTERSTOCK

Cambria & Cayucos

BEACHES | CULTURE | FARM-TO-TABLE FOOD

GETTING AROUND

Most travelers drive, but the fairly flat, straight coast road (Hwy 1) makes it relatively easy to cycle from Cambria to Piedras Blancas or Hearst Castle. Infrequent RTA buses connect Morro Bay, Cayucos, Cambria and San Simeon, but time your travels with care.

Cayucos is straddled along the beach; easy to walk between the shore, local restaurants and hotels. Meanwhile Cambria's downtown is 2 miles inland, so you might need to drive (rideshares are expensive and thin on the ground.)

TOP TIP

See what's in season at Cambria's food-only **farmers market** *(@cambria farmersmarket)*. This cornucopia of artichokes, avocados, flowers, berries, honey and more occupies the parking lot by the Veterans Hall every Friday afternoon year-round.

Between the southern end of Big Sur and Morro Bay is a surf-kissed coast anchored by two quintessentially California seaside towns. Both are convenient springboards to Hearst Castle, the masterpiece estate of erstwhile media tycoon William Randolph Hearst, and the nearby elephant-seal rookery.

Cambria was built in the 1860s from leftover slabs of wood, giving it the nickname 'Slabtown.' When the timber industry came to a halt, tourism quickly took over as Cambria's moneymaker, and today it's rife with arty shops and farm-to-table restaurants.

Fourteen miles south is Cayucos, an unpretentious surf town with a Wild West feel, thanks to its old-timey bars and vintage ambience. Named after fishing canoes used by the Chumash people, today it's popular with families for its long beach and 1872 pier. This is where Californians go on vacation for the full bucket-and-spade, takeout pizza on the beach experience. It's a friendly spot to base yourself for cliffside walks and day trips.

Golden Cliffs & Shipwrecked Shores

Walk dramatic bluffs in Cayucos

Yes, there's **Cayucos State Beach**, filled with families paddling in the gentle surf. But untamed Pacific drama is on show just north at two rugged parks, each with trails along the sea-smashed shore.

Between Cayucos and the tiny town of Harmony is the 784-acre **Harmony Headlands State Park**. Follow the **Headlands Trail** for 1.5 miles through a gentle valley, descending past a ravine that's alive with croaking frogs and overhung by mossy trees. Beyond, the dirt trail snakes alongside golden bluffs with endless views of foaming ocean. Do it as an out-and-back trail (3 miles) or continue to trail's end (Alapay Way, total 2 miles), where you'll need a ride back to town.

HIGHLIGHTS
1 Elephant Seal Vista Point
2 Hearst Castle

SIGHTS
3 Cayucos State Beach
4 Estero Bluffs State Park
5 Harmony Cellars
6 Harmony Headlands State Park
7 Hearst Ranch Winery
8 Moonstone Beach
9 Piedras Blancas Light Station
10 William Randolph Hearst Memorial State Beach

SLEEPING
11 Cayucos Sunset Inn
see 8 Fogcatcher Inn
12 Morgan
13 Pacific Motel

EATING
14 Brown Butter Cookie Co
15 French Corner Bakery
16 Hidden Kitchen
see 15 Linn's Easy as Pie Cafe
17 Lunada Garden Bistro
see 15 Robin's
see 8 Sea Chest Oyster Bar
see 7 Sebastian's General Store

DRINKING & NIGHTLIFE
see 13 Salty Tiger
18 Schooners

NORTHERN CHUMASH MARINE PROTECTED AREA

When 156 miles of California's coast were designated a marine protected area in October 2024, there were reasons to celebrate. The protected status of 4543 sq miles (south of Morro Bay to the northern edge of the Channel Islands) would allow whales, turtles, seabirds and more to thrive without threats of pollution or natural gas extraction. It was also a victory for Northern Chumash Tribes, who comanage the reserve. They campaigned for decades for community control over the area's ocean management. The **Northern Chumash Heritage National Marine Sanctuary** *(sanctuaries.noaa.gov/chumash-heritage)* is also good news for visitors, who flock to these shores to witness the abundant marine life.

BRYCIA JAMES/GETTY IMAGES

Moonstone Beach

Head back south towards Cayucos and take the turnoff to little **Estero Bluffs State Park**. The path to the bluffs (0.25 miles) has views of sea stacks, lazing seals and a rusty shipwreck. Stay away from the cliff edge, especially after rainfall. Estero Bluffs is less than a mile from Cayucos State Beach.

Historic Harmony, Population 18

Visit the tiniest town

Swiss founders made this one-block town, between Cambria and Cayucos, feel like a little corner of the Alps – complete with cow-speckled fields and rustic businesses. Start by sipping riesling, zinfandel and syrah with abandon at friendly **Harmony Cellars** *(harmonycellars.com)*, a boutique winery open 10am to 5pm that stays close to 19th-century wine-making traditions. On weekends food trucks show up, like **Harmony Valley Creamery** *(harmonyvalleycreamery.com)*; try the butter pecan. There's also a **pottery** store and **glassworks**; the latter is especially fun when resident artists blow glowing-hot glass into marvelous shapes.

EATING & DRINKING IN CAMBRIA & CAYUCOS: LOCAL FAVORITES

French Corner Bakery: Cambria's croissant enthusiasts rave about the golden buttery goodies prepared at this casual cafe. *6.30am-6pm* $

Schooners: For discerning diners (halibut with peanut slaw, rare ahi tuna...) this boozer in Cayucos delivers. *11am-10pm Sun-Thu, to 11pm Fri & Sat* $$

Lunada Garden Bistro: Enjoy dishes from French-style duck to coffee-glazed pork in Cayucos' enchanting garden. *11am-1:45pm & 5-8pm Tue-Sun* $$$

Salty Tiger: A secret speakeasy tucked into an upscale motel? We're in. Ask at Cayucos' Pacific Motel (p336) about its jauntily decorated one-room bar. *hours vary*

Gem-Studded Moonstone Beach

Mosey along Cambria's multicolor shore

The literal jewel in Cambria's crown, **Moonstone Beach** glitters with colored pebbles. Walk down to the beach to admire smooth colorful gems washing ashore (look, don't take.) The boardwalk follows the shore for roughly 1.5 miles through coastal prairies. You'll see ground squirrels racing past and enjoy exhilarating views of the bluffs.

Time your walk for late afternoon, when the sun casts a coppery glaze across the pebble beaches. Then you're just in time for dinner at the nautical-themed **Sea Chest Oyster Bar** *(seachestoysterbar.com; 5.30-9pm Wed-Mon; cash only).*

Squabbling Elephant Seals

Watch family feuds at a rookery in San Simeon

While female northern elephant seals rarely exceed 12ft in length, males can be 16ft long and weigh a mighty 5000lb. Seeing one of these beasts rear up, its super-schnozz trembling as it bellows at a rival, is nothing short of astonishing – and this drama unfolds, at a viewing station 1.5 miles south of **Piedras Blancas Light Station**.

The observation deck at the **Elephant Seal Vista Point** *(elephantseal.org; free)* overlooks a beach that elephant seals have adopted as their primary ground for snoozing, fighting and mating, depending on the season. Rampant hunting of elephant seals in the 18th century, fueling a trade in their skin and blubber, nearly drove them to extinction but the population has slowly grown back since they won protected status in 1900.

During breeding season (November to March), elephant seals arrive en masse and clash for female attention in violent, snorting standoffs. From January you can see pups and the havoc dies down by March, when you're more likely to see elephant seals dozing or flipping sand.

WINDSWEPT WALKS & RIDES

Boucher Trail: A 4-mile there-and-back walk between Piedras Blancas Light Station and the **Elephant Seal Vista Point**.

San Simeon Point Trail: This 2.5-mile round-trip hike (under two hours) from **William Randolph Hearst Memorial State Beach** has views of eucalyptus trees and foaming sea.

San Simeon Trail–Washburn Campground: A 3.5-mile backcountry loop trail along boardwalks and tangled trails.

Ragged Point Route: Challenging 37-mile return bike route along Hwy 1 between San Simeon and Ragged Point (p309).

Cambria–Cayucos Loop: A 47-mile cycling loop from Cambria; tough hill-country ascents to Cayucos, then back along the coast to Cambria.

EATING IN CAMBRIA & CAYUCOS: SIGNATURE DISHES

Hidden Kitchen: Who knew the formula for happiness was blue corn waffles, piled with avocado and cheese? In both Cayucos and Cambria. *9am-3pm* $

Linn's Easy as Pie Cafe: A wedge of olallieberry pie, made with juicy hybrid blackberries, has been Cambria's iconic dessert since the 1980s. *10am-6pm* $

Robin's: Moreish salmon bisque is reason enough to settle in at this tranquil indoor-outdoor restaurant in Cambria with an international menu. *hours vary* $$

Brown Butter Cookie Co: Rich and buttery with a hint of sea salt, cookies from this sibling-owned Cayucos bakery are vital road-trip sustenance. *9am-6pm* $

TOP EXPERIENCE

Hearst Castle

With a celestial hilltop setting and artworks to rival the Louvre, Hearst Castle is the opulent passion project of media mogul William Randolph Hearst (1863–1951). No expense was spared to build this 165-room hilltop estate. A menu of different guided tours leads you through the labyrinthine palace and its hidden corners.

PAUL R. JONES/SHUTTERSTOCK

TOP TIPS

- Hearst turned his grounds into a safari park. Ask staff where the zebras, descendants of Hearst's originals, were last seen; you can still spot them.
- Across the highway, **Hearst Ranch Winery** is an upscale place to sip/sample estate wines next door at **Sebastian's General Store**.

PRACTICALITIES

- hearstcastle.org
- Tours 9am-4pm
- Adult/child from $35/18

The Mogul & The Architect

After inheriting the *San Francisco Examiner* from his father in 1887, Hearst built a lucrative news empire; it's thought he inspired the tycoon in *Citizen Kane*. He hired the visionary architect Julia Morgan (1872–1957) to turn his 250,000-acre ranching estate into a luxurious retreat. Morgan was the first woman admitted to Paris' prestigious École Nationale Supérieure des Beaux-Arts to study architecture, and California's first licensed female architect. From Venetian balconies to lampshades made from 18th-century parchments, Morgan's pioneering designs fill every corner of the estate. Hearst's frequent changes of heart kept Morgan on her toes and despite 28 years of construction, the estate remains incomplete.

Choosing a Tour

The **Grand Rooms Tour** is ideal for first-time visitors but we love the **Upstairs Suites Tour**, which climbs to ornate guest rooms like the tower-top 'Celestial Bedroom' (367 steps in total). Not your first visit? The **Cottages & Kitchen Tour** reveals the mind-bending property management, while the **Julia Morgan Tour** focuses on the architect. All tours show you the **Neptune Pool**, 345,000 gallons of piped spring water against a Roman temple facade (a dip would cost a *sizable* donation). You'll also see **Casa Grande**, styled like a Renaissance Spanish plaza, made from poured concrete to withstand California's earthquakes.

Paso Robles

WINE | DINING | ECLECTIC ART

Natural springs made Paso Robles a reviving rest stop for Spanish missionaries, and by the mid-19th century ranchers, farmers and winemakers were arriving to grow their fortunes among its woodlands and grassy hills. Today the wine scene dominates: Paso Robles is adored by in-the-know Californians for its 200-plus wineries, many with tasting rooms in its walkable downtown. Just 25 miles inland, it's far enough from the tourist trail to escape international attention, meaning you'll enjoy more laid-back (and more affordable) wining and dining than leading destinations like Napa Valley.

The longer you spend here, the more you'll realize there are two Pasos: there's the city that most travelers see, with wine tastings, upscale hotels and bougie boutiques, but also an industrious community deeply in touch with its ranching roots. Get a flavor of both by lingering not only for wine tastings but local history, art and Paso's romantically remote surroundings.

TOP TIP

Visiting on a weekday? Check restaurant times and make reservations ahead (many only open between Thursday and Sunday). Wineries are often happy with walk-ins but it's worth calling ahead or booking online; some are small-scale operations with fluctuating opening hours.

Art until Sundown

MAP P320

Immerse yourself in Paso Robles' art scene

Paso Robles has all the ingredients for an eclectic art scene: rolling hills that beg to be captured in watercolors and a collision of Native American, Spanish and cowboy aesthetics.

continued on p320

GETTING AROUND

Downtown Paso Robles is walkable and you can manage without a car if you stick to urban wineries and use the occasional rideshare to Tin City or Sensorio. The **Amtrak station**, on the line from Oakland to LA, is also in walking distance of downtown. Bike and e-bikes are a delightful option; reserve them through **Central Coast Bike Rental** (*centralcoastbikerental.com; one-day bike/e-bike rental from $63.60/79.50*). It's possible to wander around wineries along the **North Paso Garden Loop** but plan your route carefully to avoid highways and busy downtown roads.

Paso Robles Wineries

There's wine country in every direction surrounding Paso Robles, 40,000 acres of vineyards divided into 11 different American Viticultural Areas (AVAs). Spanish settlers planted the first vines, but wine-making gathered momentum in the late 19th century. First came jammy zinfandels, followed by cabernet sauvignon and syrah. By the 1990s, wine makers were hitting their stride with Rhône varieties, while local wineries racked up awards. The range is astonishing; pick your pleasure from this list.

Where to sip if you like...

Immersive Tastings

Thacher Winery (MAP p322) Unpretentious winery producing zinfandels and chenin blancs with a hint of salty sea air. Book a slot on 'Funky Fridays' *($30)* to try uncommon varietals like valdigué and cinsault, or get VIP treatment on its Stables Tour *($80)*.

Tablas Creek Vineyard (MAP p322) As if their sun-soaked patio wasn't enough of a draw, Tablas Creek has daily guided tours *(10am; free)* of its organic vineyards with glimpses into its wine-making process. Settle in for a tasting *(from $25)* of its flagship red and white blends.

MEANDERING TRAIL MEDIA/SHUTTERSTOCK

Wine tasting, Tablas Creek Vineyard

French-Style flavors

Paix Sur Terre (MAP p322) Good vibes, games of bocce ball, and plenty of picpoul blanc. Biodynamic wines aged in French oak barrels conjure up old-world flavors in an informal and distinctly Californian setting. Tastings $25.

Dilecta Wines (MAP p322) This red wine specialist in the Adelaida District wins us over with its Rhône and Bordeaux varietals. Meanwhile the artwork gives a splash of surreality; its colorful bottles make excellent gifts. Tastings $30.

Trailblazing Winemakers

DAOU Family Estates French-born Daniel Daou keeps raising his winemaking game: barrels made from rare wood, cultivating his own native yeast, and continual testing and refinement. The result: midnight-dark and intensely flavored cabernet sauvignons and straight-outta-Bordeaux red blends. Tastings from $50.

Indigène Cellars (MAP p320) The small tasting room of one of few Black-owned and operated wineries, Indigène in downtown Paso Robles excels at hearty red blends and pinot noir rosés. Founder Raymond Smith invests some of the profits back into community projects. Tastings $25.

Anything but Wine

Willow Creek Distillery (MAP p322) Swig French oak–aged chamomile liqueur, plum brandy that's heady with vanilla, or smooth coffee liqueur made from grape brandy. Inspired by European recipes, this distillery is part of the zinfandel-focused Opolo Vineyards complex. Tastings $20.

Re:Find Distillery (MAP p322) Instead of discarding the *saignée* (literally the 'bleeding off,' or wine by-product), this innovative distillery decided to ferment and distill it into rich rye whiskeys and barrel-finished vodkas that you can sip by the flight. Wine and spirit tastings $40.

DANIEL TORRES_310/SHUTTERSTOCK

Paso Robles vineyards

HOW TO

When to go Reserve tastings year-round or time your visit for a wine festival if you want to attend exclusive events and winemaker dinners.

Cost Tastings start at $25 but check costs ahead: some are twice the price. Most wineries waive the fee if you buy a couple of bottles (expensive strategy!)

Booking ahead Reserve for weekends and if you're a large group. Most wineries offer online booking. Booking multiple in a day? Allow an hour for a leisurely tasting.

Winging it Walk-ins are often possible for solo sippers and small groups. Have alternative wineries in mind, in case your chosen spot is full or closed.

Self-driving and tours in Paso wine country

With more than 200 wineries within Paso Robles' different AVAs, choosing a region or a wine experience can feel overwhelming. Our favorite districts with quick access from Paso Robles are Adelaida, Willow Creek and Estrella. You can also head to Tin City (p322) to avoid figuring out transportation.

The Adelaida District spreads west of Paso Robles in the Santa Lucia foothills; drive a loop along Adelaida Rd and back along Peachy Canyon Rd. Or you can widen the loop south along Vineyard Dr, which skirts the Willow Creek District.

East of Paso Robles (and just north of Rte 46) extends the Estrella District, with upscale wineries like **Allegretto Wines** and sustainability-minded **J Lohr**. This region is ideal if you're planning a day out with multiple activities, as it's close to the Estrella Warbirds Museum (p321) and Sensorio's Field of Light (p320).

It's easy to get a rideshare from Paso Robles to a winery. However, you'll wait a long time for a pickup back to town. Private transportation services like **Designated Wine Driver** *(designatedwinedriver.com)* and **Destination Drivers** *(destinationdrivers.com)* can drive you in your own rental car *(per hour from $50)*. Private operators like **Uncorked Wine Tours** *(uncorkedwinetours.net)* can handle transportation and itinerary.

SIGHTS
1 Indigené Cellars
2 Pioneer Museum
3 Studios on the Park

EATING
4 Aliyah's Kitchen
5 In Bloom
6 Jeffry's Wine Country BBQ
7 Les Petites Canailles
8 Paso Market Walk
9 Paso Robles Farmers Market
10 Somm's Kitchen

DRINKING & NIGHTLIFE
11 Alchemists' Garden

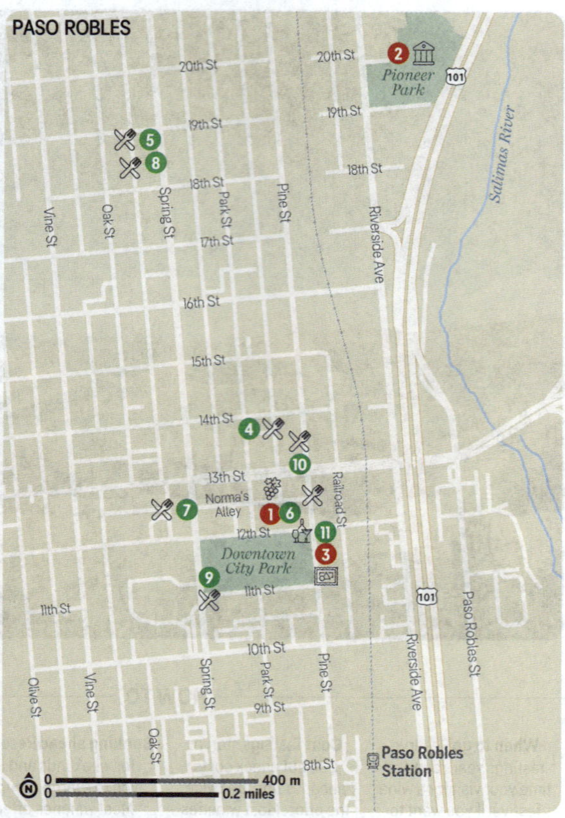

UNEXPECTED ATTRACTIONS IN PASO ROBLES

Franklin Hot Springs (p322)**:** This natural spring *(adult/child $10/5)* is where locals slather on mud.

Pioneer Museum: Outlandish taxidermy and branding irons...this free museum *(1-4pm Thu-Sun)* is a wild ride.

Vina Robles Amphitheatre (p322)**:** Full-blown concert venue in the middle of a winery? We're in. Events April to November.

Sculpterra Winery & Sculpture Garden (p322)**:** Chicago-born artist John Jagger's granite and bronze animal sculptures enliven this winery's gardens, 7 miles east of downtown.

River Oaks Spa (p322)**:** Wine-tasting in a hot tub *($65)* at this rejuvenating spot 2 miles north of downtown.

continued from p317

Studios on the Park *(studiosonthepark.org; free)* is an excellent porthole into the multifaceted scene. Step inside to muse at photography, pottery and glass art, and contemplate dropping a few hundred dollars on a bejeweled buffalo skull. With luck you can meet artists in residence. Check ahead for events and art workshops for kids. It's open noon to 4pm, Sunday to Thursday; and to 9pm on Friday and Saturday.

As the sun dips, see the hills sparkle at **Sensorio** *(sensoriopaso.com; tickets adult/child from $45/22)*, an outdoor art hub where Bruce Munro's *Field of Light* installation is in indefinite residence. Entranced by the light of more than 100,000 bulbs, you'll meander around fields turned multicolor. Dance into a kaleidoscope of spinning orbs and watch them cast lacy shadows on the ground. Five miles northeast of Paso (Rte 46); book ahead. It's open 6.30 pm to 10.30pm Thursday to Sunday from May through August, and 6 pm to 10pm Thursday to Sunday in April.

Machines of War

MAP P322

Confront tremendous trucks and planes in a giant musuem

Under a blazing blue sky, you walk across an airplane hangar. Vietnam War–era gun trucks are to your left, Navy warplanes to your right, and a jaunty soundtrack of swing and retro pop is piped across the grounds. This is the scene at **Estrella Warbirds Museum** *(ewarbirds.org; adult/child $18/8)*, where American manufacturing and military transportation is showcased through red, white and blue-tinted glasses.

Whether it leaves you misty-eyed or slack-jawed, this is a colossus of a museum. The indoor galleries, with uniformed mannequins, model warplanes and written displays on various conflicts, are informative if not cutting-edge. But the outdoors, where you can stand nose-to-wing with a VC-10 Challenger aircraft or peep inside an M-60 tank training turret, is impressive (and excellent selfie material). It's open 10am to 4pm, Thursday to Sunday.

Urban Wine Tasting

MAP P322

Sip your way around Tin City

You need your own wheels to explore Paso Robles' expansive **wine country** (p318) but you can embark on an urban wine-tasting quest by heading to **Tin City**. Less than 10 minutes by rideshare along Hwy 101, this postindustrial cluster of tasting rooms and distilleries doesn't have rolling green views but it's walkable and the wineries are friendly and small-scale.

Start at **Union Sacré Winery** *(unionsacre.com; tastings $20)*. Passionate about wine from France's Alsace region, winemakers Philip Muzzy and Xavier Arnaudin wanted to inject bright and zesty whites into Paso Robles' red-heavy scene. Along the way, they established this welcoming tasting room and managed to make riesling cool again. Open 11am to 5pm.

Head one block west along Marquita Ave and turn right on Limestone Way. Around the corner is **Field Recordings** *(fieldrecordingswine.com; tastings $25)*, which prides itself on sourcing exceptional grapes from underrated vineyards around the Central Coast. It's a rewarding spot to taste wildly different drops, from ramato-style pinot gris (Italian-style blush) through to cabernets that pack a heck of a punch. Open noon to 5pm Sunday to Wednesday; to 6pm Thursday to Saturday.

Stroll east to join Blue Rock Rd, then north until you swing right on Limestone Way. At **ONX Wines** *(onxwines.com;*

BEST FESTIVALS AROUND PASO ROBLES

Spring Release Month: Month-long program of winemaker dinners, talks, tours and more. *Mar; pasowine.com*

Art in the Park: Dozens of artists assemble in Paso's Downtown Square to showcase their wares for a weekend. *Apr & Nov; pasoroblesart inthepark.com*

Paso Wine Fest: Live DJ sets at this celebration of good wine and good living. *mid-May; pasowine. com/winefest*

Atascadero Lakeside WineFest: Wine, craft beer, live music, family-friendly fun at Atascadero's Lake Park. *mid-Jun; atascaderolakeside winefestival.com*

Paderewski Festival: Concerts celebrating the visionary composer Ignacy Paderewski (1860–1941), Polish musician turned Paso rancher. *late Oct–early Nov; paderewskifest.com*

EATING IN PASO ROBLES: BUDGET OPTIONS

MAP P320

Paso Market Walk: Mini food court with Common Grounds coffee, vegan cheeses from The Vreamery, mini cupcakes from Just Baked. *hours vary* $

Farmers Market: Behold the local bounty! Grab-and-go food, from tacos to gluten-free donuts, along with seasonal fruits and veggies. *9am-1pm Sat* $

Jeffry's Wine Country BBQ: Dry-rubbed and wood-fire smoked, the tri-tip and chicken are moreish. Veggie burgers too. *11am-8pm Thu-Mon* $$

Aliyah's Kitchen: Want to feel full? Try seafood towers, heaped combo plates and $2 taco Tuesday. *10am-9pm Mon-Thu, to 1am Fri & Sat, 8am-9pm Sun* $

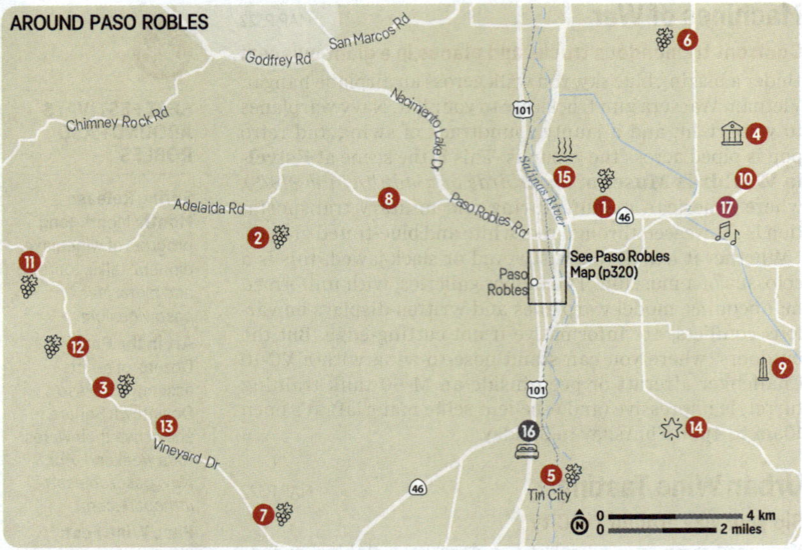

AROUND PASO ROBLES

SIGHTS
1 Allegretto Wines
2 DAOU Family Estates
3 Dilecta Wines
4 Estrella Warbirds Museum
5 Field Recordings
6 J Lohr Vineyards & Wines
see 5 ONX Wines
7 Paix Sur Terre
8 Re:Find Distillery
9 Sculpterra Winery & Sculpture Garden
10 Sensorio
11 Tablas Creek Vineyard
12 Thacher Winery
see 5 Union Sacré Winery
13 Willow Creek Distillery

ACTIVITIES
14 Franklin Hot Springs
15 River Oaks Spa

SLEEPING
see 1 Allegretto Vineyard Resort
16 River Lodge

DRINKING & NIGHTLIFE
see 5 Tin City Cider Co

ENTERTAINMENT
17 Vina Robles Amphitheatre

tastings $25), the fruit-forward zinfandels slip down very easily at its terrace with a babbling fountain. Look out for The Reckoning, an extravagantly bold and bolshy red blend. Open 10am to 5pm.

All wine'd out? Close out the experience at **Tin City Cider Co** *(tincitycider.com; tasting paddle $20)*, three blocks west along Limestone Way. At this lively bar, hand-harvested apples yield silky, not-too-sweet ciders. Pick from limited release flavors, from cinnamon to watermelon, to curate your own tasting paddle. Our favorites unite cider with local wines, blended for a uniquely deep and fruity flavor. Open 11am to 7pm Sunday to Wednesday; to 8pm Thursday to Saturday.

EATING & DRINKING IN PASO ROBLES: OUR PICKS

MAP P320

Les Petites Canailles: French flavors in a chic California dining room: yes to beef bouguignon, *moules frites*, crème brûlée. *5-9pm Thu-Mon* $$$	**In Bloom:** Share-plate menus globe-trot from Korean-style pork shank to confit duck wings, always using locally sourced ingredients. *5-9pm Wed-Sun* $$$	**Somm's Kitchen:** Intimate space. Tasting menus with elevated takes on rustic dishes, from onion soup to venison with blackberries. *11.30am-2pm & 5-9pm Thu-Sun* $$$	**Alchemists' Garden:** House-infused spirits, dashes of spice and citrus, and mixologists with a magic touch. *11am-2.30pm Thu-Sun, 5-10.30pm daily* $$$

Beyond Paso Robles

Offbeat towns and cities, some bonus wine country: Paso Robles' surroundings are worth a stop-off for travelers seeking smalltown life.

Heading north from Paso Robles? San Miguel, founded by Spanish colonists who built the stately Mission San Miguel Arcángel (1797), has a frontier feel. This is a sleepy place where you can clap eyes on centuries-old religious art or swirl syrah in a wood-lined tasting room.

If you're driving south, swing by Atascadero's elegant City Hall, framed by the Sunken Gardens. There's a seam of arty boutiques and novel places to dine. Atascadero is also a convenient base for day trips to Paso Robles, San Luis Obispo and Morro Bay (less than 30 minutes' drive from each). Just 8 miles further south along Hwy 101, a dose of Old California awaits in Santa Margarita, a former ranching town with quirky stores and untrampled nature.

Places

GETTING AROUND

The No 9 bus *(slorta.org)* travels between San Miguel and San Luis Obispo, stopping at Paso Robles, Atascadero and Santa Margarita. They're less than hourly and only a handful service San Miguel. Both destinations are easier to visit on a road trip, or as a half-day trip from Paso Robles. San Miguel is a great half- or full-day trip but Atascadero's bars and restaurants beg for an overnight stay.

San Miguel

TIME FROM PASO ROBLES: **15 MINS**

Get acquainted with Spanish mission history

Surrounded by ranches, oak valleys and farmland, San Miguel bears a strong imprint of past Spanish settlement. Half a day is enough to take a spin around its main sights.

A striking brick tower with three tiers of bells greets you as you drive in. The **Wieland Bell Tower** memorializes WWII US Navy Chaplain Fidelis Wieland and its brick arches are emblematic of old San Miguel's architecture.

Park your car and check out the nearby **Rios-Caledonia Adobe** *(historic-rios-caledonia.org; free)*, a treasured historic site (1835) with an original inn (now converted into a museum of mission life). Inside are artifacts from the daily lives of T'epot'aha'l people (or 'People of the Oaks'), the original stewards of the land around the Salinas River, as well as rooms furnished with 19th-century photographs illustrating mission life. It's open noon to 3pm, Friday to Sunday; stay awhile to putter around the gardens, which have century-old cacti and eucalyptus trees, a 1900s wishing well and a section of the old stage road (used up until 1938).

The town's focal point is a block north: the **Mission San Miguel Arcángel** *(by donation)*, a 1797 adobe complex framed by a spiky garden of cactus and aloe plants. Walk through the vaulted arcade toward the church, which is still in use today. Its 1820s frescoes of flowers, angels and the *ojo de Dios* (eye

THE MORAL MAZE OF VISITING MISSIONS

The beautiful churches and museums of 18th-century life at California's missions are popular with visitors, but they have complex and often disturbing histories. A common narrative is that kindly Franciscan priests coexisted happily with Native American people in missions. Less openly discussed is the linguistic and cultural erasure by missionaries, a deliberate strategy by the Spanish crown. There were countless deaths from diseases introduced by European colonists. Elias Castillo's book *A Cross of Thorns: The Enslavement of California's Indians by the Spanish Missions* (2017) presents evidence of violence and forced labor from Spanish government archives and letters.

JAMES MATTIL/SHUTTERSTOCK

Mission San Miguel Arcángel (p323)

of God) were completed by Spanish-born trader and artist Esteban Carlos Munràs. The San Simeon Earthquake in 2003 caused critical damage to the mission, but the incredibly well-preserved artwork on display still rivals some of California's better-known sites. It's open 10am to 4pm, Thursday to Monday. Outside is a historic cemetery; note the guardian statue of patron saint Miguel taking a stab at Lucifer.

Round off your visit with a bite to eat; we love the shrimp tacos and gigantic burritos at **Taco Mafia**.

Become an olive oil connoisseur

You examine the pastel yellow liquid in front of you. With a deep sniff, inhale an entire bouquet – floral, grassy and peppery – as you raise it to your lips. But this isn't wine tasting, it's the liquid gold produced at **San Miguel Olive Farm** (*sanmiguelolivefarm.com; private tastings & tours by reservation only*), a 1200-tree grove just 2 miles west of San Miguel.

Husband-and-wife team Richard and Myrna Meisler retired from the music industry to farm these gold-green globules and turn them into polyphenol-packed oils, keeping standards high with pesticide-free production and hand-harvested olives. Their sparkling enthusiasm for olive oil and its health benefits means you'll have farm stories and recipes to go with the bottles of EVOO you'll inevitably buy. Tours and tastings take around 1½ hours. It's a working farm, so it's open to visitors early summer to fall, and reservations by phone, ideally weeks in advance, are essential.

SPANISH MISSIONS

To see more relics of California's Spanish missions, **San Juan Bautista** (p293) is a must-see if you're heading north. Midway between Monterey and San Jose, SJB has an atmospheric state park conserving numerous historic buildings.

Red wine in cowboy country

Time to chill out at rustic tasting rooms out in the San Miguel AVA, one of Paso Robles' lesser visited wine zones. Welcoming **Locatelli Vineyards** *(locatelliwinery.com)* sets you up with zinfandel, cabernet sauvignon and award-winning red blends at its ranch-chic tasting room just east of San Miguel. Open 11am to 5pm, Thursday to Monday.

Atascadero

TIME FROM PASO ROBLES: **10 MINS**

Thrifts & gifts at uncommon boutiques

Atascadero has exceptional taste, especially in gently used and upcycled fashion. If you're looking for unique souvenirs, or a bargain-hunting stop to break up the drive between Paso and SLO or Santa Barbara, here's how to leave with a full trunk of interesting finds.

Start at **Ernest Grace** *(ernestgrace.com)*, open 11am to 5pm, just opposite Atascadero's centerpiece **Sunken Gardens**. This upscale thrift store has changing rooms that feel almost spa-like, with corsages and vintage fittings. There are high standards for donated goods, so it's a classy place to rifle the racks for high-fashion cast-offs and recent trends. Two short blocks northwest along El Camino, duck right onto Entrada Ave where you'll find **Black Sheep**, a smaller boutique selling striking handmade jewelry *(from around $40)*, along with plenty of attention-grabbing preloved clothes. Its opening hours vary.

Traffic Ave, another block northwest, is home to another two gems: the **Book Odyssey** *(@thebookodyssey)*, open 10am to 5.30pm Monday to Saturday, stacked with used books; and local legend **Traffic Records** *(trafficrecordstore.com)* – open 11am to 7pm Monday to Saturday, and 11am to 5pm Sunday – going strong since 2018. Come here to grab flyers for local shows, flick through vinyl, grab a T-shirt and gaze up at Grateful Dead posters.

Take a look into the **Pottery Studio** *(thepotteryatascadero.com)* before you get back in your car: when we last passed through, it was in the process of setting up a boutique. Sign up for one of its classes if you're staying locally.

SMALL-TOWN CHARM IN SANTA MARGARITA

Holli Rae, owner of **Giddy Up** *(giddyuphut.com)*, shares what makes Santa Margarita special.

Santa Margarita has historic ranches and Old West roots. Downtown, the **Barn Antiques** is full of treasures and history, and the **Porch** is a great community cafe and watering hole. You can ride horses through open landscapes with **Central Coast Trailrides** *(cctrailrides.com)*.

One of my favourite places is **Santa Margarita Lake** for hiking, kayaking and fishing; it also has boat-in campsites. Past the lake there's a winery in the middle of nowhere called **Vintage Cowboy Winery** *(vintagecowboywinery.com)*.

In spring, **Shell Creek Rd** becomes really popular, often there's a super-bloom of poppies and lupines.

EATING & DRINKING IN ATASCADERO: OUR PICKS

Barley and Boar: Short food menu, long drink menu, steeped in Euro flavor (burgers with Gruyère, barley panna cotta...). Try the fat-washed gin. *5-9pm* **$$$**

Poisoned Apple: Rock 'n' roll style, excellent cider and mead, plus tacos and Thursday trivia nights. *4-9pm Mon-Wed, to 10pm Thu & Fri, 3-10pm Sat, 3-8pm Sun* **$$**

AMSTRDM Coffee House: Minimalist-chic caffeine temple that nails its espresso drinks. Small brunch menu too. There's another one in Paso Robles. *7am-4pm* **$**

Emporio Alle-Pia: Swing by for road-trip snacks: its salamis, 'nduja spreads and other goodies are authentically Italian and made with love. *9am-4pm Mon-Fri* **$**

San Luis Obispo

HIKING | HILL-SCAPES | CHARMING DOWNTOWN

GETTING AROUND

Greyhound buses travel to SLO from San Francisco (4½ hours) and Los Angeles (5¼ hours) and the *Pacific Surfliner* train between Los Angeles and Oakland (San Francisco) stops in SLO.

Reserve a bike online from **Foothill Cyclery** *(foothillcyclery.com; 10am-6pm Mon, Tue & Thu-Sat; 24hr e-/road bike from $100/80)*; they can drop your rental at your hotel or even a trailhead. Find maps of cycle lanes on *bikeslocounty.org*. Rideshare apps make it easy to get to wineries, trailheads and the Madonna Inn.

TOP TIP

Don't miss the Thursday evening **farmers market** along Higuera St (btwn Nipomo & Osos Sts). Arrive by vintage transportation: on Thursday only the **Old SLO Trolley** *($0.50c)* rattles up and down Monterey St from La Cuesta Inn to Monterey & Osos (downtown SLO).

People who know San Luis Obispo can't utter its name without a faraway smile. SLO (pronounce it 'slow') captures California's many charms in a petite package. Snuggled among the volcanic 'Nine Sisters' peaks, the city is in easy reach of hiking trails, wine country and beach towns. Downtown SLO is safe and walkable with tree-lined streets and dozens of farm-to-table restaurants, many of them dotted along pretty San Luis Obispo Creek. Student life keeps things fresh by endlessly reinventing the local arts and music scenes.

Local architecture has a strong Spanish accent. SLO was founded by Spanish colonists in 1772 when the mission was built under orders of Junípero Serra, a key player in the Spanish Empire's expansion. Exploring the city's mosaic of Spanish Mission style, art deco and the rosy-pink confection of the Madonna Inn is a sweet experience; savor it.

SLO's Highest Point

Hike to panoramic views at Bishop Peak

San Luis Obispo County's craggy beauty is a gift of the 'Nine Sisters,' a daisy chain of volcanic peaks stretching from Islay Hill, southeast of SLO, northwest to the coast at Morro Bay (p331). The tallest is **Bishop Peak** (1559ft), and trails switchbacking up this volcanic plug start 2.5 miles northwest of downtown SLO.

To hike the **Summit Trail** (4 miles return, intermediate to advanced, 1180ft elevation) get over to Patricia Dr (plenty of street parking). There's a gentle incline after the **trailhead gate**, then take the left fork to follow the Summit Trail. Make your way up to the rocky summit – take care, it's a clamber – for expansive views of SLO, a tapestry of green meadows and the Santa Lucia Mountains beyond. Extend your ramble by adding the **Felsman Loop** (1.6 miles, easy to intermediate, 580ft elevation); a connector trail is well signposted.

SAN LUIS OBISPO

Foothill Cyclery (0.8mi); Summit Trail (2.1mi); Bishop Peak Trailhead (2.7mi); **Bishop Peak (3.6mi)**

La Quinta Inn (0.2mi); Apple Farm Inn (0.4mi)

Madonna Inn (1.8mi)

Mission San Luis Obispo de Tolosa
Mission Plaza
Bubblegum Alley
Public Parking Garage
Mitchell Park
San Luis Obispo Creek
Amtrak Station

0 400 m
0 0.2 miles

SLEEPING
1 Hotel San Luis Obispo

EATING
2 Ebony
3 Kiko
4 Luna Red
5 Novo

DRINKING & NIGHTLIFE
6 Feral
see 1 High Bar
7 Libertine Brewing Company
8 Sidecar

SHOPPING
9 Bizarre Antiques & Oddities
10 Blackwater
11 Buen Dia Market
12 Hands Gallery
13 Mama Ganache

EATING IN SLO: BEST OUTDOOR DINING

Ebony: Sop up lentil stew with injera (teff flour bread) at this vegan counter-serve Ethiopian spot. Peaceful terrace. *11am-8pm Thu-Sat, 10am-3pm Sun* **$**

Kiko: Tucked in the Central Market arcade, this colorful Peruvian place has a patio perfect for tangy ceviche, as well as slow-cooked beef with a view. *5-9pm* **$$**

Novo: The tree-shaded patio is a place to fall in love...with your companion, or with pork carnitas and lamb shank. *11am-9pm Mon-Sat, from 10am Sun* **$$$**

Luna Red: Buzzing outdoor terrace. The menu travels from Mexico to Spain via mole tacos and seafood paella. *11am-9pm Sun-Thu, to 10pm Fri & Sat* **$$**

UNIQUE SHOPS & SOUVENIRS

Blackwater: Nothing you need but everything you want: shirts, sarcastic greetings cards, needlepoint cushions and vintage signs.

Buen Dia Market: Grocery store or art gallery? Be amazed by meticulously curated delicacies, then shop for art prints at its sister store (790 Higuera St).

Bizarre Antiques & Oddities: Rummage crystals and curios for your home here.

Hands Gallery: Upscale boutique selling mosaic art, locally made jewelry and novelty socks.

Mama Ganache: Ethically sourced small-batch chocolate, including vegan truffles and cashew chews. Chocolate bark is durable enough for your journey home.

PAUL R JONES/SHUTTERSTOCK

Madonna Inn

The Palace of Pink

Sip kitschy cocktails at the Madonna Inn

Picture Dolly Parton firing a glitter cannon over a Swiss chalet and you're close to visualizing the **Madonna Inn** *(madonnainn.com)*, a labor of love by entrepreneur Alex Madonna. It's a fiesta of floral patterned carpets, cerise barstools and hot-pink dining booths. No wonder this 1958-built icon is the setting for *Vogue* fashion shoots and music videos, from Roxette to Grimes. You can also stay here.

For the full experience, book a table at **Alex Madonna's Gold Rush Steakhouse** *(5-10pm Sun-Thu, 4-10pm Sat & Sun)* or rock up to the **Copper Cafe** *(7am-10pm)* for a slice of Pink Champagne Cake, a fairy-tale of Bavarian cream and curls of pink chocolate. Our favorite is settling into a wingback armchair at the **Silver Bar** *(10am to midnight)* for a glittery Pink Cloud, available alcohol-free or with strawberry vodka.

DRINKING IN SLO: OUR PICKS

Sidecar: Our favorite spot for a yarn with locals, this sleek saloon-style bar knows how to sling a classy drink. Burgers and bar snacks too. *4pm-late Wed-Sat*

Feral: Imagine a hunting enthusiast won the lottery and blew it on taxidermy and premium spirits. Precise cocktails, short-rib tacos. *3-10pm Sun-Wed, to 2am Thu-Sat*

High Bar: Come for sunset, the upscale beach-bar-style rooftop of Hotel San Luis Obispo has dreamy views over the hills. *2-9pm*

Libertine Brewing Company: Laid-back vibes lubricated by barrel-aged sours. More than 70 beers on tap. *11am-midnight Wed-Sat, shorter hours Sun & Mon*

HISTORIC DOWNTOWN SLO ON FOOT

Take in SLO's Spanish colonial history and rollicking 19th-century heyday on a promenade through its fun-loving downtown.

START	END	LENGTH
Fremont Theater	Wineman Building	1 mile; 45 mins to 1 hr

Start at the 1 **Fremont Theater**, opened in 1942, mere months after the US entered WWII. Continue southwest past 2 **Andrews Hotel**; rebuilt after a fire in 1886, it was the first brick building in SLO's new, less flammable, downtown. Two blocks further southwest is the 3 **Sinsheimer Building**. This 1884 landmark is unique in town for its elegant cast-iron columns. Next you reach the 4 **Mission San Luis Obispo de Tolosa** *(missionsanluisobispo.org; 11am-4pm Wed-Sun; by donation)*, founded in 1772. Check out Chumash baskets in the small museum and admire Peruvian paintings and trompe l'oeil columns in the church. At the corner of Broad and Monterey Sts, the 5 **County Historical Museum** is a look-back at the days when cowhides were currency.

Modern-day aesthetics are on show across the street at the 6 **Museum of Art** *(sloma.org; 11am-5pm Thu-Mon; free)*. Kids in tow? Then tire them out at the toy-filled 7 **Children's Museum** *(slocm.org; 11am-5pm Thu-Mon; adult/under-2 $10/free)* on the corner of Nipomo St. Turn left (east) on Higuera St, SLO's main shopping drag since the late 19th century, named after a Spanish founding family, and look for 8 **Bubblegum Alley**, a graveyard of gum since the '60s (leaning not advised). Continue along Higuera St to finish at the imposing 1930s 9 **Wineman Building** and its emblematic sign.

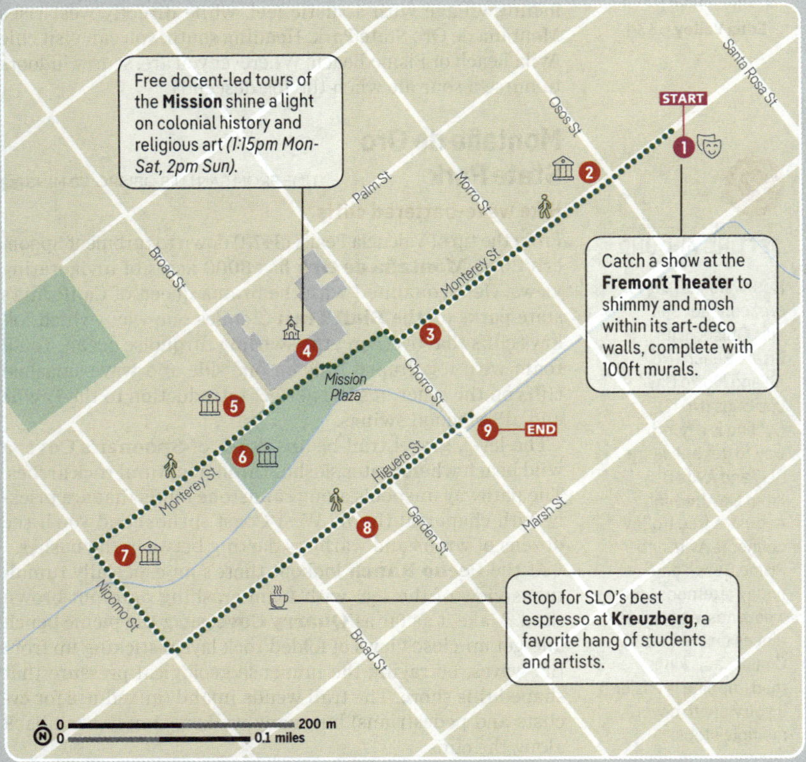

Free docent-led tours of the **Mission** shine a light on colonial history and religious art *(1:15pm Mon-Sat, 2pm Sun)*.

Catch a show at the **Fremont Theater** to shimmy and mosh within its art-deco walls, complete with 100ft murals.

Stop for SLO's best espresso at **Kreuzberg**, a favorite hang of students and artists.

START
END
Santa Rosa St
Osos St
Morro St
Palm St
Broad St
Monterey St
Mission Plaza
Chorro St
Higuera St
Garden St
Marsh St
Nipomo St
0 200 m
0 0.1 miles

Beyond San Luis Obispo

Beaches, hot springs and quaint seafront towns: day trips are part of the joy of staying in San Luis Obispo.

Places

GETTING AROUND

Hourly buses *(slorta.org)* connect San Luis Obispo with Pismo Beach (No 10) and Morro Bay/ Los Osos (No 12). Cycling is a good way to get between SLO and Avila Beach. From May through August, a free trolley connects Avila and Pismo Beach on Friday afternoons and weekends. As in most places on the Central Coast, car is king: road-tripping is easier if you want to cover multiple stops.

San Luis Obispo's enviable location gives it the best of California's coast, from Pacific-lashed beaches to ancient peaks. These remarkable surroundings make SLO much greater than the sum of its parts: the variety of day trips is truly a delight.

From SLO, it's 15 minutes' drive to the coast. Don't expect Malibu: this stretch of coast has more eucalyptus trees than sun-kissed palms, and has as many creaky, vintage seafronts as polished promenades. Northwest is Morro Bay, a popular fishing village with a rustic feel, while directly west rises Montaña de Oro State Park. Heading south, you can visit chic Avila Beach or Pismo Beach. Wherever you are, scurry indoors to nurse a sour ale when the fog descends.

Montaña de Oro State Park

TIME FROM SAN LUIS OBISPO: **30 MINS**

Hike wave-battered cliffs

From the tip of Valencia Peak (1347ft) down to turbulent Spooner's Cove, **Montaña de Oro** has 8000 acres of invigorating views. Get acquainted with the drama queen of California's state parks on the **Bluff Trail** (2 miles one-way), which follows cliffs that overhang the swirling turquoise ocean. You'll roam with fog-draped hills on one side and wave-smashed cliffs on the other; it's the perfect introduction to the Pacific and all its mood swings.

The level, gravel trail begins north of **Spooner's Cove**, a wild beach where water sloshes through natural rock arches. The pathway unspools along sandstone bluffs that are prickly with chaparral (hardy West Coast shrubs) and you'll see dozens of wrens and warblers darting between the bushes.

At the **Pecho Ranch** lookout there's an especially tumultuous view of the sea, with foam crashing onto nut-brown sand. Make it as far as **Quarry Cove**, snag the picnic bench and get up-close views of folded rock layers sticking up from the waves, betraying the immense geological pressure that shaped this shore. The trail wends inland (mixed-use for cyclists and pedestrians) but many walkers simply head back along the cliffs.

MANUELA DURSON/SHUTTERSTOCK

Morro Rock

Morro Bay

TIME FROM SAN LUIS OBISPO: **20 MINS**

Paddle beneath a volcanic rock

The bay is as still as glass, with only a few otters and somersaulting seals casting ripples across the surface. Fishers drop their lines from the pier. But one sight steals all the attention: dead ahead is **Morro Rock**, a volcanic plug that sprouts 576ft out of the water. Formed 23 million years ago, it's one of more than 20 ancient volcanic rocks that form a chain from Morro Bay to Edna Valley, known as the 'Nine Sisters' (someone miscounted).

Emerging from the ocean like a mythical being, Morro Rock is the most striking of the Sisters. It's easy to walk right up to the rock by taking Embarcadero and Coleman Dr, but this granite colossus looks most dramatic when you're out on the water. **Morro Bay Paddlesports** *(paddlemorrobay.com; kayak or SUP 1-/2hr rental $30/50)* can do more than rent you a kayak: it doubles as a cafe, and it's happy to launch you into the bay with oar in hand and a latte planted firmly in the kayak's cupholder. It's open Thursday to Tuesday.

You'll feel a drag from the current as you paddle away from the kayak launch, as though Morro Rock is reeling you in... resist! Paddle west along the spit and watch for preening herons and red-eyed grebes, as well as the sea lions that pop curious heads above the waterline.

MORRO BAY'S SLOWER PACE

Abby Ahlgrim, a surfer who creates colorful jewelry from surfboard by-products, explains the tranquil magic of Morro Bay. *surfgems.com*

In cities, you move fast. But Morro Bay is an opportunity to detach from our phones and pay attention to the landscape, the people and the wildlife. Compared to Southern California it's a pretty cold, tumultuous ocean. Morro Bay's landscape is so sensational, so start with a sense of wonder and curiosity: slow down! Go on a walk and the people working in any of the shops you walk into will be happy to chat and share about their day.

SCALE A VOLCANIC MOUNTAIN

The tallest of the Nine Sisters volcanic mountain chain is **Bishop Peak** (p326); reaching the top of this 1559ft plug is a popular hike from San Luis Obispo.

BEST BAY ACTIVITIES

Chablis Cruises: Chowder cruises, floating brunch, or sunset... This 50ft boat *(chabliscruises.com)* has wildlife-spotting with refreshments.

Morro Bay State Park Boardwalk: Feathered friends flit up close on this wooden boardwalk.

Museum of Natural History: Small, informative museum *(10am-5pm; adult/child $3/free)* overhanging glorious bay views.

Kayak Shack: Kayaking by Morro Rock (p331) yields views, but locals launch beneath the museum for peaceful waters and wildlife-watching.

Black Hill Trail: Want to see Morro Rock look like a distant marble? Walk the 20-minute switchbacking ascent from the tiny parking lot at the northern end of Upper State Park Rd.

Baywood & Los Osos

TIME FROM SAN LUIS OBISPO: **20 MINS**

Feel like a giant among pygmy trees

The 90-acre **Elfin Forest Natural Area** is an enchanting tangle of chaparral scrub and pygmy oak trees, skirting the southeastern shore of Morro Bay State Marine Reserve. The 0.8-mile boardwalk is an accessible and easy walk through a unique concoction of natural environments: salty estuary marshland mingles with dune scrub, and pygmy oaks extend their gnarled branches like witchy fingers.

Thriving in this jigsaw puzzle of ecosystems are more than 110 species of birds; watch for the emerald flash from blue-winged teals or the elegant white bodies of great egrets strutting in the shallows. There are more than a dozen kinds of reptile and amphibian, and you might see ground squirrels and skittish jackrabbits along the way.

Avila Beach

TIME FROM SAN LUIS OBISPO: **15 MINS**

Simmer in hot springs

Ever since the chance discovery of piping-hot mineral springs in the early 20th century, visitors to Avila Beach have been sitting back and saying, 'Ahh...'

Slip into a private outdoor hot tub at **Sycamore Mineral Springs** *(sycamoresprings.com; from $23 per hr; reserve ahead)*, taking breaks from the toasty water and sulphurous steam with cool showers in the wooden booths. Steam will cloud your vision as you slide into a mosaic-tiled tub, while sunshine dapples the palm fronds above you.

Want a more communal experience? The same geothermally heated waters feed **Avila Hot Springs** *(avilahotsprings.com; day pass adult/child $29/26)*. It's open 8am to 9pm. Behind the Olympic-sized heated pool (80°F) is a 20ft soaking pool that stays a simmering 104°F. Bargain seekers, come between 8am and noon or 5pm and 9pm (*$18*).

Cycle a tree-shaded trail to the sea

This gentle there-and-back mixed-use trail follows the old Pacific Railroad between the hot springs inland and the dainty seaside town of Avila Beach. It's around 6 miles there and back.

Grab a rental bike from Avila Hot Springs *(avilahotsprings.com; half-/full day $25/30)* and wheel over to the trailhead, north of Avila Beach Dr (just 0.3 miles north of Avila Hot Springs); the trail runs creekside beneath shady trees. A mile and a half

EATING IN MORRO BAY: BEST SEAFOOD

Taco Temple: Tacos so generously laden with fish that you have to hunt for the tortilla. Our favorite of the Mexican spots north of town. *11am-9pm* $

Galley: Bayfront views and primo seafood. No reservations; put your name down then listen to sea lions while you wait. *11.30am-8pm Wed-Mon* $$

Dorn's Breakers Cafe: Dorn's (1948) dishes up comfort foods fresh from the sea. Try for a deck table with rock views. Expect a wait for weekend brunch. *7am-9pm* $$

Tognazzini's Dockside: We always feel at home in Tognazzini's: Italian-accented meals and just-like-family service. Tequila-splash salmon! *7am-9pm* $$

GARY SAXE/SHUTTERSTOCK

Monarch butterflies, Pismo Beach Monarch Butterfly Grove

in, the trail joins Blue Heron Dr, between a rocky escarpment and the widening San Luis Obispo Creek.

Pedal south after another half-mile, crossing the bridge to enter the heart of Avila Beach. Finish up along Front St for views of blonde beauty **Avila City Beach**. On the way back, a mile before you're back at the bike rental, pause at the **Secret Garden** – open 10am to 5pm, summer only – for a wine or a craft beer in an idyllic little grove. You can also buy produce from the harvest stand.

Starting the trail at the Avila Beach end? Then rent from **BoltAbout Electric Bike Rentals** *(boltabout.com; per hr/day $30/90)*, open 10am to 5pm, and ride the route in reverse.

Pismo Beach

TIME FROM SAN LUIS OBISPO: **15 MINS**

Watch multitudes of monarch butterflies

The freshening scent of eucalyptus fills your lungs as soon as you reach **Pismo Beach Monarch Butterfly Grove**. Follow the sound of awed murmurs; the craned necks of visitors, gazing into the treetops, are signs of a monarch butterfly sighting.

BEST BEACHES AROUND SLO

Avila City Beach: The showpiece of the namesake town is this cove of caramel-colored sand. Best for: swimming in gentle waves.

Spooner's Cove: Sandy beach with staggering sea-stacks. Best for: tide-pooling and wave-watching.

Pismo Beach: Stroll the boardwalk, paddle or watch surfers from beneath an umbrella. Best for: families who want amenities.

Pirate's Cove: There's a steep, nerve-jangling trail down to secluded shores. Best for: photos; the upper cave offers rock-framed views of the water.

Oceano Dunes State Park: This 'vehicular recreation area' allows 4WDs along its hard-packed sandy shores. Best for: travelers who checked their car insurance fine print.

EATING IN BAYWOOD & LOS OSOS: OUR PICKS

Caliwala: Colorful signs point the way to this adorable neighborhood bakery. Organic sourdough plus at least one vegan and gluten-free option. *8am-4pm Sat-Mon* $

Beerwood: Sun-trap patio for beer, Mexi-Cali food and surfer chitchat. Dog-friendly; well-behaved humans are welcome too. *11am-9pm Mon-Sat, 10am-8pm Sun* $

Nautical Bean: Adorned with surfboards, this hut by the shore has outdoor tables for 'kitchen sink burritos.' *6am-2pm Tue-Fri, from 7am Sat & Sun, 6am-4pm Mon* $

Mirazur: Old-fashioned flower-topped tablecloths and nostalgic music. Many winning choices; the smoky pork chop is ours. *11.30am-2pm & 4-8pm Tue-Sun* $$$

A DRIVE THROUGH EDNA VALLEY'S WINERIES

Get a driver (p319) and explore the Edna Valley, an offbeat wine region adored by in-the-know chardonnay and pinot noir connoisseurs.

START	END	LENGTH
Baileyana	Tolosa Winery	10 miles; 3 to 6 hrs

No wine snobbery here, just unpretentious tasting rooms and terraces that gaze at the Santa Lucia Mountains. Begin at 1 **Baileyana**, 5 miles southeast of SLO. We especially love its plethora of chardonnays, from creamy and tropical to crisp and mineral-forward. Continue another 3 miles southeast along Orcutt Rd to 2 **Chamisal Vineyards**, which prides itself on pinot noir. Its vineyards were among the first planted in the Edna Valley and it's SIP-certified (Sustainability in Practice). Its sparkling whites have a zesty, floral quality reminiscent of France's Champagne region (it's something in the chalky soil, they say...).

Continue another mile down Orcutt Rd and then turn right along tree-lined Tiffany Ranch Rd. Take another right up Corbett Canyon Rd and after half a mile you'll see the turnoff to (SIP-certified) 3 **Center of Effort**, where wine-makers go wine tasting. Continue north along Corbett Canyon Rd and after 1½ miles, turn right on Carpenter Canyon Rd to 4 **Claiborne & Churchill Winery**, which has noteworthy riesling. Get a tasting paddle and cheese plate to enjoy at a tree-shaded table. One more? 5 **Tolosa Winery** has elegant architecture and manicured gardens to taste bright berry notes in its rosés, along with flagship, full-bodied pinot noirs. Its premium wines are priced accordingly, but we think your designated driver deserves a take-home bottle to enjoy once you're back in SLO.

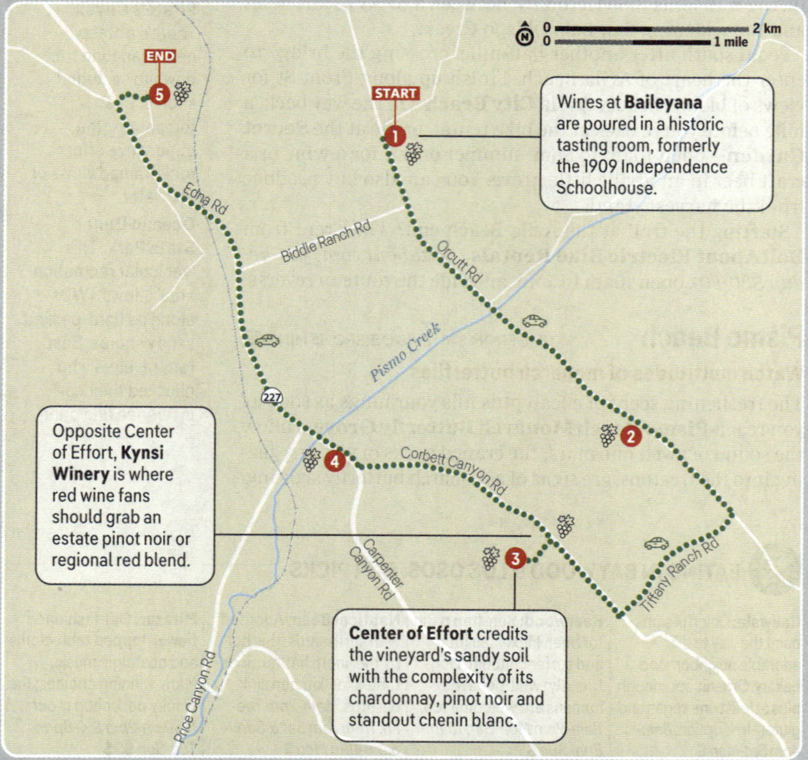

These orange-and-black beauties fly 10,000ft high and as far as 2000 miles on their annual migrations, guided by the planet's magnetic pull and the position of the sun. These odysseys lead to balmy overwintering sites along the California coast from Santa Cruz to San Diego. Pismo is one such place: between November and the end of February, this grove is their temporary home. You might initially mistake them for leaves, until a breeze exposes the orange flash of their wings, or a few of them take off into the skies.

Now for the bad news... The number of migrating monarchs has been creeping down since the 1980s, despite a temporary resurgence in 2021–22, and the butterflies' critical role in pollination has knock-on effects on other wildlife. Pismo locals sounded the alarm in the winter of 2024 when butterfly numbers were counted in the hundreds, when once they would have been thousands. Call or check online with Pismo Beach's visitor information center *(experiencepismobeach.com; 805-556-7397)* before making a special trip.

RUGGED HIKING TERRAIN

If your feet are itchy for a hikes, **Pinnacles National Park** (p305), less than two hours north of San Luis Obispo, is paradise for ramblers and climbers.

The battle for Pismo's Soul

Listen long enough at any bar around SLO County and you're sure to hear sardonic words about Pismo Beach. On our last trip, we heard 'Hawaii for Bakersfield' and 'the Starbucks of beach towns.'

Sure, Pismo lacks the postcard-worthy cove of Avila, and has none of Morro's rustic charm – but it does have long beaches, tide pools, playgrounds, bike and kayak rentals, all of which make it intensely popular with families on beach breaks. Local misgivings stem from the pace of development and the summertime crowds. Travelers will certainly find it more built-up and less walkable than other spots: choose accommodation wisely or you'll be playing parking ping-pong between different short-term lots.

EATING & DRINKING IN AVILA BEACH: OUR PICKS

Mersea's: At the end of Harford Pier (3 miles west) is our favorite spot for blackened snapper, fish tacos and satisfying chowder. *11am-8pm* **$$**

Blue Moon Over Avila: Swish service, French wine, refined entrees. Try croque monsieur or scallops in Cognac, ideally on a sea-facing table. *11.30am-8pm* **$$$**

Alapay Cellars: Taste oak-aged wines and tap toes to occasional live music in a den that's part surfy, part arty. *10.30am-6.30pm Sun-Thu, to 7pm Fri & Sat* **$$**

Locals Taproom: Founded by two SLO locals, this brewpub trades in oatmeal stouts, pale ales and good vibes. *3-9pm Wed & Thu, 1-10pm Fri & Sat, to 9pm Sun* **$**

Places We Love to Stay

$ Budget $$ Midrange $$$ Top End

Santa Cruz

MAP p285

Hotel Paradox $$ Top choice among the midrange hotels on Ocean St. Sleek and modern, marrying business functionality with surfy artwork and wicker furniture. Swish bar and oasis-like pool.

Pacific Blue Inn $$$ Between downtown and the boardwalk, this courtyard B&B with earth-tone rooms prides itself on a light carbon footprint, complete with upcycled wood and energy-efficient lighting.

Moss Landing & San Juan Bautista

Captain's Inn at Moss Landing $ Ship's wheels and nautical curios decorate this converted Pacific Coast Steamship Company building. Choose from pricier contemporary rooms or old-school maritime (with chandeliers and ship art).

Posada de San Juan $$ San Juan Bautista's standout boutique hotel has soothing woodsy rooms inside a Colonial Revival–style building (archways, terracotta tiles and a fountain).

Monterey

MAP p295

Martine Inn $$ Old-fashioned elegance in Pacific Grove. Twenty-five antique-dotted rooms fill an early-20th-century estate. Made-to-order breakfasts are served overlooking the ocean.

Spindrift Inn $$$ On Cannery Row and overlooking small McAbee Beach, the boutique Spindrift has romantic rooms with fireplaces, marble bathrooms and window nooks. Free wine and cheese happy hour.

Jabberwock Inn $$$ Follow the white rabbit to a Craftsman-style mansion (1911). Individually decorated rooms include the standalone 'Tumtum Tree' cottage nestled in cypress and redwood trees.

Carmel-by-the-Sea & Carmel Valley

Hidden Valley Inn $$ Tasteful motel with wooden floors and earthy decor, tucked away at the leafy northern end of Carmel Valley. Walking distance from wineries. Small pool, takeout breakfast pastries.

Pine Inn $$$ Leaning into its 1889 origins, this elegant hotel in Carmel-by-the-Sea has rooms with baroque prints and barrel armchairs. Splurge on an ocean-view room.

Salinas & Pinnacles National Park

Chateau Coralini $$ Five miles south of downtown Salinas, this late-19th-century inn has hands-off service but sumptuous rooms with vintage lamps and peaceful green views.

Inn at the Pinnacles $$$ Neat rooms inspired by the blue skies and terracotta tones of the national park, just 2 miles south of Pinnacles's west entrance. Vineyard views and a secluded feel.

Big Sur

MAP p307

Fernwood Resort $$ Stay in woodsy rooms with outdoor hot tubs or snug glamping tents at this friendly, few-frills resort with a cozy tavern.

Glen Oaks Big Sur $$$ Imagine an earthy national park lodge got a makeover and you're getting close to Glen Oaks' organic chic. Recycled stone floors and bamboo furniture feel ecofriendly and close to nature.

Post Ranch Inn $$$ Big Sur's luxurious adults-only resort isn't worth blowing your budget, right? On the other hand, we pine for vast rooms that make remarkable use of space and light, and fine dining with floor-to-ceiling ocean views...

Cambria & Cayucos

MAP p313

Morgan $ The undoubted best of the budget options near Hearst Castle and the elephant-seal viewpoint, this gently faded hotel has big rooms within steps of the ocean.

Cayucos Sunset Inn $$ Rooms with romantic flourish, top-quality bedsheets and Jacuzzi tubs. Even better: an eager-to-please host and made-to-order breakfasts.

Pacific Motel $$ Nautical and a little naughty, this Cayucos motel is a standout, thanks to the crisply modern rooms, sociable firepit and secret speakeasy.

Fogcatcher Inn $$ Elegant and plush, the design is all earth tones and driftwood at this inn on Cambria's Moonstone Beach. Oceanfront firepit and sea-view balconies.

Paso Robles & Around

MAPs p320 & 322

Carlton Hotel $$ A grande dame in Atascadero, the Carlton has rooms fine-tuned in baroque style, from marble-floored bathrooms to damask pillows.

River Lodge $$ We've never loved a motel more than the beach-chic River Lodge, complete with poolside bar and hammock gardens for every room. Between downtown Paso Robles and Tin City.

Allegretto Vineyard Resort $$$ Old-world elegance, on-site wine tasting and spa treatments. Rooms are adorned with velvet and chandeliers…waltz around and imagine you're in a Tuscan villa!

San Luis Obispo

MAP P327

Apple Farm Inn $ A whimsical tree-shaded complex surrounding a century-old millhouse. Rooms at the inn are more luxurious, cheaper Trellis Court is closer to road noise. Staff are wonderful, ask about wine happy hour!

La Quinta Inn $$ This chain hotel does everything right: big rooms, free bike rental, pool, walkable to downtown, and excellent bar-restaurant 1865 Kitchen next door.

Hotel San Luis Obispo $$$ Bringing a beachy aesthetic to the heart of downtown, trendy Hotel SLO wins us over with ranch-chic rooms (colorful cushions and rugs, oak floors) and rooftop bar.

Madonna Inn $$$ A palace of kitsch (p328), where themed rooms range from glittering Mardi Gras to cave dwellers and wilderness. It's the Madonna Inn, so go pink if you can (the 'Love Nest' and 'Madonna Suite' are astounding.)

Morro Bay & Los Osos

Blufftop Inn & Suites $$ A modern motel within steps of Morro Bay's waterfront. Comfy beds, monochrome decor and clean as a whistle.

Baywood Inn $$ Baywood–Los Osos is a convenient, and sleepy, alternative to staying in Morro Bay (5 miles north) and this characterful B&B has old-fashioned charm and individually decorated rooms (some themed!). Hearty hiking-fuel breakfasts next door at the Mexican restaurant.

Anderson Inn $$$ Boutique waterfront inn with contemporary nautical flair. Rooms have fireplaces and full or partial ocean views…cozy and classy!

Avila Beach

Inn at Avila Beach $ Sunbaked tones and touches of Spanish Colonial Revival style at an agreeably rustic beachfront inn. Lots of perks: free Popsicles, bike rental and barista-led breakfasts on the ocean-facing roof-deck.

Sycamore Mineral Springs Resort $$$ A spa retreat tucked away in the trees, rooms are classically elegant with flashes of vintage flair (Tiffany-style lamps, embroidered armchairs). The scent of sulfur from the hot springs is part of the experience

MARK READ/LONELY PLANET

Madonna Inn

Researched by
Wendy Yanagihara

Santa Barbara County

SPANISH COLONIAL COASTAL BEAUTY

Hike, bike and surf year-round in a Mediterranean climate where pinot noir, Pixie tangerines and avocados thrive, on the southern end of California's Central Coast.

The Santa Barbara coastline was originally inhabited by the Chumash people, who harvested and hunted from the oak-studded hills and the rich waters of the Santa Barbara Channel. Using tar from natural beach seeps, they built seafaring canoes that allowed them to settle on the northernmost of the Channel Islands.

In 1786, Spanish Franciscan missionaries dedicated the tenth California mission on the feast day of Santa Barbara, thereby blessing the city with its name and one of its most famous landmarks. With its island-sheltered beaches, front-country foothills and mild year-round climate, SB has forever attracted visitors and new residents. Over the last two decades, Santa Barbara County has developed into a wine country destination. With its transverse mountain range and unique patterns of fog and diurnal shift, a wealth of high-quality, small-production wines are yet another pleasure to savor.

RON THOMAS/GETTY IMAGES

Besides wine, the region's bountiful produce is celebrated with local festivals centered around the lemon and avocado. Appreciation for farmers, and what they literally bring to the table, continues to be an undercurrent of life here. That, and a commitment to the land and ocean in which 'Santa Barbarians' love to play. Join the locals in enjoying a slower pace of life, watching dolphins leap, and squinting for the green flash at sunset, unfussed by tar blobs staining their toes.

THE MAIN AREAS

SANTA BARBARA
What California dreaming is made of. **p344**

SOLVANG
Danish-kitsch gateway to wine country. **p354**

VENTURA
SB's secret cute sister city. **p365**

For places to stay in Santa Barbara County, see p372

EMSON/GETTY IMAGES

Left: Old Mission Santa Barbara (p345); Above: Stearns Wharf (p348)

Find Your Way

Santa Barbara occupies an easily navigable slice of coastal plain between mountains and ocean. Outlying areas of interest are reached by scenic drives along the coast or through the foothills of the Santa Ynez and Topatopa mountain ranges.

Solvang, p354

Danish-heritage tourist destination that has evolved into a serious but perenially fun intro to Santa Barbara wine country.

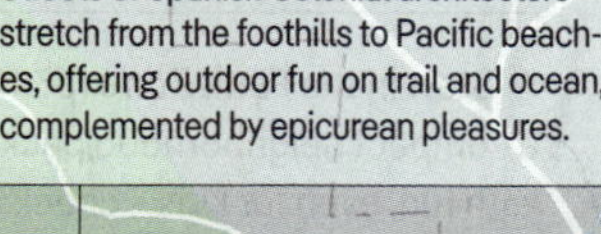

Santa Barbara, p344

Streets of Spanish Colonial architecture stretch from the foothills to Pacific beaches, offering outdoor fun on trail and ocean, complemented by epicurean pleasures.

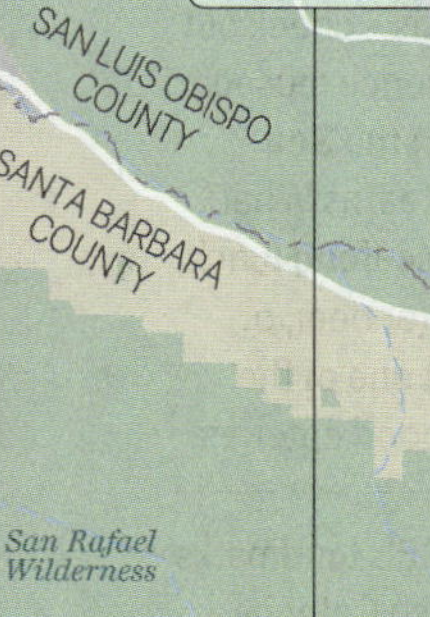

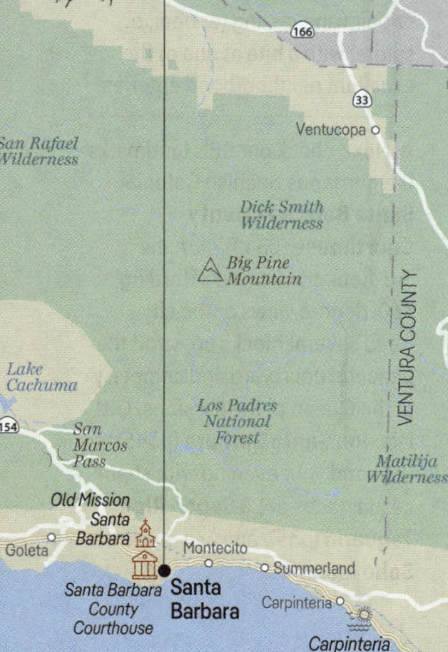

BUS

Santa Barbara MTD buses cover the city proper, with service as far as Goleta and Carpinteria. Santa Ynez Valley Transit runs buses between Buellton and the town of Santa Ynez, while Gold Coast Transit has a route between Ventura and Ojai.

BICYCLE

The city of Santa Barbara has bicycle-friendly crosstown routes with painted bike lanes on some major streets, but for the most part its bike lanes are narrow or shared with vehicle traffic. Santa Ynez Valley is more spread out and suitable for bicycle touring.

CAR

To visit outlying destinations from Santa Barbara, it's most convenient to drive, although most towns are small enough to explore on foot once you've arrived. Street parking is free or inexpensive throughout the region.

Ventura, p365

Alluringly retro beach town with under-the-radar appeal in its beaches, harbor and downtown; and it's the launch point for Channel Islands National Park.

Plan Your Time

Santa Barbara makes the most beautiful base for easy access to beach, foothills and city. Stay in Solvang or Los Olivos if wine tasting is your mission, or retreat in low-profile style to Ojai.

NADEZDA AUDIGIE/SHUTTERSTOCK

Butterfly Beach (p353)

If You Have Only One Day

- Start in the **Funk Zone** (p349), a compact neighborhood packed with fun, even for kids – check out the **MOXI** (p349) science museum and pet some rays at the **Sea Center** (p348) on Stearns Wharf. Savor an ocean-air seafood lunch, or pair wine tasting (or beer, or spirits) with a bite at one of the excellent neighborhood eateries.

- Next, check out SB's landmarks: the gorgeous Spanish Colonial **Santa Barbara County Courthouse** (p344), with the 3rd-floor clock tower affording 360-degree views of the city. Head several blocks up, stroll the peaceful courtyard and cemetery at the Queen of the Missions, **Old Mission Santa Barbara** (p345), then end your evening with super-casual tacos at **La Super-Rica Taquería** (p351) and live music at **Soho** (p351).

Seasonal Highlights

California poppies start bursting in joyous orange in mid-February or March, followed in April or May by the jacaranda trees. Year-round, different whale species travel through the Santa Barbara Channel.

FEBRUARY

The **Santa Barbara International Film Festival** (p350) lights up the historic Arlington Theatre with red-carpet screenings and talks with filmmakers and celebrities.

MAY

Artists create a patchwork of amazing chalk art squares at the Santa Barbara Mission for the **I Madonnari Italian street painting festival** (p345). The artwork remains until it gets scuffed or rained away.

JUNE

Since 1974, the only-in-SB **solstice celebration** (p351) revolves around a whimsically artsy parade continuing into a weekend festival in the park.

A Long Weekend to Play

- After exploring **Santa Barbara** (p344) on the first day, head farther afield the next.

- Take a country drive to an estate winery or two in the **Santa Ynez Valley** (p358), or to the small towns of **Los Alamos** (p362) or **Los Olivos** (p359) for sipping and exploring on foot; don't forget to pick up a tin of Danish cookies in **Solvang** (p354).

- Or, while away a day in **Ojai** (p370) to soak up sunshiny, new-agey vibes and diverse, healthy cuisine. Make time to venture outdoors to hike Santa Barbara's front country, or paddle a kayak or stand-up paddleboard (SUP) around the **harbor** (p348) for close encounters with seals, pelicans and bat rays.

Five Days or More to Explore

- Spend a day or two exploring **Santa Barbara** (p344) and get on the water, whether it's with a surf lesson, a paddle around the harbor or a whale-watching cruise. Try catching an SB farmers market on Tuesday afternoon or Saturday morning to pick up snacks and see locals at their most relaxed.

- Take advantage of a longer stay with forays to **Ojai** (p370) for hiking, horseback riding or a spa day. Consider hiring a local guide for a wine-tasting tour in the **Santa Ynez Valley** (p358), and stop in **Solvang** (p354) to feed ostriches, find the taproom speakeasy and feast like a California-style Viking.

AUGUST

Santa Barbara's biggest annual fiesta, **Old Spanish Days** (p351) celebrates the city's Spanish, Mexican and Chumash heritage with parades, street food and traditional performances at the Courthouse sunken garden, the Mission and De La Guerra Plaza.

SEPTEMBER

Kick up your dancing clogs at **Danish Days** (p356) in Solvang with music, parades, food and celebration of all things Danish.

OCTOBER

Little Carpinteria swells with visitors in early October for the **California Avocado Festival** *(carpinteriaca.gov/visitor-info/california-avocado-festival/)*, which of course features bountiful guacamole, tri-tip sandwiches and free live music.

DECEMBER

Winter is a wonderful time to be in the region, when tourist crowds have ebbed significantly. The coastal climate remains pleasantly cool, while the inland valleys aren't as blazingly hot as in summer.

Santa Barbara

RED-TILE ARCHITECTURE | BEACHES & FOOTHILLS | COASTAL CHIC

TOP TIP
Check your feet after beach visits, as SB shores have naturally occurring tar seeps that ooze up through the sand. If you've been tarred, give it a good dab of sunscreen and wipe it off with a paper towel. Plain cooking oil works best if you happen to have some handy.

Santa Barbara has long been a weekend getaway for Angelenos, for obvious reasons – only an hour-and-a-half drive up the coast from LA, it's cozily nestled between the picturesque Santa Ynez Mountains and the Pacific Ocean, with tiled Spanish Colonial architecture and chill, beach-town vibes. The self-branded American Riviera inarguably hits a sweet spot of beautiful natural setting, plentiful outdoor and cultural activities, and great dining experiences. In one day it's easy to hike into sunshine above the marine layer, frolic in the ocean and rinse off your sweaty, sandy day with world-class wine tasting. SB retains a small-town feel while still being a university city with diverse cultural events, a gorgeous outdoor music venue and thriving arts scene. The city's background is rooted in agriculture and a vibrant Mexican heritage, both of which remain proudly and visibly integral to its identity today.

Classic Santa Barbara Landmarks

Architecture, gardens and natural history

Does it sound weird that the **Santa Barbara County Courthouse** *(sbcourthouse.org; free)* is a must-visit? Once you see

GETTING AROUND

The **Amtrak station** conveniently places passengers a couple of blocks from Stearns Wharf, the beach, downtown and the Funk Zone. In this part of town, most visitors get around on foot or bike; traveling further afield within SB or outside city limits, rideshare or driving yourself gets you where you need to go. Getting to and from LAX is a breeze on the **Santa Barbara Airbus** *(www.sbairbus.com; per person one-way prepaid $60)*, which stops in Goleta, Santa Barbara, Carpinteria and Camarillo (Ventura County). The trip between SB and LAX takes 2½ hours.

Downtown SB is crisscrossed with one-way streets parallel and perpendicular to State St. Look out for wrong-way drivers, whizzing e-bikes and pedestrians crossing streets in out-of-office mode. Parking at city lots is free for the first 75 minutes, after which it's $3 an hour (or any part thereof).

NAGEL PHOTOGRAPHY/SHUTTERSTOCK

Santa Barbara County Courthouse

it, you'll understand why couples plan courthouse weddings here. Taking up an entire city block, the Spanish Colonial Revival stunner is surrounded by inviting lawn and sunken garden. **Docent-led tours** *(weekdays at 10.30am, except for court holidays)* give details on the Moorish-style tile work and intricately painted Mural Room (where former VP Kamala Harris got hitched). You can simply turn up during the day and ride up to the 3rd-story clock tower to take in 360-degree views of the surrounding city, ocean and foothills.

Next up: the Queen of the Missions. Founded in 1786, **Old Mission Santa Barbara** *(santabarbaramission.org; adult/youth $17/12)* is only one of two California missions that have continuously operated since their establishment. Self-guided and docent-led tours explore the church, courtyard garden and cemetery where white settlers and unnamed Chumash lie. The Mission lawn and rose garden below are a local favorite for picnics. If you're here during Memorial Day weekend, be sure to check out the chalk-painting festival **I Madonnari** *(@imadonnari)* as it transforms the Mission sidewalk into art.

Head a little farther toward the foothills to the **Santa Barbara Museum of Natural History** *(sbnature.org; adult/child $19/14)* in its creekside nook amid oak habitat. Find natural context in exhibits ranging from Chumash culture, indigenous wildlife and geology, then complement it with forest bathing at the nearby **Santa Barbara Botanic Garden** *(sbbotanic garden.org; adult/child $20/12)* – reservations required. The Channel Islands sector offers spectacular views and native island flora if you can't get to the islands themselves.

BUILDING A CHUMASH CANOE

Alan Salazar, Ventureño Chumash and Tataviam Tribal Elder.

We established the Chumash Maritime Association in January 1997 to oversee construction of a *tomol* (plank canoe) for the Chumash community. We had to relearn the skills of building, paddling and navigating. In 1912 Fernando Librado Kitsepawit, whose family was of the *tomol* brotherhood, built one as a demonstration; our research relied on extensive notes taken by anthropologist JP Harrington from interviews with Librado.

In 1997 we built the first working *tomol* in modern times, with the help of the Santa Barbara Maritime Museum, and paddled it across the Santa Barbara Channel in 2001. Our goal was to revitalize the Chumash maritime culture, especially to involve our young people. Conditions permitting, we now do the channel crossing annually.

HIGHLIGHTS
1 Santa Barbara County Courthouse

SIGHTS
2 Leadbetter Beach
3 MOXI
4 Santa Barbara Maritime Museum
5 Santa Barbara Museum of Art
6 Sea Center
7 Sullivan Goss

ACTIVITIES
8 Condor Express
9 Paddle Sports Center
10 Santa Barbara Sailing Center

SLEEPING
11 Canary
12 Castillo Inn
13 Harbor House Inn
14 Hotel Californian
15 Marina Beach Motel

EATING
16 Arigato Sushi
17 Barbareño
18 Bibi ji
19 Corazón Cocina
20 Helena Avenue Bakery
21 La Super-Rica Taquería
22 Loquita
23 Sama Sama Kitchen
24 The Black Sheep
25 The Lark
26 Zaytoon

DRINKING & NIGHTLIFE
27 Cajé
28 Cutler's Artisan Spirits
29 Draughtsmen Aleworks
30 Dune
31 EOS Lounge
32 Handlebar Coffee Roasters
33 Lama Dog Tap Room
34 M Special
35 Margerum Wine Company
36 Municipal Winemakers
37 Night Lizard
38 Santa Barbara Roasting Company
39 Test Pilot

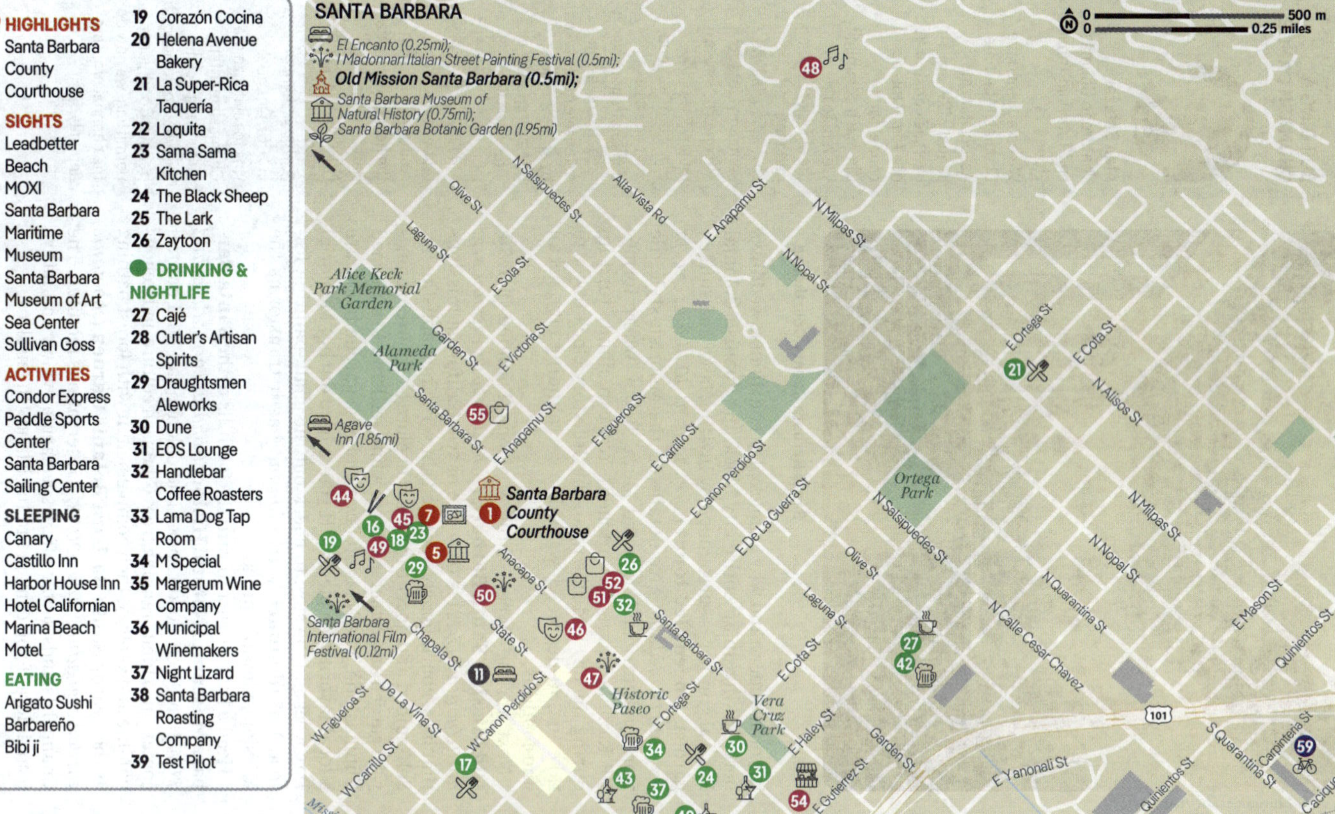

40 The Red Piano
41 The Valley Project
42 Third Window Brewing
43 Wildcat Lounge

ENTERTAINMENT

44 Arlington Theatre
45 Granada Theatre
46 Lobero Theatre
47 Old Spanish Days
48 Santa Barbara Bowl
49 Soho
50 Summer Solstice Celebration

SHOPPING

51 Farmer and the Flea
52 Mujeres Makers Market
53 Santa Barbara Arts & Crafts Show
54 Santa Barbara Certified Farmers Market
55 Santa Barbara Company
56 Shopkeepers
57 The Blue Door

TRANSPORT

58 Amtrak
59 Cal Coast Adventures
60 Wheel Fun Rentals

ARCHITECTURE WALKS

For an exceptionally insightful look at Santa Barbara's architectural highlights, take a walking tour with a docent from the **Architectural Foundation of Santa Barbara** *(afsb.org; suggested donation $20)*. Reserve a two-hour walk and talk every Saturday and Sunday at 10am. The DIY **Red Tile Walking Tour** *(santabarbaraca.com/itinerary/red-tile-walking-tour)* stops at the most significant historical sites downtown, including El Presidio de Santa Bárbara, with remnants of its original adobe structure.

Lest you think the American Riviera takes its red tile too seriously, check out a few of the playful, Seussian takes on the local vernacular with architect **Jeff Shelton** *(jeffsheltonarchitect.com/santa-barbara-map)*. Download a walking tour map or book a guided tour that includes a visit to Shelton's studio.

GERI LAVROV/GETTY IMAGES

Leadbetter Beach

Pacific Ocean Pleasures

Swim, surf, paddle, whale-watch

You could visit Santa Barbara without dipping a toe in the ocean…but why would you? Buffered from open ocean by the Channel Islands, the south-facing coastline offers a string of beautiful protected beaches for free saltwater therapy.

Novice surfers will appreciate the smaller swell of summer; most surf spots are best during the winter. **Leadbetter Beach** has a slow-rolling wave that makes it popular for lessons and beginners. Book surf lessons with **Santa Barbara Surf School** *(santabarbarasurfschool.com)* or **Surf Happens** *(surfhappens.com)* to feel the stoke. **Arroyo Burro Beach** – also known as Hendry's – is a consistent surf spot with both rights and lefts. Added bonuses: it's SB's sanctioned **dog beach**, and the **Boathouse** *(boathousesb.com)* provides the perfect setting for post-beach lunch or happy hour.

At the harbor, rent an SUP or a kayak at **Paddle Sports Center** *(paddlesportsca.com)*. Even within the breakwater, you'll encounter harbor seals, pelicans and rays on your paddle. Explore farther, steering between the pilings of **Stearns Wharf**, or upwind toward Leadbetter Beach. Wildlife-watchers can book a whale-watching tour on the *Double Dolphin* of the **Santa Barbara Sailing Center** *(sbsail.com)* or with **Condor Express** *(condorexpress.com)*, to cruise the Santa Barbara Channel in search of over 30 species of cetaceans, including migrating humpbacks, blue or gray whales and orcas (depending on the season).

Back on land, learn about SB's marine history, going back to its Chumash heritage, at the **Santa Barbara Maritime Museum** *(sbmm.org; adult/child $12/6)*. On Stearns Wharf, get to know the local marine life in the touch tanks and try out some actual research tools on the Wet Deck at the Santa Barbara Museum of Natural History's **Sea Center** *(sbnature.org; adult/child $15/12)*.

Tasting in the Funk Zone

Santa Barbara's urban wine trail

While the Funk Zone is ground zero for SB wine tasting, consider it a starting point (maybe also an ending point – your mileage may vary). The high concentration of tasting rooms, eateries, breweries and galleries could entrap you for an entire day.

There's limited street parking but large pre-pay lots are on Garden St and Cabrillo Blvd. Pick up divine pastries and coffee at **Helena Avenue Bakery** *(helenaavenuebakery.com)* and pop into vintage shops like **The Blue Door** *(thebluedoorsb.com)* and lifestyle purveyors **Shopkeepers** *(shopkeeperssb.com)*. If you've got kids with you, the excellent museum of science and innovation **MOXI** *(moxi.org; adult/child $20/15)* is a delight, with sensory exhibits and interactive exploration for all ages.

If you don't have specific wineries in mind, start at **The Valley Project** *(thevalleyprojectwines.com)* on Yanonali St, where the chalkboard art gives a quick primer on the lay of the wine-country land. Nearby, **Margerum Wine Company** *(margerumwines.com)* has an elegant feel while **Municipal Winemakers** *(municipalwinemakers.com)* offers a fun, approachable vibe. Ask your tasting room host for onward recommendations based on your tastes.

Not into wine? **Lama Dog Tap Room** *(lamadog.com)* pours a rotating selection of craft beers, with a bottle shop and convivial little patio to boot. Sample cocktails made with house-distilled bourbon, vodka and gin at **Cutler's Artisan Spirits** *(cutlersartisan.com)*. And mingle with the beautiful people at postmodern tiki bar **Test Pilot** *(testpilotcocktails.com)*, serving tropical-themed cocktails and seasonal, shrub-based non-alcoholic mocktails.

Reservations are recommended if you're set on dining at **The Lark** *(thelarksb.com)* or **Loquita** *(loquitasb.com)*.

OUTSIDE THE ZONE

The Funk Zone may be the densest, but other tasting nooks are clustered around SB's downtown area. Pick up a **Santa Barbara Urban Wine Trail map** *(urbanwinetrailsb.com)* to find worthwhile gems along the Haley St corridor, along State St and around the bougainvillea-laced **El Paseo arcade** on Anacapa St.

The purchase of an Urban Wine Trail tasting card *($200)* entitles you to one-time free tastings at participating wineries as well as day-of-tasting discounts. You can also simply use the map as an orientation tool, as many worthwhile wineries aren't part of the Urban Wine Trail program but are located in the highlighted neighborhoods.

Arts & Culture

Theater, live music, visual art

Local landmarks themselves, many of SB's arts venues enhance their events with their own architectural beauty.

Entering the historic **Arlington Theatre** *(thearlingtontheatre.com)* under its archways and sitting in a trompe l'oeil courtyard almost makes it feel like you're watching performances under a Spanish sky, complete with twinkling ceiling

DRINKING IN SANTA BARBARA: CRAFT BEER

Third Window Brewing: Beautiful Belgian-style beers, and smashburgers using beef from the family ranch. *11.30am-9pm Mon-Thu, to 11pm Fri, 11am-11pm Sat, to 10pm Sun*

Night Lizard: Great selection of beer styles named for endangered species, plus occasional live music. *3-9pm Mon, noon-10pm Tue-Thu, noon-midnight Fri & Sat, noon-8pm Sun*

M Special: Good beer, regular live music and Mexican eats from the Beast Taquería window in back. *noon-9pm Tue, Wed & Sun, to 10pm Thu, to 11pm Fri & Sat*

Draughtsmen Aleworks: Up State St in the theater district, you'll find this taproom in the Mosaic Locale food and beverage collective. *11.30am-8pm Sun-Wed, to 9pm Thu-Sun*

BEST SPOTS TO SHOP LOCAL

Santa Barbara Arts & Crafts Show: Every Sunday since 1965, along half a mile of beachfront Chase Palm Park, artists and craftspeople sell their creative work.

Mujeres Makers Market: Regularly scheduled pop-up market run by women of color, fostering community and celebrating seasonality at El Presídio de Santa Bárbara.

Farmer and the Flea: Another beautifully curated pop-up also taking place at the Presídio, on a quarterly schedule.

Santa Barbara Company: Find locally made gifts, edible goodies and flowers at this cute little cottage on East Victoria St.

Santa Barbara Certified Farmers Market: Downtown on Tuesdays and Saturdays. Locally grown bounty includes chile-spiked pistachios, toffee-studded almond butter and sage honey.

LOGAN BUSH/SHUTTERSTOCK

Granada Theatre

stars. Or you can come out to watch film stars walk the red carpet here at the **Santa Barbara International Film Festival** *(sbiff.org)* every February.

On the next block, the ornate Spanish Moorish-style **Granada Theatre** *(granadasb.org)* occupies the ground floor of the low-scale city's tallest building, topping out at 116ft, and is home to local institutions like the **State Street Ballet** *(statestreetballet.com)* and **Santa Barbara Symphony** *(thesymphony.org)*.

A little farther down State St, the elegant neoclassical **Santa Barbara Museum of Art** *(sbma.net)* houses visual inspiration, occasionally holding workshops and events. Nearby, the art gallery **Sullivan Goss** *(sullivangoss.com)* focuses on American artists of varying genres.

The **Lobero Theatre** *(lobero.org)*, a few blocks down, is the oldest continuously operating theater in California. Originally founded in 1873, it was renovated in Spanish Colonial Revival style in 1924, and its acoustics make it perfect for chamber, folk and jazz performances.

From spring to fall, it's a special treat to see a show at the **Santa Barbara Bowl** *(sbbowl.com)*, the city's beloved outdoor music venue tucked into a residential hillside. A shuttle runs from the entrance to the amphitheater, but part of the magic is walking up the woodsy path in shared anticipation with your fellow concertgoers.

DRINKING IN SANTA BARBARA: CAFFEINATION STATIONS

Dune: Minimalist, light-flooded space with a spacious patio and excellent coffee in the Lower State area. *6am-5pm Mon-Sat, from 7am Sun*

Handlebar Coffee Roasters: Friendly, efficient espresso bar established by former cycling pros, with an appealing interior and a street-side patio. *6.30am-5pm*

Cajé: This cozy space along the Haley St corridor concocts elaborate, craft-cocktail-style coffee drinks as well as the basics. *7am-6pm*

Santa Barbara Roasting Company: Since 1989, this old-school coffeehouse has been roasting beans and keeping SB whirring. *6.30am-6pm Mon-Sat, from 7am Sun*

SB's unique cultural celebrations are the biggest community parties of the year. The **Santa Barbara Summer Solstice** *(solsticeparade.com)* sambas and sashays up State St in riotous color and creativity in June, while **Old Spanish Days** *(sbfiesta.org)* – known simply as 'Fiesta' locally – celebrates the city's Chumash, Mexican and Spanish heritage with parades, dance, music and food in early August.

Check the **UCSB Arts & Lectures** *(artsandlectures.ucsb.edu)* website for current listings, or keep it casual and discover the lively local music scene at the many breweries and cafes around town.

Cycle Santa Barbara

See SB on two wheels

Santa Barbara is a great place to pedal around, whether meandering along the Cabrillo Blvd beachfront or taking a serious road tour into the foothills. Downtown SB is generally flat with some gentle climbs, and you can rent a bicycle to stitch together sightseeing stops.

Cal Coast Adventures *(calcoastadventures.com)* rents bicycles and also runs guided bike tours around the city. Additionally, their website links to bike maps of longer road cycling tours, mountain-biking trails and a great self-guided tour of downtown and the waterfront.

For short, low-commitment jaunts, **Santa Barbara BCycles** *(santabarbara.bcycle.com)* rents e-bikes for $8.70 per 30 minutes, with docks located in multiple locations around town.

Rent a bike at **Wheel Fun Rentals** *(wheelfunrentals.com; beach cruiser half-day $34)* in the Funk Zone and ride along the palm-lined Cabrillo bike path southward about 2½ miles to local favorite Butterfly Beach, or north past the harbor about a mile to Leadbetter Beach and on to Shoreline Park on the Mesa.

Mountain bikers will find plenty of technical singletrack to negotiate after the thigh-burning climbs. Etiquette tip: pick up and drop off a bike bell at the trailhead, as trails in the front country are multiuse and very popular with hikers.

BEST LIVE-MUSIC VENUES

Santa Barbara Bowl: Even the nosebleeds are a sweet place to be, with spectacular views of city and ocean from the upper bar.

Soho: Going strong since 1994, this intimate venue hosts live local and touring bands.

The Red Piano: It does have a red piano, with 'Church on Monday' blues and live music every night of the week.

EOS Lounge: Long-running club with DJs spinning a range of styles – this being SB, the vibe is casual.

Wildcat Lounge: Teeny, busy and always a winner for people-watching in the wild. Sister lounge **Bobcat**, out back, is a more chilled-out space.

EATING IN SANTA BARBARA: FROM A TO Z

Arigato Sushi: Popular Arigato has been around for decades and still pulls them in. *5.30-9:45pm Sun-Thu, to 10:15pm Fri & Sat* $$

Barbareño: Showcasing fresh, locally harvested produce, seafood and meats. Lunch is a more casual affair. *5-8.30pm Sun-Thu, to 9pm Fri & Sat* $$$

Bibi ji: Santa Barbara-style Indian food, with an extensive natural-wine list. *5-10pm Thu-Tue* $$

Corazón Cocina: It's worth the long line at SB Public Market for bright, fresh ceviches and regional-specialty tacos. *11am-9pm* $

La Super-Rica Taquería: There's always a line at this cash-only shack beloved by Julia Child. *11am-9pm Mon, Thu & Sun, to 9.30pm Fri & Sat* $

Sama Sama Kitchen: Southeast Asian fusion, paired with cocktails. *noon-3pm Tue-Sun & 5-9.30pm Tue-Thu & Sun, to 10.30pm Fri & Sat* $$

The Black Sheep: French-style cuisine with a California accent. The tasting menu is a solid bet. *5-9pm Wed, Thu & Sun, to 10pm Fri & Sat* $$$

Zaytoon: Good Middle Eastern food and a romantic, twinkling ambience. *5-9pm Tue-Thu & Sun, to 10pm Fri & Sat* $$

Beyond Santa Barbara

Hwy 101 north opens up to coastline ranches, while to the south you'll discover some of the county's best underrated small towns.

Places

GETTING AROUND

It's easiest to drive, whether heading north to the Gaviota Coast or to Montecito and Summerland, but once there you can explore on foot. Santa Barbara MTD runs regular express buses through to Carpinteria. Less frequently, you can catch local train services on Amtrak, with a platform mere blocks from Carpinteria State Beach.

Note that the Santa Barbara coastline runs east–west, but locals give directions in reference to Hwy 101 – putting Summerland south and Goleta north of SB.

Northbound 101 moves through Goleta – 'The Good Land' – and branches off to Santa Barbara Municipal Airport, the University of California, Santa Barbara (UCSB) and the community of Isla Vista. After that it rolls through scenic ranchlands and the wild Gaviota coastline before turning inland to Buellton and Santa Ynez Valley wine country.

Southbound, the highway cuts through the rarefied enclave of Montecito, land of low-key lavish estates but accessible foothill trails and village restaurants. A smidge south is hillside Summerland, with its crescent of gorgeous beach and strip of cute boutiques, followed by the throwback beach town of Carpinteria. Easy to bypass on your way elsewhere, these small towns have their allures for those who detour through.

Gaviota Coast

TIME FROM SANTA BARBARA: **25 MINS**

Windswept tidepools & trails

The wild coast north of Goleta is a wealth of coastal open space, much of it privately owned, working ranchland with some parcels purchased by conservation organizations to protect these rare oceanfront lands from future development.

Of three state parks along Hwy 101, the first is **El Capitán State Beach** *(parks.ca.gov)*. The campground is closed for renovation through 2025, but the beach is open to pedestrian access for day use. Explore tidepools, the nature trail along El Capitán Creek and miles of empty beach, stretching east and west from a south-facing point. A paved trail from the west leads all the way to **Refugio State Beach** *(parks.ca.gov; vehicle entry $10)*, about 3 miles further northbound on Hwy 101. This crescent of beach is lined with stately palm trees and has over 60 campsites.

Furthest north, at the coastline where Hwy 101 veers inland, find **Gaviota State Park** *(parks.ca.gov; vehicle entry $10)*, with interesting tilted shale beds embedded in the beach sand. Offshore, the park's waters form part of the **Kashtayit State Marine Conservation Area**. The trestle bridge above the beach is still used by Amtrak and freight trains, and camping is also available here.

Day hikers can access the **Gaviota Wind Caves trail** from the green gate past the state park entrance; the five-mile out-and-back takes you up to the caves for beautiful windswept views of the coast below.

WAYNE VIA/SHUTTERSTOCK

El Capitán State Beach

South County

TIME FROM SANTA BARBARA: **10 MINS**

Not-so-secret small towns

Begin in Montecito with coffee and real French croissants at **Bree'osh** *(breeosh.com)* or **Renaud's** *(renaudsbistro.com)* and stroll **Coast Village Rd** boutiques, keeping an eye out for mononymous luminaries like Oprah, Harry and Meghan roaming under the radar. Cross over the freeway at Olive Mill Rd and walk to **Butterfly Beach** to while away your morning before a wood-fired pizza at **Bettina** *(bettinapizzeria.com)* or Mexican favorite **Los Arroyos** *(losarroyos.net/montecito)*.

Then head into the foothills for a hike through front-country ceanothus and chaparral to reach views of the coastline as far south as Malibu. Find trail information at the website of the **Montecito Trails Foundation** *(montecitotrailsfoundation.info)*. Pursue more meditative walks through the wondrous landscape of **Lotusland** *(lotusland.org; adult/youth $60/25)* – by appointment only – a lavish, eccentric botanical garden on the former estate of opera singer Ganna Walska. End with a fancy cocktail at **Honor Bar** *(honorbar.com)* or **Lucky's** *(luckys-steakhouse.com)*.

A few miles further south lies the hillside beach town of **Summerland**, where Lillie Ave boutiques like **Porch** *(porchsb.com)* and **Botanik** *(botanikinc.com)* are stuffed with chic coastal decor and succulent art. On the ocean side of the freeway, bluff-top **Lookout Park** *(countyofsb.org/822/Lookout-Park)* has a great playground, bocce court, picnic tables and path down to the beautiful slice of **Summerland Beach**.

Beyond Summerland, the little beach town of **Carpinteria** is at heart an agricultural community, growing avocados, citrus and cherimoyas, and celebrating the **California Avocado Festival** *(avofest.org)* every October.

Downshift into small-town gear and cruise **Linden Ave** down to **Carpinteria State Beach** *(parks.ca.gov)*, browsing the indie shops and homegrown restaurants. Little kids love running around the **Tomol play area**, after which you can grab burgers at old-timey shack **The Spot** and take them over to **Island Brewing Co** *(islandbrewingcompany.com)* to enjoy with a sunset beer.

CARPINTERIA FERMENTATION OPERATIONS

Bordering the **Carpinteria Salt Marsh**, the industrial park at the west end of Carpinteria Ave is not visually inspiring. But walk around the back alley and you'll find a bubbly social zone with miniscule tasting rooms, empanadas, a specialty wine store and boutique chocolate.

The dreamy **Apiary** *(theapiary.co)* brews beautiful and complex mead, cider and kombucha from local honey, flowers, herbs and fruit.

Next door, nanobrewery **BrewLAB** *(brewlab craft.com)* always has a creative selection of top-notch small-batch beers on tap, from sours to stouts brewed with locally grown flora.

At the end of the line, **Rincon Mountain Winery** *(rinconmtn.com)* pours tastings of their Carpinteria-farmed and -produced wine. Weekends are liveliest with food trucks, live tunes and kids running around underfoot.

Solvang

DANISH KITSCH | WALKABLE VILLAGE | WINE-COUNTRY BASE

GETTING AROUND

Solvang has an eminently walkable downtown – park in one of the free public lots south of Mission Dr and roam on foot. Copenhagen Dr is the main shopping and restaurant strip, with the surrounding streets fanning out to tasting rooms, hotels and the residential area to the south. Many local lodgings offer free bicycles for their guests to borrow.

☑ TOP TIP

Solvang makes a great base for exploring Santa Barbara's wine country, but if you're seeking a more low-key vibe during your stay, the nearby towns of Santa Ynez and Los Olivos are stellar choices. Los Alamos is another option, though it's slightly more removed.

From red-tiled Spanish Colonial Santa Barbara, arriving in Solvang ('sunny fields' in Danish) is like experiencing a mildly kooky bout of culture shock. Founded in 1911 by three Danish-American educators, Solvang shows its authentic Danish influence even if the decorative motif is over the top. Before the Danes, the Spanish established Mission Santa Inés here in 1804, and before that, it was the ancestral land of the Native Chumash people.

Nowadays the Chumash tribe not only runs the nearby casino resort, but also tends vineyards and makes wine, as is the contemporary tradition of the Santa Ynez Valley. Long a destination for its butter cookies and Disneyfied Scandinavian window dressing, Solvang does make a convenient central base for exploring Santa Ynez Valley wine country. And don't worry, there's plenty of good food besides *aebleskiver* and *pandekager* (Danish fritters and pancakes).

Solvang's Danish Heritage

Local insight into Danish culture

Solvang's Danishness runs deeper than the scent of sugary confections and its ersatz windmills – details like stork statues on rooftops and the gabled rooftops themselves are nods to the town's actual Danish roots. Learn more at the charming **Elverhøj Museum of History & Art** *(elverhoj.org; adult/child $5/free)*, open Thursday to Monday. It was formerly the residence of an artist couple; the beautiful tongue-and-groove construction of the home was modeled after an 18th-century Danish farmhouse design and is itself a work of art.

Back on main drag Mission Dr (Rte 246), you'll find the **Hans Christian Andersen Museum** *(bookloftsolvang.com; free)* upstairs at The Book Loft bookstore. The museum houses a small collection of the author's handwritten letters, first-edition copies of his illustrated books and a model of

HIGHLIGHTS
1 Elverhøj Museum of History & Art

SIGHTS
2 Bethania Lutheran Church
3 California Nature Art Museum
4 Hans Christian Andersen Museum
5 Hans Christian Andersen Park
6 Old Mission Santa Ínes
7 Rundetaarn

SLEEPING
8 Hamlet Inn
9 Hotel Corque
10 The Landsby
11 Viking Inn

EATING
12 peasants FEAST
13 Ramen Kotori
14 The Gathering Table

DRINKING & NIGHTLIFE
15 Lost Chord Guitars
16 The Backroom
17 Vaquero Bar

ENTERTAINMENT
18 Danish Days

SHOPPING
19 Copenhagen House

his childhood home. A scaled-down replica of Copenhagen's *Little Mermaid* statue sits in contemplative repose in the fountain across the road.

On narrow Copenhagen Dr, the **Copenhagen House** (*thecopenhagenhouse.com*) imports Danish furniture and jewelry as well as high-end kitchenware and designy trinkets. The shop's comings and goings are supervised by the stern-faced wooden figures of Solvang's founders, Reverend Benedict Nordentoft, Reverend JM Gregersen and Professor PP Hornsyld, standing sentry out front.

Several notable buildings around town were also inspired by monuments in Denmark, including **Bethania Lutheran**

AEBLESKIVER

Translated as 'apple slice,' Solvang's ubiquitous *aebleskiver* is a round, sweet fritter with a crispy exterior and a tender, doughy bite. Fresh from the pan, they're usually dusted with powdered sugar and served with jam.

It takes some technique to make the perfect *aebleskiver*, as they need to be turned evenly on their special stovetop pan to get uniform doneness on all sides. You can buy cast-iron *aebleskiver* pans in town to make these festive balls of carby happiness at home.

Church *(bethanialutheran.net)* whose stucco design echoes the more elaborate Gruntvig's Church in Copenhagen but also incorporates a Spanish-style red-tiled roof. Also taking inspiration from Copenhagen is Solvang's one-third-scale replica of the **Rundetaarn**. The stately brick round tower doesn't have an astronomical observatory but does house a pizzeria.

If you're visiting Solvang in the latter half of September, you can join in celebrating **Danish Days** *(solvangdanishdays.org)*, a cultural festival replete with *aebleskiver* eating, beer drinking, parade spectating and some friendly axe throwing. You can also throw your name into the drawing for a trip to the real Denmark, in case Solvang piques your interest in Scandinavia.

Slow Solvang

Low-speed sights and delights

As tourist-saturated as Solvang can get, it has quiet corners worth finding. East of downtown along Mission Dr, the driveway to Solvang's **Old Mission Santa Inés** *(missionsantaines.org; free)* is an immediate escape. Fringed with olive trees, the mission garden is a peaceful spot to retreat for a moment. Pause in the cemetery to remember the Chumash people who were conscripted to build the mission here.

EATING & DRINKING IN SOLVANG: OUR PICKS

peasants FEAST: Seasonal, local American classics with an emphasis on freshness; superb picnic takeout at their deli across the street. *11am-6pm Wed-Sun* $

Ramen Kotori: Authentic ramen, gyoza and Japanese-style small plates like poke with fresh local seafood and farmers-market produce. *noon-3pm & 4.30-8pm Wed-Sun* $

The Gathering Table: Chef Budi Kazali's Asian-inflected French menu is executed beautifully for memorable seasonal cuisine. *5-9pm Wed, Thu & Sun, 8am-2pm & 5-9.30pm Fri & Sat* $$$

Vaquero Bar: Squeeze in at the bar for a cocktail, and order a grilled artichoke or rib-sticking ribeye off the Coast Range menu. *10am-midnight Wed-Mon, from 5pm Tue*

TRAVELVIEW/SHUTTERSTOCK

Solvang

At the other end of town, visit with room-sized troll Lulu Hyggelig at the nonprofit **California Nature Art Museum** *(calnatureartmuseum.org; adult/child $5/free)*, formerly the Wildling Museum. Lulu is the museum's latest ambassador who, in her inimitably enchanting selfness, explores how art can foster a closer relationship with nature. The troll, one in a worldwide series (see *trollmap.com*) by Danish recycling artist Thomas Dambo, will remain in residence until 2035. After visiting with Lulu, wander off through the museum's current exhibits, often featuring local artists whose work is deeply connected with nature.

One block over, turn off of Mission Dr at 4th Pl and leave the tourist traffic behind. Stop into the home-brewing supply shop **Valley Brewers**, where the carboys and bags of hops may not hold any thrall for you. But you're here to pass the owner a fiver for the privilege of being led down the hallway of illusory bookshelves and let in – speakeasy-style – to **The Backroom** *(valleybrewers.com/the-backroom; over-21 adult entry $5)*. This tiny taproom always has interesting craft beers, meads and ciders on rotation and a quiet patio to enjoy them in the sunshine.

End your evening with first-rate live music of the singer-songwriter bent at **Lost Chord Guitars** *(lostchordguitars.com; cover varies)*, a guitar shop and music venue on Copenhagen Dr.

BEST SANTA YNEZ VALLEY KIDS FUN

Ostrichland: Few thrills are cheaper than $1 feed bowls for the resident ostriches and emus that will come calling, all legs and necks and delightfully prehistoric *(ostrichlandusa.com; adult/child $7/3)*.

Vega Vineyard: For more animal encounters, stop at family-friendly Vega Vineyard, where kids can feed all sorts of animals: look for rabbits, sheep, llamas, potbellied pigs and a mini Highland bull *(vegavineyard andfarm.com; free)*.

Hans Christian Andersen Park: Let the kids enjoy themselves at this lovely Solvang park, with an oak-shaded, creekside trail, a playground, skate park and interactive sensory play areas. Take Atterdag Rd north from Mission Dr, veering left onto Chalk Hill Rd. A castle gate marks the entrance in true Solvang style.

EATING & DRINKING IN BUELLTON: MORNING TO NIGHT

Ellen's Danish Pancake House: Established in 1947, this comfortingly old-timey diner is where locals come for the best Danish pancakes and all-day breakfasts. *6am-2pm* $

Industrial Eats: Wood-fired pizzas with ever-changing toppings, innovative small plates and creative specials concocted from locally sourced producers. A must. *noon-8pm* $$

Hitching Post 2: Dark-paneled chophouse serving oak-grilled steaks, rack of lamb, quail and such. Pair with one of their own popular Hitching Post wines. *4.30-9pm Wed-Mon* $$

Firestone Walker: This gastropub, taproom and barrel room celebrates wild ferments. A Buellton beer institution. *noon-8pm Mon-Thu, to 9pm Fri, 11am-9pm Sat, to 8pm Sun*

Beyond Solvang

All roads lead to wine from gingerbread village Solvang. Westward, the landscape opens into the rolling hills of the Santa Ynez Valley.

Places

GETTING AROUND

Regular bus services with **Santa Ynez Valley Transit** *(syvt.com)* connect Buellton, Solvang, Santa Ynez and Los Olivos from Monday through Saturday. If you're roaming beyond town, you'll need private transportation to explore the rest of the Santa Ynez Valley.

Santa Barbara wine country fans out from the Solvang area, its local appellations ranging west along Santa Rosa Rd to Lompoc and northward through Los Olivos, Los Alamos and Santa Maria. Each of the little hamlets anchoring the Santa Ynez Valley have their own look and vibe – Los Alamos with its Old Western storefronts that include a Michelin-starred restaurant among its good culinary company, and Los Olivos' clapboard-ranch-chic aesthetic and oak-lined lanes. A drive along Santa Rosa Rd or Rte 246 is the simplest way to visit some of the region's best wineries while also enjoying a slow day trip through the valley's picturesque rolling hills cultivated in rows of vines.

Santa Ynez Valley

TIME FROM SOLVANG: **7 MINS**

Un-wine in the SYV

Wine is queen around here, but there are other pleasures to savor in the Santa Ynez Valley. These rolling hills have traditionally sustained the Chumash people and supported agriculture and ranching that have nothing to do with the relatively new fermented-grape industry.

Begin with an introduction to the region's indigenous background at the newly-opened **Chumash Cultural Center** *(sychumashmuseum.org; adult/teen/child $15/12/10)* in Santa Ynez. The museum's contemporary architecture incorporates the dome shape of the traditional Chumash *'ap* house, and has a garden element landscaped with grasses, herbs and other native flora used for medicine and weaving. Inside, the wonderful interactive exhibits teach visitors about Chumash folklore, Samala language, maritime culture, history and the many cultural contributions of its tribal members. Even the tile work leading to the museum entrance features illustrations of native animals with their Samala names.

Then, inhabit your inner *vaquero/a* (cowboy/girl) on a horseback ride with **Vino Vaqueros** *(vinovaqueros.com)*. To be fair, the ride does end with a wine tasting, but the main event is riding through ranch and vineyard with experienced guides and horses; kids eight and up can ride, too. Reservations must be made in advance; walk-ins are not accommodated.

Local tasting isn't limited to wine: try lavender honey and pick up lavender baking mixes and teas at **Clairmont Farms**

BILLYHANKEJR/SHUTTERSTOCK

Vineyard, Los Olivos

(clairmontfarms.com). Its small shop also sells housemade skincare and mists, and visitors are free to enjoy the shade and walk amid the lavender; blooming season is in June and July.

Local olive farmers offer estate-grown tastings of their grassy, fruity and peppery olive oils in beautiful ranch settings, including at **Rancho Olivos** *(rancholivos.com)* just outside of downtown Los Olivos.

Los Olivos

TIME FROM SOLVANG: **11 MINS**

Walking & wine tasting

Wine tasting in Los Olivos is a delicious reminder that life is good. Its petite size makes this appealing town the perfect choice if you've only got an afternoon to taste in the valley, as you can walk to two dozen tasting rooms within a few blocks. Tastings generally run around $25, and wineries may waive the tasting fee if you purchase multiple bottles – policies vary by individual business.

Although there's no need to drive anywhere once you've parked, do plan ahead for getting safely to your onward destination. If you're cruising around with others, a good strategy for hitting several wineries is to split your tastings with someone so you're not consuming the entirety of each pour. When tasting solo, sip and spit. (The dump bucket is there for a reason; no one will be offended if you use it.)

THE SIDEWAYS EFFECT

In the 2004 film *Sideways*, whose story took place in the Santa Ynez Valley, wine-snob protagonist Miles famously declared he didn't want to drink merlot, and almost as famously helped trigger a real-world decline in merlot sales. But though the 'Sideways Effect' did contribute to the 2% drop, a glut of merlot plantings and subsequent production of lower-quality wines had already set that effect in motion.

Though pinot noir is still a local darling around here, it's worth giving a good merlot another try. Either way, you can follow in the fictional footsteps of the wayward Miles and Jack on your own *Sideways*-based tour *(solvangusa.com/solvang-wine-country/sideways)* for tasting stops, scenic drives and ostrich encounters.

EATING & DRINKING IN SANTA YNEZ: OUR PICKS

Santa Ynez Billiards & Café: A falafel or shawarma wrap plus cool drink on the shaded patio: the best deal in town. *11am-8pm Sun, to 9pm Mon, Tue, Thu-Sat* $

Maverick Saloon: Santa Ynez's go-to for late-night cocktails, live music and line dancing with the locals. *11am-midnight Sun-Thu, to 2am Fri & Sat* $

SY Kitchen: Reservations recommended for standout, authentic Italian farm-to-table cuisine in the bustling modern farmhouse dining room or fairy-lit veranda. *11.30am-2pm & 4.30-9pm* $$

Pony Cocktails + Kitchen: Get a coffee fix and brunch in the morning, craft cocktails and fresh takes on comfort food later on. *8am-2.30pm daily & 4.30-10pm Tue-Sat* $$

PUTTING THE OLIVES BACK IN LOS OLIVOS

Los Olivos comes by its name honestly. In the 1880s, a young rancher planted 5000 olive trees near Ballard. When the Pacific Coast Railway built its rail line from Los Alamos down to its new station, it eventually bequeathed the stop with the name Los Olivos in homage to the trees. Unfortunately, a harsh winter in 1889 killed most of the young olive trees.

In the mid-1990s, observing that the latitude and climate are similar to olive-growing regions in Spain and Italy, a few intrepid souls began planting olive trees in the Santa Ynez Valley expressly to produce olive oil. The happy, full-circle result is that you can now taste olive oil in Los Olivos.

If you have no clue where to start, you'll find a super-approachable vibe at **Carhartt Family Wines** *(carharttvineyard.com)*, which is open 11am to 6pm and often has live music on their spacious patio, or at family-run **Saarloos + Sons** *(saarloosandsons.com)*, who also do cupcake pairings *(open 11am to 5pm)*. Try the region's cool-climate Burgundian and Rhône varietals like chardonnay, pinot noir and syrah at the amazing small producers here. These include **Blair Fox Cellars** *(blairfoxcellars.com)*, open noon to 5pm Sunday to Thursday and to 6pm Friday and Saturday, **Storm Wines** *(stormwines.com)*, open 11am to 5pm Wednesday to Monday, **Liquid Farm** *(liquidfarm.com)*, open from 11am, and women-run **Holus Bolus** *(holusboluswine.com)*, open noon to 5pm, and **Story of Soil** *(storyofsoilwine.com)*, by reservation only Monday to Thursday. Sample less common varietals like interesting Austrian skin-contact grüner veltliner at **Solminer** *(solminer.com)*, open 11am to 5pm Sunday to Friday, to 6pm Saturday, and be sure to taste at heavy-hitters like **Brewer-Clifton** *(bygregbrewer.com)*, open 10am to 4pm Thursday to Tuesday, and **Stolpman** *(stolpmanvineyards.com)*, open 11am to 4pm.

This town is mostly (OK, all) about the wine, but Los Olivos has boutiques and galleries to browse between tastings. Weekends often feel like a block party, with live bands and a festive atmosphere. Arrive early to find parking closer in.

Lompoc

TIME FROM SOLVANG: **30 MINS**

Tasting at the Wine Ghetto

There's nothing hidden about Lompoc's **Wine Ghetto**, but it feels like you've discovered a local secret when you park among the nondescript industrial buildings in this warehouse complex. It's just off the intersection of Hwy 1 and 12th St in the city of Lompoc (pronounced 'Lom-poke'); you could easily spend a day here tasting a representative spectrum of Santa Rita Hills terroir.

Each tasting room has its own creative feel reflective of its resident winemaker: from the self-effacing cartoon goats of **Flying Goat Cellars** *(flyinggoatcellars.com)* labels (belying the artistry inside the bottle), to the bright and friendly **Fiddlehead Cellars** *(fiddleheadcellars.com)*, pouring estate-grown wines made by pioneering winemaker Kathy Joseph.

Family-run **Ampelos Cellars** *(ampeloscellars.com)* uses grapes from organically and biodynamically farmed vineyards to make their pinot noir and Rhône varietals. Also sourcing from

EATING IN LOS OLIVOS: WINE-COUNTRY PAIRINGS

Panino: Take a break from tasting with a takeout sandwich and a cool non-alcoholic beverage. *10am-4pm* $

Mattei's Tavern: There's cozy elegance at the coffee shop, atmospheric bar and tavern serving California cuisine. *6.30am-2pm & 5-9pm* $$

Los Olivos Wine Merchant & Cafe: Elevated but relaxed dining created with organic ingredients from the restaurant's own farm. *11.30am-8.30pm Sun-Thu, to 9pm Fri & Sat* $$

Bar Le Côte: The couple who brought us Bell's in Los Alamos has set up shop here, with Euro-style seafood on the menu. *noon-8.30pm* $$

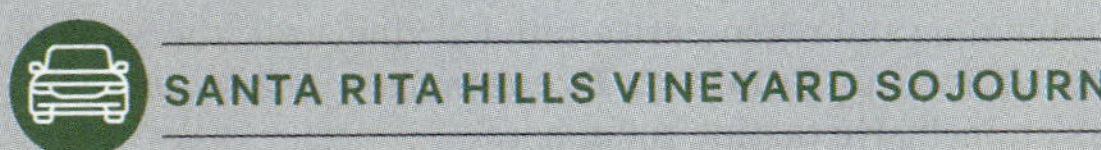

SANTA RITA HILLS VINEYARD SOJOURN

Roll through the terroir of the green hills and curves of the Santa Rita Hills AVA (American Viticultural Area).

START	END	LENGTH
Buellton	Melville Winery	29 miles; 50 mins

Drink in the beauty of these vineyards, planted mostly with pinot noir and chardonnay, though other varietals like grenache, syrah and viognier are cultivated. Start the loop in ❶ **Buellton** with your picnic fixings packed, taking Santa Rosa Rd to the west. About 6 miles down the bucolic, winding road, stop to taste at ❷ **Peake Ranch**, in its contemporary, airy tasting room with an outdoor patio looking out to the vineyard. On the same road offshoot, try the beautiful wines of ❸ **Alma Rosa Winery & Vineyards** (reservations required), which organically farms its grapes in an intentional commitment to sustainability. Alma Rosa was founded by Richard Sanford, the first vintner to plant pinot noir in Santa Barbara County in 1971.

Just before Santa Rosa Rd intersects with Hwy 1, ❹ **The Hilt Estate** offers sublime tastings (appointment only). Turn right on Hwy 1 to drive the two miles to Lompoc's industrial ❺ **Wine Ghetto**, where you can sample multiple wineries' offerings efficiently if you're pressed for time. Return to Buellton on Rte 246 heading east. You'll find the tasting experience to be relaxed and playful at the multigenerational, family-run ❻ **Babcock Winery**, which often has live music and other fun events. Next-door neighbor stalwart ❼ **Melville Winery** offers a more elegant setting, either in the civilized tasting room or in the front vineyard.

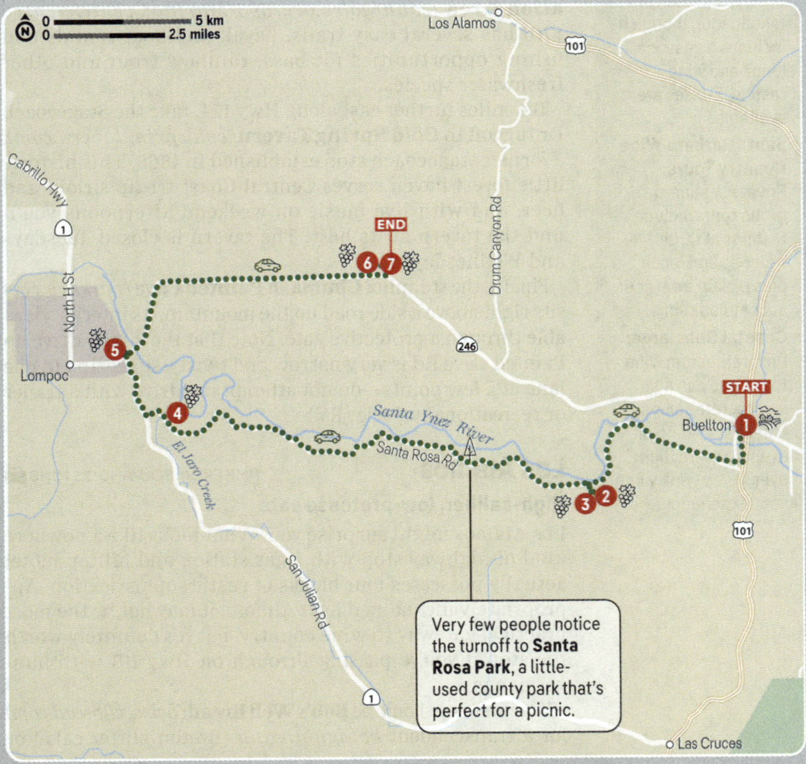

Very few people notice the turnoff to **Santa Rosa Park**, a little-used county park that's perfect for a picnic.

BEST WINE TOURS

Sustainable Wine Tours: This small company brings guests to private tastings at wineries that aren't open to the public.

Destination Vine: A concierge-style outfit with personable guides and customizable tours, run by two women who have long-standing relationships with valley wineries.

Santa Barbara Wine Country Cycling Tours: More of a cycling than a tasting tour, though it includes a seasonal lunch and wine tasting. E-bikes are available.

Santa Barbara Wine Country Tours: Private or shared group tours include tastings at three wineries and lunch, plus pickup from your accommodations.

Coastal Concierge: Private, custom wine tours; you can also incorporate sailing, horseback riding or even a private flight over wine country into your experience.

biodynamic and regenerative-minded vineyards, the women- and Native-run **Camins 2 Dreams** *(camins2dreams.com)* has an inclusive tasting room here.

Find a map of the Wine Ghetto at *explorelompoc.com*, and let your tasting-room hosts suggest neighboring wineries to discover something new to you, just steps away.

At some point you'll probably want to grab a bite, in which case you should head straight to **Eye on I** *(theeyeoni.com)*, about 1.5 miles from the Ghetto on North I St. A cousin to local fave **Industrial Eats** (p357), it consistently offers wood-fired pizza on the menu, which otherwise changes seasonally and is hand-written on butcher paper on the wall. Open Tuesday through Saturday, it has a cluttered, industrial feel that extends to its funky back patio.

San Marcos Pass

TIME FROM SOLVANG: **20 MINS**

Detours off Highway 154

The drive over San Marcos Pass (Hwy 154) between Santa Barbara and the Santa Ynez Valley is a gorgeous one, with a few detours worth making if you have time for a relaxed drive. Along much of the way, the winding mountain pass has only two lanes, so it's particularly important to be or designate a sober driver.

About 12 miles from Solvang, **Cachuma Lake Recreation Area** *(countyofsb.org/693/Marina; vehicle entry $10)* has several easy trails, kayak and boat rentals and fishing opportunities for bass, rainbow trout and other freshwater species.

Ten miles further east along Hwy 154, take the Stagecoach Dr turnoff to **Cold Spring Tavern** *(coldspringtavern.com)*, a former stagecoach stop established in 1868. This historic little forest haven serves Central Coast tri-tip sirloin and beer, and with live music on weekend afternoons you'll find the tavern at its best. The tavern is closed Tuesdays and Wednesdays.

Finally, the stunning **Chumash Painted Cave** *(parks.ca.gov)* sits right above a side road up the mountain, its interior viewable through a protective gate. Note that the 2-mile drive up Painted Cave Rd is very narrow and twisty, squeezing to one lane at a few points – do not attempt the drive with a trailer or recreational vehicle (RV).

Los Alamos

TIME FROM SOLVANG: **25 MINS**

High-caliber, low-pretense eats

Los Alamos might surprise you. What looks like a nowhere kind of highway stop with a gas station and hilltop motel actually possesses four blocks of rustic sophistication. Appropriately nicknamed Lost Almost, it may not be the most practical gateway to wine country, but it's definitely worth the stop if you're passing through on Hwy 101 with hunger pangs.

Your first stop should be **Bob's Well Bread** *(bobswellbread.com)* for a transcendent *kouign amann* (Breton butter cake) or

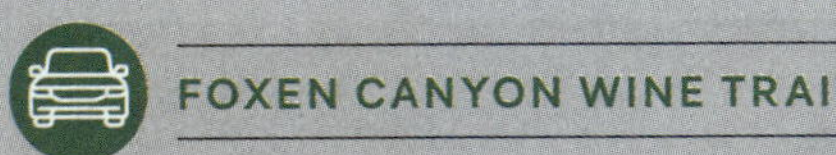

FOXEN CANYON WINE TRAIL

The winding Foxen Canyon Rd invites you to drink in the scenery of bucolic ranches and a sea of vineyard rows.

START	END	LENGTH
Demetria Estate	Presqu'ile	27 miles; 1 hr

Foxen Canyon, the region's oldest AVA (American Viticultural Area), is home to some of Santa Barbara County's most venerable vineyards. Its hilly topography and microclimates create ideal conditions for different varietals to thrive: you'll travel from Rhône-heavy territory to a Burgundian clime as you head closer to the coast.

Tastings at 1 **Demetria Estate** are by appointment only, but visiting this estate is like scoring the cheapest ticket to Tuscany you'll ever find. Grapes here are organically and biodynamically grown, an added bonus at this gorgeous estate tasting experience. Next on the road northward, one of the oldest wineries in the Santa Maria AVA, 2 **Foxen Winery** runs a sustainable operation and a ranch-style, solar-powered tasting room serving spectacular pinot noir, syrah and chardonnay. Half a mile up the road, their 3 **Shack** pours Bordeaux and Italian varietals. Continue almost two miles to the sharp right onward to 4 **Rancho Sisquoc Winery** – reserve picnic boxes ahead of your tasting and soak in the historic atmosphere. End by pairing a picnic with delicate pinot noir and/or pinot bubbles at peaceful, female-run 5 **Riverbench Vineyard & Winery**. The cozy ranch house and outdoor tables are lovely settings. Or opt for a more energizing finish to your day with live music, bites and wine at 6 **Presqu'ile**, whose scene-stealing tasting room and amphitheater complement their beautiful wines.

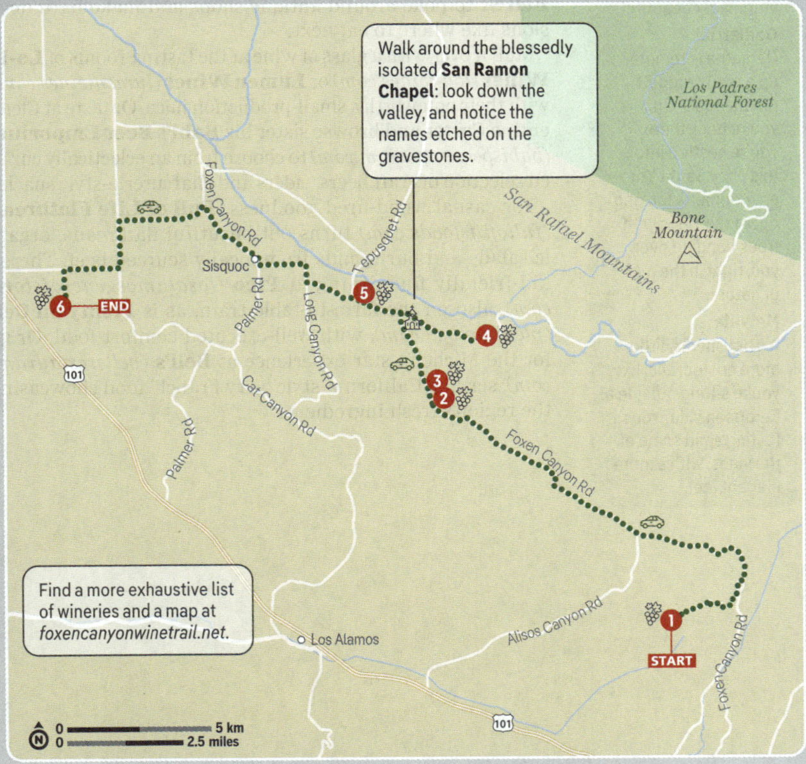

Walk around the blessedly isolated **San Ramon Chapel**: look down the valley, and notice the names etched on the gravestones.

Find a more exhaustive list of wineries and a map at *foxencanyonwinetrail.net*.

PICNICKING AT ESTATE WINERIES

Amy Christine, co-owner and winemaker at Holus Bolus & The Joy Fantastic, shares her picks for winery picnics.

Peake Ranch
Their tasting room is in the vineyard, which is not the case everywhere. So you're sitting in the vines, away from the highway – it's quiet, modern, very comfortable and stunningly beautiful.

Demetria
Demetria is remote, up a really rugged private road. Once you're back there you're nestled into this cozy Santa Ynez environment, looking out at the vines with trees hanging over you, right in the midst of nature.

Melville
It's polished, a little more aristocratic, like you're sitting outside a European villa. You're tasting amid some of the vines, with a more elegant feel.

BUYENLARGE/GETTY IMAGES

Chumash Painted Cave (p362)

sit-down breakfast. For the gluten-free, the hearty brick of seeded GF bread is worth picking up. From here, roam along **Bell St** to poke around antique shops and make hard decisions like where to eat next.

Mull it over with a glass of wine at the tasting rooms of **Lo-Fi Wines** *(lofi-wines.com)* or **Lumen Wines** *(lumenwines.com)*, with their noteworthy, small-production juice. Or taste at Clementine Carter and browse sister biz **Babi's Beer Emporium** *(babisbeeremporium.com)* to choose from an eclectically curated selection of craft beers, ciders and charcuterie-style snacks.

For casual wood-fired goodness, **Full of Life Flatbread** *(fulloflifefoods.com)* turns out beautiful flatbreads, organic salads and burnt ends from locally sourced beef. There's kid-friendly fine dining at **Pico** *(losalamosgeneralstore.com)*, also on the farm-to-table train, as is **Plenty on Bell** *(plentyonbell.com)*, with well-executed comfort food. Or go for the Michelin-star experience at **Bell's** *(bellsrestaurant.com)*, serving California-style 'very Franch' food showcasing the region's fresh ingredients.

Ventura

LOW-KEY VIBES | COASTAL CULTURE | OCEAN RECREATION

Often overlooked by visitors in favor of Santa Barbara, Ventura is SB's more salt-of-the-earth sister, underrated only because she lacks the movie-star sheen. This coastal city (officially known as San Buenaventura) has an attractive old town anchored by the Mission San Buenaventura, plus a beachfront promenade and slightly retro little harbor village.

Ventura and its surrounding area were originally occupied by the Ventureño Chumash people, who built seafaring canoes and were skilled at spear-fishing. During the era of Spanish colonialization, Junípero Serra established Mission San Buenaventura in 1782, the last of the California missions. In the early 1900s, oil drilling boomed, and some of East Main St's architecture has survived from that period.

Ventura harbor is the jumping-off point for Channel Islands National Park, about an hour's boat ride across the Santa Barbara Channel. It's also the coastal gateway to Ojai, nestled in the Topatopa mountain range.

GETTING AROUND

Downtown Ventura is walkable, with plenty of free or cheap parking. Because so many people who work in Santa Barbara live in Ventura County, the $4 (one-way) Coastal Express bus runs several trips daily during commuting hours from Ventura to Santa Barbara. It's also possible to take the local Amtrak service between Ventura and Santa Barbara County towns.

TOP TIP

Adjacent to Ventura, the agricultural city of Oxnard is California's biggest strawberry producer. Pick up super-fresh, juicy berries from local farmstands, such as those at the T-junction of Telephone Rd and Olivas Park Dr.

Old-Town Ventura

Visit the mission, old town and botanical garden

Ventura's retro old town lies along East Main St, with the beaux-arts **City Hall** looming on the hill above and the beach

EATING IN VENTURA: SEAFOOD SPOTS

Spencer Makenzie's: This casual counter-service joint slings ceviche, fish tacos, ahi pockets and poke a little eastward of old town. *11am-8pm* $

Brophy Bros: Upstairs institution with harbor views and a busy, boisterous atmosphere for huge platters of seafood and strong drinks. *11am-9pm Sun-Thu, to 10pm Fri & Sat* $$

Rumfish y Vino: Lovely patio whisks you to coastal Spain, with excellent seafood and a Latin twist in old-town Ventura. *from 11.30am Mon-Sat, from 11am Sun* $$

Lure Fish House: Sustainably caught fresh fish, organic regional farm produce and California wines. *11.30am-9pm Sun-Thu, to 10pm Fri & Sat* $$

SIGHTS
1 Mission San Buenaventura
2 San Buenaventura State Beach
3 Surfers Point
4 Ventura Botanical Gardens
5 Ventura River Estuary

ACTIVITIES
6 Ventura Promenade

SLEEPING
7 Crowne Plaza Ventura Beach
8 Hotel San Buena

EATING
9 Jolly Oyster
10 Lure Fish House
11 Rumfish y Vino
12 Spencer Makenzie's

DRINKING & NIGHTLIFE
13 Bank of Italy Cocktail Trust
14 Leashless Brewing
15 Rocks & Drams
16 Topa Topa Brewing Company

SHOPPING
17 Patagonia

a few blocks below. Closed to vehicle traffic, this section of East Main St is a pleasant stretch for window-shopping, with gobs of indie and thrift shops, and places for a bite of Thai food or tacos.

Mission San Buenaventura welcomes visitors on the western end of Main St and remains a community parish church. In the peaceful garden area, its olive mill and brick filtering tank from the mission's aqueduct still stand.

For a short hike you can do right from downtown, **Ventura Botanical Gardens** *(venturabotanicalgardens.com; $7)* – free on Fridays, closed on Mondays – has a 2-mile graded trail zigzagging up a ridge. The steep path shows off expansive views of the city and ocean as you climb through South American and South African garden areas.

Otherwise, walk along the **Ventura Promenade** to soak up salt air with the cyclists, skaters, joggers and dog-walkers enjoying the paved pathway. A bike and pedestrian path begins off Main St (park in the small lot just west of the Hwy 33 overpass), following the Ventura River down to the **Ventura River Estuary** before heading east along the beach. Watch the surfers – or paddle out into the lineup yourself – at **Surfers Point**. From here, you can walk two to three miles to **San Buenaventura State Beach**, where on weekends you can top off your beach day with freshly shucked oysters at the **Jolly Oyster** *(thejollyoyster.com)*, a seafood shack in the state park.

GREAT PACIFIC ENV(IRON)MENTAL WORKS

Yvon Chouinard founded pioneering outdoor clothing brand **Patagonia** *(patagonia.com)* in Ventura. In 1972, he set up shop in the distinctive yellow **Great Pacific Iron Works** building, where Patagonia's HQ still operates today, as does its flagship retail shop.

Chouinard's unconventional business practices always dovetailed with his core beliefs – he is an environmentalist to his bones.

The nonprofit 1% for the Planet was co-founded in 2002; its member companies donate 1% of their profits to collectively support environmental causes. In 2022 Patagonia announced its partnership with the purpose-built nonprofit Holdfast Collective to which Patagonia's excess profits are plowed, to fund environmental conservation and address climate change.

DRINKING IN VENTURA: DOWNTOWN

Bank of Italy Cocktail Trust: Named for the historic building it occupies; also serves Italian-style bites. *4pm-midnight Mon-Thu, 2pm-1am Fri & Sat, 2pm-midnight Sun*

Rocks & Drams: Craft cocktails, great happy hour specials and regularly programmed live music and DJs. *5-10pm Mon-Thu, 5pm-midnight Fri, 3pm-midnight Sat, 3-9pm Sun*

Leashless Brewing: Organic, beer in the Belgian style, including gluten-free options. Occasional live music. *4-9pm Tue & Wed, 4-10pm Thu, 4-11pm Fri, 1-11pm Sat, 1-8pm Sun*

Topa Topa Brewing Company: Good vibes and ethics on so many levels besides the great beer; check the calendar for events. *noon-9pm Mon-Thu, to 10pm Fri & Sat, to 8pm Sun*

Beyond Ventura

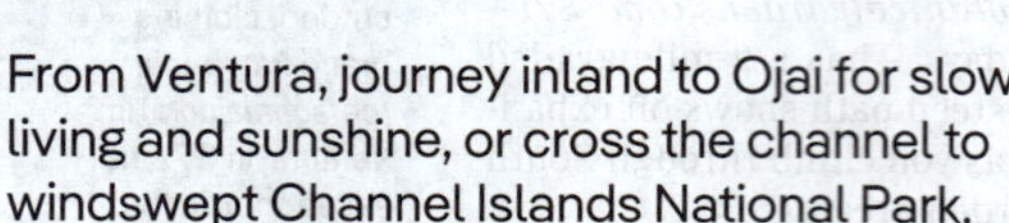

From Ventura, journey inland to Ojai for slow living and sunshine, or cross the channel to windswept Channel Islands National Park.

Places

GETTING AROUND

Downtown Ojai is small enough to explore on foot once you've arrived (it's a 25-minute drive from Ventura). Journeys beyond, from Meiners Oaks (3 miles) to nearby trailheads, require a car drive or bicycle ride.

On the Channel Islands, you'll rely on your own feet on land or paddle power on the water.

When the coast is cool and tinged with fog, chances are good that the sun is shining in Ojai. About 20 minutes' drive into the oaky inland valley transports you to a different world altogether, where citrus groves and horse country meet spiritual seekers and Hollywood refugees. The lovely nest of a valley exudes good energy for rejuvenating and recreating.

Offshore, the Channel Islands topography defines the horizon line. Traveling across the channel is a 1½-hour journey over marine wilderness, where dolphin and whale encounters are the norm. Hiking on the wild, windswept islands is witnessing what the coastal mainland might have looked like a thousand years ago.

Channel Islands National Park

TIME FROM VENTURA: **1½ HRS**

Day-tripping to Santa Cruz Island

Harbor seals bark your way out as your boat departs Ventura Harbor into the **Santa Barbara Channel**. From there, it's all eyes on the ocean's surface as you scan for whale spouts or dolphins racing your vessel. It's not that unusual to find your boat in the middle of a superpod of dolphins numbering in the hundreds, or to have a curious humpback whale approach as the boat idles.

Once you dock at the island, it's yours to explore on foot. **Santa Cruz Island** is the most accessible of the five-island chain, with the most frequent boats making daily trips in high season. At **Scorpion Anchorage**, displays explain the island's human history, flanked with antique ranching equipment rusting in the sun. The 2-mile **Cavern Point Loop** heads through the campground and up to a bluff trail to a lovely overlook of offshore arches, ocean and distant mainland California. A longer 5-miler goes to a viewpoint on **Potato Harbor** and the islands beyond.

Alternatively, meet up with your guide and suit up for **kayaking** into sea caves and isolated coves, exploring the ecosystem on the island's fringe. As you paddle, you'll marvel at the coppery blades of kelp swaying in contrast with the clear blue water, poppy-orange garibaldi (California's state marine fish) darting within the kelp bed and bristling reef beneath.

BRAM REUSEN/SHUTTERSTOCK

Scorpion Anchorage

Island camping

Imagine waking up to the tranquility of central California's landscape as it was when wild and in ecological balance. Camping on the Channel Islands gifts you with the luxury of immersing yourself in something akin to that.

Exploring one of these offshore sanctuaries after day-trippers have departed for the mainland you'll get a taste of the rugged survival of the original Channel Islands people and the peace with which they lived. In fact, the name Chumash is derived from these island inhabitants, who were the 'makers of shell-bead money.'

In the Chumash creation story, the first people lived on **Limuw** (Santa Cruz Island) but had become too numerous to all remain there. Hutash (Mother Earth) told the people that they must cross over to the mainland on a rainbow she had created for them. Some of the people looked down as they crossed the rainbow bridge and were dizzied by the height, falling into the water. Hutash, not wishing to see them perish, turned them into dolphins, now considered by the Chumash as family – beautiful context for your channel passage.

Scorpion Canyon Campground on Santa Cruz Island has the most campsites (31), only a half-mile from the boat dock with potable water and vault toilets. If you're backcountry camping, you'll have to bring your own water and haul it to the designated campgrounds. Reserve campsites up to six months ahead at recreation.gov; cancellations do happen, so keep checking in.

Regardless of location, the super-intelligent ravens know how to unzip zippers and fearless little island foxes will steal silently away with unattended snacks, so it's key for wildlife health to lock down your food in the fox boxes.

ISLAND TOUR OPERATORS

Island Packers Cruises is the national park concessionaire running public transportation to and from the Channel Islands, departing from Ventura Harbor. If you rent or bring your own kayaks, they can also transport them with prior notice. They're also a fantastic choice for whale-watching trips on the channel.

To explore the waters of the national park, you can arrange kayaking and snorkeling day trips with **Channel Islands Adventure Company**. For divers and those with the time for deeper exploration, **Channel Islands Expeditions** operate their own vessels for multiday liveaboard trips to several of the islands.

BEST DAY SPAS

Spa Ojai: The full-on, decadent resort experience at Ojai Valley Inn, with private outdoor terraces, desert clay mud treatment, guided meditation and light-flooded common areas.

Day Spa of Ojai: Owner Kim Wachter's Chumash heritage influences her treatments at this cozy downtown spa offering massages and skincare.

Ojai Garden Spa: Gazebo massages outdoors in the garden of the Lavender Inn downtown; also offers skincare treatments.

Ojai Massage: Experienced professionals providing a range of bodywork and therapeutic massage. Outcalls to your accommodations can also be arranged.

Ojai Skin Revision: With a customized approach to skincare, Ojai's oldest day spa (formerly known as Body Essentials) has an infrared sauna and offers facial treatments and massage.

Ojai

TIME FROM VENTURA: **25 MINS**

Roaming the valley of the moon

Holiday with Hollywood escapees in the magical place that is Ojai. Taking its name from the Chumash word *'awhay'* for 'moon' (some say 'nest'), this valley has always attracted seekers, from spiritual philosopher Krishnamurti to contemporary urban dwellers lured, possibly, by the spiritual energy of Ojai's vortexes.

Downtown is defined by Ojai Ave. **Libbey Park**, with its pretty archways, has a fantastic playground, walking paths and picnic tables under the trees. Further back, catch outdoor concerts at **Libbey Bowl** *(libbeybowl.org)* amphitheater.

Along this side of Ojai Ave and its side streets you'll find wine-tasting rooms, local boutiques like the indoor/outdoor **Fig** *(figojai.com)*, and the gallery and theater of the **Ojai Art Center** *(ojaiartcenter.org)*, established in 1939.

People-watch from the corner patio of **Topa Topa Brewing Company** *(topatopa.beer)* with Asian pub fusion food (like *okonomiyaki* tots) from **Little Sama Ojai**. Try the Burmese tea-leaf salad at the sustainably minded **Dutchess** *(thedutchessojai.com)*, which also tempts with sumptuous pastries and an excellent wine list.

Across Ojai Ave, find art galleries, shops and honey tastings along the **Ojai Arcade**, which opens out to a plaza behind. The spectacular, cheerfully jam-packed Sunday morning **farmers market** sets up shop in the parking lot on East Matilija St just beyond the plaza. Stroll a few more blocks west along East Matilija St to browse the maze of aisles at cherished landmark **Bart's Books** *(bartsbooksojai.com)*, known as the 'world's largest outdoor bookstore,' founded in 1964.

Oh hi, outdoors

Hiking is the leisure activity of choice in Ojai, backed as it is by the Topatopa Mountains and Los Padres National Forest.

Easily accessed from town is the **Shelf Rd Trail** in the **Valley View Preserve** *(ovlc.org/valley-view-preserve)*, at the north end of Signal Rd in Ojai. This is a mostly flat hike with excellent views of the valley; make it an out-and-back or return through town. You'll also find the **Fox Canyon Trail** in the preserve, which you can connect with others for a more challenging loop hike.

Use your America the Beautiful parks pass or pay the day-use fee *($10)* for the easy, short hike to a waterfall (best in springtime) on the **Rose Valley Falls Trail** in the Sespe

EATING & DRINKING IN OJAI: OUR PICKS

Ojai Tortilla House: The window of opening hours at this authentic, hole-in-the-wall Mexican spot is limited, as is the menu. Cash only. *11am-2pm* **$**

Ojai Beverage Company: OBC is the place to refuel post-hike with a salmon salad or burger and a beer. *11am-9pm Tue-Thu & Sun, to 10pm Fri & Sat* **$**

Ojai Rôtie: Farm-to-picnic-table fare shines here, with housemade sourdough, roast chicken and local wine. *7.30-11am Sun, noon-3pm & 4-8pm Wed-Sun, to 8.30pm Fri & Sat* **$$**

Rory's Place: Locally sourced, fresh ingredients assembled in simple, sophisticated style. Oysters, roasted beets, salt-and-vinegar martinis: yes please. *5-10pm Wed-Mon* **$$**

JAY L CLENDENIN VIA GETTY IMAGES

Ventura River, Ojai

Wilderness, about 15 miles from Ojai on Hwy 33. Another Sespe hike is the **Piedra Blanca Trail**, with beautiful white sandstone boulders at the end, about 5 miles round trip with a creek crossing. Call or visit the **Ojai ranger station** *(fs.usda.gov/detail/lpnf)* for detailed info.

Closer to town, a kid-friendly trail is the flat, close to 1-mile hike at **Ojai Meadows Preserve** *(ovlc.org/omp)* that's good for birding as it passes wetlands and meadows with views of the mountains.

Rent bicycles at the **Mob Shop** *(themobshop.com)* on W Ojai Ave and ride along the **Ojai Valley Trail**, the Ojai section of the Ventura River Parkway Trail. Or take a trail-only sunset horseback ride in the Ventura River Valley Preserve to enjoy Ojai's 'pink moment' with **Ojai Valley Trail Riding Company** *(ojaivalleytrailridingcompany.com)*.

VENTURA RIVER PARKWAY TRAIL

Cycling the 16-mile **Ventura River Parkway Trail** from the Ventura River Estuary to Ojai is a fantastic way to experience the changing landscape from coast to inland valley. Running through local parks and natural preserve lands, the pedestrian-and-bike trail passes historical sites such as the **Ortega Adobe** and **mission aqueduct** along the way. Climbing through agricultural and open space before emerging into oak chaparral woodland, the trail eventually connects with the Ojai Valley Trail and heads into the heart of Ojai. Find a trail map at *friendsofventurariver.org*.

EATING IN MEINERS OAKS: RURAL GEMS

Farmer & the Cook: Run by an Ojai farmer/poet and cook couple, serving some of the most direct farm-to-table food at its cafe/market. *8am-4pm Mon-Wed, to 8pm Thu-Sun* $

Ojai Noodle House: Vietnamese food (not just noodles), with a covered patio and moody Southeast Asian bar. *11am-3pm & 4-9pm Wed-Sun* $

Ojai Deer Lodge: Ojai's oldest restaurant, serving panzanella and shishito peppers alongside burgers. *noon-8pm Wed-Thu, noon-9pm Fri, 11am-9pm Sat, 11am-8pm Sun* $$

The Ranch House: The original owners' ethos purportedly inspired Alice Waters' farm-to-table philosophy. Reservation only. *5-9pm Tue-Sun* $$$

Places We Love to Stay

$** Budget **$$** Midrange **$$$ Top End

Santa Barbara

MAP p346

Agave Inn $ Playful Mexican accents and a sun-splashed color palette create warm ambience in this updated Uptown motel. Family-size rooms have a kitchenette and pullout sofa beds.

Marina Beach Motel $ This whitewashed, pet-friendly motor lodge is a block from the beach, with tidy remodeled rooms, some with kitchenette, and complimentary beach cruisers to borrow.

Castillo Inn $ One of the best of the West Beach bunch. Rooms are large and bright, some with private terraces, with the Funk Zone, Stearns Wharf and harbor a short walk away.

Harbor House Inn $ Two blocks from the beach, this meticulously run inn offers bright, individually decorated studios and rooms, plus free loaner beach gear and bicycles.

Canary $$$ Stylish downtown Kimpton joint with rooftop pool and sunset-watching perch for cocktails. In-room spa services and Saturday yoga soothe away stress, but be aware of ambient street noise.

Hotel Californian $$$ This upscale spot puts the Funk Zone and waterfront within strolling distance, with a glamorous blend of Spanish Colonial and North African Moorish style.

El Encanto $$$ This enchanting 1920s classic in the Riviera neighborhood looks out over the city from its foothill perch, a real Santa Barbara refuge.

Gaviota Coast

Refugio State Beach Campground $ A lovely beachside campground with palms fringing the beach and tidepools to poke around in at low tide. Walk-in only from December 1 to March 31.

El Capitan Canyon $$ Glamp in cedar cabins with covered porches, or in canvas yurts with skylights for stargazing. All have picnic tables and firepits for barbecuing.

South County

Inn on Summer Hill $$ This cute Summerland B&B has a prime location with ocean views on one side, but be aware that it also overlooks the freeway and Amtrak railway.

Rosewood Miramar Beach $$$ An exceedingly enviable beachfront locale on Miramar Beach for a truly splurgy Montecito stay, with a range of luxurious garden and beachside rooms.

Solvang

MAP p355

Viking Inn $ A friendly little family-run motel done up in in bright white and astroturf lawn with Adirondack chairs on the western end of main street, Mission Dr.

Hamlet Inn $ A modern motel makeover with a bit of Danish flavor, crisp, comfortable rooms and a location right on Mission Dr in the heart of Solvang.

Hotel Corque $$ On the eastern end of town and adjacent to open space, the Corque has spacious and quiet rooms and a pool, and offers a visual break from all things Scandinavian.

The Landsby $$ Contemporary style and spacious suites surround a welcoming courtyard, with live music often featured at the lobby bar. Central location on Mission Dr.

Buellton & Santa Ynez

Flying Flags $ Hook up your own RV, check into a kitted-out Airstream, or choose a glamping tent, cabin or cottage at this Buellton RV resort that feels like summer camp.

Sideways Inn $ The Scandinavian design ends with the big windmill out front – enjoy modern accommodations, a pool, firepit and lounge after a day exploring.

Pea Soup Andersen's Inn $ The neighboring historic restaurant may have closed, but this Buellton hotel is still a great, reasonably priced choice for families, with a pool and outdoor games.

Hotel Ynez $$ Upstyled wine-country motel with an airy ranch feel and a relaxed garden setting between Santa Ynez and Solvang, with bocce, an adults-only pool and outdoor spaces for lounging.

Los Olivos

Fess Parker Wine Country Inn $$$ Find low-key luxury in the center of Los Olivos, where fireplaces come standard in spacious rooms, as do breakfast and a wine tasting.

The Inn at Mattei's Tavern $$$ Originally a stagecoach stop, Mattei's is now an eminently softer landing spot if you can swing it. It's also de rigueur for morning coffee.

Los Alamos

Alamo Motel $ A hip little Western-themed spot, centrally located on Bell St, with an inviting lawn, a firepit and a bar shack for socializing outdoors.

Skyview Los Alamos $$ Another remodeled retro number, this hilltop motel has a pool, restaurant and bar – it's near Bell St, but across the highway.

Victorian Mansion B&B $$ This attractive Victorian has a unique and ornate interior with themed rooms that go all-in, from a pirate lair to a hobbit hole.

Ventura

MAP p366

Crowne Plaza Ventura Beach $$ Yes, it's a chain hotel, but pickings are slim in Ventura, and you can't argue with beachfront property and easy access to old-town Ventura.

Hotel San Buena $$ From the bones of a former Elks Lodge springs a blend of modern and Spanish Revival design at this lovely boutique hotel, steps from old-town Ventura.

Ojai

Ojai Rancho Inn $ On the western approach into Ojai, this modernized mid-century motel has a pool and sauna, plus free bicycles that are useful for getting into town.

Hummingbird Inn $ A peaceful stucco-and-tile inn at the eastern end of Ojai on the edge of a residential neighborhood, with a pool, shaded lawn and little outdoor sitting nooks.

Caravan Outpost $$ Airstreams outfitted with modern comforts and a Southwestern aesthetic are arranged within little garden havens for privacy, with communal showers and toilets, a firepit and a fun community vibe.

Emerald Iguana Inn $$ Close to downtown Ojai, this boutique inn has comfortably boho rooms and standalone cottages in an attractive woodsy setting, with a pool and Jacuzzi.

Ojai Valley Inn & Spa $$$ A relaxed luxury resort with Spanish Colonial architectural style, a golf course and a dreamy spa, but also culinary classes and events celebrating regional bounty.

STEVE CUKROV/SHUTTERSTOCK

Hotel Californian

For places to stay in Los Angeles, see p438

UVL/SHUTTERSTOCK

Above: Downtown Los Angeles (p386); Right: Hollywood Boulevard (p380)

THE MAIN AREAS

Researched by
Ryan Ver Berkmoes

Los Angeles

CITY OF DREAMS

Balmy weather warms wave-kissed beaches at the Pacific edge of a vast tapestry of neighborhoods, holding sights and surprises that endlessly delight.

Los Angeles is many things to many people. It is a city of dreams, but has too much traffic. It enjoys perfect weather, but there are so many wildfires. It has the best sunsets, but the smog is terrible. And while all of this rings true in this vast metropolis, what's absolutely for sure is that nothing beats the pulsating, vivacious and infamous flair of Los Angeles.

For many, LA is Hollywood. The sign on a hillside. Famous faces behind sunglasses. The studio magic that captures hearts and minds. LA is also home to music legends: rap is synonymous with South LA and rock and roll is symbiotic with the Sunset Strip. It's where creatives bivouac in Downtown and the Arts District. Melrose is where shopping trends begin, while Koreatown never sleeps. Free-spirit vibes flourish in Venice and everyone celebrates the beaches over 75 miles of coast all the way to Malibu.

LA is also a kaleidoscope of cultures from over 140 countries, with nearly 220 languages spoken, creating an intricate web of diversity that connects deep beneath the surface. Can't travel abroad? Travel north, south, east and west in LA and you'll find a vibrant enclave for almost any culture you can name.

And that's part of LA's endless appeal for any visitor – it's so many places in one. Boyle Heights is not like Pasadena, Burbank is different from Compton, Los Feliz is not Beverly Hills and Chinatown is not West Hollywood. You get the idea. You can experience so many different places and never leave LA. Once you get the hang of the Metro and the freeways, you can range wide and you'll make the startling discovery that LA is one of the great walkable cities. Yes! Pick a neighborhood and you'll likely find a compact center with shops, sights, history and food and drink and, probably, more than one famous film location.

Looking ahead, LA is working hard to shake off 2025's wildfire and prep for the 2028 Summer Olympics. It has an incredible new building coming at LACMA and more exciting developments in its ceaseless reinvention.

SEAN PAVONE/SHUTTERSTOCK

Find Your Way

Los Angeles is a vast city known for its traffic with a side of chaos. It's simply not easy to get from here to there. In late afternoon, Santa Monica to Los Feliz (14 miles) can take 90 minutes. Use the expanding network of subways and light rail when possible.

Burbank & Universal Cit
p430
Universal Studios Hollywood

West Hollywood & Beverly Hills
p415
Academy Museu of Motion Picture
LACM

Santa Monica & Malibu
p421
Getty Center
Getty Villa
Santa Monica Pier
Venice Boardwalk

Venice & South Coast Beaches
p425
Los Angeles International Airport
Santa Monica Bay

0 — 5 km
0 — 2.5 miles

Warner Bros Studio Tour

Hollywood Bowl

Hollywood
p380

Griffith Park, Los Feliz & Echo Park
p396

Pasadena
p434

Huntington

Paramount Pictures

Los Angeles Dodgers

Koreatown, Miracle Mile & Fairfax
p407

Walt Disney Concert Hall

Broad

Grammy Museum

Downtown
p386

Exposition Park & South LA
p402

FROM THE AIRPORT

Huge Los Angeles International Airport (LAX) is the main airport, located in Inglewood. It's right off the I-405, which is often traffic-choked. The new Metro Rail K Line, due to open in 2026, will connect to the airport's elevated shuttle.

CAR

A car offers flexibility and the freedom to travel to the many corners of LA that are not easily reached by public transportation. But it also handcuffs you to being stuck in traffic, paying usurious parking lot rates or simply trying to find parking.

PUBLIC TRANSPORTATION

Billions are being spent to stitch together LA with a network of subways, light rail and commuter trains. Buses fill in the gaps and the entire system can be surprisingly efficient. Use map apps to plan trips. Use the TAP app to pay for rides.

RIDESHARE

Services like Uber and Lyft are great for providing the last mile of transportation after you've covered the bulk of the distance on Metro Rail. Once you see the cost of car rental and parking, rideshare fees become palatable.

Plan Your Days

Los Angeles is like the best of burritos: it's huge and filled with delights, so go slow and enjoy it one bite at a time.

PANDORA PICTURES/SHUTTERSTOCK

Venice Boardwalk (p425)

Day 1

Morning

- Walk all over your favorite stars on the **Hollywood Walk of Fame** (p380) and size up their handprints outside the **TCL Chinese Theatre** (p382).

Afternoon

- Hasten over to the **Original Farmers Market** (p412) and graze your way to a fresh and wonderful lunch. Just south, dig into movie magic at the extraordinary **Academy Museum of Motion Pictures** (p409). Next door, get a dose of fine art in the striking new building at **LACMA** (p409).

Evening

- After dinner at historic old Hollywood **Musso & Frank Grill** (p383), laugh it up with live comedy at the **Laugh Factory** (p417) or **Improv** (p414).

You'll Also Want To...

With about a million things to do in LA, here are a few things to do that give an idea of all the options.

HIT THE PIÑATA DISTRICT

Head to the busy **Piñata District** (p395), just south of the Arts District. The high ceilings are loaded with colorful characters and you can have lunch, a snack or a drink in the big open-air cafeterias.

GO ON A STUDIO TOUR

See where they filmed *Casablanca* and hundreds of other films and TV shows like *Friends* on the **Warner Bros Studio Tour** (p431) in Burbank. It's the best of the offerings from the major studios.

SEE AFRICAN AMERICAN LA ART

See what's on at **CAAM** (California African American Museum; p404), which has ever-changing exhibits by top artists and photographers. Then get wowed at the nearby California Science Center.

Day 2

Morning

● Explore Downtown LA (DTLA), reserving tickets in advance to the spectacular modern art at **Broad** (p387) and discover the city's Spanish heritage at **El Pueblo de Los Ángeles** (p393).

Afternoon

● Following lunch at **Grand Central Market** (p393), wander **Little Tokyo** (p394) and walk the busy streets of **Chinatown** (p391). Browse the galleries and shops in the **Arts District** and **Row DTLA** (p395).

Evening

● Have cocktails at **Everson Royce Bar** (p393) and then a sublime, modern meal at **Bavel** (p390). Enjoy an evening of music in the great acoustics of **Walt Disney Concert Hall** (p390). Book your tickets in advance.

Day 3

Morning

● Spend the morning using your prebooked admission at the **Getty Center** (p420), a spectacular synergy of art, architecture, landscaping and panoramic views.

Afternoon

● Have lunch at the innovative, produce-driven **Gjusta** (p427) in ever-eclectic Venice. Satiated, hunt down unique fashion, accessories and art along **Abbot Kinney Boulevard** (p427), then stroll, pedal or skate along the **Venice Boardwalk** (p425), taking in its street art, goofball souvenirs and acres of powdery sand.

Evening

● Wrap up the day in neighboring Santa Monica, catching a perfect SoCal sunset from **Santa Monica Pier** (p421) before heading up the coast to dinner with a view at **Nobu Malibu** (p424).

OBSERVE THE SUNSET

Head up to the landmark **Griffith Observatory** (p396) to watch the sun sink over the city in sprawling Griffith Park. It's a famous LA architectural treasure – and a good place to see the cosmos too.

WALK EVER-CHANGING BOYLE HEIGHTS

Go for a walk near Downtown in **Boyle Heights** (p391), the neighborhood built by waves of immigrants over the decades. See how it evolved from Eastern European Jews 100 years ago to Mexican Americans today.

CATCH A DODGERS GAME

Play ball! Get your tickets well ahead, then go see LA's much-loved **Dodgers** (p401) play at Dodger Stadium near Echo Park. Have a Dodger Dog in the park.

TOUR LA ON FOOT OR BIKE

See LA on a bike or on a hike with a tour by **Bikes & Hikes LA** (p419). One of its most popular is a 32-mile cycling jaunt that shows you 'LA in a Day.'

Hollywood

THE DREAM, THE REALITY, THE FAME

TOP TIP
Come early to Hollywood Blvd for the strictly Hollywood sights (Walk of Fame, forecourt of the Chinese Theatre), then skedaddle before the crowds swell during the day, filling the many attractions that aren't unique to the area (wax museums and the like).

The Hollywood area might be past its heyday, but its history is rich in stories of Californian glamour. The neighborhood is filled with iconic monuments, including the Egyptian and TCL Chinese Theatres, that even the excessive souvenir shops and tour buses can't taint. The Walk of Fame is part of the bread and butter of Hollywood and millions of visitors come each year to stroll down the tawdry but bustling city blocks to see the terrazzo sidewalks with their celebrity stars.

Look beyond the tourist-magnet landmarks of Hollywood Blvd and you'll discover a nuanced, multifaceted neighborhood where sometimes gritty streets are punctuated by edgy galleries, swinging bistros and the homes of long-gone movie stars. There are good restaurants and bars to be found here. And, yes, you can see a great movie – new or classic – in a golden-age movie palace or join Angelinos at a beloved venue like the Hollywood Bowl.

GETTING AROUND

Hollywood is well-served by the Metro Rail B Line with three stations along Hollywood Blvd, including iconic Hollywood/Vine.

Otherwise, Hollywood is easily walked. And you'll want to be on foot for spotting some of those 2800 names on the Walk of Fame. The only hills are the Hollywood Hills, where the stars live. Street parking is competitive and parking lots are expensive.

Hollywood's Galaxy of Stars

Follow the Walk of Fame

Hollywood Blvd is just tawdry enough that having an excuse to stare at the ground can be a good thing. The **Hollywood Walk of Fame** *(walkoffame.com)* gives you over 2800 reasons to keep your eyes down.

Jennifer Lopez, Bob Hope, Marilyn Monroe and Aretha Franklin are among the luminaries being sought out, worshipped, photographed and stepped on. Or, in the case of many names, pondered over, since production staff and writers are also honored. They've been adding the brass and pink-terrazzo stars since 1960.

Follow the galaxy along Hollywood Blvd between La Brea Ave and Gower St and on Vine St between Yucca St and Sunset Blvd. At least 30 new stars are added each year and the ceremonies often draw famous faces. Check the website for the schedule.

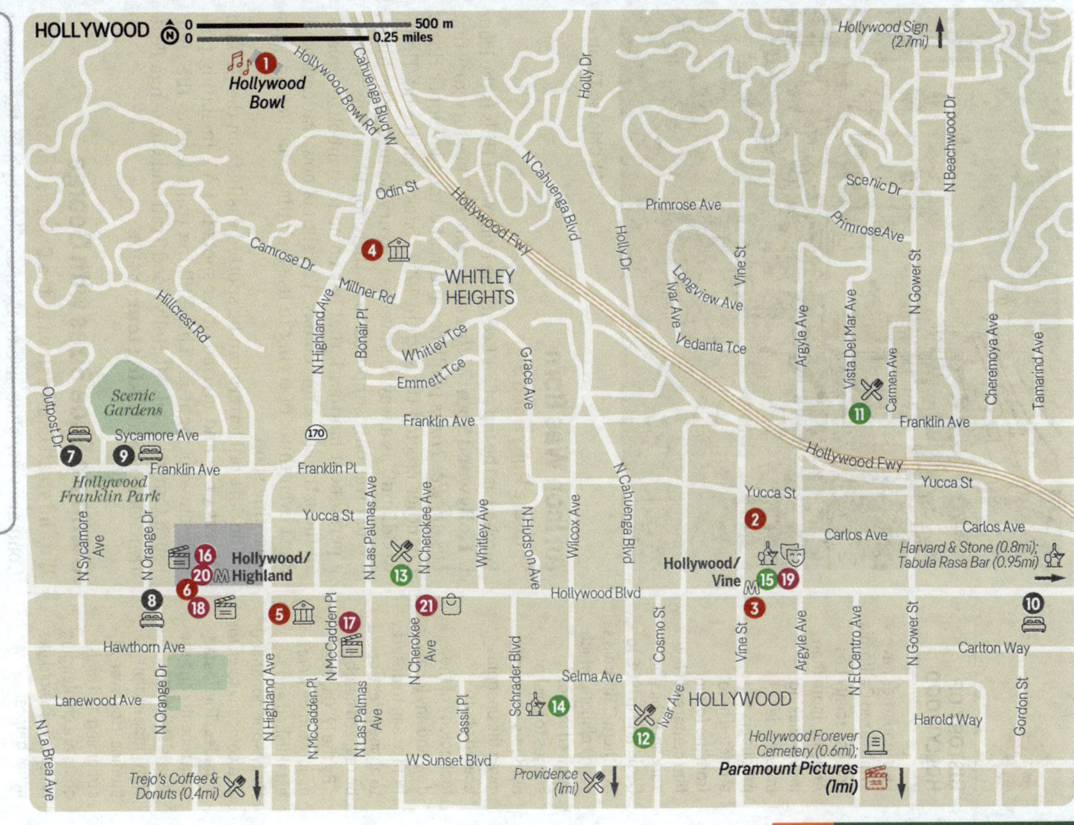

★ **HIGHLIGHTS**
1 Hollywood Bowl

SIGHTS
2 Capitol Records
3 Hollywood & Vine
4 Hollywood Heritage Museum
5 Hollywood Museum
6 Hollywood Walk of Fame
see 3 Taft Building

SLEEPING
7 Highland Gardens Hotel
8 Hollywood Roosevelt
9 Magic Castle Hotel
10 Vibe Hotel Hollywood

EATING
11 Clark Street Diner
12 Grandmaster Recorders
13 Musso & Frank Grill

DRINKING & NIGHTLIFE
14 Bar Lis
15 Frolic Room

ENTERTAINMENT
16 Dolby Theatre
17 Egyptian Theatre
18 El Capitan Theatre
19 Pantages Theatre
20 TCL Chinese Theatre

SHOPPING
21 Larry Edmunds Bookshop

HISTORY OF HOLLYWOOD

Few industries have symbolized California, and especially Los Angeles, more than movie-making. Independent producers were attracted here from the former film centers of New York and Chicago beginning in 1908 for Southern California's sunny climate, which allowed indoor scenes to be shot outdoors – essential given the unsophisticated photo technology of the day. And any location, from ocean to desert to alpine forest, could be realized nearby.

By the 1920s, the major studios were established and Hollywood continued as a company town for decades. This lasted until recently and the area is still dotted with independent studios. However, AI, streaming and high costs are challenging Hollywood's hold like never before.

GABRIELE MALTINTI/SHUTTERSTOCK

TCL Chinese Theatre

An Icon Was Born

Spot the Hollywood Sign

Perched at the top of Mt Lee in the Hollywood Hills is the iconic **Hollywood Sign** *(hollywoodsign.org)*. The story goes that *Los Angeles Times* publisher and real estate developer Harry Chandler erected the sign in 1923 (back then it said 'Hollywoodland') as a way to advertise luxury homes in the hills.

What was only supposed to be there for 18 months became a permanent landmark that has come to symbolize a place, an industry and a mythology. The sign is now trademarked; don't even think of trying to use a similar typeface for your smoothie shop.

The 50ft-tall letters can be spotted easily from the Griffith Observatory and myriad other spots in LA – including possibly on your flight in. Three hiking trails lead to the sign: Brush Canyon Trail, Mt Hollywood Trail and Cahuenga Peak Trail. Or go on a **hiking tour** (p419).

Compare Shoe Sizes with George

Big and small impressions at the Chinese Theatre

Compare your shoe size to George Clooney's in the famous forecourt of **TCL Chinese Theatre** *(tclchinesetheatres.com; forecourt free)*. Or why not try standing in Tom Hanks' shoes? Just find his footprints among the many in front of this world-famous movie palace. The exotic pagoda theater once known as Grauman's (first name Sid, who you'll see mentioned in the older imprints) – complete with temple bells and stone heaven dogs from China – has shown movies since 1927, when Cecil B DeMille's *The King of Kings* first flickered across the screen.

And it's not all feet. There's Betty Grable's legs, Whoopi Goldberg's braids, Daniel Radcliffe's wand and R2-D2's wheels. Inside, the cinema lives up to the promise. The main theater is one of the world's few that can show 70mm film prints on an Imax screen.

Dine Like a Star

Famous Musso & Frank

Hollywood history hangs in the thick air at **Musso & Frank Grill** *(mussoandfrank.com)*, Tinseltown's oldest eatery (since 1919). Charlie Chaplin came here to knock back vodka gimlets, Raymond Chandler penned scripts in the high-backed booths and movie deals were made on the old phone at the back. The menu favors old American classics like steaks, lobster thermidor and huge salads. It's in constant use as a shooting location; recent appearances include *Once Upon a Time in Hollywood* and anything associated with writer Michael Connelly and his detective Harry Bosch.

Mixed drinks like the famous martinis come with sidecars on ice so your chaser is right at hand. Note that Musso's has never been more popular, so be sure to book ahead. It's open from 5pm to 10pm Tuesdays through Sundays.

Hear Stars under the Stars

The magical Hollywood Bowl

The Hollywood Hills stalwart **Hollywood Bowl** *(hollywoodbowl.com)* hosted its first concert in 1922. Top headliners have ranged from Billie Holiday to the Beatles and it's still the summer home of the LA Philharmonic. The amphitheater stands out for its silhouette, which is reminiscent of – you guessed it – a bowl, with concentric shell-like arches. This is a live-show summer haven for Angelenos and although food and beverage prices can hit a high note (you can bring your own), the Hollywood Hills backdrop, the acoustics and the views make up for it all.

Tinseltown's Unmissable Attic

Star at the Hollywood Museum

Something of Hollywood's attic, the musty **Hollywood Museum** *(thehollywoodmuseum.com; adult/child $15/5)* is a temple to the stars and a mishmash of props, memorabilia and movie and TV costumes chaotically spread across four floors. The museum is housed inside the Max Factor Building, which launched in 1935 as a glamorous beauty salon for Hollywood's leading ladies. Track down the toupees worn by Frank Sinatra and John Wayne. A must-see is the 'Real to Reel' exhibit on LGBTQ+ issues in the industry. You'll also encounter various props, scripts, movie posters and even Marilyn Monroe's million-dollar dress, in addition to changing exhibits.

HOLLYWOOD'S BEST THEATERS

TCL Chinese Theatre: This legendary 1927 cinema is one of the world's few that can show 70mm film prints on an Imax screen. *tclchinesetheatres.com*

El Capitan Theatre: Disney premieres blockbusters at this 1926 movie palace and the *Jimmy Kimmel Show* is produced here – book tickets at *liota.com.*

Pantages Theatre: A 1930 art deco showplace and home of the Oscars through the 1950s. *broadwayinhollywood.com*

Egyptian Theatre: The first of Hollywood's opulent movie palaces. Lavishly restored, with hieroglyphs and sphinx heads. Netflix uses it for premieres and classic films. *egyptiantheatre.com*

Dolby Theatre: State-of-the-art theater in a shopping mall. The Oscars have been held here since 2001. *dolbytheatre.com*

DRINKING IN HOLLYWOOD: OUR PICKS

Frolic Room: This Hollywood dive has served everyone from Judy Garland to Charles Bukowski. Toast the fabulous cartoon mural. *11am-2am*

Harvard & Stone: Lures partiers with bands, DJs and burlesque troops working their saucy magic. It's ski lodge meets steampunk factory, with a rockabilly soul. *9pm-2am*

Bar Lis: Hollywood's all around the rooftop lounge of the hip Thompson Hollywood. There's a bit of a posh Med vibe (Cannes, anyone?). *6pm-midnight*

Tabula Rasa Bar: Away from the glitz, this unpretentious wine bar gets everything right with well-picked tunes and regular live gigs. Rear terrace. *2pm-midnight*

THE 'FIRST' BEVERLY HILLS

For a taste of Old Hollywood, walk north up Ivar Ave from Hollywood Blvd to the narrow streets of **Whitley Heights**, an area peppered with beautiful Moorish, Renaissance and Italianate-style villas. This was the city's first 'Beverly Hills' and it was close to the silent-era movie studios. Developed in the early 1900s, the neighborhood was home to all the A-listers of silent-era Hollywood. Stories abound of famous names racing horses on the hilly streets and tying them up in front of Hollywood Blvd watering holes. By the 1930s, Beverly Hills was luring everyone west. Innumerable films were shot here. The Alto Nido Apartments (1851 N Ivar Ave) were used for the initial home of the ill-fated Joe Gillis in *Sunset Boulevard*.

Hollywood's Last Great Studio

Tour Paramount Studios

Indiana Jones, The Godfather and *Ironman* are among the blockbuster series that originated at **Paramount Pictures**, the country's second-oldest movie studio (1914) and the only major one still in Hollywood proper.

Two-hour golf-cart **tours** *(paramountstudiotour.com; from $69)* of the studio complex are offered year-round, taking in the back lots and sound stages. Passionate, knowledgeable guides offer fascinating insights into the studio's history and the movie-making process in general. VIP tours include a meal, but are not worth the much higher fee. Fans of *Star Trek* will want to follow Leonard Nimoy Way to the sound stages where the original TV show was shot.

Resting Place for the Stars

Stroll Hollywood Forever Cemetery

Paradisiacal landscaping, vainglorious tombstones and epic mausoleums (plus a view of Paramount Studios over the wall) at **Hollywood Forever Cemetery** *(hollywoodforever.com; free)* make for an appropriate resting place for some of Hollywood's most iconic dearly departed. Residents include Rudolph Valentino, Cecil B DeMille, Mel Blanc (his tombstone reads, 'That's all folks'), Jayne Mansfield, Judy Garland, punk rockers Johnny and Dee Dee Ramone, *Golden Girls* star Estelle Getty, Burt Reynolds and David Lynch.

Recalling Hollywood's Early Days

When movies were silent

Hollywood's first feature-length film, Cecil B DeMille's *The Squaw Man* (1914), was shot in this building, which was originally set at the corner of Selma and Vine Sts. DeMille went on to co-found Paramount and had the barn moved to the lot in the '20s. The building is now the fascinating **Hollywood Heritage Museum** *(hollywoodheritage.org; adult/child $14/free)*, which does a deep dive into pre-talkie history.

Mid-Century Landmark

Spot the Capitol Records building

You'll have no trouble recognizing the iconic 1956 **Capitol Records** tower, one of LA's great mid-century buildings. Designed by Welton Becket, it resembles a stack of records

EATING IN HOLLYWOOD: OUR PICKS

Providence: Michael Cimarusti's fine dining is the ultimate LA experience, offering the finest seafood, service and stunt-free cuisine. *6-9pm Tue-Sat* **$$$**

Grandmaster Recorders: Buzzing bistro with Italian flavors; the airy dining room was once home to the namesake recording studio. Rooftop bar. *5-10pm Tue-Sat* **$$$**

Clark Street Diner: Legendary coffee shop has been in movies *(Swingers)* and served actors and writers nursing bottomless cups of java. *7am-9pm* **$$**

Trejo's Coffee & Donuts: Standout in a town known for doughnuts. Owned by Danny Trejo *(Heat)*, the goods reflect his Mexican heritage. *7am-4pm* **$**

ALEX MILLAUER/SHUTTERSTOCK

Paramount Pictures

topped by a stylus blinking out 'Hollywood' in Morse code. Some of music's biggest stars have recorded hits in the building's basement studios, including Nat King Cole, Frank Sinatra, the Beatles, Katy Perry and Sam Smith. Outside on the sidewalk, Garth Brooks and John Lennon have their stars.

Hollywood's Literary Hub

Find it at Larry Edmunds Bookshop

For decades, the **Larry Edmunds Bookshop** *(larryedmunds.com)*, a cluttered old-school shop, has been the place to go for all types of entertainment industry books, new and used. You can find out-of-print bios of long-dead celebs mixed with classic tomes on acting and scriptwriting techniques. Browse the bins of lobby cards for classic films and studio stills. They have a huge range of TV and movie scripts.

It hosts events with industry luminaries who have books to sign. Look on the walls for notable mementos, such as a check for a book purchase from Lucille Ball.

Find a Famous Corner

Hollywood and Vine

If you'd turned on the radio in the 1920s and '30s, chances were you'd hear a broadcast 'brought to you from **Hollywood and Vine**.' The corner still has some cachet even if the reality pales. However, take a moment at the southeast corner of the intersection for Hollywood's first high-rise office tower, the 12-story **Taft Building**. Dating back to 1923, its former tenants include Charlie Chaplin and the Academy of Motion Picture Arts and Sciences.

BEST FILMS ABOUT HOLLYWOOD

Sunset Boulevard (1950): Director and screenwriter Billy Wilder at his best, plumbing the dark side of fame and Hollywood's delusions.

The Player (1992): Robert Altman brings decades of experience on the front lines to this biting satire about the moral rot at the heart of studio execs.

La La Land (2016): Timeless musical of plucky kids hoping to make it big in Hollywood.

The Artist (2011): Won the Oscar for best picture for its story of the often-brutal late-1920s transition from silent pictures to talkies.

A Star Is Born: Pick your version (1937, 1954, 1976, 2018) of the classic drama about fame and tragedy.

Downtown

HISTORY, CULTURE, STROLLING AND FOOD

TOP TIP

LA's intractable housing issues manifest fully here. There are many people living on the streets. This is also the original home of Skid Row (it's the neighborhood between 4th and 7th Sts east of Los Angeles St). The usual cautions about personal safety apply across Downtown.

Downtown Los Angeles is not your typical downtown area: it's relatively small compared to others in the US and is made up of smaller, diverse neighborhoods that all converge together.

Take Manhattan, add a splash of Mexico City, a dash of Tokyo, shake and pour. Your drink: Downtown LA. Rapidly evolving, DTLA (the preferred moniker) is the city's most intriguing patch, where cutting-edge architecture and killer modern-art museums contrast sharply with blaring mariachi tunes, Chinese grocers, abject poverty, old architectural gems and intriguing restaurants, bars, galleries and boutiques, especially in the Arts District.

It's a place of surprises: one corner can be full of life, the next could be struggling; another turn could lead you to spectacular museums and art exhibits and still another could take you to what feels like a different country and time. It's a place where shops hawking $99 suits mix with an artist's personal vision for the future.

GETTING AROUND

Downtown is the hub of LA's transit. All the Metro Rail Lines come together here, from the subways to the light rail. At beautiful Union Station, there are regional Metrolink commuter trains and local Amtrak trains north to Santa Barbara and south to San Diego, plus various long-distance trains.

Pricey parking is easily found, although the surrounding freeways are often traffic-clogged – try to take Metro Rail. LA's center is flat and walkable, although distances can add up, like from the Arts District to Chinatown (2½ miles). DASH buses provide local service around Downtown (50¢).

CHIZHEVSKAYA EKATERINA/SHUTTERSTOCK

Walt Disney Concert Hall (p390) and the Broad

DTLA's Striking Museum

Be dazzled at the Broad

The **Broad** (rhymes with 'road'; *thebroad.org; free*) is a must-visit for anyone with the slightest interest in postwar and contemporary artworks. It houses the world-class collection of the Broads, local philanthropists and billionaire real-estate developers. They amassed more than 2000 postwar pieces by dozens of heavy hitters, including Cindy Sherman, Jeff Koons, Andy Warhol, Roy Lichtenstein, Robert Rauschenberg, Keith Haring and Kara Walker.

Among the many blockbuster exhibits here is Yayoi Kusama's immersive **Infinity Mirrored Room**. When it's your turn to view the installation, you'll enter a room that's both an artwork and an entire world of light and color. With your reservation to see the work, you can tour the museum and you'll receive a text message when there's an opening for you to go in. Wait times are dynamic, as some people spend less time inside than you'd think.

Once you've eyed up the temporary exhibitions on the lobby floor, an escalator whisks you up through a narrow tunnel to the 35,000-sq-ft 3rd-floor gallery, where Jeff Koons charms visitors with his giant bunch of stainless-steel tulips. The surrounding galleries rotate works from the Broad's permanent collection, considered one of the world's most prominent holdings of postwar and contemporary artworks. These include a second interactive installation by Yayoi Kusama.

Longing for Eternity.
The museum docents are knowledgeable. The Broad has an excellent website geared toward the browsers on phones that

continued on p390

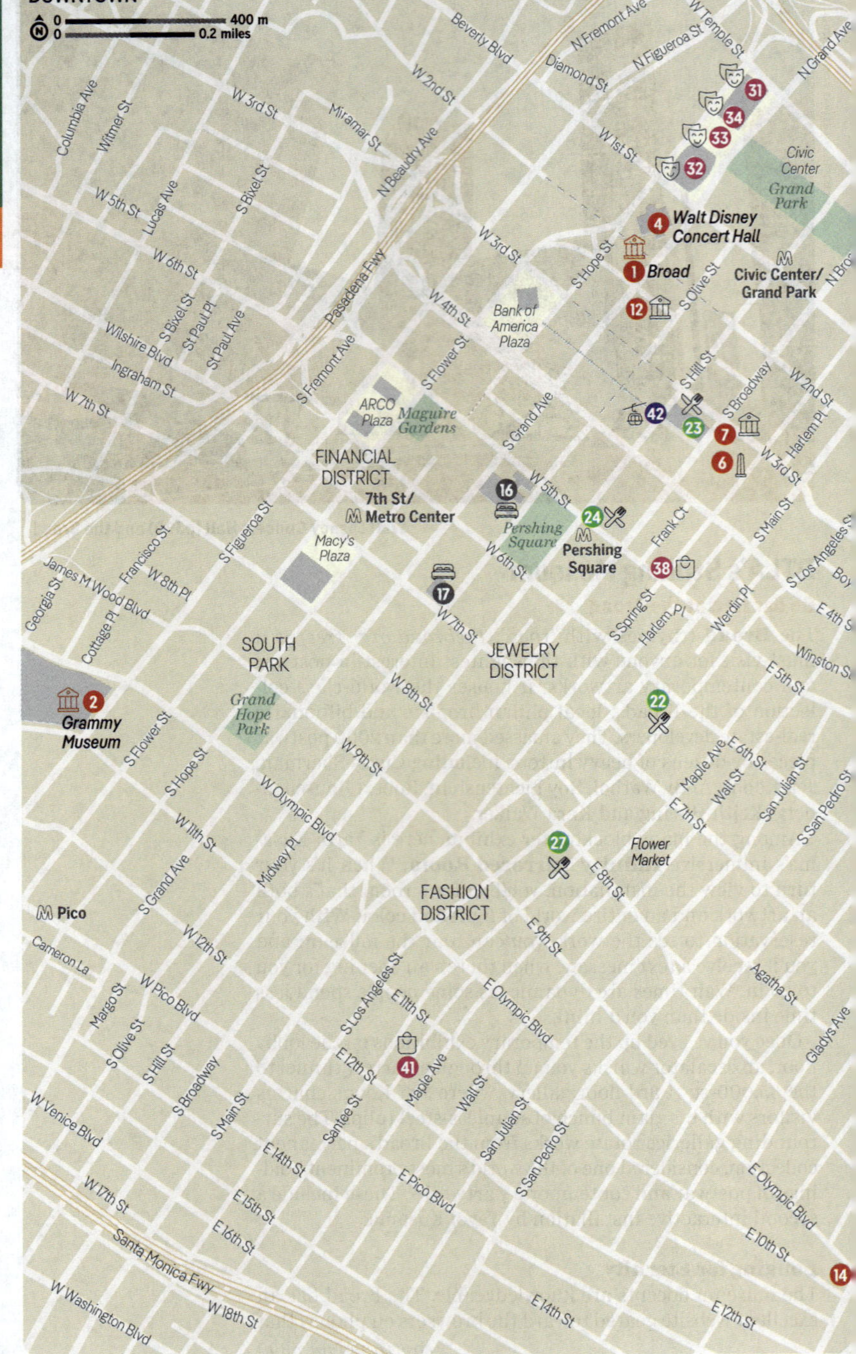
DOWNTOWN
0 400 m
0 0.2 miles
Walt Disney Concert Hall
Broad
Civic Center/ Grand Park
Civic Center
Grand Park
Bank of America Plaza
ARCO Plaza
Maguire Gardens
FINANCIAL DISTRICT
7th St/ Metro Center
Pershing Square
Macy's Plaza
SOUTH PARK
Grand Hope Park
JEWELRY DISTRICT
Grammy Museum
Flower Market
FASHION DISTRICT
Pico

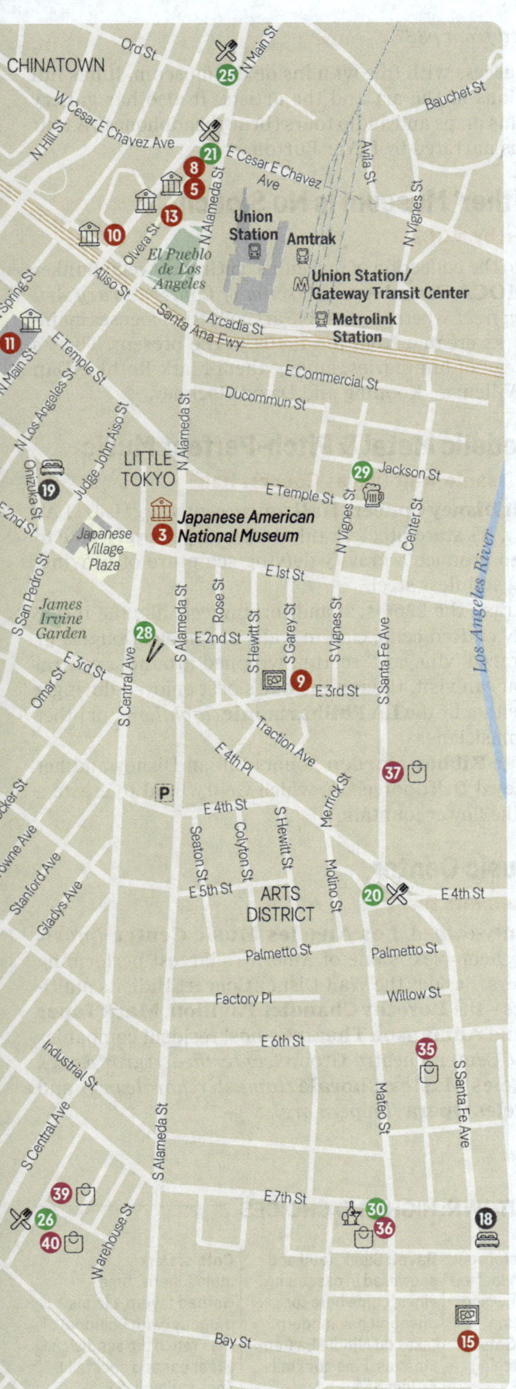

HIGHLIGHTS
1 Broad
2 Grammy Museum
3 Japanese American National Museum
4 Walt Disney Concert Hall

SIGHTS
5 Avila Adobe
6 Biddy Mason Memorial Park
7 Bradbury Building
8 El Pueblo de Los Ángeles
9 Hauser & Wirth
10 LA Plaza
11 Los Angeles City Hall
12 MOCA Grand Ave
13 Museum of Social Justice
14 Piñata District
15 Webber 939

SLEEPING
16 Biltmore Los Angeles
17 Hotel Per La
18 Kodō Hotel
19 Miyako Hotel Los Angeles

EATING
20 Bavel
21 Cielito Lindo
22 Cole's
see 23 Eggslut
23 Grand Central Market
24 Perch
25 Philippe the Original
26 Pizzeria Bianco
27 Sonoratown
see 23 Sticky Rice
28 Sushi Gen

DRINKING & NIGHTLIFE
29 Boomtown Brewery
30 Everson Royce Bar

ENTERTAINMENT
31 Ahmanson Theatre
32 Dorothy Chandler Pavilion
33 Los Angeles Music Center
34 Mark Taper Forum

SHOPPING
35 Dover Street Market
36 Good Liver
37 Hennessey + Ingalls
38 Last Bookstore
39 Omami Mini
40 Row DTLA
41 Santee Alley

TRANSPORTATION
42 Angels Flight

THE BROAD'S ARTFUL ARCHITECTURE

The **Broad's building** (p387) is as much a talking piece as the collection within. Costing $140 million, the 120,000-sq-ft showpiece was completed in 2015. It's 'shrouded' in a white lattice-like shell, complete with a dimple (an oculus looking out onto Grand Ave) and corners that lift sharply at street level to let art lovers and the curious in and out. Inside, the building bucks the museum tradition of hiding away its storage facilities. Here, the Vault becomes an integral part of the visit. Hovering between the 1st- and 3rd-floor galleries, it's pierced by the 105ft escalator connecting the gallery floors and visible through glass panels, offering visitors a voyeuristic peek at hibernating artworks.

continued from p387

you can access with free wi-fi inside the museum. It has full descriptions of the art and the artists. It also has gallery guides plus maps and audio tours (bring headphones). A tour for kids is narrated by LaVar Burton.

The 'Other' Museum Is No Slouch

Be moved by MOCA

Adding to the collection of museums on Grand Ave in Bunker Hill is **MOCA Grand Ave** *(Museum of Contemporary Art; moca.org; free)*, where the notable art collection focuses mainly on works created from the 1940s to the present. There's no shortage of luminaries, among them Mark Rothko, Dan Flavin, Willem de Kooning and David Hockney.

Psychedelic Metal & Pitch-Perfect Music

The unmissable Walt Disney Concert Hall

The **Walt Disney Concert Hall** *(musiccenter.org)* is DTLA's eye candy. It's starchitect, Frank Gehry, played every note to the hilt to produce a gravity-defying sculpture of heaving, billowing stainless steel.

In contrast, the 2265-seat auditorium feels like the inside of a finely crafted cello, clad in walls of smooth Douglas fir with terraced 'vineyard' seating wrapped around a central stage. You can visit, though the hall's best enjoyed during a concert, either by the **LA Philharmonic** *(laphil.org)* or other visiting musicians.

The **Blue Ribbon Garden** honors Lillian Disney and her love of Royal Delft porcelain, which Gehry used to create a mosaic-like flower fountain.

LA's Music Center

The venues with Disney

The county-owned **Los Angeles Music Center** *(musiccenter.org)* complex is one of America's largest performing arts centers. Besides the Walt Disney Concert Hall, its multiple venues – the **Dorothy Chandler Pavilion**, **Mark Taper Forum** and **Ahmanson Theatre** – host resident companies including Center Theatre Group *(centertheatregroup.org)*, **Los Angeles Master Chorale** *(lamasterchorale.org)* and **Los Angeles Opera** *(laopera.org)*.

EATING & DRINKING DOWNTOWN: HIGH-END CHOICES

Sushi Gen: Grab a lunch seat in Little Tokyo; chefs carve slabs of the freshest fish. Dinner is less frenetic. *11am-2pm & 5-8.30pm Tue-Sat* **$$**

Perch: Two-elevators get you to this French rooftop bar-restaurant crowning the vintage Pershing Square Building. Gatsby-esque vibe; bewitching views. *4pm-1am* **$$**

Bavel: Sleek, loud and showered in cascading vines, come here for phenomenal, modern takes on Middle Eastern classics. Fine cocktails. *5-11pm* **$$$**

Cole's: Dark, atmospheric, time-warped tavern, claims progeny (with Philippe) of the French dip sandwich. Great bar and cocktails. *3pm-midnight* **$$**

STROLLING DOWNTOWN'S CHINATOWN

Discover today's Chinatown and its vibrant mix of shops, restaurants and galleries on this walking tour, which stops for treats.

START	END	LENGTH
Union Station	Chinatown Metro Rail stop	1.85 miles; 2hr

In the 1920s, LA's white leaders maneuvered to replace the city's Chinatown, which was deemed too close to the center of power, with a new 1 **Union Station**. The Chinese population was moved several blocks north to today's Chinatown. From the station, cross through **El Pueblo de Los Ángeles** (p393) to N Broadway, where there's the dragon-topped 2 **Gateway Monument** (2001). Cut around to N Spring St and 3 **Long's Family Pastry**, where people line up for the $1.50 leek cakes.

Return to Broadway and walk north. Note the vendors, some with little more on offer than oranges they may have found on a tree. 4 **Far East Plaza** is worth a pause for the Now Serving cookbook store, the vintage muumuu of your dreams at the East/West Shop, the fanatical coffee preparation at Endorffeine and the exciting Filipino fare at Lasita Rotisserie & Natural Wine.

Continue on Broadway until you see the 5 **East Gate**. Enter 6 **Central Plaza** (1938). Note the Bruce Lee Statue (his martial arts studio was at 628 W College St). Cross Hill St to 7 **West Plaza**, an appealing collection of small galleries. Back on Broadway, stop at 8 **Phoenix Bakery** for a slice of its famous strawberry cake. Across the street, 9 **Steep LA** holds regular tea ceremonies and classes. Finish at the 10 **Chinatown Metro Rail stop**.

You might see baseball fans walking to nearby **Dodgers Stadium**. It also was used as a form of urban renewal.

The final shot in *Chinatown* – 'Forget it, Jake, it's Chinatown' – was filmed looking south in front of **Long's Family Pastry**.

The **Chinese American Museum** (*camla.org; adult/child $3/2*) near Union Station has full details on LA's Chinatown. It's in the 1890 Garnier Building.

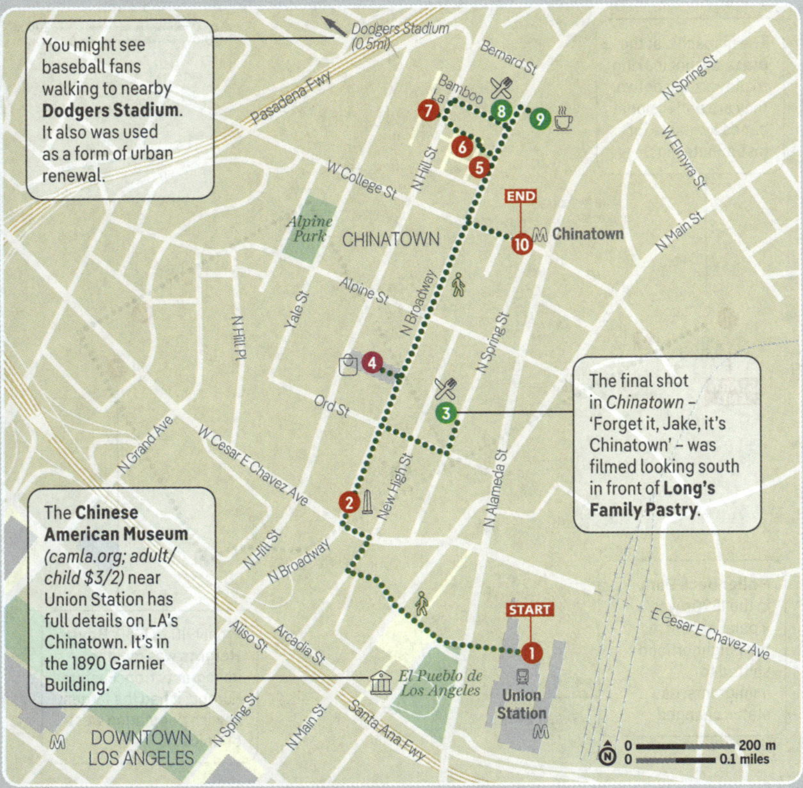

GETTING TO KNOW BOYLE HEIGHTS

See where LA's mariachi bands wait for gigs, then wander a neighborhood built on immigration, filled with unique businesses run with heart.

START	END	LENGTH
Mariachi Plaza Metro Rail stop	Mariachi Plaza Metro Rail stop	1.6 miles; 2hr

Begin at 1 **Mariachi Plaza Metro Rail stop**, where mariachi bands often wait in the shade of the gazebo for work. Hungry? 2 **Un Solo Sol** serves vegan Latin American dishes. The banana date shakes are a rich treat. Nearly next door, the glittery House of Trophies and Awards produces mantelpieces for amateur leagues. Another couple of doors down, you can see where the mariachis get their embroidered suits at La Casa del Mariachi. Across 1st St, 3 **Espacio 1839** is a community arts space.

Back across the street, the 4 **Women's March Store** supports the group's political activities with merch, including ever-popular tote bags. Cross under I-5 and walk up the 1920s residential Cummings St to Cesar Chavez Ave and turn east. 5 **Other Books** is packed with comics and zines. A series of blocks follow packed with mom-and-pop retail. 6 **Las Fotos Project** *(lasfotosproject.org)* teaches teenage women of color about the power of photography.

Turn south on N Breed St to step back to a previous era at the 7 **Breed Street Shul Project**, which is restoring the 1922 Byzantine synagogue. Back at 1st St, turn west and go two blocks. Tiny 8 **Al & Bea's Mexican Food** is so old (1966) it was a burrito pioneer in LA. Close by, Botanica Olokun stocks spiritual candles. Return to Mariachi Plaza Metro Rail stop.

The mariachis at the **plaza** are not looking to play a song or two, they are professional bands available for last-minute gigs.

Hollenbeck Park in the 1890s was a palatial gem. As the neighborhood shifted to immigrants, its status changed.

From 1910 to 1950, **Boyle Heights** was mostly immigrants from Eastern Europe; it had the largest Jewish population west of Chicago.

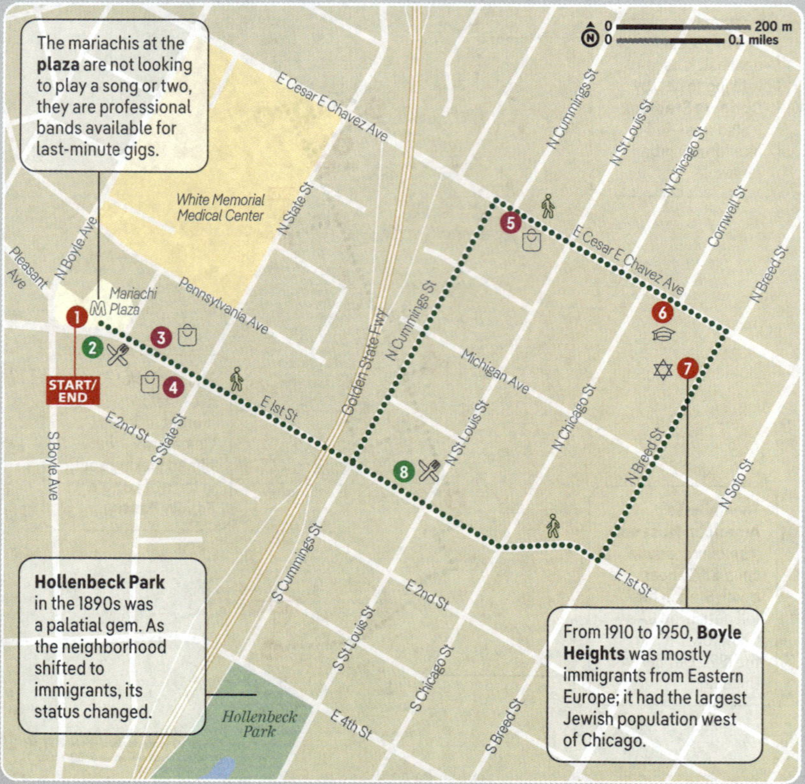

Taste Grand Central Market

A global culinary feast

Designed by prolific architect John Parkinson and once home to an office occupied by Frank Lloyd Wright, LA's beaux arts **Grand Central Market** *(grandcentralmarket.com; hours vary)* has been satisfying appetites since 1917 and today is DTLA's always-busy hub of food culture. Lose yourself in its bustle of neon signs, stalls and counters, which peddle everything from fresh produce to sizzling Thai street food at **Sticky Rice**, hipster breakfasts at **Eggslut**, modern deli classics, artisanal pasta and specialty coffee.

For a digestive interlude, exit and cross S Hill St for a quick ride on **Angels Flight** *(angelsflight.org; $1)*, the famous short funicular up to Bunker Hill. It's another local star in many TV and film productions.

Two Iconic Stars

Gaze at the Bradbury and City Hall

The **Bradbury Building** (1893) is one of LA's heritage jewels. Behind its Romanesque-lite facade lies a whimsical galleried atrium that wouldn't look out of place in New Orleans. Inky filigree grillwork, rickety birdcage elevators and yellow-brick walls glisten golden in the afternoon light, which filters through the peaked glass roof. Such striking beauty hasn't been lost on Hollywood; it's been used in hundreds of productions, including *Blade Runner.*

Two blocks north is another instantly recognizable icon, **Los Angeles City Hall** (1928), the phallic-shaped star of *Dragnet, LA Confidential* and countless other films and TV shows. It hides a surprise on its 27th floor: a free **observation deck** with incredible views of the city – when the smog allows. The observation deck is open from 9am to 5pm, Monday through Friday.

Where Modern LA Was Born

Dig down in El Pueblo

Compact and popular, **El Pueblo de Los Ángeles** *(elpueblo.lacity.org)* is the historic district where LA's first colonists settled in 1781. Wander through narrow **Olvera St**'s vibrant and family-owned Mexican-themed stalls and check out the district's museums, the best of which is **LA Plaza** *(lapca.org; free)*, offering snapshots of the local Mexican American

DTLA'S BEST SHOPPING

Last Bookstore: LA's largest new-and-used bookstore. Rare tomes, terrific vinyl, good prices and staff recs. Display of books banned in parts of the US.

Omami Mini: In Row DTLA, fashion-forward clothing for the under-12 set (though it's really aimed at parents).

Hennessey + Ingalls: Light-filled new-and-used bookstore focuses on design, from architecture to graphics and photography.

Good Liver: Carefully curated, museum-like space sells beautiful artisan objects you're unlikely to find elsewhere; each displayed with its story and craftsmanship.

Santee Alley: Scores of alley vendors with bargains in clothing, bling and eyewear between Santee St and Maple Ave, from Olympic Blvd to 12th St.

TOP CHOICES FOR AFFORDABLE EATING & DRINKING DOWNTOWN

Boomtown Brewery: Great brews served inside and out downtown, with a parade of food trucks turning up. Pool tables, party atmosphere and local art. *4-10pm* **$**

Philippe the Original: Famous old-fashioned joint renowned for French dip sandwich (try the pastrami instead). Always busy; don't miss beets on the side. *6am-10pm* **$**

Sonoratown: Straddles the Fashion District and DTLA. Superb northern Mexican street food, like buttery tortillas with succulent, mesquite-grilled meats. *11am-10pm* **$**

Everson Royce Bar: Arts District bar that puts the happy in happy hour. Suitably artful cocktails, best enjoyed in the shady backyard. *4-10pm* **$$**

AN INCREDIBLE LIFE

Stretching along a green, inviting alley behind the Bradbury Building and across from Grand Central Market, the easily overlooked **Biddy Mason Memorial Park** tells the remarkable story of an early LA resident. Historical displays detail the incredible life of Bridget 'Biddy' Mason, who was born an enslaved person in Mississippi in 1818. She eventually moved to California, walking much of the way, where she won a landmark court case in 1856 confirming her freedom. Working as a midwife and nurse, she saved her money and began buying land – including this part of DTLA. As her wealth grew, she became a philanthropist to African Americans, the poor and the sick and founded an elementary school. Before she died in 1891, she was worth $3 million.

experience. The **Avila Adobe**, built in 1818, is one of the region's oldest buildings. The heartfelt **Museum of Social Justice** *(museumofsocialjustice.org; free)* examines LA's history through the filters of poverty, women's suffrage and civil rights. Have a *taquito* (rolled taco, fried crispy) at the **Cielito Lindo** *(9am-8pm)*, the stand that claims their invention in 1923.

One of LA's First Communities

Deeply enriching Little Tokyo

To the north of Downtown lies Little Tokyo, a robust Japanese community that's been around since the early 1900s. Scores of shops and restaurants thrive across several blocks and there is a traditional Buddhist temple. It's a rewarding cultural immersion to stroll, browse and dine.

At the center is the impressive **Japanese American National Museum** *(janm.org)*, which focuses on the evolution of Japanese American culture and gives moving insight into the mass incarceration of over 125,000 American citizens of Japanese descent in remote internment camps during WWII. Watch for temporary exhibitions; it's undergoing renovations through late 2026.

LA's Sound of Music

Listen in at the Grammy Museum

The highlight of the LA Live entertainment complex, the **Grammy Museum**'s *(grammymuseum.org; adult/child $23/free)* features interactive exhibits that explore the evolution of popular music and the famous awards. Rotating exhibits might include iconic threads worn by Whitney Houston,

RUBEN A MARTINEZ/SHUTTERSTOCK

Arts District

HISTORY OF LA: PART 1

LA's human history begins with the Gabrielino and Chumash, who roamed the area as early as 6000 BCE. Their hunter-gatherer existence ended in the late 18th century with the arrival of Spanish missionaries and Mexican settlers who founded **El Pueblo de Los Ángeles** (p393). The Gold Rush in Northern California also opened up LA to US influence, which soon forcibly pushed aside the Mexicans. The city was incorporated on April 4, 1850. A series of seminal events caused LA's population to grow exponentially: the railroad's arrival in the 1870s, the birth of the citrus industry in the late 1800s and the discovery of oil in 1892. But that was nothing compared to the 20th century (p437).

Peggy Lee and Beyoncé; scribbled words from the hands of Count Basie and Taylor Swift; and instruments once played by music legends. Top names often perform.

Where the Surprises Never Stop

Explore the Arts District

The **Arts District** is one of DTLA's most intriguing places. Blocks of old warehouses and gritty industrial areas have been cleaned up and you never know what you'll find behind those big metal roller doors: a gallery? A designer shop? Or perhaps something more esoteric?

Start at the vast **Row DTLA** *(rowdtla.com)*, a curated garden of specialty retail and dining delights across several big warehouses next to a produce market. Among the chic boutiques is beloved **Pizzeria Bianco** *(11am-9pm)*. Less elevated is **Dover Street Market** *(doverstreetmarket.com)*, a sprawling, off-the-radar warehouse in which bleeding-edge fashion and art collide to spectacular effect and TikTok kids shoot videos out front.

Among the swanky galleries, **Hauser & Wirth** *(hauserwirth.com)* displays contemporary art; **Webber 939** *(webberrepresents.com)* has exhibits by famous names like Yorgos Lanthimos.

For the ultimate in single-use colorful art, head to the busy **Piñata District**, where high-ceiling emporiums display legions of aliens, animals and other characters waiting for the big moment to spew forth candy when burst with a stick. It's a carnival for the eyes; the other senses also get in on the action as stores sell treats and there are several delicious open-air Mexican cafeterias with full bars.

Griffith Park, Los Feliz & Echo Park

FAMILY FUN, NATURE, HIPSTER FUN AND NIGHTLIFE

TOP TIP

Enjoy touring Griffith Park by bike, from the flat trails near the river to the hillsides. Rent all types of bikes at **Spokes 'N Stuff**, located just southwest of the LA Zoo. The bike paths are geared to all levels and are family-friendly.

GETTING AROUND

Individual portions of this large area are walkable. Overall, it is hilly, especially in Griffith Park. Each of the neighborhoods is good for strolling.

Transit access is mostly by bus with the exception of Los Feliz, which is near the Metro Rail B station Vermont/Sunset. Outside of the parks, parking is mostly on streets and is always at a premium.

From the natural heights and artificial diversions of Griffith Park, the trendy neighborhoods of Los Feliz, Silver Lake and Echo Park offer hipsterism, laid-back vibes and urban charms unlike anywhere else in the sprawling city.

Griffith Park, one of the US largest municipal parks, is a refreshing escape from the hustle and bustle, with its rugged, trail-laced hills and iconic Griffith Observatory offering some of the best views of the Hollywood sign and the LA Basin.

South is walkable Los Feliz with its shops and nightlife along Vermont Ave and Sunset Blvd. The latter flows right into ever-trendy Silver Lake. Its diversity of food, people, LGBTQ+ history and constant reinvigoration keep residents staying put.

Echo Park nears Downtown and mixes heritage with natural beauty and funky urban charms. Its many independent shops, beautiful architectural monuments and namesake lake offer a great excuse to plunge deep – even if you don't get wet.

Observe LA!

And the universe from the Griffith Observatory

The universe aside, the rooftop viewing platform of the **Griffith Observatory** *(griffithobservatory.org; free)* offers boffo – and free – views of LA and the Hollywood Hills. The uber-popular art deco observatory is no stranger to the spotlight itself, having made cameos in numerous movies and TV shows, among them *La La Land, Terminator, 24* and *Alias*. The film it's most associated with, however, remains *Rebel Without a Cause,* commemorated with a bust of James Dean on the west side of the observatory lawn.

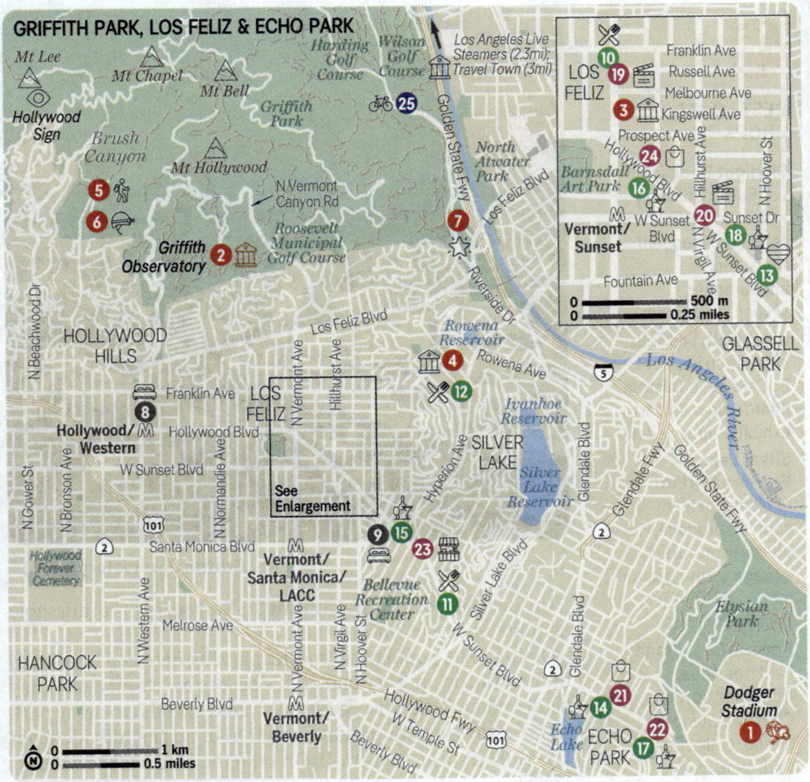

GRIFFITH PARK, LOS FELIZ & ECHO PARK

HIGHLIGHTS
1 Dodger Stadium
2 Griffith Observatory

SIGHTS
3 Disney's First Studio
4 Snow White Cottages

ACTIVITIES
5 Bronson Canyon
6 Bronson Caves
7 Griffith Park & Southern Railroad

SLEEPING
8 Cara Hotel
9 Silver Lake Pool & Inn

EATING
see 19 Figaro Bistrot
10 House of Pies
see 20 Pam's Coffy
11 Playita Mariscos
12 Speranza

DRINKING & NIGHTLIFE
13 Akbar
14 Bar Flores
15 Black Cat
16 Covell
see 3 Dresden Lounge
17 Ototo
18 Tiki-Ti

ENTERTAINMENT
19 Los Feliz Theatre
20 Vista Theater

SHOPPING
see 3 Kingswell
21 Reverie Bookstand
22 Sick City Records
23 Silver Lake Farmers Market
see 19 Skylight Books
24 Wacko

TRANSPORTATION
25 Spokes 'N Stuff

WHERE TO EAT & DRINK IN LOS FELIZ: OUR PICKS

Figaro Bistrot: A culinary trio includes a boulangerie, bistro and lounge. Figaro channels Paris with sidewalk tables and Gallic-inspired fare. *8am-midnight* **$$**

House of Pies: Indomitable survivor of a chain that once swept California, the House serves top diner fare plus its namesake desserts. *7am-1am* **$$**

Covell: Over 150 wines by the glass, showcasing interesting producers, unusual grapes and lesser-known regions. *4pm-midnight* **$$**

Tiki-Ti: Channeling Waikiki since 1961, this tiny tropical tavern packs in everyone from stylish slummers to 'non-ironic' partiers in Hawaiian shirts. *6pm-midnight Wed-Sat* **$$**

BEST LOCAL SHOPS

Skylight Books: Los Feliz institution with an incredible selection. Frequent top author appearances. *skylightbooks.com*

Kingswell: Los Feliz skate shop is one of SoCal's best. Custom boards, gear and art exhibits. *kingswell.tv*

Silver Lake Farmers Market: The best locally sourced produce, plus artisan coffee, vintage clothing and more. *1.30-7pm Tue, 6am-1.30pm Sat*

Reverie Bookstand: Find treasures, from used Joyce to Chekov's *Guide to Acting*, at this Echo Park gem. *reverie bookstand.com*

Sick City Records: Get your punk groove on at this used album shop in Echo Park.

Wacko: Sprawling Los Feliz carnival of pop, kitsch and camp is always a fun browse. *wackola.com*

ENGEL CHING/SHUTTERSTOCK

Griffith Observatory (p396)

Inside, there's a **planetarium** and all sorts of unmissable exhibits on the cosmos.

Owing to its popularity, finding parking here can be akin to finding life on another planet. It's best to arrive on a weekday before noon. Otherwise, especially on weekends, you may park so far away that you might as well hike up the hillside from Los Feliz (it *is* a great trail). Or, take the DASH Observatory/Los Feliz shuttle bus from the Vermont/Sunset metro station.

Famed Film Location in the Park

Hike to Bronson Caves

With more than 50 miles of trails, **Griffith Park** is LA's great hub of hiking. It's accessible from all directions and offers all types of experiences. A good start is the family-friendly jaunt (0.75 miles one-way) up **Bronson Canyon** off Canyon Dr to **Bronson Caves**. The latter are legit stars: among many appearances, they served as the Bat Cave in the old *Batman* TV series and were the climactic location in the still-relevant *Invasion of the Body Snatchers* (1956). From here, more challenging trails lead to sights like the Hollywood Sign (p382).

Choose Your Choo-Choo

Griffith Park has three train rides

Families can spend a day riding miniature trains in Griffith Park; each of the three options comes with a distinct appeal.

Closest to Los Feliz, the **Griffith Park & Southern Railroad** *(griffithparktrainrides.com; adult/child $4/3)* has ferried generations of parents and kids on pint-sized trains around a 1-mile loop past an old Western town since 1948. Everyone loves the soft-serve ice cream stand.

Travel Town *(traveltown.org; free)* is the park's railroad museum, with a collection of moth-eaten railcars and locomotives that once rolled along the tracks that crossed the Western US. There's a **miniature train** *(griffithparktrainrides.com; adult/child $4/3)* you can ride that meanders around the full-size collection.

Right next door, **Los Angeles Live Steamers** *(lalsrm.org; $4)* is a group of hobbyists who give rides most Sundays on their own miniature loop of track.

Screen Gems

Feel the magic of classic cinemas

Dating back to 1923, the single-screen **Vista Theater** *(vistatheaterhollywood.com)* received a 100-year anniversary revamp of its wonderfully kitsch 'ancient Egyptian' interior from owner Quentin Tarantino. Like his other cinema, the acclaimed New Beverly (p413), he programs an eclectic lineup of mostly classic films (many from his own collection) projected in 35mm as opposed to digital. The director also runs the adjoining **Pam's Coffy** *(8am-7pm)*, a cafe dedicated to the actor Pam Grier.

For more movie magic just up the road, the century-old **Los Feliz Theatre** *(vintagecinemas.com)* is a gem of a neighborhood cinema. It screens first-run movies and a good mix of classics and arthouse films.

Lounge Acts

Hear timeless tunes at the Dresden

This institution has been serving the LA crowds since 1954. You may have seen it in the film *Swingers*, where the line, 'You're so money' was made famous. The **Dresden** *(thedresden.com; no cover)* is an old-school, retro-style bar and restaurant with dimly lit rooms, arched walkways and red-wine-colored booths. Once known for singers Marty and Elayne, today their tuneful traditions are carried on nightly by an array of talented crooners. This is definitely the place to savor a traditional cocktail – try the Sidecar. It's open 5pm to midnight.

Iconic Bar

Make your own history at the Black Cat

New York City has the Stonewall Inn, Los Angeles has the **Black Cat**. Look for the winsome logo on Sunset Blvd in

SNOW WHITE'S INSPIRATION

LA had a secret love for storybook and fairy-tale houses between the 1920s and '30s – look no further than the **Snow White Cottages**. Built by fantastical developer Ben Sherwood in 1931, the eight white houses have thatched roofs, sweet window boxes and chimneys. They are said to be the inspiration for *Snow White and the Seven Dwarfs* (1937) and were built in ersatz Tudor style. Coincidentally (!), the cottages stand just around the corner from the site of Walt Disney's studios on Hyperion Ave from 1926 until 1940 (now a supermarket).

Disney's first studio, however, still stands modestly at 4647 Kingswell Ave in Los Feliz. Now a copy shop, Mickey's face peers out the window. Employees claim they sense the ghost of Walt every day.

EATING & DRINKING IN SILVER LAKE & ECHO PARK

Playita Mariscos: Homemade tortillas and fresh seafood star at a simple Mexican cafe with a short menu. Plenty of seating outside. *11am-9pm* $

Speranza: Feels like a secret club but it's not – it's just sign-challenged. The verdant patio is the spot for Italian fare like handmade pastas. *5.30-11pm* $$

Ototo: Japanese craft beer bar does big business with Dodgers fans pre-game. Great snacks; vaunted Tsubaki restaurant adjoins. *5-10pm* $$

Bar Flores: Upstairs cantina faces Sunset Blvd, providing views of the 'hood with a candlelit glow. Mellow vibe, delicious drinks and snacks. *4pm-2am* $$

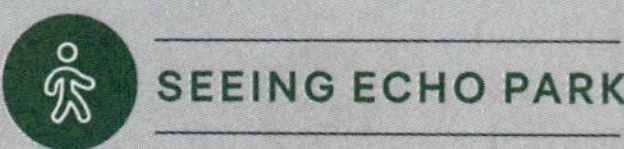

SEEING ECHO PARK

From old Victorians to an iconic lake, Echo Park is a star on screen and off. Its shops and views are bonuses.

START	END	LENGTH
Bob's Market	Angels Point	3.1 miles; 3hr

Begin at ❶ **Bob's Market** (1913), aka Toretto's Market & Deli, owned by Vin Diesel's character in the *Fast & Furious* franchise. Look for the shelf of merch. It was also in *LA Confidential*. Walk uphill to Angelino Heights, established in the mid-1880s as one of LA's first suburbs. Its most charming street is the ❷ **1300 Block of Carroll Avenue**, home to the largest concentration of Victorian-era homes in the city. A few house numbers of note: 1300 is the grandest on the block; 1316 captures the look of the 1880s with its old-style drapes; 1329 is the most original and was Halliwell Manor in the TV series *Charmed;* 1330 has Asian details like the lion dogs below the arch; and 1337 is the oldest house on the block (1872).

Walk down via Bellevue Ave to ❸ **Echo Park Lake**, anchor of the namesake park. One block of Sunset Blvd has a thicket of cool retail like the literature-rich ❹ **Stories** and the indescribable Time Travel Mart, where the slogan is 'Whenever you are, we're already there.' You won't regret a minute you spend inside.

Walk north up Portia St and use your map app to wander through leafy ❺ **Elysian Park** and up to ❻ **Angels Point**. Under towering public art, you'll enjoy uncommon views of LA, including Dodger Stadium, downtown and Hollywood.

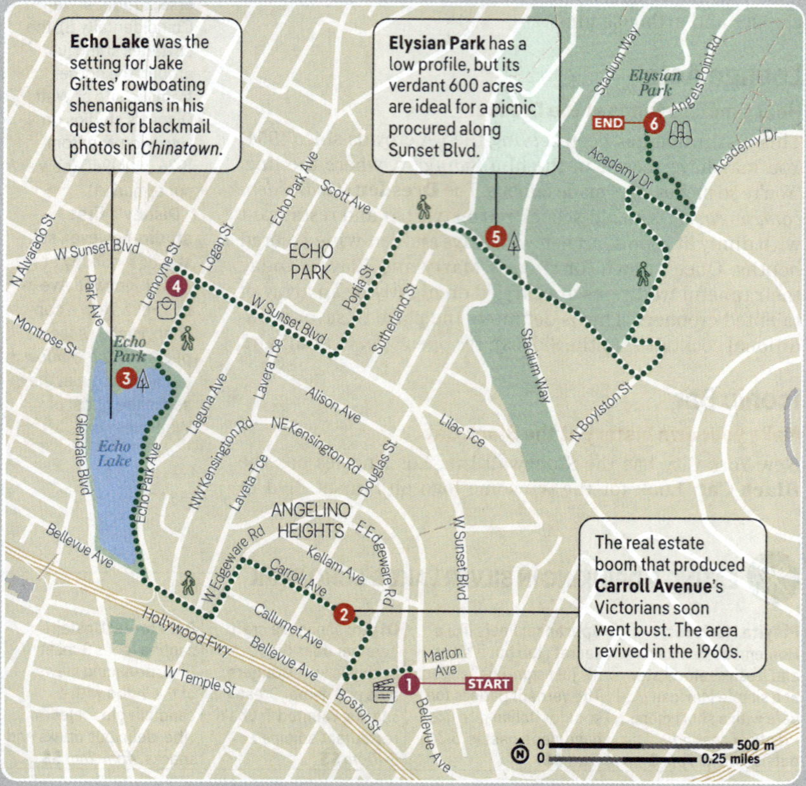

Echo Lake was the setting for Jake Gittes' rowboating shenanigans in his quest for blackmail photos in *Chinatown*.

Elysian Park has a low profile, but its verdant 600 acres are ideal for a picnic procured along Sunset Blvd.

The real estate boom that produced **Carroll Avenue**'s Victorians soon went bust. The area revived in the 1960s.

Silver Lake, which leads to this historic tavern, which became a symbol for LGBTQ+ civil rights.

The Black Cat was the site of an early LGBTQ+ civil rights demonstration in 1967 after being raided by the LA police during New Year's Eve celebrations. Now recognized as a Los Angeles Historic-Cultural Monument for its significant role in the LGBTQ+ movement, look for the plaque outside the building that honors the tavern's place in the fight for human rights.

Today, the Black Cat continues to be an inclusive neighborhood hangout with a loyal following. Casual bar food is paired with great cocktails in a woodsy, vintage interior with seating for fab people-watching out front.

After a visit, head to nearby **Akbar** to dance the rest of the night away. Both Black Cat and Akbar are open from 4pm to 2am.

Take Me Out to the Ballgame

LA is crazy for the Dodgers

Few teams can match the **Los Angeles Dodgers** *(mlb.com/dodgers)* for history (Jackie Robinson, Sandy Koufax, Fernando Valenzuela and sportscaster Vin Scully), success and fan loyalty, especially after they won an eighth World Series title in 2024. You see Dodger blue everywhere and current sensation Shohei Ohtani is LA's most popular person.

Mid-century **Dodger Stadium**, between Echo Park and Chinatown (built on what was once the vibrant Mexican American neighborhood of Chavez Ravine), is considered one of baseball's most scenic, framed by views of palm trees and the San Gabriel Mountains. Buy tickets well ahead as games sell out.

THE FATE OF CHAVEZ RAVINE

Chavez Ravine, the piece of land where Dodger Stadium sits, has the sort of tangled past that's not uncommon in LA.

In the 1940s, it was a Mexican American neighborhood, filled with residents who'd been unable to own homes elsewhere due to racist land covenants. Eyeing this prime land near downtown, the city declared it 'blighted' (it wasn't) and bought out homeowners with the claim that the land would be used for public housing (it wasn't).

Repeating the fate of the old Chinatown in the 1930s, Chavez Ravine was bulldozed and some homes were sold to the studios for their backlots. In 1958, the land was given to Walter O'Malley, who broke a million Brooklyn hearts and moved the Dodgers to LA.

Exposition Park & South LA

MUSEUMS, SPORTS, MUSIC, ARTS AND CULTURE

TOP TIP

For a wonderful read that transports you back to South Central in 1948, check out *Devil in the Blue Dress,* the first of the best-selling, hardboiled Easy Rawlins novels by South LA native Walter Mosley.

GETTING AROUND

The Metro Rail E Line has stops at Expo Park. There is also a DASH bus route from downtown (50¢). The A Line serves Compton and Watts. The K Line serves Downtown Inglewood and the LAX area.

Otherwise, South LA is the stereotypical Southern California sprawl of suburbia. You'll need a car to get around. None of the privately built stadiums in the SoFi Stadium area were located near mass transit. Expo Park is the one ideal place for extended walking.

The massive area south of the I-10 Fwy and straddling the I-110 Fwy comprises dozens of neighborhoods collectively called South LA. On its north end is Exposition Park, home to LA's iconic Memorial Coliseum, popular museums and the University of Southern California (USC).

A couple of miles west, Leimert Park is the thriving, beating heart of LA's African American community and east of the 110 is Watts, known for Watts Towers, a masterpiece of folk art.

South LA (formerly known as South Central) burst into global consciousness with the rat-a-tat-tat rhythm and rhyme of some of hip-hop's greatest pioneers. With infectious beats and sharp tongues, folks such as Ice T, Ice Cube, Eazy E, Dr Dre and Tupac Shakur broadcast gangsta life to the suburbs and beyond.

Today, as transit lines snake into the area and vast projects like SoFi Stadium spawn further investment, South LA continues its evolution.

LA's Olympic Games Home

Get lost in Exposition Park

Exposition Park – or Expo Park – began as an agricultural fairground in 1872, devolved into a magnet for the down-and-out, before finally emerging as a patch of public greenery in 1913. It contains three big-time museums (the California Science Center, California African American Museum and Natural History Museum) and will soon host a fourth (p406).

The centerpiece is the grand 1923 **Los Angeles Memorial Coliseum** *(lacoliseum.com)*. This vast bowl has hosted the 1932 and 1984 Summer Olympic Games, various Super Bowls, NFL teams and the USC Trojans college football team. It's due for another round of international fame in 2028 when the Olympics return to town. **Guided tours** *(adult/child $28/22)* are available.

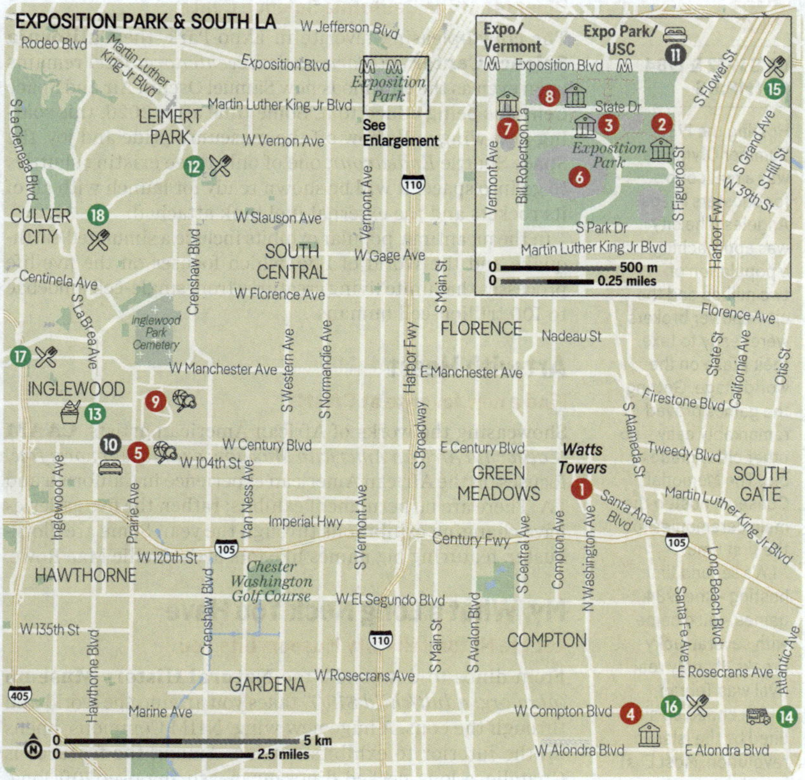

EXPOSITION PARK & SOUTH LA

HIGHLIGHTS
1 Watts Towers

SIGHTS
2 CAAM
3 California Science Center
4 Compton Art and History Museum
see 4 Compton City Hall
5 Intuit Dome
6 Los Angeles Memorial Coliseum
7 Lucas Museum of Narrative Art
see 4 Martin Luther King Memorial
8 Natural History Museum
9 SoFi Stadium

SLEEPING
10 Crestridge Inn
11 USC Hotel

EATING
see 4 Alma's Place
12 Dulan's On Crenshaw
13 Foster's Freeze
14 Kitchen's Corner
15 Mercado La Paloma
16 Patria Coffee Roasters
17 Randy's Donuts
18 Somerville

TOP CHOICES FOR EATING & DRINKING IN SOUTH LA

Dulan's On Crenshaw: Soul food mainstay in a lovely space near Leimert Park. Great mac 'n cheese. *11am-8pm* $$

Kitchen's Corner: This top Compton BBQ food truck is so popular it's double-size. Texas-style fall-off-the-bone: enjoy at the big park across Atlantic Ave. *11am-7pm* $$

Alma's Place: Near Compton City Hall, Alma cooks 'food for the soul' and her pork chops and catfish are just that. Lunch specials. *11am-5pm* $$

Somerville: Evoking a 1940s supper club, elegance is the theme where soul meets steakhouse and cool jazz plays. Book well ahead. *6-11pm Wed-Sun* $$

LA'S 1932 & 1984 OLYMPICS

Hosting the 1932 Summer Olympics was a real coup for boosters in Los Angeles. The city was approaching a population of two million and the city's power brokers were ready to take their place on the world stage. Getting the games proved remarkably easy – no other cities made a bid. The Memorial Coliseum hosted the main ceremonies for the first time.

LA's second time hosting – the 1984 games – also came with several lucky breaks. Its only real rival was Tehran, which ended up sidelined by the Islamic revolution. Most Eastern Bloc countries wound up boycotting the games, which ensured that the US won the most medals. In addition, minimal new construction and tight budgets meant that the games turned a sizable profit.

From Amoebae to the Stars

Blast off at the California Science Center

The crowd-pleasing favorite in Expo Park, the **California Science Center** *(californiasciencecenter.org; free)* remains open even as the enormous new Samuel Oschin Air and Space Center is being added to it. Some time after 2026, this soaring new wing will show off the museum's pride and joy, the Space Shuttle *Endeavour,* one of only three existing shuttles to go into space. It will be shown ready for launch with all of its rockets and the external fuel tank attached.

In the meantime, popular exhibits include a simulated earthquake and the World of Life, which focuses on the five life processes that unite living creatures from single-cell amoebae to 100 trillion-cell humans.

Art with Heart

Find a new favorite at CAAM

Showcasing the works of African American artists, **CAAM** *(California African American Museum; caamuseum.org; free)* focuses on the African American experience in California and LA. There are no permanent exhibits; rather, the five galleries have changing exhibitions through the year. Some are blockbuster, featuring big names like folk artist Nellie Mae Rowe.

My, What a Long Neck You Have

Let the Natural History Museum bite you

From dinos to diamonds, the **Natural History Museum** *(nhm.org; adult/child $18/7)* takes you around the world and through the eons. A huge new wing, NHM Commons, opens up the interior to exhibits outside. Among the features is Gnatalie, a long-necked dinosaur measuring over 70ft long. It's all housed in a beautiful 1913 Spanish Renaissance-style building that stood in for Columbia University in the first Tobey Maguire *Spider-Man* movie – where Peter Parker was bitten by the radioactive arachnid.

All That Glitters Isn't Good

SoFi Stadium and Intuit Dome

Flying into LAX, you'll likely spot the new and growing complex of corporate-financed stadiums east of the airport in Inglewood. Largest is **SoFi Stadium** *(sofistadium.com),* a huge, flashy NFL stadium that some would say has a split personality and others would say has no personality. That's because the 70,200-seat arena serves two teams, the LA Rams and the LA Chargers, and thus can't show allegiance to either. So while Lambeau Field is all about the Green Bay Packers and Arrowhead Stadium is all about the Kansas City Chiefs, SoFi Stadium isn't about anything (SoFi is a 'financial technology company').

Just south, past a growing mall, the glitzy **Intuit Dome** *(intuitdome.com)* puts on a nighttime light show and is home to the NBA's LA Clippers. By day, you can see that when they

WALTER CICCHETTI/SHUTTERSTOCK

SoFi Stadium

bought up the land to build the arena, they didn't buy up all the land, eg there's an old cut-rate liquor store near the entrance as well as a tawdry mini-storage facility.

Soaring Folk Art

Marvel at the Watts Towers

The three 'Gothic' (or is it Gaudí-esque?) spires of the fabulous **Watts Towers** *(wattstowers.org; tour adult/child $7/3)* rank among the world's greatest monuments of folk art. In 1921, Italian immigrant Simon Rodia set out to 'make something big' and then spent 33 years cobbling together this whimsical free-form sculpture from concrete, steel and a motley assortment of found objects: green 7-Up bottles, seashells, tiles, rocks and pottery.

The towers reach up to 99.5ft in height, just below the city's legal limit of 100ft. You can admire Watts Towers from beyond the fence 24/7 (and there's good explanatory signage), but to get inside, you must take the tour.

The adjacent **Watts Towers Art Center** has rotating exhibitions of important artists such as David G Brown, who created searing political cartoons. The campus is a short walk from the Metro Line A 103rd St/Watts Towers station.

THE 2028 OLYMPICS

For its Summer Olympics hat trick *(la28.org)*, the city once again had great luck. It came down to just two candidates for the 2024 games – LA and Paris – and so the International Olympic Committee suggested a compromise: Paris in 2024 and LA in 2028. *Voila!*

Like the profitable 1984 games, events will be held at existing venues, including the **SoFi Field** (Opening Ceremony, Swimming), the **Memorial Coliseum** (Track & Field, Closing Ceremony), the **Expo Park 1932 Pool** (Diving), along with the **Intuit Dome**, **Crypto.com Arena**, **Dodger Stadium**, **UCLA** and the **Pasadena Rosa Bowl**. The games will be held in LA July 14–30. Besides prepping venues and finishing new transit lines, many hope the city will scrub itself up.

TOP CHOICES FOR A QUICK BITE IN SOUTH LA

Mercado La Paloma: A walk under the I-110 from Expo Park, this fabulous food hall has everything from Yucatán cuisine to Thai. *9am-9pm* $

Patria Coffee Roasters: Only a block from Compton's City Hall, this art-filled coffee house is a standout for top-end coffee drinks. Next to a park. *8am-3pm* $

Foster's Freeze: Time-warp Inglewood soft-serve emporium. Order a hot fudge sundae and enjoy it at a picnic table. *10am-8pm* $

Randy's Donuts: Famously excellent doughnuts are your first or last memory of LA going to/from LAX. Simple flavors, like glazed old-fashioned, are best. *24hr* $

THE LUCAS MUSEUM OF NARRATIVE ART

An enormous, sinuous blob rising west of the Coliseum, the **Lucas Museum of Narrative Art** *(lucasmuseum.org)* is the dream of George Lucas, creator of *Star Wars*. However, exactly what his hundreds of millions of dollars will buy is more labyrinthine than the plot of *The Phantom Menace*.

Both San Francisco and Chicago rebuffed efforts to locate the museum in those cities. Ground was broken in Expo Park in 2018. However, the original 2021 opening has been pushed back repeatedly amid massive staff upheavals and layoffs. As for what will be inside the metallic shell, the official line is that the mission is 'to inspire and connect people through the exploration of visual stories and their influences in society.'

WALTER CICCHETTI/SHUTTERSTOCK

Watts Towers (p405)

Compton's Anthem

See the site of 'Not Like Us'

West Coast rap and hip-hop have been part of Southern California since NWA's 1988 album *Straight Outta Compton* launched the careers of Eazy E, Ice Cube and Dr Dre and established gangsta rap.

Jump ahead and Compton remains relevant, as megastar Kendrick Lamar showed in 2024 with his music video 'Not Like Us.' Viewed millions of times, it features scenes shot at the striking modernist **Martin Luther King Memorial** on the wide open plaza at the **Compton City Hall**.

Lamar invited the people of Compton to show up for the shoot and they did. The results are joyous and vivacious. It's worth visiting the location while watching the video on your phone. After, cross S Acacia Ave and see what's on at the **Compton Art and History Museum** *(comptonmuseum.org; adult/child $5/3)*. Exhibits regularly change.

Koreatown, Miracle Mile & Fairfax

NONSTOP DELIGHT, TOP MUSEUMS AND EDGY SHOPPING

And the Oscar goes to...the swath of gridded streets from Koreatown in the east to the trendy zone butting up against Beverly Hills in the west. This area claims some of LA's top cultural and retail assets. It's here that you'll find the 'Miracle Mile' and its string of blockbuster museums, the Orthodox Jewish-meets-hipster Fairfax district and once-trendy-now-funky Melrose Ave.

Sometimes called Mid-City, though that's really a specific neighborhood down by the Santa Monica Fwy, you'll find every aspect of LA here. The unbeatable cluster of museums includes the Academy Museum of Motion Pictures, otherwise known as the Oscar Museum, and the city's boffo main art museum, LACMA, which has a stunning new building. Running through the middle of it all is a new subway line that's been years in the digging.

The eating, drinking, shopping and entertainment run almost around-the-clock, especially in Koreatown, LA's tireless enclave of frenetic day and night action.

TOP TIP

With many LA neighborhoods and nightspots going quiet by midnight, Koreatown remains the city's most vibrant and exciting nightlife district. An ever-changing line-up of bars and clubs keeps the action going well past the witching hour. As the venues of choice are always changing, ask around for what's hot.

GETTING AROUND

Metro's D (Purple) Line subway serves Koreatown with the Wilshire/Normandie and Wilshire/Western stations. The big news is the extension that was due to open in 2025 covering stops on Wilshire at La Brea Ave, Fairfax Ave and La Cienega Blvd. The Wilshire/Fairfax stop promises to be the best transit development in LA for visitors in decades as it will serve several top sights like the Oscar museum and LACMA. Further extensions will serve Rodeo Dr in Beverly Hills (by 2027) and Westwood (before the 2028 Olympics). Individual neighborhoods in this area, such as Koreatown, are all enjoyably walkable.

HIGHLIGHTS
1 Academy Museum of Motion Pictures
2 LACMA

SIGHTS
3 La Brea Tar Pits & Museum
4 Little Ethiopia
5 Petersen Automotive Museum

SLEEPING
6 Banana Bungalows Hotel and Hostel West Hollywood
7 Hotel Normandie LA
see 7 Line Los Angeles
8 Palihouse West Hollywood

EATING
9 Ahgassi Gopchang
see 4 Buna
10 Canter's
11 Danbi
12 Guelaguetza Restaurant
see 16 Happy Ice
13 My 2 Cents LA
14 Pink's Hot Dogs
15 République

DRINKING & NIGHTLIFE
16 Be Bright Coffee
17 Dan Sung Sa
18 El Carmen
19 Lock & Key
see 7 Normandie Club
20 Pips on La Brea
21 Rosen Karaoke
22 Snake Pit
23 Stir Crazy

ENTERTAINMENT
24 El Rey Theatre
see 16 Groundlings
25 Improv
26 Largo at the Coronet
27 New Beverly Cinema

SHOPPING
28 Golf Wang
29 Melrose Trading Post
30 Original Farmers Market
31 Polkadots & Moonbeams
32 Posers Hollywood
33 Ripndip

Stunning New Home for Art

Take in the wealth at LACMA

Soaring across Wilshire Blvd, the new **LACMA** *(Los Angeles County Museum of Art; lacma.org; adult/child $28/13)* is set to open for visitors by mid-2026. The $720 million David Geffen Galleries will replace the museum's four aging buildings and with the new real estate will come an entirely new philosophy for exhibiting the largest collection of art in the western United States.

The depth and wealth of LACMA's collection is stunning. It includes millennia worth of Chinese, Japanese, pre-Columbian and ancient Greek, Roman and Egyptian sculpture, plus treasures across media from every continent except Antarctica. From Europe and North America come stars like Rembrandt, Cézanne, Magritte, Mary Cassatt and Ansel Adams.

Permanent collection highlights include Chris Burden's outdoor installation *Urban Light* (a surreal selfie backdrop of hundreds of vintage LA street lamps) and Michael Heizer's *Levitated Mass,* a surprisingly inspirational 340-ton boulder perched over a walkway. Other high points: *Cold Shoulder* by Roy Lichtenstein and *Flower Day* by Diego Rivera. Two works are iconic LA: *Mulholland Drive* by David Hockney and *105 Freeway* by Catherine Opie.

LACMA's Zen-like **Pavilion for Japanese Art** houses pieces ranging in origin from 3000 BCE to the 21st century. Several cafes are planned for admission-free public spaces on both sides of Wilshire Blvd once the new galleries open.

DISPLAYING ART IN A NEW WAY

LACMA's new building is the bold vision of Swiss architect Peter Zumthor. The curvaceous, airy, cantilevered galleries straddle Wilshire Blvd and floor-to-ceiling windows will make the most of LA's natural beauty, highlighting its hills and celebrated natural light.

Inside, LACMA's curators have challenged themselves to utterly rethink how their huge and rich collection is displayed. They want to dispense with the Eurocentric and chronological narrative that dominates art museums and instead show how works spanning mediums, cultures and time interrelate. As they readily admit in interviews, this new paradigm is a 'challenge.'

Movie Magic's Home

See the blockbuster Academy Museum of Motion Pictures

You'll be channeling your inner movie-lover at LA's lavish **Academy Museum of Motion Pictures** *(academymuseum.org; adult/child $25/free)*. Spectacular and expansive, it's a cutting-edge ode to film, with thought-provoking exhibits, priceless memorabilia and a dynamic program of movie screenings and talks delving deep into celluloid culture. If you only have time for one museum in town, make it this one.

Designed by Italian starchitect Renzo Piano, this 300,000-sq-ft blockbuster's permanent exhibition offers an immersive, state-of-the-art journey through cinema's evolution. The core **Stories of Cinema** galleries explore the many aspects of filmmaking, as well as showcasing movie memorabilia that includes Dorothy's ruby slippers from *The Wizard of*

EATING IN MIRACLE MILE & FAIRFAX: OUR PICKS

République: Artisan bakery, light-filled cafe and bistro. The kitchen whips up delectable French-accented dishes and desserts. *8am-2pm & 5.30-10pm* $$

Canter's: The veteran deli isn't closed despite the appearance. Legendary pastrami and other standards. Comfy booths, knowing servers and parking. *6am-11.30pm* $$

My 2 Cents LA: Acclaimed restaurant of TV-chef Alisa Reynolds has a loyal, A-lister following for her Southern fusion fare. Book. *11.30am-9.30pm Thu-Sun* $$$

Pink's Hot Dogs: Famous doggeria (since 1939) with glacially moving lines thanks to the garlicky all-beef frankfurters drenched in chili. *9.30am-midnight* $

BEST SHOPPING

Golf Wang: Tyler, the Creator, known for his alternative hip-hop, owns this clothing store that reflects his vision of cool. *golfwang.com*

Polkadots & Moonbeams: Whimsical vintage shop stocked with affordable designer dresses, shades, scarves and hats. *polkadotsandmoonbeams.com*

Ripndip: Streetwear, skatewear and skateboards. The witty logo will look familiar to tire buyers. *ripndipclothing. com*

Melrose Trading Post: Every Sunday, over 250 vendors sell threads, jewelry, crafts and other offbeat items in the Fairfax High parking lot. *melrosetradingpost.org*

Posers Hollywood: Embodies the old Melrose Ave. Dr Martens, Fred Perry and other punkish wear. *posersonline.com*

Oz. Iconic items from films are all here, including a surviving Rosebud sled from *Citizen Kane*. Scripts for blockbusters are dissected and annotated to explain the creative process. Temporary exhibitions have depth, such as Oscar-winner Bong Joon Ho (*Parasite*; 2019) detailing how he creates his films.

The Academy Museum occupies two sharply contrasting buildings. Entry is via the restored **Saban Building**, a 1939 Streamline Moderne landmark that once housed a May Company department store, which was a popular shopping location for many of the stars now memorialized within. Directly behind it is Piano's addition, a commanding space-age sphere featuring a dome with 1500 glass panels. A terrace offers sweeping views of the Hollywood Hills.

The museum's theaters host year-round film screenings and discussions. Oscar Sundays brings out award-winning blockbusters, while Silent Sundays screens long-forgotten classics. Branch Selects sees Academy members curating films significant to their specific craft. Watch for films hosted by Academy members who worked on them.

Use the Bloomberg Connects app, which offers insight to greatly enhance your experience in the galleries. There's a good cafe-restaurant with outdoor seating.

Smell the Ice Age

Get stuck at the La Brea Tar Pits

Mammoths, saber-toothed cats and other critters roamed LA's savanna in prehistoric times. The **La Brea Tar Pits & Museum** *(tarpits.org; adult/child $18/7)* preserve a trove of skulls and bones and are one of the world's most famous fossil sites. Generations of young dino hunters have come to learn about paleontology in the museum.

Outside, the smell of asphalt permeates the air as the tar pits still bubble away and beloved models show mammoths stuck in the gooey crude oil bubbling up from deep below Wilshire Blvd. A life-size diorama of a mammoth family dramatizes the cruel fate of countless thousands of animals between 50,000 and 10,000 years ago. Nearby, you can observe pits where fossils are still being discovered.

Not Just for Gearheads

Zoom into the Petersen Automotive Museum

The **Petersen Automotive Museum** *(petersen.org; adult/child $21/12)* is a treat even for those who can't tell a piston from a crankshaft. Inside the museum's body of undulating

DRINKING IN MIRACLE MILE & FAIRFAX: OUR PICKS

El Carmen: Loud, dimly lit and festooned with bull heads and *lucha libre* wrestling memorabilia, this tequila tavern pulls in an industry-heavy crowd. *5pm-2am*

Stir Crazy: Neighborhood favorite with sociable tables out front and rare California wines by the glass. Daily specials and small plates. *5-11pm Mon-Fri*

Be Bright Coffee: Storefront cafe roasts its own beans, used by restaurants across LA. Expertly crafted coffee drinks; plenty of tea options. *8am-4pm*

Snake Pit: Long-running dive bar serving the Dr Martens crowd on Melrose. Good drink prices and big selection of whiskey. Popular burgers. *3am-midnight*

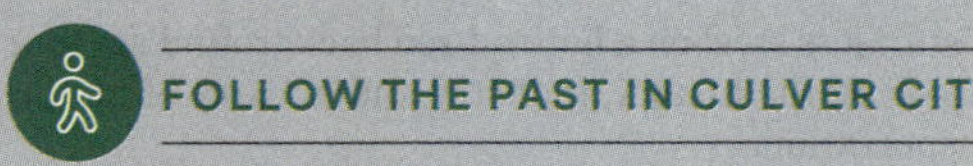

FOLLOW THE PAST IN CULVER CITY

Hollywood's workaday sibling, Culver City, produced scores of movies. Now a burgeoning tech hub, it's a walkable pleasure.

START	END	LENGTH
Metro E Line, Culver City Station	Sony Pictures	2 miles; 2hr

Cross over from the Metro line E, Culver City Station ❶ **Platform**, a buzzing outdoor development that harbors niche boutiques and eateries. Loqui offers creative Mexican you can enjoy on the back patio. Hidden behind an inconspicuous door on Venice Blvd, the ❷ **Museum of Jurassic Technology** *(mjt.org; $15)* is LA's most idiosyncratic museum. Its labyrinth of curiosities would be right at home in a carnival sideshow. Book ahead.

Many iconic movies were filmed at ❸ **Culver Studios**, including the original *A Star Is Born*. It's now home to Amazon Studios. The ❹ **Culver Hotel** (1924) is a National Historic Landmark. From here, Washington Blvd is lined with many shaded cafes. A striking example of Streamline Moderne architecture, the 1946 ❺ **Kirk Douglas Theatre** *(centertheatregroup.org)* showcases new works by local playwrights. Across the intersection, diminutive Village Well Books attracts writers who tap away at communal tables. Stop into the ❻ **Backstage Bar & Grill**, the long-running dive bar popular with studio workers in for a shot.

MGM, arguably the most storied of the old major studios, was not in Hollywood but in Culver City. Today, it's known as ❼ **Sony Pictures** and you can visit the locations of famous films. In-depth tours *(sonypicturesstudiostours.com; from $55)* depart from Overland Gate on Overland Ave.

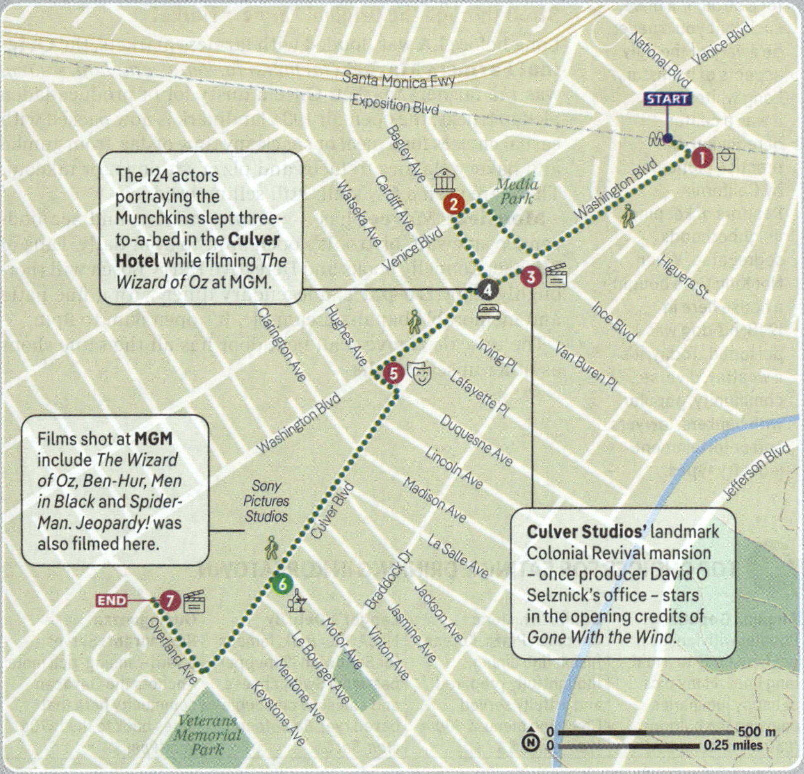

The 124 actors portraying the Munchkins slept three-to-a-bed in the **Culver Hotel** while filming *The Wizard of Oz* at MGM.

Films shot at **MGM** include *The Wizard of Oz, Ben-Hur, Men in Black* and *Spider-Man. Jeopardy!* was also filmed here.

Culver Studios' landmark Colonial Revival mansion – once producer David O Selznick's office – stars in the opening credits of *Gone With the Wind.*

HANCOCK PARK

Century-old mansions flank the tree-lined streets of **Hancock Park**, a genteel neighborhood roughly bounded by Highland, Rossmore and Melrose Aves and Wilshire Blvd. In the 1920s, LA's leading families, including the Dohenys and Chandlers, hired famous architects to build their cribs and numerous celebrities have lived here amid the curving lawns.

It's a lovely area for a stroll or a drive, such that you'd never be aware of the ugly aspects of its history. Long whites-only, it was a center of redlining, the practice pioneered by California Realtors of keeping neighborhoods segregated. When Nat King Cole bought a house here in 1948, his dog was poisoned. Today, it's a wealthy, diverse community, popular with bankers, lawyers and entertainment industry types.

bands of stainless steel on a hot-rod-red background are four floors exploring the history, industry and artistry of motorized transportation.

Vehicles are rotated through the exhibitions regularly. Start your visit on the history floor, loaded with classic and concept cars. In the Cars of Film and Television gallery, you might see the DeLorean from *Back to the Future,* the Durango 95 from *A Clockwork Orange* and a Batmobile or two.

The industry floor is devoted to how cars are designed and built. The kids' section is inspired by Disney's *Cars;* there's a custom-built Lightning McQueen. The ground floor focuses on the art of the automobile, mostly in special exhibits.

New for 2025, the extra-admission basement **Vault** *(adult/child $28/12)* displays over 300 rare cars and motorcycles. Here you won't find cars that ran on the open road; rather, you'll discover rare concept cars and vehicles designed for special purposes. Many are exquisite works of art. Expect anything from Pope John Paul II's Popemobile to cars decades ahead of their time, like the 1953 Cadillac Series 62 by Ghia.

The Petersen is the perfect stop if you've arrived in LA via Route 66, which passes to the north on Santa Monica Blvd and ends at the Santa Monica Pier.

Taste Delight

Stroll through the Original Farmers Market

Long before LA was flooded with farmers markets, the **Original Farmers Market** *(farmersmarketla.com; hours vary)* was *the* farmers market. Once a dusty lot of produce-laden pickup trucks, the open-air 1934 landmark is now packed with casual choices for a meal or snack any time of day, from gumbo and bakery classics to tacos and pizza, sit-down or takeout. There are even a few stalls still selling produce.

Monsieur Marcel has a gourmet market and seafood-centric sidewalk bistro. It's open 9am to 9pm daily. Fans of Michael Connelly books and Detective Harry Bosch will thoroughly enjoy **Du-par's**, a legendary diner with a fine patio and memorable banana cream pie. It's open 6am to 9pm.

The upscale **Grove** mall next door has all the same shops as other upscale malls.

TOP CHOICES FOR EATING & DRINKING IN KOREATOWN

Ahgassi Gopchang: Popular with families; get here early to avoid long lines. Many pics of happy luminaries enjoying the bulgogi. *11.30am-midnight* $$

Danbi: In historic Chapman Plaza, Korean fusion fine dining, thoughtfully prepared and artfully served. Changing menu. *6-10pm Wed-Sun* $$$

Langer's Deli: By MacArthur Park, famous for Sandwich 19 (peppery pastrami, Swiss cheese and coleslaw on double-baked rye). *8am-4pm Mon-Sat* $$

Guelaguetza Restaurant: Serves award-winning, rich mole. Anchors the Oaxacan community here that dates back to the 1990s. *9am-9pm* $$

KIT LEONG/SHUTTERSTOCK

Original Farmers Market

High Style & Street Pleasures

Prowl Melrose Ave and 3rd St

This legendary rock-and-roll shopping strip is as famous for its epic people-watching as it is for its retail pleasures. The strip between N Poinsettia Pl and N Fairfax Ave gets a lot of the buzz thanks to the boutiques stuck together like block-long hedgerows. Most of its gear is rather low-end, so amuse yourself browsing, then get sweet at **Happy Ice**, which is open from noon to 9pm.

If you're after hipper, higher-end stuff, explore the long stretch of Melrose between N Crescent Heights Blvd and Santa Monica Blvd. Stop for selfie joy at the Paul Smith clothing store's Barbie-pink wall. Or hit 3rd St in the same area, which is the current place to find attitude outpacing style and cars with sticker prices beyond the means of the 99% idling in traffic.

Tarantino's Features

Nightly film fests at New Beverly Cinema

Quentin Tarantino owns the vintage 1920s **New Beverly Cinema** *(thenewbev.com)*, which screens classic, cult, current and art films. All are projected in 35mm, with many of the restored prints from the owner's collection. He also owns the Vista Theater (p399) in Los Feliz. Some programs are double

VIBRANT LITTLE ETHIOPIA

Starting with Little Armenia near Los Feliz, you can run right through the alphabet of LA's great diversity of cultures. Ever-changing, these enclaves are both old (Downtown's Little Tokyo) and new, like **Little Ethiopia**. Along a block of Fairfax Ave south of Olympic Blvd, it started with one shop around 1990. As is often the case, this attracted other immigrants and everyone's success became symbiotic. Soon, it was a hub for LA's Ethiopian community and in 2002 the city officially named the neighborhood Little Ethiopia. Browsing the many stores, cafes and markets makes for a fine walk. The green, yellow and red of the Ethiopian flag colors storefronts. Sidewalk displays offer yams and other staples. Cafes like **Buna** are indicative of the neighborhood's vibrancy.

TOP CHOICES FOR EATING & DRINKING IN KOREATOWN

Normandie Club: This dimly lit bar is cool and approachable. Talented staff whip up creative cocktails for pre-dinner imbibers and first dates. *6pm-2am*

Rosen Karaoke: Popular spot for great service and private rooms in varying sizes. Sing, snack and drink yourself happy. Good tunes selection. *7pm-2am*

Dan Sung Sa: In a tatty strip mall, mimics a Seoul street bar with tight wooden booths, potent soju cocktails and ribald revelry. *4pm-2am*

Lock & Key: Look for the neon key sign and enter. Classy, with candles on tables and a cool dance patio. The dress code eschews most bro-wear. *7pm-2am*

HUN YOUNG LEE/SHUTTERSTOCK

Koreatown

features and many include classic Bugs Bunny cartoons. The crowd is heavy with industry types who stand up front before the lights go down, discussing projects and deals.

No Ending to the Happy

Prowl the action in Koreatown

Koreatown is as close as LA gets to being the 'city that never sleeps.' Sprawling and vibrant, it's a platter of sizzling BBQ joints, buzzing malls and karaoke bars, all splashed with a dash of glorious Moderne architecture from the area's gilded past when it was a bastion of Golden Age Hollywood.

Koreatown is roughly bounded by Beverly and Olympic Blvds north and south, plus Western Ave on the west. The east side abuts MacArthur Park, the one that 'melts in the dark' in the eponymous Jimmy Webb song made famous by Donna Summer. Wilshire Blvd is the main artery, along with W 6th St, S Vermont Ave and W 8th St.

Koreatown has a vast number of eateries. Enjoy *soju-* (rice alcohol) or *makgeolli-* (rice wine) fueled swilling at a sweaty drinking den or in a *noraebang* (private karaoke room) hangout.

And, just to keep things geographically off-kilter, there's a cluster of superb Oaxacan restaurants.

BEST VENUES FOR LIVE ACTS

Groundlings: Improv alums include Will Ferrell, Maya Rudolph and Melissa McCarthy. On Thursdays, the main company and surprise guests riff together. *groundlings.com*

Improv: Launch pad for countless stand-up comics from Richard Pryor to Ellen DeGeneres. Mixes headlines with improv. *improv.com*

El Rey Theatre: This 1936 art deco dance hall is a brilliant live-music venue, with a killer sound system. *theelrey.com*

Pips on La Brea: Beautiful heated patio in Mid-City that's the scene for near-nightly jazz. Trees with fairy lights add to the date-night ambience. *pipsonlabrea.com*

Largo at the Coronet: Incubator of high-minded pop culture. It features edgy comedy and nourishing night music. *largo-la.com*

West Hollywood & Beverly Hills

WEALTH, LGBTQ+ LIFE AND FABLED SHOPPING

Famous worldwide, the 90210 zip code is a symbol for wealthy A-list celebrities, luxe hotels and top-of-the-line shopping. In the 1920s, actors Douglas Fairbanks and Mary Pickford built their home in Beverly Hills, turning the neighborhood into an immediate status symbol. Today, visitors flock here to get a taste of the fantasy and to take in the opulent real estate and swaying palm trees.

Nudging up alongside, but a world apart, West Hollywood (aka WeHo) is distinctly, proudly independent. With some of LA's finest bars, renowned live music, hedonistic nightlife and the famous (albeit faded) Sunset Strip, WeHo has a draw to rival the famous zip code. More importantly, WeHo is a thriving LGBTQ+ community, making West Hollywood one of the nation's most influential cities on LGBTQ+ issues. Of course, there is a little fun to be had; just drop by in June for Pride and October for Halloween.

TOP TIP

Superb walking tours of Rodeo Dr and celebrity homes are easily followed in the free **Beverly Hills Experience** app from the Beverly Hills Historical Society. The fact-filled routes are clearly marked. The home tour includes houses used by Frank Sinatra, Barbra Streisand, Eddie Murphy, Lucille Ball, George Clooney and many others.

GETTING AROUND

When the Metro Rail Line D Wilshire/Rodeo station opens – possibly in 2026 – it will revolutionize public transit access to Beverly Hills. Until then, Metro Bus Line 4 runs frequently along Santa Monica Blvd in West Hollywood and Beverly Hills, also reaching Hollywood, Silver Lake, Echo Park and Downtown LA. Metro Bus Line 2 connects Sunset Blvd in West Hollywood to Westwood, Hollywood, Silver Lake, Echo Park and Downtown LA.

Parking in WeHo and Beverly Hills is never easy and usually expensive. Both areas are enjoyably walkable, although WeHo is hilly at the edges.

SIGHTS
1 Greystone Mansion & Gardens

ACTIVITIES
see 13 Bikes & Hikes LA

SLEEPING
2 Andaz West Hollywood
3 Beverly Hills Hotel
4 Beverly Wilshire
5 Chateau Marmont
6 Crescent Hotel Beverly Hills
7 Mondrian Los Angeles
8 Sunset Tower Hotel

EATING
9 Hamburger Mary's
10 Nate'n Al's
11 Spago
12 Sugarfish
13 Tail O' the Pup
see 8 Tower Bar
14 Wally's Beverly Hills

DRINKING & NIGHTLIFE
15 Bar Next Door
16 Barney's Beanery
17 Micky's WeHo
18 The Abbey

ENTERTAINMENT
19 Comedy Store
20 Jazz Café at Cipriani Beverly Hills
21 Laugh Factory
22 Roxy Theatre
23 Whisky-a-Go-Go

SHOPPING
24 Book Soup
25 Cheese Store
26 Edelweiss Chocolates
see 24 Mystery Pier Books
27 Pleasure Chest

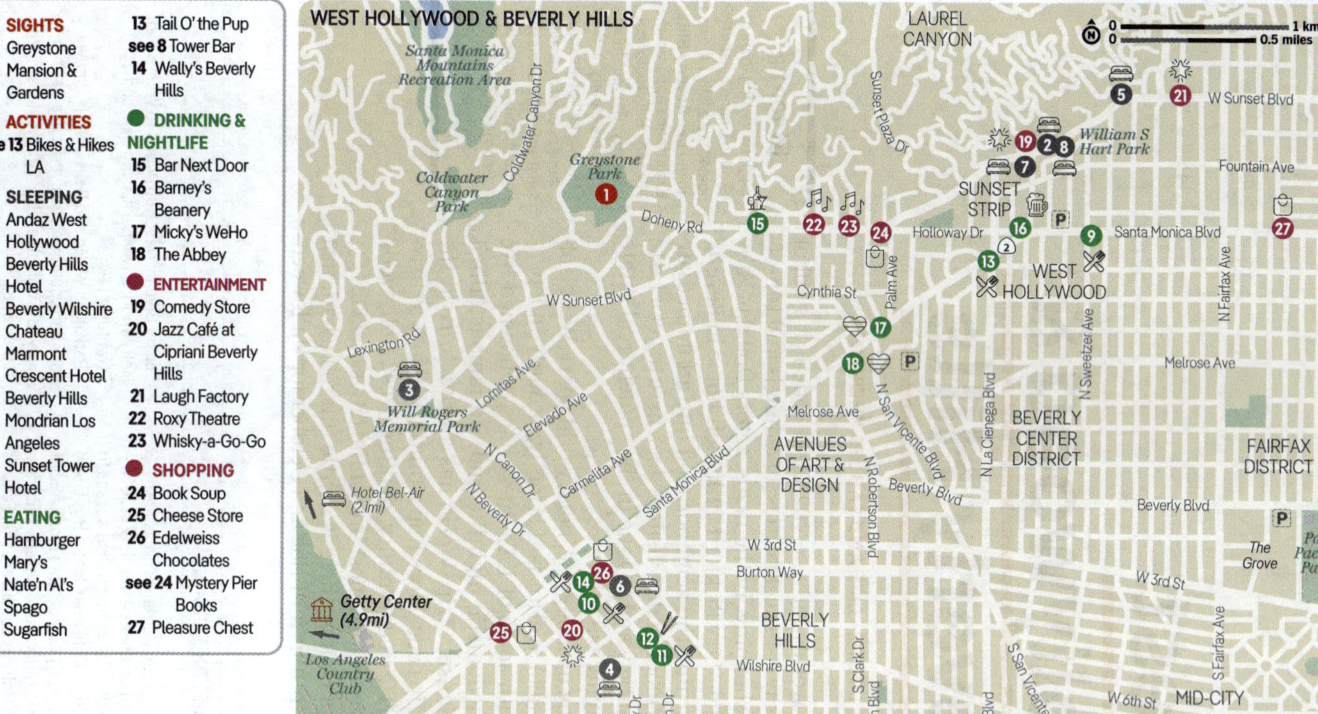

A Neighborhood Like No Other

Do the West Hollywood Walk

Santa Monica Boulevard is the main drag of West Hollywood (WeHo) and barhopping its length is one of the LA region's great joys. The LGBTQ+-centric bars and clubs heave through the weekends, with Sunday brunch being a must. Weeknights are busy as well.

Central to WeHo is one of the most iconic gay nightclubs on the West Coast today, **The Abbey**, which serves the community as a cultural center as well as being a bar and nightclub. With over three decades in the game, it's been called the best gay bar in the world. Match your mood to the space: thumping dance floor, outdoor patios, Goth lounge or chill space. It's open from 11am to 2am daily.

The boulevard abounds with choices like the iconic **Micky's Weho**, with long-running drag shows and great DJ sets. It's open noon to 2am. **Hamburger Mary's** is the Sunday afternoon brunch go-to. It's open from 11am to 10 pm.

If You Were Rich & Famous

The Beverly Hills experience

Beverly Hills is as much a state of mind as a place. Its name is so often used as shorthand for ostentatious wealth, conspicuous consumption and celebrity that it can get reduced to cliché. Ultimately, however, it's a rich, tidy place without a plethora of must-see sights; rather, you go to soak up the vibe, nibble off a bit of the fantasy and think about what life would be like if that was your Lamborghini parked on Rodeo Dr.

On a short walk (p418), you can take in the heart of Beverly Hills, including Rodeo Dr. Spoiler alert: the big-name retailers here all exist to serve free-spending tourists; the rich and/or famous shop at the private boutiques.

Stop at the **Beverly Hills Hotel**, the famed 'pink palace' that's never lost its sheen of glamour and where the **Polo Lounge** or **Cabana Cafe** remain the ultimate Beverly Hills experience. Have a martini and mourn the arrival of cell phones, which ended the tradition of fading celebs calling the hotel and having themselves paged to remind producers of their existence.

Note: don't bother with **Bel Air**, which is all 16ft hedges and fences.

WEHO'S BEST LIVE VENUES

Whisky-a-Go-Go: Trades on its legendary status when the Doors were the house band and go-go dancing was invented here. *whiskyagogo.com*

Roxy Theatre: A Sunset Strip fixture since 1973. This small venue puts you close to the bands, with some big-name surprises. *theroxy.com*

Comedy Store: The club with cred. Richard Pryor, George Carlin, Eddie Murphy and Robin Williams were all nurtured here. *thecomedystore.com*

Laugh Factory: The Marx Brothers used to keep offices at this institution. Gets big names, up-and-comers and surprise celebs. *laughfactory.com*

Jazz Café at Cipriani Beverly Hills: In Beverly Hills this luxe jazz bar caters to a refined crowd in the swank Cipriani Hotel. Top acts. *cipriani.com*

WHERE TO EAT & DRINK IN WEHO

Tail O' the Pup: Look for the big weenie in a bun – it's right beside the road. Hot dogs served in myriad ways. *noon-10pm* $

Barney's Beanery: Burger and beer bar that has fronted Santa Monica Blvd since it was known as Route 66 and Studebakers steamed out front. *11am-2am* $$

Tower Bar: Old-school Hollywood luxury in an indoor-outdoor setting at the swank Sunset Tower Hotel. Vaunted martinis and high-end burgers. *7am-10pm* $$$

Bar Next Door: Enticing cocktail bar with a solid backlist of creations going back more than a century. Has rare libations; cheery, mellow vibe. *5pm-2am* $$

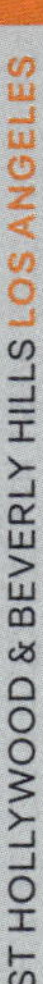

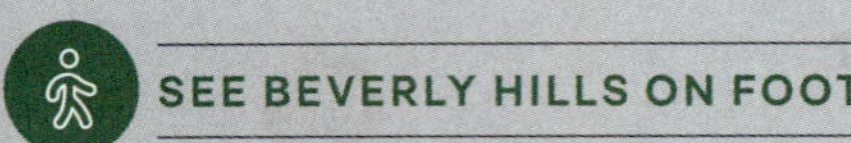

SEE BEVERLY HILLS ON FOOT

Stroll Rodeo Dr and discover notable art and iconic architecture and get your picture taken: yep, you're in Beverly Hills!

START	END	LENGTH
Rodeo Dr and Wilshire Blvd	Beverly Gardens Park	0.75 miles; 2hr

Standing at the corner of 1 **Rodeo Drive and Wilshire Boulevard**, begin your walk up the three-block ribbon of consumption that features every major luxury brand on the planet. Architecturally, nothing is especially noteworthy – even the Frank Lloyd Wright 2 **Anderton Court Shops** at number 328 are ho-hum. Rather, a successful day here is measured by the number of glossy brand-name shopping bags you can carry. Note: celebs go to private boutiques, so don't expect to see any famous faces.

When you reach inner-Santa Monica Blvd, turn right for one block. 3 **Mr Brainwash Art Museum** *(mrbrainwashartmuseum.com; adult/child $20/free)* is the namesake project of the French-born Banksy protege who's based in LA. It's crammed with his whimsical kitsch-meets-fine art; eg, the Hollywood Sign pops up in a Van Gogh.

Two streets east is a mid-century icon: the 4 **Union 76 Gas Station**. Its swooping, back-to-the-future canopy is a world-famous example of Googie architecture and is spectacular at night. Swing around to Rexford Dr and the 5 **Beverly Hills Civic Center**, a grand 1932 Spanish Revival edifice. Cross into 6 **Beverly Gardens Park**. At nearly 2 miles, this green swath is the manicured, flower-filled border to commercial Beverly Hills. The 40ft-long 'Beverly Hills' sign might as well spell s-e-l-f-i-e.

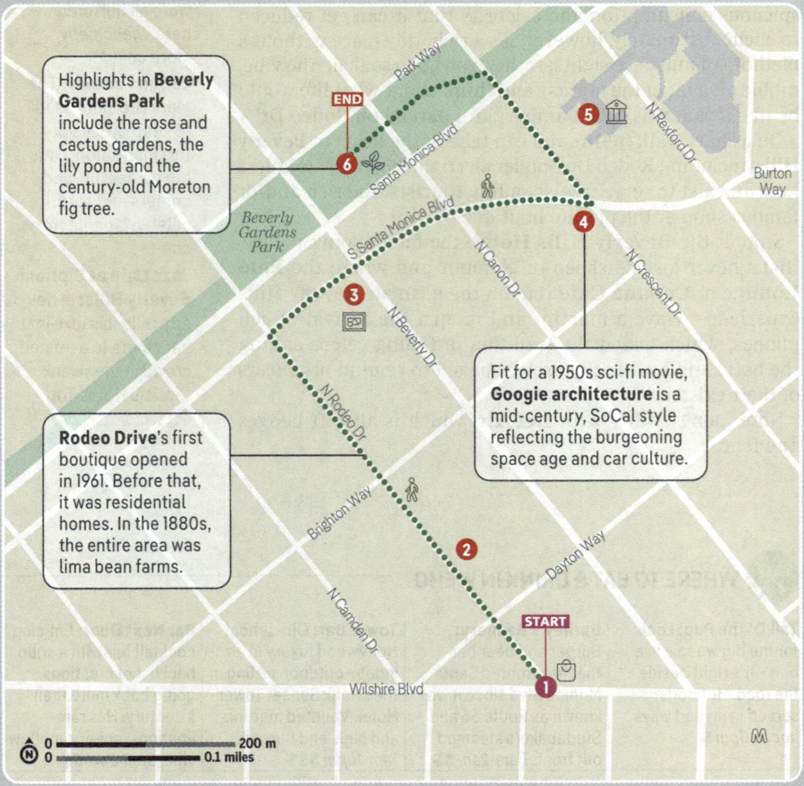

Touring the Active Way

Hiking and biking the sights

See Hollywood, Beverly Hills and greater LA on highly recommended tours with **Bikes & Hikes LA** *(bikesandhikesla.com)*. Its signature ride is the 32-mile 'LA in a Day,' which takes in celebrity homes, swank shopping streets, inspiring architecture and the Pacific *(from $187 on an e-bike)*. Other options include shorter tours and e-bikes. Hiking tours include a 1½-hour jaunt to the Hollywood Sign (p382).

A Vital Experience

The compelling Museum of Tolerance

Learning the hard lessons of humanity's past so they aren't repeated is at the core of the **Museum of Tolerance** *(museumoftolerance.com; adult/child $18/13.50)*. The human cost of intolerance is relentlessly detailed on each floor. Among the museum's many fascinating artifacts are original diary entries written by Anne Frank as well as the first record of Hitler's anti-Semitic beliefs.

Visitors, including many school groups, are given the persona of a child who died in the **Holocaust** and then follow an effective and gripping exhibit about the events that shows the influence of major donor Steven Spielberg. In the basement, the **Social Lab** is an immersive and interactive exploration of how we are driven apart through prejudice and bigotry. It's effective and timely.

One BIG House

Be dazzled at Greystone Mansion & Gardens

Looking just like you'd expect a Beverly Hills mansion to look, the **Greystone Mansion & Gardens** *(free)* has featured in countless movies and TV shows *(The Big Lebowski, There Will Be Blood)*. This 1927 Tudor Revival pile was a gift from oil tycoon Edward Doheny to his son Ned. In 1929, the oil heir and his male secretary were both found dead in an alleged murder-suicide – a notorious mystery that has been debated endlessly ever since.

The elegant grounds with their perfectly coiffed lawns, Italian Renaissance fountains and 166ft walkway with enormous cypress trees offer commanding views of LA. The lavish interior is often open the first Saturday or Sunday each month.

THE BEST NON-DESIGNER SHOPPING

Cheese Store: Featured in one of the final episodes of *Curb Your Enthusiasm;* has a section for 'Larry David's cheese.' *cheesestore.com*

Edelweiss Chocolates: Old-school shop; that woman buying chocolates looks like the one who played Mom on a classic sitcom. *edelweiss chocolates.com*

Pleasure Chest: The perfect boutique to accessorize your soiree in WeHo. Most tastes are catered for in this adult novelty store. *thepleasure chest.com*

Book Soup: Great indie bookstore with thoughtful staff recs. The source for eclectic, edgy and LA-based fiction. *booksoup.com*

Mystery Pier Books: Signed scripts from blockbusters and rare 1st editions. Curated selection of mystery and detective fiction. *mysterypierbooks.com*

EATING IN BEVERLY HILLS: TOP CHOICES

Spago: Wolfgang Puck's heart remains where his empire started and most evenings he still turns up. The smoked salmon pizza is an icon. *5.30-9.30pm* $$$

Sugarfish: Quality sushi in a small space; always packed with talent agents and local residents. The 20-course tasting menu is pure pleasure. *11.30am-10pm* $$$

Nate'n Al's: Get a bowl of piping-hot matzo-ball soup and a Brentwood sandwich at this Beverly Hills institution, which shines after a refresh. *8am-9pm* $$

Wally's Beverly Hills: Wine bar and restaurant with outdoor seating and a huge choice of wine, mescal and champagne. Cheese platters too. *10am-12.30am* $$

GETTY CENTER TIPS

- Book a timed entry reservation in advance. Parking is $25 ($15 after 3pm); a space is reserved for all reservation holders.
- Visit early morning or mid-afternoon. Sunsets create a remarkable alchemy of light and shadow. Saturday nights are usually less crowded.
- Get the essential GettyGuide app. Free audioguides are available in the lobby. Bring a photo ID.
- There's a modern American restaurant and two casual cafes. The food is fine, but consider bringing a picnic lunch to enjoy on the beautiful grounds.
- The 16,000 tons of travertine cladding the Getty came from the same Italian quarry used for Rome's ancient Colosseum. Look closely to spot fossilized shells, fish and foliage.
- Tours and special events are invariably worth the time.

WALTER CICCHETTI/SHUTTERSTOCK

Getty Center

Treasures on a Hill

Experience the Getty Center

Straddling a hilltop in the Santa Monica Mountains off the 405, the palatial **Getty Center** *(getty.edu; entry free)* offers an irresistible feast of art, design and botanical beauty. Ponder the myths and landscapes of Dossi, Van Gogh and Cézanne, gaze out over the City of Angels and kick back in a verdant wonderland of gurgling water, lush lawns and world-famous sculptures.

The Getty's collections focus on European art, with a concentration on works from the 19th and 20th centuries. There are genuine treasures here. In the east pavilion, seek out Gentileschi's *Danaë and the Shower of Gold* and Rembrandt's self-portrait, *Rembrandt Laughing*. In the west pavilion, look for Van Gogh's *Irises*, Monet's *Wheatstacks, Snow Effect, Morning*, Manet's *Jeanne (Spring)* and Turner's *Modern Rome – Campo Vaccino*. The south pavilion's outdoor terrace is home to Marino Marini's excitable bronze *Angel of the Citadel*, while the grounds themselves are studded with prized sculptures, including three works by Henry Moore.

On Saturday evenings in summer, the center hosts **Off the 405**, a popular series featuring top progressive pop and world-music acts in the Getty courtyard.

Santa Monica & Malibu

SUNSETS, FUN PIERS, BEACHES, SURFING AND LIFESTYLE

Santa Monica is LA's little sister: its smaller, beachier twin, with glass towers abutting the famous pier and amusement park. Surrounded by the city on three sides and the Pacific on the fourth, here boarders bob in the waves, laid-back dudes sip hazy brews next to martini-swilling Hollywood producers and celebrity chefs rub elbows with on-point soccer moms at bountiful farmers markets.

With the Pacific as the canvas, the vermilion spectacle at sunset extends along the Pacific Coast Hwy (PCH) to Malibu, the fabled beach town. Although the entire region is working hard to recover from the devastating 2025 Palisades wildfires, there is much to engage the visitor. Unmissable sights like the Getty Villa and the Malibu Pier still amaze and delight. And the near-endless ribbon of beaches are as welcoming as ever with famous names like Zuma ready to allow any comer to join in the Southern California dream.

TOP TIP

Tour LA's world-famous beaches by riding the 22-mile-long **Marvin Braude Bike Trail**. The paved coastal path starts at Will Rogers Beach in Santa Monica and passes through Venice, Hermosa and Redondo Beaches before ending at Torrance Beach. Rent a cruiser or an e-bike from **Joyride** *(joyridesantamonica.com; all-day rentals from $30)*.

Go for a Ride

The unmissable Santa Monica Pier

No visit to LA is complete without a stroll on historic **Santa Monica Pier** *(santamonicapier.org; free)* that features on just about every LA tourist ad. Stretching almost a quarter-mile

GETTING AROUND

Santa Monica is well-served by the Metro Rail E Line, which goes right downtown and provides easy links to LAX and beyond. Going north, transit options dwindle quickly to one Metro bus line, the 134 along the Pacific Coast Hwy to Malibu. There's a stop for the Getty Villa. Topanga Canyon has no service.

Beachside parking fees add up quickly along the coast. For Santa Monica, take the train. Santa Monica is also enjoyably walkable, especially on the bluff overlooking the beaches, which seamlessly flow right into Venice. Malibu sprawls, with no real center to walk.

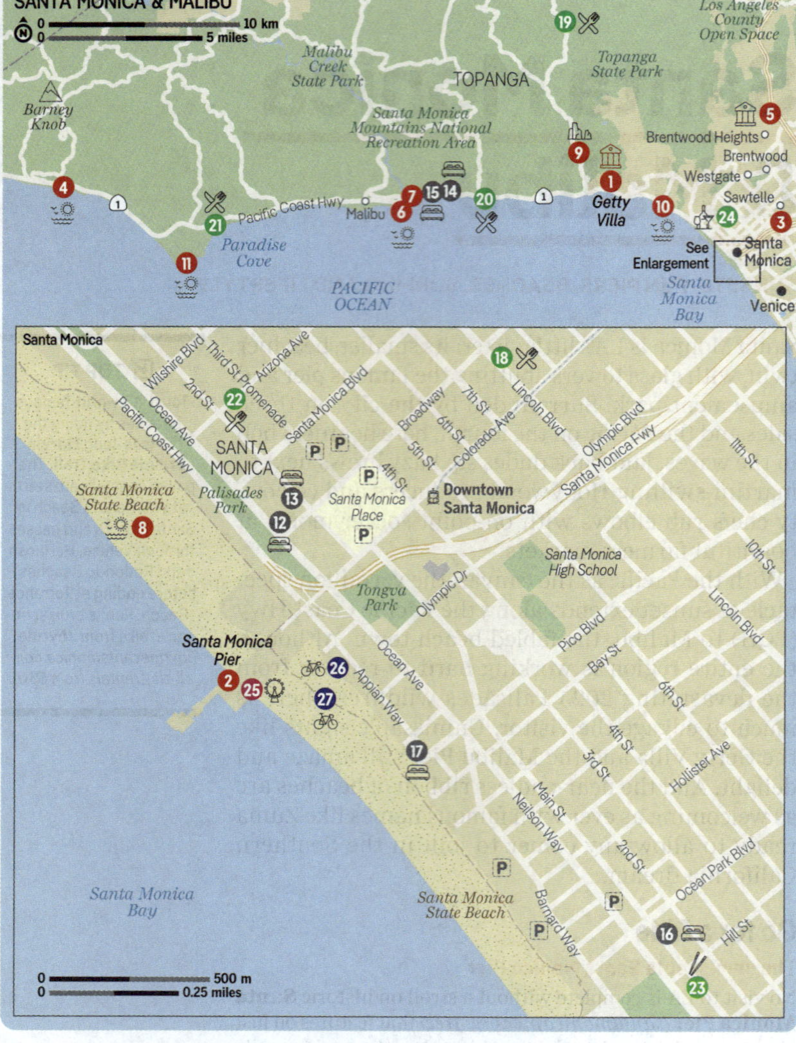

HIGHLIGHTS
1 Getty Villa
2 Santa Monica Pier

SIGHTS
3 Bergamot Station Arts Center
4 El Matador State Beach
5 Getty Center
6 Malibu Lagoon State Beach
7 Malibu Pier
8 Santa Monica State Beach
9 Topanga Canyon
10 Will Rogers State Beach
11 Zuma Beach

SLEEPING
12 Georgian Hotel
13 HI Los Angeles Santa Monica Hostel
14 M Malibu
15 Malibu Beach Inn
16 Sea Shore Motel
17 Shutters on the Beach

EATING
18 Bay Cities Italian Deli & Bakery
19 Cafe on 27
20 Duke's Malibu
see 7 Malibu Farm Restaurant
see 15 Nobu Malibu
21 Paradise Cove
22 Santa Monica Farmers Markets
23 Sunny Blue

DRINKING & NIGHTLIFE
24 Divine Vintage

ENTERTAINMENT
25 Pacific Park

TRANSPORTATION
26 Joyride
27 Marvin Braude Bike Trail

over the Pacific, it's the exclamation point on iconic Route 66, which began 2400 miles east in Chicago.

Dating to 1908, the pier is the city's most compelling landmark. Every angle is dominated by the **Pacific Park** *(pacpark.com; rides from $8)* amusement park and its family-friendly arcades, carnival games, soaring **Ferris wheel** and tame roller coaster. Nearby is a vintage 1922 carousel and an aquarium. The pier is most photogenic when framed by California sunsets and when it comes alive with free concerts and outdoor movies in the summertime.

Year-Round Creative Festival

Discover the Bergamot Station Arts Center

A former trolley yard, **Bergamot Station Arts Center** *(bergamotstation.com)*, has been converted to one of LA's best arts centers. More than 20 private galleries show the works of well-regarded (and often famous) artists and photographers. The free exhibitions are always changing, so just wander around to see what's on. The Metro E Line stops right outside.

Ancient Treasures by the Sea

Visit the extraordinary Getty Villa

Located just north of Santa Monica in Pacific Palisades is the remarkable **Getty Villa** *(getty.edu; entry free)*. This stunning place was built in 1974 when billionaire J Paul Getty decided to recreate Herculaneum's Villa dei Papiri, a Roman villa that was buried in the eruption of Mt Vesuvius in 79 CE. The focus here is on the art and cultures of ancient Greece, Rome and Etruria and there's also a vast collection of classical and Renaissance-era artworks on display. Corinthian columns surround perfectly manicured gardens and an elongated pool. Don't miss the Pompeii fountain and Temple of Herakles.

An advance, timed ticket is required; parking costs $25 ($15 after 3pm). Note: the **Getty Center** (p420) is one of LA's premier cultural highlights. The parking fee can be used at both institutions on the same day.

Back to a Beautiful Past

Drive Topanga Canyon

The sinuous 12 miles of Hwy 27 that cut north through **Topanga Canyon** from the namesake beach to Woodland Hills in the San Fernando Valley are a scenic time warp. The road

BEST BEACHES: SANTA MONICA TO MALIBU

El Matador State Beach: Park on the bluffs and stroll down to sandstone rock towers rising from emerald coves.

Zuma Beach: Easily accessed from the PCH (and Metro bus), with parking and long stretches of sand. Find privacy at Pirate's Cove.

Malibu Lagoon State Beach: Where Malibu Creek meets the ocean, migratory birds proliferate, attracting human spotters. To the north are popular surf breaks.

Will Rogers State Beach: The quiet alternative to the famous strands to the south. This was the beach used for *Baywatch*.

Santa Monica State Beach: There are endless ways to enjoy this 3.5-mile stretch of sand, running seamlessly into Venice Beach (p427) in the south.

EATING & DRINKING IN SANTA MONICA: OUR PICKS

Bay Cities Italian Deli & Bakery: Best Italian deli in LA, period. Signature sandwich is the spicy Godmother (piled with Italian meats). *9am-6pm Wed-Sun* $

Sunny Blue: *Omusubi* (rice balls, aka *onigiri*) made to order from dozens of filling choices, from seaweed to salmon. One of the best waterfront options. *11am-8pm* $$

Santa Monica Farmers Markets: You haven't really experienced Santa Monica until you've explored one of its outdoor farmers markets. *8am-1pm Wed & Sat* $

Divine Vintage: Charming wine bar in a cute cottage. Most choices are organic. Nearby is Father's Office, a welcoming gastropub. *noon-8pm* $$

THE 2025 PALISADES FIRE

On January 7, 2025, a small brush fire near Pacific Palisades, fueled by drought and high winds, erupted into a raging inferno. Before the end of the month, the fire had burned nearly 23,500 acres, destroyed over 6800 structures and killed at least 12 people. Much of the affluent community of Pacific Palisades and parts of Malibu were destroyed. The flames reached the beaches and entire swaths of the famous cheek-to-jowl oceanfront homes along the Pacific Coast Hwy (Hwy 1) burned. In the aftermath of LA's worst wildfire to date, the region struggled with recovery. The cleanup lasted for months and many beloved businesses that weren't destroyed went bankrupt during the months the PCH was closed.

CHIZHEVSKAYA EKATERINA/SHUTTERSTOCK

Malibu Pier

first passes through a primordial cleft cut deep in the Santa Monica Mountains before reaching heights that afford sweeping views of the valley.

The road is shadowed by lazy oaks and glimmering sycamores and the whole thing smells of wind-blown black sage and 'cowboy cologne' (artemisia). Along the way, you'll pass vendors selling new-agey wares and signs depicting pigs with wings.

About halfway to the pass, the cute country town of **Topanga** sprouts on both sides of the road. A bit further on, popular **Cafe on 27** has tables in the trees. The cafe is open from 9am to 5pm.

Gangway to the Pacific

Stroll Malibu's great little pier

Besides the extraordinary beaches, Malibu's one real highlight is its namesake wooden **pier**, which traces its history to 1905. Strolling its 700ft length is a delight and there is a good restaurant, **Malibu Farm** at the base. Some of the best views of the Malibu coast are from the pier, as the wall-to-wall beach houses (even after the 2025 fires destroyed so many) cut off views from the Pacific Coast Hwy.

EATING & DRINKING WITH A VIEW IN MALIBU

Malibu Farm Restaurant: Dining rooms at Malibu Pier are a perfect place to munch on farm-to-table brunches, lunches and snacks. *9am-7pm* $$

Duke's Malibu: A beachfront legend known to employ minor Malibu celebs. The cocktail-seafood-steak menu is a crowd-pleaser. *11.30am-9pm* $$

Paradise Cove: Famous semi-private beach with expensive parking controlled by this cafe. Have lunch on the sand to avoid high fees. *8am-9pm* $$

Nobu Malibu: Chef Nobu Matsuhisa's empire of luxe Japanese restaurants includes this celeb-favored hotspot where tables overlook the sea. *noon-10pm* $$$

Venice & South Coast Beaches

BOHEMIAN BOARDWALKS, CANALS, STREET ART AND THE BEACH

For many, Venice Beach is synonymous with the Boardwalk. It embodies a clichéd California vibe that mixes carefree beach life, post-hippie weirdness and general funkitude. And that's all true, but Venice is much more. It's about good food and drink, good shopping and adapting hip trends to your own good life. You'll discover that the name isn't random as there really are canals and, in their own way, they embody all of Venice's qualities.

Heading south, you pass through the string of South Bay beach towns for which LA is also famous. The long sandy swath never ends as you pass through one volleyball-and-bacchanalia haven after another.

Manhattan Beach has so much to offer that it's hard to leave. Hermosa Beach and Redondo Beach add their own unique charms. At the south end, the Palos Verdes Peninsula crowns the coastline as it angles from south to east.

TOP TIP

Get gear for the boardwalk, the coastal Marvin Braude Bike Trail and getting around town at **Venice Boardwalk Bike Rental** *(veniceboardwalkbikerental.com)*. It rents all types of bikes, skateboards and in-line skates.

Living Life on the Sand

Venice's beach and boardwalk

Prepare for a sensory overload on the **Venice Boardwalk**, one of LA's essential experiences. Buff bodybuilders brush elbows with street performers and sellers of sunglasses, ribald

GETTING AROUND

The Metro Rail E Line to Downtown Santa Monica is a nice beach stroll 1.5 miles north of Venice. Otherwise, take Metro Bus Line 33 and Santa Monica's Big Blue Bus Lines 1, 3 and 18 from the station south into Venice. The South Bay beach towns all have minimal bus service and are best reached by car, which also allows you to bounce from one town to the next along the PCH.

Venice is wonderfully walkable and that's one of the prime reasons for coming. Use the 22-mile-long Marvin Braude Bike Trail to cycle the entire coast.

HIGHLIGHTS
1 Abbot Kinney Blvd
2 Venice Boardwalk
3 Venice Canals
4 Venice Skate Park

SIGHTS
5 Bruce's Beach
6 Dockweiler State Beach
7 El Porto Beach
8 George Freeth Memorial
9 Hermosa Beach
10 Manhattan Beach
11 Marina Mother's Beach
12 Redondo Beach
13 Venice Beach
14 Venice Beach Art Walls

SLEEPING
see 9 Beach House Hermosa Beach
15 Hotel Erwin
16 Inn at Venice Beach
see 10 ITH Hermosa Beach Surf Hostel LAX
17 Samesun Venice Beach
18 Sea View Inn at the Beach
19 Venice Breeze Suites

EATING
20 Café Gratitude
21 Felix Trattoria
22 Gjusta
see 10 Manhattan Beach Creamery
23 Martha's Hermosa Beach
see 8 Quality Seafood

DRINKING & NIGHTLIFE
see 10 Ercoles 1101
see 9 Pier Plaza
24 Townhouse & Del Monte Speakeasy

SHOPPING
25 Aviator Nation
26 Principessa

TRANSPORTATION
27 Venice Boardwalk Bike Rental

underwear, Mexican ponchos and cannabis, while cyclists and in-line skaters whiz by on the bike path and skateboarders and graffiti sprayers get their own domains.

Venice Beach has long been associated with street art. Proof are the tagged-up towers and the freestanding concrete wall of the **Venice Beach Art Walls** *(veniceartwalls.com)* that have been covered by graffiti painters from 1961 to the present.

Gym rats with an exhibitionist streak can get a tan and a workout at this famous **outdoor gym** right on the Venice Boardwalk, where Arnold Schwarzenegger and Franco Columbu once bulked up. Nearby **volleyball nets** and **basketball courts** also get a workout.

When Angelenos drained their swimming pools during a 1970s drought, board-toting teens made their not-quite-welcome invasion and modern skateboarding culture was born. Today, the public 17,000-sq-ft ocean-view **skate park** is a destination for both high flyers and gawking spectators. There are regular competitions.

Venice's Characterful Shopping Strip

Browse Abbot Kinney Blvd

Abbot Kinney Boulevard between Venice Blvd and Main St is full of upscale boutiques (both indie and chain), galleries, lofts and cafes and restaurants. Many shops are housed in reconstructed old wooden beach shacks. Favored shops include **Aviator Nation** *(aviatornation.com)* and **Principessa** *(principessavenice.com)*. The parallel stretch of Lincoln Blvd four blocks north is also good shopping territory.

Home of Beach Volleyball

Surf and sand at Manhattan Beach

A bastion of surf music and the birthplace of beach volleyball, **Manhattan Beach** may have gone chic, but that salty-dog heart still beats. Downtown's trendy restaurants and boutiques still mix with dive bars.

Ditch the shoes on the wide sweep of golden sand at the **beach**. You'll find pick-up **volleyball courts**, a **pier** with sweeping sea views and a consistent sandy bottom. The volleyball nets start here and run right through Hermosa Beach.

Founded in 1912, **Bruce's Beach** was a popular private African American beach. Driven by racism, the town of Manhattan Beach seized the beach from the Bruce family in 1924. In 2022, LA County returned the area bounded by Highland

VENICE CANALS

The **Venice Canals** are uniquely embedded in the heart of a now desirable residential area. The picturesque canals were created in 1905 by developer and conservationist Abbot Kinney, who wanted to replicate Italy's famed waterways, dubbing the area the 'Venice of America.'

What was once an expansive place of bridges and canals has shrunk in size, with only six canals remaining, comprising a length of 3 miles. Having become decrepit after WWII, the canals have reclaimed their beauty and charm, especially with the architecturally diverse homes that line the canalside paths.

A popular film and TV location, the canals' apex may have been toward the end of *Touch of Evil* (1958) when a dissolute Orson Wells dies, flopping around in the then-polluted waters.

BEST PLACES TO EAT & DRINK IN VENICE

Felix Trattoria: People flock here for maestro chef Evan Funke's *rigatoni all'amatriciana* and other artfully invented new forms of pasta. *5-9.30pm* **$$$**

Café Gratitude: Cutting-edge vegan dishes are paired with an open patio and fresh sea breezes. Sustainable, locavore and always surprising. *10am-9pm* **$$**

Gjusta: A *very* local bakery, cafe and deli behind a nondescript storefront on a hidden side street. Great patio. Food to go is ideal for picnics. *7am-4pm* **$$**

Townhouse & Del Monte Speakeasy: Upstairs: a cool, dark bar with a history dating to 1915. Downstairs: a speakeasy with DJs and bands. *5pm-2am* **$**

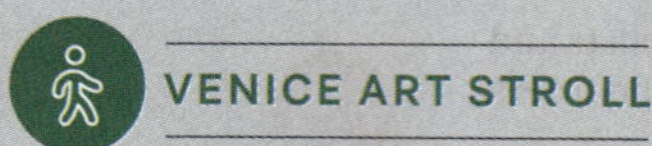

VENICE ART STROLL

Step into the Venice lifestyle and see the art that helps give the area its idiosyncratic vibe.

START	END	LENGTH
Venice Pier	Venice Ale House	2¼ miles; 2hr

Start at 1 **Venice Pier**. Here nature's golden sands unfurl and the blue sea churns. Walk inland to the 2 **Venice Canals** (p427). This idyllic neighborhood preserves 3 miles of waterways lined with a warren of cool waterside houses with cute little gardens, many featuring outdoor sculptures. Take time to wander at will. Exit the enclave and turn left on S Venice Blvd.

Pause at 3 **LA Louver**, a modern and contemporary art gallery featuring rotating, museum-quality exhibitions. Now, it's time for the main event, the 4 **Venice Boardwalk** (p425), where free expression is de rigueur. Look for Rip Cronk's epic 30ft-tall 5 **Jim Morrison Mural** on your right. Then see the Cronks of tomorrow in action at 6 **Venice Beach Art Walls** (p427), a vortex for the loony, the free-spirited and the hip. Head away from the sand briefly on Windward Ave until you see 7 **Venice Reconstituted**, a Cronk ode to Botticelli's *Birth of Venus*.

Back on the boardwalk, stop into 8 **Small World Books** and its artfully curated stock. Continuing north, nose around the 9 **narrow lanes** just off the walk between Wavecrest Ave and Brooks Ave; the area is rich with ever-changing murals. Finish at the 10 **Venice Ale House**, which has boardwalk seating.

In 1965, Jim Morrison was crashing at his friend Ray Manzarek's Venice apartment, where they plotted to start **The Doors**.

Since 1994, **LA Louver** – one of LA's top galleries – has been housed in a landmark building designed by Frederick Fisher.

The **Venice Art Walls** are part of a public foundation that maintains them. Permits are free; apply online.

JW_PNW/SHUTTERSTOCK

Hermosa Beach Pier Plaza

Ave and 27th St to the family, who then sold it back to the county so it can continue to serve as the popular public park it is today. Markers recall the saga.

Fun Day & Night

Party in Hermosa Beach

Strolling down **Hermosa Beach Pier Plaza** on a summer weekend, you'll notice everyone's wearing flip-flops, tiny tees and a tan and they all seem to be having way too much fun. The short, car-free strip is the South Bay's party central. Out on the **sand**, watch for international volleyball contests throughout the year.

Sandy Joy for Everyone

Diverse Redondo Beach

Redondo Beach is the most economically and ethnically diverse beach town and the largest in the South Bay. King Harbor interrupts the sweep of sand and is the place to find info about excursions on the bay. To the south, the **Palos Verdes Peninsula** is wealthy and notorious for having a land-slip problem that is causing an enormous portion of it to slowly erode into the ocean.

BEST BEACHES OF THE SOUTH BAY

Marina Mother's Beach: Childminders love it: a wave-free, half-crescent of sand that's safe for the tiniest of tots.

Dockweiler State Beach: Almost 4 miles of sand in the shadow of departing LAX jets. Backed by dunes, it's a rare beach with fire rings.

El Porto Beach: At the north end of Manhattan Beach, this is a good patch of sand for surf lessons, or renting a lounger and doing nothing.

Redondo Beach: Surfing was brought here from Hawai'i by George Freeth in 1907. Look for his memorial on the pier.

Rat Beach: Standing for Right-After-Torrance, this beautiful sandy patch (aka Malaga Cove) is right against the start of the Palos Verdes Peninsula.

EATING & DRINKING IN THE SOUTH BAY: OUR PICKS

Manhattan Beach Creamery: Housemade ice creams served in cones or pressed between two cookies for a 'Cream'wich.' Worth the line. *10am-9pm* $

Ercoles 1101: In Manhattan Beach; dark, neon-lit and cozy. Beloved by everyone from salty barflies to yuppie pub crawlers to volleyball stars since 1927. *10am-2am*

Martha's Hermosa Beach: The first stop before a day on the sand. Residents swear by the omelets at this beachside patio joint. *7am-3pm* $

Quality Seafood: Big seafood market on the Redondo pier, since 1953. Choose from a huge selection and they'll cook it your way. *10.30am-8pm* $$

Burbank & Universal City

STUDIOS, THEME PARK AND CULTURE

TOP TIP

California's microclimates are on full display in summer when moderating ocean breezes can't penetrate the valley. On sunny days, temps can be 20°F (11°C) higher – and pollution levels worse – than on the Downtown and Hollywood side of the Hollywood Hills.

GETTING AROUND

Take the Metro B Line from Downtown LA and Hollywood to the Universal City/Studio City and the North Hollywood Stations. The former has shuttle buses up the steep hill to the Universal Studios theme park.

Much of the San Fernando Valley is flat, but it defines suburbia and is so spread out that there are few areas that are worth walking. When Dionne Warwick sang 'LA is a great big freeway...,' she could have been describing the Valley.

Angelenos from the other side of the Hollywood Hills think of two things first when it comes to 'the Valley': major studios and urban sprawl. One, they think, is worth visiting. The other, not so much.

Snootiness aside, the Valley (principally the communities of Sherman Oaks, Studio City, Universal City, North Hollywood, Burbank and Glendale) does sprawl. It's the place where car culture was invented, along with the mini-mall, drive-in movie theater, drive-in bank and drive-in restaurant.

But look closer and you'll see there's a lot of there's a lot of the real here. This is where the real folk live, making it more laid-back and down-to-earth than other areas in the city. There's plenty of culture, to the extent that North Hollywood has its own moniker, 'NoHo,' and its own arts district. One of the studios offers an excellent tour, while the other comprises a major theme park.

Harry Potter, Mario & Bart

Thrill to Universal Studios Hollywood

Although Universal is one of the world's oldest continuously operating movie studios (since 1912), it's best known for the theme park in and around the studio's backlot. Despite the ebbs and flows of showbiz, the park has remained a draw for generations of visitors and residents alike, thanks to an entertaining, ever-changing mix of thrill rides, live-action shows and a tram tour.

The theme park is officially known as **Universal Studios Hollywood** *(universalstudioshollywood.com)* to differentiate it from the other parks around the globe – many of which are much larger, if you're an aficionado. Here, the most popular ride is the **Flight of the Hippogriff** roller coaster and the 3-D **Harry Potter and the Forbidden Journey**. Buy wizarding equipment and 'every-flavour' beans in the fantasy-themed shops, then quaff mugs of butterbeer at **Three Broomsticks** restaurant.

HIGHLIGHTS
1 Universal Studios Hollywood
2 Warner Bros Studio Tour

SLEEPING
3 BLVD Hotel & Studios
4 Hotel Amarano Burbank-Hollywood

EATING
5 Bob's Big Boy
6 Daichan
7 Smoke House
8 Tuning Fork LA

ENTERTAINMENT
9 Baked Potato
10 El Portal
11 Zombie Joe's Underground Theatre

SHOPPING
12 It's a Wrap!

Over in **Super Nintendo World**, the big ride is **Mario Kart: Bowser's Challenge**, which uses virtual reality to put riders inside the game. Elsewhere, the **Jurassic World** ride is a float back to dinosaur days before a tumble through a land of raptors and T rexes. A ride based on **The Simpsons** goes rocketing along through Springfield. While in this area, stop off for the top-notch doughnuts at **Lard Lad** (get the Big Pink).

The theme park also includes the original **tram tour of the studio backlot**, although over the years this has morphed into more of a theme-park ride than an actual behind-the-scenes tour.

Flashing video screens, oversized facades and garish color combos (think *Blade Runner* meets *Willy Wonka*) animate **Universal CityWalk**, the outdoor shopping concourse adjacent to Universal Studios. Under the glitz, CityWalk's shops and restaurants will be mostly familiar to anyone who has visited a US suburban mall, although the **Hello Kitty and Friends Cafe** is a hit.

Tour It Again, Sam

Thrill to the Warner Bros Studio Tour

The **Warner Bros Studio Tour** *(wbstudiotour.com; tours adult/child from $76/65)* offers a fun, mostly authentic look behind the scenes of a major movie studio. Much of the lot dates

TIPS FOR UNIVERSAL STUDIOS HOLLYWOOD

Universal Studios Hollywood uses demand pricing, which varies significantly throughout the year. At non-peak times, one-day admission is adult/child $109/103. At peak times, such as school holidays, it's adult/child $154/148. Buy tickets online for possible savings and watch for two-for-one offers, which give you free admission on a second non-consecutive day. Once the park reaches capacity, the ticket booths will close. You can cut the often long lines for rides at busy times by purchasing an Express Pass one-day admission for a significant premium: $329 at peak periods.

Parking costs $35 to $75. The Metro Rail B Line to Universal City/Studio City and the free shuttle combo is efficient and traffic-free.

back to 1926 and large parts of it feel surprisingly unchanged since the days when Jack Warner was cutting deals and trying to steal credit from his brothers.

The two-hour standard tour kicks off with a video of WB's greatest hits (*Rebel Without a Cause,* many versions of *Batman*), before a tram whisks you around 110 acres of sound stages, legacy sets for TV shows like *Friends* and the *Big Bang Theory* and technical departments, including props, costumes and a collection of Batmobiles. It's awe-inspiring as you encounter the places where legendary films like *The Big Sleep, Blade Runner* and *La La Land* were shot.

Tour variations include our favorite, the **TCM Classic Films Tour** *(adult/child $99/85),* which focuses on the studio's history and the production of films like *Casablanca.* The six-hour **Deluxe Tour** *($330)* includes an in-depth guided tour and lunch.

Nightlife in the Valley

NoHo is where you want to be

The **NoHo** (aka North Hollywood) **Arts District** along Lankershim Blvd is sprinkled with theaters and venues known for their edgy live theater, music and comedy.

Dating to 1926, **El Portal** *(elportaltheatre.com)* is a three-stage mainstay of the district with top-name acts. **Zombie Joe's Underground Theatre** *(zombiejoes.com)* is part theater, part haunted house. Shows are at turns creepy, campy, deranged and critically lauded.

ATTILA ADAM/SHUTTERSTOCK

NoHo Arts District

A bit south, **Baked Potato** *(thebakedpotato.com)* is an intimate jazz-and-blues hall – LA's oldest – where the schedule mixes no-names with big-timers.

Dress Like a Star

Browse wardrobes at It's a Wrap!

Industry legend **It's a Wrap!** *(itsawraphollywood.com)* is the outlet used to unload on-screen wardrobes and props. Besides the cachet, you get great prices on designer labels. Items are racked by show affiliation. Near Halloween, there are displays of authentic costumes from productions.

GUIDE TO STUDIO TOURS

Four of the five surviving major studios in LA offer public tours. Some are better than others.

Paramount Pictures: Unfussy tours of the historic Hollywood lot, which is pretty quiet these days.

Sony Pictures: Once the MGM Studios, but not an overwhelming sense of history with all the intellectual rights musical chairs.

Universal Studios: Turned its tours into a theme park in the 1970s. The 'backlot' really isn't, but it's a spectacle.

Warner Bros: Fascinating tours of a busy studio with palpable history all around.

Walt Disney Studios: In Burbank, it now includes 20th Century Studios. It only rarely gives tours.

EATING IN BURBANK & THE VALLEY: TOP CHOICES

Bob's Big Boy: Famous survivor of a once-ubiquitous chain of diners renowned for a winsome mascot plus a burger that's like a Big Mac. *6am-midnight* **$**

Daichan: Ventura Blvd's Sushi Row in Studio City is a hub of top choices, including this affordable Japanese diner. *11.30am-2.30pm & 5.30-8.30pm Mon-Sat* **$$**

Tuning Fork LA: Has a music industry vibe; staff spin tunes most nights. Casual bistro defines the California cuisine ethos: fresh, simple and creative. *5-9.30pm* **$$**

Smoke House: Located just outside Warner Bros and serving luminaries since 1948. George Clooney allegedly started his production company here. *11.30am-10pm* **$$**

Pasadena

GENTEEL, ART, CULTURED AND PLEASANT

TOP TIP
Old Pasadena is a 20-block downtown shopping and entertainment district of historic brick buildings south and east of Walnut St and Pasadena Ave. It mixes national chains with local businesses. In the 1950s, Route 66 came from the east on Colorado Blvd before turning south on Arroyo Pkwy.

GETTING AROUND

The Metro Rail A Line serves Pasadena and connects it to Downtown LA. Stations are on the west and north edges of downtown. Metro bus line 662 serves the Rose Bowl. The Huntington is not near transit; you'll need a rideshare from a transit stop.

Downtown Pasadena is pleasantly walkable and mostly level, though some distances, such as to the Rose Bowl (2.5 miles), are long.

You'll find a lot of things in Pasadena: a community with a button-down soul, a historical perspective, an appreciation for art and jazz, an old-school conservative undercurrent and a reverence for tradition. Its Rose Bowl college football game has been played annually since 1916, the namesake stadium dates to 1923 and the Rose Parade that perfumes the streets before the game began in 1890.

Pasadena's genteel streets are the home of old money, some of it from fortunes made in California, which funded two extraordinary local museums. Some of it came from fortunes made elsewhere and were brought here for the warmer climes (you'll find old mansions with names like Wrigley and Gamble).

On clear days, the San Gabriel Mountains to the north are a stunning backdrop, although they also hold peril. In January 2025, the Eaton fire began in the hills and went on to destroy the vibrant community of Altadena and threaten Pasadena.

A Wealth of Beauty

Be awe-struck by the Huntington

One of the most delightful, inspirational spots in LA is the century-old **Huntington** *(huntington.org; adult/child $29/13)*. It is rightly a highlight of any trip to California, thanks to a world-class mix of art, literary history and over 120 acres of themed gardens (any one of which would be worth a visit on its own), all set amid stately grounds. There's so much to see and do that it's hard to know where to begin; allow three to four hours for a basic visit.

Start at the **Orientation Gallery**, where you can try to prioritize your visit. Pick up the laughably misnamed 'I have an hour tour' guide, which takes at least two hours.

The **library** could be next. Only a fraction of the six million rare books are on display at any one time, but the highlights are impressive: a Gutenberg Bible, a manuscript of *The Canterbury Tales* by Geoffrey Chaucer, plus books by Marco Polo and Christopher Columbus.

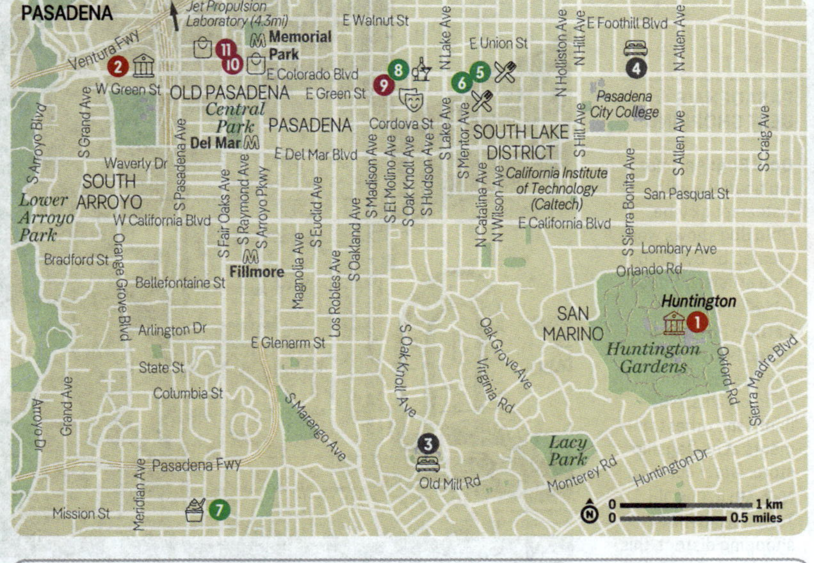

HIGHLIGHTS
1 Huntington

SIGHTS
2 Norton Simon Museum

SLEEPING
3 Langham Huntington Pasadena
4 Saga Motor Hotel

EATING
5 Artisanal Goods by CAR
6 Bistro 45
7 Fair Oaks Pharmacy

DRINKING & NIGHTLIFE
8 The 1894

ENTERTAINMENT
9 Pasadena Playhouse

SHOPPING
10 Gold Bug
11 Homage
see 10 Lather
see 10 Neo 39
see 8 Vroman's Bookstore

In the **galleries** of European and American art, you can lose yourself in the brushstrokes of Thomas Gainsborough's *The Blue Boy* and Thomas Lawrence's *Pinkie*. Other artists here include Mary Cassatt, Edward Hopper, Andy Warhol and Frank Stella.

Note the dour portraits of the patrons Henry and Arabella Huntington. They partly made their immense fortune by owning the 'Red Cars,' the trolley system that stitched the LA region together 100 years ago (and which is now being partly reconstituted for untold billions).

The extensive **gardens** – about a dozen – are as meticulously curated as the museums themselves. Don't miss the roses, the Chinese Garden, the Japanese Garden and the lush Jungle Garden.

Reserve your visit in advance at busy times.

Pasadena's Treasure

Savor the Norton Simon Museum

Rodin's *The Burghers of Calais* and *The Thinker* near the entrance are only an overture to the full symphony of art in store at the exquisite **Norton Simon Museum** *(nortonsimon.org; adult/child $20/free)*. Norton Simon (1907–93) was an

PASADENA'S BEST SHOPPING

Gold Bug: An amazing boutique with a steampunk vibe, Gold Bug shows work created by over 100 area artists. *goldbugpasadena.com*

Lather: Pasadena-based body-care showcases natural hand creams, exfoliants and other treatments at its flagship store. *lather.com*

Neo 39: In the Old Town Pasadena shopping district, this sneaker depot stocks the rare, the imported and the stylish. *neo39.com*

Vroman's Bookstore: Since 1894, Vroman's claims to be the largest and oldest bookstore in SoCal. Regular events. *vromansbookstore.com*

Homage: A Pasadena treasure with a selection of gifts, stationery, jewelry, accessories and more that includes many local items. *homagepasadena.com*

entrepreneur with a passion for art who parlayed his fortune into a remarkable collection.

The galleries teem with choice works by Renaissance and impressionist artists, including Rembrandt (eg *Self-Portrait*), Renoir *(Young Woman in Black)*, Canaletto *(Piazzetta in Venice Looking North)* and Van Gogh, as well as an outstanding array of works by Degas. Twentieth-century masterpieces span Picasso and LA's own Sam Francis.

Asian sculpture – principally Buddhist and Hindu imagery in stone, bronze and copper – is another highpoint. The outdoor **sculpture garden** inspired by Monet's home in Giverny, France, is superb. A massive revamp of the museum's external grounds began in 2025.

EATING & DRINKING IN PASADENA: TOP CHOICES

Artisanal Goods by CAR: The best $6 chocolate croissant you'll ever eat. The cafe does other treats too, as well as coffee. *8.30am-5pm Tue-Sun* $

Fair Oaks Pharmacy: Nostalgic 1915 ice cream fountain where 'soda jerks' dish out 'phosphates' (flavored syrup and soda water) and malts. *9am-5pm Mon-Sat* $

Bistro 45: Sample fine California cuisine in an art deco–inspired dining room. Elegant yet not stiff, with the best local ingredients. Lovely patio. *5-8.30pm Tue-Sun* $$$

The 1894: Excellent wine bar adjoining Vroman's Bookstore, with literary-themed cocktails, microbrews and a quality selection of California wines. *3-9pm Wed-Sun* $$

ANGEL DIBILIO/SHUTTERSTOCK

Pasadena Playhouse

California's State Theater

Thrill to the Pasadena Playhouse

Fully deserving of the word legend, the **Pasadena Playhouse** *(pasadenaplayhouse.org)*, an attractive Spanish Colonial complex, was founded in 1917 and by 1937 had developed such a reputation that it was named the State Theater of California. It ran a lauded acting school in the 1930s and 1940s and has premiered hundreds of works. Grads include Dustin Hoffman, Gene Hackman and Leonard Nimoy. It won the Tony Award in 2023 for the best regional theater in the US.

Far Out

Visit other worlds at NASA's JPL

The world's premier space exploration agency, the **Jet Propulsion Laboratory** *(JPL; jpl.nasa.gov; free)*, has commanded robot explorers on Mars and interplanetary probes leaving our solar system from this campus on the north side of Pasadena.

The accomplishments of the scientists and engineers here, working in conjunction with CalTech and, at times, international space agencies, are extraordinary. And it's all done with cool professionalism and a lack of bombast or overhyped claims. Fascinating tours of the facility that birthed the Mars rovers and which is plotting the first ever return of Martian soil – among other feats – can be arranged at least three weeks in advance via the website.

HISTORY OF LA: PART 2

The opening of the LA aqueduct in 1913 turned the spigot on the region's growth. The bounty of water procured by dubious means (there's plenty of truth in the movie *Chinatown*) fueled fortunes like that of the Huntingtons in Pasadena.

During WWI, the Lockheed brothers and Donald Douglas established aircraft manufacturing plants in LA. Two decades later, aviation and then aerospace – helped along by billions of federal dollars for contracts first for WWII, then for the Cold War and then the space race – were among the industries that contributed to a real-estate boom and sparked suburban sprawl. And freeways and more freeways. And more...

Then there's the film biz, which took root in 1908 and gave LA and Hollywood their public persona.

Places We Love to Stay

$ Budget $$ Midrange $$$ Top End

Hollywood

MAP p381

Vibe Hotel Hollywood $ Blue-hued motel-style units come with a tiki-style outdoor lounge. Some have kitchens; Hollywood Blvd is out front.

Highland Gardens Hotel $ Famous landing spot for future celebs. Motel-style accommodations are only one block from the first star on the Walk of Fame.

Magic Castle Hotel $$ Solid hotel comes with an unmatched perk: access to the members-only Magic Castle private club where magicians ply their trade.

Hollywood Roosevelt $$ Hollywood lore lives large at its most famous hotel (tip: get a pool room). Celebrity stories abound.

Downtown

MAP p388

Biltmore Los Angeles $$ Grand old dame awash with history, grandeur and legend. The Academy Awards were founded in the Crystal Ballroom in 1927.

Kodō Hotel $$ A treasure in the Arts District. It blends Japanese and Western sensibilities in eight serene rooms.

Miyako Hotel Los Angeles $$ In the heart of Little Tokyo, right Downtown. Modern rooms with Japanese style have serene comfort and good transit connections.

Hotel Per La $$$ Vintage interiors and a rooftop pool in a restored Downtown palazzo that was once the grand digs of the Bank of Italy. Plush rooms.

Los Feliz & Silver Lake

MAP p397

Cara Hotel $$ Med-style in a small courtyard hotel on a quieter street with a convenient location between Los Feliz and Hollywood. Good, jazzy bar.

Silver Lake Pool & Inn $$$ Channeling Palm Springs, effortlessly hip, chilled and awash in SoCal light. The design credentials include locally produced art and bright rooms.

Exposition Park & South LA

MAP p403

Crestridge Inn $ Good, indie motel in Inglewood that's convenient to the SoFi Stadium area and LAX. Basic, budget-friendly rooms.

USC Hotel $$$ Wear your Trojan gear with pride at this luxe campus hotel in the shadow of Exposition Park. Rooms are comfortable.

Koreatown

MAP p408

Line Los Angeles $$ In the heart of Koreatown, this mid-century high-rise has exposed concrete walls and smallish rooms (some with sweeping views).

Hotel Normandie LA $$ Dating to 1926 when the neighborhood was awash in movie swells, the Normandie has vintage luxuries and a famous bar (p413).

Fairfax & Mid-City

MAP p408

Banana Bungalows Hotel and Hostel West Hollywood $ Budget digs in a primo location. Private rooms are a great deal, especially those with full kitchens.

Palihouse West Hollywood $$$ In the W 3rd St shopping district. Everything here is calming. Lovely pool area; some rooms are on the courtyard and offer watery serenity.

Culver City

Palihotel Culver City $$ What was a 1920s boarding house is now a fashionable boutique hotel. Art deco accents, smallish rooms and eclectic artwork.

Culver Hotel $$$ A 1924 heritage hotel with a tradition of serving MGM and the other Culver City studios. Renovated and luxurious.

West Hollywood

MAP p416

Andaz West Hollywood $$ Known as the Riot House in the '60s and '70s for the rock stars who partied hard and the hotel still has an industry vibe.

Mondrian Los Angeles $$$ Celeb-magnet landmark. The rooftop pool has the sweeping views you'd expect, and the cream-and-blue rooms welcome you home after a long day.

Sunset Tower Hotel $$$ A striking high-rise icon rich in showbiz history – it was once luxury apartments for the stars. Has a restaurant (p417) lauded for its martinis.

Chateau Marmont $$$ Where else? Looming over the Sunset Strip, storied hotel mixes Gothic details with a mishmash of French Loire Valley chateau inspiration.

Beverly Hills

MAP p416

Crescent Hotel Beverly Hills $$ Basic hotel with limited service and smallish rooms, but it's an incredible value near Rodeo Dr. Part of the Sonder chain.

Beverly Wilshire $$$ Has corked Rodeo Dr since 1928. It exudes a formal elegance in the original Wilshire wing. Less of a laid-back LA vibe.

Beverly Hills Hotel $$$ The revered 'Pink Palace' packs more Hollywood lore than any other hotel in town. Slumber in an elegantly appointed hotel room or self-contained bungalow.

Hotel Bel-Air $$$ Tranquil, 12-acre Spanish Colonial estate that's a popular hideaway for royalty – Hollywood or otherwise.

Santa Monica

MAP p422

HI Los Angeles Santa Monica Hostel $ Near the beach and promenade, these budget-friendly digs rival facilities at properties costing many times more. Single-sex dorms and private rooms.

Sea Shore Motel $$ Family-run lodgings at this comfy motel put you a Frisbee toss from the beach.

Shutters on the Beach $$$ A New England–style retreat in Santa Monica. Slink into a lounge chair on the ocean-view deck around the pool.

Georgian Hotel $$$ Across the street from Palisades Park and the Pacific beyond, the eye-catching 1933 art deco landmark has a snug ocean-view veranda.

Malibu

MAP p422

M Malibu $$ Minimalist cool, the 2nd- and 3rd-floor rooms have views of the ocean across the street (which provides some noise).

Malibu Beach Inn $$$ Adult-oriented hacienda with coveted art and ocean views. Interiors make designers rave. First-floor rooms have decks.

Venice

MAP p426

Samesun Venice Beach $ In a refurbished 1904 building with spectacular rooftop views of Venice Beach. Dorms, private rooms and a cool travelers' vibe.

Hotel Erwin $$ Unremarkable-seeming 1970s beachfront hotel offers fab place for sunset at the High Rooftop Lounge. Guests get bikes, coolers and volleyballs.

Inn at Venice Beach $$ Close to the beach, the Venice Canals, bars and restaurants. This mid-century-themed motel is comfortable and has a central courtyard.

Venice Breeze Suites $$$ Beachfront studios and suites right on the boardwalk. Good rates out of peak season. The Rooftop features big views and a communal barbecue area with sofas.

South Coast Beaches

MAP p426

ITH Hermosa Beach Surf Hostel LAX $ In the heart of Hermosa Beach's party zone. The pier, the sand and the shots are all close by. Dorms and private rooms.

Sea View Inn at the Beach $$ Low-key motel with a variety of rooms spread over several buildings close to the sand in a low-key part of Manhattan Beach.

Beach House Hermosa Beach $$$ Upscale beachfront inn epitomizing California's laid-back lifestyle. Ocean-view suites let in the breezes. Located away from the frenetic center of Hermosa Beach.

Burbank & Universal City

MAP p431

BLVD Hotel & Studios $$ A fun boutique property that's walking distance to Universal Studios. Large rooms and a heated indoor pool.

Hotel Amarano Burbank-Hollywood $$ Close to Warner Bros; rooms at this boutique hotel are inspired by movie sets.

Pasadena

MAP p431

Saga Motor Hotel $ East of the center, this Route 66–era motel boasts a cool sign and comfortable rooms around a relaxing, palm-shaded pool.

Langham Huntington Pasadena $$$ Dating to 1906, this elegant 23-acre, palm-dappled, beaux-arts country estate has every luxury, from rambling gardens to a giant swimming pool.

Researched by
Julie Tremaine

Disneyland & Orange County

A QUINTESSENTIALLY CALIFORNIA EXPERIENCE

Laid-back and ultra-chic, Orange County shines with the magic of Disneyland and gem-like beaches.

Orange County is the most glamorized part of California. You've almost definitely seen it on television before, whether it's in reality shows like *The Hills* or *The Real Housewives of Orange County,* dramas like *The OC* or comedies like *Orange County.* Once you get there, you'll realize some important things: nothing you've seen on a screen compares to the stunning beauty of the iconic coastline and nothing – absolutely nothing – beats a day traveling up and down the Pacific Coast Hwy, whether you're driving, biking or simply walking and taking in the beaches and the ocean beyond.

Those beach vibes infuse every inch of Orange County and you'll likely feel an instant serotonin boost from the massive dose of 'vitamin sea.' If you can tear yourself away from the water's edge, the area offers a lot more, like strollable historic downtown areas, art and culture museums, scenic hiking and biking routes and unmissable events. There's also a little matter of the Happiest Place on Earth – Disneyland is the state's biggest tourist draw, attracting 28 million visitors annually and could be a whole vacation unto itself. The 1955 attraction is worth a visit, even if you think you're not a theme park person. The Disney magic just might surprise you.

DISNEYLAND RESORT

THE MAIN AREAS

DISNEYLAND
A destination for kids and kids at heart.
p446

NEWPORT BEACH
A chic destination to see and be seen.
p458

LAGUNA BEACH
An artist colony turned beach oasis.
p466

For places to stay in Disneyland & Orange County, see p472

JON BILOUS/SHUTTERSTOCK

Left: Disneyland, (p446); Above: Laguna Beach (p466)

KNOTT'S BERRY FARM

Sierra Sidewinder, Knott's Berry Farm (p456)

Find Your Way

There's no wrong way to spend time in Orange County, but if you've only got a day or two, you'll likely want to stick to the coastal cities to maximize your ability to soak in the sun, sand and surf.

Newport Beach, p458

Don't be fooled by the megamansions and yachts: Newport Beach also has laid-back beaches and charming old-school boardwalk attractions.

Disneyland, p446

The Happiest Place on Earth has endless diversions for kids and adults. Nearby, Knott's Berry Farm is a theme park with a lot of delicious history.

Laguna Beach, p466

The artistic center of Orange County, Laguna Beach was founded as an artists colony and has become a destination for art, theater and singular events.

CAR

To make the most of your time, you'll need your own vehicle in order to explore more than one or two places in Orange County. Traffic can be intense, so use predictive software to gauge drive times as you're planning your itinerary.

METROLINK

Los Angeles's Metrolink trains go as far north as Ventura and Lancaster and as far south as San Diego County. There are no train stops at area airports, but there are bus connections. Use the Metrolink Mobile app to plan your route.

BUS

If you'd rather skip traffic and parking fees, try the robust bus system. Anaheim Regional Transportation (the ART bus) has easy access to Disneyland and local attractions. For other locations in OC, use the Orange County Transportation Authority (OCTA) app, called Transit Royale.

Plan Your Time

Orange County has a summer vibe all year long. Plan to bring layers, though: the mornings and evenings can be surprisingly chilly, especially near the water.

JON BILOUS/SHUTTERSTOCK

Balboa Pier (p458)

One Day in Orange County

- Spend the day exploring the Pacific Coast Hwy (PCH). Start in **Laguna Beach** (p466), spending the morning walking the scenic paths high above the beach, or down in the sand. The seaside shops are lovely to browse, but you'll get just as much enjoyment out of walking around downtown and seeing all the **public art** (p466).

- In the afternoon, head north to **Newport Beach** (p458). Stroll the Balboa Peninsula, especially the **Newport Beach Pier** (p461) and **Balboa Fun Zone** (p458), which is an old-time amusement park. Head to **Balboa Island** (p458) to sample one of the area's famous frozen bananas, or stroll the waterfront park in **Corona del Mar** (p461). Whatever you do, make sure you're somewhere for the sunset, whether that's the beach itself or a waterfront restaurant in **Mariner's Mile** (p458).

Seasonal Highlights

Orange County in the off-season is a delight, with smaller crowds, lower hotel prices and seasonal events.

MARCH

The superbloom is one of California's most elusive and unforgettable experiences, when massive swaths of wildflowers bloom at once. Try the **Laguna Coast Wilderness Parks** (p469) in Laguna Beach.

APRIL

You can watch surfers in Huntington Beach every day, but the **Jack's Surfboards Pro** (p462) is your chance to see some of the world's top surfers hit the waves as part of the World Surf League's qualifying series.

JULY

Laguna Beach's **Sawdust Art Festival** (p466), **Festival of Arts** (p466) and **Pageant of the Masters** (p469) happen every July and August. Browse works by hundreds of artists and see people immerse themselves in actual paintings.

A Weekend or More

- Before or after your PCH day, give yourself – and your inner child – an overnight at **Disneyland** (p446). While you can definitely get a lot out of a one-day visit, the best experience involves the nighttime shows like fireworks and parades, depending on the time of year. After a long park day, your body will thank you for booking a nearby hotel and not having to make a long drive.

- The Disneyland Resort has two parks, which can be accessed via single park tickets or a park hopper for same-day access to both. For classic attractions and pure nostalgia, head to **Disneyland Park** (p446). For thrill rides, excellent food and movie magic, choose **Disney California Adventure Park** (p449).

A Full SoCal Experience

- If you're planning to spend several days in Orange County, do yourself a favor and take it as slowly as possible – which means exploring by foot or bicycle. While a drive on the PCH is a supreme delight, it's easy to miss the small details that make places like **Seal Beach** (p464) and **Huntington Beach** (p462) truly memorable.

- Taking your time will give you opportunities to appreciate the surf monuments in Huntington, the public art in **Laguna** (p466), **Noguchi Garden** (p465) in Costa Mesa, the harbor boardwalks in **Dana Point** (p470) and a million other little details it's easy to overlook when you're trying to squeeze the most out of a short time. In **Newport** (p458), give yourself some time to get out on the water, whether it's on a whale watch or a sunset harbor tour.

AUGUST

Over a million people head to the **OC Fair** (p465) in Costa Mesa, which happens annually in July and August and includes concerts, a carnival, culinary demonstrations, agricultural contests and all the festival food you can handle.

SEPTEMBER

Halloween starts early at OC theme parks. Disneyland's **Oogie Boogie Bash** (p452) is a delightfully spooky and kid-friendly event, while the **Knott's Scary Farm** (p457) event is purely terrifying, in the best way.

OCTOBER

The **Newport Beach Film Festival** (p460) brings in nearly 60,000 attendees for red carpet events, film screenings, filmmaking Q&As and more. Expect to see early looks at movies that will end up at next year's Oscars.

DECEMBER

It doesn't get more OC than yachts decked out in holiday lights. The iconic Newport Beach **Christmas Boat Parade** (p460) usually happens the week before Christmas, but there are harbor tours of festive home and boat decor all month.

Disneyland

PURE NOSTALGIA | IMMERSIVE RIDES | MICKEY-SHAPED FOOD

TOP TIP

Bring a power bank for your smartphone. The Disneyland app is a must-have to keep track of wait times, book Lightning Lane passes, order food, make dining reservations and lots more.

GETTING AROUND

If you're not planning to rent a car – which, for a Disneyland-only trip, you likely won't need – the closest airports to Disneyland are Long Beach and John Wayne Airport in Santa Ana. Your flight will likely have a connection and cost more than the direct options into Los Angeles International Airport, about an hour away. Everything near Disneyland is walkable or easily accessible via rideshare or the ART Bus, and grocery delivery from nearby Target and Walmart is a cinch.

'Here you leave today,' the sign reads over the entrance into Disneyland Park, 'and enter the world of yesterday, tomorrow and fantasy.' It's easy to dismiss Disney as an only-for-kids attraction, but it's truly the kind of place where you can fully immerse yourself in the magic and take a break from the real world for a little while.

Walt Disney opened Disneyland in 1955, when it was just one park and admission cost $1. The idea was to create a place where kids and adults could have fun together, with everyone enjoying the same experience. It revolutionized family entertainment and set the standard for theme parks around the world. Today, the Disneyland Resort includes two separate parks – Disneyland Park and Disney California Adventure Park (DCA) – as well as three hotels and a shopping and dining district called Downtown Disney, which doesn't require a ticket to enjoy.

The Magic of Disneyland Park

Step into yesterday, tomorrow and fantasy

Walking into **Disneyland Park** *(disneyland.disney.go.com; from $104 per person for a single day ticket)* it's easy to see glimpses of Walt Disney's original park. The Disneyland Railroad puffs its way above the entrance and once you're walking down **Main Street USA**, there's joyful music, balloons flying overhead, the smell of popcorn and churros in the air, and cartoon mice waving at you as they walk by. Look to the left and you'll see a lamp in the window of the Disney family's personal apartment, lit in remembrance of Walt the day he died in 1966 and never turned off since. Look ahead and you'll see **Sleeping Beauty Castle**, a pink and blue dream that's the gateway to **Fantasyland**, where original opening-day rides like Peter Pan's Flight and the King Arthur Carrousel still spin today.

DISNEYLAND

HIGHLIGHTS
1 Disney California Adventure Park (DCA)
2 Disneyland Park
3 Star Wars: Galaxy's Edge

SIGHTS
4 Adventureland
5 Cars Land
6 Fantasyland
7 Frontierland
8 Grizzly Peak
9 Hollywood Land
10 Main Street USA
11 New Orleans Square
12 Pixar Pier
13 Sleeping Beauty Castle
14 Tomorrowland

SLEEPING
15 Alpine Inn
16 Anaheim Hotel
17 Candy Cane Inn
18 Disneyland Hotel
19 Disney's Grand Californian Hotel & Spa
20 Howard Johnson by Wyndham Anaheim Hotel
21 Pixar Place Hotel
22 Westin Anaheim

EATING
23 Blue Bayou
24 Carnation Cafe
25 Carthay Circle
26 Craftsman Grill
27 Goofy's Kitchen
28 Lamplight Lounge
29 Napa Rose
30 Paradise Garden Grill
31 Plaza Inn
32 Pym Test Kitchen
33 Ronto Roasters
34 Storytellers Cafe
35 Tiana's Palace

DRINKING & NIGHTLIFE
36 Broken Spell Lounge
37 Hearthstone Lounge
38 Trader Sam's Enchanted Tiki Bar

ENTERTAINMENT
39 Avengers Campus
40 Mickey's Toontown

TOP EXPERIENCE

Downtown Disney

A ticket to Disneyland has a hefty price tag, but there's an element of the Disneyland Resort that you can enjoy for free. Downtown Disney is the shopping and dining district that connects the two theme parks to the resort hotels. If a Disneyland day isn't in the cards for you on this trip, this outdoor pedestrian mall will give you a taste of the experience.

KIT LEONG/SHUTTERSTOCK

Disney Magic Without Disney Tickets

Downtown Disney has the same theming and feel as being inside the parks. There are character topiaries, fountains that do magic tricks and music wafting from the sky. During festival and holiday seasons, the area is also decorated the same way the parks are and sometimes has roving seasonal performers in addition to the nightly concerts at its performance stage. Downtown Disney is also the only place you can buy official Disney merchandise outside of the parks and hotel gift shops.

The Flavor of Downtown Disney

Downtown Disney has 26 dining options and has seriously upped its culinary game over the past few years. A trio of restaurants from Michelin-starred chef Carlos Gaytan (Paseo, Centrico, Tiendita) offer gourmet Mexican food at different price points and an outpost of the wildly popular dim sum restaurant **Din Tai Fung** serves 10,000 dumplings daily. Its newest restaurant, **Parkside Market**, is a food hall with an upstairs cocktail bar that has views of the Monorail and the Disneyland fireworks. Two more restaurants are coming: a fine dining steakhouse and a barbecue joint.

TOP TIPS

- $10 validated parking is available in the Simba Lot for four hours with validation from a store, or six hours with validation from a table-service restaurant.
- There's easy access into the Disneyland Hotel and Grand Californian Hotel to see and shop.
- Parking for the theme parks is not allowed.

PRACTICALITIES

Scan the QR code for more information on Downtown Disney.

The other lands of Disneyland aren't quite as storybook-like, but they are just as transportive. **Adventureland** is tropical-themed, with attractions like the delightfully punny Jungle Cruise and thrilling Indiana Jones Adventure: Temple of the Forbidden Eye. The Wild West–themed **Frontierland** has Big Thunder Mountain Railroad, a coaster where you escape an exploding mine. **New Orleans Square** has Pirates of the Caribbean (complete with a restaurant, Blue Bayou, inside the ride) and Haunted Mansion, the first truly immersive haunted house ever built. The retro-futuristic **Tomorrowland** offers a ride on Space Mountain and **Toontown** has the trackless dark ride Mickey and Minnie's Runaway Railway, the only ride dedicated to the mouse himself. The park's newest land, **Star Wars: Galaxy's Edge**, has the park's most technologically advanced ride: the 18-minute Star Wars: Rise of the Resistance. In this land, the park's nighttime fireworks have a special Star Wars projection show to match.

The Thrills of Disney California Adventure

A movie multiverse, with even bigger rides

If Disneyland is about making dreams real, then **Disney California Adventure Park** *(DCA; disneyland.disney.go.com; from $104 per person for a single day ticket)* is about making movies come to life. Instead of a Main Street USA modeled after Walt Disney's childhood, the land that greets you through the gates of DCA is the **Buena Vista Street** of 1920s Hollywood, when the Walt Disney Studios rose to prominence for making *Snow White and the Seven Dwarfs,* the first-ever full-length animated film.

Note: this is a separate park from Disneyland and requires separate admission or a park hopper ticket. It's not recommended that you visit both parks on the same day.

In **Hollywood Land**, which mimics Hollywood Blvd, there are meet-and-greets with Mickey and friends in Old Hollywood garb and the Animation Academy where you can learn to draw Disney characters. **Avengers Campus**, the Marvel-themed land, has rides like WEB SLINGERS: A Spider-Man Adventure and Guardians of the Galaxy – Mission: Breakout! That land, currently under expansion, is set to open a King Thanos multiverse ride and an Iron Man ride, likely in 2026.

On **Pixar Pier**, the Incredicoaster rockets you into the air with the Incredibles family and, in **Cars Land**, you can zoom through Ornament Valley on Radiator Springs Racers, a thrilling but kid-friendly car race ride. On **Grizzly Peak**, one of the

PLANNING AHEAD & SKIPPING LINES

Disneyland uses a reservation system to manage capacity, so while you can still buy a ticket in person, it's not a guarantee that you'll be able to go the same day. The much better way is to buy your tickets in advance online at *disneyland.disney.go.com.* Many Disney vacation planning sites offer discounted tickets.

On busy days, waits for the most in-demand rides can range from one to two hours, but the Lightning Lane Multi-Pass ($35 per day per person) allows priority access on many rides. For the most popular rides, including Star Wars: Rise of the Resistance and Radiator Springs Racers, there's an additional Individual Lightning Lane cost per ride – the good news is that you can purchase those without having to buy a Multi-Pass.

EATING AT DISNEYLAND: CHARACTER DINING

Goofy's Kitchen: In the Disneyland Hotel, this is a huge, kid-friendly buffet, with friends like Minnie and Pluto and a photo op with Chef Goofy. $$

Storytellers Cafe: An elevated buffet in the Grand Californian, serving wild Bloody Marys and an adventure theme. Mickey and friends come to every table. $$

Napa Rose: The Grand Californian's fine dining restaurant has an elegant Princess Breakfast, with high tea–like service and visits from Cinderella, Tiana and Elsa. $$$

Plaza Inn: Minnie and Friends Breakfast in the Park, inside Disneyland Park, is a morning buffet at Plaza Inn offering Minnie (not Mickey) waffles and comfort foods. $$

DISNEYLAND TURNS 70

Disneyland celebrates 70 years in May 2025 through summer 2026 with special entertainment, food and parades. Two additional nighttime spectaculars form part of the celebration: DCA debuted World of Color–Happiness, a fountain show with projections that include the Muppets and characters from Inside Out; and Disneyland brought back the fan favorite Wondrous Journeys fireworks show along with the Paint the Night parade. Disneyland 70 also marked the debut of a new show at the Main Street Opera House. In *Walt Disney: A Magical Life,* Disneyland debuted the first-ever Audio Animatronic figure representing Walt himself, using actual clips of Disney speaking as narration.

original lands from the park's 2001 opening, you can make a splash on the Grizzly River Run, or fly above the clouds on Soarin' Across the World, a 4D movie experience.

Disneyland Festivals

Lunar New Year Celebration (January & February)

Disney California Adventure marks the Lunar New Year with a celebration of East Asian food, culture and heritage. Food booths offer Disney takes on Chinese, Vietnamese and Korean street foods; and there are parades and musical performances. The year 2026 celebrates the Year of the Horse and 2027 marks the Year of the Goat.

California Adventure Food & Wine Festival (March & April)

The vast and varied landscape of California's regional cuisines are the spotlight for this highly anticipated annual festival at DCA. Not only are there food booths themed to different regions and iconic California foods – think an entire booth

EATING AT DISNEY CALIFORNIA ADVENTURE: OUR PICKS

Lamplight Lounge: Reserve this Pixar Pier place when World of Color is showing. The prime view is even sweeter with a bite and a cocktail. $$

Paradise Garden Grill: The Mexican food at this Paradise Gardens spot is always a winner, especially for its vegetarian fare and rotating menus. $$

Pym Test Kitchen: Avengers Campus spot inspired by Ant-Man's size: think tiny pasta with one giant, plant-based 'meatball' served in a huge spoon. $$

Craftsman Grill: This poolside restaurant is just through the Grand's dedicated park entrance. Its gourmet hot dogs (really!) and pizzas are the perfect break. $$

DISNEYLAND RESORT

Pixar Pier (p449), Disneyland

devoted to garlic, one of California's biggest crops – there are special dining events and chef demonstrations throughout the festival. As a special homage to its home state, the park brings back **Soarin' over California**, the original version of the ride, which showcases Golden State scenery like the Golden Gate Bridge and Big Sur.

Season of the Force (April & May)

If the phrase 'May the Force be with you' means anything to you, you might want to time your visit for Disneyland's **Season of the Force**, which celebrates Star Wars with specialty foods in Tomorrowland and a Star Wars overlay of Space Mountain, which becomes Hyperspace Mountain and puts riders in the battle between the Resistance and the First Order. During this time, Disneyland hosts **Star Wars Nite**, a specially ticketed after-hours event for fans who dress up as their favorite characters and wield their lightsabers with abandon. The dates vary, but there's always one on, you guessed it, May the Fourth.

HOW TO SKIP THE WAIT FOR NIGHTTIME SHOWS

On nights when Disneyland will have Wondrous Journeys fireworks, or DCA is showing World of Color, you'll likely see people staking out the best spots several hours in advance. If you only have a short time at the park, that's not the best way to utilize your time. There are two ways to guarantee prime viewing spots without the wait. Disneyland offers dessert parties, which are an additional cost, but come with seating for nighttime shows and parades. The parks also offer dining packages at certain restaurants: when you dine there with the package menu (just ask for it when you arrive), you'll receive a voucher for entry into a reserved viewing area for the nighttime Fantasmic! show or the Paint the Night parade.

DRINKING AT DISNEYLAND: BEST FOR COCKTAILS

Broken Spell Lounge: Sleeping Beauty–themed spot in the Disneyland Hotel; cozy couches, woodland-inspired cocktails and nightly live music.

Carthay Circle: Downstairs from the fine-dining restaurant, the lounge offers classic cocktails, including an unforgettable espresso martini.

Trader Sam's Enchanted Tiki Bar: Order the right drink at this Disneyland Hotel bar and it might do a magic trick. Bartenders are tiki aficionados.

Hearthstone Lounge: This Grand Californian spot has an excellent whiskey selection, a walk-up bar for drinks to enjoy by the lobby fireplace and a casual menu.

MUST-TRY SNACKS

Churros: A signature Disneyland treat, this cinnamon-sugar fried dough has endlessly delicious seasonal variations like s'mores and pumpkin spice. Snack carts open daily.

Dole Whip: No Disney day is complete without this frozen treat, in flavors like original pineapple and raspberry, best enjoyed sitting in Walt Disney's Enchanted Tiki Room.

Popcorn: Each cart has an adorable Roastie-Toastie animatronic inside that's themed to a specific land. The refillable popcorn buckets are seriously fun souvenirs.

Mickey-Shaped Foods: It's a proven fact that everything tastes better Mickey-shaped, including ice cream bars, hot pretzels, cookies and caramel apples.

DISNEYLAND RESORT

Tiana's Bayou Adventure, Disneyland

Halloween Time (September & October)

For those who love a spooky good time, there is no better season at Disneyland than **Halloween Time**. Both parks are fully decorated for the holiday, including an entire makeover of Cars Land with incredibly inventive Halloween decorations from auto parts: it includes a 'Haul-o-Ween' ride overlay for Mater's Junkyard Jamboree and Cars like Lightning McQueen and Mater dressed in Halloween costumes. Also in DCA, the Avengers Campus Guardians of the Galaxy – Mission: Breakout! becomes Monsters After Dark, an even more terrifying version of the drop ride. **Oogie Boogie Bash** is a highly anticipated, separately ticketed Halloween party with Disney villains and trick-or-treating. It sells out months in advance every year.

Halloween also brings the popular holiday overlay of Haunted Mansion, which becomes **The Nightmare Before Christmas**-themed and has a huge gingerbread house that changes every year. In past years, it has featured a guillotine that really dropped a blade and a moving gingerbread zombie.

National Hispanic and Latin American Heritage Month & Dia de los Muertos (September–November)

National Hispanic and Latin American Heritage Month brings musical performances, special characters and incredible

EATING AT DISNEYLAND PARK: OUR PICKS

Blue Bayou: There's no more quintessentially Disneyland restaurant than Blue Bayou, inside Pirates of the Caribbean. Boats glide by as you enjoy your meal. $$$

Carnation Cafe: Southern-inspired comfort food is the order of the day at Carnation Cafe, famous for its fried pickles and Walt's Chili. $$

Ronto Roasters: Quick-service stand serving inexpensive, delicious sausage and veg 'Ronto Wraps' but the plant-based Rontoless Wrap is the star. $

Tiana's Palace: A counterpart to the new Tiana's Bayou Adventure ride, Tiana's Palace serves New Orleans–inspired food like jambalaya and muffaletta. $$

Mexican-inspired food to both parks. **Dia de Los Muertos** celebrates those who have passed with a huge, walk-through ofrenda in Disneyland's Frontierland. At The Tree of Life in the Paradise Gardens area of DCA, you can write a message to a departed loved one and hang it on the tree. By the end of the celebration, there are thousands of beautiful, moving messages.

The Holidays at Disneyland (November–January)

When it's snowing in Anaheim, it must be the **Holidays at Disneyland**. There's nothing like Disneyland Park at the Holidays, when Sleeping Beauty Castle's halls are decked with ornate decorations and, during the nightly fireworks, gingerbread-scented snow falls over Main Street. A **Christmas Fantasy Parade** brings Disney princesses through the streets, surrounded by dancing snowflakes and festive holiday music, followed by an appearance by Santa himself. The most in-demand treats at this time of year are the Mickey gingerbread cookies, which people buy by the dozen, and the hand-pulled candy canes, made fresh on a few select days: people arrive at the park hours early to make sure they'll be able to snag one.

During this time, It's a Small World becomes It's a Small World Holiday, a sweet celebration of holidays around the world and Haunted Mansion Holiday is still around after Halloween.

California Adventure Festival of Holidays (November–January)

Just like in Disneyland, DCA is absolutely laden with festive decor during the holiday months. While all the rides with holiday overlays are in Disneyland Park, DCA has a few special things going on during this season, like Santa appearing in the Redwood Creek Challenge Trail for holiday photos. The biggest event, though, is the **Festival of Holidays**, which celebrates Christmas, Hanukkah, Kwanzaa, Navidad, Diwali and Three Kings Day through food, musical performances and character appearances.

BEHIND THE SCENES

For fans who can't get enough of the mouse, Disneyland offers special ticketed tours that take guests into inaccessible areas like Walt Disney's personal apartment or the Lilly Belle, the Disneyland Railroad car reserved for visiting dignitaries. Those tours are add-ons to park admission and generally cost between $120 and $160 per person, depending on the experience. The multihour experience usually includes a snack, a collectible souvenir and Lightning Lane access to a ride. For the ultimate access, a VIP tour with a private guide allows you to skip all the lines and get priority access to shows. Book these experiences through the Disneyland website or at the Tour Booth inside the Town Square.

HELP ME PICK:

Hotels Near Disneyland

Unlike Walt Disney World® in Florida, which is the size of San Francisco and has multitudes of on-property hotels, Disneyland only has three of its own accommodations. The experience of staying at a Disneyland hotel definitely adds to the immersive experience, but it can be pricey. Within easy walking distance of the park, there are dozens of 'good neighbor' hotels, which tend to be more affordable and sometimes come with perks like free breakfast.

The main hotels

Disneyland Hotel

Disneyland Hotel is the resort's mid-tier property, but it absolutely has the most Disney magic, with touches like headboards that light up with Tinkerbell flying over the castle and playing *When You Wish Upon a Star* and luxury suites with pirate, jungle and Mickey themes. The hotel has four towers: the Fantasy Tower, the Adventure Tower and the Frontier Tower all match the theming of areas in Disneyland and those three have a huge central pool with hot tubs and Monorail-themed water slides. The newest tower, the Villas at the Disneyland Hotel, is an homage to animation with a smaller pool (still open to all hotel guests) with a Steamboat Willie-themed splash pad.

Disney's Grand Californian Hotel

With the ultimate convenience and the highest price tag, **Disney's Grand Californian Hotel** has an entrance directly into Disney California Adventure Park, which is especially convenient if you've got little kids who need to go back to the room to nap in the middle of the day. The Grand Californian has Craftsman-style architecture, woodsy Chip 'n Dale theming in the rooms and a rock waterfall in its pool area. Even if you aren't staying there, it's supremely pleasant to go sit in the soaring lobby with its overstuffed couches and rocking chairs by the fireplace and listen to music from the grand piano or enjoy a glass of wine.

Pixar Place Hotel

Formerly Paradise Pier Hotel, **Pixar Place** got a huge makeover in 2024 and is now themed to Disney's Pixar films like *Inside Out, Cars* and *Monsters, Inc.* The hotel is across the street from the main resort, but is still a very short walk and is the most affordable of the three. The Finding Nemo-themed waterslide and splash pad complex is fun and there's a patio area with lawn games for kids and adults to play together. The rooftop pool area offers some of the best fireworks viewing outside the parks. In the afternoons, Bing Bong from *Inside Out* makes appearances throughout the hotel and, in the evenings, Joe from *Soul* plays piano and tells stories in the lobby.

Disneyland Hotel

Disney's Grand Californian Hotel

Pixar Place Hotel

FROM LEFT: SIPA USA/ALAMY LIVE NEWS/ALAMY, JASON O. WATSON (USA: CALIFORNIA PHOTOGRAPHS)/ALAMY, SIPA USA/ALAMY LIVE NEWS/ALAMY

FELIPE SANCHEZ/SHUTTERSTOCK

Westin Anaheim

HOW TO

When to go The busiest, most expensive times are school vacations and the Halloween and holiday festivities. If price is a factor, choose an off-time.

Book ahead Disneyland hotel reservations can be made 180 days in advance, while local good neighbor hotels generally offer longer booking windows.

Before you go Necessities like refillable water bottles and bandages are pricey in the park; either pack them or order from a delivery service.

Budget If you're willing to book a few blocks further away, the good neighbor hotel prices drop dramatically and often have less expensive parking.

Affordable nearby options

The **Westin Anaheim** is newly renovated as of 2024 and the **JW Marriott Anaheim** opened in 2021. Both are excellent, higher-end options that have rooftop lounges where you can see the Disneyland fireworks. Slightly outside of walking distance, the **Hyatt Regency Orange County** offers similar quality for slightly more attractive prices, though without the rooftop.

For the ultimate in theming, choose the **Anaheim Hotel**, across the street from Disneyland's Harbor Boulevard entrance, which has mid-century vibes and mid-tier room rates. The **Anaheim Majestic Garden Hotel** has castle-inspired architecture and room decor; while it's not exactly walkable, the hotel offers a shuttle for a fee and has family suites for larger parties. The **Howard Johnson by Wyndham Anaheim Hotel** has a pirate-themed water park and a suite themed after one of Disney's long-gone attractions. The House of the Retro Future looks like the Monsanto House of the Future that was in Tomorrowland from 1957 to 1967.

Both **Alpine Inn** and **Candy Cane Inn** are directly adjacent to Disney California Adventure. Alpine has European theming that feels like it could be in the park right next to the Matterhorn and offers free parking. The Candy Cane Inn is even closer and offers free breakfast, free parking and a complimentary shuttle.

Find more places to stay on p472.

KNOTT'S BERRY FARM/SEAN TEEGARDEN PHOTOGRAPHY

Calico Mine Train

TOP EXPERIENCE

Knott's Berry Farm

What started as an actual berry farm in Buena Park in 1920 is now one of California's most beloved attractions. Today, Knott's Berry Farm is a hugely popular theme park with thrill rides, an Old West ghost town (which is more real than you might think) and unmissable seasonal events – but, at its core, the place is still all about the berries.

DON'T MISS

- Mrs Knott's Chicken Dinner Restaurant
- Calico Saloon
- Ghost Rider
- Calico Mine Ride
- Birdcage Theater

A Berry Amusing Park

Knott's Berry Farm has four main lands, all elements of the California experience. Calico Ghost Town is a fun version of the Old West. Fiesta Village, inspired by California's history as part of Mexico, celebrates the state's Mexican heritage and culture. The Boardwalk is a coastal-themed land with thrill rides like Hang Time, an intense plunge coaster inspired by surfing. Camp Snoopy, evocative of Northern California's redwood forests, is full of kid-friendly rides and Peanuts characters.

PRACTICALITIES

Scan the QR code for details of upcoming Knott's Berry Farm events and prices.

Calico Ghost Town

The centerpiece of Knott's Berry Farm is **Calico Ghost Town**, based on a real silver mining town in the Mojave Desert. Calico Ghost Town is the true heart of Knott's Berry Farm, not just because it feels so transportive, but because Walter Knott once lived in the real Calico and brought in historic buildings from the town (and other ghost towns across the West) to create the most immersive feeling.

The land includes **Calico Mine Train**, a dark ride through 'gold mines' complete with animatronic miners; the **Calico Railroad**, a real train that chugs around the park and has an unusually high rate of bandits aboard; a **Pony Express** coaster; and even real stagecoaches pulled by horses. Ghost Town is also home to **Ghost Rider**, the tallest, oldest, wooden roller coaster in the West.

Catch a 'burle-q revue' at the **Birdcage Theater**, visit the **Calico Saloon** or livery with live animals and go to 'school' and learn about the pioneer days of California. During the **Ghost Town Alive!** event, the town is full of characters like outlaws and sheriffs who give you interactive storylines to follow and solve.

It's Always Boysenberry Season

Visit the park on any day and you can get a taste of the berry that made the farm famous. Knotts' boysenberry funnel cakes, topped with boysenberry preserves and boysenberry soft serve, are legendary, as are the freshly made boysenberry-filled churros, boysenberry pie, even boysenberry beer. But during March and April the park takes it to another level with its annual **Boysenberry Festival**, which incorporates the berry into foods in unexpected ways: think boysenberry beef chili over mac 'n cheese, boysenberry BBQ pulled pork over boysenberry corn bread, boysenberry lavender lemonade and boysenberry vanilla double hazy IPA.

A Taste of Knott's Outside the Park Gates

Cordelia Knott's restaurant has come a long way from its start. Now, **Mrs Knott's Chicken Dinner Restaurant** feeds 1000 people daily. The restaurant is open to the public, so you can get a taste of the food that started one of California's most iconic destinations without paying admission. Even better: a chicken dinner includes chicken soup or cherry rhubarb, salad, vegetables, biscuits and preserves and a piece of boysenberry or apple pie for under $30.

A Halloween Scream

Knott's Spooky Farm is a kid-friendly Halloween experience, where rides like the Timber Mountain Log Ride and Calico Mine Train get festive seasonal makeovers. At night, the terror starts. **Knott's Scary Farm** is a separately ticketed event with intense haunted house mazes, delightfully creepy foods and fog-filled walkways where monsters emerge at any moment.

IT ALL STARTED WITH A BERRY

When Walter and Cordelia Knott introduced the boysenberry – a mix of red raspberry, blackberry and loganberry – to their farm, the business took off. In 1934, they started serving fried chicken dinners and soon people were lining up for hours to dine. Walter started building small attractions to keep them busy. Soon, they had an Old West town and, by 1968, they had a bona fide theme park.

TOP TIPS

- Knott's Berry Farm doesn't require advance park reservations and sells tickets at the gate, but they're cheaper if you buy online.
- Add a Fast Lane entry for an additional fee and you can skip the standby queues and use the speedier Fast Lanes on attractions.
- You can also pre-purchase meal packages online, which are a good value if you're planning on being at the park all day.

Newport Beach

PRISTINE BEACHES | LIVELY WATERFRONT | CHIC ATMOSPHERE

There's no city in California quite like Newport Beach. The upscale beach community has 10 distinct neighborhoods ranging from quiet and residential to bustling tourist draws. You'll likely spend most of your time at Balboa Island, the Balboa Peninsula, Lido Marina Village, Corona del Mar and Mariner's Mile, as they have the highest concentration of attractions for visitors.

So much of Newport Beach's allure involves the water. The city is home to the largest recreational harbor on the West Coast, with 10 miles of waterfront that offers boating and fishing, water sports and endless views. An enormous ecological wetland preserve is home to more than 200 endangered species. Beyond the shore, Newport Beach has some of California's most sought-after golf courses, beloved annual cultural events and shopping at Fashion Island that rivals Beverly Hills.

TOP TIP

Get a taste of the luxury life by doing a day rental of a sports car like a Ferrari or Aston Martin from one of Newport Beach's exotic car rental businesses.

GETTING AROUND

The closest Metrolink station is Tustin to the east. To access Newport Beach by bus from John Wayne Airport, take the bus to Huntington Beach and connect south from there. Since Newport Beach's main areas are somewhat spread out, you'll likely need to fill in some gaps with rideshare or bike/scooter rentals. If you're renting a car, expect to pay for parking most places; many restaurants offer valet parking for a fee.

Beach Vibes at Balboa Peninsula

A quintessentially beachy OC experience

Balboa Peninsula is where to head if you want a quintessential beach town experience. Stroll **Balboa Pier**, rent a bike and traverse the boardwalk, soaking in the sunshine and salt air. From here, you can hop the ferry to **Balboa Island** (also accessible by car or foot) or catch the **Catalina Flyer** *(catalinainfo.com)* to Catalina Island, a short sail away. In Balboa Village, there's **Balboa Fun Zone** *(balboafunzone.com)*, an old-time amusement park, with rides and midway games.

Make a Splash

If you don't get on the water, you didn't visit Newport

For an adventure by sea – or just to see the superyachts docked nearby – head to **Mariner's Mile**. This is where you'll disembark for water excursions like harbor tours, gondola rides

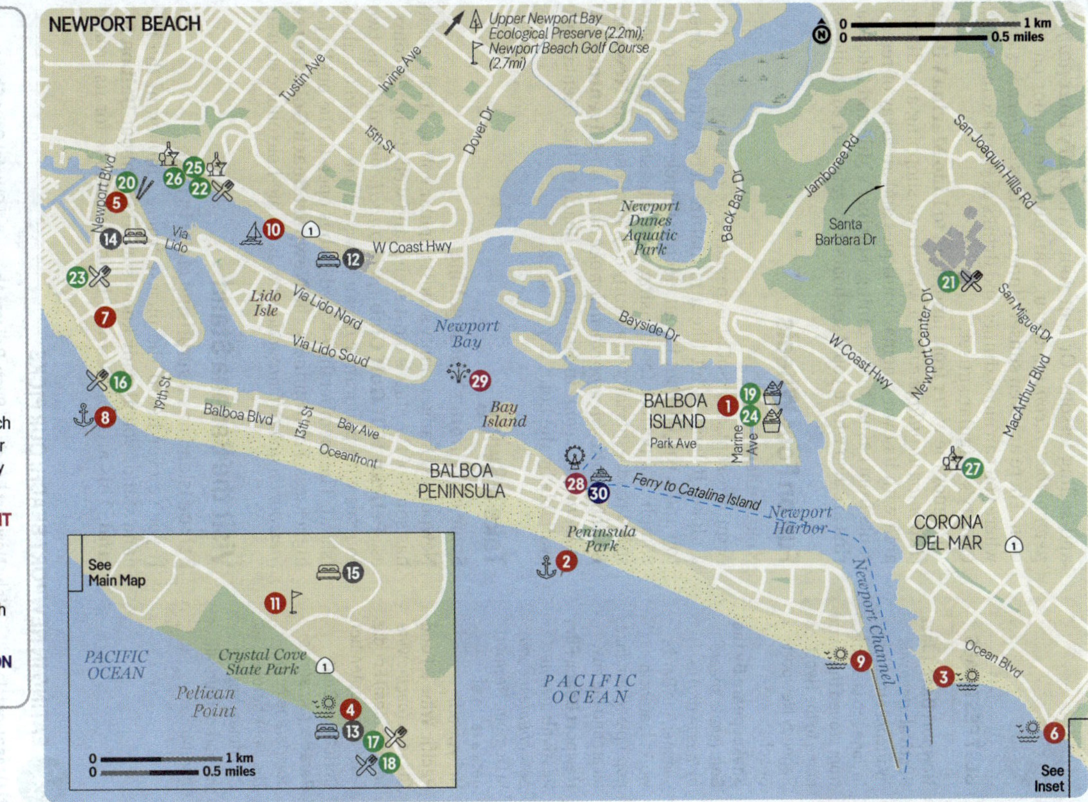

SIGHTS
1 Balboa Island
2 Balboa Pier
3 Corona del Mar State Beach
4 Crystal Cove State Park
5 Lido Marina Village
6 Little Corona del Mar Beach
7 Newport Beach Moke
8 Newport Beach Pier
9 The Wedge

ACTIVITIES
10 Duffy Electric Boat Rentals
11 Pelican Hill Golf Club

SLEEPING
12 Balboa Bay Resort
13 Crystal Cove Beach Cottages
14 Lido House
15 Resort at Pelican Hill

EATING
16 21 Oceanfront
17 Beachcomber Café
18 Crystal Cove Shake Shack
19 Dad's Donut & Bakery Shop
20 Nobu Newport Beach
21 RH Ocean Grill
22 Rusty Pelican
23 Sancho's Tacos
24 Sugar n' Spice
see 14 Topside

DRINKING & NIGHTLIFE
25 Billy's at the Beach
see 17 Bootlegger Bar
26 Louie's by the Bay
27 Under CdM

ENTERTAINMENT
28 Balboa Fun Zone
29 Christmas Boat Parade
see 5 Newport Beach Film Festival

TRANSPORTATION
30 Catalina Flyer

BEST FESTIVALS

Newport Beach Jazz Festival: *(festivals.hyattconcerts.com)* In June top jazz acts from around the world come to the Hyatt Regency Newport Beach.

Shakespeare By the Sea: *(shakespearebythesea.org)* In summer, the Bard's works feature in pop-up performances all around the city.

Newport Beach Film Festival: *(newportbeachfilmfest.com)* In October, Newport gets a taste of Hollywood.

Pacific Wine & Food Classic: *(pacificwineandfood.com)* Foodie festival in September.

Christmas Boat Parade: *(christmasboatparade.com)* The week before Christmas, but there are harbor tours all month.

and sailing lessons. Or rent your own **Duffy boat** *(duffyofnewportbeach.com)* and cruise around the harbor on your own. There are even sunset dinner **cruises** *(citycruises.com)* where you can enjoy dinner and drinks as you take in Orange County's singular sunset.

To enjoy the water from land, head to **Lido Marina Village** *(lidomarinavillage.com),* a waterfront shopping and dining area with its own cinema, boutiques and an array of restaurants from casual to fine dining. Mariner's Mile and Lido Marina are also where you'll see boats decorated for the holidays.

Fun on Four Wheels

Moke cruising

A quintessentially SoCal experience is cruising around in a Moke. It looks a bit like a miniature Jeep, with an open top and a roll bar, but it's an electric vehicle that tops out at 25mph. It's perfect for cruising along the shore or any low-speed road, especially on a sunny day. Rent one from **Newport Beach Moke** *(newportbeachmoke.com)* or **Adventure OC** *(adventureoc.com)* in Huntington Beach (p462). Rentals are available by the hour, day or week.

Take a Swing

Some of California's best golfing

Newport is Orange County's most popular golf destination and has some of the state's most scenic and well-designed courses. **Pelican Hill Golf Club** *(pelicanhill.com/golf)* has two courses with panoramic ocean views all the way to Catalina Island. The membership-based club is open to the public for higher fees. For beginners, the **Newport Beach Golf Course** *(newportbeachgolfcoursellc.com)* is a nine-hole public course.

Visit the Banana Stand

Balboa Island has a surprising claim to fame

If you've ever heard the phrase 'there's money in the banana stand,' you already know something about **Balboa Island**. This area of Newport Beach is famous for its frozen

EATING IN NEWPORT BEACH: OUR PICKS

21 Oceanfront: In Doryman's Oceanfront Inn, this fine-dining seafood and steak restaurant serves up unparalleled beach views. *4pm-late* $$$

Nobu Newport Beach: Outpost of the legendary Japanese with two floors of water views. *noon-3pm Fri-Sun, Tanoshi 5-7pm Mon-Thu, dinner from 5pm* $$$

Rusty Pelican: An institution in Mariner's Mile since 1972, this harborside restaurant serves creative fish preparations with a robust wine list. *11am-10pm* $$$

Crystal Cove Shake Shack: Serving burgers and shakes on the beach since 1945; eat them on picnic tables and head straight back to the sand. *7am-9pm* $$

RH Ocean Grill: Elegant rooftop destination in Fashion Island housed in an all-season greenhouse lit with chandeliers. *10am-9pm* $$$

Sancho's Tacos: Once a backyard project but now with several OC locations, including Balboa Peninsula. Tacos on the patio, or take them to the beach. *9am-9pm* $$

Beachcomber Café: This lively, casual cafe at Crystal Cove is ideal for hungry diners walking in off the beach or wanting beach vibes. *7am-9.30pm* $$

Topside: On the roof at Lido House, Topside is a place to see and be seen with coastal-inspired small bites. *4-10pm Mon-Thu, to 11pm Fri, 2-11pm Sat, 11am-11pm Sun* $$

JON BILOUS/SHUTTERSTOCK

Corona del Mar State Beach

chocolate-dipped bananas, which inspired the family business on *Arrested Development.* Visit the 80-year-old original **Sugar n' Spice** *(sugarnspice.co)* or **Dad's Donut & Bakery Shop** for a taste. A note: in addition to getting there by ferry from Balboa Peninsula, the quaint island is easily accessible by foot, bike or car – but parking can be hard in the cozy community.

Nature, Preserved at Back Bay

This enormous ecological reserve is a natural dream

What's really the **Upper Newport Bay Ecological Preserve** *(ocparks.com)* is colloquially called Back Bay, with more than 1000 acres of protected coastal wetland and a 10.5-mile hiking and biking trail running through it. Admission to its Peter and Mary Muth **Interpretive Center** *(newportbay.org),* dedicated to local wildlife programming and education, is free.

NEWPORT BEACH'S BEST BEACHES

Crystal Cove State Park: Appealing destination with three beaches, campsites, cabins and an underwater park for snorkeling and diving.

Corona del Mar State Beach: Known as Big Corona, this beach is family- and pet-friendly. If it looks familiar, you might recognize the beach from *Gilligan's Island.*

Newport Beach Pier: The stretch of sand on Balboa Peninsula around the Newport Beach Pier has fine sand and views and proximity to many shops and cafes.

Little Corona del Mar Beach: Calm beach known for snorkeling and tide pools, with no steps down to the sand.

The Wedge: This scenic beach's waves make it popular with surfers. In the summer, boards are prohibited between 10am and 5pm.

DRINKING IN NEWPORT BEACH: BEST COCKTAILS

Billy's at the Beach: Grab a seat at the harborside bar, watch boats pull up and get food and drinks to go. *11am-9pm Tue-Sat, to midnight Thu-Sat*

Bootlegger Bar: This casual bar at Crystal Cove State Park serves creative margaritas and a legendary Bloody Mary. *11am-9.30pm Mon-Fri, 10am-9.30pm Sat & Sun*

Under CdM: Under CdM is a speakeasy designed for tipplers who love an elevated smoked or infused cocktail. *by availability Thu-Sun*

Louie's by the Bay: Italian steakhouse offering refined cocktails like barrel-aged bourbon and gin drinks, plus a signature caviar martini. *happy hour 4-6pm, to late Wed*

Beyond Newport Beach

Places

GETTING AROUND

The closest Metrolink stations to Huntington Beach and Seal Beach are in Orange and Santa Ana, inland from the coast. Grab a rideshare or hop on an OCTA Bus to reach your final seaside destination. Costa Mesa is a short bus ride away. Find routes and timetables via the Metrolink Mobile app or the OCTA Transit Royale app. If you're driving, there are paid public lots on the Pacific Coast Hwy, but you can often get lucky and snag street parking, especially in the off season.

Head north on the Pacific Coast Hwy for incredible stretches of beach and the surfing capital of America.

Centrally located in Orange County's waterfront, Newport Beach is a great homebase to explore other areas up and down the PCH. North of Newport you'll find Huntington Beach, a haven for surfers and sun worshippers, where beach vibes are an entire lifestyle. Above that, Seal Beach is an idyllic postage stamp of a beach town with a very different vibe from the highly trafficked Huntington and Newport Beaches. It's perfect for people hoping to avoid crowds. Slightly inland, Costa Mesa offers a fun, artistic vibe, with must-see museums and performance spaces.

Huntington Beach

TIME FROM NEWPORT BEACH: **15MIN**

Welcome to Surf City, USA

There's no place in Orange County more closely associated with surfing than **Huntington Beach**, also known as Surf City, USA. It's where surfing first became popular in California and it's where the sport is celebrated every day by pros and first-timers alike, both on water and on land. There's an **International Surfing Museum** *(huntingtonbeachsurfingmuseum.org)* just blocks off the shore and a **Surfers' Hall of Fame** outside **Huntington Surf & Sport** *(hsssurf.com)*. Outside **Jack's Surfboards**, which has been an institution since the 1950s, is the **Surfing Walk of Fame** *(surfingwalkoffame.com)*. The Walk of Fame hosts an induction ceremony during the **US Open of Surfing** *(redbull.com/us-en/events/vans-us-open-of-surfing)*, the world's largest surfing competition, which happens in Huntington Beach in July. In April, Jack's hosts its own major surf competition, **Jack's Surfboards Pro** *(jackssurfboards.com)*, a qualifying event for the World Surfing League.

But you don't have to be a pro to surf in Huntington: many surf schools offer beginner's lessons. Head toward the water and you'll find one.

KK STOCK/SHUTTERSTOCK

Plaza, Huntington Beach Pier

Stroll the pier

At 1850ft long, **Huntington Beach Pier** is one of the largest piers on the West Coast. The pier has shops and dining and often artists selling their wares and street musicians performing. Before you arrive in Huntington Beach, you can scope out the scenery on the live-streamed webcam *(huntingtonbeachca.gov)*.

Beach all day, beach all night

Your beach vacation isn't complete without a beach bonfire. Three of Huntington's five beaches have fire pits available on a first-come, first-served basis: **Huntington City Beach**, **Huntington State Beach** and **Bolsa Chica State Beach**. Even though there are more than 500 available, they can be hard to come by in peak season, when people stake them out early in the day. However, there's a trick – rent a picnic spot through **California State Parks** *(parks.ca.gov)* and a fire pit comes with the rental. Be warned, though, the rentals can range from $200 to $300 a day, but are big enough to accommodate a larger group.

Appreciating the outdoors

Huntington's gorgeous scenery goes way beyond the beach. The 1300-acre **Bolsa Chica Ecological Reserve** *(bolsachica.org)* is the largest saltwater marsh in Southern California and has 5 miles of walking trails with scenic overlooks. Bird lovers flock here to see the more than 300 avian species that have been spotted in the last decade.

The 350-acre **Huntington Central Park** *(huntingtonbeachca.gov)* has horseback-riding trails, a playground, disc golf, a dog park and horseshoes, as well as a nature center showcasing local flora and fauna and three restaurants.

BEST BEACHES IN HUNTINGTON

Huntington State Beach: This 3-mile stretch of beach is popular with sunbathers, surfers, anglers and bird-watchers.

Huntington City Beach: Home to the Huntington Beach Pier; this beach is where the pro surfing happens.

Huntington Dog Beach: Unlike other OC beaches, you can have your pup here anytime. The Dog Beach has an annual SoCal Corgi Beach Day.

Bolsa Chica State Beach: Camping available across from Bolsa Chica Ecological Reserve and a visitors center with kid-friendly marine exhibits.

Sunset Beach: Ideal place to catch a perfect OC sunset. An attached park, the Green Belt, has a playground.

DEBBIE ECKERT/SHUTTERSTOCK

Huntington Central Park (p463)

Make a splash

Huntington Harbor is a must-see destination in the city. The harbor area is a collection of five human-made islands surrounded by more than 500 houses, many with truly remarkable (and remarkably quirky) architecture. During the holiday season, harbor homes are decked out for the **Huntington Harbor Cruise of Lights** *(cruiseoflights.org; adult/child $26/19)*, a narrated boat tour of the festive decorations that has been going on for more than 60 years.

The harbor area is an ideal place to get on the water if you're interested in water sports other than surfing. The calm waters are perfect for kayaking or stand-up paddleboarding and rental equipment is readily available at locations throughout. Private charters and electric boats are also available for hire.

Seal Beach

TIME FROM NEWPORT BEACH: **30MIN**

Sea the wildlife

Seal Beach gets its name from the seals that dot its shores. On any given day, you might spot them from the town's small pier or its quaint waterfront promenade. Many day-trippers bike to Seal Beach via the **San Gabriel River Bike Trail** *(trails.lacounty.gov/Trail/265/san-gabriel-river-trail)*, a 28-mile stretch of bike path next to the San Gabriel River that

EATING IN HUNTINGTON BEACH: OUR PICKS

Duke's: Founded by Duke Kahanamoku, surfer and Olympian, Duke's serves Hawaiian-inspired food on the beach. *11.30am-9pm Tue-Sat, 10am-8.30pm Sun* $$$

Jolie: Jolie has an elevated seafood menu and stunning water views. The Belle is a lively rooftop bar. *11am-10pm, to 11pm Fri-Sun* $$$

LSXO: This 28-seat restaurant is hidden within the Bluegold and serves refined Vietnamese cuisine and cocktails. *4-9.30pm Mon-Wed, 11am-10pm Thu-Sun* $$$

Pacific Hideaway: In the Kimpton Shorebreak Hotel, serves Asian- and Latin-influenced cuisine and has a dog menu. *7am-10pm* $$$

separates the city from Los Angeles County. Another attraction is the 965-acre **Seal Beach Wildlife Preserve** *(fws.gov/refuge/seal-beach),* on the grounds of the Naval Weapons Station Seal Beach military base. On the last Saturday morning of the month, you can take a free guided tour of the salt marsh. Aside from those tours, the refuge is not open to the public.

Shop and stroll

The charming town of Seal Beach is very small and walkable, which means you can take in most of it in an afternoon. After you've explored the beach, take some time to stroll and peruse independent seaside shops selling seashells, chocolates and beachy fashion. Because it's tucked away in the furthest northwest part of Orange County, Seal Beach tends to be less crowded than larger destinations.

Costa Mesa

TIME FROM NEWPORT BEACH: **15MIN**

A Renaissance city

Costa Mesa is a cultural hub in Orange County, with theater and fine art attractions worth detouring for. The **Orange County Museum of Art** *(ocma.org)* opened in its current home in 2022, with a collection focusing on California art, and is free to the public. The **Segerstrom Center for the Arts** *(sctfa.org)* has six venues. It's home to the Pacific Symphony and the Philharmonic Society of Orange County and hosts traveling Broadway productions. **South Coast Repertory** *(scr.org)* is a theater that has been debuting new works since 1966 and hosts an annual **Pacific Playwrights Festival**. The city is also known for its festivals: the **OC Fair** *(ocfair.com)* happens every July and August for food, festivities and concerts.

BEST FOR PUBLIC ART

Center Tower: This office building has several large-scale sculptures in the courtyard and lobby.

Noguchi Garden: At the Pacific Arts Plaza is this serene art garden.

19th Street & Wallace Avenue: Murals celebrate Dolly Parton and LA Lakers legend Kobe Bryant and his daughter Gianna.

Segerstrom Center for the Arts: The courtyard of this performance center has a striking 65ft steel sculpture.

South Coast Plaza: This huge shopping center has an enormous, vivid outdoor sculpture by Charles O Perry and a stained-glass dome skylight made of 7200 pieces of glass.

DINING IN COSTA MESA: OUR PICKS

Folks Pizzeria: Small but mighty pizzeria serving up inventive small plates and pies. *4-9pm Mon-Thu, 3-9.30pm Fri, noon-9.30pm Sat, noon-9pm Sun* **$$**

Descanso: Refined Mexican served a la carte, or meals cooked 'à la plancha' at a grill directly at your table. *3-9pm Mon, 11.30am-10.30pm Tue-Sun* **$$**

AnQi by House of An: AnQi is a stylish restaurant that serves elevated California Asian cuisine. *noon-9pm* **$$$**

El Matador: A local favorite since 1966. Mexican classics are served alongside its 'wall of tequila' which has more than 400 selections. *11.30am-9pm* **$$**

Laguna Beach

LAID-BACK BEACHES | ARTISTIC VIBE | UNMISSABLE FESTIVALS

TOP TIP

Parking can be limited in the quaint downtown. In high season, consider taking the Laguna Beach Trolley, which services North Laguna, South Laguna and Dana Point. Download the Trolley Tracker app or access it online at *visitlagunabeach.com.*

GETTING AROUND

One of the supreme pleasures of an Orange County visit is biking along the Pacific Coast Hwy, a stretch of waterfront road about 40 miles long. It's also the single best way to beat the traffic and parking in crowded places like Laguna Beach and Newport. You can easily find bike rental shops up and down the PCH in beach towns like Laguna Beach, Huntington Beach and Newport Beach. Nearby Laguna Niguel is accessible via Metrolink; Laguna Beach is accessible by OCTA Bus.

Laguna Beach has a singular energy all its own. Founded as an artist colony over a century ago, the city has evolved into a vibrant cultural center with events that draw visitors from near and far. But more than that, Laguna is just beautiful: there is public art nearly everywhere you look and where there isn't, there is some of the most scenic coastline imaginable. Its seven miles of beach is mostly connected and is easily accessible from the city's main waterfront thoroughfare. Watersports like surfing and kayaking are popular in Laguna, but the mountains and canyons offer outdoor recreation away from the shore. In short, there's a lot more to do than just hang out at the beach.

A City of Art

Just walk around and you'll soak up creativity

Even if you're not into art, the city's artsy vibe is infectious. Stroll through downtown **Laguna Village** and you'll quickly notice that there's street art almost everywhere: phone booths, parking meters, alleyways, fences. Anywhere that can be made more beautiful has been made more beautiful by the city's artistic community.

The city is home to **Laguna Art Museum** *(lagunaartmuseum.org)*, which is a storied cultural institution that houses an all-Californian art collection. Throughout the city, there are over 80 art galleries and artists workspaces. Every first Thursday of the month, more than half of them open their doors on **First Thursdays Art Walks** *(firstthursdaysartwalk.org; free)*, an open gallery event with artist receptions and live performances, with free trolley transportation.

Every summer, two major art festivals light up Laguna Beach. The **Sawdust Art Festival** *(sawdustartfestival.org)* has been happening annually since 1967 and offers 500 art classes during its June, July and August event. The **Festival of Arts** *(foapom.org)* happens in July and August – the visual art portion of the festival showcases the works of more than 100 Orange County artists.

SIGHTS
1 Laguna Art Museum
2 Laguna Beach Cultural Arts Center
3 Main Beach
4 Thousand Steps Beach
5 Victoria Beach

ACTIVITIES
6 Aliso & Wood Canyons Wilderness Park
7 Divers Cove

SLEEPING
8 La Casa del Camino
9 Montage Laguna Beach
10 Ranch at Laguna Beach

EATING
11 La Sirena Grill
12 Larsen
13 Lost Pier Cafe
14 The Cliff
15 The Deck on Laguna

DRINKING & NIGHTLIFE
16 Laguna Beach Beer Company
17 Las Brisas
see 8 Rooftop Lounge

ENTERTAINMENT
18 Festival of Arts
see 1 First Thursdays Gallery Art Walk
19 Laguna Playhouse
see 18 Pageant of the Masters
20 Sawdust Art Festival

PREP FOR THE BEACH...OR DON'T

Don't stress about packing beach gear in Orange County. There are shops up and down Pacific Coast Highway that rent everything you need for the beach, including beach chairs, sand toys and boogie boards, in addition to selling items like sunblock and goggles. Some even sell bonfire kits for beach firepits once the sun goes down.

If you'd rather make it easier, there are companies all over Orange County that will deliver beach rentals to you and offer daily and weekly rentals, or longer. Try **Bliss Beach** *(blissbeach.co)*, which delivers gear packed in a wagon, or **Beach Bros** *(beachbrosssharing.com)* or **SoCal Beach to You** *(socalbeach2you.com)*, which both hand-deliver supplies.

SUNFLOWERMOMMA/SHUTTERSTOCK

Thousand Steps Beach

The Beach & Beyond

Over 30 strips of sand to explore

Each of Laguna's 30-plus beaches has something unique. **Main Beach**, across from Laguna Village, is the one you might have seen on television before. It's famous for its scenery, beach volleyball and surfers and boardwalk. **Crescent Bay Beach** is popular with surfers; the adjacent **Crescent Bay Cove** is a green space with expansive views and tide pools. If that's the easiest to access, then **Thousand Steps Beach** is the hardest. Descend 218 steps to get to a secluded beach that has deep tide pools and a sea cave you can walk all the way through at low tide. **Diver's Cove** is ideal for snorkeling and has mild waves. **Victoria Beach** has a 'pirate tower' and a community-maintained swimming pool fed by ocean surf.

Most of the coves on Laguna's coast have tide pools that are protected environments, so they're thriving marine-life habitats which you can explore (look but don't touch). The best time to visit is at low tide, usually in the morning and evening.

EATING & DRINKING IN LAGUNA BEACH: WATERFRONT DINING

The Deck on Laguna: Dine at tables directly in the sand; also serves food and cocktails to the rentable beach bungalows next door. *11am-9pm* **$$$**

Larsen: Housed in the historic Laguna Hotel, this restaurant overlooks Main Beach and has outdoor tables and couches for lounging. *from 11am* **$$$**

Las Brisas: The water views are gorgeous at this Mexican-meets-Californian fine dining restaurant. *8am-10pm Sun-Thu, to 11pm Fri & Sat* **$$$**

Rooftop Lounge: On the roof of La Casa del Camino Hotel, the Rooftop serves creative cocktails and shared plates. Weekday happy hour. *11am-10pm* **$$**

A Haven of Performing Arts

The creative side of Laguna

Visual art isn't the only artistic medium prized in Laguna Beach. The **Laguna Beach Cultural Arts Center** *(lbculturalartscenter.org)* offers various events almost every day, from film screenings to gallery shows to opera and theater performances. The **Laguna Playhouse** *(lagunaplayhouse.com)* has been in continuous operation for over a century and regularly hosts world-premiere works and brings Hollywood celebrities to its stage.

The July and August Festival of Arts (p466) includes an art show, but also one of the most unique art events in the country: **Pageant of the Masters**. During this singular event, people create living dioramas of famous works of art. (If you've watched *Gilmore Girls*, you've seen this before – Stars Hollow hosts a Pageant of the Masters on the show.)

Take a Hike

Explore the coast and mountains

Much of Laguna Beach is high up above beach cliffs, making for stunning scenery and especially good visibility up and down the coast. The city has 20,000 acres of protected wilderness to explore in the **Laguna Green Belt** *(lagunagreenbelt.org)*, which is a series of linked parks: **Laguna Coast Wilderness Parks**, **Aliso & Wood Canyon Parks** and **Crystal Cove State Park**. Laguna Coast has more than 40 trails; in the spring, you might catch a wildflower superbloom. Crystal Cove has beaches, but also mountain biking trails that will bring you up to some of the best views in the city. Aliso and Wood Canyons have shadier trails through woodland.

TRAVELING WITH PETS

While many coastal communities in California are pet-friendly, Laguna Beach is especially accommodating for four-legged family members. Many places are open to well-behaved dogs and there are an abundance of shops that leave water bowls out on the sidewalk. On beaches, leashed dogs are allowed before 9am and after 6pm in the summer and all day the rest of the year.

Finding a pet-friendly hotel isn't challenging, either. **Visit Laguna Beach** *(visitlagunabeach.com)* offers an extensive and continuously updated list of accommodations that welcome dogs and sometimes other pets. Keep in mind that most hotels charge a pet fee, which can vary from $100 per stay to $50 or more per night.

EATING IN LAGUNA BEACH: PET-FRIENDLY RESTAURANTS

The Cliff: Terraced patio with water views and a dog-specific menu with choices like chicken breast or salmon with rice. *11am-9pm Mon-Thu, 8.30am-10pm Fri-Sun* $$$

Laguna Beach Beer Company: This brewery and kitchen serves seasonal beers along with pizza and tacos. Large dog-friendly patio. *noon-9pm, to 10pm Fri & Sat* $$

La Sirena Grill: This downtown Mexican kitchen prioritizes sustainability and welcomes dogs at its outdoor tables. *8am-8pm Mon-Sat* $$

Lost Pier Cafe: Beach cafe with casual vibe, upscale casual food and rentable fire pits to enjoy on the beach. *8am-6pm* $$

Beyond Laguna Beach

Places

Head south on the Pacific Coast Hwy to find quieter shores, or escape to an island.

Driving (or biking) south from Laguna Beach on the PCH, the next beach town you'll reach is Dana Point. Known for its laid-back surf culture, it's also a destination for golfers and people looking for quiet, pristine beaches. But beyond the beach, Dana Point is full of attractions, from historic tall ships to an aquarium and public art. The city has a creativity all its own and hosts unusual and fascinating annual events like the Ocean Institute Maritime Festival and the Festival of Whales – in addition to Pearl Jam frontman Eddie Vedder's Ohana Festival, which brings in huge musical acts for beachfront concerts.

Dana Point

TIME FROM LAGUNA BEACH: **15MIN**

Set sail for adventure

If you've always wanted to learn to sail, **Dana Point** might be the place to do it. **Dana Point Charters** *(danapointcharters.com)* offers private sails for up to six people; you can even participate in the operating of the ship and learn from the captain and crew while aboard. The **Ocean Institute** *(oceaninstitute.org)* is home to *Spirit of Dana Point,* a replica of a 1770s privateer schooner that offers tall-ship sails where

GETTING AROUND

Driving or biking south along the coast, Dana Point is so close to Laguna Beach that you might not even notice that you've left one and entered the other. The Laguna Beach Trolley services North Laguna, South Laguna and Dana Point. Download the Trolley Tracker app or access it online via *visitlagunabeach.com.* If you're driving, expect to pay a nominal fee in public lots.

If you're headed to Catalina Island, there are only two places to hop on a ferry from Orange County. One is in Newport Beach and the other is in Dana Point. Once aboard the **Catalina Express** *(catalinaexpress.com),* it's about 90 minutes from Dana Point to Avalon on Catalina.

guests can help with the rigging, sunset sails and adventure sails where they fire off a real cannon.

The Ocean Institute also offers sails on the Research Vessel *Sea Explorer*: take a whale watch in an area especially known for whale sightings, or go on a nighttime bioluminescence cruise in the summer months.

The organization hosts an annual **Maritime Festival** every September, which brings in other tall ships to Dana Point and features cannon battles, pirate school, sailor camp and a mermaid swim show.

Take a surfing lesson or learn to kayak

If watching all the surfers has you inspired to hit the waves, sign up for a lesson with **Girl in the Curl** *(girlinthecurl.com; from $150)*. This **Doheny Beach** surf shop offers private surf lessons for groups and individuals and provides all the equipment you need for the day.

Because of its calm water, Dana Point's **Baby Beach** is an easy place to try your hand at kayaking or stand-up paddleboarding. Many surf and sail shops by the beach offer day rentals of equipment with no reservations necessary – feel free to pop in and give it a shot.

Celebrate sea life

Dana Point has a front-row seat to the seasonal migration of gray whales from the colder waters of the West Coast to the warmer waters of Baja California. Every March, the city hosts a **Festival of Whales** *(festivalofwhales.com)* celebrating that unique gift, which includes whale-watching excursions, family entertainment and marine-themed activities.

Gather with your ohana

Founded by Eddie Vedder in 2016, the **Ohana Fest** *(ohanafest.com)* is a multiday music festival with a special mission: to educate people about conservation and environmental issues between performances from huge headliners like Stevie Nicks, Jack White, P!nk and Green Day.

The city also hosts the **Palm Tree Music Festival** *(palmtreemusicfestival.com)* in October, which features huge EDM acts like Martin Garrix and Calvin Harris.

Learn about the natural world

The **Headlands Conservation Area** *(danapoint.org)* has a network of easy and moderate hikes ranging from 1 to 2.5 miles, with scenic views from cliffs above the ocean and access to tide pools. The area is also home to the **Dana Point Nature Interpretive Center**, open every day but Monday, which has kid-friendly exhibits about the local environment and wildlife.

The **Ocean Institute** is also home to an aquarium that allows families to learn about the ocean, even if they don't want to sail. The aquarium has touch tanks, including one with sharks and rays and interactive exhibits.

THE BEST BEACHES IN DANA POINT

Doheny State Beach: A renowned surfing location that's also a popular camping spot; tide pools to explore at low tide.

Baby Beach: This family-friendly beach has a roped-off section of calm water perfect for kids to swim in.

Capistrano Beach: There's more to do than luxuriate in the sand: Capistrano Beach has beach volleyball courts and a boardwalk.

Dana Strand Beach: This beach, far below the parking lot, has a funicular that transports people down to the water.

Salt Creek Beach: Expect to see lots of surfers at Salt Creek Beach, where surf conditions are almost always ideal.

Places We Love to Stay

$** Budget **$$** Midrange **$$$ Top End

Disneyland & Anaheim

MAP p447

Alpine Inn $ An affordable motel very close to the park. Alpine Inn has the same aesthetic as Disneyland's signature Matterhorn. Free parking and free coffee in the morning.

Anaheim Hotel $$ This hotel matches Disneyland's retro vibe with mid-century chic decor and affordable room rates. It's located directly across from an entrance to Downtown Disney.

Anaheim Majestic Garden Hotel $$ This Fantasyland-inspired hotel has castle-like architecture both inside and outside. Not quite walking distance to the park, but offers a paid shuttle.

Howard Johnson by Wyndham Anaheim Hotel $$ Directly across from an entrance to Downtown Disney, this hotel has a pirate-themed water park attached and a singular Disneyland-inspired, art-filled suite.

Candy Cane Inn $$ Independently owned motel with free breakfast and free parking, which was recently refurbished. Very short walk to parks, or a free shuttle.

Disneyland Hotel (p454) $$$ Original Disneyland hotel, with four highly themed towers, two pools and Monorail-themed waterslides. Food options include a coffee shop and five restaurants.

Disney's Grand Californian Hotel (p454) $$$ The most convenient of the on-property hotels, the Grand Californian has a direct entrance into the park, plus a themed pool area, five restaurants and a soaring lobby with couches and a fireplace.

Pixar Place Hotel (p454) $$$ Newly renovated in 2024, Pixar Place has a themed pool, waterslide and lawn games area, plus excellent fireworks viewing and three restaurants.

Westin Anaheim $$$ A short walk from Disneyland, the newly renovated Westin has a luxury feel and a rooftop bar with fireworks views, plus attached restaurants including Fleming's.

JW Marriott Anaheim $$$ Opened in 2021, this hotel is attached to the Anaheim GardenWalk, an outdoor pedestrian mall with restaurants and entertainment. The hotel has a fine dining restaurant and a rooftop lounge with fireworks views.

Knott's Berry Farm

Knott's Hotel $$ The only hotel on Knott's Berry Farm property recently reopened with a top-to-bottom renovation, including a new restaurant showcasing the park's signature boysenberry.

Hilton Buena Park Anaheim $$ Close to Knott's, this Hilton has a heated rooftop pool, full-service breakfast and a 24-hour grab-and-go market.

Newport Beach

MAP p459

Crystal Cove Beach Cottages $$ These cottages in Crystal Cove State Park are unusually affordable for their beachside location between Newport Beach and Laguna Beach, but they sell out immediately when the six-month window opens.

Lido House Newport Beach $$$ This Autograph Collection hotel in the Lido Marina Village area has a fine dining restaurant, a rooftop lounge, a luxury spa and separate cottages apart from the main building.

Resort at Pelican Hill $$$ This sprawling oceanside resort has five restaurants and two golf courses and has been rated best resort in the country by Forbes Travel Guide. Accommodations go up to four-bedroom villas.

Balboa Bay Resort $$$ This AAA Four Diamond waterfront hotel has a lavish spa, on-site fine dining restaurant and a marina with boat rentals.

Huntington Beach

Surf City Inn $$ This quiet boutique hotel has harbor views and a short walk to Sunset Beach. Some rooms have Jacuzzi tubs.

Ocean Surf Inn & Suites $$ A quaint 30-room inn steps from the beach. Some rooms come with Jacuzzi tubs and water-view balconies.

Paséa Hotel & Spa $$$ Stylish beachfront hotel with a rooftop restaurant ideal for watching the sunset over the ocean.

Kimpton Shorebreak Hotel $$$ Get the daily surf report in this stylish hotel with lobby games and courtyard firepits, plus free breakfast.

Waterfront Beach Resort $$$ Relaxing Hilton resort with a spa and rooftop lounge, plus two waterslides in the lagoon-style pool.

Hyatt Regency Huntington Beach Resort & Spa $$$ Large beachfront hotel with two pools and amenities like bike rentals and beach bonfire packages.

Seal Beach

Pacific Inn $$ This beachside hotel offers free breakfast and provides a free local shuttle daily until 9pm.

Water Tower House $$$ Perched 85ft above the beach, this three-story rental is accessible via private elevator. It has four bedrooms and amenities including in-unit laundry.

Costa Mesa

The Westin South Coast Plaza $$ Extremely close to South Coast Plaza's shopping and dining, plus the Segerstrom Center for the Arts. This hotel has two restaurants and a market.

Avenue of the Arts $$ Tribute Portfolio Hotel overlooking Avenue of the Arts Lake and sculptures; a free airport shuttle and free pool cabanas.

Laguna Beach

MAP p467

La Casa del Camino $ The historic La Casa del Camino has water views, Mediterranean-themed rooms and a rooftop lounge.

Montage Laguna Beach $$$ An immersive resort with three pools, a spa, several restaurants and a museum-quality fine art collection.

Ranch at Laguna Beach $$$ California's only National Geographic Lodge of the World feels rustic yet refined in a secluded canyon and has beach access.

Dana Point

Waldorf Astoria Monarch Beach $$$ One of OC's most luxurious accommodations has its own beach club and golf course, plus six restaurants, including from acclaimed chef Michael Mina.

Laguna Cliffs Marriott Resort & Spa $$$ This resort is a short walk from Doheny Beach and offers beach gear for guests, as well as the ability to book gourmet lunches to-go. Three restaurants and a spa are on property.

STEVE CUKROV/SHUTTERSTOCK

Hyatt Regency Huntington Beach Resort & Spa

For places to stay in San Diego and Around, see p510

TOKAR/SHUTTERSTOCK

Above: Mission Beach (p492), San Diego; Right: Balboa Park (p486)

Researched by
Julie Tremaine

San Diego & Around

CALIFORNIA'S MOST LAID-BACK CITY

The southernmost city in California is a low-stress paradise. San Diego's relaxed, beachy energy is more than a vibe – it's a lifestyle.

San Diego is a city unlike any other in California. The second-largest in the state by population, San Diego has everything you could ask for in a metropolis: vibrant arts and culture, diverse and varied neighborhoods, incredible food and one of the best zoos in America. But even with all that, the city manages to always feel relaxed. The chill coastal vibes and endless sunshine are ingrained in every corner of this Southern California paradise.

Part of what makes San Diego so different is that it sits on the Mexican border and there's a real cultural influence from Tijuana, its neighbor to the south, in everything from food and festivals to art galleries showcasing Chicano and Latino works. Another thing that deeply influences the city's character: the beach. Nowhere in San Diego is more than a short drive from its 17 miles of coastline. There are beaches for families and for surfers, ocean caves to explore, tide pools to observe, boats to be chartered, seaside boardwalks to stroll and stunning sunsets to appreciate. Outside San Diego proper, smaller beach communities like La Jolla and Carlsbad have characters all their own and attractions worth driving to. And while Northern California is better known for its wine, the southernmost wine destination in California is worth a taste. Temecula is a wine lover's paradise, with idyllic scenery and hot-air balloons in the sky.

DANCESTROKES/SHUTTERSTOCK

THE MAIN AREAS

KYLE SPRAGUE/SHUTTERSTOCK

La Jolla (p494)

Find Your Way

San Diego International Airport (SAN) is in the city center and is easily accessible from almost anywhere. Amtrak's Pacific Surfliner train travels daily between Santa Barbara, Los Angeles and San Diego, with stops in between.

Temecula, p504

There are more than 50 wineries in Temecula Valley, an epicurean's destination with excellent dining and skies dotted with hot-air balloons.

San Diego, p480

The second-most-populous city in California, San Diego has plenty of sandy beaches and sunny neighborhoods worth exploring.

Carlsbad, p497

A beach town known for its Legoland theme park, expansive fields of flowers and pristine waterfront.

BICYCLE

The San Diego County Bicycle Coalition *(sdbikecoalition.org)* has extensive resources about the best, safest bicycle routes. If you're planning to get around on two wheels, you'll be well-covered.

TROLLEY & BUS

San Diego has a network of trolleys and buses. Not only do they get you where you need to go, but the trolleys also provide a fair bit of history and an overview of local points of interest as you ride.

CAR

If you plan to stay in and around San Diego, you can get away with not having a car. However, but if you plan to explore some of the surrounding areas or venture up into the mountains, you'll want to drive.

Plan Your Time

Exploring San Diego means going from the ocean all the way up into the mountains. Be prepared for a variety of climates, especially at higher elevations, where it can be chilly even in summer.

LARISA GRIB/SHUTTERSTOCK

Temecula

If You Only Do One Thing

- Give yourself one perfect day in **San Diego** (p480). Start with a morning on Imperial Beach, where you can take a serene walk on the **Silver Strand** (p490) watching the birds, take a swim in the surf or sit in the sand with a book.

- In the afternoon, head to **Balboa Park** (p486) and explore one or two of the many attractions there, from the **San Diego Zoo** (p486) and the art and science museums to the 34 different **International Cottages** (p487).

- Head to **Coronado** (p490) for dinner, where you can get a waterfront table at one of the restaurants at the **Hotel del Coronado** (p491) to watch the sunset. Then, follow up at a speakeasy with a secret entrance – San Diego has a lot of them – for a **nightcap** (p483).

Seasonal Highlights

When it feels like summer every day, you don't have to confine your travel to July and August. Any month of the year is a good time to visit San Diego.

MARCH

The superbloom at the **Flower Fields** (p497) at Carlsbad Ranch starts at the beginning of this month, when 55 acres of flowers burst into living color.

APRIL

The **Mission Fed ArtWalk** (p492) in San Diego's Little Italy is the largest art event on the West Coast, with proceeds going to nonprofit art education.

MAY

Arguably the most beautiful time to visit an already beautiful place is during the **Temecula Valley Balloon & Wine Festival**, when hot-air balloons fill the sky.

Three Days to Travel Around

- Depending on whether you're flying into San Diego or driving down from the north, take a few days to go up or down the Pacific Coast Hwy. Either start in the city and make your way north to **La Jolla** (p494) and **Carlsbad** (p497), or start in a **smaller beach town** (p502) and finish in San Diego. Either way, you'll have a nice mix of laid-back time on the coast and an entertaining time in the city.

- Stay at least one night in a beachfront hotel and one night in the city center to truly give yourself a taste of everything San Diego has to offer.

If You Have More Time

- Venture out into the mountains around **Temecula** (p504). The idyllic city is only about 60 miles from San Diego, but the scenery is a world away. As the state's southernmost wine destination, Temecula Valley has over 50 **wineries and tasting rooms** (p508). Many of them are spread out in the hills and it's easy to hire a tour company to drive you around and spend a day tasting.

- Spend another day on two wheels taking in the scenery: with its 90 miles of bicycle trails, Temecula is especially suited to **cycling enthusiasts** (p507). Then there's the historic town center that has destination-worthy restaurants, antiques shopping and a **country music venue** (p507) known throughout the state for its line dancing and live bands.

JUNE

Make your way to Del Mar for the **San Diego County Fair** (p495), a month-long celebration with carnival games, concerts, festivals, performances and agricultural events.

SEPTEMBER

The **Festival of Sail** (p483) attracts tall ships from around the world to San Diego Bay, complete with food, games, pirates and a cannon battle.

NOVEMBER

Oceanside's **Dia de los Muertos** (p484) is a citywide celebration of Mexican culture, with live music, entertainment, food and altars remembering those who have passed.

DECEMBER

Celebrate the holidays SoCal style with the San Diego Bay **Parade of Lights** (p483), where sailing vessels are bedecked with thousands of Christmas lights.

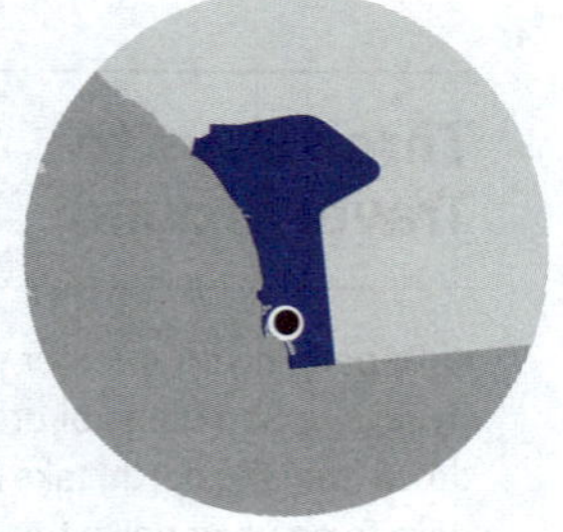

San Diego

CULTURE | WALKABLE HISTORY | BEACHES

TOP TIP

San Diego's huge waterfront isn't just for the Navy; it's also a busy port for cruises. About 75 cruise ships dock in San Diego Bay every year and 10 cruise lines either stop as a port of call or start or end here. Many hotels offer cruise-related deals.

San Diego is unlike any other city in California. It's huge – the second-most populous city in the state, just after Los Angeles – but the southerly city is a starkly different experience. Somehow, despite its size and how much it packs in, San Diego manages to exude a relaxed, sunny vibe no matter where you are or what you're doing.

And there's a lot to do: it has far more than you could possibly fit into a short visit. A stunning collection of museums in Balboa Park, the world-famous San Diego Zoo, the San Diego Padres baseball team and one of the largest naval bases in the country are just scratching the surface. Beyond the city center, there are a number of vibrant neighborhoods worth exploring, each with a character all its own. On top of that, the food and drink – especially the local craft beer – are divine. Is San Diego California's coolest city? You'll just have to visit to find out.

GETTING AROUND

San Diego's public transportation makes getting around the city without a car easy. The San Diego Metropolitan Transit System (MTS) has a network of buses and trolleys that service most of the city and has a route planner on its website *(sdmts.com; day pass $6)* that makes it simple to navigate. Even the airport is easy to reach on public transit: both bus route 992 and the Old Town Airport Shuttle offer frequent daily access; it's about a 15-minute ride.

Savor the Gaslamp District

MAP P482

Dine, drink and shop downtown

The downtown **Gaslamp District** was named for the gas street lights installed here in the late 1800s. The glowing neon signs welcoming you to this historic neighborhood tell you exactly what you need to know: while the buildings are from the Victorian era, what's inside is totally modern. There are more than 100 places to eat, drink, shop and dance in the district's 16 square blocks – this is the place to come if you're just looking to walk around, explore and stumble on places that look enticing to stop for a bite or a drink. This is also where you'll head if you're looking for nightlife, or to have a cocktail on a rooftop lounge. Rumors of ghost sightings swirl throughout the neighborhood, especially at the **Gaslamp Museum at the Davis-Horton House** *(gaslampfoundation.org; admission $8)*, which offers walking ghost tours.

HIGHLIGHTS

1 Old Town San Diego State Historic Park

SIGHTS

see 1 Bazaar del Mundo

2 Cabrillo National Monument

see 1 Casa de Estudillo

3 Chicano Park

see 10 Heritage Park

4 Juniper Canyon

5 Junípero Serra Museum

6 Marston House

7 Mission Bay Park

8 North Park

9 South Park

10 Whaley House Museum

ACTIVITIES

11 Coronado Historical Association

12 Waterhorse Charters

SLEEPING

13 Hotel del Coronado

14 Humphrey's Half-Moon Inn

15 Kona Kai Resort & Spa

16 Mission Bay Resort

17 Wayfarer San Diego

EATING

18 Roberto's Taco Shop

DRINKING & NIGHTLIFE

19 Eppig Brewing Waterfront Biergarten

20 Hillcrest Brewing Company

21 North Park Flavordome

22 Part Time Lover

ENTERTAINMENT

23 Belmont Park

24 Lamb's Players Theatre

25 Parade of Lights

SHOPPING

26 Coronado Ferry Landing

TRANSPORTATION

27 San Diego International Airport

DOWNTOWN SAN DIEGO

HIGHLIGHTS
1 New Children's Museum
2 USS Midway Museum

SIGHTS
3 Gaslamp Museum at the Davis-Horton House
4 Maritime Museum
5 Petco Park
6 San Diego Waterfront Park

ACTIVITIES
7 Flagship Cruises

SLEEPING
8 Guild Hotel
9 Ocean Park Inn
10 Omni San Diego
11 Pendry San Diego

EATING
12 Animae
13 Civico 1845
14 Fish Market
15 Headquarters at Seaport
16 Juniper & Ivy
17 Mona Lisa Italian Foods
18 Morning Glory
19 Werewolf

DRINKING & NIGHTLIFE
20 False Idol
21 Noble Experiment
22 Prohibition Lounge

ENTERTAINMENT
23 San Diego Comic-Con

SHOPPING
24 Seaport Village

Anchors Aweigh

MAP P482

Maritime history at the Embarcadero

Embarcadero, the waterfront area of downtown San Diego, has a lot to explore, especially when it comes to maritime history. Tour the **USS Midway Museum** *(midway.org; adult/child $39/26)*, a decommissioned aircraft carrier that served for 47 years. Independence Day is an especially good time to visit, when the museum hosts a July 4 Fireworks Viewing Party during the city's annual **Big Bay Boom** celebration.

The **Maritime Museum** *(sdmaritime.org; adult/child $24/from $12)* is a collection of historic ships that includes the 150-year-old *Star of India,* the oldest active sailing ship in the world. Families can even stay overnight on the ship and the museum offers an interactive pirate show. In September, the museum hosts the **Festival of Sail**, an enormous tall ships festival.

If you'd rather get out on the open water, it's easy to hop on a ship. **Flagship Cruises** *(flagshipsd.com)* offers seasonal whale watches, daily harbor tours, weekly dinner cruises, champagne brunch cruises and more.

Every December, more than 80 boats are aglow on San Diego Bay during the **Parade of Lights** *(sdparadeoflights.org)*, when owners decorate their vessels with holiday lights and set sail.

If you'd prefer to enjoy the harbor from dry land, **San Diego Waterfront Park** *(sdparks.org)* is a public space with grassy areas for picnics, splash pads and water features to cool off in and seriously gorgeous water views. The **New Children's Museum** *(thinkplaycreate.org; adult/child $24/20)* has fun, interactive science exhibits where kids can play and learn. **Seaport Village** *(seaportvillage.com)* is a waterfront shopping and dining district that looks like a harbor village from a century ago, with live music every weekend.

More Than Baseball

MAP P482

Petco Park is a community gathering place

Petco Park *(petcoparkevents.com)*, the home of the San Diego Padres, is located where the Gaslamp and East Village meet. Petco Park encompasses the stadium along with **Gallagher Square**, which is an outdoor concert venue that brings in huge national touring acts and is also a popular gathering spot on game days. Petco Park offers daily guided **stadium tours** *(mlb.com/padres; $43)* that take guests into the press box, the Hall of Fame, a luxury suite and down onto the field's warning track.

VISITING MEXICO

San Diego shares an international border with Tijuana and it's easy for US citizens with passports to head south and explore the Mexican border town. There's even a Cross Border Xpress skybridge connecting the Tijuana International Airport to San Diego. International visitors can also cross the border, but need a valid passport as well as a valid I-94 form or multiple entry visa or visa waiver, which can be managed through the US Customs & Border Patrol's CBP One app.

In TJ, as locals call it, you can shop duty-free, eat Mexican food and explore the city's sights, like **Tijuana Cultural Center**, which combines art galleries with a botanical garden, performance stages and an aquarium.

DRINKING IN SAN DIEGO: SPEAKEASIES

MAP P482

Prohibition Lounge: Open the door to 'Law Office, Eddie O'Hare, Esq' to find a Gatsby-esque lounge with elevated cocktails and live music. *8pm-1.30am*

Noble Experiment: Head to the back of Neighborhood, then push open the wall of kegs to reveal a cabinet of cocktail curiosities. *6pm-2am*

Part Time Lover: Walk into Purity & Accuracy Records and you'll find this vinyl listening bar and record store where guests can spin their favorites. *4pm-2am*

False Idol: San Diego's most-lauded tiki bar also happens to be a speakeasy, hidden behind a walk-in cooler at Craft & Commerce. *5pm-1am*

THE BIRTHPLACE OF CALIFORNIA

San Diego holds the distinction of being the first place in California that European explorers settled, on land belonging to the Native American Kumeyaay people. Portuguese explorer Juan Rodríguez Cabrillo first came ashore in 1542 in what's now Point Loma: you can visit the site of his landing at the **Cabrillo National Monument** *(nps.gov/cabr)*. The Mission San Diego de Alcalá was established in the 1769 in what's now the Old Town and was the first of 21 Spanish missions that stretched along the California coast, from San Diego to Sonoma. Today, you can still see buildings that date back to that earliest settlement in the Old Town, along with tributes to the Kumeyaay people.

Celebrate Chicano Culture

MAP P481

Explore Logan Heights and Barrio Logan

The city's oldest Mexican-American neighborhood is a living tribute to Chicano culture, especially in **Barrio Logan**, an art-filled neighborhood that represents the city's vibrant identity. The second Saturday of every month, the **Barrio Art Crawl** *(allforlogan.com)* is a self-guided tour through the cultural district's public art and galleries, with food and live music. Make sure to stop by SI=, which has more than 100 Chicano murals and sculptures, plus gardens and green space.

Discover Old Town San Diego

MAP P481

Step back in time

Old Town San Diego State Historic Park *(oldtownmarketsandiego.com)* is a cluster of 19th-century buildings northwest of downtown, many of which date from San Diego's Mexican and early American eras. Arguably the most iconic of Old Town's historic buildings is the **Whaley House Museum** *(whaleyhousesandiego.com; adult/child $13.30/9.50)*, constructed in 1856 on the site where public hangings once took place. Today, it's rumored to be so haunted that it's been featured on many ghost-hunting television shows. At night, they offer ghost tours and after-hours paranormal investigations.

Casa de Estudillo is an original adobe building dating back to 1825 and is furnished with antiques from the 16th to the 20th century. **Heritage Park** nearby has a collection of preserved Victorian homes. The **Junípero Serra Museum** *(sandiegohistory.org; suggested donation $10)* commemorates Spanish Franciscan missionary Father Junípero Serra, who established the state's first mission; the event is widely considered to be the founding of California.

You can also make your own candles, buy penny candy and visit **Bazaar del Mundo**, which brings together merchants selling everything from jewelry to pottery.

Old Town is also the location of must-see events like May's **Fiesta Old Town Cinco de Mayo** *(oldtowncincodemayo.com)*, with *lucha libre* wrestling, music and entertainment. In November, Old Town celebrates one of the most important holidays in Mexican culture with a **Dia de los Muertos** *(dayofthedeadsd.com)* parade, music and entertainment in the streets and public *ofrendas* remembering those who have

continued on p490

DRINKING IN SAN DIEGO: CRAFT BREWERIES

MAP P481

Hillcrest Brewing Company: This beer haven and pizzeria claims to be 'the first gay brewery in the world.' *2-9pm Mon-Fri, 11am-10pm Sat, 10am-8pm Sun*

North Park Flavordome: Modern Times' tasting room is in the heart of the North Park beer neighborhood and has 20 brews on tap. *noon-9pm Sun-Thu, to 10pm Fri & Sat*

AleSmith: One of San Diego's biggest and most popular tasting rooms, Alesmith is kid- and dog-friendly. Food trucks too. *11am-10pm Mon-Thu, to 11pm Fri & Sat, to 9pm Sun*

Eppig Brewing Waterfront Biergarten: This Point Loma alfresco spot is BYOF, or you can hit up the on-site food trucks. *noon-9pm Mon-Fri, from 11am Sat & Sun*

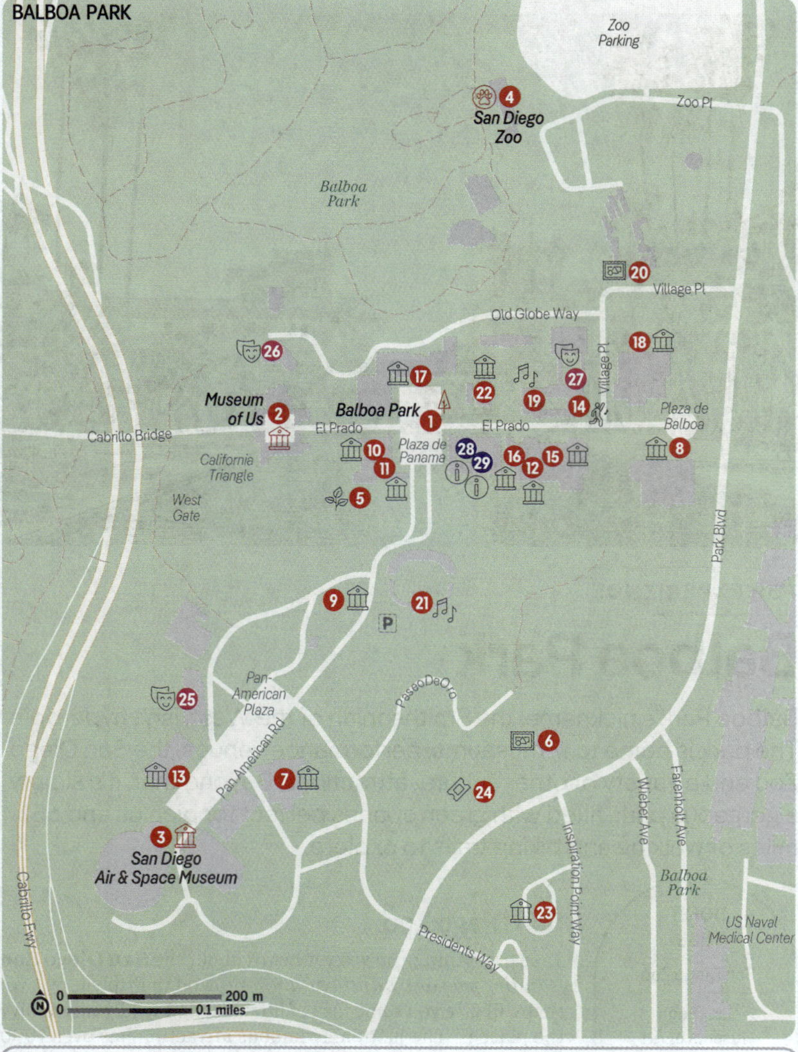

HIGHLIGHTS
1 Balboa Park
2 Museum of Us
3 San Diego Air & Space Museum
4 San Diego Zoo

SIGHTS
5 Balboa Park Gardens
6 Centro Cultural de la Raza
7 Comic-Con Museum
8 Fleet Science Center
9 House of Pacific Relations International Cottages
10 Institute of Contemporary Art, San Diego
11 Mingei International Museum
12 Museum of Photographic Arts
13 San Diego Automotive Museum
14 San Diego Civic Youth Ballet
15 San Diego History Center
16 San Diego Model Railroad Museum
17 San Diego Museum of Art
18 San Diego Natural History Museum
19 San Diego Youth Symphony
20 Spanish Village Arts Center
21 Spreckels Organ Pavilion
22 Timken Museum of Art
23 Veterans Museum of Balboa Park
24 WorldBeat Cultural Center

ENTERTAINMENT
25 Marie Hitchcock Puppet Theater
26 Old Globe
27 San Diego Junior Theatre

INFORMATION
28 Balboa Park Visitor Center
29 Park Ambassador Information Tent

VALERIA VENEZIA/SHUTTERSTOCK

TOP EXPERIENCE

Balboa Park

Balboa Park's nickname, the Smithsonian of the West, isn't hyperbole. The park is home to 17 museums, performance venues, the San Diego Zoo and a variety of other cultural attractions. Beyond that, it's simply a gorgeous park, filled with green spaces perfect for picnics and 65 miles of walking and biking trails to explore.

DON'T MISS

- San Diego Zoo
- San Diego Museum of Art
- Centro Cultural de la Raza
- Museum of Us
- The Old Globe
- Air & Space Museum
- Natural History Museum
- International Cottages

San Diego Zoo

Take everything you've ever heard about the **San Diego Zoo** *(sandiegozoo.org; adult/child $76/66)* and multiply it by two: that will give you some idea of how vast and wildly impressive the place is. The justifiably famous attraction has over 4000 animals representing more than 650 species in a beautifully landscaped setting. Typical enclosures replicate a species' natural habitat.

Specialized bioclimatic environments like the Elephant Odyssey, Panda Canyon and Monkey Trail are home to the zoo's many inhabitants: big cats (cheetahs, jaguars and leopards), elephants, giraffes, grizzly bears, red pandas, king cobras and much, much more.

PRACTICALITIES

Scan the QR code for details of upcoming Balboa Park events.

The San Diego Zoo has been instrumental in saving the endangered California condor, which you can also see while you're there.

Wear comfortable shoes: walking is the best way to get close to the animals. Alternatively, you can hop on a double-decker bus for a 35-minute narrative overview tour (free with your ticket): sitting downstairs puts you closer to the animals. Another option for those unable to walk far is the Kangaroo Bus, which lets you hop on and off at four stops. The **Skyfari** aerial tram flies from one side of the zoo to the other, with beautiful views of the rest of the park.

Arts Appreciation

For those who love the fine arts, there are several museums in Balboa Park worth checking out. The **Museum of Photographic Arts** *(mopa.org; by donation)* has a vast collection, ranging from Ansel Adams to avant-garde cell-phone photography. The **San Diego Museum of Art** *(sdma.org; adult/child $20/free)* has international exhibits that range from El Greco to Japanese woodblock prints, as well as an outdoor sculpture garden. The **Timken Museum of Art** *(timkenmuseum.org; free)* has a collection of works by European old masters like Rembrandt.

The **Centro Cultural de la Raza** *(centrodelaraza.com; free)* is an arts center highlighting Mexican, Indigenous and Latino art and performance. The **Institute of Contemporary Art, San Diego** *(icasandiego.org; by donation)* exhibits the works of artists in Southern California from Los Angeles to Tijuana and has a second outpost in Encinitas. The round, steel building, originally a water tank, is impressively painted with 240ft of murals. The folk-art focused **Mingei International Museum** *(mingei.org; adult/child $15/free)* has exhibits showcasing handmade arts and craft from people and cultures around the world.

The **Spanish Village Arts Center** *(villageartscenter.org)* is a community of more than 200 local artists showing their works, with open studios and art demonstrations in a vibrant recreation of a Spanish village. It's also home to the **San Diego Mineral and Gem Societies' Museum** *(sdmg.org; free)*.

Science & Technology

To learn about the world, try the **Museum of Us** *(museumofus.org; adult/child $19.95/16.95)*, dedicated to anthropology, human history and a deeper understanding of what makes us 'us.' Exhibits hopscotch from ancient Egypt to the Native American Kumeyaay people and from beer to the long-running cannibals exhibition. The **San Diego Air & Space Museum** *(san diegoairandspace.org; adult/child $35/22)* has the real *Apollo 9* Command Module and artifacts from Amelia Earhart and Charles Lindbergh. The **Fleet Science Center** *(fleetscience.org; adult/child $24.95/19.95)* has 100 interactive science exhibits that aren't just for kids; every month, the center hosts an adults-only 'after dark' event.

SAFARI PARK

In northern San Diego County is the San Diego Zoo's **Safari Park** *(sdzsafaripark.org; adult/child $76/66)*, where animals roam freely in savannas. There are a variety of experiences, ranging from the Sun Up Cheetah Safari – see cheetahs sprinting through the park before it opens for the day – to the Roar & Snore, where you camp in the park overnight.

INTERNATIONAL COTTAGES

If Disneyland's It's A Small World ride were a walk-through attraction, it would be the **House of Pacific Relations International Cottages** *(sdhpr.org)*. A gathering of 33 different 'houses,' each represents the traditions of its host country (from South Korea to Ukraine) through music, art, dance and food.

FINDING YOUR WAY

At more than 1200 acres, Balboa Park can be overwhelming to navigate – but there are two places that can help you get started. Pop into the **Visitor Center** at the House of Hospitality or the **Park Ambassador Information Tent** in the Plaza de Panama to get maps, recommendations and more information.

'The Nat,' as the **San Diego Natural History Museum** *(sdnhm.org; adult/child $24/14)* is called, offers a summer Fridays deal: admission is half-price after 5pm, the museum stays open until 10pm and there are special events throughout the night and dining on the rooftop. In addition to dinosaur fossils and a 'living lab,' the Nat offers lectures, events and hikes led by 'Canyoneers.'

For the Fun of It

Since 1970, the **San Diego Comic-Con** in late July has been a standard bearer for fandom events; its **Comic-Con Museum** *(comic-con.org/museum; adult/child $30/15)* celebrates all things superhero and fan culture. The **Marie Hitchcock Puppet Theater** *(balboaparkpuppets.com; $5)* stages whimsical performances every weekend. The park is also home to a 1910 carousel with hand-carved animals and a miniature, rideable antique railroad train.

History & Transportation

The **Marston House** *(sohosandiego.org; adult/child $20/7)* is a beautifully preserved example of California's signature arts-and-crafts architecture. The **San Diego History Center** *(sandiegohistory.org; by donation)* focuses on local history. The **Veterans Museum of Balboa Park** *(veteranmuseum.org; adult/child $5/free)* is housed in the former chapel of the naval hospital and is devoted to local military history.

For transportation nerds, there's the **San Diego Automotive Museum** *(sdautomuseum.org; adult/child $19.50/15)* that

ARTAZUM/SHUTTERSTOCK

Marston House

FIIPHOTO/SHUTTERSTOCK

Public gardens

delves into car culture, and the **San Diego Model Railroad Museum** *(sdmrm.org; adult/child $20/free)*, which has the world's largest operating model railroad running through a miniature California.

Public Gardens

Balboa Park started as a public garden and grew into what it is today thanks to the World's Fairs of 1915–16 and 1935–36. The natural landscape is still the heart of the park experience. The park has remarkable **public gardens**, including Palm Canyon, with 58 species of palm trees; Trees for Health, a medicinal plant garden; the Kate O Sessions Cactus Garden; the Inez Grant Parker Memorial Rose Garden, which has 130 varieties of rose and is in bloom almost all year; and the Zoro Garden, which was once a nudist colony and is now a butterfly garden.

All the Park's a Stage

Balboa Park hosts an incredible number of live performances, from the international dance-focused **WorldBeat Cultural Center** *(worldbeatcenter.org)* to the **San Diego Civic Youth Ballet** *(sdcyb.org)*, **San Diego Junior Theatre** *(juniortheatre.com)* and **San Diego Youth Symphony** *(keynotemusic.org)*. The **Old Globe** *(theoldglobe.org)*, based on the original theater in London, has three stages and hosts productions that often head to Broadway.

One of the most engaging things to do in San Diego is to attend a free Sunday afternoon organ concert at the **Spreckels Organ Pavilion** *(spreckelsorgan.org)*, which has the largest outdoor organ in the world, with more than 5000 pipes.

FREE GUIDED TOURS

Every Tuesday and Friday morning, Balboa Park offers free guided tours *(foreverbalboapark.org)* of the Central Mesa. Guides talk about the history of the park, the attractions it holds and what events are currently on. Once a month, the park also offers a botanical tour, digging deep into the park's varied landscape.

TOP TIPS

- Save on admission fees by buying a Balboa Park Explorer Pass *(explorer.balboapark.org; adult/child from $60/39)*. They're available for four museums in a single day or unlimited admission for a week.
- Give yourself plenty of time to explore. Balboa Park has miles of walking and biking trails and no matter what attraction you're going to see, you're almost guaranteed to see something else that catches your interest.
- Parking in the park is free, but the lots near attractions fill up quickly. Use the in-park shuttle system to catch a ride from a more distant lot.

SAN DIEGO'S BEST BIKE PATHS

San Diego has over 1800 miles of bikeways – use the *San Diego Regional Bike Map (sandag.org)* to find your route.

Bayshore Bikeway: A 24-mile loop from Coronado to Chula Vista, but you can stick to the beachside Silver Strand (p490) for a bike path-only route.

Mission Bay Bike Loop: Mission Bay, between SD and La Jolla, has a flat 12-mile bike path with gorgeous views.

Balboa Park Loop: Cruising around the park on two wheels offers a new perspective.

San Diego River Bike Path: This 20-mile car-free path follows the San Diego River from Mission Valley to Ocean Beach.

Los Penasquitos Canyon: This mountainous area has hiking and biking paths for all levels.

continued from p484

passed. December's **Old Town Las Posadas** is a Mexican celebration honoring biblical Christmas stories.

A Delicious Departure

MAP P481

Craft beers and vintage shopping in North and South Park

If you truly want to experience San Diego like a local, head to **North Park** and **South Park**, just beyond Balboa Park. North Park is often called the best beer neighborhood in the country because of the number of craft beer bars and breweries along University Ave and 30th St, like **North Park Brewing** and **Thorn Street Beer**. South Park has a distinctly indie vibe, with interesting, forward-thinking galleries and vintage shopping. Between the two, **Juniper Canyon** is an urban park with an easy 1-mile hike with gorgeous views.

Find the Silver Lining in Coronado

MAP P481

A sparkling beach destination

Dr Beach praised **Silver Strand State Beach** in **Coronado** as one of the best in the country – but if we're being honest, all of Coronado seems to shine. This coastal neighborhood, on a peninsula on the opposite side of San Diego Bay from the mainland, is connected to downtown San Diego via bridges.

EATING IN SAN DIEGO: GASLAMP & EMBARCADERO

MAP P482

Headquarters at Seaport: Village San Diego's old police HQ now offers food stalls, fine dining and shopping. *10am-9pm Mon-Sat, to 8pm Sun* $$

Fish Market: Freshly caught fish; straight from the sea to your plate at this Embarcadero restaurant. Del Mar outpost too. *11am-8.30pm Sun-Thu, to 9pm Fri & Sat* $$

Animae: Steakhouse infused with Japanese and Filipino influences from chef Tara Monsod. Seriously chic, art-filled dining room. *5-9pm Sun-Thu, to 9.30pm Fri & Sat* $$$

Werewolf: This lively brewpub in the Gaslamp is a high-energy destination serving brunch and elevated bar food. Nightly karaoke. *8am-2am* $$

MATTHEW JAMES FERGUSON/SHUTTERSTOCK

Coronado

It's an easy escape that's just a few minutes away. The area is full of beach cottages and boutiques. **Ferry Landing** is a strollable collection of shops, restaurants and galleries. **Lamb's Players Theatre** *(lambsplayers.com)* stages five productions a year and the **Coronado Historical Association** *(coronadohistory.org; adult/child $25/10)* offers daily walking tours of the island.

Coronado's best-known resident is the **Hotel del Coronado** *(hoteldel.com)*, one of the most famous hotels in California. The 1888 hotel was originally built for wealthy Victorians looking to take in the ocean air and has grown over the years to become a destination beloved for its location, historic architecture and, some say, its hauntings. Rooms can be very pricey, especially during high season. But the good news is that you don't have to be a guest to enjoy many of the hotel's attractions and restaurants, including year-round ghost tours and wintertime ice skating by the beach.

Ocean Trash, Ocean Treasure

MAP P481

Go diving at Wreck Alley

A global destination for scuba enthusiasts, **Wreck Alley** is an artificial reef a few miles off the coast of Mission Beach. A collection of intentionally scuttled boats, including an old

THE CALIFORNIA BURRITO

If you've ever had a California burrito outside of California, you've likely had one made with meat, beans, rice, cheese and guacamole. But that's actually a Mission burrito, invented in San Francisco. A real California burrito is a signature San Diego food and it's a must-try while you're in town. It features *carne asada* (grilled steak), *pico de gallo* salsa, guacamole, cheese and...french fries? Don't knock it until you've tried it.

Roberto's Taco Shop *(robertostacoshop.com)* is credited with inventing the California burrito in the 1980s – the local chain has locations across the city and beyond – but you'll find it's widely available at many taco shops and Mexican restaurants throughout the region.

EATING IN SAN DIEGO: LITTLE ITALY

MAP P482

Juniper & Ivy: One of the most decorated restaurants in San Diego, Juniper & Ivy has a seasonally driven fine-dining menu. *5-9pm Sun-Thu, to 10pm Fri & Sat* $$$

Mona Lisa Italian Foods: This grocery and restaurant is like the local version of Eataly. *deli 9am-10pm, restaurant 11am-9.30pm Mon-Sat, from noon Sun* $$

Civico 1845: In addition to freshly made pasta and Calabrian cuisine, this restaurant has a full slate of vegan offerings. *4-9pm Sun-Thu, to 10pm Fri, noon-10pm Sat & Sun* $$

Morning Glory: Whimsical brunch restaurant with a roving Bloody Mary cart and breakfast carbonara and chilaquiles. *8am-3pm Mon-Fri, to 4pm Sat & Sun* $$

OLD TOWN TROLLEY TOURS

One of the most entertaining and stress-free ways to see the city is on the **Old Town Trolley** *(trolleytours.com; $52/33)*, which is a hop-on, hop-off transportation that spans 25 miles over 11 stops. A two-hour loop on the Old Town Trolley will take you from Old Town to locations like the Gaslamp District, Barrio Logan, Seaport Village, the Embarcadero, Balboa Park and Coronado, and the tour guide provides local history and information about each area as you go. The best part: you do it on your own schedule. Trolleys run all day, so you can hop on and off the trolley to explore on your own, then catch a ride back when you're ready.

ROSAMAR/SHUTTERSTOCK

Mission Bay

Coast Guard ship and a Canadian naval destroyer, plus pieces of a former city bridge, have formed an artificial reef that's rich in marine biodiversity and perfect for diving. **Waterhorse Charters** *(waterhorsecharters.com; dives from $175)* takes divers out to the wrecks on public and private charters. Because there are both shallow and deep dive sites, the alley is suitable for divers of all levels.

On a Mission for Fun

MAP P481

Make a splash at Mission Bay and Mission Beach

Mission Bay Park, half waterfront and half water, is the place to go for water sports. This area offers everything from kayaking to water skiing, sailing and kitesurfing. If you want to charter a fishing or sailing excursion, this is the place to do it. **Mission Beach** has a classic beachside boardwalk with a vintage roller coaster, midway games, restaurants and beach bars at the 100-year-old **Belmont Park** *(belmontpark.com)*. Admission is free and each ride or game is paid individually.

Get a Taste of Italy in SoCal

MAP P482

Little Italy is a lifestyle

If you think the city's historic Italian neighborhood is just a place to go when you're craving pasta, think again. Just blocks from the harbor, **Little Italy** is full of art, outdoor markets and pedestrian spaces like Piazza della Famiglia, which really does feel like Europe. There's also, of course, a lot of pasta. Every April, Little Italy hosts the **Mission Fed ArtWalk** *(artwalksandiego.org)*, which brings together over 250 artists, performers and food vendors for a celebration of creativity.

Beyond San Diego

Coastal cities around San Diego have a charm all their own: explore an arts haven, a beach sanctuary and a superb aquarium.

Places

You could spend an entire vacation within San Diego city limits and still not see everything the city has to offer – but you'd also be missing out on some truly special destinations that are a short distance away, whether you're driving, biking or taking the trolley.

La Jolla is similar to the Spanish phrase *la joya*, meaning 'the jewel.' Pronounced la-*hoy*-yah, the name may actually date from Native Americans who called the place *'mut la hoya, la hoya'* – the place of many caves.

Del Mar and Chula Vista are also easily reachable from San Diego without relocating your hotel accommodations or investing too much time in transit. Even if you only head to one of these destinations for an hour or two, it will be time well spent.

GETTING AROUND

The San Diego Metropolitan Transit System *(sdmts.com)* has trolley and bus services that connect the city to La Jolla, Chula Vista and Del Mar. Within the towns themselves, there are easy-to-navigate public transit systems. La Jolla has a hop-on, hop-off trolley *(trolleytours.com)* and Chula Vista has shuttle service on demand *(chulavistaca.gov)*.

Chula Vista

TIME FROM SAN DIEGO: **15MIN**

Sunny days, chasing the clouds away

Everyone's favorite monster-filled street comes to life at **Sesame Place San Diego** *(sesameplace.com; entry $95)*, a *Sesame Street* theme park for young kids in Chula Vista. There are parades and character meet-and-greets with Big Bird and friends, rides like Super Grover's Box Car Derby and experiences like Dine with Elmo. Water features like the Count's Splash Castle will help you stay cool. Pro tip: online tickets are substantially discounted from gate ticket prices.

How the other half trains

Future Olympians often find themselves at the **Chula Vista Elite Athlete Training Center** *(trainatchulavista.com)*, a massive campus that works with up-and-coming athletes at the highest level. The campus is open for tours; either take a self-guided tour and explore on your own or reserve spots on a guided tour on golf carts.

TAKE A SWING AT TORREY PINES

This neighborhood in northern La Jolla has some of the city's most iconic destinations: **Torrey Pines Golf Course** *(torreypines.com)* and **Torrey Pines State Natural Reserve** *(torreypine.org; parking $10-25)*. The golf course, open to the public, is widely regarded as one of the best destinations in the country because of its sweeping cliffside location and the quality of its terrain. The natural reserve is a popular hiking spot prized for those same views. It's also home to a rare species of pine tree – *Pinus torreyana*, or Torrey pine – once prevalent in California and now preserved only in this reserve and on one island off Santa Barbara.

La Jolla

TIME FROM SAN DIEGO: **20MIN**

Stroll the Village

The Village is a picturesque collection of strollable shops and restaurants and includes many of **La Jolla**'s most notable attractions – including the sea lions the city is famous for. **Scripps Park** is especially picturesque. Most days you'll see street vendors set up in and around Scripps Park, selling everything from handmade jewelry to art painted in front of you.

Directly below Scripps Park in **La Jolla Village** is **La Jolla Cove**, one of the most famous beaches in Southern California, where you can swim and spot sea lions. Remember to keep your distance; some days, there are ropes in place to ensure the sea lions have enough space to themselves.

One of the most unusual places to check out is the **Cave Store** *(cavestore.com)*. This jewelry and gift shop is the entrance to a tunnel where you'll descend 144 steps carved out of pure rock, walking down and down until you arrive at **Sunny Jim's Sea Cave**, the only sea cave in California that's accessible by land. The tunnel has been open since 1902; legend has it that bootleggers smuggled alcohol through the cave during Prohibition.

One final note: don't confuse the Village with La Jolla Village, a more residential inland area.

The artful side of La Jolla

La Jolla has a robust art scene. On the **La Jolla Village Art Walk** *(lajollabythesea.com)*, you'll pass the Madison Gallery, Martin Lawrence Galleries and Peter Lik Gallery; the latter is one of the showrooms of the artist who allegedly sold the world's most expensive photograph, *Phantom,* in 2014 for $6.5 million.

La Jolla is also home to a standout local theater company, **La Jolla Playhouse** *(lajollaplayhouse.org)*, which is nationally renowned for the quality of its works and the star power it attracts. The playhouse hosts world premieres of innovative and forward-thinking works and brings in luminaries like Matthew Broderick to star in its productions.

Explore the ocean

La Jolla has two offshore marine reserves: the **San Diego-Scripps Coastal Marine Conservation Area** and the **Matlahuayl State Marine Reserve**. Both are ideal locations for snorkeling and scuba diving, but if you'd rather see marine

DINING IN LA JOLLA: OUR PICKS

George's at the Cove: This waterfront seafood restaurant has a dining room and a more casual rooftop terrace with gorgeous ocean views. *11am-10pm* **$$$**

Marine Room: A coastal seafood restaurant that's so close to the water that waves crash against the expansive windows at high tide. *5-9.30pm Wed-Sun* **$$$**

The Taco Stand: The first location of the Taco Stand serves killer tacos with handmade tortillas and slow-roasted and braised meats. *9am-9pm Sun-Thu, to 10pm Fri & Sat* **$**

Wayfarer Bread and Pastry: This bakery is beloved for its breakfast pastries and sandwiches perfect for the beach. *8am-2.30pm Tue-Sun, 4.30-8.30pm Tue-Sat* **$$**

CHRIS LABASCO/SHUTTERSTOCK

La Jolla Cove

life on land, then head to the **Birch Aquarium at Scripps** *(aquarium.ucsd.edu; adult/child $35/30).* Part of University of California San Diego's **Scripps Institution of Oceanography**, the aquarium has more than 60 marine habitats on display, including an enormous two-story kelp forest. Among Birch's most famous residents: a pod of blue penguins, leopard sharks, seahorses and seadragons. The aquarium also has hands-on outdoor tide pool tanks and offers guided explorations of natural tide pools led by an aquarium naturalist, generally in the winter and early spring. Once per month, Birch hosts **Ocean at Night**, an after-hours event that celebrates bioluminescence in all its forms (including glowing cocktails).

Another part of Scripps that puts you close to the ocean is the **Ellen Browning Scripps Memorial Pier**, where oceanographic research takes place daily. You can only access the pier via student-led tours *(scripps.ucsd.edu/about/tours).*

THE MURALS OF LA JOLLA

La Jolla sits atop bluffs with the ocean on three sides. But the city's natural beauty isn't the only thing worth admiring here. A massive public art program has been tasked with beautifying the city since 2010. Today, there are 16 large-scale **murals** on display and more than 50 pieces of public art. The Murals of La Jolla website *(muralsoflajolla.com)* details the art and the artists and offers a walking tour so you can see them for yourself.

Del Mar

TIME FROM SAN DIEGO: **25MIN**

Visit the county fair

One of the most highly anticipated events of the year is the **San Diego County Fair** *(sdfair.com),* which is so huge that it lasts a month. More than a million people visit the Del Mar Fairgrounds in June and July for the fair, which has

BEST COCKTAIL BARS IN LA JOLLA

Le Coq After Hours: A bistro menu complements the next-level cocktails while DJs spin vinyl at this new-wave French restaurant. *5pm-midnight Tue-Sun*

Raised by Wolves: Make a reservation for this stylish cocktail bar with sophisticated libations. *11.30am-11pm Sun-Wed, to midnight Thu, to 1am Fri & Sat*

The Whaling Bar: Inside La Valencia Hotel, this swanky lounge revives a much-missed meeting spot, with original art and a daily martini hour. *3-11pm*

Birdseye: This rooftop restaurant and lounge serves bright, herbaceous cocktails. *11am-10pm Mon-Thu, 11am-11pm Fri, 10am-11pm Sat, 10am-10pm Sun*

HORSE RACING IN DEL MAR

Besides the San Diego County Fair, the Del Mar Fairgrounds are also home to the **Del Mar Racetrack** *(dmtc.com)*. Bing Crosby was an original owner and instrumental in getting the track built; on its opening day in 1937, the crooner was at the gate greeting the first guests. The first-ever nationally broadcast horserace was at Del Mar, where Seabiscuit won by a nose. Today, the thoroughbred racing season takes place from late summer to early fall.

KALJUNIOR/SHUTTERSTOCK

Del Mar

more than 2000 attractions and 1700 performers. There's a midway with carnival rides and games, concerts with major headliners, art and flower exhibitions, animal encounters, artisan craft demonstrations and wine, beer and spirits festivals. And that's just for starters.

Learn to surf

Because of its reliable surf conditions and less busy beaches, **Del Mar** is ideal if you've always wanted to take a surf lesson but never got around to it. Many surf shops and surf schools in Del Mar offer lessons that include board rentals, including **Rusty Del Mar Surfboards** *(rustydelmar.com; lesson $150, board and wetsuit rental $80)*, **Del Mar Surf Sessions** *(delmarsurfsessions.com; lesson $150)*, **Del Mar Surf School** *(delmarsurfschool.com; lesson $150)* and **Progressive Surf Academy** *(progressivesurfacademy.com; lesson $115)*.

DINING IN DEL MAR: OUR PICKS

Addison: The three Michelin-starred Addison offers tasting menus focused on local, seasonal ingredients and the flavors of Southern California. *6-9pm* **$$$**

Poseidon: This stylish seafood restaurant has incredible water views and a Mediterranean-inspired menu. *10am-9pm Sat & Sun, 4.30pm-9pm Mon, 11am-9pm Tue-Fri* **$$$**

Jake's Del Mar: Serves the same Hawaiian spirit of aloha as its sister restaurant Duke's, including its signature hula pie. *hours vary* **$$**

Viewpoint Brewing: This casual, fun brewery has swinging seats and water views, plus a huge selection of house-brewed beers. *noon-9pm Tue-Fri, from 10am Sat & Sun* **$$**

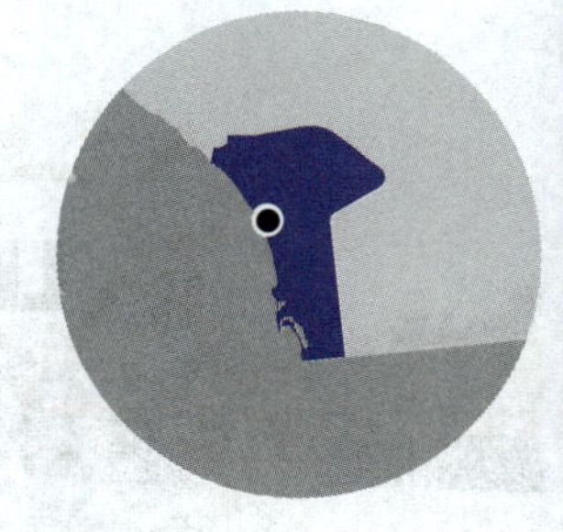

Carlsbad

MUSEUMS | NATURE | BEACHES

Beachside locales like Carlsbad are the strongest endorsement there is for taking the scenic route. If you travel exclusively on the I-5 freeway, you'll miss some of the most charming parts of Southern California. But if you take the more leisurely Pacific Coast Hwy, you'll pass through the kinds of places that stick with you long after you've left. Moving further north from La Jolla up the PCH, you'll reach Carlsbad, another oceanfront city with gorgeous beaches but very different attractions.

Carlsbad came into being in the 1880s when John Frazier, an early homesteader, sank a well and found water that had a high mineral content, supposedly identical to that of the spa water in Karlsbad, Bohemia (now in Czechia).

The city today is home to an aquarium, a gem institute, several intriguing museums and the first-ever Legoland theme park. Carlsbad also has some of the area's best golf courses.

Carlsbad in Flower

Where the superbloom hits different

There's no bad time to visit Carlsbad, but the best time is probably spring, when the **Carlsbad Ranch Flower Fields** *(theflowerfields.com; adult/child $27/17)* burst into vivid color. These 55 acres of carefully cultivated flowers bloom from March to May every year. Beyond the sea of color, there's also a floral hedge maze and kids' activities.

Where Learning Is Fun

One-of-a-kind museums

The city is home to a host of irresistible attractions, like the **Museum of Making Music** *(museumofmakingmusic.org; adult/child $15/10)*, which explores the history of music

continued on p500

TOP TIP

To help manage traffic and reduce emissions and help people find the best way of getting from Point A to Point B, the City of Carlsbad designed the Carlsbad Commuter app and website *(carlsbadcommuter.com)*

GETTING AROUND

Carlsbad is only about a 40-minute drive from San Diego International Airport, but if you'd rather take public transportation, it's very easy. The North County Transit San Diego Railroad *(gonctd.com; ticket $6.50)* connects Carlsbad and Oceanside to the north to downtown SD. If you're staying in Carlsbad and planning to explore on two wheels, the city is very bikeable, especially on the Coastal Rail Trail.

LEGOLAND CALIFORNIA

TOP EXPERIENCE

Legoland

This builder's paradise is more than just a theme park – it's an immersive land where Legos are life-sized, dragons are real and the only limit is your imagination. The first Legoland theme park in the country, Carlsbad's main attraction has two hotels, a separately ticketed aquarium and water park and a full schedule of fun seasonal events.

DON'T MISS

- Dino Valley Explorer River Quest
- Miniland USA
- Legoland Water Park
- Sea Life Aquarium
- Brick-or-Treat Monster Party
- Legoland Castle Hotel

Orientation

Just like Lego bricks themselves, the Legoland California park is small but mighty. The easily navigable campus includes the Legoland theme park, an attached Legoland water park and a separate Sea Life Aquarium – plus two themed hotels – all within a very short walk of one another. While there's fun for everyone, this is an ideal theme park to visit when your kids are younger (12 and under). The rides are fun but not too intense and many ride queues and waiting areas (even in the restaurants) have Lego play areas where kids can burn off extra energy during the boring parts when parents are

PRACTICALITIES

Scan the QR code for Legoland tickets and passes.

waiting in line. Everything from the food to the hotels (with free breakfasts) to the online ticket deals are a good value at this family resort.

Legoland Park

There are over 60 rides and attractions at **Legoland Park**, ranging from gentle rides for young kids to thrill coasters – but even the thrill coasters are still family-friendly. In Dino Valley, the park's newest land, you can search for dinosaurs on Explorer River Quest or escape the Coastersaurus. Search for treasure in the Lost Kingdom Adventure dark ride in the Land of Adventure, or tame the Dragon coaster on Castle Hill.

The central land at Legoland, **Miniland USA**, is a jaw-dropping attraction made of millions of Lego bricks. The enormous installation features scenery from Los Angeles, San Diego, San Francisco, New York, Washington, DC and Las Vegas. You can walk around and explore – there are even motorized functions like moving cars – or take the Coast Cruise, a boat ride across the park's central lake, to get a water's-edge view.

In addition to rides, Legoland has interactive shows and parades, like 'Once Upon a Brick – Tale of the Unicorn Knight' storytime and the Legoland Jam dance party. Meet characters from entertainment like *The Lego Movie* and *Lego Ninjago*.

Legoland's **Water Park** is within the gates of the theme park, but there's an additional charge for admission (note: there's no access without Legoland admission; it's an extra $35 if you buy discounted tickets online). Inside the water park, there are six waterslides, a pirate boat flume ride, a lazy river and Orange Rush, a raft slide half-pipe.

Sea Life Aquarium

Legoland's **Sea Life Aquarium** shares a central plaza with the theme park, but you can purchase a separate ticket for entry *($25, less if you have a park ticket)* without having to enter Legoland itself. Inside are over 350 species of marine creatures, most of them native to Southern California, and outdoor touch tanks.

Brick or Treat

In September and October, Legoland celebrates Halloween with **Brick or Treat**, featuring special entertainment like a dance party with Lego Dracula and in-park trick or treating. Costumes are encouraged and not even the zombie cheerleader Lego characters are too scary.

Accommodations

There are two Lego hotels here. The **Legoland Resort Hotel** has pirate- and adventure-themed rooms and the **Legoland Castle Hotel** is full of wizards and dragons. Both offer separate kids' sleeping areas in every room, a box of Legos to play with in the room, free breakfast and nightly family entertainment, like poolside movies.

GRANNY'S APPLE FRIES

If you know someone who's been to Legoland, they've likely said one thing to you: under no circumstances should you skip the apple fries. To confirm, they are 100% correct. The legendary apple fries are French fry–cut slices of apple, dredged in cinnamon sugar and lightly fried just long enough to crisp them up, served with whipped cream.

TOP TIPS

- Legoland is a Certified Autism Center. Its accommodations for neurodivergent guests, including sensory guides and quiet spaces, are top-notch.
- Single-park tickets can cost as much as $129 per person when purchased at the park, but online deals can be as much as 40% off.
- Both hotels share a small plaza with the front gate of Legoland and Sea Life Aquarium, so it's less than a minute's walk to get in and out of the attractions.
- From I-5, take the Legoland/Cannon Rd exit and follow the signs. Parking is $35.

HIGHLIGHTS
1 Legoland California Resort

SIGHTS
2 Carlsbad Barrio & Museum
3 Carlsbad Ranch Flower Fields
4 Gemological Institute of America
5 Miniature Engineering Craftsmanship Museum
6 Museum of Making Music

ACTIVITIES
7 Aviara Trail System
8 Carlsbad Golf Center
9 Lake Calavera Preserve
10 Omni La Costa Golf Course
11 Park Hyatt Aviara Golf Club
12 Rancho Carlsbad Golf Course
13 Rancho La Costa Preserve

SLEEPING
14 Beach Terrace Inn
15 Cape Rey Carlsbad by Hilton
16 Legoland Castle Hotel
17 Legoland Resort Hotel

EATING
18 Campfire
19 Jeune et Jolie
20 Lilo
21 Same Same

continued from p497

and musical instruments. It hosts a concert series all year long. The **Carlsbad Barrio & Museum** *(carlsbadhistoricalsociety.com; free)* celebrates the city's Mexican heritage and the families who established the area as a center of agriculture more than a century ago. The **Gemological Institute of America** *(gia.edu; free; reservations required)* houses a vast collection of stones, including the Tower of Brilliance, the world's largest crystal octahedron. The tiniest exhibits ever are at the **Miniature Engineering Craftsmanship Museum** *(craftsmanshipmuseum.com; free)*, which showcases teeny models.

Hike Carlsbad

Over 65 miles of trails

This oceanfront city has an abundance of scenic, relatively easy hiking trails. The **Lake Calavera Preserve**, adjacent to the Carlsbad Highlands Ecological Reserve, is a series of shorter trails, some going around the lake and others circling

NAYADADARA/SHUTTERSTOCK

Lake Calavera Preserve

its green space. The **Aviara Trail System**'s Lagoon Trail is a mostly flat 2.7-mile loop around its lagoon, with signage about the area's wildlife and flora. The more challenging **Rancho La Costa Preserve** is a 4-mile trail system that has some rugged spots, especially through Box Canyon.

Fore!

Carlsbad's top golf courses

Carlsbad is well known for its golfing and is even hosting the NCAA Division 1 Golf Championships through 2028. The **Carlsbad Golf Center** *(carlsbadgolfcenter.com)* has been consistently ranked as a top public range for more than 20 years and the **Rancho Carlsbad Golf Club** *(ranchocarlsbad golf.com)* is another excellent public course. Arnold Palmer designed the course at **Park Hyatt Aviara Golf Club** *(parkhyattaviara.com)* and legends like Jack Nicklaus and Tiger Woods have played at **Omni La Costa Golf Course** *(theclubatlacosta.com)*.

THE BIRTH OF MODERN SKATEBOARDING

In the 1970s, skateboarding was making a comeback from a lull in popularity and Southern California was the epicenter. In 1975, Del Mar hosted an enormous skateboarding competition, the Del Mar National Championships. The following year, Carlsbad opened one of the first skate parks in the world. Today, skateboarding is inextricable from Southern California's worldwide image, thanks to generations of skate kids who turned the pastime into a bona fide sport, like Carlsbad native Tony Hawk, who was just eight years old when the park opened. Widely hailed as one of the best skateboarders of all time, Hawk held the title of vertical skateboarding world champion for 12 straight years and inspired a skateboarding video game empire.

WHERE TO EAT IN CARLSBAD: OUR PICKS

Same Same: Modern Thai paired with Thai-tinged drinks, like nitro draft cocktails with tiki inspiration. *4pm-midnight Sun-Thu, to 1am Fri & Sat* $$

Campfire: New American restaurant serving a menu of wood-fired foods with an upscale rustic camping theme. *5-10pm Mon, Wed & Thu, 4:45-11pm Fri & Sat, 4-9pm Sun* $$$

Jeune et Jolie: A modern French restaurant serving four-course tasting menus, plus a more casual seafood-forward bar menu. *5-10pm Wed-Sun* $$$

Lilo: A truly curated dining experience, with a multicourse California coastal tasting menu served at an intimate chef's counter. *5-10pm Tue-Sat* $$$

Beyond Carlsbad

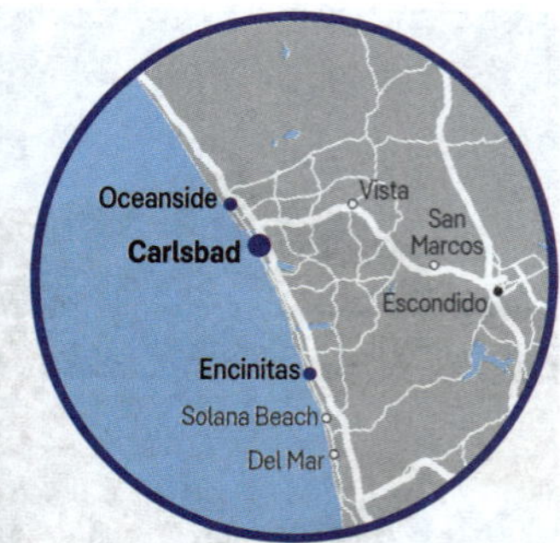

Oceanside and Encinitas are two charming beach towns that require you to slow down and enjoy the view.

Places

GETTING AROUND

The North County Transit San Diego Railroad *(gonctd.com; ticket $6.50)* connects Oceanside, Carlsbad and Encinitas to San Diego. Oceanside's gO'side shuttles are electric vehicles that you can request on-demand through the Ride Circuit app. A single passenger costs $3 and a group of riders is capped at $6 total.

When you're traveling, it's too easy to get caught up in wanting to see as much as possible and use every possible minute of your time. While that's tempting, especially in a place like California with its parade of unmissable attractions, it's antithetical to the spirit of the Pacific Coast Hwy. The coastal drive forces you to slow down and savor every moment – especially in smaller spots like Oceanside and Encinitas. Use your time in these beach havens as an antidote to the rush of city life. Take a walk, ride a bike, soak up the sun and let the laid-back Southern California energy take over.

Oceanside

TIME FROM CARLSBAD: **10MIN**

A California Cultural District

One of only 14 designated Cultural Districts in California, the **Oceanside Cultural District** is buzzing with local art, especially in Artist Alley. On the first Friday of every month, the district hosts **Art Walk Oceanside** *(oceansideartwalk.org)*, where galleries and artists' studios open their doors and offer demos, live music and refreshments. Every October, the district hosts the **O'Arts Festival**, which features visual art, performers, tattoo artists and culinary arts.

A short walk on a long pier

The **Oceanside Pier**, first constructed in 1888 and rebuilt through the centuries, is a must-stop in the city. Fishing is allowed without a license on the pier and there's a bait shop mid-pier that rents equipment. If you're just taking in the scenery, make sure to watch for sea mammals: dolphins and sea lions often swim up close, while it's not out of the question to spot a humpback whale in the distance. The amphitheater at the foot of the pier regularly hosts concerts and festivals.

A love affair with surfing

Every September, Oceanside hosts the **Super Girl Surf Pro** *(supergirlsurfpro.com)*, a three-day event that's the largest all-female surf contest in the world. In addition to surf events, there are also concerts, a female art expo, beach sports and a festival village.

Oceanside is also home to the **California Surf Museum** *(surfmuseum.org; adult/child $7/free)*, which is a tribute both to the sport and the distinctive SoCal surf culture that has grown from it. The museum regularly hosts film screenings and events like the Silver Skater Awards.

Encinitas

TIME FROM CARLSBAD: **15MIN**

Smell the flowers

Encinitas might be known for its beaches, but it's also got incredible scenery off the sand – specifically in the 37-acre **San Diego Botanic Garden** *(sdbg.org; adult/child $18/10)*. It has 4 miles of walking trails and 29 different themed gardens, including the largest bamboo collection on the continent and the biggest children's garden on the West Coast, with interactive features and things to climb. Inside the enormous glass conservatory, plant islands hang from the ceiling.

The most fun on four wheels

On the third Thursday of the month during the summer, classic cars line up on Encinitas' Main St for **Classic Car Nights** *(encinitias101.com)*, when hundreds of hot rods and vintage autos are on display; there's throwback live music, too. Every September for nearly five decades, the **Wavecraft Woodie Car Show** *(sandiegoassociationofcarclubs.org)* has been held on Moonlight Beach, where owners and enthusiasts of wood-paneled cars gather to talk shop.

TAKE MY BREATH AWAY

While it's not hard to find *Top Gun* filming locations in and around San Diego, arguably the most iconic – and inarguably the most delicious – is the **High Pie** *(highpief10.com)* in Oceanside. The historic bungalow that was used as Charlie's (Kelly McGillis') house in the movie is now a bakery and pie shop, filled with *Top Gun* set photos and movie memorabilia, plus memorable art installations. The hand pies are small enough that you'll feel fine ordering one of every flavor, especially the ones that come warm with still-frozen ice cream inside. Outside, there's a Maverick-approved motorcycle to pose on and a waterfront porch where you can sit and enjoy the views.

DINING IN OCEANSIDE: OUR PICKS

Valle: This Michelin-starred Mexican restaurant has a seasonal tasting menu, plus a more casual bar experience. *5-9pm Tue-Sat* **$$$**

Little Fox Cups + Cones: To try Choco Tacos head to Little Fox for gourmet ice cream tacos alongside its sophisticated sweet and savory flavors. *11.30am-9pm* **$**

Wrench & Rodent Seabasstropub: This sushi gastropub offers inventive seafood- and plant-based rolls. *4-9pm Wed-Sun* **$$**

Dija Mara: Serves Balinese cuisine, like tofu *rendang* and *mie goreng*, with fun cocktails using ingredients like roasted pineapple and pandan. *5-9pm Tue-Sun* **$$**

Temecula

WINERIES | OLD TOWN | HOT-AIR BALLOONS

TOP TIP

The **De Portola Wine Trail** is a collection of 10 family-owned wineries along De Portola Rd in Temecula Valley and is a great place to start your tasting journey.

GETTING AROUND

About 60 miles from San Diego, Temecula isn't as easily accessed by public transit as other coastal locations. You might want to plan on driving to this sunny inland destination. Once you arrive, plan on leaving the car behind and use rideshares, bicycles or your feet instead.

Most people associate Napa Valley and Sonoma County with the best wines coming out of California – but the truth is that the entire state is littered with prime grape-growing areas, even down in the southernmost parts of SoCal. Temecula is only about an hour north of San Diego, but it feels like an entirely different world. Pull into Temecula Valley and you'll see row after row of grapevines dotted with picturesque tasting rooms, with the Temescal and Santa Ana Mountains rising up in the distance.

While you might be tempted to spend all of your time in Temecula tasting wine, you'd be missing much of what makes the valley great. Beyond the wineries (over 50), there are destination-worthy golf courses, 90 miles of bicycle trails, a children's museum and the Temecula Valley Symphony. Hot-air balloons are so popular in the area that there's an annual Temecula Valley Wine & Balloon Festival every May, with food, wine, concerts and 50 vividly colored balloons floating through the air.

A Taste of the Old West

Old Town Temecula is a place out of time

The heart of Temecula Valley was an important location in the Old West: after Mexico ceded California to the United States, Temecula served as a stagecoach stop and was also home to California's second-ever post office, after San Francisco. Following the Civil War, the town experienced an influx of settlers from the East. In 1882, the area saw the establishment of the Pechanga Reservation and the construction of a train station. The **Temecula Valley Museum** *(temeculavalleymuseum.org)* explores local history from the Native Luiseno

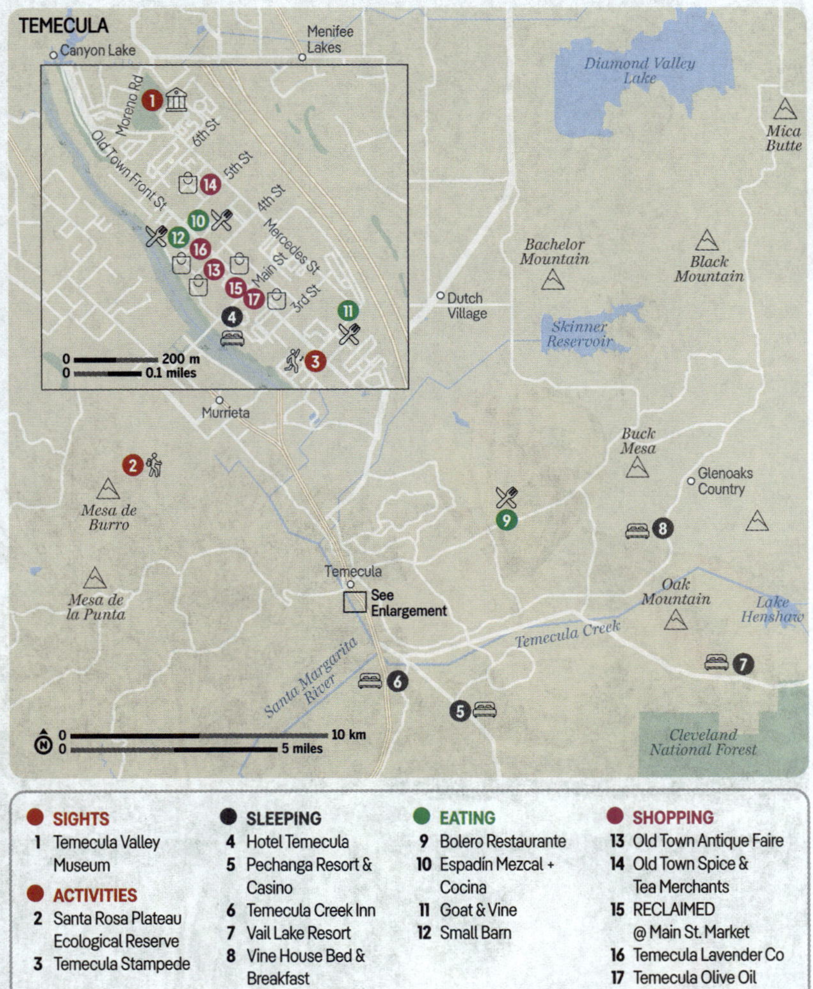

tribe to Mission San Luis Rey (1798), with a miniature street scene for kids to play in.

Walking into Temecula's **Old Town** today recalls the late 1800s: there are still plenty of historic Old West buildings along Front St, but now they're home to antiques stores, boutiques, craft breweries and restaurants. **Temecula Olive Oil Company** *(temeculaoliveoil.com)* grows its own olives and presses them into robust olive oils; tastings are free in the shop. **Old Town Spice & Tea Merchants** *(spiceandtea merchants.com)* sells 350 spices and 100 loose-leaf teas. **Temecula Lavender Company** *(temeculalavernderco.com)* sells products made from flowers grown on its own local lavender

TIME STOOD STILL PHOTO/SHUTTERSTOCK

Temecula Valley

farm. One block on Fourth St holds several antiques shops, like **Old Town Antique Faire** and **RECLAIMED @ Main Street Market**, which refurbishes vintage furniture.

The largest country music venue on the West Coast, the **Stampede** *(thetemeculastampede.com)*, has line dancing, bull riding and live music every weekend. It's located in the Old Town.

Explore the Outdoors

Cycle and hike the hills

Temecula Valley is a popular spot for cyclists, with more than 90 miles of biking trails and trail maps provided by the **Bike Temecula Valley** *(tvbikecoalition.com)* coalition.

In the **Santa Rosa Plateau Ecological Reserve** *(rivcoparks.org/srp)*, you'll find a variety of terrains and ecosystems that are home to 200 species of native birds and 49 endangered or rare animal and plant species, including one that exists nowhere else on earth: the fairy shrimp.

WHY I LOVE TEMECULA

Denise and Stephen Otico are travel content creators. *@partyof4sometimes2*

We've called Temecula home for nearly 18 years and love how it's the perfect mix of peaceful living and vibrant experiences. From scenic wineries and outdoor adventures to the charm of Old Town dining and lively nightlife, there's always something to enjoy here. Whether we're exploring as a family or going out for a date – Temecula has a little bit of everything we love!

DINING IN TEMECULA: OUR PICKS

Bolero Restaurante: Serves Spanish tapas with a gourmet sensibility. Chef Hany Ali trained and cooked throughout Europe before arriving in California. *8am-9pm* $$

Small Barn: This farm-to-table restaurant and boutique winery evolved from the owners' backyard winemaking operation. *hours vary* $$

Espadín Mezcal + Cocina: Take a break from wine with inspired regional Mexican food and agave-based cocktails. *11am-9pm Sun-Thu, 11am-10pm Fri & Sat* $$

Goat & Vine: This stone-hearth kitchen might be casual, but its food is not: everything, from the pizza dough to the sauces, is made in-house daily. *11am-9pm* $$

HELP ME PICK:

Temecula Valley Wineries

Because the weather here is similar to a Mediterranean climate, Temecula is especially well-suited to growing Spanish, French and Italian grape varietals. Expect to sip Sangiovese, Montepulciano and Syrah – though vineyards cultivate more than two dozen different grapes.

Where to sip if you love...

Old World Wines

Doffo Winery At Doffo Winery, Marcelo channels his Argentine and Italian heritage to make outstanding Zinfandel and red blends. He also has a collection of vintage motorcycles at the winery.

Miramonte Winery Another standout, the Miramonte focuses on Spanish- and Portuguese-influenced styles like Tempranillo and medium-bodied red blends.

Robert Renzoni Vineyards A fourth-generation winemaker. Robert's great-grandfather worked in vineyards in northern Italy.

An Immersive Atmosphere

Briar Rose Winery If Disneyland owned a winery, it would be Briar Rose, which looks like it came straight out of *Snow White*. The compound was built by Beldon Fields, a former Walt Disney Imagineer, who designed it to look like his own fairy tale. Now owned by the Linkogle family, Briar Rose makes wines like Tempranillo, Syrah and Viognier.

Carter Estate Winery Known for its French-style sparkling wines, Carter Estate Winery is surrounded by blocks of vines and has an inn on site.

Palumbo Family Vineyards Known for its bigger reds like Cabernet Sauvignon and Cabernet Franc, Palumbo offers a 'Dirt to Bottle' tour of the winemaking process.

Europa Village This wine lover's compound has Spanish-influenced Bolero, French C'est La Vie and Italian Vienza wineries on site, as well as a Spanish restaurant and Italian market, an inn and casitas.

Wine & Food Pairings

Bottaia Winery Has wine and charcuterie pairings. If that's not enough, go to its wine blending lab and create your own custom bottle.

Herzog Wine Cellars At this winery's restaurant, Tierra Sur, every dish is prepared with a Herzog wine.

Leoness Cellars At the restaurant at Leoness, the menu changes with the seasons and takes into account what complements their new vintages and single vineyard reds.

Live Music & Entertainment

Ponte Winery There's a lot to keep you lingering at this Italian wine-focused estate, which has an inn, a restaurant and live music on Friday and Saturday evenings.

Rancho Guejito Vineyard Focuses on lighter-body reds and interesting whites and has live music on Sunday afternoons at its estate winery.

Callaway Vineyard & Winery Callaway brings in bands and a food truck for summer evening concerts. Sip wines like Sangiovese, Petite Sirah and Sauvignon Blanc.

THE IMAGE PARTY/SHUTTERSTOCK

Callaway Vineyard & Winery

HOW TO

When to go Every September, Temecula celebrates California Wine Month with events and live entertainment. Expect tasting tours, culinary events...even grape stomping!

Before you go Many wineries require reservations, so make sure to check in advance – or ask the tasting room staff for their recommendations on your next stop.

Remember to hydrate The Inland Empire is hot and dry, especially in the summer and fall. Make sure you've got a bottle of water and don't forget to drink it!

Budget Most wineries charge a tasting fee per person, but many also waive that fee with the purchase of a few bottles of wine.

Leave the keys at home

While driving is definitely the easiest way to get to Temecula Valley, once you're there, you might want to park your car and forget about it...especially if you're planning to go wine tasting. There are plenty of options for local wine tours and car services that will leave the responsibility of designated driving to a professional.

The **Temecula Wine Trolley** *(temeculawinetrolley.com; from $129)* has daily wine tours to three wineries; either buy a seat on a trolley or book a whole trolley for a private party. **Grapeline Wine Tours** *(gogrape.com; from $159)* runs wine tours and vineyard picnic tours. **Cable Car Wine Tours** *(temeculacablecar.com; from $110)* transports people in a restored 1914 San Francisco cable car.

Borrow Our Bikes *(borrowourbikes.com; from $53)* and **Temecula Wine Country E-Bikes** *(uyswines.com; from $60)* arrange e-bike rentals. Sidecar Tours *(sidecar toursinc.com; from $210)* has something totally unique: vintage motorcycles with sidecars modified to fit two people, which will transport you anywhere in the valley. There are even horse-drawn carriage wine tours courtesy of **Temecula Carriage Company** *(temeculacarriageco.com; from $215)*.

Places We Love to Stay

$ Budget $$ Midrange $$$ Top End

San Diego

MAPS p481, 482

Omni San Diego $$ High-rise hotel in the Gaslamp, connected to Petco Park and the San Diego Convention Center.

Wayfarer San Diego $$ On Pacific Beach, this newly renovated hotel has suites and rooms with gorgeous ocean views.

Mission Bay Resort $$ A newly renovated resort with a pool complex, beach access, spa treatments and three waterfront restaurants.

Ocean Park Inn $$ This mid-century modern hotel offers all-suite accommodations, many with kitchenettes and water views.

Kona Kai Resort & Spa $$ Shelter Island hotel with a private beach – a rarity in San Diego – and a tropical island feel.

Humphrey's Half-Moon Inn $$ This delightfully mid-century-inspired Shelter Island hotel radiates 'golden age of Hawaii travel.'

Guild Hotel $$$ Boutique hotel in a century-old building that was once a YMCA, with original architectural details.

Pendry San Diego $$$ Luxury hotel in the Gaslamp District with six restaurants and elegant decor.

Loews Coronado Bay Resort $$$ This luxury hotel has a private marina and offers shuttle service to Silver Strand Beach.

Hotel del Coronado $$$ One of the most historically significant and beautiful hotels in California, directly on the beach.

La Jolla

San Diego Marriott La Jolla $$ Closer to UCSD and Torrey Pines, this hotel has two restaurants and an outdoor pool.

Grande Colonial $$ Historic 1913 hotel with a Michelin-recommended restaurant and upscale accommodations and water views.

Estancia La Jolla Hotel & Spa $$$ AAA Four Diamond boutique hotel with luxury amenities and 10 acres of gardens and courtyards.

La Jolla Shores Hotel $$$ Request a water view at this oceanfront hotel that has easy access to the beach.

La Valencia Hotel $$$ Iconic pink hotel with Mediterranean inspiration and beach access, with pet-friendly rooms and dining.

Orli La Jolla $$$ Thirteen-room boutique hotel in a historic building, with thoughtful touches and a fun vibe.

Chula Vista

The Rambler Motel $$ This vibrant mid-century-inspired motel has bright colors and fun room decor, plus a pool.

Gaylord Pacific Resort $$$ On the Chula Vista Marina, this huge hotel has an expansive pool complex with waterslides.

Del Mar

L'Auberge Del Mar $$$ A luxury hotel with beach access, a spa, a fine-dining restaurant and pet-friendly accommodations.

Fairmont Grand Del Mar $$$ Next to Los Peñasquitos Canyon Preserve, this luxury accommodations has horseback riding, yoga and archery, plus a spa and golf.

Del Mar Beach Hotel $$$ The only beachfront hotel in Del Mar recently got a huge renovation; it's now a modern example of mid-century California architecture.

Carlsbad

MAP p500

Beach Terrace Inn $$ This renovated beachfront hotel in Carlsbad has gorgeous views and easy access to the sand.

Cape Rey Carlsbad Beach $$ Carlsbad hotel with beach access and a large pool for when you've had enough of the ocean.

Legoland Resort Hotel (p499) **$$** Attached to Legoland theme park, this family hotel offers separate bunkbeds for kids, in-room Legos, free breakfast and pirate- and adventure-themed rooms.

Legoland Castle Hotel (p499) **$$** Also attached to Legoland, this property has the same amenities as the Legoland Hotel, but with a medieval fantasy theme.

Oceanside

The Seabird Ocean Resort & Spa $$ An elevated pool allows you to soak in the water while watching the waves roll in, which is especially perfect at sunset.

The Fin Hotel $$ A totally rehabbed 1920s hotel that's part of the Hilton Tapestry Collection – the Fin feels like a piece of California history.

Pacific Beach Resort $$$ Recently named *Travel + Leisure's* top US resort, this place is steps from the beach and has a fine-dining Mexican restaurant.

Encinitas

Surfhouse Boutique Hotel $$ Chic surf motel vibes combine with amenities like complimentary beach cruiser bikes and surfboards for guest use.

Alila Marea Beach Resort $$$ Luxurious rooms overlooking the ocean and Pacific Coast Hwy, with unparalleled sunset views.

Temecula

MAP p505

Hotel Temecula $$ Old West vibes abound at this 1891 historic hotel in the heart of Old Town.

Vine House Bed & Breakfast $$ Luxury inn with vineyard views and complimentary breakfast, within walking distance to several wineries.

Pechanga Resort & Casino $$ One of the largest casinos in the country, Pechanga is a AAA Four Diamond property with fine dining and a huge pool complex.

Vail Lake Resort $$ This resort has campsites and cabins for rent, plus an enormous bass fishing lake, horseback riding, a mountain-bike park and 40 miles of hiking trails.

Temecula Creek Inn $$$ Idyllic resort with a 27-hole golf course, fine dining and complimentary shuttle service.

MANUELA DURSON/SHUTTERSTOCK

Hotel del Coronado

Van Ness Ave., California
49
& Market
Streets

TOOLKIT

The chapters in this section cover the most important topics you'll need to know about in Coastal California. They're full of nuts-and-bolts information and valuable insights to help you understand and navigate Coastal California and get the most out of your trip.

Cable car, San Francisco (p75)

S.BORISOV/SHUTTERSTOCK

Arriving

California has a dozen airports with flights from out of state. Many have international services, including LAX, San Diego and airports in the San Francisco Bay Area. You can also reach California by train from neighboring states and beyond. Many travelers roll into Cali in their own vehicles via interstate freeways – road trip!

Easier Visas

Check *travel.state.gov* for rules about the US Visa Waiver Program (VWP), whereby citizens of 42 countries can stay up to 90 days with an approved passport and Electronic System for Travel Authorization (ESTA).

Complex Visas

Regulations for non-VWP visas change regularly. For up-to-date information about requirements and eligibility, check the visa section on the **US Department of State** *(travel.state.gov)* website or contact a US embassy or consulate in your home country.

Cell Phones

Foreign phones usually work in California. Buy prepaid SIM cards locally or get an e-SIM. Coverage can be spotty in remote areas such as the far northern coast, and in the mountains and Sierra Nevada.

Wi-Fi

Wi-fi is nearly ubiquitous in the state that is home to Silicon Valley. Free networks abound in civic centers, restaurants, cafes, hotels and more.

Public Transport from Airports to City Centers

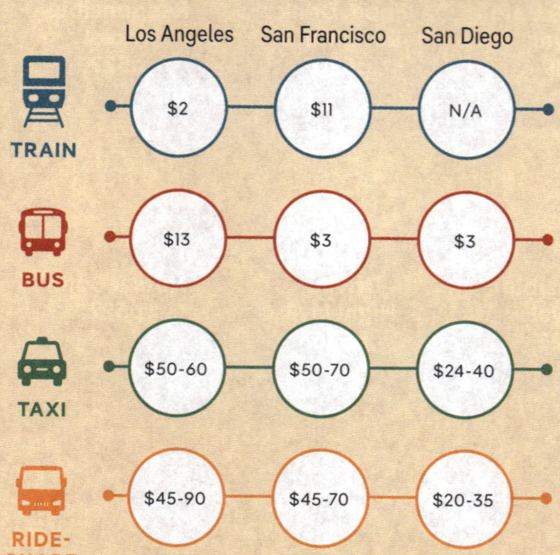

	Los Angeles	San Francisco	San Diego
TRAIN	$2	$11	N/A
BUS	$13	$3	$3
TAXI	$50-60	$50-70	$24-40
RIDE-SHARE	$45-90	$45-70	$20-35

THE SCENIC WAY TO CALIFORNIA

There are four Amtrak routes to California from the rest of the USA. Each offers superb scenery.

From Seattle and Portland, the **Coast Starlight** serves Sacramento, the Bay Area and Santa Barbara, en route to Los Angeles. The ride along the coast is stunning.

From Chicago and Denver to the Bay Area, the **California Zephyr** traces the route of the first Transcontinental Railroad as it enters the state at Truckee high in the Sierras.

Also from Chicago, the **Southwest Chief** reaches LA via beautifully stark desert, as does the **Sunset Limited** from New Orleans, Houston and Tucson.

Getting Around

The car is king in California. But while the road trips are legendary so, too, is the city traffic. There are many regional options to get around by train, bus, bike and trail.

TRAVEL COSTS

Car rental
$35-160/day

Gas
Approx $5/ gallon

EV charging
$0.45/kWh

Train ticket from LA to San Diego
From $35

Hiring a Car

There's no inherent advantage between airport and city location rates for rental cars. Both vary widely depending on season and demand. Don't rent a car if all you'll do is park it in the pricey hotel garage – for example, ride BART into San Francisco, then get a one-day rental for Napa.

Road Conditions

After years of neglect due to fractured state finances, California's voters approved an extra gas tax that is funding repair, rebuilding and construction of roads statewide. You may get caught in work-related delays. But the result is that road conditions in the state are rapidly improving.

TIP

Download the **Caltrans QuickMap** *(quickmap.dot.ca .gov/QM/app.htm)* app, which shows road conditions statewide.

Scan to find out more

ROAD HABITS

Californians spend a lot of time in their cars. Certain rules and habits are enshrined in the state's road culture that may not be immediately apparent to visitors.

- On scenic and mountainous roads, pull over so that residents can whiz past.
- Motorcycles are allowed to ride between cars on freeways. It's called lane-splitting.
- Car-pool lanes are tightly regulated. If you have the correct number of passengers, use them and fly past coagulated traffic.

DRIVING ESSENTIALS

Drive on the right

Speed limit is usually 65mph on freeways, 55mph on two-lane highways and 35mph in cities

.08

Blood alcohol limit is 0.08%

Bus, Train & Ferry

California has more public transit than many think. The LA region is well covered with a dense network as is the Bay Area. Whether it's a ferry to Sausalito or Catalina Island, the ride is part of the adventure. Amtrak's regional trains are fast and reasonably frequent.

Public Transit Tickets

In LA, it's the TAP app, in the Bay Area it's the Clipper Card app. Both let you ride the various forms of transit in their respective regions with a tap of your phone. Refill their stored value online or just use your phone's payment options.

Plane

Californians use planes the way people in other places use trains. The environmental cost aside, service between the state's 12 major airports and numerous smaller ones is frequent and cheap, especially for tickets bought ahead. One downside is that barring a clear day and a window seat, you miss the scenery.

LEFT TO RIGHT: FUSE/GETTY IMAGES, GOGLIK83/GETTY IMAGES

Money

CURRENCY: DOLLAR ($)

Credit & Debit Cards

Visa and Mastercard are accepted everywhere, American Express and Discover are spottier. Regular visitors from abroad will cheer that the US has finally fully adopted chip-and-pin systems for cards, although some small businesses have not. Debit cards may require extra security checks at gas stations, rental car counters etc.

Digital Payments

After a surprising lag compared with Europe and Asia, the home to Apple and Google has finally caught up with digital payments. Residents commonly pay for everything with a tap of their phone and can go weeks without ever using cash. (Save $1 bills for the tip jars in coffee bars etc.)

Taxes & Refunds

- California state sales tax (7.25%) is added to the retail price of most goods and services (groceries are exceptions).
- Local sales taxes may add on up to 3%.
- Tourist lodging taxes vary statewide, but average 10.5% to 14% in major cities.
- No tax refunds are available to international visitors.

HOW MUCH FOR...

Beach parking **Free–$15**

Bridge toll **$9**

Driving Hwy 1 **Free**

ATM fee **$3.50**

HOW TO... Save Some Dollars

Buy an **America the Beautiful Pass** *(store.usgs.gov/recreational-passes)*, which costs $80 and grants unlimited entry to all US national parks – 28 of which are in California – plus national wildlife refuges and more. It's good for one year from the purchase date and is incredible value considering that it can pay for itself after visiting just three parks. (The vehicle entrance fee at Yosemite alone is $35.)

Scan to find out more

WHAT TO TIP

Tipping is not optional, it's part of the workers' wages.

- **Bartenders** 15% to 20% per round, minimum $1 per drink.
- **Concierges** Nothing for simple info, up to $20 for securing last-minute restaurant reservations etc.
- **Hotel bellhops** $2 or $3 per bag, minimum $5 per cart.
- **Housekeeping staff** $2 to $4 daily.
- **Parking valets** From $2 to $5 when your car keys are handed back.
- **Restaurant servers** 15% to 25%.
- **Counter service** Optional. Generally 10%, $1 or nothing.
- **Taxi/rideshare drivers** 10% to 15% of the fare, rounded up to the next dollar.

LOCAL TIP

Most passes for California's 280 **state parks** *(parks.ca.gov)* are best for year-round residents, but some are good outside of summer. Without a pass, for the parks that charge, park outside and walk in.

Accommodations

A Bed for Every Taste

With its many beautiful destinations and innovative spirit, California has hundreds of cool, unique accommodations. Find solitude at a desert campsite or feed all your desires with decadent city luxury. Aside from the usual motels and hotels, there are offbeat options like retro motels, vacation rentals right on the beach, campsites perched in dramatic locations and myriad forms of glamping.

Retro Motels

The humble motel has been revitalized over the last few years, with many tired models receiving makeovers that have given them a second act. Designed with an eye to the mid-century aesthetic and consciously addressing contemporary needs, these roadside spots are hot little properties that can be stylish but affordable options. Look for brilliantly restored neon signs.

Estate Wineries

Immerse yourself in a wine-country retreat with views of vineyard rows. Go big at a high-end château, complete with spa treatments and South of France ambience, or choose from a wide range of more low-key winery digs. California's wine regions aren't limited to Napa and Sonoma Counties and accommodation styles can be as individual as their winegrowers and makers.

Don't Camp, Glamp

California may not have invented glamping, but it has perfect backdrops and set pieces for the concept. Iconic national parks and private entities alike have placed canvas safari tents and yurts in gorgeous settings like Yosemite, Kings Canyon and Big Sur. Much of the state maintains a fairly temperate climate for most of the year, making glamping a realistic option almost everywhere.

HOW MUCH FOR A NIGHT IN...

a hotel
$100-300 or more

a hostel
from $40

a campsite
$25-45 or more

See the Forest from the Trees

Commune with the redwoods in a treehouse. Widely viewed on Instagram, human-size nests and birdhouse-clad pods are some of the more feral-feeling luxury aeries you can settle into for the night. Some meet the definition of shelter better than others, so check details, weather reports and your comfort zone before committing. Confirm basic details such as sanitation and water availability.

VACATION RENTAL LIMITS

Vacation rentals are a charged topic in California. In a state with a catastrophic shortage of affordable housing, any housing stock removed from availability for the masses provokes strong reactions. Once-affordable rural areas have become weekend retreats for the urban affluent, forcing residents who work in the shops and cafes to scramble for housing they can afford. In wealthy areas, residents have grown weary of beach houses turned into party pads for tech bros. In response, cities and towns statewide have imposed limits on vacation rentals, especially ones listed on Airbnb.

FROM LEFT: RED HERRING/SHUTTERSTOCK, JOSEPH SOHM/SHUTTERSTOCK

Family Travel

California is a tailor-made destination for family travel. The kids will be begging to go to theme parks and teens to celebrity hot spots. Then take 'em into the great outdoors – from sunny beaches shaded by palm trees to misty redwood forests and four-seasons mountain playgrounds. Even getting around is fun, from stops at roadside diversions to the adventure of a train or ferry.

Prams, Strollers & Babies

Urban areas are great for strollers but if you plan on enjoying the great outdoors, child carriers are definitely a better option. Some attractions offer rental strollers. Basics are available in supermarkets and drugstores 24/7, while organics and specialty items can be found at higher-end supermarkets, big-box stores and boutiques. Bathrooms with changing facilities are common, as are family bathrooms.

Dining Out

Casual eateries typically have high chairs and children's menus available. More clever eateries won't just cut down on portions for small-size diners but will offer special kid-tested items so that everybody at the table feels special. Roadside restaurants on tourist routes often have extra inducements for families to stop, such as playgrounds, amusing displays or a chance to pet a winsome barnyard animal.

KID-FRIENDLY PICKS

Disneyland Resort (p446)
Kids, even teens and the young-at-heart adore the 'Magic Kingdom.'

Monterey Bay Activities (p299)
Meet jellyfish at a national marine sanctuary then go tide-pooling and kayaking.

Santa Cruz Beach Boardwalk (p286)
Old-timey amusement park on a great beach.

Pier 39 Sea Lions (p55)
Listen to the honking chorus of San Francisco's resident sea lions.

Fort Bragg Skunk Train (p242)
Munch popcorn chugging through Mendocino countryside.

Knott's Berry Farm (p456)
SoCal's original theme park offers thrills-a-minute.

Don't Get Caught Short

Some amusement-park rides have minimum height and/or age requirements. Let younger kids know about possible limitations in advance to avoid disappointment – or tears – when standing in front of the cut-out clown with the 'riders must be this tall' requirement.

Car Travel

Any child aged under eight must be buckled up in the car's back seat in a child/infant safety seat; children under two must be in a rear-facing safety seat – reserve one ahead when renting a car. Bring in-car distractions for inevitable traffic delays.

KEEPING COSTS DOWN

California is not cheap. Cost-conscious families need help avoiding sticker shock.

- In hotels and motels, look for 'kids stay free' and/or 'free breakfast' promotions.
- Motels are cheaper on average, most have two queen- or king-size beds and many have fridges and microwaves.
- If you're visiting theme parks, carry a cooler in the car and have a picnic in the parking lot (ensure you have park reentry permission before you do) to avoid expensive and often junk-foodie options inside.
- With endless beaches, mountains and urban parks for frolicking, some of the most family-friendly activities in California are free.

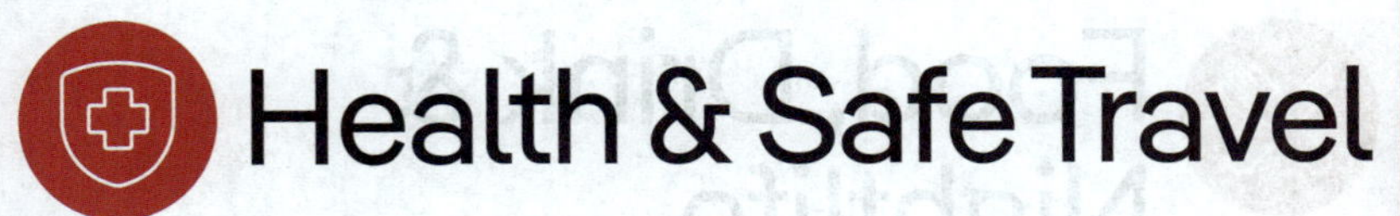

Health & Safe Travel

INSURANCE

Travel insurance to cover theft, loss and medical problems is essential, especially for international visitors. Domestic visitors should confirm they have proper coverage: injuries or maladies from altitude sickness to COVID-19 can strike unexpectedly. Some policies do not cover 'risky' activities such as scuba diving, motorcycling and skiing, so read the fine print. Trip-cancellation insurance can be a worthwhile expense, too.

Earthquakes

Earthquakes happen all the time, but most are so tiny they're undetectable. If you're caught in a serious temblor:

- If possible, stay in an open outdoor space.
- If indoors, get under a desk or table or stand in a doorway.
- Protect your head and stay clear of windows, mirrors or anything that might fall.
- Don't head for elevators or go running into the street.

Wildfires

The wildfire season gets ever-longer (at least June through November). Fires limit access to roads and parks and can cause vacationers and residents to flee for their lives. Of late, fires have affected Los Angeles, the Santa Cruz Mountains, Napa and Sonoma Wine Country, Big Sur, Sequoia and Kings Canyon National Parks, Lake Tahoe and all the national forests.

MARIJUANA

Cannabis is legal in California for medicinal and 21-plus recreational use. Shops sell myriad forms of marijuana. Driving under the influence is illegal.

WILDFIRE DANGER RATINGS

LOW

Control of fires is generally easy

MODERATE

Fires can start from accidental causes

HIGH

Fires can start easily from most causes

VERY HIGH

Fires start easily and spread rapidly

EXTREME

Fires start quickly, burn intensely and are hard to control

Smoking

Smoking (tobacco, marijuana, vapes, anything) is prohibited inside all public buildings, including airports, malls, stadiums and transport stations. No smoking is allowed inside restaurants, although lighting up may be tolerated at outdoor patios or sidewalk tables (ask first). As of 2024 hotels no longer have smoking rooms. In some areas you can't smoke outside near a business.

THOUSANDS WITHOUT HOMES

Despite billions spent annually to combat California's homelessness crisis, the number of people living on the streets keeps inexorably growing. You'll see unhoused people – the current descriptor of choice – in large cities and small towns, living in tents, under tarps, in battered RVs etc. Solving the causes, which include housing costs, mental health and substance-abuse problems, is an elusive goal.

Food, Drink & Nightlife

When to Eat

Breakfast Usually between 7:30am and 11am. Residents often grab this meal on the go, except on weekends.

Brunch Enjoyed from 11am until 3pm on weekends. Often boozy.

Lunch Generally served between 11:30am and 2:30pm. Lunch out tends to be for social or business purposes. Alcohol is less consumed than in Europe.

Dinner Between 5pm and 9pm.

MENU DECODER

Californian casual Few restaurants require more than a dressy shirt, slacks and shoes that aren't flip-flops. At most places, T-shirts, shorts and sandals are fine.

Corkage You can bring your own wine to most restaurants; a 'corkage' fee of $15 to $30 usually applies.

Entrée Always confusing to non-Americans – the word for the main course.

Heirloom Trendy term for types of produce meant to evoke varieties grown in the past.

Split-plate If you ask the kitchen to divide a plate between two (or more) people, there may be a small split-plate surcharge.

Allergies and vegetarian/vegan Travelers with food allergies or dietary restrictions are in luck – vegetarian and vegan fare is routine in California and many restaurants are used to catering to specific dietary needs.

Where to Eat

Whether you're into fine dining or searching for the ultimate surf-shack taco, California will spoil you. Make reservations online at least a month ahead for top tables.

Cafes and diners Historically, diners were often called 'coffee shops.' Hours vary, but expect breakfasts and comfort food.

Farmers markets Vendors selling superb local produce and prepared foods.

Food trucks Get fresh, imaginative food to go, often in a parking lot.

Destination dining Top restaurants in high-end hotels and wine-country resorts.

CDRIN/SHUTTERSTOCK

Tips & Tricks of California Dining

Californians love to swipe right with restaurants, especially places deemed new and unmissable. It's essential to reserve a table as far in advance as possible at restaurants with buzz or perennial popularity. Hot tables in a trend-loving place like West Hollywood will be booked up weeks in advance.

Destination restaurants like the Napa Valley's French Laundry have become tick boxes for some diners whose main interest is bagging another famous meal. An entire market has been created for secondary sales of table reservations – people pay hundreds of dollars for a booking. Trust us, there's always a fine alternative restaurant.

What to tip (p216) is already a minefield for non-Americans not used to the practice. Now some restaurants in the Bay Area and LA have introduced mandatory tip fees. But they often leave the door open to additional tipping (!), meaning the 'service fee' is the equivalent of the hated mandatory resort fee. So inquire if the waitstaff will actually get the 'service fee.'

HOW MUCH FOR A...

Coffee
$3-7

Glass of local wine
$8 and up

Craft beer
$7-10

Burrito
$9-12

Bowl of cioppino
$30-50

Dungeness crab sandwich
$18 and up

California sushi roll
$9.50

Cup of artisanal ice cream
$5.50

HOW TO... Eat & Drink Like a Californian

Start your morning with a pricey coffee. Some have it black, most adulterate their brew with something like oat milk and various flavorings. Breakfast might be a Greek-style yogurt or something simple from an artisan bakery; fare like omelets and hash browns is saved for a special occasion or weekend brunch.

Lunch can easily be from a food truck near work; Mexican food trucks or 'taco trucks' are the most popular, often superb and relatively cheap, but there are plenty of other types, too. Lunch might also be something light like a sandwich or salad consumed at one's desk. And while many tend to ignore this, ubiquitous fast-food joints prove that all California meals aren't created healthily.

After-work drinks outside on a patio at a brewery or bar are popular 12 months a year. Sure, sometimes temperatures might get down into the 50s, but that's what overhead heaters are for.

Dinner at home might feature whatever is fresh at the local farmers market (many are open year-round). Favorite dining-out choices are Japanese, regional Chinese, Vietnamese, Italian, the catch-all Mediterranean (which is a lot like Californian!), regional Mexican (of course), other Central American cuisines and regional American. A trendy cocktail and/or a local wine is a favorite accompaniment. Restaurants are uniformly casual and, since COVID-19, many feature year-round outside dining.

Bars tend to close early, so even in cities like San Francisco or LA the streets get quiet by midnight.

Food Trucks

California has about 1000 food trucks (p33) operating across the state. Some are found in clusters, others operate alone. Some are in the same spot every day, others move around. Sample widely!

HOW TO TASTE WINE

- **Clutch your wallet** The days of free tastings are long gone at the vaunted vineyards of Napa and Sonoma Counties (and elsewhere), where a 45-minute tasting costs $30 or more. At many Napa Valley wineries, it's much more.
- **Swirl** Before tasting a just-opened bottle of wine, swirl your glass to oxygenate the wine and release the flavors.
- **Sniff** Dip your nose (without getting it wet) into the glass for a good whiff. This sniff prompts your senses and your salivary glands to fully appreciate the wine.
- **Swish** Take a swig and roll it over the front of your gums and sides of your tongue to get the full effect of complex flavors and textures on all your taste buds. After you swallow, breathe out through your nose to appreciate the finish.
- **If you're driving or cycling, don't swallow** Sips are hard to keep track of at tastings, so perfect your graceful arc into the spit bucket.
- **Take it easy** There's no need for speed, even if the winery seems to be hurrying you along. Plan to visit three wineries a day maximum.
- **No need to buy** No one expects you to buy, especially if you're paying to taste or take a tour – but it's customary to buy a bottle before winery picnics and tasting fees are sometimes refunded with purchases.

Join the club? Many wineries push their own 'wine clubs' with promises of free future tastings and discounts of bottles. Before plunking down the dough, ask yourself: 'Will I ever come here again?'

Responsible Travel

Climate Change & Travel

It's impossible to ignore the impact we have when traveling; Lonely Planet urges all travelers to engage with their travel carbon footprint, which will mainly come from air travel. While there often isn't an alternative, travelers can look to minimize the number of flights they take, opt for newer aircraft and use cleaner ground transport, such as trains. One proposed solution – purchasing carbon offsets – unfortunately does not cancel out the impact of individual flights. While most destinations will depend on air travel for the foreseeable future, for now, pursuing ground-based travel where possible is the best course of action.

The **UN Carbon Footprint Calculator** shows how flying impacts a household's emissions.

The **ICAO's Carbon Emissions Calculator** allows visitors to analyze the CO_2 generated by point-to-point journeys.

Rent an Electric or Hybrid Car

California car rental companies have embraced hybrid and electric vehicles. If rates seem high, shop around as discounts do pop up. The state has thousands of charging stations *(afdc.energy.gov/fuels/electricity_locations.html)*.

Train It!

Within California, Amtrak is excellent, timely, efficient and often faster than clogged freeways. Don't forget regional rail and metro like Marin and Sonoma Counties' SMART train, SF Bay Area's Caltrain and BART, and LA's Metrolink and Metro.

California's near-permanent drought means that everybody can help save water, including visitors. The state has a list of easy things we all can do to reduce our use *(saveourwater.com)*.

A thicket of federal and state regulations governs California's fishing industry. Learn about the most sustainable seafood to buy at *seafoodwatch.org* or learn sustainable practices and fish with **Sea Forager Expeditions** in San Francisco.

WHERE & HOW TO CYCLE

Bikes, e-bikes and e-scooters are easily rented at all of California's main tourist areas. **CalBike** *(calbike.org/go_for_a_ride/map_routes)* has dozens of links to online and downloadable maps of bike routes, lanes and paths statewide.

Get Cash for Containers

Look for 'CA CASH REFUND' or 'CA CRV' on beverage containers sold in California (although not wine bottles). Refunds range from 5¢ to 10¢. Find recycling points to collect the cash at *calrecycle.ca.gov/BevContainer/RecyclingCenters*.

Combat Overtourism

Crowds during high season at California's popular spots impact the environment and cause friction between residents and visitors. Visit in low season or join initiatives like **Yosemite Facelift** or take a cooking class at **Sonoma Family Meal**.

California has great drinking water and many water fountains have spigots for refilling water bottles easily.

Help the beaches: adopt any trash you see as your own and toss it – this works elsewhere too!

Save on Plastics

Rinse out resealable beverage containers and fill them with tap water. One plastic bottle will last the duration of your trip. If you're given a plastic straw (banned in many parts of California), rinse and reuse it.

Carbon Emissions

Driving between San Francisco and LA emits about 150kg of carbon dioxide for an average-size car and 20kg for an e-vehicle; flying emits 160kg per passenger, buses emit 20kg per passenger and trains 40kg. Calculate your trip: *native.eco/for-individuals/calculators/#Travel.*

RESOURCES

greenbusinessca.org
Search for green businesses by category.

happycow.net
Vegetarian and vegan restaurants in California and beyond.

saveourshores.org
Sponsors events to improve Monterey Bay National Marine Sanctuary's beaches.

CLOCKWISE FROM TOP LEFT: ANGEL DIBILIO/SHUTTERSTOCK, PEOPLEIMAGES.COM - YURI A/SHUTTERSTOCK, TYEU/SHUTTERSTOCK

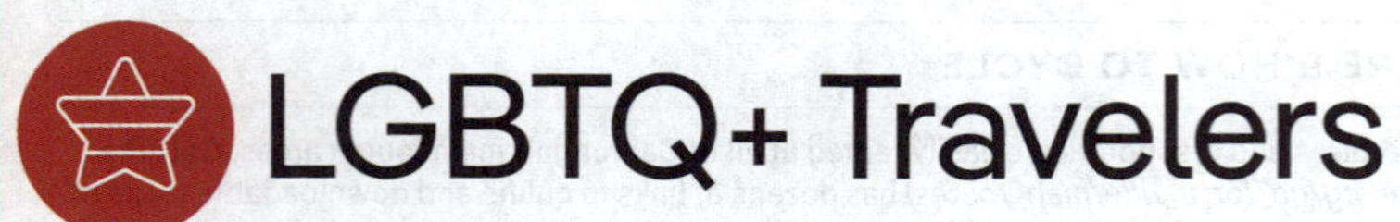

LGBTQ+ Travelers

Inclusivity tends to be the norm in California and its embrace of all things LGBTQ+ is cause for both admiration and ridicule in other parts of the US. But it's a large and diverse state in terms of demographics and culture. Though largely progressive, attitudes vary from region to region. To generalize, the rural parts of the state can be less tolerant.

Notable Times for LGBTQ+ Travel

There's no bad time for LGBTQ+ travel in California, but there are months famous for their special events. First is June, when pride events and fabulous parades fill cities like LA (p415) and San Francisco (p69), with Soul of Pride, too and Disneyland. Palm Springs lets its great weather shine for its November pride. Head to Russian River for **Women's Weekend** (p217) in May and **Lazy Bear Week** (p216) in late July/early August.

QUEER HAVENS

Many places in California are queer-friendly but the following are at another level: San Francisco's Castro District (p101), home of the rainbow flag and the Mission (p92), a hub for lesbian and transgender folks; West Hollywood (p415) and its extraordinary culture; Guerneville (p215) for redwood escapes;and Santa Cruz (p284).

Get Married in California

Though it's legal across the USA, many LGBTQ+ couples prefer to marry in a state known for its queer welcome. In California, you needn't be a citizen or take a blood test. Just fill out a form at a county clerk's office, pay a fee and get a license. Then get hitched!

DISCOVER LGBTQ+ HISTORY

For insight into LA's fascinating queer history, download the free **Pride Explorer** *(https://thelavendereffect.org/virtual-tour/)* smartphone app, which offers self-guided walking tours of Hollywood and Downtown LA. In San Francisco, visit the **Leather & LGBTQ** and Trans Districts (p66).

LGBTQ+ RESOURCES

Advocate *(advocate.com/travel)* News, LGBTIQ+ travel features and destination guides.
Damron *(damron.com)* Long-running, advertiser-driven gay travel guides and app.
LGBT National Help Center *(lgbthotline.org)* Counseling, information and referrals for people of all ages; special resources for youths.
Out Traveler *(outtraveler.com)* Free online magazine articles with travel tips, destination guides and resort reviews.
Strut *(sfaf.org)* San Francisco clinic for inclusive sexual health services.

 NITO/SHUTTERSTOCK

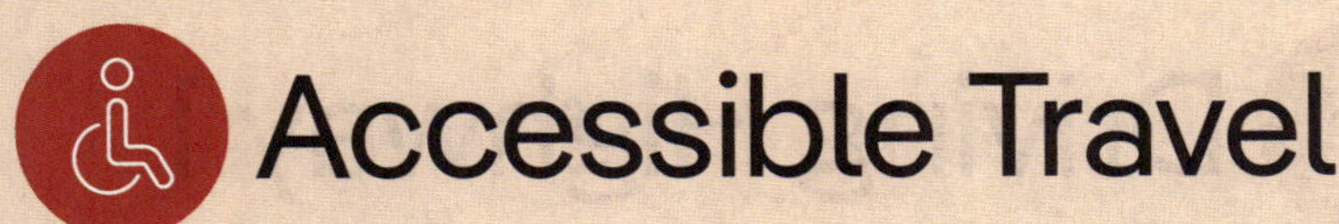

Accessible Travel

The USA leads the way on accessibility and California is among the best states in the USA. More populated areas of California are reasonably well equipped for travelers with disabilities, although older properties may have limitations.

Airport

California's airports comply with accessibility laws. Assistance is available through your airline.

Park Passes

US residents with a permanent disability quality for a free lifetime pass, which waives entry fees to all national parks. California State Parks' disabled discount pass ($3.50) gives 50% off parking and camping fees.

Accommodation

Hotels built since 1993 must meet modern accessibility requirements. Major chains usually have rooms adapted for accessibility needs, but book in advance and double-check they have what you require. Holiday rentals and vintage properties may not be accessible.

Buses

Public transit buses are all wheelchair accessible by law. Ramps deploying automatically when buses are lowered to the curb are the norm. Drivers may have to assist with securing wheelchairs once inside buses.

Trains

In the Bay Area, BART is fully wheelchair accessible; Caltrain has four minor stations that aren't accessible. In Southern California, Metro trains and stations are all accessible. Amtrak requires advance notice for accessibility service.

DISABILITY RIGHTS

The US Department of Justice enforces the Americans with Disabilities Act (ADA; *ada.gov*). Its comprehensive website says 'Disability rights are civil rights.' The act covers many areas of public life including employment, transportation, accommodations and telecommunications.

RESOURCES

Search for the name of your destination plus 'accessibility' – for example, 'Disneyland accessibility' brings up comprehensive information.

Access Northern California *(accessnca.org)* Extensive links to accessible-travel resources, including outdoor recreation opportunities, lodgings, tours and transportation.

California State Parks *(parks.ca.gov/)* Searchable online map and database of accessible features at state parks.

Travelability *(travelability.net/destination/california)* Curates accessible itineraries and travel inspiration across the Golden State.

Service Dogs

Fully-trained service dogs are welcomed on flights for no extra charge; they're also allowed on trains and buses. This does not apply to emotional support animals: additional fees apply on planes and they may only be permitted on select Amtrak services.

Driving Highway 1

Resplendent Hwy 1, the Pacific Coast Highway, unfurls for 656 miles along some of the world's most beautiful shoreline. Take in dramatic sea cliffs, sun-soaked surfing towns, untrodden beaches and the Golden Gate Bridge en route to buzzing Santa Monica and the bling of the beaches in Orange County and San Diego beyond.

The Route

Hwy 1 starts out a mere redwood-lined lane and snakes along craggy coast in Northern California. Approaching San Francisco, it loops across the Marin Headlands (p214) and the Golden Gate Bridge. It's less curvy as it wends through Santa Cruz (p284) and is occasionally even a highway en route to Santa Barbara (p344), Los Angeles (Santa Monica; p421) and San Diego (p480). Landslides or fire occasionally causes closures; check *dot.ca.gov.*

Wildlife-Spotting

Elk roam the Lost Coast (p251) and Point Reyes (p128), which is also home to myriad sea birds. Marine life is rich throughout, with highlights in Point Reyes, Rodeo Beach, Monterey Bay (p294), Morro Bay (p331) and Crystal Cove. Elephant seals and sea lions (pictured) dwell in Point Reyes, Año Nuevo and Piedras Blancas (p315). Glancing offshore anywhere along the coast can reveal whales migrating.

Stop for the Night

If you're driving the whole highway, you'll need to break for the night along the way. Beyond obvious large cities, other top spots include Eureka (p259), Fort Bragg (p242), Mendocino (p234), Santa Cruz (p284), Monterey (p294), Carmel (p302), Big Sur (p306), Cambria (p312) and Laguna Beach (p466). State parks have campgrounds – some where you reserve in advance.

It's Longer Than You Think

Short as some of the distances may seem, beyond slow-driving travelers (you?) certain areas can bottleneck. This is especially true of the area just north of and through San Francisco, the corridor south of Santa Cruz (rough in rush hours) and certainly the Los Angeles fringes. Time your journey accordingly.

PULL OVER

There are plenty of reasons to pull off Hwy 1. Turnouts abound. And, you'll let locals continue on their way as you happily dawdle.

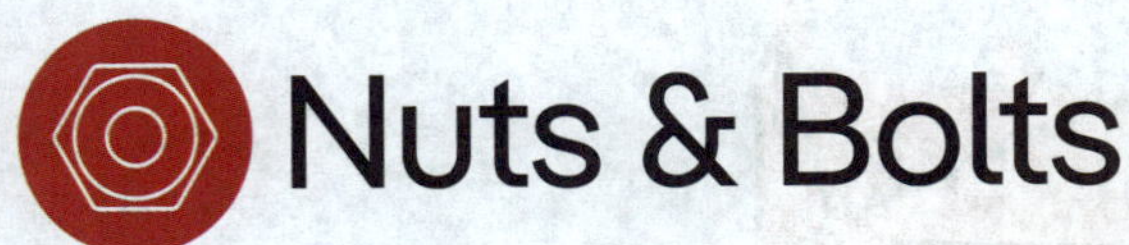

Nuts & Bolts

OPENING HOURS

Businesses, restaurants and shops in tourist areas may close earlier and on additional days during the winter off-season (November to March). Standard hours include:

Banks 9:30am–5pm weekdays

Bars 4pm–2am

Restaurants 11am–3pm and 5:30pm–10pm daily, some open later Friday and Saturday

Shops 10am–7pm Monday to Saturday, 11am–6pm Sunday (many open later)

Toilets

Free public restrooms are easy to find inside shopping malls, public buildings, libraries, gas stations and some transportation hubs, as well as at parks and beaches.

Weights & Measures

Imperial (except 1 US gallon equals 0.83 imperial gallons).

Electricity 120V/60Hz

GOOD TO KNOW

Time zone
Pacific Standard Time (GMT/UTC - 8 hours)

Country calling code
1

Emergency number
911

Population
40 million (California)

Water

Tap water in California is good quality and is safe to drink. (San Francisco's comes mostly from snowmelt and is excellent.)

PUBLIC HOLIDAYS

On the following holidays, banks, schools and government offices (including post offices) are closed and transportation, museums and other services may operate on a Sunday schedule. Holidays falling on a weekend are usually observed the following Monday.

New Year's Day January 1

Martin Luther King Jr Day Third Monday in January

Presidents' Day Third Monday in February

Cesar Chavez Day March 31

Memorial Day Last Monday in May

Independence Day July 4

Labor Day First Monday in September

Veterans Day November 11

Thanksgiving Fourth Thursday in November

Christmas Day December 25

OPPOSITE TOP-BOTTOM: IRIS VAN DEN BROEK/SHUTTERSTOCK, NURIA KREUSER/SHUTTERSTOCK

STORYBOOK

Our writers delve deep into different aspects of Coastal Californian life

Golden Gate Bridge (p56), San Francisco

LUCIANO MORTULA · LGM/SHUTTERSTOCK

A HISTORY OF COASTAL CALIFORNIA IN 15 PLACES

California is forever dreamin', the dream just changes shape over time. Indigenous tribes, pious colonists, starry-eyed gold prospectors and Hollywood movie stars have all called Coastal California home. Vast, beautiful and teeming with resources, it's long been attractive for settlement and exploitation – and rapid innovation persists for both good and ill. By Anita Isalska

THE EARLIEST MIGRANTS to the Americas came from Asia by sea 12,000 to 15,000 years ago following the 'Kelp Highway,' a biodiverse band of kelp forest rich in shellfish and edible seaweeds. Thousands of years later, European settlers made landfall – but 'California' existed as an ideal even before they arrived. The Spanish writer Garci Rodríguez de Montalvo's 1510 romance novel *Las Sergas de Esplandián* described the 'island of California' as an elysian place where Amazonian women lived in harmony with nature. This inspired 16th-century Spanish explorers to use the name 'California' when they landed on a long Pacific peninsula – now Baja ('Lower') California in Mexico. The name later extended north to what we now call the Golden State.

Spanish conquistadors and priests soon relinquished their flea-plagued missions and ill-equipped *presidios* (forts) to Mexico. Their main legacy? The near-extermination of Indigenous peoples. The unruly territory was handed off to the USA in the Treaty of Guadalupe Hidalgo mere months before gold was discovered in 1848, prompting a virtual flood of prospectors and settlers to wash over California. Generations have made the trek to these Pacific shores for gold, glory and self-determination, making homes and history on America's most fabled frontier.

1. Alaxuluxen (Chumash Painted Cave)

MILLENNIA OF CIVILIZATION

Stone tools unearthed in Santa Barbara and Scotts Valley (Santa Cruz) confirm that human life has thrived along the coast for thousands of years. One of these Native American peoples are the Chumash: their land extends across what modern maps call the Central Coast and Santa Barbara County, and place names like Ojai and Pismo Beach descend from their language. There is still-vivid Chumash rock art at Alaxuluxen (the Chumash Painted Cave). Protected as a state park, the land is honeycombed with sandstone and has a small cave where sunburst-like patterns in mineral pigments hint at ancient Chumash cosmological beliefs. Archaeologists believe these cave paintings could be 1000 years old.

For more, see p362.

2. Mission San Miguel Arcángel

CHURCHES AND CULTURAL ERASURE

When a simple wooden cross was raised by the mouth of the San Diego River in 1769, it was the start of a sea change for the religious, cultural and physical landscape of coastal California. Initially led by the Franciscan friar Junípero Serra, Spanish colonists established 21 missions from San Diego to Sonoma. Their stated aim was conversion of Native American people to Christianity; along the way they consolidated claims on territory and enriched themselves from local labor. One of the best-preserved sites is the Mission San Miguel Arcángel (1797), whose cactus gardens and frescoed church remain a focal point for the town, as well as a reminder of a sad legacy of dominance and cultural erasure.

For more, see p323.

3. Jack London State Historic Park

CHANGING TIMES AND FORTUNES

If there's one quality Californians share, it's resilience in turbulent times – and the resourcefulness to change your life, career or location when opportunity knocks. Take the now-notorious writer Jack London: tough circumstances denied him the chance to graduate from the University of California, so he joined the Klondike Gold Rush before turning to social activism and hard-scrabbling his way to publishing his work. After launching his feted work The *Call of the Wild* (1903), a stint as a war reporter and a marriage or two, London changed once lanes again. He purchased a ranch in Glen Ellen; its ruins are now protected as a state historic park.

For more, see p196.

4.Mendocino's Water Towers

GROWING INDUSTRY, THIRSTY TIMES

Water, water, everywhere...or not. In the 1870s Ulysses G Grant commissioned an investigation to solve the thorny problem of irrigation in California. In forested areas in northern California, where the water table was shallow, the solution was water towers. Today California's water towers, some more than a century old, are visible remnants of the logging industries that drew settlers to California's northerly forests. With more than 100 redwood water towers and windmills, Mendocino gained the name The Town of Water Towers. Many of them are still dotted along Mendocino's Main St, some even repurposed into accommodation.

For more, see p237.

Angel Island Immigration Station (p125)

MICHAEL VI/SHUTTERSTOCK

5. Angel Island Immigration Station

WEST COAST ELLIS ISLAND

Denied gold rush mining claims, many Chinese prospectors opened service-based businesses that became the basis for the Chinatowns that were once found in nearly every California city and town. However, discriminatory Californian laws restricting housing, employment and citizenship for anyone born in China were codified with the 1882 US Chinese Exclusion Act, which remained US law until 1943. One legacy of the law can be found on Angel Island in the San Francisco Bay where the Immigration Station operated from 1910 to 1940. It was a detention center for Chinese immigrants and many were cruelly held for long periods before ultimately being sent back to China. Many left only mournful graffiti behind.

For more, see p125.

6. Dolores Park

REFUGE FROM EARTHQUAKE FLAMES

California's 'robber barons' (Leland Stanford et al) built Nob Hill mansions in San Francisco with their fortunes. The City by the Bay dominated the West Coast but San Francisco's grand ambitions came crashing down on April 18, 1906, when earthquake and fire reduced the city to rubble. With flames destroying what the shaking didn't, thousands escaped the inferno in Dolores Park. Cross 20th St to the fire hydrant (still painted golden) that saved the neighborhood, and take in the view of the city's skyline today.

For more, see p92.

7. Hearst Castle

LUCK, FOLLY AND GENIUS

George Hearst (1820–1891) had a Midas touch – though it was quartz and silver ore, not just gold, that grew his fortune. While he was busily building his mining empire, the *San*

Francisco Examiner practically fell into his hands; he accepted it as payment for a gambling debt. When he passed the newspaper to his only son, William Randolph Hearst (1863–1951), the publication was the first building block of a newspaper chain that out-sensationalized all its competitors. With unimaginable riches at his disposal, the younger Hearst commissioned a talented architect, Julia Morgan, to build the ultimate ranch retreat: La Cuesta Encantada ('The Enchanted Hill'). The hilltop property still defies all measures of extravagance with its vast gardens, fairy-tale towers, priceless artwork and Roman-style pool.

For more, see p316.

8. Hollywood Sign

NO BUSINESS LIKE SHOW BUSINESS

The 1906 earthquake had hobbled San Francisco, opening the door for Los Angeles. SoCal boosters like Los Angeles Times publisher and real estate developer Harry Chandler (1864–1944) were busy building an empire out of what had been Spanish and Mexican land-grant ranches and desert. In 1923, Chandler had a 'Hollywoodland' sign erected in the hills to advertise a luxury home development (the first of many!). Conceived as temporary, the sign arrived with the meteoric rise of the film studios. Soon 'land' decayed away and, as they say, a star was born as the sign became the literal symbol for the entertainment industry, known generically as Hollywood.

For more, see p382.

9. Cannery Row

HEAVY INDUSTRY AND MARINE LIFE

During the 1930s and '40s Monterey's Cannery Row emanated a throat-clinging stench of sardines. The sound of fish-canning factories was almost deafening, as workers toiled day and night to vacuum sardines from the oceans and cram them into hundreds of thousands of tin cans annually. It was a short-lived hey-day for coastal California's fishing industry because they rapidly fished themselves out of business. By the early '70s there were simply no more sardines to can. Today Monterey Bay is a marine conservation success story, known for whale-watching excursions and a huge aquarium.

For more, see p296.

10. Rosie the Riveter WWII Home Front National Historic Park

ALL HANDS ON DECK

No place better symbolizes the win-at-any-cost WWII war effort than the old Kaiser shipyards on the San Francisco Bay in Richmond. From 1942 until 1946, a whopping 747 ships were built here – an extraordinary accomplishment, made more so because much of the vast workforce had been marginalized before the war: women and African Americans. The societal changes caused by this upheaval of the social order are still felt today, as detailed at the Rosie the Riveter WWII Home Front National Historic Park. Meanwhile, names like Douglas and Lockheed created the Southern California aerospace industry, which fueled California's first post-war boom.

For more, see p146.

11. Disneyland

HEY MICKEY, YOU'RE SO FINE

It was the dawn of the California dream in 1955, when California's middle class exploded along with the population. Increased wages allowed the whole family to take a holiday and drive the Chevy on a new freeway to Disneyland, Walt's new idealized fantasyland. Families flocked here from their new tract houses spreading like crabgrass in suburbs across the LA Basin, the San Fernando Valley, across San Jose up north and all around the San Francisco Bay and beyond. Today, Disneyland is yet another California first and, at its core, remarkably unchanged from Walt's original vision for Main Street USA, Sleeping Beauty Castle, Frontierland, Adventureland and Tomorrowland.

For more, see p446.

12. Golden Gate Park

TURN ON, TUNE IN, DROP OUT

The Summer of Love really started on January 14, 1967, in San Francisco's Golden Gate Park, when Human Be-In blew minds, gave Timothy Leary a stage and celebrated all things psychedelic. Free speech was the mantra and Haight-Ashbury became the place to be. Passions soon turned to racial injustice and the Vietnam War. Starting with UC Berkeley, college campuses across the US were roiled by unrestrained, at times violent, protests. Yet the social upheavals also jump-started the careers

DORI CHRONICLES/SHUTTERSTOCK

Historic Harvey Milk office and camera store, the Castro (p101)

of California's 'law and order' politicians Ronald Reagan (who was elected governor in 1966) and Richard Nixon (elected president in 1968).

For more, see p105.

13. Henry Miller Memorial Library

ARTISTIC MINDS IN THE WILD

No single stretch of coast has inspired the clacking of typewriters quite like Big Sur, and its untamable scenery was the perfect muse for the raw, spotaneous writing style of the Beat Generation. When renegade writer Henry Miller moved to Big Sur in 1944 he considered it his 'first real home in America,' a place he would describe as mystical and uncategorizable in his memoir Big Sur and the Oranges of Hieronymus Bosch (1957). Activist poet Lawrence Ferlinghetti also owned a cabin in Big Sur's Bixby Canyon, and invited fellow writer Jack Kerouac to use it as a solitary writing retreat; Kerouac produced his own homage, the novel *Big Sur* (1962).

For more, see p306.

14. Transgender Cultural District

A LONG HISTORY OF QUEER SPACES

San Francisco Supervisor Harvey Milk became the first openly gay man elected to public office in California in 1977. He lived in the Castro, where a plaza now carries his name, and sponsored a gay-rights bill before his murder by a political opponent in SF's iconic City Hall. But while the Castro is SF's most visible epicenter of LGBTQ+ life, the community's history goes back even further in the Tenderloin. Six blocks in the neighbourhood's southeast have been legally recognized as SF's Transgender District (a world first), encompassing venerable LGBTQ+ bars and the site of 1966 riots against police harassment of trans people.

For more, see p101.

15. Computer History Museum

THE PACE (AND PRICE) OF PROGRESS

At the 1977 West Coast Computer Faire, Steve Jobs and Steve Wozniak, then in their 20s, introduced the Apple II, a personal computer with unfathomable memory (4KB of RAM!) and microprocessor speed (1MHz!). The question remained: what would ordinary people do with all that computing power? The rest, of course, is history. What's now known as Silicon Valley has spawned countless millionaires and products that have transformed lives (and attention spans) worldwide. Boom-and-bust cycles are the norm, and the pace of technological advancement is still breakneck – worth remembering as you stroll from 1970s color displays to exhibits on AI chatbots at the Computer History Museum. What a difference a few decades make?

For more, see p151.

MEET THE COASTAL CALIFORNIANS

Self-belief defines this diverse coast. Though the California dream eludes many, this is a promised land for entrepreneurs in pursuit of the good life. ANITA ISALSKA introduces the Coastal Californians.

COASTAL CALIFORNIA PROMISES wealth and natural abundance. But when prosperity doesn't materialize, Californians do what they do best: adapt fast, and dream up a new scheme.

Take California's Gold Rush (1848–55), which brought hundreds of thousands of fortune-seekers almost overnight. A few became wealthy but most had to quickly change tack, turning to farming, fishing, ranching and vine-growing. When the Prohibition era temporarily halted wine-making and Monterey overfished their lucrative sardine-canning industry, locals were forced once again to adapt.

'Pivoting' is still an art form for Californians. The term is bandied around, especially in Bay Area tech circles, to mean abrupt reinvention when circumstances change. Everywhere you go, you'll hear about life pivots: burned-out executives turning to wine-making, software engineers finding themselves as surf or ski bums, and – the most common story – new arrivals irresistibly drawn from out of state, or across the world, to build a life in California.

In California, fortune favors the brazen as much as the bold. Hollywood's origins as a global movie-making center germinated in the early 20th century when film-makers tried to evade enforcement of Thomas Edison's patents (which included the Kinetograph, his motion picture device). Arguably the same cowboy opportunism exists today in Silicon Valley, the Bay Area's nucleus of technology and innovation.

Californians have a fraught relationship with their own hot-blooded genius. Innovations cause new economies to appear overnight, like ride-sharing and delivery driving – but these can deflate or disappear just as quickly, leaving people suddenly without work.

The changing climate intensifies the difficulties of making ends meet. Southern California's devastating wildfires in January 2025 not only tore through parts of Los Angeles and San Diego County, they also severely impacted a major source of revenue: tourism. Elsewhere ongoing road closures – like the years-long landslides blocking access to parts of Big Sur – can cut off entire communities from their primary money-makers.

This compounds the pressure of Coastal California's high living costs, a struggle for all but the most privileged people. And the 0.01% sure are doing well: some of the country's most valuable real estate is here (San Francisco's SoMa is most expensive per square foot, if you have a few mill to burn).

But although the ultra-wealthy guard their resources, there's increasing openness to acknowledging past wrongs. California has been a leading supporter of the return of ancestral land to tribal custodians, with the state awarding more than $107 million for tribal land projects in 2024 – many of them along the coast.

By and large, coastal Californians feel blessed to be here and will defend life in their diversely beautiful communities. When President Trump ramped up 'immigration raids' in June 2025, large-scale operations to imprison and deport non-US citizens – including families and their children – it was in Los Angeles that protests brought major highways to a standstill. It was an outpouring of defiance against rising nationalism and a show of support for their migrant neighbors – swiftly followed by protests in Santa Ana, San Francisco and Oakland, where thousands more locals flooded the streets. Californians know that diversity is their strength, and they show up for one another.

CLOCKWISE FROM TOP LEFT: PEOPLEIMAGES/GETTY IMAGES, GERI LAVROV/GETTY IMAGES, ANADOLU VIA GETTY IMAGES, CAROLINE SCHIFF/GETTY IMAGES

Richly Diverse

40% of California residents are Latinx. Just over one-third are white and the Black population is roughly 6%. Approximately 27% of Californians are foreign born, more than double compared to other states.

TYPICAL CALIFORNIAN?

I grew up in Oakland, a child of two people with wildly different backgrounds. My mother's family has been here for seven generations. One of my ancestors on her side was among the first female Spanish-land-grant-holders in the Los Angeles area. She in turn married a German immigrant. My father's family arrived from Eastern Europe via NYC to East LA (Boyle Heights, to be specific) in the 1940s. They were Jewish communists who were persecuted during Joseph McCarthy's Red Scare. Proof that California's institutions are actually not always tolerant.

My parents were both teachers and during my youth we spent many years living overseas, speaking other languages, but always returned to Oakland.

California is a land of immigration, innovation and change, and my family history is as multivalent as many people here. So, really, all it shows is that the only thing typical in California is that there is no such thing as a typical Californian.

CRUISING CALIFORNIA

Turning on some tunes, finding a glorious stretch of open road and going for a drive just might be the state's most quintessential activity. By Amelia Mularz

NATIVE CALIFORNIAN Joan Didion famously described the experience of driving on LA's freeways as 'the only secular communion Los Angeles has.' The 2004 film *Sideways* turned the rural routes of Santa Barbara's wine country into big-screen stars, while the hit HBO series *Big Little Lies* elevated maneuvering the throughways of Big Sur to an art form.

The Birthplace of Car Culture

Practically speaking, driving in the Golden State is all too often a headache. Traffic-riddled freeways around every major metropolis devour our time. Rural roads navigate coastal, mountainous and sometimes windswept desert stretches, requiring the utmost concentration and speeds much slower than some would prefer. And then there's the pain that come with parking (limited spaces, impossible-to-comprehend signs, expensive tickets, the list goes on...). But culturally speaking, driving in California is a phenomenon. Dubbed the world's first 'auto-civilization,' California is obsessed with driving. And that obsession has shaped not only how the state's residents live, but how people across the country live.

Many point to the Arroyo Seco Parkway (aka the 110), which connects Los Angeles with Pasadena, as the birthplace of California's car culture. Dedicated on December

Pictured clockwise from top left: Intercity freeway, San Diego (p480); Tesla factory, Fremont; Highway intersection, Los Angeles (p375); In-N-Out Burger, Ventura (p365)

30, 1940, this was the first freeway in the US and considered an engineering marvel at the time. City plans preceding the Arroyo's unveiling, back in the early 1900s, had included Parisian-style grand boulevards. But because California and especially LA, came of age at the same time as the car, the boulevards were scrapped and plans featuring massive, limited-access highways to alleviate car congestion were chosen instead. This freeway system would soon become a model for urban roadways around the world.

Freeways enabled Californians to live even farther from work and while the state can't claim to be the birthplace of the modern-day suburb (most give that honor to New York), residential sprawl has certainly flourished here. California was also an early adopter of suburban America's favorite amenity: the drive-thru. In-N-Out Burger opened one of the very first drive-thrus, complete with two-way speakers, at their Baldwin Park location in 1948.

Because they were spending so much time in their cars, Californians naturally began to use the automobile as a means of entertainment and self-expression. Drag racing got its start on the dry lake beds of California's Mojave Desert. Lowriders, with their bold custom paint jobs and ground-grazing bodies, have their roots in the Mexican-American communities of Southern California.

From Smog to Sustainability

Never ones to rest on their low-riding laurels, Californians have continued to innovate car culture, zeroing in on zero-emission rides in recent decades. In the early 1990s, the state issued a Zero-Emission Vehicle (ZEV) mandate as part of a move to improve air quality. The mandate required all automakers to sell a small percentage of ZEVs in the state. And while car technology wasn't quite up to the task, the mandate did inspire some feats of engineering. In 1997, a San Dimas car company called AC Propulsion unveiled the first electric sports car, called the tZero.

It's probably no wonder then that the Golden State was also the base for a small Silicon Valley startup called Tesla Motors. In 2006, the company announced it was starting production of a luxury electric sports car that could get 200 miles on a single charge. Another California car company, Rivian, based in Irvine, became a pioneer in the industry 15 years later when they released the first electric pickup truck in 2021.

Today, California leads the country in both electric vehicle ownership and charging locations. According to the US Department of Energy, 35 percent of the country's electric vehicles are registered in California. So should you rent an electric ride on your visit, you'll be in good company and well accommodated.

Beyond electric cars, the state has also been a leader in rethinking how car culture affects wildlife. At the time of publication, the Wallis Annenberg Wildlife Crossing outside of Los Angeles was on track to open in early 2026. When it does, it will be the largest wildlife corridor in the world. Covered in vegetation and reaching across Hwy 101, the bridge will provide safe passage for many wildlife species – including bobcats, mountain lions, mule deer and gray foxes – between the Santa Monica Mountains and the Sierra Madre Range.

This is welcome news for nature lovers who, like so many of us, feel the paradox of wanting to see and celebrate as much of the environment as we can, while also striving to protect it.

Scenic Byways

Speaking of seeing some awe-inspiring environments, California has a number of iconic roadways that'll run you past countless natural wonders. The legendary Route 66 enters the state in the Mojave Desert near Needles and drops off drivers right by the beach in Santa Monica. Yosemite's seasonal Tioga Road, only open in the summer, is the highest elevation highway in the state: a scenic 47-mile journey past meadows, forests and granite domes. Then there's the Pacific Coast Highway (aka Route 1), which is road trip royalty. Hugging the Pacific along some breathtaking stretches, the state's longest route runs 656 miles from Dana Point in Orange County to Leggett in Mendocino County.

And if you're the one behind the wheel and terrified of tackling California's notoriously wide freeways (Orange County has an interchange with a whopping 26 lanes), take some advice from Didion herself and think only about where you are, instead of where you're going. Then all that's left to do is enjoy the ride.

CLOCKWISE FROM TOP LEFT: DOGORA SUN/SHUTTERSTOCK, FELIX MIZIOZNIKOV/SHUTTERSTOCK, TIERNEYMJ/SHUTTERSTOCK, ROBERT V SCHWEMMER/SHUTTERSTOCK

Boudin Bakery, San Francisco

PACK-SHOT/SHUTTERSTOCK

BREAD CULTURE IN THE BAY AREA

A bevy of bakers is drawing people from near and far to revel in the rich culture around artisanal bread. By Lisa Park

HEAD OVER TO Acme Bread Company in Berkeley any day of the week and you'll find a line of customers that's sometimes 30-plus deep, eagerly waiting to get inside. Hand-drawn signs touting savory creations such as 'hella wet levain' and 'multigrain spelt' border the bakery's picture window, which offers a tantalizing glimpse of the arts-and-crafts loaves that have earned Acme accolades and a devoted following. Meanwhile, the yeasty aroma of freshly baked bread keeps customers enthralled until it's their turn to pick and choose from crusty baguettes, buns, rounds and rolls – like a kid in a candy store.

Not too shabby for a bakery that's been around for over 40 years. But Acme's not alone when it comes to getting this kind of steadfast attention. Artisanal bakeries across the San Francisco Bay Area are drawing big crowds and fostering communities keen on indulging their appetite for – and love of – handcrafted, high-quality bread.

Artisanal Bread's Ups & Downs

Bay Area breadmaking goes back to the mid-1800s when Isadore Boudin of Boudin Bakery used a sourdough starter given to him by a gold miner to create his classic French bread. While the rest of the country moved toward ultra-processing bread post WWII (using commercially made cake yeast and chemicals such as emulsifiers to speed up production), Boudin Bakery resisted. Staying true to old-world traditions, it still makes bread with just flour, water and salt, using the same starter or mother dough from 176 years ago.

Even as Boudin flourished, many artisanal bakeries gave way to large, industrial operations mass-producing cheap, bland, chemically enhanced white bread. It wasn't until the 1970s when a new breed of bread makers, including Zen monks, hippies and counterculture kids, decided they'd had enough of Wonder Bread. They started making bread the old-fashioned way – kneaded and shaped by hand then baked in wood-fired ovens – fusing classic techniques focusing on texture and flavor development with modern values emphasizing good, clean and nourishing food.

Over the next few decades, bakers at Tassajara, Cheeseboard Collective, Acme, Semifreddi's and the San Francisco Baking Institute (SFBI) each had a hand in 'laying the groundwork for people to enjoy arts-and-crafts style bread,' says Miyuki Togi, SFBI baking instructor. Their success helped elevate people's appreciation for, as Togi explains, 'handmade bread that takes time and is made with care.' And it also helped make artisanal bread accessible – via storefronts, restaurants and grocery outlets – throughout the Bay Area.

JUNE
SEPTEMBER
NOVEMBER

Tartine's Outsize Impact

Then along came Tartine in the early aughts. Its novel bakes experimenting with longer fermentation, higher hydration, whole grains and a super-dark crust blew the Bay Area bread scene wide open. The now-famous brand snagged the ultimate endorsement from New York Times food writer Mark Bittman who called Tartine his 'favorite bakery in the United States.'

Artisanal bakeries inspired by Tartine's spirit of innovation and excellence started popping up all over the Bay, each investing the time and resources toward creating delicious, nutritious bread. Consider San Francisco favorite the Mill, whose owner and head baker Josey Baker specializes in freshly milled (in house, no less) wholegrain sourdough breads that need up to 40 hours to complete – 'because good things take time,' according to Baker on his website.

At Fournée Bakery in Berkeley, the mission is to 'make the best possible product consistently using the best possible ingredients sourced from local farms and purveyors.' Meanwhile, Mountain View–based the Midwife and the Baker is all about cultivating 'craft and community,' baking only with organic flour and seeds from sustainable farms to create quality products for its customers.

'THERE'S A REAL SYMBIOTIC RELATIONSHIP BETWEEN MAKING BREAD THAT'S BEAUTIFUL AND HAVING PEOPLE WHO VALUE YOU AND THE ART OF BAKING.' AZIKIWEE ANDERSON, RIZE UP BAKERY FOUNDER

Tartine Bakery
GADO IMAGES/ALAMY

Love for Craft & Community

With Tartine's meteoric rise, 'customers got more serious about what they were looking for in bread,' says Togi. In addition, 'people in the Bay Area are more open to paying more for better quality food. So they don't mind paying more for a loaf of really good bread from a small bakery.'

Theo Dolarian, fellow SFBI baking instructor and Mill alumnus, agrees and adds that 'people are also more open to new flavor profiles. They will try different things... The wonderful thing about the San Francisco Bay Area is that if there's a style of bread you're interested in, there's a place that does it and probably does it really well.'

Case in point: home-based-project-turned-growing-commercial-operation Rize Up Bakery, whose inventive sourdough breads – ube, masala and K-pop (aka gochujang) – have struck a resounding chord. Says founder Azikiwee Anderson (who was previously a chef), 'the only reason I get to innovate is because I have customers who care enough to support what I'm doing. There's a real symbiotic relationship between making bread that's beautiful and having people who value you and the art of baking.'

Adds Anderson, Rize Up is a reflection of the San Francisco Bay Area, 'where there's a lot more we than I. Breadmaking is about being part of a community of different cultures. It's about representing and including those cultures so that they feel seen and cared about.'

'When you ask me what makes bread culture in the Bay Area special, I really do think it's the community. We're part of something bigger. And when you're surrounded by people who care and are down to do the hard work, that makes our bread untouchable.'

Baking is a labor of love for the craft and for the community, says Anderson, whose North Star questions include things like: 'Would you stand in line for our bread? Would you buy it special to share at a dinner? When you bite into it, do you do a little happy dance? Does it talk to your soul?'

Yes, yes and so much yes.

INDEX

A

B

Map Pages **000**

Map Pages **000**

I

Map Pages **000**

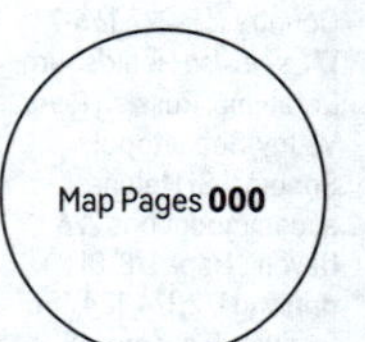

Map Pages **000**

Map Pages **000**

"San Francisco (p43) is the threshold between fact and fiction, past and future, body and soul."

ALISON BING

"Mendocino Village (p234) was saved from economic disaster by artists in the 1960s. Today it feels simultaneously suitable for a well-journeyed sea captain and a bohemian poet."

AMELIA MULARZ

FROM LEFT: ANTON_IVANOV/SHUTTERSTOCK, ALESSANDRARC/SHUTTERSTOCK

All rights reserved. No part of this publication may be copied, stored in a retrieval system, or transmitted in any form by any means, electronic, mechanical, recording or otherwise, except brief extracts for the purpose of review, and no part of this publication may be sold or hired, without the written permission of the publisher. Lonely Planet and the Lonely Planet logo are trademarks of Lonely Planet and are registered in the US Patent and Trademark Office and in other countries. Lonely Planet does not allow its name or logo to be appropriated by commercial establishments, such as retailers, restaurants or hotels. Please let us know of any misuses: lonelyplanet.com/legal/intellectual-property.

Mapping data sources:
© Lonely Planet
© OpenStreetMap http://openstreetmap.org/copyright

THIS BOOK

Destination Editor Melissa Yeager

Production Editor Jeremy Toynbee

Image Editors Megan Cassidy, Dermot Hegarty

Cartographers Julie Dodkins, Corey Hutchison

Coordinating Editor Gabrielle Innes

Assisting Editors Peterjon Cresswell, Fionnuala Twomey

Cover Researcher Katelyn Perry

Thanks Michelle Bennett, Melanie Dankel, Kevin Ebbutt, Alison Killilea, Kellie Langdon, Chris Lee-Ack, Ailbhe MacMahon, Jennifer McCann, Anne Mulvaney, Anthony Phelan, Saralinda Turner

Paper in this book is certified against the Forest Stewardship Council™ standards. FSC™ promotes environmentally responsible, socially beneficial and economically viable management of the world's forests.

Published by Lonely Planet Global Limited
CRN 554153
7th edition – Jan 2026
ISBN 978 1 78701 678 1
© Lonely Planet 2026
10 9 8 7 6 5 4 3 2 1
Printed in Malaysia